ASIAN DEVELOPMENT

Outlook 2003

Special Chapter
Competitiveness in Developing Asia

**Published for the Asian Development Bank
by the Oxford University Press**

OXFORD
UNIVERSITY PRESS

Oxford University Press is a department of the University of Oxford.
It furthers the University's objective of excellence in research, scholarship,
and education by publishing worldwide in

Oxford New York

Auckland Bangkok Buenos Aires Cape Town Chennai
Dar es Salaam Delhi Hong Kong Istanbul Karachi Kolkata
Kuala Lumpur Madrid Melbourne Mexico City Mumbai Nairobi
São Paulo Shanghai Taipei Tokyo Toronto

Oxford is a registered trade mark of Oxford University Press

Published in the United States
by Oxford University Press Inc., New York

© Asian Development Bank 2003

First published in 2003
This impression (lowest digit)
1 3 5 7 9 10 8 6 4 2

Published for the Asian Development Bank by
Oxford University Press

British Library Cataloguing in Publication Data
available

Library of Congress Cataloging-in-Publication-Data
available

ISBN 0-19-596278-8
ISSN 0117-0481

Printed in Hong Kong
Published by Oxford University Press (China) Ltd
18th Floor, Warwick House East, Taikoo Place, 979 King's Road, Quarry Bay
Hong Kong

Foreword

The *Asian Development Outlook 2003* is the 15th edition of the annual comprehensive economic report on the developing member countries of the Asian Development Bank (ADB).

The *Outlook* provides a detailed analysis and assessment of macroeconomic trends, including fiscal, monetary, and balance-of-payments developments, for 41 Asian and Pacific economies for 2002, as well as projections for 2003 and 2004. It also provides a broad diagnosis of macroeconomic conditions, future growth prospects, and progress in poverty reduction in the economies of the region.

After a marked slowdown in 2001, both the world economy and developing Asia got off to a strong start in 2002. As the year advanced, however, the pace of growth in the major industrial countries slowed and became more uneven. The United States' economy showed strong growth in the first and third quarters of 2002, but weaker performance toward the end of the year kept its overall recovery below expectations. Economies in the euro area did not perform as vigorously as projected at the beginning of the year. In Japan, despite stronger than expected growth in gross domestic product in the second half of the year, the economy expanded only slightly in 2002.

In contrast to the industrial countries, economic growth in developing Asia generally strengthened, accelerating further in the second half of 2002 as export demand picked up. Expansionary fiscal policies and accommodative monetary policies, mainly in East and Southeast Asia, contributed to the strengthening of aggregate demand, particularly consumption, while firmer export markets provided a boost to industrial production.

Growth projections for the global economy for 2003 have recently been adjusted downward, reflecting economic slowdown in industrial countries in the early part of the year, concerns about the consequences of the severe acute respiratory syndrome (SARS) epidemic in Asia, and uncertainties, though diminished, relating to the situation in Iraq. Sound policies and structural reforms remain essential for achieving robust, sustainable economic growth.

In developing Asia, aggregate growth projections have been reduced from those made at the end of last year. Revised estimated growth of 5.3% for developing Asia, with steady domestic and export demand in most countries, will still be robust in 2003 compared with all other regions in the world. Macroeconomic policies are expected to remain generally supportive. However, the economic outlook for Asia is highly dependent on the trends in the global economy, and susceptible to the risks associated with disruptions in tourism as well as other regional and international markets resulting from current uncertainties, including the SARS epidemic.

This year's *Outlook* contains a theme chapter addressing the issue of competitiveness, a topic high on the agenda of policy makers in Asia and the Pacific whose economies face rapid globalization, constant changes in technology, and increasing competition. The chapter analyzes the nature and role of competitiveness in national economic development, emphasizing that competition is first and foremost a firm-level issue. At the same time, governments play a key role in developing appropriate policy measures and creating a conducive environment that will enable the private sector to compete in the global market place.

The preparation of the *Outlook* was made possible through the efforts of many individuals both inside and outside of ADB. I would like to thank external economists and policy makers for their valuable insights and inputs. I would like to acknowledge the contribution of the economists from ADB's five regional departments and the resident missions as well as those from the Economics and Research Department. The publication would not have been possible without the support of ADB's Office of Administrative Services and the Office of Information Systems and Technology. Finally, the advice and assistance of the Office of External Relations in disseminating the *Outlook* are gratefully acknowledged.

Tadao Chino

TADAO CHINO
President

Acknowledgments

The *Asian Development Outlook 2003* was prepared by the staff of the Asian Development Bank (ADB) from East and Central Asia Department, Mekong Department, Pacific Department, South Asia Department, Southeast Asia Department, the various resident missions of ADB, and the Economics and Research Department (ERD).

The economists who contributed the country chapters are: Ramesh Adhikari and Dao Viet Dung (Viet Nam), Douglas Brooks (Republic of Korea), Johanna Boestel (Tajikistan), Giovanni Capannelli (Cook Islands, Democratic Republic of Timor-Leste, Republic of the Marshall Islands, Federated States of Micronesia, and Nauru), Emma Xiaoqin Fan (Hong Kong, China), Yolanda Fernandez (Mongolia), Manabu Fujimura (Afghanistan), Bahodir Ganiev (Azerbaijan), David Green and Amanah Abdulkadir (Indonesia), Naved Hamid and Safiya Aftab (Pakistan), Francis Harrigan (Myanmar), Hideaki Imamura (Maldives), Yun-Hwan Kim (Malaysia and Singapore), Rajiv Kumar (Turkmenistan), Mandar Jayawant (Uzbekistan), Sukanda Lewis (Cambodia and the Lao People's Democratic Republic), Yeo Lin (Taipei,China), Xuelin Liu (Philippines), Jayant Menon (Thailand), Aliya Mukhamedyarova (Kazakhstan), Sudipto Mundle and Hiranya Mukhopadhyay (India), Soo-Nam Oh and Abid Hussain (Bhutan), Sungsup Ra (Nepal), Purnima Rajapakse (Bangladesh), Diwesh Sharan (Fiji Islands, Papua New Guinea, Samoa, Solomon Islands, and Tonga), Min Tang and Jian Zhuang (People's Republic of China), V. B. Tulasidhar (Kyrgyz Republic), Umaporn Wongwatanasin (Kiribati, Tuvalu, and Vanuatu), and Joseph Ernest Zveglich (Sri Lanka). The subregional coordinators were Frank Harrigan and Tao Zhang on Southeast Asia, Rajiv Kumar on Central Asia, Sultan Hafeez Rahman and Narhari Rao on South Asia, and Diwesh Sharan on the Pacific.

In ERD, the *Outlook* team was led by J.P. Verbiest, Assistant Chief Economist, Macroeconomics and Financial Research Division, assisted by Charissa N. Castillo and James P. Villafuerte. The chapter on Developing Asia and the World was contributed by J.P. Verbiest together with Douglas Brooks and Akiko Hagiwara while the chapter on Fiscal Policy Issues in Asia was contributed by Emma Xiaoqin Fan. The special chapter on Competitiveness in Developing Asia was prepared by Jesus Felipe. It benefited from extensive comments from Gerry Adams, Rana Hasan, Mike Hobday, Alejandro Nieto, and Josef Yap.

The initial drafts and various background papers were discussed at the *Asian Development Outlook Conference 2003* in January 2003 by leading economists from the academic world and the private sector, as well as policy makers from ADB's developing member countries and ADB economists. Staff from the International Monetary Fund, the Organisation for Economic Co-operation and Development, the United Nations Economic and Social Commission for Asia and the Pacific, and the World Bank participated in the Conference.

Technical and research support was provided by Roshan Ara, Emma Banaria, Veronica Bayangos, Laura Britt-Fermo, Benjamin Endriga, Heidee Lozari, Maritess Manalo, Aldalyn Nada-Bere, Aludia Pardo, Marife Principe, Pilipinas Quising, Cynthia Reyes, Sinha Roy Saikat, and Lea Sumulong.

John Malcolm Dowling, Gonzalo Jurado, John McCombie, and Richard Niebuhr as the economic editors made substantive as well as advisory contributions. Jonathan Aspin did the copy editing and Elizabeth Leuterio was responsible for book design; she was assisted in typesetting by Mercedita Cabañeros. Mike Svegfors developed the cross-system data-linking facilities. Eva Olanda, assisted by Patricia Baysa and Susan Torres, provided administrative and secretarial support. The publication would not have been possible without the cooperation of the Printing Unit under the supervision of Raveendranath Rajan. Charissa N. Castillo coordinated the overall publication of the *Outlook*.

Robert H. Salamon, Ann Quon, Tsukasa Maekawa, Lynette Mallery, and Penelope Price of the Office of External Relations planned and conducted the dissemination of the *Outlook*.

IFZAL ALI
Chief Economist
Economics and Research Department

Contents

Boxes

Figures

Tables

Statistical Appendix Tables

Acronyms and Abbreviations

AFTA	ASEAN Free Trade Area
AMC	asset management company
ASEAN	Association of Southeast Asian Nations
AusAID	Australian Agency for International Development
CPI	consumer price index
DMC	developing member country
EU	European Union
FATF	Financial Action Task Force
FDI	foreign direct investment
FEZ	free economic zone
GDP	gross domestic product
GNP	gross national product
GVC	global value chain
ICT	information and communications technology
IT	information technology
IMF	International Monetary Fund
Lao PDR	Lao People's Democratic Republic
MNC	multinational corporation
NIE	newly industrializing economy
NPL	nonperforming loan
ODM	own design and manufacture
OECD	Organisation for Economic Co-operation and Development
OEM	original equipment manufacture
OPEC	Organization of Petroleum Exporting Countries
PBC	People's Bank of China
PRC	People's Republic of China
PICTA	Pacific Island Countries Trade Agreement
PRGF	Poverty Reduction and Growth Facility
R&D	research and development
SARS	severe acute respiratory syndrome
SME	small and medium enterprise
SOCB	state-owned commercial bank
UNIDO	United Nations Industrial Development Organization
UK	United Kingdom
US	United States
VAT	value-added tax
WTO	World Trade Organization

Definitions

The economies discussed in the *Asian Development Outlook 2003* are classified by major analytic or geographic groupings, such as industrial countries, developing Asia, and transition economies.

For purposes of *ADO 2003*, the following apply:

- **Association of Southeast Asian Nations (ASEAN)** comprises Brunei Darussalam, Cambodia, Indonesia, Lao People's Democratic Republic, Malaysia, Myanmar, Philippines, Singapore, Thailand, and Viet Nam.
- **Developing Asia** refers to 41 developing member countries (DMCs) of the Asian Development Bank discussed in *ADO 2003*.
- **East Asia** comprises People's Republic of China; Hong Kong, China; Republic of Korea; Mongolia; and Taipei,China.
- **Industrial countries** refer to the high-income OECD countries defined in World Bank, available: www.worldbank.org/data/countryclass/classgroups.htm#High-income.
- **Newly industrialized economies (NIEs)** comprise Hong Kong, China; Republic of Korea; Singapore; and Taipei,China.
- **Southeast Asia** comprises Cambodia, Indonesia, Lao People's Democratic Republic, Malaysia, Myanmar, Philippines, Singapore, Thailand, and Viet Nam.
- **South Asia** comprises Afghanistan, Bangladesh, Bhutan, India, Maldives, Nepal, Pakistan, and Sri Lanka.
- **Central Asia** comprises Azerbaijan, Kazakhstan, Kyrgyz Republic, Tajikistan, Turkmenistan, and Uzbekistan.
- **The Pacific** comprises Cook Islands, Fiji Islands, Kiribati, Republic of the Marshall Islands, Federated States of Micronesia, Nauru, Papua New Guinea, Samoa, Solomon Islands, Democratic Republic of Timor-Leste, Tonga, Tuvalu, and Vanuatu.
- **Transition economies** refer to the countries of Central Asia, Mongolia, Cambodia, Lao PDR, and Viet Nam.
- The **euro area** comprises Austria, Belgium, Finland, France, Germany, Greece, Ireland, Italy, Luxembourg, Netherlands, Portugal, and Spain.
- Unless otherwise specified, the symbol "$" and the word "dollar" refer to US dollars. Currency abbreviations are given in Statistical Appendix Table A20.

The *Statistical Notes* give a detailed explanation of how data are derived.

ADO 2003 is based on data available up to 21 March 2003.

ASIAN DEVELOPMENT
Outlook
2003

Part 1 Developing Asia and the World

ASIAN DEVELOPMENT
Outlook
2003

Developing Asia and the World

Developing Asia and the World

Overview of Economic Trends and Prospects

The world economy and developing Asia began 2002 quite strongly as the recovery from the slowdown of 2001 continued, though as the year advanced the pace of growth in industrial countries slowed and became more uneven. The United States (US) economy showed strong growth in the first and third quarters of 2002, but weaker performance toward the end of the year kept overall recovery below expectations. Economies in the euro area performed poorly in comparison with estimates made at the beginning of the year. In Japan, despite stronger than expected gross domestic product (GDP) growth in the second half, the economy expanded only slightly over the course of the year.

In contrast, in developing Asia (the developing member countries—DMCs—of the Asian Development Bank), growth in most countries strengthened; it accelerated further in the second half of the year as export demand began to pick up. Expansionary fiscal and accommodative monetary policy, mainly in East and Southeast Asia, contributed to strengthening aggregate demand—particularly consumption—while somewhat firmer external markets provided a boost to industrial production (Figure 1.1).

Prospects for 2003 are clouded by economic weaknesses in the industrial countries and uncertainties relating to the conflict in Iraq and the recent outbreak of severe acute respiratory syndrome (SARS) in Asia. As a result, forecasts have all been adjusted downward in early 2003. In industrial countries, growth divergences between the US, euro area, and Japan will remain significant, with growth in the US at around the 2002 outcome, and weak GDP growth in the euro area and Japan.

In developing Asia, aggregate growth projections have been reduced from those at the end of 2002. In most DMCs, domestic demand will remain robust and exports will continue to expand. Macroeconomic policies will generally remain supportive, although both fiscal and monetary policy will need to tighten somewhat in many countries.

At the start of the second quarter of 2003, the economic outlook for Asia is highly vulnerable to the risks of a further weakening in the outlook for industrial countries, volatility in oil prices, disruptions in tourism, the negative impacts on regional and international markets due to the conflict in Iraq, and the as yet uncertain consequences of SARS.

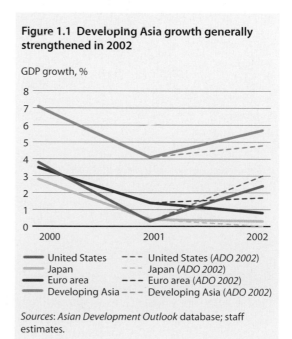

Figure 1.1 Developing Asia growth generally strengthened in 2002

GDP growth, %

Sources: Asian Development Outlook database; staff estimates.

Overview of Economic Trends in Developing Asia in 2002

In 2002, growth in developing Asia strengthened compared with the previous year, and economic performance gained momentum as the year unfolded (Table 1.1). In most countries, export growth accelerated and domestic demand remained strong while, except in the Pacific, inflation subsided. Consumption expenditures grew strongly in the People's Republic of China (PRC), Republic of Korea (Korea), India, Indonesia, Malaysia, Philippines, Thailand, and Viet Nam. In contrast, business investment continued to decline in most East and Southeast Asian economies, due to a combination of uncertainty and overcapacity. Notable exceptions were the PRC, Korea, Lao People's Democratic Republic (Lao PDR), Malaysia, Viet Nam, and to a lesser extent, Thailand. In South

Asia, investment showed positive growth except in the Maldives and Pakistan. Export growth, which increased more rapidly in the second half of the year, was also notable in largely the same economies, particularly Cambodia; PRC; India; Korea; Malaysia; Philippines; Taipei,China; Thailand; Viet Nam; and several Central Asian republics (CARs). The US dollar value of exports increased by 9.4%, a substantial reversal from the almost 7% decline in 2001 and nearly double the Asian Development Bank (ADB) forecasts made in early 2002. In terms of overall growth performance, the PRC and Korea had the best record in East Asia; Lao PDR, Thailand, and Viet Nam in Southeast Asia; Bhutan in South Asia; and Azerbaijan, Kazakhstan, Tajikistan, and Turkmenistan in Central Asia. In the Pacific, the performance of the Fiji Islands and the Marshall Islands stood out. In 19 DMCs, output grew at a rate of 4.0% or more. Still, in spite of this perfor-

Table 1.1 Selected Economic Indicators, Developing Asia, 2000–2004

	2000	2001	2002	2003	2004
Gross Domestic Product (annual % change)					
Developing Asia	7.1	4.1	5.7	5.3	5.9
East Asia	8.1	4.4	6.5	5.6	6.2
Southeast Asia	6.2	1.7	4.1	4.0	4.8
South Asia	4.5	5.0	4.2	5.7	6.1
Central Asia	8.5	10.9	7.7	5.8	5.8
The Pacific	-0.5	0.4	0.9	2.4	2.5
Consumer Price Index (annual % change)					
Developing Asia	2.2	2.4	1.4	2.5	2.7
East Asia	0.6	1.1	-0.1	1.1	1.4
Southeast Asia	2.4	4.6	4.3	4.2	4.0
South Asia[a]	6.3	3.7	3.0	4.9	5.0
Central Asia	17.2	13.6	12.3	13.9	14.2
The Pacific	9.1	6.9	7.1	6.3	-
Current Account Balance (% of GDP)					
Developing Asia	2.8	2.9	3.6	2.9	2.6
East Asia	2.5	2.8	3.6	3.0	2.7
Southeast Asia	8.1	7.0	7.2	6.3	6.0
South Asia	-0.8	0.0	0.8	0.0	0.0
Central Asia	1.6	-3.3	-2.1	-4.2	-5.1
The Pacific	3.9	2.8	-1.9	-	-

- Not available. [a] India reports on a wholesale price index basis.
Sources: Asian Development Outlook database; staff estimates.

mance, growth in most DMCs remained below its long-term potential, and in many of the smaller and poorer DMCs, growth was insufficient to substantially raise income and reduce poverty. This was also true in a few of the large countries.

Inflation in developing Asia remained low despite the acceleration in growth, averaging 1.4% compared with 2.4% in 2001. There was high inflation in a few countries such as Indonesia, Lao PDR, Papua New Guinea, Sri Lanka, Tajikistan, Tonga, and Uzbekistan.

Fiscal deficits remained common throughout Asia. The economies most affected by the 1997–98 financial crisis continued fiscal expansion to strengthen their recovery, while structural deficits persisted in some countries. Throughout the region, budgetary stances are coming under increasing scrutiny and efforts are under way toward fiscal consolidation (see the section, *An Overview of Fiscal Policy in Developing Asia*, below).

With the exception of the Pacific, external balances improved in 2002 as surpluses on both the trade and current accounts increased, and the deficits in Central Asia narrowed. Exports grew faster than imports, and the region's aggregate current account surplus increased from 2.9% of GDP in 2001 to 3.6% in 2002. The region thus continued to accumulate international reserves in 2002 (Box 1.1). One of the important reasons for the buoyancy of

exports in several countries appears to be rapidly increasing exports to the PRC, partly as a result of the reforms associated with World Trade Organization (WTO) entry of the PRC (Box 1.2).

Macroeconomic Conditions in 2002

Major External Markets
Industrial countries remain by far the largest market for DMC exports, a market that strengthened significantly in 2002. In the US, the destination for about one fifth of developing Asia's exports, consumer spending, particularly on cars and housing, was buoyant. Along with a modest revival in equipment and software investment as well as restocking, this served to sustain the growth momentum. However, by the end of the third quarter some of the steam had gone out of consumer spending, suggesting that growth would be slowing over the next few quarters (Figure 1.2). In the last months of the year, consumer confidence indicators dipped and investment spending slowed. Concern over conflict with Iraq, weak stock and job markets, and uncertainty over the form of fiscal stimulus all served to shake consumer confidence.

Both the euro area and Japan depended to a significant extent on external markets to drive economic growth in 2002. In the euro area, weak domestic demand conditions combined with

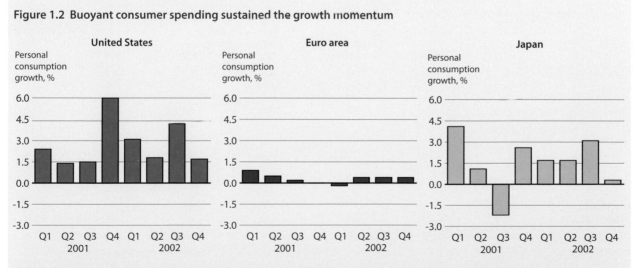

Figure 1.2 Buoyant consumer spending sustained the growth momentum

Sources: US Department of Commerce, Bureau of Economic Analysis, BEA News Releases, available: www.bea.doc.gov/bea/dn/nipaweb/; Statistics Bureau & Statistics Center of Japan, available: www.esri.cao.go.jp/en/sna/menu.html; Eurostat Euro Indicators, available: www.europa.eu.int/comm/eurostat/.

Box 1.1   Asia's International Reserves: Prudent or Overcautious?

During the Asian financial crisis, economies with the largest international reserves were able to hold their exchange rates steady (e.g., the PRC) or suffered only modest currency depreciations (e.g., Singapore and Taipei,China) while other emerging economies suffered severe devaluations. The Box Table shows how reserves have increased in several economies to precrisis levels and, in others, much higher. Total reserves for the economies in the Box Table doubled between 1996 and 2002, from $486 billion to $952 billion.

There are several ways to measure the adequacy of international reserves. First, an import reserve cover of 3 months has traditionally been seen as a minimum level of adequacy. With the exception of Korea, the crisis-hit economies had reserves equivalent to more than 3 months of import cover before the crisis. Second, empirical work[1] suggests that the ratio of reserves to short-term external debt is the most important indicator of reserve adequacy in economies with uncertain access to capital markets. A ratio of 1 is adequate. At the end of 2002, the ratio averaged 2.8 for the crisis-hit economies.

A more relevant exercise would be to assess the adequacy of the level of reserves, given the amount of short-term debt, and assuming the existing level of current account deficits and a complete cut-off from capital markets. Such an analysis suggests that, except for Malaysia and the Philippines, the crisis-hit economies could not have covered their short-term obligations before the crisis.

Since the crisis, the countries of the region have substantially improved their risk-bearing capacity for external shocks. The risks of such shocks are not negligible today. In addition, many DMCs are projected to continue running significant current account surpluses and to further accumulate reserves over the medium term.

While a prudent level of reserves supports macroeconomic stability, there is genuine concern that excessive reserves might be counterproductive and keep economic growth below potential. Excessive reserves could be accumulated at the cost of forgone imports and associated investment opportunities. Some of these reserves could be used to prepay expensive external debt or facilitate the import of new technology to stimulate productivity increases.

The difficult issue for policy makers is of course what a "prudent" level of reserves is. While the broad criteria discussed above are one consideration, every economy must basically determine the prudent minimum level of reserves required, depending on a critical assessment of its sources and uses of foreign exchange. This assessment should also involve an analysis of a series of reasonable external shock scenarios to assess the ability to meet trade requirements and debt-servicing obligations, and reduce exchange rate volatility. An important consideration is that of continued access to capital markets in the event of an external shock. The experience of developing Asia in the financial crisis, and more recently that of Argentina, can serve as important lessons in this regard. Finally, in this context, reserve pooling initiatives should be strengthened and expanded.

[1] See, for instance, Rodrik, Dani and Andrés Velasco. 1999. "Short-Term Capital Flows." NBER Working Paper 7364.

Box Table.   International Reserves of Selected Asian Economies

	International Reserves[a] ($ billion)		As Months of Goods and Services Imports		As Ratio to Short-Term External Debt[b]	
	1996	2002	1996	2002	1996	2002
Crisis-Hit Asian Economies	**130.1**	**242.6**	**3.9**	**6.5**	**0.9**	**2.8**
Indonesia	19.3	31.6	4.4	8.8	0.5	1.9
Korea	33.2	121.3	2.3	7.9	0.3	2.2
Malaysia	27.1	34.6	4.0	4.8	1.8	4.4
Philippines	11.7	16.2	3.4	4.7	1.2	1.8
Thailand	38.7	38.9	5.6	6.3	0.8	3.6
Other Asian Economies	**356.1**	**709.6**	**6.1**	**10.0**	**3.0**	**5.8**
China, People's Rep. of	105.0	286.4	8.2	10.5	2.4	7.1
Hong Kong, China	63.8	111.9	3.5[c]	5.9[c]	-	-
India	22.4	69.9	5.1	12.4	1.8	5.3
Singapore	76.8	79.7	6.0	6.3[d]	-	-
Taipei,China	88.0	161.7	7.6	14.9	4.7	5.0[e]

- Not available. [a] Excluding gold except for Indonesia, Malaysia, Philippines, and Thailand. [b] As reserves include those of the banking sector, this is not a suitable measure for countries with large international banking sectors. [c] From national income accounts as balance-of-payments data are not available before 1997. [d] Imports of goods, services, and income. [e] Short-term external debt as of September 2002.

Sources: Central Bank of China, available: www.cbc.gov.tw; Hong Kong Monetary Authority, available: www.info.gov.hk/hkma; Singapore Department of Statistics; World Bank, *Global Development Finance*, available: http://publications.worldbank.org/GDF; Institute of International Finance, Inc., available: www.iif.com; Asian Development Bank, *Key Indicators 2002; Asian Development Outlook* database.

slowing external demand toward the end of the year to produce very modest economic growth of less than 1% for the year. In Japan, consumer spending and exports strengthened in the second and third quarters. However, later in the year the yen strengthened, export performance deteriorated, unemployment increased, and consumer confidence fell. Growth for the year was minimal.

Consumer price inflation remained very low in 2002. Indeed there was some concern that a deflationary cycle might arise in some countries. Inflation in the US and the euro area was low, averaging around 2% in both cases. Prices continued to fall in Japan for the third year in a row, although the trend was toward greater price stability throughout the year. Several factors contributed to a low level of inflation, including stiff price competition among exporters, generally strong supplies of primary products (aside from oil toward the end of the year), and innovations that continue to lower the costs of technologically based goods and transportation.

Fiscal policy in most industrial countries became more accommodating and then expansive as the year unfolded and the recovery turned more tentative. Government deficits in Organisation for Economic Co-operation and Development (OECD) countries generally increased as a percentage of GDP—from 1.4% in 2001 to 2.9% in 2002—most strongly in the US, where the deficit increased from

0.7% of GDP in 2001 to over 3% in 2002. While the stability and growth pact limits the deficit to 3% of GDP in the euro area, Germany and France were approaching that limit. In Japan, the deficit, which was already high at 7.2% of GDP at the end of 2001, widened somewhat further.

Likewise, monetary policy remained accommodative throughout the year in industrial countries. In the US, the Federal Funds rate remained at 1.75% for nearly a year and was reduced further to 1.25% in November 2002. Policy rates in other OECD countries also remained largely unchanged through the year—zero or close to zero in Japan, 3.25% for the euro area until early December when it was reduced by 0.5%, and 4% in the United Kingdom (UK). Long-term interest rates have fallen, particularly after the first quarter, as the weakness of the overall recovery became more apparent and inflationary expectations continued to abate.

World Trade in Goods and Services

Developments in external markets are critical for DMCs since their exports respond very quickly to changes in the pattern of world import demand. Growth in the world economy and in import demand improved in 2002, albeit at a modest pace (Figure 1.3). Import demand of industrial countries grew by 3% and economic growth in this group of countries accelerated to 1.4% from 0.8%

Figure 1.3 Growth in industrial countries improved modestly in 2002

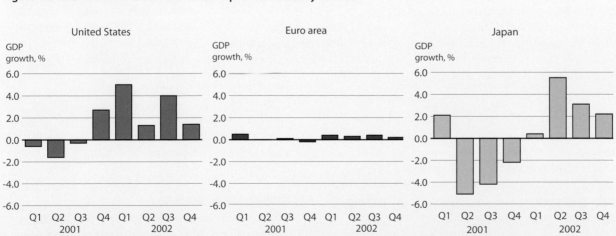

Sources: US Department of Commerce, Bureau of Economic Analysis, BEA News Releases, available: www.bea.doc.gov/bea/dn/nipaweb/; Statistics Bureau & Statistics Center of Japan, available: www.esri.cao.go.jp/en/sna/menu.html; Eurostat Euro Indicators, available: www.europa.eu.int/comm/eurostat/.

Box 1.2 Changing Patterns of International Trade in East and Southeast Asia

The pattern of international trade has changed fundamentally in the past few years as the impact of globalization has become stronger. Outsourcing and greater complexity in the production chain, which involves the internalization of manufacturing in a global value chain (see Part 3 for greater detail on this), have contributed to rapid growth in trade both among countries in the Asian region and Asian trade with the rest of the world. The emergence of the PRC as a major trading power has also had a significant impact on the recent pattern and growth of trade, especially in East and Southeast Asia.

Total merchandise trade of DMCs to the rest of the world increased rapidly from January to September 2002. The region was an aggregate net exporter of goods with a 31.3% hike in exports by September from $50.6 billion in January. Moreover, the September 2002 exports of $66.4 billion reflect a roughly 14% gain from the same month in 2001. Imported goods from the rest of the world also increased but only by a moderate $1.4 billion or 3.0% from their level of $46.0 billion in September 2001.

The magnitude and direction of these changes are evident from looking at trade patterns both within East and Southeast Asia and between those subregions and the rest of the world in 1990 and in 2001 (Box Figure). The country groupings in the figure aggregate the PRC and Hong Kong, China; the rest of the world includes all economies except the PRC and Hong Kong, China; Korea and Mongolia; and Southeast Asia, and thus includes some other DMCs.

Several developments are of interest. First, between 1990 and 2001, trade between the PRC and Hong Kong, China and the rest of the world more than tripled, and trade between Southeast Asia and the rest of the world roughly doubled, as did trade between Korea and Mongolia and the rest of the world. Second, Korea and Mongolia; the PRC and Hong Kong, China; and Southeast Asia each continue to run a trade surplus with the rest of the world. Third, trade between Korea and Mongolia and Southeast Asia has about tripled, and remains roughly in balance between imports and exports. Fourth, Southeast Asia's exports to the PRC and Hong Kong, China have grown more rapidly than exports in the other direction.

Finally, and perhaps of greatest interest, both Southeast Asia and Korea and Mongolia export far more to the PRC and Hong Kong, China than they import from them. Exports of Korea and Mongolia to the PRC and Hong Kong, China have grown only slightly more slowly, but remain much greater, than their imports from the PRC and Hong Kong, China.

The overall trade figures show that the other countries in the region benefited from the dynamism of the PRC and Hong Kong, China to the extent that their trade with them increased rapidly and they are (in aggregate) net exporters to the PRC and Hong Kong, China.

One concern has been that the PRC is becoming an important producer and exporter of a wide range of manufactured goods and that it will displace other economies in the region that are also exporting these goods in global markets. To explore this issue, one should consider changes in the breakdown of trade components between the two periods. Has there been a significant increase in raw and semifinished imports into the PRC from the rest of Asia at the expense of finished goods, particularly manufactures?

Data on the PRC's imports from Asian economies are not readily available, but general information on PRC imports and exports has been compiled by stage of production for the late 1990s.[1] These data show that PRC imports are predominantly intermediate goods (almost two thirds), including parts

---

in 2001. As the world economy recovered, some commodity prices firmed somewhat. Despite the uncertainties associated with the conflict in the Middle East, average oil prices increased by only 2.25% in 2002 compared with the 2001 level. Other commodity prices that are sensitive to increasing uncertainty, such as rare metals, also increased. Overall, prices for manufactured goods remained weak in 2002, but prices for many food and agricultural products, grains in particular, increased significantly for various reasons, including adverse weather conditions (e.g., drought in major wheat-producing countries) and civil disturbances in some commodity-producing countries (e.g., Cote d'Ivoire).

Global Financial Markets

Worldwide equity markets continued to trend downward in 2002. A combination of lower corporate earnings, fallout from accounting irregularities, and concern about geopolitical instability and its impact on petroleum prices were responsible for

and components and semifinished
goods, while exports are predominantly finished goods (also just less
than two thirds). The remainder
of both imports and exports are
mostly final goods, with capital
goods accounting for 20% of final
goods imports and 15% of final
goods exports. Less than 10% of
both the PRC's imports and exports
are primary goods.

Assuming that this overall trade
pattern is typical of the PRC's trade
pattern with its Asian neighbors,
and combining it with the changing
pattern of trade discussed above, it
appears that the bulk of the PRC's
imports from its Asian neighbors
are manufactured inputs while
its exports are weighted toward
finished goods.

Hence, the shift in the balance of
trade is the result of a more rapid
growth in trade of intermediate
parts and components. This is in
keeping with the general pattern
of growth in outsourcing and the
development of global value chains
in electronics, telecommunications,
and other subsectors of manufacturing within East and Southeast
Asia over the past several decades.

[1] Françoise Lemoine and Deniz Unal-
Kesenci. 2002. "China in the International Segmentation of Production
Processes." CEPII Working Paper 2002-
02. March.

Box Figure. Intraregional and Interregional Trade Flows, 1990 and 2001

Source: International Monetary Fund, *Direction of Trade Statistics*, CD-ROM, February 2003.

continued weakness. By the end of the year, the
Nikkei 225 index, the Dow Jones Industrial Average,
and the FTSE All-Share index were down, respectively, by 19%, 17%, and 32%, for the year.

In credit markets, short-term interest rates
remained at historically low levels for the year,
having fallen substantially from the previous year's
level. The yield curve flattened out, reflecting a
continuation of a low inflation environment and
weaker equity markets.

Emerging market sovereign risk spreads

widened slightly in the middle of 2002, and then
narrowed in the second half of the year. By the end
of the year they were very close to their levels of the
end of 2001. Spreads were highest for Latin American countries at over 900 basis points while the
spreads for African, European, and Asian sovereign
risk were 400–500 basis points lower.

During the first 2 months of 2002, the US dollar
strengthened against a trade-weighted basket of
currencies—the Federal Reserve's "broad index".
Subsequently, the dollar weakened as capital inflows

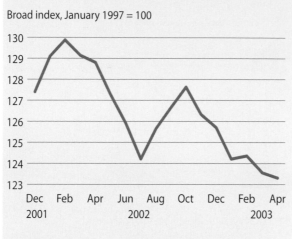

Figure 1.4 The dollar weakened as capital inflows slowed

Broad index, January 1997 = 100

Note: The broad index is a weighted average of the foreign exchange values of the US dollar against currencies of major US trading partners.
Source: www.federalreserve.gov/releases/h10/Summary.

slowed (Figure 1.4). By the end of the year, the dollar had fallen by 2.6% against this broad index. The dollar depreciated by 17.6% against the euro and by 10.2% against the yen in 2002 (Figure 1.5). The dollar's weakness reflected low nominal interest rates on treasury securities relative to those of other OECD countries. It also reflected a reappraisal of investment returns in the US equity market following weak earnings reports and a decline in corporate profits, lower returns on foreign direct investment (FDI), and continued concern following auditing irregularities and the need to finance a growing US current account deficit.

Outlook for Industrial Countries

The growth momentum of the world economy was clearly slowing in the closing months of 2002 and growth is likely to remain subdued during the first half of 2003, and possibly into the third quarter. Nevertheless, barring major catastrophes affecting the world economy, a modest upturn is likely to start in the second half of the year in response to additional policy stimulus in industrial countries, particularly in the US, euro area, and Japan (Table 1.2). Consumption demand has played an important role in the past few years in supporting economic growth in industrial countries, particu-

larly in the US. With the possible exception of the euro area, consumer demand is, however, likely to be weaker during most of 2003 than it was in 2002. The upturn projected in the latter part of 2003 in industrial countries critically relies on an improvement in business investment, which should start contributing positively to growth after 2 years of a negative contribution. The upturn in industrial countries is projected to further strengthen in 2004 as uncertainties in the world economy abate. Hence, GDP growth for industrial countries is forecast at 1.5–1.7% in 2003 and 2.7–2.9% in 2004. This compares with an outcome of 1.4% in 2002.

Baseline Assumptions on External Conditions

Many economic indicators in the US (car, home, and retail sales; business investment on equipment and software; job creation) weakened in the fourth quarter of 2002 and GDP growth dipped to an annual rate of 1.4%. Slow growth is likely to continue at least for the first half of 2003. Prospects for the US economy continue to be affected by the hangover of the investment bubble of the past decade, the estimated $6 trillion decline in household net worth (since early 2000), and concerns about continued increasing unemployment rates. Other uncertainties relate to a possible retrenchment in the housing market and negative wealth effect, the impact of uncertainty related to the conflict in Iraq and its aftermath, and the prospects of a sharply deteriorating fiscal situation over the medium term.

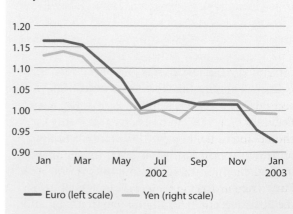

Figure 1.5 The dollar depreciated against the euro and yen in 2002

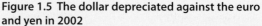

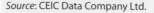

— Euro (left scale)   — Yen (right scale)

Source: CEIC Data Company Ltd.

Table 1.2 GDP Growth, Selected Economies, 2001–2004

	2001	2002	2003	2004
GDP Growth (%)				
Industrial countries	0.8	1.4	1.5–1.7	2.7–2.9
United States	0.3	2.4	2.2–2.4	3.4–3.6
Euro area	1.4	0.8	0.9–1.4	2.4–2.7
Japan	0.4	0.3	0.5–0.7	1.3–1.6
Memorandum Items[a]				
United States Federal Funds rate (%)	3.9	1.7	1.4–1.6	2.8–3.2
Brent crude oil spot prices ($/bbl)	24.4	25.0	25.0–27.0	21.0–23.0
Global trade volume (% change)	0.4	3.0	5.0–6.0	7.0–8.0

Note: Staff projections are based on the Oxford Economic Forecasting World Macroeconomic model.

Sources: US Department of Commerce, Bureau of Economic Analysis, BEA News Releases, available: www.bea.doc.gov/bea/dn/ nipaweb/; Statistics Bureau & Statistics Center of Japan, available: www.esri.cao.go.jp/en/sna/menu.html; Eurostat Euro Indicators, available: www.europa.eu.int/comm/eurostat/; World Bank Development Economics Prospects Group; US Federal Reserve, available: www.federalreserve.gov/releases/n15/data/fedfund.txt.

In March 2003, the Conference Board's Consumer Confidence Index reached its lowest level in nearly a decade. On the positive side, however, corporate profitability appears to be improving as a result of restructuring efforts, substantial improvements in productivity, and tax cuts, thus eventually leading to an anticipated revival in corporate investment. The improvement in corporate balance sheets over the past year has resulted in a reduction in interest rate spreads and the cost of capital for corporate borrowing. Already there are some signs of this improvement—business investment picked up in the fourth quarter of 2002 for the first time in 2 years. A positive factor is productivity growth, which should result in increasing real wages and provide some support for growth in consumption spending in 2003. Hence, a progressive improvement in business investment offsetting somewhat weaker consumption demand is a key element in the improving US outlook in the second half of 2003 and in 2004. The November Federal Funds rate cut of 50 basis points to 1.25% should add to the impact of the cumulative cuts of the past years, further supporting spending and investment. In the baseline scenario, the Federal Funds rate in 2003 is projected somewhat below the 2002 average before rising in 2004 as inflation picks up a little and as the fiscal deficit deteriorates further. US fiscal policy will be expansionary in 2003–2004 as tax cuts are implemented. Finally, a weaker exchange rate for the dollar might provide some stimulus for exports. Generally, US growth in 2003 should be more evenly balanced between consumption and investment growth as nonresidential investment begins to improve after 2 years of decline while private consumption and residential investment moderate somewhat. The baseline growth forecast for the US economy in 2003 is 2.2–2.4%, increasing to a range of 3.4–3.6% in 2004.

The economic performance of the euro area is likely to remain disappointing in 2003 after a particularly poor outcome in 2002. Stock market declines (which have generally surpassed those in the US), high unemployment, weak consumer spending, and more fundamental structural weaknesses will continue to weigh on the euro area economies. In addition, the largest economy, Germany, and the second largest, France, are running up against the EU stability and growth pact limit of 3.0% of GDP on budget deficits, and might have to cut back expenditures in 2003. At the beginning of 2003, many consumer and business indicators, particularly in Germany, continued to show a declining trend pointing toward slow growth in the euro area in the first part of 2003. The European Central Bank is likely to cut interest rates further, following a 0.5% cut in December 2002 and a 0.25% cut in February 2003.

The euro area's growth momentum in 2003 will probably shift from reliance on exports toward final domestic demand. Combined with a more accommodating monetary policy, these developments should enable the euro area to post growth of 0.9–1.4% in 2003, further increasing to 2.4–2.7% in 2004. Similarly, in the UK, despite depressed consumer confidence at the end of 2002 and in the first months of 2003, as well as low investment spending, growth should improve in 2003 as the uncertainties associated with the Iraq conflict abate. It is expected that a supportive policy environment in the UK, both fiscal but mainly monetary (interest rates are expected to be reduced further) should lead to a significant recovery in corporate investment later in the year. GDP growth is thus forecast at 2–2.3% in 2003, further improving to about 3% in 2004.

Growth in the Japanese economy appeared to slow substantially toward the end of 2002. With sluggish growth expected in the US and euro area in the first half of 2003, the Japanese economy will recover only slowly. Deflationary expectations, stagnant nominal wages, and growing unemployment will continue to depress private consumption. Nevertheless, continued expansion in liquidity, supplementary budgetary spending, and further progress in resolving the nonperforming loan issue should allow the economy to post modest GDP growth for 2003 as a whole. Baseline assumptions are for 0.5–0.7% growth in 2003, rising to 1.3–1.6% in 2004.

The Australian and New Zealand economies are likely to continue their robust growth over the next 2 years, albeit at a slower pace than in 2002. In Australia, GDP growth is projected at 3.5% and 3.7% in 2003 and 2004, respectively, compared with 3.8% growth in 2002. Business investment, particularly nonresidential construction investment, will continue expanding rapidly in the next 2 years, while household consumption might slow somewhat. The economic slowdown is partly predicated on the continued impact of the severe drought that affected the economy in 2002.

A more marked slowdown is forecast for New Zealand, with GDP expected to expand by an annual 2.8–3% in 2003–2004 as consumption spending softens substantially and exports grow more slowly. Investment, particularly in 2003, will continue to grow faster than GDP.

Baseline Assumptions on World Trade and Key International Commodity Prices

World trade as measured by export volume rose in 2002, at a rate of 3%, sharply above the rate recorded in 2001. This upward trend is expected to continue in 2003, with growth strengthening in the range of 5–6%. Export volumes of both developed and developing countries are forecast to accelerate somewhat in 2003.

Oil prices, which averaged $25 per barrel (/bbl) in 2002 (Brent Crude Spot price) increased sharply during the first quarter of 2003, averaging $31.40/bbl, due to uncertainties related to conflict in Iraq. The increase occurred in spite of a rise in OPEC production. As the conflict started, oil prices dropped substantially. There remain considerable uncertainties related to developments in the conflict in Iraq, but it appears that major supply disruptions are unlikely. Seasonal demand for oil will also decrease in the second and third quarters of the year, at the same time that supplies from Venezuela are restored. However, commercial oil inventories at the end of the first quarter are at a 10-year low and restocking will be accelerated over the remainder of 2003. Taking all of these factors into account, oil prices are not forecast to increase significantly in 2003 compared with the 2002 average. Although the oil market could remain volatile, prices are projected on average in the range of $25–27/bbl in 2003, and to settle in a range of $21–23/bbl in 2004. The probability of a prolonged higher oil price scenario in the range of $35–40 has significantly decreased over March–April 2003.

Prices of metals and minerals (aluminum, copper, gold) strengthened a little in the closing months of 2002, and this rally continued in the early part of 2003. On average, the prices of nonprecious metals will likely be slightly higher in 2003 than in 2002.

The outlook for agricultural commodity prices is positive. Vegetable oil prices, in particular palm oil, have risen and should remain strong, supported by continued import demand from the PRC. Rice prices (Thai, 5% broken) that averaged $198.80/metric ton in the first 2 months of 2003 are expected to increase by about 5% over the rest of 2003. Grain prices, which increased sharply in 2002, are projected to remain firm in 2003. Between January 2001 and February 2003, cocoa prices more than doubled, due to continued supply disruptions in Cote d'Ivoire; prices will probably remain at current high levels in 2003. Stocks are high for coffee, cotton, and sugar, and so further price increases are unlikely. Overall, food and agricultural prices are expected to continue growing at double-digit rates in 2003 with industrial raw material prices also growing somewhat faster than in 2002, in the range of 4–5%.

Financial Market Developments

Consumer price inflation in OECD countries, estimated at 1.5% in 2002, was at a historically low level. With the strength of the recovery in industrial countries projected to be relatively weak in 2003, inflation is forecast to pick up only slightly in the OECD (to around 2%), in spite of higher oil prices in the first quarter of 2003. In the US, consumer prices rose by 3.0% in February 2003 compared with February 2002, a significant increase caused mainly by higher oil prices. The impact of higher energy prices should, however, weaken in the second and third quarters, in part as a result of lower seasonal energy demand.

Consequently, monetary policies in industrial countries will remain accommodative for most of 2003, with benchmark policy interest rates declining further in the first part of the year, particularly in the euro area. The baseline assumption is therefore for the Federal Funds rate, which averaged 1.7% in 2002, to average 1.4–1.6% in 2003.

Developments in the bond markets closely reflected expectations on monetary policies as well as the overall sentiments of weakness in the global economy. In the US, the yield curve moved down during the second half of 2002. Comparing end-June 2002 yields with those at end-March 2003 (Figure 1.6), the March curve, though still relatively steep, was flatter at the short end and the difference between the two curves was much larger at the long end. For maturities of less than 1 year, the curve dips slightly after June 2002, indicating that markets continue to expect lower rates. However, the upward slope, which is rather steep, indicates that markets expect a significant increase in rates over the medium and longer term.

The euro benchmark yield curve shows an even stronger inverted shape, downward sloping at the short end and upward sloping for maturities beyond 1 year (Figure 1.7). The market expectation is for further rate cuts by the European Central

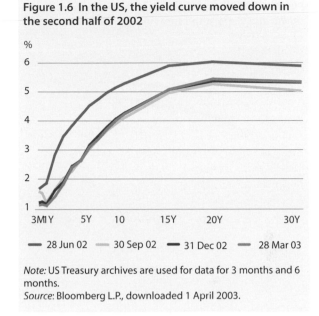

Figure 1.6 In the US, the yield curve moved down in the second half of 2002

Legend: 28 Jun 02 — 30 Sep 02 — 31 Dec 02 — 28 Mar 03

Note: US Treasury archives are used for data for 3 months and 6 months.
Source: Bloomberg L.P., downloaded 1 April 2003.

Bank. Higher yields are, however, contemplated for intermediate and longer maturities.

Over the medium term, the monetary easing might be reversed (hence the steepness of the curves) but the prospects for this appear to have receded, particularly in the US where the whole yield curve has dropped substantially since June 2002. Even with low interest rates, markets seem to expect a slow return to firmer economic growth rates.

In emerging markets, sovereign risk spreads converged in early 2003 as European and African sovereign risk fell toward Asian levels (Figure 1.8). However, the spreads for Asian markets remained somewhat below those of other emerging markets, particularly in Latin America, at the end of 2002. Hence the Asian market remains relatively attractive for investors. In the first months of 2003, substantial uncertainty and volatility continued to dominate financial markets but some improvement is likely as the year progresses.

While the PRC will continue to attract large capital flows, mainly in the form of FDI, capital flows to most other Asian countries should also improve from the 2002 rate (Box 1.3). The Institute of International Finance estimates that net private financial flows to emerging markets in the Asia-Pacific region will increase from $61.8 billion in 2002 to $62.5 billion in 2003. Of that, flows to

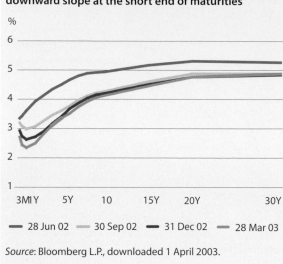

Figure 1.7 The euro benchmark yield curve shows a downward slope at the short end of maturities

— 28 Jun 02 — 30 Sep 02 — 31 Dec 02 — 28 Mar 03

Source: Bloomberg L.P., downloaded 1 April 2003.

Indonesia, Korea, Malaysia, Philippines, and Thailand would total $5.7 billion, up from $2.9 billion in 2002, though this is still well below the total of $17.2 billion recorded in 2000. Official flows are expected to remain negative as repayments exceed new inflows. While investor confidence in the region is likely to improve in 2003–2004, substantial risks still exist and FDI flows in particular will have to be closely monitored.

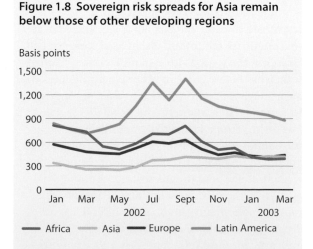

Figure 1.8 Sovereign risk spreads for Asia remain below those of other developing regions

— Africa — Asia — Europe — Latin America

Note: Sovereign risk spreads are yield spreads of sovereign bonds over US treasury bonds.
Source: J. P. Morgan's Emerging Markets Bond Index, available: www.jpmorgan.com.

Developing Asia: Subregional Trends and Prospects

Following an outcome for 2002 which was significantly stronger than expected, growth projections for 2003–2004 show the Asia-Pacific region to continue to expand at a robust rate (Table 1.1). Despite the softness in the world economy expected for the first part of 2003 and uncertainties linked to the conflict in Iraq and the outbreak of the SARS epidemic, aggregate GDP growth of 5.3% for 2003 is only slightly below the projections made in the September 2002 *ADO Update*. The Asia-Pacific region will thus remain a bright spot on the world economic map. There will be diversity, but continued strong domestic demand, sustained export performance partly linked to greater diversification and to dynamism of intraregional trade, as well as a continuing supportive policy environment, in particular fiscal and monetary policies, will be the main driving forces of Asian economic dynamism over the next 2 years. This partly results from the strong fundamentals of the region as shown by the high level of reserves (Box 1.1) and generally low inflation rates. While international reserves are estimated at about $1 trillion at the end of 2002, the aggregate current account surplus for developing Asia is projected at $99 billion for 2003, further adding to the region's remaining reserves. Average inflation for the region is estimated at 2.5% in 2003, about a percentage point higher than in 2002, but still a fairly low average rate. The positive outlook is also predicated on the continuation and often acceleration of major economic reforms in finance, trade, industry, small and medium enterprises, and economic governance in most countries of the region. Governments are also making determined policy efforts to raise productivity and competitiveness of Asian firms.

East Asia

The East Asian subregion posted a solid performance in 2002, with GDP growth averaging 6.5%, though performance varied considerably among countries. The PRC continued its rapid expansion bolstered by strong exports, surging FDI, buoyant domestic demand, and expansionary macroeconomic policies. Korea's brisk recovery was underpinned by both strong external and domestic demand. While exports in the second half of 2002 moderately lifted economic growth in Hong Kong, China and Taipei,China, both economies continued to face weak domestic demand. After 2 years of stagnation, expansion in industry and services and a mild winter saw growth return to Mongolia.

Despite strong overall growth in the subregion, some economies still had to grapple with deflation and high unemployment. Deflation in the PRC occurred because of cheaper imports following WTO accession, productivity growth, and excess capacity. Rising unemployment, intensified competition, and increased economic integration with the PRC caused deflationary pressure in Hong Kong, China and Taipei,China. Falling prices in Hong Kong, China also reflected the post-financial crisis decline in property prices. Weak domestic demand dampened labor market performance in Hong Kong, China while economic restructuring pushed unemployment higher in the PRC. Strong economic growth has helped Korea's unemployment rate decline each year since 1998. Mongolia's official unemployment rate dropped from 4.6% in 2001 to 3.6% in 2002, though incomplete registration may mask the actual figure.

Robust economic growth is likely in 2003–2004 if the global economic environment strengthens, geopolitical stability prevails, and the recent outbreak of SARS is brought under control quickly. Growth is expected to be lower than in 2002, however, averaging 5.6% in 2003 and 6.2% in 2004 (Figure 1.9). In the PRC, rising unemployment, an expanding fiscal deficit, and lagging development in poor interior provinces are likely to constrain expansion. The 2003 outlook for Korea reflects significantly more moderate growth than in 2002, due primarily to the slowdown in consumer credit expansion and a deterioration in investor sentiment stemming from geopolitical uncertainties, including those on the Korean peninsula. While economic performance will improve in Hong Kong, China and Taipei,China in the second half of 2003 and in 2004, domestic recovery will lag behind due to ongoing structural adjustments. In Mongolia, growth is expected to strengthen as mining and labor-intensive industries expand. In contrast, the agriculture sector is likely to struggle.

Consumption growth will vary among economies in East Asia. Consumption in the PRC will

Box 1.3 Shifts in Foreign Direct Investment Flows to Developing Asia

In recent decades, FDI inflows to countries in developing Asia have soared, from $3.7 billion in 1980 to $132.5 billion in 2000. All Asian subregions (except the Pacific) had higher inflows in 2000 than in 1980. However, the distribution of those inflows has changed dramatically, with Southeast Asia's share falling from roughly two thirds of the total to less than one tenth, while East Asia's share (including the PRC) jumped from 26% to 88% (Box Figure). Rough estimates indicate the shift would appear less dramatic, but still substantial, if the "round-tripping" of PRC domestic investments coursed through Hong Kong, China were excluded.

After the Asian financial crisis of 1997–98, absolute gross FDI inflows to East Asia increased substantially until 2000, before declining in 2001, primarily due to reduced flows to Korea and Taipei,China. Inflows to Southeast Asia have generally continued to decline since the crisis.

The lumpiness of investments makes discerning trends over short periods difficult and quantitative data do not necessarily reflect the quality of investments. However, the postcrisis data, together with partial-year data for 2002, suggest that the postcrisis trends of generally rising inflows to East Asia and generally declining inflows to Southeast Asia may continue unless Southeast Asian nations find ways to improve their institutional infrastructure to boost the competitiveness of their firms (see Part 3).

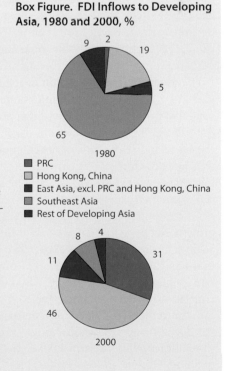

Box Figure. FDI Inflows to Developing Asia, 1980 and 2000, %

1980

2000

- ■ PRC
- ☐ Hong Kong, China
- ■ East Asia, excl. PRC and Hong Kong, China
- ▨ Southeast Asia
- ■ Rest of Developing Asia

expand on the back of continued enthusiasm in the emerging markets for housing and cars. High unemployment will partly offset this expansion, however. Korea's consumption growth is likely to remain firm because of strong real wage growth and low unemployment, although tighter consumer credit and mortgage terms will restrain growth somewhat. High unemployment in Hong Kong, China and Taipei,China will constrain consumer spending there. Additionally in Hong Kong, China, falling property prices and deteriorating household balance sheets will dampen consumption growth. The recent outbreak of SARS will further delay the pace of economic recovery in the first half of 2003.

Private investment will, however, firm up over the next 2 years. In the PRC it is likely to gather momentum as economic reforms continue, rural incomes grow moderately, and substantial FDI inflows continue. Korea's 200 largest corporations plan to increase investment in 2003 as corporate indebtedness declines, and the successful promotion of broadband Internet usage boosts high value-added technology sectors. Investment spending in Hong Kong, China and Taipei,China is expected to rebound moderately, with renewed acquisition of machinery and equipment to boost productive capacity. However, building and construction may decline again in Hong Kong, China, with few new projects planned and a public housing construction cutback.

Trade has increased within East Asia. In particular, the PRC is emerging as one of the largest export markets for the other economies in the subregion. Strong growth in the PRC should, therefore, help exporters in developing Asia to weather slowdowns in other markets, though East Asian export growth will still be affected by economic performance beyond the region. Strong price competitiveness will support PRC export growth, but growth may not match the 2002 level as only modest demand is expected in its biggest markets, the US and Japan. Hong Kong, China and Taipei,China for their part should experience an export-led recovery, fueled by strong growth in the PRC. This will eventually feed into the domestic economies, although ongoing structural adjustments will continue to curb domestic demand. Growth in tourism (and in the services sector in Hong Kong, China) is likely to slow in the subregion as a result of mounting concerns

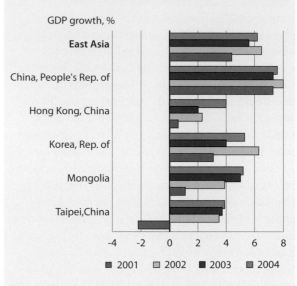

Figure 1.9 East Asia's performance will remain strong

GDP growth, %

Sources: Asian Development Outlook database; staff estimates.

over the emergence of SARS. The impact of a short epidemic of SARS on Hong Kong, China's economy is estimated at about 0.6% of GDP in 2003.

Fiscal expansion has played an important role in stimulating East Asian growth, though concerns about rising deficits and debt are likely to constrain expansion in 2003–2004. In the PRC, there is a growing need to reduce the fiscal deficit and debt as the Government contemplates another huge bank bailout as well as ways to fund its fledgling pension system. Reining in the deficit is the top priority for the authorities in Hong Kong, China. Although legislation in Taipei,China has cleared the way for fiscal expansion if necessary, the authorities remain cautious about implementing such policies. Concerns are also mounting over Mongolia's short- to medium-term debt sustainability. Although structured as long-term debt, repayments are due to start soon. Korea's healthy fiscal position has given the Government leeway to carry out desired spending.

With the exception of Korea and Mongolia, price pressures are likely to remain subdued in East Asia. Monetary policy in most subregional economies is thus expected to remain expansionary, while interest rates in the US, and so in Hong Kong, China, are likely to remain low for most of 2003.

Tackling unemployment has become a major issue for PRC; Hong Kong, China; and

Taipei,China. Unemployment is a particularly pressing problem in the PRC. More workers from state-owned enterprises will be laid off as reforms continue, swelling the ranks of the 8 million new labor-market entrants and rural migrants seeking work each year. These challenges add urgency to the task of fostering the conditions that promote private sector development. Developing an urban social safety net and social security reforms are also needed to ameliorate the social costs of economic reform.

East Asia's growth hinges on global economic recovery and continued robust growth in the PRC. Considerable downside risks are evident in this regard since the global economic recovery remains uncertain. The aftermath of the conflict in Iraq and the potential instability stemming from developments in the Korean peninsula could lead to a significant economic deterioration. All East Asian economies are net oil importers, which makes any significant rise in oil prices harmful to them.

The recent outbreak of SARS has already affected the economy of Hong Kong, China, and, to a lesser extent, those of the PRC and Taipei,China. Any further spread of SARS would pose a serious threat to the subregion's economic outlook. The forecasts are based on the assumption that SARS will be brought under control quickly.

Southeast Asia

The recovery in the economies of Southeast Asia was generally much stronger in 2002 than anticipated earlier in the year. Indeed, GDP growth at 4.1% in 2002 was about 1% above that forecast in *ADO 2002*. Malaysia, Thailand and, to some extent, the Philippines showed a strong recovery in growth in 2002 while Singapore moved out of recession. The economies of Indonesia, Lao PDR, and Viet Nam improved only marginally from the 2001 levels. In contrast, GDP growth fell from 6.3% in 2001 to 4.5% in Cambodia, one of the poorest countries in Southeast Asia.

The recovery in Southeast Asia was the outcome of a combination of factors. Although business investment remained generally depressed due to overcapacity, domestic demand through the subregion, mainly consumption (both private and public), gained strength during the year. At the same time, the subregion experienced a significant improvement in exports, particularly in the second

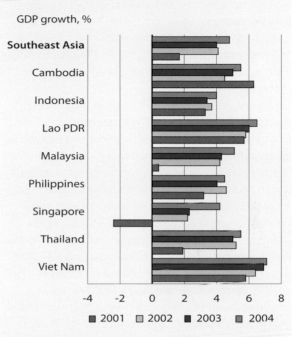

Figure 1.10 Southeast Asia's growth is driven by strong domestic demand

GDP growth, %

Southeast Asia
Cambodia
Indonesia
Lao PDR
Malaysia
Philippines
Singapore
Thailand
Viet Nam

■ 2001   ☐ 2002   ■ 2003   ■ 2004

Sources: Asian Development Outlook database; staff estimates.

half of the year. For many countries, high export growth to the PRC appears to have played an important role in this favorable outturn (Box 1.2). With inflation generally low—except in Indonesia and the Lao PDR—monetary policies remained accommodative while fiscal policies maintained a generally strong expansionary stance.

Given the momentum of strong domestic demand and solid export performance, GDP growth in Southeast Asia is projected at 4.0% in 2003. As the world economy recovers from the uncertainties and weaknesses experienced in 2001–2002, prospects are somewhat better for 2004, with a forecast of 4.8% GDP growth. Still, many countries are expected to grow at a rate well below their potential. This is particularly the case for Indonesia (Figure 1.10).

In most Southeast Asian countries, domestic demand is expected to remain strong in 2003–2004, particularly private and public consumption. In early 2003, consumer expenditure strengthened in several countries, including Singapore, Thailand, and Viet Nam. In Indonesia, Malaysia, and Philippines, consumption growth is, however, expected to decelerate somewhat in 2003 as fiscal policies become less expansionary. With few exceptions, fiscal policy stances will be less expansionary in 2003 because of governments' concerns—to varying degrees—over increasing fiscal deficits in the past few years and rising public debt burdens. In Cambodia, Lao PDR, Malaysia, Philippines, and Viet Nam, fiscal deficits are a particular concern that will be addressed.

In the outlook for 2003–2004, a progressive strengthening of private investment is indicated as capacity utilization rates improve and financial sector reforms are accelerated. The vigorous pursuit of financial sector reforms will be particularly critical in Indonesia, Philippines, and to some extent Thailand. In the subregional economies in transition of Cambodia, Lao PDR, and Viet Nam, the momentum of market-oriented reforms accelerated in 2002 and is expected to continue in 2003–2004, thereby stimulating private sector investment.

Accommodative monetary policies will continue to support resilience of domestic demand. With the exception of Indonesia and the Philippines, nominal interest rates are projected to remain low and in some cases to be reduced further in 2003, before increasing in 2004. In the Philippines, real interest rates will remain high in 2003, further dampening investment prospects. Inflation is projected to remain relatively low in most countries of Southeast Asia, with the exception of Indonesia and the Lao PDR.

A critical factor in the outlook is the continued strength of exports. Despite a softening of growth in industrial economies expected during the first half of 2003, exports are forecast to keep their momentum in 2003–2004, and data in the first months of 2003 appear to confirm this trend. Greater diversification in export production, restructuring of regional manufacturing production, and increases in trade among subregions linked to continued strong domestic demand in the East and Southeast Asian economies are supporting the forecast for sustained export growth. A driving force for the subregion's exports will be the PRC market, which will absorb a rapidly rising share of the subregion's exports (Box 1.2). The governments in virtually all countries in the subregion have been concerned over the past 2 years about a possible loss of competitiveness of their economies (Part 3) and are implementing measures to address this issue. For instance, Singapore strongly supports the

development of biotechnology; Malaysia and Thailand have both initiated national competitiveness programs over the past year; and the Philippines is pursuing a Medium-Term National Action Agenda for Productivity. For the oil exporters of the subregion (Indonesia, Malaysia, and Viet Nam), higher oil prices were a windfall, although countries like Viet Nam, which is a large exporter of rice and tea to Iraq, and countries receiving substantial overseas remittances from workers in the Middle East (the Philippines and Viet Nam) will be adversely affected by the conflict in Iraq.

Imports in Southeast Asia are projected to grow more rapidly in 2003 and 2004 (by 7.8% and 9.6%, respectively), partly due to higher average oil prices in 2003. Overall, as current account surpluses shrink or deficits increase, trade will likely contribute less to GDP in 2003–2004 than in 2002.

In the first few months of 2003, downside risks have significantly increased for many Southeast Asian economies as prospects for industrial countries have weakened for the first half of 2003, thus possibly dampening stronger export prospects. Several of the Southeast Asian economies are vulnerable to volatile oil prices, the loss of export markets in the Middle East, and reduced remittances from overseas workers (see the section *Impact of Conflict in Iraq*, below). Finally, and more importantly, the outbreak of the SARS epidemic might substantially affect tourism and the other services sectors of the subregion if prolonged. Already, it is estimated that SARS will lower GDP growth in Indonesia and Singapore by about half a percent and that of Malaysia by somewhat less.

South Asia

In recent years, South Asia has experienced relatively low growth in per capita income. Relative to its population, the subregion accounts for a very low share of global GDP (less than 3%) and an even lower share of global exports (about 1%). The economies in the subregion are relatively closed on average, with the subregion's ratios of merchandise exports and imports to GDP lower than any other major subregion in the world. Government revenues tend to be low in relation to GDP while expenditures continue to be higher than revenues, resulting in persistent fiscal deficits.

Savings and investment rates vary widely across countries, with gross domestic savings reaching about 46% of GDP in the Maldives and only about 15% in Pakistan. Similarly, gross domestic investment as a share of GDP ranges from under 14% in Pakistan to 48% in Bangladesh. In India, 2002 savings and investment rates were about 24% of GDP—substantial, but less than would contribute to more rapid poverty reduction.

In 2002, South Asia was affected somewhat less than other subregions by global developments due to its relatively low levels of trade and financial integration with the rest of the world. The subregion's export growth rate continued to exceed the import growth rate, further reducing the trade deficit. Domestic factors played a more important role, such as the security situation in Nepal, tensions between India and Pakistan, and progress on peace talks in Sri Lanka. With the relatively high importance of agriculture to GDP and to food security, floods and droughts in different parts of the subregion impacted significantly on economic growth and development.

Growth in GDP for the subregion declined to 4.2% from 5.0% in 2001, instead of increasing as forecast in *ADO 2002*, primarily as a result of adverse weather conditions in Bangladesh, India, and Nepal. In addition, the economies of Bangladesh and Nepal suffered from extremely weak external demand. In contrast, Bhutan, Maldives, Pakistan, and Sri Lanka experienced stronger growth in 2002 compared with the previous year. Strong construction growth in Bhutan, tourism recovery in Maldives, robust consumption in Pakistan, and services recovery in Sri Lanka contributed to dampen the negative effects of insufficient rainfall in other parts of the subregion.

Inflation remained generally mild at 3.0%, as most economies in the subregion adopted macroeconomic policies that kept prices stable. While Sri Lanka still had double-digit inflation in 2002, it was an improvement from the previous year's 12.1%. Export growth in the subregion picked up to 7.0% in 2002 as India's exports recovered, in spite of weak external demand in some major markets. Import growth also recovered to 2.5% on account of India's strong demand.

The medium-term outlook for South Asia is based on an assumed acceleration in global economic growth, improved political stability and security in the countries of the subregion, and normal weather conditions. In this context, growth

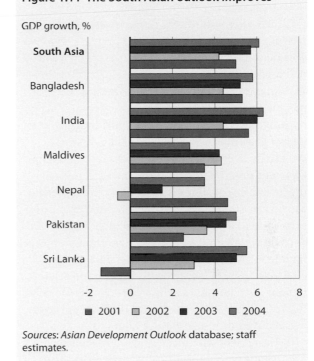

Figure 1.11 The South Asian outlook improves

GDP growth, %

Sources: *Asian Development Outlook* database; staff estimates.

is expected to increase to 5.7% in 2003 and to 6.1% in 2004, led by strong expansion in India which accounts for roughly three fourths of the subregion's economy (Figure 1.11). Growth in Pakistan and Sri Lanka is expected to accelerate substantially, benefiting from continued macroeconomic stability and favorable developments on both supply and demand sides. In addition, domestic demand recovery in Bangladesh, plus continued construction expansion in Bhutan, should contribute to the subregion's growth. Per capita income growth of 4.1% and 4.4% in 2003 and 2004, respectively, will contribute to poverty reduction.

With continued economic liberalization and private sector-led growth, gross domestic investment as a share of GDP is expected to increase in most countries, contributing to rising labor productivity and future growth. With the stronger growth and accommodative monetary policy, prices are expected to rise in South Asia, to 4.9% in 2003 and to 5.0% in 2004, though these rises are still moderate.

Agricultural production, a key for poverty reduction in the subregion, is expected to increase moderately over the medium term on the assumption of less inclement weather. Industrial output and services, which already account for the bulk of value added in South Asian economies, are expected to continue expanding more robustly.

With strengthening recovery in major markets outside the subregion, merchandise export growth will accelerate to double-digit levels in 2003–2004 and exceed import growth, contributing to a narrowing of the subregional trade deficit. This is particularly true for Bangladesh and India, where export growth is projected to surpass import growth by over 3 percentage points in 2003. While there are significant variations across countries, the balance-of-payments surplus on the current account is expected to significantly decline for the subregion as a whole to about $620 million in 2003 and about $130 million in 2004, assuming oil prices remain fairly stable. However, as a percentage of GDP, the aggregate current account is projected to remain near zero in the medium term, as the deficits in Bangladesh, Nepal, and Sri Lanka are offset by surpluses in India and Pakistan.

Fiscal consolidation may again make slow progress because of political uncertainties. The revenue-to-GDP ratio in most countries is expected to moderately rise, but restraint of expenditure is expected to continue to be difficult. Consequently, government share in the economy will increase and fiscal deficits are projected to persist. The external debt service ratio is already high in several South Asian countries, and may increase to the extent that the persistent fiscal deficits are financed from external sources.

The medium-term outlook is subject to several risks. Political uncertainty could affect the scope and pace of economic reforms, and volatile oil prices would adversely affect growth. Remittances from overseas workers could decline substantially as a result of the conflict in Iraq. In addition, growth will remain fragile unless governments pursue fiscal consolidation with determination. Prudent exchange rate management will be necessary to take advantage of the revival in global growth, and enhanced foreign reserve management is becoming increasingly important as the subregion's reserves rise.

Central Asia

Economic growth for 2002 in the six Central Asian republics (CARs) as a group is estimated to be 7.7%, somewhat better than the 5.7% rate forecast in *ADO 2002*. While growth had been expected to moderate from the strong 10.9% expansion in 2001, GDP growth weakened by more than predicted in two countries due to unexpected events—in the Kyrgyz Republic an accident that closed the important Kumtor gold mine, and in Turkmenistan an extremely poor cotton harvest. On the other hand, this was more than offset by faster than expected growth in Azerbaijan, Kazakhstan, and Tajikistan at rates of 9–11%. Growth in Azerbaijan and Kazakhstan continued to be driven by large-scale investments in the oil sector, largely funded by FDI, while in Tajikistan it reflected continued strong post-civil war recovery in aluminum, agriculture, and electricity.

Export gains, at rates of 9–13% in dollar terms, boosted growth in Azerbaijan, Kazakhstan, and Turkmenistan (the large oil/gas producers), and in Tajikistan where the gain in part reflected a bounceback from a sharp drop in 2001.

Unemployment and underemployment were little improved in 2002, even in the fast-growing oil/gas-producing economies, due to the capital-intensive nature of oil and gas development.

As countries in transition to market economies, the CARs have faced—and to varying degrees effectively dealt with—a legacy of issues including large structural and pricing distortions, off-budget spending, and incomplete statistics that make macroeconomic assessment and comparison between countries difficult. However, some broad developments in 2002 can be highlighted.

Progress continued on the inflation front. Monetary policy in Azerbaijan, Kazakhstan, and Kyrgyz Republic maintained relative price stability in 2002, while strong adjustment efforts reduced average inflation in Tajikistan to 14.5% from the very high levels associated with the civil war and its aftermath. In Uzbekistan, monetary policy remains largely oriented to meeting the credit needs of state-owned enterprises and inflation has remained high at about 28%. Policy is similar in Turkmenistan where inflation increased to 8.8%. In both Uzbekistan and Turkmenistan, price structures are heavily affected by state provision of commodities and services, and distorted by the multiple exchange rate regime with highly overvalued fixed official rates. Uzbekistan, however, adjusted the official rate over 2002 to reduce the spread between the official and market rates.

Financial policies kept floating exchange rates in Azerbaijan, Kazakhstan, Kyrgyz Republic, and Tajikistan roughly stable, or marginally depreciating, in real terms. In Azerbaijan and Kazakhstan, accumulation of part of the governments' large oil/gas revenues in oil funds (to be used for economic diversification) led to overall government budget surpluses and aided sterilization efforts to prevent excessive appreciation of the exchange rate that would stunt development in the non-oil sector ("Dutch disease").

Regarding structural reforms, significant actions were taken to improve budget management and transparency in Azerbaijan, Kazakhstan, and Kyrgyz Republic; reduce energy subsidies in Azerbaijan, Kyrgyz Republic, and Tajikistan; and improve the tax system while enhancing incentives in Kazakhstan and Kyrgyz Republic. Action to strengthen bank supervision was taken in Kazakhstan and the Kyrgyz Republic. Deposit mobilization from the private sector improved in Kazakhstan and Tajikistan, but there as elsewhere in the CARs the bulk of deposits remained denominated in foreign exchange. The banking system needs to be strengthened and the public's confidence in it lifted if the low levels of savings and financial intermediation in the system are to be raised.

In April 2002, four of the CARs—Azerbaijan, Kyrgyz Republic, Tajikistan, and Uzbekistan—together with three other low-income Commonwealth of Independent States (CIS) countries joined with bilateral donors, and four international financial institutions—ADB, European Bank for Reconstruction and Development (EBRD), International Bank for Reconstruction and Development (IBRD), and International Monetary Fund (IMF)—to create the CIS-7 Initiative. The Initiative seeks to create a collaborative effort to enhance economic growth and poverty reduction. Azerbaijan unveiled its Program on Poverty Reduction and Economic Development for 2003–2005 in October 2002. Moreover, the Kyrgyz Republic and Tajikistan have developed plans in the context of IMF's Poverty Reduction and Growth Facility, implementing macroeconomic stabilization programs during 2002 and continuing in 2003–2004.

The outlook for the CARs is for a moderate slowing in growth for the subregion as whole to an annual 5.8% in 2003–2004 from 7.7% in 2002 (Figure 1.12). This is because growth in the oil/

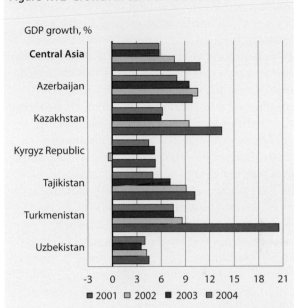

Figure 1.12 Growth in Central Asia slows

GDP growth, %

Sources: Asian Development Outlook database; staff estimates.

gas producers is expected to be somewhat below recent rates, while present policies indicate that the economy of Uzbekistan can be expected to grow by only 3.5–4%, marginally lower than in recent years. The Kyrgyz economy should recover from its 2002 setback and grow at about 5%, while Tajikistan is likely to slow gradually since the recovery phase is now ending and new investment has been small.

The Pacific

After 2 years of stagnation, the Pacific subregion witnessed a subdued recovery in economic growth in 2002 as GDP grew by about 1.0% (Figure 1.13). The recovery reflected the strengthening of international commodity prices, a rise in tourist arrivals, and generally expansionary fiscal policies accompanied by accommodative monetary policies in most countries. As a result, domestic demand strengthened. The external environment also improved slightly with some strengthening of global trade in 2002 compared with the previous year.

Tourists' perceptions of the Pacific as a safe destination due to global and regional security concerns seem to have benefited tourism in the subregion. However, the Pacific is still suffering from the after-effects of ethnic tension that erupted in mid-2000 in the Fiji Islands and Solomon

Islands. Internal problems accompanied by weak macroeconomic management in many countries prevented the Pacific from posting a stronger recovery. With an annual population growth rate of 2.7%, per capita GDP declined in 2002 for the third year in a row. Labor market conditions improved slightly in some countries but unemployment among educated young people remained a concern and continued causing social tensions.

Fiscal outcomes in 2002 were disappointing, particularly among the larger countries. As a result, nearly all the countries are facing fiscal difficulties. In some of them, the situation is approaching crisis proportions. The average inflation rate increased from 6.9% in 2001 to 7.1% in 2002, reflecting a weakening of most Pacific currencies, and higher local food and transport prices in some countries. Despite some rise in most countries, merchandise exports declined by 9.7% for the subregion as a whole, largely reflecting a sharp fall in exports from Papua New Guinea due to declining oil production. Exports also declined in the Cook Islands and Samoa. Imports into the region fell, by 5.8%, reflecting high costs as currencies depreciated in value. The overall current account for the subregion recorded a deficit for the first time since 1997, primarily reflecting a deterioration on the current account in Papua New Guinea. The current account as a share of GDP also worsened in Fiji Islands, Kiribati, and Timor-Leste. The flow of remittances, which is very important for some countries including Samoa and Tonga, remained strong in 2002. In several countries, trust funds suffered capital losses, reflecting weakness in global equity markets.

Medium-term prospects are for a modest rebound in economic performance in the Pacific. Factors contributing to the positive outlook include rising tourist levels, favorable commodity prices, and prospects of a more stable macroeconomy. GDP is forecast to grow at a weighted average rate of 2.4% in 2003, with all countries projected to record growth, except for Timor-Leste where the international presence will continue to wind down. Papua New Guinea and Solomon Islands are expected to emerge from recession and the Fiji Islands is expected to experience much faster growth with a strong boost from tourism. In 2004, the subregion is projected to grow by 2.5%, with all Pacific countries experiencing growth. Inflation is

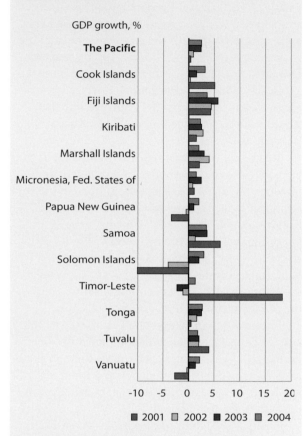

Figure 1.13 Political stability improves the Pacific economic outlook

GDP growth, %

Sources: Asian Development Outlook database; staff estimates.

forecast to decline to 6.3% in 2003, largely reflecting lower inflation in Papua New Guinea and modest or no increases in most other countries. Inflation is projected to decline further in 2004, mainly due to yet slower inflation in Papua New Guinea with expected currency stabilization.

The difficult fiscal situation in 2002 caused many countries to present more responsible budgets for 2003, which were mostly accompanied by frameworks for gradual adjustments toward fiscal consolidation. Accordingly, some progress is projected for an improvement in fiscal balances over the medium term.

Risks to these projections arise from the continuing possibility of sociopolitical instability, weakening of commitment to reforms, adverse commodity price movements, natural disasters, and external shocks. The credibility of fiscal measures and complementary policies announced in budgets for 2003 and their likely success also remain to be seen. Further, with the free-trade Pacific Island Countries Trade Agreement (PICTA) expected to come into force soon, PICTA will likely have an adverse impact on tax revenue of countries relying heavily on trade taxes; it will require them to make necessary adjustments, such as greater reliance on value-added-type taxes and excise taxes. Some countries face very demanding fiscal adjustments in both the medium and longer terms. In some cases, there are good signs that comprehensive economic and public sector reform programs will continue to be developed and implemented, but in other cases weak government commitment or slow progress is likely to continue to be a major constraint in achieving higher standards of living.

Developing Asia: Risks and Uncertainties

Two broad kinds of risk underlie the forecast for the next 2 years. The first set concerns threats to the macroeconomic assumptions underpinning the forecast. The second set is related to geopolitical uncertainties associated with the possibility of terrorism and its impact on tourism, a major source of revenue for the region. Among these risks, the possible consequences of the conflict in Iraq on oil prices, trade, and remittances remain highly uncertain. In addition to these two risks, very recently the outbreak of what could become a major epidemic of SARS in several areas in Asia might have a substantial negative impact on several economies of the region by further discouraging tourism and slowing trade and business activity.

Global Economic Uncertainties
Failure of Global Investment to Revive. Investment in the OECD could remain weak given the weight of low equity prices, geopolitical uncertainties, and higher oil prices. In previous recoveries in the US, for example, equity prices rebounded quite strongly following the end of the recession as measured by the bottom of the trough. In the current recovery, however, this trend has been strongly reversed. Equity prices fell by 19.4% (to 31 March 2003) from the end of the recession (i.e., 31 January 2002). The conflict in Iraq appears to be the main reason for possibly low stock prices in the next year according to a survey of European retail investors conducted

by Gallup and the Swiss bank, UBS. However, investor uncertainty has also increased because of the series of accounting and other examples of corporate malfeasance, as well as concerns about oil prices and the growth potential of industrial countries. Should these developments, plus low capacity utilization and weakening consumption demand, lead the industrial countries to put off capital spending, it would have a depressing effect on economic growth in these countries with knock-on effects for developing Asia.

Deflation. There has been growing concern in several countries about the problem of deflation—a general fall in the price level for some sustained period of time (Box 1.4 discusses additional aspects of deflation). Among industrial countries, Japan has been in such a situation on and off for the past few years and both Hong Kong, China and the PRC have experienced deflationary pressure. There are several possible negative effects of deflation. Some of them are psychological while others have real effects on the economy. From the psychological point of view, if lower prices are anticipated in the future, consumers may hold off consuming until a later date. That will have a depressing effect on aggregate demand and contribute to a possible acceleration in a downward spiral of decreasing prices. In a country with a large debt overhang, deflation increases the cost of servicing as well as the real value of debt. It makes fiscal consolidation difficult and jeopardizes the loan portfolios of the financial system as corporations experience difficulty in servicing debt. The burden of addressing the problem of deflation is complicated when normal policy options such as devaluing the currency, increasing the money supply, lowering interest rates, and undertaking fiscal stimulus are limited. This could occur in circumstances where the banking system is already burdened with a large volume of nonperforming loans, where government deficits and existing debt are already high or legally constrained, and where the exchange rate is fixed.

Rapid Adjustment in the US Current Account Balance and Dollar Exchange Rate. The problem of the so-called "twin deficits" of the US fiscal and current account balances has been cited as a risk in previous *ADO* forecasts as well as by the World Bank, IMF, and others. However, these risks have

Box 1.4 Deflation

Deflation refers to a fall in prices, leading to a negative change in a major price index over a sustained period. Recently, there has been growing concern about deflation in particular countries and the possibility of deflation at the global level. However, the causes and consequences of deflation are not the same everywhere.

At present, economists and policy makers disagree whether or not there is an imminent threat of global deflation, but there is broad agreement that the possibility of deflation should not be dismissed.

Over the past 4 years, the rate of consumer price inflation has averaged a relatively low 2.5% in the US and 2.0% in the euro area, and showed a negative 0.7% in Japan and a negative 0.3% in the PRC. East Asia, taken as a whole, has an inflation rate of just 0.2% for the same period.

Causes and Consequences of Deflation

The nature of deflation depends on its cause, while the consequences and appropriate policy responses depend on its nature and factors influencing the possibility for monetary or fiscal stimuli (Brooks and Quising 2002). A fall in general prices can result from improvements in productivity, changes in

the policy environment, a drop in prices of major inputs, excess capacity, or weak demand. Deflation associated with the first three of these causes is normally benign, since increased aggregate supply due to factors lowering costs of production can be accompanied by strong economic growth.

Deflation may also arise if aggregate demand decreases more rapidly than aggregate supply, such as when consumers reduce their spending because they expect prices to fall or they become more concerned about future economic security. When price declines result from severe contractions in aggregate demand, or from competition in industries with excess capacity from overinvestment, deflation can reinforce the fall in output and demand. Declining prices can then lead to shrinking profit margins, business failures, and resulting unemployment, reducing aggregate demand further.

A country's financial system may fall prey to, and reinforce, damaging effects of deflation. As prices fall, the real value of the currency rises in terms of the amount of goods and services that it can purchase. Consequently, the real value of debt and debt servicing rises. The increased cost to debtors may lead to higher loan default levels, particularly when the share of nonperforming

loans is already high and collateral values fall, threatening financial system soundness and possibly the corporate sector as well.

As uncertainty and expectations of falling prices take hold in this case, even buyers not dependent on credit and investors reduce spending. Unemployment rises, output contracts further, and deflation persists. Faced with greater uncertainty and possible loss of income, some depositors withdraw funds from the banking system, forcing solvent but illiquid banks to fail. The spiral of deflation then continues to depress the economy until measures are undertaken to restore solvency of the banking system and stop price speculation.

Current low levels of inflation (and in cases, deflation) are due to several factors, some country specific and others structural, defining the current global economy.

Current Conditions in the Global Economy and Asia

Although the global economy improved in 2002, return to vigorous global growth will likely be slower than expected earlier. Pressure from excess capacity remains as the output gap is still significant for the Group of Seven industrial economies, exerting downward pressure on prices.

not materialized. In 2002, the value of the dollar fell by 2.6% against a trade-weighted basket of currencies which should, other things equal, result in a tendency for the US current account deficit to narrow. After posting a surplus in the last years of the Clinton administration, the fiscal position of the US has recently deteriorated substantially following the onset of the recession at the end of 2000 and in the early months of 2001, as a result of higher spending following the events of September 11, 2001, and more recently the conflict in Iraq.

Has the twin deficit challenge reemerged as a significant risk? First, the chances of a downward spiraling of the dollar following capital flight are low. This scenario is unlikely because it would create a situation from which none of the major regions of the world economy would benefit, in particular Europe and Japan. Flight from the dollar would require a major reassessment of the risk-return trade off in holding US assets. This appears unlikely, as US assets seem an even stronger safe haven in a period of increasing global

In Japan, financial problems in the banking and corporate sectors and increasing government debt have muted monetary and fiscal policies implemented to stimulate growth and address the problem of deflation. However, political constraints have also limited the Government's ability to deal with deflation.

In the PRC in contrast, the continuous decline of prices is partly due to recent declines in global commodity prices and its growing integration with global markets. However, per capita income continues to rise and the economy continues to grow strongly. In this context, deflation contributes to poverty reduction.

In general, declines in nontraded goods such as housing account for most of the falls in consumer price indices for Hong Kong, China; Singapore; and Taipei,China with negative wealth effects. Further, as private consumption remains weak, profits are squeezed. Unemployment has been relatively high in these countries, reflecting actions taken by firms to support profit margins and this contributes to dampening investment spending.

Policy Responses

Monetary policy effectiveness depends primarily on the current level of interest rates, financial system soundness (particularly the level of nonperforming loans), and corporate and household debt levels. Fiscal policy effectiveness may depend on current levels of public sector debt and deficit.

Where possible, the best response is to try to preempt deflation by cutting interest rates aggressively before inflation and interest rates fall too close to zero. If short-term interest rates are already essentially zero, purchases of securities by the central bank could still lower long-term interest and/or exchange rates, reducing real capital costs for firms to spur investment.

Direct intervention in foreign exchange markets can be undertaken to influence price levels in a country with a floating exchange rate and adequate foreign reserves. A central bank can purchase foreign currencies to raise their values relative to domestic currency and raise domestic prices of imported goods while increasing export price competitiveness. If a country has a fixed exchange rate, monetary policy options to fight deflation are limited since it cannot freely expand the money supply without raising pressure for currency devaluation and disturbing household and business expenditure plans.

Expansionary fiscal policy can be effective in boosting demand to fight deflation if the government's budget deficit and debt load are not high. When debt and deficit levels are high, as in Japan, credible communication of a commitment by the central bank to persist with aggressive quantitative easing may raise expectations and hence demand. So may purchasing domestic or foreign securities. However, restoring sustained economic growth may require further structural reforms in banking and corporate sectors.

In sum, deflation can lead to a downward spiral in output, employment, and demand where normal policy options cannot be effected. This is particularly true when debt levels are already high. It can also be benign and accompanied by strong economic growth. The consequences and policy implications of deflation depend both on its cause and on the policy instruments available.

Sources:
Brooks, D. and P. Quising. 2002. Dangers of Deflation. *ERD Policy Brief Series*, Number 12. Asian Development Bank. Manila; Ha, J. and K. Fan. 2002. One Country, Two Prices? A Study of Deflationary Effect of Price Convergence on Hong Kong. Presented at the 8th Convention of the East Asian Economic Association, Kuala Lumpur, Malaysia, 4–5 November 2002; Schellekens, P. 2002. Deflation in Hong SAR. Presented at the 8th Convention of the East Asian Economic Association, Kuala Lumpur, Malaysia, 4–5 November 2002.

uncertainty, even factoring in the threat of international terrorism. A flight from the dollar would help make US manufacturing more competitive in international markets and that would promote US exports. However, it would have strong negative domestic effects, putting upward pressure on prices and interest rates and possibly discouraging investment. It would also hurt the exports of Japan and the EU and their stock markets, and thus their growth prospects. Developing countries would also be adversely affected. Particularly in Asia, exchange rates of several currencies could come under severe pressure. For these reasons it is unlikely that the required adjustments in external and domestic imbalances in the US will take place sharply.

A more likely outcome is that the recent downward adjustment in equity prices will have a dampening effect on consumption, leading to a greater balance between the forces of investment and consumption sustaining growth. However, if very large unexpected fiscal deficits, partly resulting from tax cuts, add to the already high US federal debt held by the public ($3,711 billion, as of 31 March 2003), upward pressure on interest rates will intensify, possibly affecting a revival in investment and pulling down growth.

Geopolitical Uncertainties

Terrorism and Shortfall in Tourism. As the attack on the Indonesian island of Bali showed, terrorism can have a significant impact on tourism in Asia. For many DMCs, tourism is a major source of external revenue and economic growth. Tourism accounts for about 9% of developing Asia's GDP and 7% of employment (see Box 1.1 "Tourism Trends in Developing Asia", *ADO 2002*). In Southeast Asia, tourism accounts for nearly 11% of GDP (9.9% in Indonesia, 11.5% in Malaysia, 10.8% in Singapore, and 13.0% in Thailand). In South Asia, over 50% of the Maldives' GDP depends on tourism while for the Pacific it averages 22.2% of GDP. Similarly, employment in the tourism industry is sizable in many DMCs.

Terrorist activities could thus significantly impact many economies in the Asia-Pacific region, with GDP, employment, and the balance of payments directly affected. In the case of Indonesia, estimates of the impact of the Bali bombing on the economy range from 0.5% of GDP in 2002 to 0.5–2% of GDP in 2003, depending on the effectiveness of the government response to the security threat and the repercussions on consumer and investment confidence.

Impact of Conflict in Iraq. The conflict could affect DMCs in a number of ways. Certainly, one is the risk of terrorism and its impact as discussed above. In addition, the economic impact could be felt through three other channels: (i) a significant oil price increase; (ii) a fall in overseas worker remittances; and (iii) a sharp fall in export demand from industrial countries, the US in particular, as well as from Middle Eastern countries.

While the Asia-Pacific region includes several oil exporters (Azerbaijan, Indonesia, Kazakhstan, Malaysia, Turkmenistan), most of the DMCs are oil importers—PRC, India, and Korea particularly so. Hence, a significantly higher oil price lasting several quarters would have a substantial direct impact on the DMCs' oil importers, in terms of higher

imports and inflation. For instance, a $2.50 average increase in oil prices would cost Korea—the world's fourth largest importer of oil—over $2 billion a year in higher imports. Model simulations based on the Oxford Economic Forecasting World Macroeconomic model indicate that an oil price increase of about 20% over the 2003 baseline would cost, depending on the economies concerned, 0.2–0.3% in terms of GDP growth in 2003, and 0.3–0.5% GDP growth in 2004, even if prices returned to an average of $26/bbl by 2004. However, while somewhat higher oil prices are already factored into the baseline forecast, it appears that with the conflict unwinding, the oil market situation is such that neither significant supply disturbances nor high oil prices are expected. But high volatility might remain in the oil market.

The conflict might significantly affect the remittances of DMC workers in the Middle East. About half of Pakistan's overseas worker remittances originate in the Middle East, and so does a significant proportion of remittances to Bangladesh and Sri Lanka (India's remittances are more diversified). Remittances from the Middle East to the Philippines are also substantial (about 10% of total remittances, or about $700 million).

The conflict and its aftermath might seriously impact many of the DMCs' economies—the greatest risk appears to be that beyond a certain length of time, it will adversely impact consumer (and mainly investor) confidence in industrial economies, thus further retarding a recovery that by all measures is already anticipated to be weak. Also, the conflict will have a direct impact on the exports of DMCs to the Middle East. Some DMCs depend on the Middle Eastern markets, and on Iraq in particular, for a significant share of their exports. For instance, Iraq alone absorbs about one third of Viet Nam's exports of rice and tea (which are among Viet Nam's leading primary exports).

It is noteworthy that estimates of the impact on the overall balance of payments from the first Gulf crisis (August 1990–February 1991) point to relatively modest losses of 1–2% of GDP for Bangladesh, India, Pakistan, and Philippines; the loss was over 4% for Sri Lanka, resulting from a combination of a fall in tourist arrivals, loss of remittances, and higher oil prices.

Uncertainties Related to SARS

Increasingly, a major risk to economic growth in developing Asia, particularly East and Southeast Asia, relates to the spread of SARS. Already, the epidemic is significantly affecting travel and tourism in several countries of the region, as well as several other services subsectors, such as hotels and restaurants, retail trade, and transport—particularly air transport within the region. While it is too early to evaluate the impact of the epidemic on regional economic activity, since much will depend on how long it lasts, certain economies—PRC; Hong Kong, China; Indonesia; Malaysia; and Singapore—will be affected, even if the impact is of short duration (2–3 months). Hence GDP growth forecasts for these economies for 2003 have already been lowered.

However, if the epidemic is not brought under control by about mid-May, the economic impact on developing Asia will be much broader and deeper, for two main reasons. First, bookings for the major tourism season associated with summer holidays in Europe and elsewhere in the northern hemisphere will be lost. Second, the reduction in business travel and other transport-related cutbacks could start to affect manufacturing export orders, such that the impact of the epidemic would be felt across a broader swathe of the economies affected.

In response to these uncertainties, several governments in Southeast Asia, e.g., those of Singapore and Thailand, are considering support packages for those sectors of their economies most affected by the epidemic.

Overview of Fiscal Policy in Developing Asia

The developing member countries (DMCs) of the Asian Development Bank (ADB) have been confronted by global economic slowdown and weak external demand over the past few years. This has prompted many governments to adopt expansionary monetary and fiscal policies to stimulate economic growth and guard against further downturns. This section reviews recent fiscal policy implemented in DMCs. It shows that substantial variation in economic conditions and performance between subregions and countries has necessitated somewhat different policy frameworks. Where rising public debt burdens have become a cause for concern, efforts are now under way toward fiscal consolidation.

Fiscal Indicators and Postcrisis Policies

The 1997 Asian financial crisis and the subsequent global economic slowdown generally influenced East and Southeast Asian economies more than other subregions in Asia. The crisis directly hit a number of economies. Furthermore, the openness of these two subregions and the importance of the United States (US) as an export market made them especially vulnerable to the weakness of the US economy over the past 2 years. A slowdown in demand for information and communications technology (ICT) products also hurt both subregions' exports due to their heavy reliance on these products.

The crisis and policy responses to it formed a critical watershed for government fiscal positions in East and Southeast Asia, with fiscal balances in Southeast Asia deteriorating more dramatically. Government revenues contracted sharply in some cases. Simultaneously, greater expenditures were needed to support and rehabilitate the banking sector, meet increasing demands for social safety nets, and continue servicing foreign debt. The latter increased substantially in domestic currency terms following severe domestic currency depreciations. In addition, contingent fiscal liabilities became actual liabilities in some cases (Box 1.5).

In East Asia, some economies saw declining fiscal surpluses, while others began to register deficits. Perhaps the most dramatic turnaround occurred in Hong Kong, China. Its budget was mostly in surplus before 1997, but the financial crisis saw a surplus of 6.5% of GDP in 1997 converted into a deficit of 1.8% of GDP in 1998, and an estimated 5.5% of GDP during fiscal year

(FY) 2002, as falling property prices continued to drain government coffers and weak economic conditions exacerbated the revenue shortfall. The fiscal deficit in Taipei,China, after lingering around 1.0% of GDP in the mid-1990s, climbed to 3.0% in 2002. The deficit in the PRC increased from 1.0% of GDP in 1995 to 3.0% in 2002. Korea's budget also dipped into the red from 1997 to 1999 but strong economic growth boosted government revenues and created budget surpluses from 2000 onward.

In Southeast Asia, Indonesia, Malaysia, and Thailand had long been running surpluses before the crisis. In 1994, the Philippines achieved its first fiscal surplus in more than two decades as it adopted more of the conservative fiscal policies pursued by its neighbors. However, all four countries' budgets went into deficit in 1998 and have remained there since. Singapore's moderate deficit in 2001 was the first since 1987 (Appendix Tables A22–A24).

In response to the postcrisis slowdown, governments in East and Southeast Asia also actively implemented expansionary fiscal policies. The PRC and Malaysia have made particular use of fiscal policies as their fixed or de facto fixed exchange rate regimes reduce the scope for monetary policies. Several major stimulus packages covering a wide range of initiatives were implemented to raise government spending and encourage private investment and consumption. Even Singapore, which had traditionally resisted using fiscal policies for short-term demand management, responded to the downturn in 2001 with large fiscal stimulus packages. While these packages injected momentum in these economies, it also accentuated fiscal deficits.

With the exceptions of Malaysia and

Box 1.5 Contingent Liabilities

Contingent liabilities are commitments to take on liabilities in the future if specific unpredictable events occur. They do not involve a current cash flow, but rather an obligation regarding possible future cash flows. Examples of contingent liabilities include unfunded social security programs, government willingness to bail out state enterprises, trade and exchange guarantees, and deposit insurance for the banking system. Contingent liabilities can become real public liabilities in the event of a crisis, and may result in governments facing substantial fiscal costs. Conventional budget balances give broad indications of fiscal conditions, but do not take into account governments' contingent liabilities. As a result, deficit statistics may underestimate potential fiscal burdens.

The danger of contingent liabilities was demonstrated after the Asian financial crisis when private banking liabilities were transferred to public agencies to relieve systemic risk in the banking sector. A large number of bank loans had become nonperforming. Coping with this sudden rise in nonperforming loans (NPLs) has been a slow and difficult process for DMCs. In Indonesia, for example, the Government established the Indonesia Bank of Restructuring Agency (IBRA) in 1998 to manage assets with a face value of about Rp550 trillion. By 2002, the IBRA still retained assets with a face value of Rp475 trillion. In Thailand, the level of NPLs peaked at B2.7 trillion or 47.7% of total loans from financial institutions at the end of May 1999. In April 2001, Thailand established the national Asset Management Corporation (TAMC) to manage the impaired assets of financial institutions and to restructure debt. By the end of 2002, the TAMC had approved a total of 2,090 debtor cases with a book value of B482 billion.

Malaysia's asset management company, Danaharta, acquired its first NPL in September 1998 with a total face value of RM11.14 billion. By 31 December 2002, Danaharta's entire NPL portfolio had a total adjusted loan rights acquired value of RM52.52 billion, 57% of which it expects to recover. In Korea, the Government has spent W156 trillion on cleaning up the financial sector, equivalent to roughly one third of GDP.

The realization of contingent liabilities can create huge fiscal burdens for governments. By taking on contingent liabilities, governments may also make the occurrence of such events more likely (due to "moral hazard"—where excess insurance increases the probability that unfavorable events will occur). Preparations for potential liabilities are fraught with difficulties as the potential magnitude of a contingent liability, as well as the probability of it being realized, is difficult to fully understand and predict. The timing of a liability's realization can be even harder to foresee. Not surprisingly, governments are often underprepared for the realization of contingent expenses. However, precautionary measures can be taken to reduce both the magnitude of contingent liabilities and the likelihood of such events. Policies that ensure an efficient market economy and macroeconomic stability are essential for reducing the probability of contingent liabilities arising in the first place.

Taipei,China, growth in current expenditures has generally outpaced capital expenditures. The rise of current expenditures devoted to welfare and social security spending has been particularly noticeable in several economies since 1997 (Figure 1.14). In the PRC, for example, social security and welfare spending soared from a mere 0.2% of total expenditures in 1996 to 6% in 2002 to stimulate domestic demand and support the economic transition. In part, this has been a response to a significant increase in unemployment as a large number of state-owned enterprises have been driven to the brink of bankruptcy by increased competition. Reforms have also gradually transferred welfare responsibilities from workplaces to the Government. Because of emerging urban poverty, expenditures on the "minimum living allowance" rose 23-fold during 1998–2002 to $554.2 million.

On the revenue side, to revive economic activity in the private sector, governments in East and Southeast Asia implemented tax reductions and tax incentives. Correspondingly, revenue growth was lower in most economies from 1997 to 2001 by a significant amount as economic activity remained subdued in several of these economies. (Revenue growth in the PRC has accelerated due to improved revenue collection since tax reforms in 1994, despite the recent lowering of corporate income tax.) In Hong Kong, China, total real revenues declined sharply by 11.3% annually on

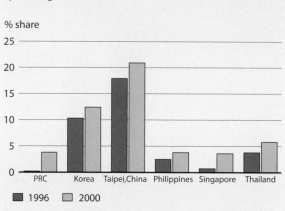

Figure 1.14 The share of social security and welfare spending increased

% share

1996   2000

Note: Data for PRC and Korea are for 1996 and 1999; those for Singapore are for 1998 and 2000.
Sources: ADB Statistical Database System; International Monetary Fund, *Government Finance Statistics Yearbook 2001.*

average from 1997 to 2002, compared with 15.3% average annual growth from 1990 to 1996. This post-1997 decline resulted from heavy reliance on property taxes and the slump in the property market, as well as countercyclical fiscal measures. In Thailand, tax breaks were provided for new businesses, home purchases, and stock exchange listings to stimulate domestic demand. Singapore's 2002 budget proposed reducing corporate and personal income tax rates, enhancing tax incentives for the financial sector, and increasing tax reductions for certain service company research and development expenses. Malaysia reduced personal income tax rates, lowered import duties on some intermediate goods, adjusted investment allowances, and introduced tax holidays. These measures, combined with weak economic growth, saw tax revenues as a share of GDP decrease significantly from 1997 to 2000. The share has increased slightly since 2000, but still remains below precrisis levels.

Most South Asian economies were less affected by the financial crisis. They have maintained moderate growth in the late 1990s, so budgetary pressure from slow growth was not a significant factor affecting their fiscal policies. Furthermore, persistent fiscal deficits have been the norm in South Asia because of weak revenue collection and governments' inability (or reluctance) to cut expenditures. This leaves little room for further fiscal expansion. As a result, most South Asian

governments have not pursued fiscal expansion over the past few years, and their revenues and expenditures as shares of GDP have remained relatively stable. Deteriorating fiscal positions, however, have prompted several governments to undertake moderate fiscal consolidation recently (see the section *Fiscal Consolidation* below). The Sri Lankan Government reduced its deficit from 10.9% to 9.0% of GDP between 2001 and 2002, primarily by cutting expenditures. In Bangladesh, the Government improved revenue collection through a renewed emphasis on administrative initiatives and close monitoring and supervision.

Several Asian transition economies face fundamental structural problems affecting their fiscal situations. Mongolia, Cambodia, and the Lao People's Democratic Republic (Lao PDR) have recorded significant government deficits almost every year during the past decade. Economic transition, and particularly the closing of inefficient state-owned enterprises and the loss of very substantial foreign assistance, has presented Mongolia with many fiscal challenges, while political instability and lackluster economic performance underlie fiscal difficulties in Cambodia and the Lao PDR.

Economic transition has been the dominant factor shaping the fiscal conditions in the Central Asian republics (CARs). The initial stage of economic transition is often accompanied by deteriorating fiscal balances. This occurs because privatization and enterprise restructuring necessitate increased spending on unemployment benefits, pensions, and other forms of welfare. Social security and welfare expenditures make up over 30% of total current spending in some economies. (The profile is similar in Mongolia, where social security and welfare spending accounted for 24.6% of total government spending in 2000.) Meanwhile, revenue collection from state-owned enterprises declines and from the nascent private sector is slow to rise (Figure 1.15).

As a result of the declining revenues and increased spending associated with the transition, large fiscal deficits emerged and persisted in most CARs in the 1990s. However, improved economic conditions and robust growth since 1999 have allowed CARs to reduce their budget deficits and assist economic performance in turn, despite a global slowdown. After undergoing vast difficulties in the initial stages of economic transition, some

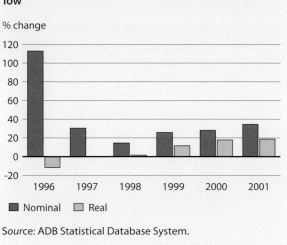

Figure 1.15 Tax revenue collection in Central Asia is low

% change

Source: ADB Statistical Database System.

of the CARs have achieved among the highest growth rates in the world in recent years. Rather than stimulating demand, government expenditures have mainly focused on long-term considerations, such as providing infrastructure. Some CAR economies have also made use of improved economic conditions to reform their fiscal systems and implement fiscal consolidation. Total expenditures as a percentage of GDP are lower now, however, than the very high level of the early 1990s, due to rapid GDP growth.

The most extreme fiscal situations may be found in the Pacific economies, which continue to face narrow economic bases, heavy reliance on aid, vulnerability to external shocks, and difficulties in fiscal and financial management. Some of these economies have also recently suffered from political instability, ethnic tension, and civil disorder. Economic growth remains low in most of them. As a result, many of these economies have persistent fiscal deficits.

Many Pacific economies are characterized by relatively large public sectors, with central government spending accounting for a large share of GDP. This makes the economies highly sensitive to changes in such spending. Domestic revenue generation in many of them remains weak and government expenditures are heavily dependent on external assistance. Heavy dependence on grants reduces the use of fiscal policies for macroeconomic management as government spending hinges on the availability of aid. Volatile fiscal balances have resulted as aid is often not as stable or sustainable as tax revenues.

Economies can suffer severe strain if grants are not forthcoming, as happened in the Marshall Islands where the Government and the economy as a whole were very reliant on provisions for US funding under the Compact of Free Association. The Government borrowed heavily, but public investments failed to deliver expected returns and the public sector became excessively large and inefficient. This, together with the scaling back of grants from the US, led to a major financial crisis in 1996 and 1997, and economic weakness since then. Similarly, with the exception of 2000, growth in the Federated States of Micronesia has been very weak since the mid-1990s following reductions in US funding under the provisions of that country's Compact. The resumption of economic growth since 1999 has been driven by expansionary fiscal policy made possible by revenue "bump-ups" from Compact funds (see the relevant country chapters in Part 2).

Fiscal Challenges Facing Developing Asia

Fiscal deficits financed by increased public borrowing can add to the public debt burden, potentially jeopardizing fiscal sustainability and hindering economic performance. The debt-to-GDP ratio has risen in most DMCs over the past few years. Rapid growth in debt can crowd out private investment and inhibit private consumption, divert resources away from development goals, constrain investment in human development and infrastructure, and create difficulties for the implementation of monetary policies. A high debt-to-GDP ratio also tends to make fiscal policy less effective in stimulating economic growth. Reducing deficits and paying off debt are essential for economic development in economies suffering persistent fiscal deficits and heavy indebtedness.

In most East Asian economies, overall debt-to-GDP ratios are still moderate but have increased significantly in recent years in line with widening or emerging fiscal deficits. In some cases, governments also face increased contingent liabilities. In the PRC, the Government moved to shift the burden of supporting state-owned enterprises to the state-owned banking sector. The potential for accumulating nonperforming loans can threaten fiscal sustainability and hinder macroeconomic stability. A combination of sharp currency depreciation, high real domestic interest rates, lower government revenues, and a drop in exports as a result of the financial crisis caused a steep increase in both the size and burden of external debt repayment in Indonesia, Malaysia, Philippines, and Thailand. Fiscal expansion has further led to increased fiscal deficit and debt accumulation.

Several South Asian economies suffer heavy indebtedness due to persistent fiscal deficits. In India, for example, combined central and local government indebtedness increased to an estimated 72.6% of GDP in 2001. In some economies, access to external finance eased the pressure on domestic credit and reduced the likelihood of deficit financing, thereby reducing the crowding out of private investment. However, excessive reliance on external finance runs the risk of increasing exposure to external shocks.

Strong economic growth has provided public finance relief for the CARs. External public debt declined in line with government intentions to limit borrowing and pay down outstanding external debt. Nevertheless, the CARs still face substantial debt burdens. For example, Tajikistan's public external debt was over 87% of GDP in 2002.

In the Pacific, reining in persistent fiscal deficits and cutting debt remain major challenges. High deficits and debt have threatened fiscal sustainability and triggered macroeconomic instability in several of them. Government debt in the Cook Islands and the Marshall Islands reached unsustainable levels in the mid-1990s, leading to fiscal and economic crises. Nauru has few funding options for its continuing budget deficits; the Government's ability to secure new funds is seriously impaired by the absence of adequate collateral, local liquidity, or future revenue sources. Some Pacific economies now face difficulties paying public sector wage and utility bills.

Mounting debt can spin into a vicious circle (Table 1.3). Rising debt has placed upward pressure on many countries' expenditures because of correspondingly higher debt interest payments, potentially leading to higher debt levels, greater pressure on interest rates, bigger budget deficits, and further increases in debt. Nearly 20% of total revenues were diverted to serve interest payments in Indonesia and the Philippines in 1999. In 2000, over 30%

of current revenues in India and Sri Lanka went to interest payments. Several economies had to reschedule bilateral debt with Paris Club members in December 2001, including Indonesia, Pakistan, and Tajikistan. To reduce debt levels, governments must achieve substantial primary budget surpluses and perhaps sell off some assets.

Increased public spending and rising public debt can restrict the credit available to the private sector, lead to higher interest rates, and crowd out private investment. Simulations using macroeconomic models for some countries indicate that the crowding-out effect has been low in East and Southeast Asia because private investors' demand for credit suffered a severe blow in the aftermath of the financial crisis, and economies in these subregions still have substantial excess capacity. If continued, however, debt accumulation will eventually impede private investment. In South Asia, simulation results suggest that high public spending has led to crowding out. In the Pacific, the public sector is large and absorbs substantial resources, stifling private sector development. Large amounts of grants may also have driven up exchange rates, handicapped export growth, and impaired the ability of domestic products to compete with imports. Rising debt can also constrain monetary policy options as perceptions about the sustainability of public debt affect financial market sentiment and interest rates. Prudent fiscal policy is necessary to ensure monetary policy credibility and avoid overburdening monetary policy with the sole responsibility for maintaining macroeconomic stability.

Fiscal Consolidation

Persistent deficits and debt accumulation may signal structural problems that require government action to carry out fiscal consolidation. Indeed, in response to fiscal imbalances, many DMCs have implemented or are contemplating such moves, and most recent DMC government budget statements vow to bring down deficits.

As economic recovery and growth continue in East and Southeast Asia, attention seems to be shifting from stimulating short-term demand toward fiscal consolidation. The PRC Government introduced measures to keep its budget deficit under control, including reducing tax evasion by

Table 1.3 External Debt, Central Government Debt, and Interest Payments, %

Subregion and Economy	Public and Publicly Guaranteed Long-Term External Debt/GDP		Central Government Debt/GDP		Interest Payments/Current Revenues	
	1996	2000	1996	2000	1996	2000
East Asia						
China, People's Rep. of	14.6	10.6	-	12.7	-	-
Korea	5.2	11.6	8.1	15.0	2.4	-
Mongolia	39.2	87.7	61.8	95.2	3.3	6.1
Southeast Asia						
Indonesia	29.7	48.9	-	88.5	7.1	21.6
Lao PDR	122.0	166.3	-	-	-	-
Malaysia	17.7	24.1	35.3	36.7	11.0	-
Philippines	36.3	43.9	53.2	65.6	18.9	27.7
Singapore	-	-	76.7	87.3	2.9	1.3
Thailand	-	-	3.7	22.8	1.2	7.5
Viet Nam	105.9	40.5	-	-	4.5	3.9
South Asia						
Bangladesh	37.3	32.5	-	40.1	-	15.7
Bhutan	36.8	45.2	-	-	10.0	1.8
India	22.5	19.8	46.8	56.5	32.4	36.4
Maldives	-	33.2	42.1	48.0	6.1	4.4
Nepal	53.4	55.5	65.2	64.5	14.5	12.0
Pakistan	37.3	45.3	-	89.0	34.0	44.5
Sri Lanka	54.2	49.9	92.3	97.1	33.5	33.7
Central Asia						
Azerbaijan	10.3	13.0	-	-	2.6	2.5
Kazakhstan	11.7	21.2	-	21.6	-	11.9
Kyrgyz Republic	42.3	98.1	71.4	114.5	4.3	10.2
Tajikistan	124.6	57.6	-	112.8	-	3.7
The Pacific						
Fiji Islands	7.4	3.9	38.3	-	11.5	-
Papua New Guinea	33.5	43.6	54.9	63.9	15.6	22.3
Vanuatu	19.5	31.4	24.4	32.3	2.5	3.7

- Not available.

Sources: World Bank, *World Development Indicators*, available: http://publications.worldbank.org/WDI, *Global Development Finance*, available: http://publications.worldbank.org/GDF; International Monetary Fund, *International Financial Statistics*, March 2003; Institute of International Finance Inc., available: www.iif.com.

strengthening collection efforts, and tightening auditing procedures for enterprises and high-income groups. Measures have also been taken to improve supervision of extrabudgetary funds and unauthorized spending. The FY2003 budget in Hong Kong, China aims to restore budgetary balance by FY2006. Measures proposed in the new budget include sales of public assets; pay cuts for civil servants; a freeze on new recruits for government positions; and increasing departure, payroll, profit, and property taxes. In Thailand, expenditures on special programs will be reduced. The Government is also considering raising the value-added tax (VAT) rate from 7% to 10%. In order to offset revenue loss from reduced income taxes, Singapore proposes to increase its goods and services tax rate from 3% to 4%. The Malaysian Government intends to balance the government budget by 2005 through containing growth in operating expenditures and scaling back noncore development projects. Indonesia has been progressively lowering fuel subsidies.

Several South Asian governments are also addressing fiscal concerns. India's Task Force on Direct and Indirect Taxes has recommended wide-ranging reforms of tax policy and tax administration, including eliminating a range of tax exemptions, raising the minimum taxable income, and simplifying the tax structure. With combined state deficits roughly equal to the central government deficit, a Medium-Term Fiscal Reform Program for States was also negotiated between the central Government and several state governments. In Pakistan, the Government has drafted a Fiscal Responsibility and Debt Limitation Ordinance, which requires it to eliminate the deficit by end-June 2007 and to lower the outstanding public debt from around the current 90% of GDP to 60% by end-June 2012. Sri Lanka's 2002 budget focused on fiscal consolidation to achieve macroeconomic stabilization. Wide-ranging changes were made to simplify tax administration and widen the tax base. The Government of Nepal approved an Immediate Action Plan in June 2002 to prioritize development expenditures and drop low-priority projects.

With strong economic growth easing the fiscal pressures in the CARs, some of these economies have taken advantage of the situation to implement active measures to strengthen their fiscal position. In 2002, for example, Kazakhstan enacted a new tax code, designed measures to monitor large taxpayers, and introduced an electronic registration system for taxpayers and tax reporting. Improved tax collection and administration helped revenues reach the budget target. The Government of Azerbaijan has taken measures to curtail implicit energy subsidies and enhance the transparency and accountability of its budget management. The Kyrgyz Republic removed many VAT exemptions in 2002, consolidated personal income tax rates, increased retail sales tax rates, raised the nonagricultural land tax and energy tariffs, initiated steps to reform and strengthen the customs administration, and created a special unit to monitor and collect taxes from large taxpayers.

Fiscal consolidation has been a difficult but serious issue in the Pacific. To reduce fiscal defi-

cits and debt, the 2003 budget of the Fiji Islands proposed increasing excise and tariff rates, raising the VAT rate from 10% to 12.5%, and reducing capital expenditures. Following the fiscal crisis of 1996, the Marshall Islands implemented a Public Sector Reform Program, reducing the civil service by about 35% between 1995 and 2000. The Papua New Guinea 2003 budget also signaled measures to help correct the fiscal position, with notably an increase in the company tax rate and an emphasis on improved tax compliance. Some cuts to expenditures were also made.

Samoa announced a raft of taxation changes for FY2003, including increasing VAT, reducing the import tariff on goods, and increasing excise rates and motor vehicle fees. Further efforts were made to corporatize and privatize state-owned enterprises, which have been a drain on public finances. The 2003 budget of the Solomon Islands proposed significant reductions in the government wage bill through civil service retrenchments with redundancy payments financed by donors and making all capital purchases subject to the discipline of the Central Tender Board. Similarly, Tonga's 2003 budget also proposes reducing public sector wages and salaries.

Notwithstanding these efforts, the Pacific economies still require substantial fiscal reforms, made even more pressing by the fact that they tend to rely heavily on trade-related revenues that will likely decline with anticipated tariff reductions. Their public financing also relies heavily on grants, which, together with the low level of private sector development, continues to pose fiscal challenges. The prospects for fiscal sustainability remain fragile while high debt burdens persist.

Fiscal consolidation assists long-term growth since countries with low deficit and debt levels can exercise more options over expenditure priorities, and allocate more resources to productive sectors. However, fiscal tightening may cause output to contract in the short term. European experience during the 1990s, however, suggests fiscal consolidation when there is a large fiscal imbalance and a high level of government debt can lead to higher output growth even in the short run. This is because deficit and debt reduction can lead to lower interest rates and increased private sector confidence, thereby boosting private investment and consumption. Thus, countries suffering from persistent fiscal deficits and high debt may benefit from fiscal consolidation both in the short and long term.

There is no easy way to carry out fiscal consolidation to eliminate fiscal deficits and debt. Several ways are at hand to finance the fiscal deficit, including higher taxation, cutting spending, domestic borrowing, external borrowing, external assistance, selling public assets, or printing money. Each one faces constraints and carries risks. Heavy domestic borrowing can raise real interest rates, reduce the credit available to the private sector, and crowd out private investment. If real interest rates exceed the real growth of public revenues, domestic debt growth can become explosive. Furthermore, domestic financial markets in developing countries are often not developed enough to provide the necessary financing. While external borrowing eases the short-term constraints on capital, increasing foreign indebtedness may result in balance of-payments or currency problems. Although fiscal deficits can be financed by external grants and aid, these sources are not always forthcoming or reliable. Selling public assets is also an unsustainable source of financing. Monetizing fiscal deficits (i.e., printing money) causes inflation and curbs private consumption. When inflation becomes very high, revenues from an inflation tax can fall because of reduced economic activity. Inflationary financing can also create uncertainties, distort prices, and lead to economic inefficiency.

The difficulties associated with financing fiscal deficits provide a strong case for countries to implement prudent fiscal policies. They also indicate that sustainable fiscal consolidation is best achieved through increasing revenues, improving revenue collection, and reducing spending. However, financing through increased taxes and spending cuts has its own problems, and needs to contend with administrative difficulties, economic cost, and political resistance. Despite these difficulties, DMCs with persistent deficits and high debt-to-GDP ratios may need to seriously consider measures to increase revenues and cut spending to bring about sustained improvements in their fiscal positions.

On the revenue side, most DMCs need to improve tax collection, tax administration and compliance, and to reduce tax evasion. DMC tax revenues as a share of GDP tend to be significantly lower than in industrial countries, often making up less than 20% of GDP, compared with more than

30% of GDP in most Organisation for Economic Co-operation and Development countries. The proportion of GDP coming from tax revenues is particularly low in South Asia, averaging about 8% in 2001 (Figure 1.16).

One reason for the low reliance on direct taxation in developing countries is that it is difficult to administer and collect taxes. This is particularly so for income tax. A greater share of national income is derived from agriculture in developing countries than in more developed ones. Without effective taxation of income from land, much of the income derived from the agriculture sector goes untaxed. Similarly, the income of the self-employed and most of the informal urban sector remains untaxed. Furthermore, low literacy rates and poor tax administration also contribute to the ineffectiveness of direct taxation.

The relatively low ratio of tax revenues to GDP in DMCs carries important macroeconomic consequences. A low tax share limits the ability of tax revenues to serve as an automatic stabilizer. Low tax-to-GDP ratios also limit governments' capacity to use countercyclical fiscal policies to stabilize economies. Many DMCs introduced VAT and reduced reliance on trade taxes in the 1980s and 1990s to broaden their tax bases. However, they still tend to have fairly low revenue shares from direct taxes, such as income taxes and corporate taxes, despite often having high top marginal tax rates. In many economies, there is still scope for further widening the tax base by broadening collection.

Figure 1.16 Tax revenue collection has improved in East Asia and Central Asia

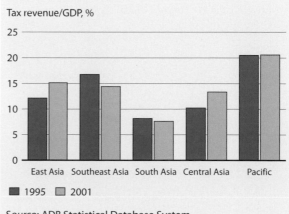

Tax revenue/GDP, %

Source: ADB Statistical Database System.

On the expenditure side, transfers to finance inefficient public enterprise investment or cover their operating losses often drain public finances. Phasing out subsidies or privatization can reduce this. Public consumption, which largely comprises the public sector wage bill, accounts for a large share of total government spending in most DMCs. Streamlining government consumption may offer another option. The budget process in some DMCs is often haphazard, with low computer capacity, and weak public accountability. There are also substantial capacity constraints in the administration of taxes, providing potential for tax evasion and avoidance. Improving budgetary planning, process, and systems offers another avenue to improve fiscal positions.

Concluding Remarks

Fiscal positions vary significantly across countries and subregions. Significant fiscal deficits and accumulation of public debt are relatively new phenomena for most East and Southeast Asian economies. However, expenditure growth outpaced revenue growth throughout the 1990s in many South Asian, CAR, and Pacific economies, leading to persistent budget deficits and high indebtedness. The situation has started to improve in the CARs over the past 2 years as expenditure growth has come more in line with revenue growth, and efforts toward improvement are under way in South Asia and the Pacific.

Fiscal consolidation is essential for reducing public debt, improving operation of monetary and exchange rate policies, and facilitating private sector-led growth. Weak fiscal positions have left little room for further fiscal expansion in most DMCs when faced by economic slowdown. Sustained fiscal deficits and debt accumulation can also hinder growth by generating higher inflation, interest rate hikes, and reductions in private investment and consumption. As economic recovery takes hold in East and Southeast Asia, attention has consequently shifted from stimulating domestic demand to fiscal consolidation. These active efforts, together with economic growth, can potentially resolve fiscal imbalances in these two subregions. Strengthened economic performance has helped the CARs improve their fiscal positions. Tackling persistent and substantial deficits in South Asian and Pacific DMCs depends on sustained commitment to overcome political and economic hurdles.

Compared with monetary policy, which is essentially a tool for short-term demand management, fiscal policy covers a greater number of issues and affects both short- and long-term economic performance. Fiscal policies contribute to long-term economic performance through creating a stable macroeconomic environment, correcting market failures, and providing public goods. Fiscal policies can also promote economic growth by helping mobilize resources, fostering capital formation, developing technology, building infrastructure, and developing human capital. Sound fiscal policies and robust economic performance go hand in hand. Prudent fiscal policies can help achieve sound economic performance and allow governments more leeway to exercise demand management and weather unfavorable international conditions. In turn, sound economic performance and buoyant long-term economic growth relieve many fiscal problems. These relationships mean that fiscal policy needs to be considered within a broad economic framework.

ASIAN DEVELOPMENT
Outlook
2003

Part 2 Economic Trends and Prospects in Developing Asia

ASIAN DEVELOPMENT
Outlook
2003

Economic Trends and Prospects in Developing Asia

East Asia
People's Republic of China
Hong Kong, China
Republic of Korea
Mongolia
Taipei,China

People's Republic of China

With a strong performance in the trade sector after World Trade Organization accession, record inflows of foreign direct investment, and large fixed investment, the country continued its rapid economic expansion in 2002, recording one of its fastest rates in 5 years. Strong economic performance is expected to continue, though growth will slow slightly in 2003–2004. However, many challenges remain, including slow growth in rural incomes, the need to create jobs and an enabling environment for the private sector, growing disparities between the coastal and interior provinces, and financial sector weaknesses.

Macroeconomic Assessment

GDP growth in the People's Republic of China (PRC) accelerated to 8.0% in 2002 from 7.3% in 2001, moving higher than the 7.8% average of the previous 5 years. This higher than expected figure resulted from exports performing better than anticipated, surging foreign direct investment (FDI), and buoyant domestic demand. Expansionary fiscal and monetary policies also played a role.

Industry (including construction) was the key engine of economic growth, with value added accelerating to 9.9% in 2002 from 8.7% in 2001. Electronic equipment, transportation equipment, and chemical products all did well. A surge in FDI and export growth resulted in the value added of foreign-funded enterprises increasing by 13.3%. Supported mainly by growth in transportation, telecommunications, and real estate, the services sector expanded by 7.3% in 2002 (though because of weaknesses in the statistical system, growth in this sector is probably underestimated). Despite a spring drought, agriculture sector performance improved slightly compared with the previous 2 years. Grain output, which dropped by 2.1% in 2001, rose by 1%.

A surge in fixed asset investment, which grew by 16.1%, stimulated domestic demand (Figure 2.1). Private investment rose by 15.7% in the year, faster than in 2001. Across sectors, investment in real estate was particularly strong, registering a 21.9% increase in 2002, as housing reforms and more housing mortgage loans led to a buoyant property market. Supported by the Government's western region development strategy, investment in that region grew by 20.6%, faster than in the central (20.0%) and eastern (16.2%) regions.

Domestic consumption strengthened by 8.8%. The steady growth in domestic spending was mainly driven by urban households, which spent 10% more than in the previous year. Rural residents' spending registered a 6.8% increase, reflecting the continued widening of urban-rural income disparities. Per capita urban disposable income grew by 13.4% in real terms to exceed CNY7,700 ($928), while per capita real rural cash income increased by only 4.8% to reach CNY2,476 ($298). The rapid increase in urban incomes triggered a purchasing boom for private cars, telecommunications equipment, and houses. In 2002, car imports increased by 77% and sales of telecommunications equipment and houses grew by 69% and 39%, respectively.

As economic restructuring continued, employment in the state-owned sector and urban collectives continued decreasing. The number of employees in the state-owned sector fell by 4.6 million in 2001 and by the end of 2002 had fallen by a further 4.8 million. Excluding smaller private and informal sector activities, employment in the nonstate-owned sector increased by

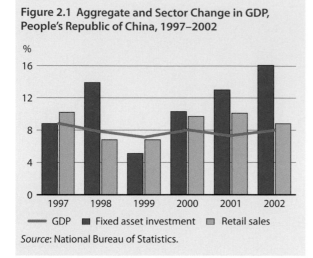

Figure 2.1 Aggregate and Sector Change in GDP, People's Republic of China, 1997–2002

Source: National Bureau of Statistics.

3.0 million in 2002. Based on official statistics, which underestimate the problem, the urban registered unemployment rate rose from 3.6% in 2001 to 4.0% in 2002. If workers at state-owned enterprises (SOEs) who had not been reemployed were included, the adjusted unemployment rate would have been more than 7%. The development of an urban social safety net and reform of social security are needed to ameliorate the social costs of the economic reform program.

The Government maintained an expansionary fiscal policy in 2002 to support economic growth. The 2002 fiscal deficit is CNY310 billion, or equivalent to 3.0% of GDP, and 0.4 percentage points higher than recorded in the previous year. However, these official figures do not reflect the true fiscal position. If the Government's social security obligations and the costs associated with the nonperforming loans (NPLs) of the four state-owned commercial banks (SOCBs) were included, the fiscal deficit would be much higher.

Total fiscal revenues grew by 15.4% while expenditures increased by 16.4% in 2002. The slower increase in revenues from the 22.3% surge in 2001 resulted from lower corporate income tax and a substantial decline in tariff revenues and stamp duty. Tariff revenues fell in 2002 due to reductions in tariffs after World Trade Organization (WTO) accession. The rise in government spending resulted mainly from expenditures on capital construction, pension and social security funds, and government administration. Because of emerging urban poverty,

expenditures on the "minimum living allowance" have risen 23-fold from CNY0.2 billion in 1998 to CNY4.6 billion in 2002. Central government expenditures on social security have increased from 1% of total budget expenditures in 1997 to 6% in 2002.

Because of the slowing revenues and rising expenditures, the Government took several measures to keep the budget deficit within target. These included reducing tax evasion by strengthening collection efforts and ensuring stricter compliance with audits of firms, foreign-funded enterprises, and high-income groups. On the expenditure side, measures focused on tightening supervision of extrabudgetary funds and unauthorized spending.

As a consequence of banking reform and strengthening financial risk control, banking credit grew moderately in 2002. Outstanding loans rose by 15.4% while outstanding deposits increased by 18.1%. To boost domestic demand, the People's Bank of China (PBC), the central bank, cut interest rates in February. The 1-year lending rate was lowered by 0.5 percentage points to 5.3%, in the first reduction since mid-1999.

Concerned about financial risks, SOCBs preferred to place funds in deposits at PBC or buy treasury bonds, rather than extend credit to the corporate sector. Broad money (M2) growth accelerated to 16.8% in 2002, from 14.4% in 2001. Due to its robust economic growth and strong balance-of-payments position, the Government maintained a stable exchange rate, allowing the currency to fluctuate in a narrow band of around CNY8.3 to the dollar.

Stock market indices increased slightly in the first half of the year and then fell in the second. As of 31 December 2002, the Shanghai and Shenzhen A-share indices gained only 0.2% and 4.8%, respectively, from their lows in 2002. The main reasons for the market weakness include poor corporate performance and a crackdown on market irregularities.

Consumer prices continued to decline in 2002. The consumer price index (CPI) was on average 0.8% lower in 2002 than in 2001, and its fall reflects three main factors: (i) as a result of tariff reductions and quota cancellations, cheaper imported products entered the domestic market, intensifying downward pressure on domestic prices; (ii) productivity in the industry sector has been improving, with statistics showing that the PRC's productivity grew

Table 2.1 Major Economic Indicators, People's Republic of China, 2000–2004, %

Item	2000	2001	2002	2003	2004
GDP growth	8.0	7.3	8.0	7.3	7.6
Gross domestic investment/GDP	37.1	38.6	38.5	38.2	38.5
Gross domestic savings/GDP	38.0	38.6	38.7	38.2	38.6
Inflation rate (consumer price index)	0.4	0.7	-0.8	0.5	1.0
Money supply (M2) growth	12.3	14.4	16.8	15.5	16.0
Fiscal balance[a]/GDP	-2.8	-2.6	-3.0	-2.8	-2.6
Merchandise export growth	27.9	6.8	22.3	10.0	12.0
Merchandise import growth	35.2	8.1	21.0	12.0	14.0
Current account balance/GDP	1.9	1.5	1.9	1.6	1.5

[a] Central and local government finance.

Sources: National Bureau of Statistics; International Monetary Fund; staff estimates.

by 6.9% annually in 1996–2001; and (iii) the relative excess supply of agricultural products.

Exports grew by 22.3% in 2002, rebounding from a disappointing performance (6.8% growth) in 2001 as more opening of the trade sector after WTO accession brought a significant increase in FDI, and a weaker dollar improved international competitiveness. A shift in exports toward high-tech products was also noticeable. The country's agricultural products achieved a trade surplus with double-digit export growth, contrary to expectations of the impact of WTO on the sector. Industrial exports of textiles, garments, and mechanical and electronic telecommunications equipment all grew rapidly. Automobile imports did not grow as rapidly as had been expected, while surging iron, steel, and fertilizer imports put pressure on domestic enterprises.

Contracted FDI grew by 19.6% to $82.8 billion, and actual FDI increased by 12.5% to $52.7 billion. In tandem with strong FDI inflows, imports rose significantly by an estimated 21.0% in 2002, compared with an 8.1% rise in 2001. As a result, the trade surplus reached an estimated $44.6 billion, equivalent to 4.0% of GDP.

With the FDI inflows and large trade surplus, foreign exchange reserves reached a record high of $286.4 billion by the end of 2002, up from $212.2 billion in 2001. Total external debt amounted to $169.1 billion by end-June 2002. Short-term debt accounted for 31% of total debt and the debt service ratio was comfortable at 7.3%.

Policy Developments

Fiscal policy has played a key role in stimulating the PRC's economic growth over the past 5 years. The Ministry of Finance estimated that four consecutive fiscal stimulus packages contributed 1.5, 2.0, 1.7, and 1.8 percentage points to GDP growth in the years 1998–2001, respectively. The Government issued CNY150 billion ($18.1 billion) in special bonds to finance the public deficit in 2002. These bonds were mainly used to finance public sector projects under construction, development projects in the western region, technological upgrading of key enterprises, projects to divert water from the south to the north, and rural infrastructure.

To promote the development of an integrated national market and fair competition between enterprises in different regions, the Government changed the methodology of income tax sharing between the central and local governments. From 1 January 2002, corporate income tax revenues were no longer divided according to the jurisdiction of the enterprise. Except for several special industries, most of the corporate income tax and all personal income tax revenue were shared between the central and local authorities at a fixed ratio. The central Government used the income tax increase resulting from the reform for transfer payments from the central budget to local authorities, especially those in the central and western regions. Government procurement procedures were also strengthened.

With WTO accession, the Government accelerated the pace of reforming the domestic economy. A series of adjustments in fiscal and tax policies was made in the first year after WTO accession including: (i) reducing tariffs on more than 5,300 commodities, resulting in the general tariff level dropping from 15.3% to 12.0% (and further to 11.0% in early 2003); (ii) eliminating different treatments between domestic and foreign enterprises, such as unifying accounting standards, by applying the same tax rate reduction on investment in encouraged sectors and in the western region; and (iii) raising the export rebate rates on cotton, rice, wheat, and corn exports from 5% to 13%.

On the monetary front, the Government adopted several measures to stimulate domestic demand and took substantial steps to fulfill its WTO commitments. Concerned that the decline in SOCB lending could aggravate deflationary pressure, PBC adopted the following measures: (i) it cut the 1-year lending rate by 0.5 percentage point to 5.3% in February; (ii) it raised the target growth rate for M2 from 13% to 14% in May; and (iii) it issued a directive in mid-2002 urging SOCBs to increase lending to consumers and small and medium enterprises (SMEs).

To strengthen financial support to SMEs, the Government passed the ADB-supported Law on the Promotion of Small and Medium-Sized Enterprises. The Law includes provision for an SME development fund, the regulations for which are being written. In October, PBC released a set of trial regulations governing automobile financing for both foreign and domestic nonbanking financial institutions. To fulfill its WTO commitments, the Government allowed foreign-funded financial institutions to conduct local currency business in five more cities. Previously, the Government had removed restrictions on the foreign exchange clients of foreign banks and allowed them to conduct local currency business in Shanghai, Shenzhen, Tianjin, and Dalian.

Facing growing competition from foreign-funded financial institutions, the domestic banking system accelerated its pace of reform. The first step was to disclose the financial position of commercial banks requested by PBC in May 2002. All commercial banks must make their annual reports available no later than 1 April each year. The reports should provide key figures, such as the capital-adequacy ratio, asset quality, and amount of profit or loss.

The NPL ratio in the SOCBs stood at 23.4% by the end of June 2002 compared with 25.4% at the end of 2001. The goal of the four banks is to reduce their NPL ratios to less than 15% by end-2004. Four asset management companies have disposed of NPLs and initiated corporate restructuring. By the end of June 2002, the general recovery ratio of the four companies reached 21.6%. At the end of 2002, the financial authority approved the first two joint-venture asset management companies to bring foreign capital and expertise into the domestic nonperforming asset market.

Apart from the policy changes in the fiscal and monetary sector, the PRC made progress in many other sectors toward meeting its WTO obligations in 2002 (Box 2.1).

In another area of domestic economic reform, the Government moved to reform monopoly industries. In May 2002, China Telecom was split into two and a number of telecom operators began to compete with one another. In October 2002, the

---

Box 2.1 One Year After World Trade Organization Accession

Assessments of the PRC's compliance with its WTO obligations in the first year are generally positive.

Progress has been made in (i) reducing import tariffs from an average of 15.3% to 11.0% by early 2003; (ii) modifying laws and regulations to make them WTO-compliant (2,300 amended, 830 abolished, 325 to be enacted); (iii) improving the legal/regulatory framework to protect intellectual property rights; (iv) easing restrictions on foreign investment (e.g., telecommunications, insurance); (v) allowing qualified foreign institutional investors to participate in the domestic stock market; and (vi) removing some restrictions on foreign banks.

Despite these achievements, many challenges need to be overcome, including a lack of transparency, a lack of independent regulators, and inadequate enforcement and regulations. In addition, concerns have been voiced over the capital registration requirements for banks and securities firms, as well as the food products regulations (e.g., sanitary and phytosanitary standards, and genetically modified grains and oil seeds).

aviation industry finished regrouping with six major groups becoming independent enterprises. Corporate governance reforms also gained momentum. The China Securities Regulatory Commission (CSRC) and the State Economic and Trade Commission implemented corporate governance inspections on listed companies, with a special focus on the behavior of state-owned controlling shareholders. The CSRC set up a committee to check irregularities in the reorganization of listed companies involving substantial acquisition, sale, and swap of assets. To strengthen the legal framework needed for SOE reform, a new draft of the bankruptcy law clarifies and streamlines bankruptcy procedures for state-owned and private enterprises.

As part of the SOE reforms, the Government made legal provision for more foreign ownership of SOEs in 2002. Work began on drafting the merger and acquisition regulations that are expected to be adopted in 2003. To comply with the PRC's commitments to WTO, a new FDI guidance catalogue puts FDI into four major categories: encouraged, permitted, restricted, and prohibited. According to the catalogue, more industries are open to foreign investors. The CSRC also released rules that allow the establishment of fund management joint ventures if the foreign companies investing in PRC fund management companies have actual paid-in capital of at least CNY300 million and fall under the Government's definition of a financial institution. The CSRC reiterated that foreign shareholders in fund management companies could hold no more than a 33% stake within 3 years of the PRC's entry into WTO, and not more than 49% after that period.

There was substantial progress in promoting regional cooperation with the PRC's neighbors. In November 2001, the Association of Southeast Asian Nations (ASEAN) and the PRC agreed to establish the world's largest free trade area with 1.7 billion people and $2 trillion in GDP. The Framework Agreement was signed in November 2002 to establish the free trade area by 2010. The PRC granted most favored nation status and will also consider debt relief to less developed non-WTO member countries such as Cambodia, Lao People's Democratic Republic, and Viet Nam.

The Declaration on the Conduct of Parties in the South China Sea and the Facilitation of Cross-Border Transport of Goods and People in the Greater Mekong Subregion were signed in 2002.

The Government adopted the Joint Declaration of ASEAN and PRC on Cooperation in the Field of Non-Traditional Security Issues and initiated a feasibility study on a free trade area among ASEAN members, plus Japan, Republic of Korea, and PRC.

According to an assessment by the ADB Institute, the PRC's economic development and membership of WTO will present many opportunities for East and Southeast Asia. The PRC will be those subregions' largest trading partner in the long term. While the country will be developing Asia's largest exporter by 2010, it will become the largest importer 5 years earlier, by 2005. The PRC is likely to develop, by 2020, a structural trade surplus with Organisation for Economic Co-operation and Development (OECD) countries and a trade deficit of about the same magnitude with East and Southeast Asia. The spillover effects from the PRC's growth and trade expansion will outweigh trade diversion effects on East and Southeast Asia.

The accuracy of PRC statistics has sometimes been questioned. The traditional comprehensive statistical reporting system is not suited to a market economy, and the Government is trying to establish a new statistical survey system. To improve statistical accuracy, the Government agreed to participate in the General Data Dissemination System of the International Monetary Fund (IMF) in April 2002. ADB, together with other international institutions (e.g., IMF, World Bank, OECD, and the Canadian International Development Agency), is assisting in strengthening the PRC's statistical capacity.

Outlook for 2003–2004

The economy will face downward pressure over the next 2 years. With a less expansionary fiscal policy, low growth in the rural sector, and the impact of severe acute respiratory syndrome (SARS), economic growth is forecast at 7.3% for 2003.

After record trade levels and government spending in 2002, exports and investment growth will slow in 2003. First, exports will not match 2002's rate of expansion as growth in import demand in its biggest markets, the US and Japan, is expected to be modest and growth of imports will exceed that of exports, resulting in a smaller trade surplus. Second, the Government's growing budget deficit will limit the continued use of fiscal stimulus packages. Worries about rising debt are expected to

Box 2.2 The Reform Agenda and New Leadership

The 16th Congress of the Communist Party of China in November 2002 and the March 2003 National People's Congress saw both continuity and change. The reins of power passed smoothly to a new generation of leaders who are experienced and well educated. Policy continuity is expected. The new Government's overriding goal is to maintain steady and rapid economic growth to improve living standards, and intends to achieve this through strategic economic restructuring and continued opening up to the outside world.

The 16th Congress set a target of quadrupling 2000 GDP by 2020. This would require GDP growth of 7.2% annually for the next two decades, and make the PRC the world's third largest economy by 2020, with per capita GDP of about $3,000. The keynote speech by the outgoing Party General Secretary, Jiang Zemin, outlined the Party's economic development and reform agenda to achieve this. Measures include: improving the market economy; accelerating modernization; sustained, rapid, and sound economic development; and steadily raising people's living standards. The agenda suggests that the growth target will be achieved through various measures.

The **macroeconomic management** framework has expanded from solely emphasizing GDP growth to including four targets: reduced unemployment; sustainable economic growth; stable prices; and a favorable balance of payments.

Job creation is particularly emphasized. The Party promises to do "everything possible to create more jobs and introduce flexible forms of employment and encourage people to find jobs on their own or become self-employed." Efforts will also be made to improve basic old-age pensions, medical and unemployment insurance, and subsistence allowances for urban residents.

The agenda encourages **private sector promotion** by setting a level playing field, and providing legal protection for private income and property. **State-owned enterprise reform** will separate government from firm management; strengthen state asset management and corporate governance; and encourage multiple shareholdings and company investment abroad. There will be a renewed focus on **industry reform**, particularly in power and telecommunications. Instead of continuing to focus on self-sufficiency, **agricultural reform** will allow and encourage farmers to switch emphasis from grain to more value-added crops such as fruits, vegetables, and flowers. The sale of land-use rights will allow increased economies of scale. Given the existence of an estimated 150 million underemployed in rural areas, rural residents will be allowed to leave the agriculture sector, assisted by **accelerating urbanization**.

Legal reform provisions will encourage courts and prosecutors to operate independently and impartially and improve enforcement of legal judgments. **Anticorruption**

initiatives require prominent officials to exercise power correctly, and crack down on all forms of corruption. Mr. Jiang's speech promises that corruption will be severely dealt with.

The growth target set by the 16th Congress faces a number of economic hurdles. Three were especially identified by the new Government: unemployment and the social security system; fiscal issues; and improperly functioning markets. Corruption, growing income disparities, and major problems in the financial sector also pose major challenges. Further economic reform and development will involve some uncomfortable choices, but the new leaders remain committed to this path. Within the reform agenda, priority will be given to the rural economy; state-owned enterprises; reform of the financial system; and government agency reform.

Some government reorganization has already been carried out to promote deregulation and competition consistent with a market economy and WTO requirements. Some existing government bodies have been merged and restructured, and several new bodies established, including the State Development and Reform Commission, State Asset Management Commission, China Regulatory Banking Commission, Ministry of Commerce, State Power Regulatory Commission, State Food and Drug Administration, and State Population and Family Planning Commission.

constrain government bond sales to finance more infrastructure and construction projects. There is a growing need to reduce debts in other sectors of the economy as the Government contemplates another huge bank bailout and ways to fund its fledging

pension system. As the effectiveness of fiscal stimulus tapers off in 2003, growth of investment in fixed assets will rely more heavily on the private sector and FDI.

Although consumption will be robust, the

consumption pattern may change with more money being spent on housing, cars, and tourism. However, services will suffer from the spread of SARS. Due to large excess capacity in many industries and cheap imports related to WTO trade liberalization, deflationary pressure will remain in 2003. CPI inflation is forecast at 0.5%. Substantial FDI inflows will partly offset the decline in the current account surplus resulting from the deteriorating trade balance. The current account surplus will be 1.6% of GDP in 2003.

If the world economy experiences a modest recovery, domestic private sector investment gathers momentum, and rural incomes rise moderately, then the economy will maintain its high growth in 2004, projected at 7.6%. With the deepening of economic reforms and industrial restructuring, excess capacity and supply should be gradually absorbed or transferred to emerging industries or sectors. Inflation will likely be moderate at 1.0%. The current account is forecast at 1.5% of GDP.

Although the 16th National Congress of the Communist Party of China outlined the Government's ambitious agenda for economic development and reform in the next two decades, such as quadrupling GDP by 2020 (Box 2.2), there are several important issues that could adversely affect economic prospects in the short and medium term.

In the next 5 years or so, the most important challenge for the PRC's policy makers is job creation, because, as the country continues its economic restructuring and reform of SOEs, more workers will be laid off. These workers will join about 8 million new labor market entrants and rural migrants in their search for jobs each year. It will not be possible for the country to reduce poverty and maintain social stability unless economic growth becomes more employment intensive, implying that the economy will need to shift from resource-extensive to labor-intensive growth.

The private sector is playing the key role in job creation, generating almost all new jobs between 1996 and 2002. To create a better enabling environment for the private sector, the Government needs to emphasize improving the legal framework and judicial system; honoring contracts; eliminating fake products and protecting intellectual property rights; converting legitimate fees and charges into taxes and abolishing illegal and arbitrary fees; reducing

administrative bureaucracy; removing local protectionism, barriers to interprovincial trade, and other factors preventing fair competition; and setting better accounting and auditing standards and improving disclosure and enforcement.

Income inequality within regions, the gap between rural and urban areas, as well as disparities between the eastern region and western region (where most of the poor live) have all widened. Addressing the issues of poverty and inequality is essential to maintain broad-based public support for the country's reform program. More jobs need to be created for the poor and economic growth promoted in rural areas and in the interior provinces. This calls for strengthening policies and institutions, developing infrastructure, addressing land degradation, and supporting human resources development. Other measures required include strengthening social safety nets and the social security system, initially in urban areas and gradually in rural areas; improving poverty reduction programs with better targeting; encouraging poor people to participate in decisions that affect them; and undertaking pro-poor fiscal reform, particularly at the provincial and subprovincial levels.

Although the economic growth rate has been impressive, the efficiency of resource use can still be improved. The financial sector does not allocate capital efficiently. A large volume of NPLs and a poorly performing banking system have hindered the development of an efficient nationwide financial system and imposed large costs on the economy, and represent a potential systemic risk. WTO entry and short-term challenges associated with trade and financial liberalization will exacerbate vulnerabilities in the financial system.

To counter these risks, the Government needs to institute regulatory reform and information disclosure mechanisms in the financial sector conforming to international standards. Other measures required in a sequenced approach to liberalizing the financial sector include resolving NPLs; diversifying ownership of financial institutions; giving more autonomy to PBC and financial regulatory agencies; liberalizing interest rates; allowing foreign participation and the development of private banks; opening the capital account in phases after strengthening domestic institutions; and establishing a sound, flexible, and resilient exchange rate regime.

Hong Kong, China

The economy continued to grapple with weak domestic demand, falling property prices, persistent defla-tion, high unemployment, and a deteriorating fiscal position in 2002. Recent statistics, however, have given rise to cautious optimism as both merchandise and services exports posted strong growth in the second half of the year. Anticipated strengthening of the global economic environment should feed through to domestic demand, and economic activity is expected to gradually pick up over the next 2 years, though the outbreak of SARS may slow the pace of recovery in the first half of 2003.

Macroeconomic Assessment

The economy of Hong Kong, China continued to face structural and cyclical problems in 2002. Recent data, however, suggest some-what firmer grounds for optimism. After weak performance in the first half of the year, GDP on a year-on-year basis grew by 3.3% in the third quarter and by 5.0% in the fourth, lifting overall growth for 2002 to 2.3%, from only 0.6% in 2001.

Growth was underpinned by strong export performance. After a sluggish start to the year, merchandise and services exports registered double-digit growth rates in the second half of the year. Exports benefited from strong demand in the PRC and other Asian economies, and growth in offshore trade and transportation services. The recent weak-ening of the Hong Kong dollar, along with the US dollar to which it is pegged, also assisted export growth. However, significant differences character-ized performance of different export components. Strong demand from Asian economies led to a 10.9% growth in the volume of reexports in 2002, while domestic exports fell by 11.3%.

In contrast, the domestic economy remained subdued. Consumer spending declined further in the third and fourth quarters of 2002 against a backdrop of falling property prices and high unem-ployment. Overall, private consumption fell by 1.6%

in 2002—the first yearly fall since 1998. Having declined for four consecutive quarters, real invest-ment spending posted marginal growth of 0.5% in the fourth quarter. Nevertheless, investment in 2002 as a whole still fell by 4.4% (Figure 2.2). Growth also varied among sectors. Output growth in services was strong while manufacturing output fell due to the continued weakness in domestic exports and relocation of labor-intensive production to the PRC.

The seasonally adjusted unemployment rate rose from 7.2% in the period November 2002–January 2003 to 7.4% for December 2002–February 2003. This rise can, in part, be attributed to a downturn in construction where there has been a slowdown in new private sector building projects, government cuts to the Public Housing Programme, and reduced work on decoration and maintenance immediately after the Lunar New Year period. The consequent sharp rise in construction sector layoffs, particularly temporary and part-time workers, outweighed the additional hiring within the retail trade and hotel sector in response to increasing inbound tourism. The current high unemployment rate is in stark contrast to the full employment norm before the Asian financial crisis.

Due to the weakness of the labor market, the nominal average wage has been falling since early 2002. Nevertheless, real wages still rose because nominal wage decreases fell short of the decline in

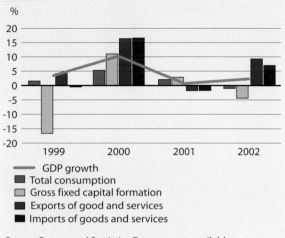

Figure 2.2 Growth of GDP and Its Demand Components, Hong Kong, China, 1999–2002

- GDP growth
- ■ Total consumption
- ■ Gross fixed capital formation
- ■ Exports of good and services
- ■ Imports of goods and services

Source: Census and Statistics Department, available: www.info.gov.hk/censtatd.

consumer prices. This stickiness in wage adjustment has contributed to the inability of the labor market to adjust to sluggish demand and to continued high rates of unemployment.

Deflation continued. The Composite Consumer Price Index fell by 3.0% in 2002, its fourth consecutive year of decline. The prime cause has been declining property prices and rentals. The residential property market slid further in 2002, with apartment prices falling by 12% and rentals by 14%. Greater integration with the Pearl River Delta has created pressures for price convergence between the two areas. Lower import prices also put downward pressure on prices. Average import prices fell by 3.9% in 2002, reflecting subdued prices in the international economy, especially in the PRC and Japan, the two leading suppliers of imports.

The current account surplus of 10.7% of GDP in 2002 was even larger than that of the 7.5% of GDP in 2001. The merchandise trade account deficit remained stable, while the services trade surplus continued expanding. The external factor income account also recorded a further surplus, though net outflows from financial non-reserve assets rose further.

Taken together, the balance of payments had a deficit of 3.5% of GDP in the fourth quarter of 2002, resulting in a corresponding fall in reserve assets, as against a deficit of 2.4% of GDP in the third quarter.

Nevertheless, the external debt position remains sound and the Government is debt free.

The new budget released on 5 March 2003 estimated a consolidated deficit of HK$70 billion for FY2002 (ended 31 March 2003), or 5.5% of GDP. Loose monetary policy in the US has kept nominal interest rates in Hong Kong, China low. Deflation, while not conducive to domestic demand, has helped external competitiveness and contributed toward the recent surge in exports.

Policy Developments

Rising fiscal deficits—deriving from the financial crisis, the restructuring of the economy, and a cyclical downturn—have become a major concern for the authorities. The bursting of the property bubble has caused a significant decline in real estate-related revenues, while ongoing relocation of production to the PRC has also weakened government revenues. With the exception of FY1999, Hong Kong, China has registered fiscal deficits every year since FY1998.

Prolonged fiscal deficits increase the risk of macroeconomic instability, though this possibility remains low due to the authorities' prudent fiscal policies and the cushion provided by the large fiscal reserves accumulated during the sustained economic boom before the financial crisis. Despite recent deficits, the fiscal reserves are expected to be over HK$300 billion at the end of March 2003 (close to US$40 billion). Foreign exchange reserves are also high.

The combination of weak economic growth and a rising fiscal deficit presents a dilemma for policy makers. In March 2002, the previous budget set medium-term targets of restoring fiscal balance by FY2006. It also proposed stimulating domestic demand through measures such as reducing charges for certain public utilities. It contained tough measures to rein in the deficit, such as pay cuts for civil servants. These cuts, however, turned out significantly smaller than assumed in the 2002 budget because of the rigidity of the civil service pay structure. The budget deficit widened in FY2002 as a result of weak economic growth, countercyclical fiscal measures, and the rigidity in reducing government expenditures.

The new budget for FY2003 suggests that containing the deficit has become the authorities'

Table 2.2 Major Economic Indicators, Hong Kong, China, 2000–2004, %

Item	2000	2001	2002	2003	2004
GDP growth[a]	10.2	0.6	2.3	2.0	4.0
Gross domestic investment/GDP	28.1	26.5	24.2	25.0	27.0
Gross domestic savings/GDP	32.9	31.6	33.9	34.0	33.5
Inflation rate (consumer price index)	-3.7	-1.6	-3.0	-1.5	0.5
Money supply (M2) growth	7.8	-2.7	-0.9	-1.0	2.0
Fiscal balance/GDP	-0.6	-5.0	-5.5	-5.7	-4.2
Merchandise export growth	16.0	-5.8	4.9	6.5	6.2
Merchandise import growth	18.6	-5.5	3.1	5.9	6.7
Current account balance/GDP	5.5	7.5	10.7	11.5	8.5

[a] In August 2002, the Census and Statistics Department released the revised GDP series. The base year of the constant price GDP was updated to 2000 and historical estimates of GDP and components were revised accordingly.

Sources: Census and Statistics Department; Hong Kong Monetary Authority; staff estimates.

top priority. The authorities committed to bring the budget into balance by FY2006 and to tackle the deficit with a three-pronged strategy: boosting economic growth, cutting public expenditures, and raising revenues. Expected economic recovery will provide some relief to the fiscal position. A series of revenue-generating measures has been proposed, including selling public assets; increasing departure, payroll, profit, and property taxes; and increasing fees and charges for public services.

Operating expenditures will be reduced from HK$213 billion (US$27.3 billion) in FY2003 to HK$200 billion (US$25.6 billion) as targeted for FY2006, by phases. Concrete measures include a 6% civil service pay cut; a 10% reduction in the civil service establishment (through a freeze on recruitment and a second phase of the voluntary retirement scheme); and an 11.1% adjustment of the Comprehensive Social Security Assistance payment, in line with deflation.

Reacting to the difficult state of the property market, the authorities introduced, in November 2002, measures to reduce the supply of new public apartments and increase demand for private apartments, while still providing public rental housing for low-income earners. While it is important to exercise fiscal discipline, the authorities need to tread a fine line between the need for fiscal restraint and the need to use fiscal policy to stimulate domestic demand.

The recent economic downturn has exposed weaknesses in the tax base. Government finances have been overly dependent on revenue from land sales and property transactions. While a broad-based goods and services tax is probably the best alternative to adopt in the future, the authorities remain cautious. Increased taxation is always unpopular and may dampen domestic demand in the short term. Furthermore, Hong Kong, China's low tax rates have long been considered an advantage for attracting skilled labor and capital. As such, the introduction of a goods and services tax is ruled out for the next few years.

The economy is generally associated with minimal government intervention, though spending on infrastructure and education has been significantly increased since the mid-1990s, partly in response to the need to upgrade facilities and the skills base as the economy matured. The authorities have also financed a large proportion of health care costs, subsidized rents for low-income earners, and provided unemployment benefits. The share of public expenditures in the economy has risen from 15.6% in 1993 to 21.5% in 2003. The FY2003 budget proposes more infrastructure upgrades, including the construction of new tourist attractions.

Although delaying or reducing infrastructure projects has been mooted, the FY2003 budget boosted annual capital expenditures, to around HK$29 billion from FY2003 to FY2007.

To facilitate economic integration between Hong Kong, China and the PRC, the Hong Kong, China authorities are considering relaxing restrictions on mainland professionals coming in to work. A Closer Economic Partnership Arrangement (CEPA) with the mainland is being pursued to boost bilateral flows of trade, services, and investment. Discussions are already under way regarding the construction of a bridge linking Hong Kong, China; Macao, China; and the western part of the Pearl River Delta, as well as a Guangzhou–Shenzhen–Hong Kong, China express railway.

Outlook for 2003–2004

Hong Kong, China may have already embarked on an export-led recovery in the second half of 2002. This process is expected to continue over the next 2 years on the back of strong growth in the PRC and a pickup in world demand. Improved exports would feed into the domestic economy. However, the recovery of the domestic economy will be gradual due to the structural transformation it is undergoing. The recent outbreak of SARS has also undermined the prospects for a rapid economy recovery. However, provided that SARS is quickly brought under control, GDP growth is likely to strengthen from the second half of 2003. GDP is expected to grow by 2.0% in 2003 and by 4.0% in 2004.

Strong export growth is likely to continue in 2003. Reexports will be bolstered by robust exports from the PRC, while exports of services should expand in conjunction with merchandise trade. However, the vibrant performance of inbound tourism in 2002 is likely to slow substantially in the first half of 2003 as a result of mounting concerns over the emergence of SARS.

SARS is also affecting domestic demand. As an economy dominated by the services sector (over 80% of GDP), Hong Kong, China is likely to feel the pinch more than other economies in this regard. Tourism, transport, retailing, and entertainment have already felt the strain. As the number of infected cases is small relative to the population, SARS is unlikely to significantly affect production capacity. However, it could have a severe impact on demand by causing uncertainty and panic. Domestic demand is thus likely to be weak in the first half of 2003.

The impact of SARS is likely to be short lived, once it is brought under control. In the second half of 2003, private consumption and investment are forecast to recover slightly, as the effects of export expansion filter through to domestic sectors. Nevertheless, consumer spending is likely to remain subdued in 2003 due to high unemployment and falling property prices. Investment spending is expected to rebound moderately. There will probably be renewed acquisition of machinery, equipment, and computer software to boost productive capacity. On the other hand, building and construction may decline again, as public housing construction is cut back and work on the KCR West Railway winds down. In addition, few new projects are planned. The persistent budget deficit will constrain government fiscal expansion.

Export growth will outpace import growth in 2003 due to weak domestic demand. The current account surplus is forecast to widen to 11.5% of GDP, before settling to 8.5% of GDP in 2004 as imports pick up.

Employment will be strained in the short term by the uncertain business outlook. The unemployment rate is expected to stay at around its current level for the immediate future. Over time, however, strong exports and strengthening domestic demand will gradually lift labor market performance. Unemployment is forecast to be around 7.4% in 2003 and to fall to 6.2% in 2004.

The ending of the earlier special relief measures by the authorities will lift prices somewhat, although deflation will only gradually abate. Further adjustment of the property market, relatively high unemployment, and ongoing price convergence between the PRC and Hong Kong, China will continue to exert downward pressure on prices. A weaker US dollar may increase import prices, although keen competition among local retailers and distributors may keep in check price rises. Furthermore, deflation in the PRC and Japan will reduce external price pressures. The Composite Consumer Price Index is forecast to fall by 1.5% in 2003, then increase by 0.5% in 2004. Interest rates in the US, and thus in Hong Kong, China, are likely to remain low for most of 2003. This should encourage consumer spending and corporate investment.

The economy will continue to face a range of longer-term structural problems. High unemployment, persistent deflation, and serious fiscal deficits are symptomatic of two interrelated phenomena:

prolonged sluggishness in the property market and increasing integration with the PRC, though the latter has proven to be a double-edged sword. It has boosted Hong Kong, China's economic growth, but also lured firms to relocate to the mainland to lower their production costs. Growing movements of goods and services between the two economies have promoted price convergence as wage and land costs rise in Guangdong province and fall in Hong Kong, China. The fact that properties in Shenzhen are only one third to one fifth the price of their Hong Kong, China equivalents means that the property market is likely to fall further, especially as border restrictions will be lowered steadily in the coming years.

Although property prices have fallen by about 60% from their peak in 1997, Hong Kong, China remains one of the world's most expensive places to buy and lease property. Labor costs are also fairly high, certainly compared with those in the PRC. Lower production costs in the PRC will place considerable pressure on Hong Kong, China and force substantial structural changes. However, the economy still possesses many advantages, including a flexible labor market, efficient public institutions, sound legal and financial systems, a good location, and a well-developed infrastructure. Nevertheless,

income and living standards between Hong Kong, China and the mainland will continue to narrow, as economic liberalization and development in the PRC proceed.

The openness of the economy makes it highly dependent on the strength of its trading partners. This is especially true when the domestic economy is beset by various structural difficulties. Reexports, which are strongly affected by economic conditions among Hong Kong, China's trading partners, have been the main driver of overall export growth. Thus, economic rebound hinges on global economic recovery, and particularly on continued robust growth in the PRC.

This forecast is based on the assumption that the global economy will slowly pick up in 2003, and strengthen in 2004. It also assumes continued strong growth in the region, especially in the PRC, and that the conflict in Iraq will not significantly affect the oil supply and dampen investor confidence. In addition, it is based on the assumption that the recent outbreak of SARS will soon be brought under control. If not controlled soon, SARS could disrupt the overall functioning of the economy, especially certain services-related industries. Any risks in these regards could significantly alter the outlook.

Republic of Korea

The economy performed strongly in 2002, led by vigorous expansion in exports of goods and services, particularly in the second half of the year. As private consumption decelerated from the second through fourth quarters, equipment investment and exports took up the slack, resulting in steady and high growth. Keeping fiscal and monetary policy supportive of moderate yet sustainable economic performance, the Government passed regulations restricting consumer loans and housing mortgages. Optimism for the future based on domestic factors is tempered by regional and global political uncertainties.

Macroeconomic Assessment

The Republic of Korea (Korea) continued its brisk recovery in 2002, with GDP expanding by 6.3%. On the demand side, private consumption made the strongest contribution to growth in the first half of the year thanks to robust income growth, the wealth effect of rising property (and hence loan collateral) values, low interest rates, and tax incentives. Consumption growth slowed in the second half, reflecting unusually bad weather, the relatively high level of accumulated debt, the end of a temporary tax exemption on certain durable goods, and stricter regulation of consumer credit. An increase in exports offset the slowdown in consumer spending and construction investment, the latter of which decelerated noticeably following completion of projects for the World Cup and Asian Games sports events.

The gross savings ratio was 29.2% while the gross domestic investment ratio was 26.1%, both slightly lower than in 2001. The increased opportunities to acquire and use consumer loans and credit cards, which boosted consumption, led to the savings rate reaching a 20-year low of 26% in the third quarter of the year (Box 2.3). The investment ratio declined amid rising global uncertainties over prospects for the world economy and continuing corporate efforts to lower debt-equity ratios.

In terms of supply, services made the strongest contribution to growth, followed by manufacturing (Figure 2.3). The services sector grew by 7.4% overall, and by 5.8% excluding finance and insurance services. Particularly noteworthy is the information technology industry, which has been the fastest growing industry sector in recent years, accounting for some 10% of GDP and 30% of total exports in 2002.

Industrial production increased by 6.1%, led by export subsectors such as semiconductors, telecommunications devices, and machinery; manufacturing's capacity utilization rate increased to 76.7%. Since the 1997–98 Asian financial crisis, the country's largest conglomerates (*chaebol*) have reduced debt and cross shareholdings, and improved corporate governance. By September 2002, the debt-equity ratio of manufacturing firms had been reduced to 131% from 398% in 1998. However, several *chaebol* continue to dominate the corporate environment, with the top 30 of them accounting for about 40% of manufacturing output and 50% of exports.

The unemployment rate has declined each year since 1998, reaching just 3.0% in 2002 as employment in the services sector particularly (especially wholesale, retail, housing, and food services) expanded and as the economy continued its rapid recovery from the financial crisis, generally benefiting from its diverse economic structure, improved

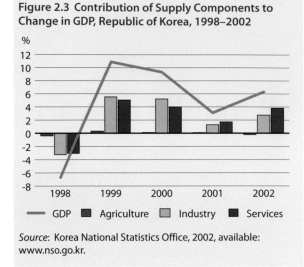

Figure 2.3 Contribution of Supply Components to Change in GDP, Republic of Korea, 1998–2002

Source: Korea National Statistics Office, 2002, available: www.nso.go.kr.

governance, financial sector rehabilitation, and enhanced flexibility. Manufacturing employment declined marginally in 2002 but manufacturing wages continued to rise as labor productivity grew by more than 10% over the year.

Central government revenues reached 26.6% of GDP and the consolidated fiscal surplus amounted to 3.9% of GDP, boosted by proceeds from the sale of the Government's stake in Korea Telecom, greater revenues from value-added tax (VAT), transferred profits from the Bank of Korea, and contributions from the National Pension Fund, as well as restraint in expenditures. Repeated budgetary surpluses since 2000 have contributed to one of the lowest ratios of public debt to GDP (42%) in the OECD and leave room for further fiscal stimulus if necessary.

The CPI edged up by 2.7% in 2002 (3.0% excluding agricultural products and oil), but producer prices rose by just 1.6%. Long-term interest rates declined throughout most of the year. After a protracted rise in response to a shift in banking behavior from lending to firms to greater lending to households, housing prices appear to have stabilized, reflecting stricter regulation of consumer credit and toughened taxation of real estate and capital gains. The positive wealth effect from higher housing values contributed to the growth in general consumption while the expansion of home ownership boosted sales of consumer durables in particular.

Credit card delinquencies rose to a record 12.2% in November 2002, and as a result, lending to house-

holds is slowing. However, the overall ratio of NPLs to total loans in the banking sector is down to 2.4% from a peak of over 16% in 1998. Banks are again placing their emphasis on corporate lending, which the Government is hoping will be increasingly directed to SMEs.

Equity market volumes continued to grow in 2002, with the values of stocks and bonds traded increasing by 51% and 232%, respectively. The KOSPI stock price index declined by 9.5%, reflecting a general weakness in equity markets in the region.

Despite a 10.5% appreciation of the won against the dollar during the year, exports increased by 7.5% as export prices on a won basis declined by 4.8%. The strong export performance reflected a 20.1% increase in shipments of ICT products, such as wireless communications devices, semiconductors, and computers, and a 3.9% increase in non-ICT exports. Korea has benefited from both more diversified export markets and a broader export base than some other developing Asian economies.

The PRC (including Hong Kong, China) has replaced the US as Korea's largest export market, taking 20.9% of exports, as well as being the favored destination for investment outflows. Direct investments in the PRC also stimulated exports of equipment and components to supply the factories associated with those investments. However, export expansion lagged the import growth rate of 7.7%. With over 50% import content in exports, robust import growth is likely to underpin continued strong export performance. Meanwhile, the current account surplus has declined steadily each year since its approximately $40 billion peak in 1998 following the onset of the financial crisis, but at around $6 billion in 2002 continued to boost the country's net creditor position (Korea has been a net creditor since 1999).

Reversing a trend of positive capital inflows, net outflows of $703 million of direct investment by foreigners and inflows of $183 million of portfolio investment were recorded. Gross FDI inflows in 2002 fell by 44.1% to $2.0 billion, as foreign investors bought only five Korean companies under major restructuring, compared with 18 in 1999, partly reflecting the previous success in postcrisis recovery. However, foreign investors' interest remains strong, particularly in finance and telecommunications, as seen in the 35.4% of Korean Stock

Table 2.3 Major Economic Indicators, Republic of Korea, 2000–2004, %

Item	2000	2001	2002	2003	2004
GDP growth	9.3	3.1	6.3	4.0	5.3
Gross domestic investment/GDP	28.3	27.0	26.1	26.0	27.0
Gross domestic savings/GDP	32.4	30.2	29.2	28.0	29.0
Inflation rate (consumer price index)	2.3	4.1	2.7	4.0	3.5
Money supply (M2) growth	25.4	13.2	10.4	15.0	15.0
Fiscal balance/GDP	1.3	1.3	3.9	1.0	2.0
Merchandise export growth	21.2	-14.0	7.5	8.0	8.0
Merchandise import growth	36.2	-13.4	7.7	9.0	9.0
Current account balance/GDP	2.7	2.0	1.3	0.0	-0.3

Sources: National Statistics Office; Bank of Korea; staff estimates.

Exchange market capitalization held by foreigners as of end-February 2003. At the same time, outward investment by Koreans has been increasing.

By the end of December 2002, total external liabilities amounted to $131.0 billion, or about 27.5% of GDP. Short-term foreign liabilities, driven mostly by external borrowing by local branches of foreign banks, were about 40% of total foreign liabilities. However, they were more than adequately covered by $121.4 billion of foreign exchange and gold reserves. Foreign exchange reserves increased in dollar terms primarily through interest revenue earned on the stock of reserves and an increase in the value of yen- and euro-denominated assets when converted into dollars. Total external assets increased to a record $185.3 billion by end-2002.

Policy Developments

The fiscal policy stance was basically neutral and remains constrained over the medium term by the need to cover costs already incurred for financial sector restructuring and precautions with regard to geopolitical uncertainties. Income tax rates were trimmed to boost household disposable income and preferential tax treatment equivalent to a 10% deduction for corporate capital investments was extended until June 2003 to help offset the tightening of consumer credit.

In the second half of 2002, the Government intervened to reduce the likelihood or magnitude of a bubble in the property and consumer credit markets. The Financial Supervisory Commission is continuing to closely monitor loans to households to prevent the higher consumer debt from disrupting the financial sector, and the ceiling for new mortgages was lowered from 80% to 60% of the value of the property. Credit card companies are being required to maintain a capital-adequacy ratio of 8%, will have to write off loans that are unpaid for more than 6 months, and will have to classify risky loans more strictly.

Despite falling international interest rates, the Monetary Policy Committee of the Bank of Korea kept its key call-rate target steady at 4.25% for the last 8 months of the year to balance the tensions between brisk economic growth and external uncertainties. Although neighboring countries are experiencing deflation and the current nominal interest rate is relatively high, the Bank of Korea has not seen the need to loosen monetary policy significantly. To protect against currency volatility, the foreign exchange equalization bond ceiling was raised from W5 trillion to W8 trillion in 2002. Increased overseas confidence in the economy was reflected in the low spreads between Korean sovereign bonds and US treasury bonds, which fell to just 95 basis points by end-November 2002.

Privatization in the banking sector continues. Banks and brokerage firms will be permitted to sell casualty and life insurance products targeted at households beginning in August 2003, with a goal of full market liberalization by 2007, including government withdrawal from the financial sector.

Box 2.3 Consumer Credit Growth in Korea

Koreans have traditionally preferred to pay for their purchases in cash, but after the Asian financial crisis, aggressive marketing efforts by financial institutions were directed toward consumers. Firms, in their efforts to rehabilitate and reduce their debt-equity ratios, resorted to equity financing instead of borrowing from banks. As a result, some banks found themselves with a lot of cash but no borrowers. They then began to tap a new market for their loan products—the household. With renewed consumer confidence in the economy, it was quite easy for financial institutions to encourage households to adopt their loan products.

While consumer borrowing remains heavily oriented toward housing, credit card use has expanded rapidly in recent years. New credit cardholders were often signed up at sidewalk stands without even a home address required. In the second half of 1999, the Government granted incentives to credit card users, including taxable income deductions for payments made via credit card and introduction of a credit card lottery service, to lift consumer spending and improve tax collection. This further fueled the credit card boom. The result was a large expansion in credit card use, effectively reducing transactions in the underground economy and boosting VAT revenues.

As the credit card industry grew and credit card use soared, adverse impacts from their reckless use began to appear. A large proportion of credit card transactions involve the cash advance facility for which cardholders can avail of non-collaterized loans from automatic teller machines. Cardholders began to use advances from one credit card to pay off debts falling due on another credit card. As a result, the debt was simply rolled over but never actually repaid. However, since cardholders can only have as many credit cards as the number of card issuers, the supply of new credit cards eventu-

Box Figure. Delinquency rate on consumer loans, by type of credit card issuer

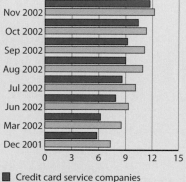

%, end-of-period

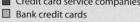
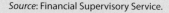

■ Credit card service companies
□ Bank credit cards

Source: Financial Supervisory Service.

ally became tight and cardholders faced the prospect of defaulting on their loans. As could be expected, the number of delinquent cardholders began to rise, with most delinquents having debts well in excess of their annual income. From only 7.3% at the end of 2001, default rates on bank-issued credit cards rose to 12.2% by end-November 2002 (Box Figure). Credit card companies also saw their rates of overdue payments double to 11.7% from only 5.8% over the same period .

This has raised concern about the bursting of the consumption credit bubble and impending mass bankruptcies of households. According to the Bank of Korea, household debt surged to three quarters of GDP as at end-2002, from less than half in 1999. In absolute terms, household credit more than doubled to W439 trillion by the end of 2002 from only W214 trillion at the end of 1999. Even as increased household

spending was fuelling inflation, the Government remained wary of increasing interest rates as this could trigger new financial turmoil, just as mounting corporate debt contributed to the 1997 financial crisis. While rising interest rates could have reined in consumer spending, they would have led to even higher loan default rates, particularly at a time when household debt had reached very high levels.

In their desire to stem the excessive use of credit cards, card issuers are now educating cardholders on personal credit management. The Government, for its part, has put pressure on banks and credit card companies to lower fees, reduce the cash advance limit for cardholders, and increase loan-loss provisions. In particular, the Government has ordered credit card issuers to set aside capital equivalent to 8.0% of outstanding loans to cover potential defaults, write off debts older than 6 months, and use a stricter yardstick to judge the creditworthiness of applicants.

The Government and credit card companies also agreed to cancel 2.1 million "dormant" cards (i.e., cards not used for 1 year) in 2003. While this will benefit card companies by freeing up the required 1.0% of the cash advance limit they have set aside for every card issued, stricter rules on credit card operations put a strain on their profitability in the second half of 2002.

In addition, financial sector shares in the stock market, which include banking shares, lost about 20% of their value between September and December 2002. Overall, the initial impact on credit card companies may be unfavorable, but the timely response of the Government to mounting household credit may be just what the industry needs to ensure its long-run viability.

Risks of disruptions to oil supplies due to conflict or political disturbances in oil-producing regions have been mitigated by the stockpiling of emergency reserves in excess of 100 days' consumption. In addition, major Korean airlines have been entering into forward contracts as defensive measures against potential oil supply disruptions.

Free economic zones (FEZs) are at the center of the Government's plans, unveiled in April 2002, to turn the country into the business hub of Northeast Asia. Five FEZs are to be set up by July 2003, offering tax incentives, "one-stop shop" investment facilities, and other amenities to attract foreign investors. The strategy aims to develop a state-of-the-art transportation and logistics network, capitalize on the nation's advanced communications infrastructure, and create a world class business environment for foreign firms.

The policy direction under the new Government appears to aim both at continuing corporate reforms (since a significant number of companies still have weak balance sheets), and at improving efficiency of the product distribution system. Corporate reforms for the *chaebol* are to be pursued on a voluntary and gradual basis, raising some concerns about the speed and effectiveness of their implementation. Among other plans are expansion of employee shareholding schemes, distribution of profits between management and workers, and introduction of class-action lawsuits to increase accountability of owners and managers. Indications that the privatization program may be put under review have cast doubts on the proposed sale of gas and rail systems.

Outlook for 2003–2004

With strong real wage growth and high employment levels, GDP growth is expected to remain firm, though declining to 4.0% in 2003 before rising somewhat to 5.3% in 2004. The slowdown in consumer spending growth arising from tighter consumer credit and mortgage terms will be largely offset by rising exports to growing world markets, the end of the global manufacturing downturn, and

a moderate revival of savings and business investment. There is, however, a downside risk stemming from rising uncertainty over developments in the north of the peninsula and the aftermath of the conflict in Iraq.

Planned capital investment by the 200 largest corporations is forecast to increase in the second half of 2003, according to the Ministry of Commerce, Industry and Energy, when global markets are expected to pick up and corporate debt-equity levels will have declined to even more comfortable levels. Automobile, machinery, and petroleum companies are expected to be the most aggressive in their investment spending. The slowdown in consumer spending is likely to cause unemployment to edge up marginally.

Exports are expected to rise by 8.0% and imports by 9.0% in both 2003 and 2004. The change in trade patterns favoring higher exports to the PRC and Hong Kong, China should help export performance weather any slowdown in the US or EU. Nevertheless, the current account is expected to slip back into the red as the services account deficit and recovery-driven imports increase.

Domestically, the successful promotion of broadband Internet usage will continue to spur the development of higher value-added sectors and to maintain competitiveness. Slowing domestic consumption is expected to feed into growth of only 1.7% for the industry sector. Government efforts to expand the housing supply and spending on social infrastructure projects will continue to support construction investment, while support for SMEs is aimed to counter the consumption slowdown.

With housing prices stabilized and growth in consumer debt slowing, inflation is expected to remain within—but near the top of—the Bank of Korea's target range of 2–4%. To contain inflation, the Government plans to minimize increases in charges for public services. In the financial sector, the interest rate spread between loans and deposits is expected to widen slightly as stricter lending guidelines and greater credit risks push up loan rates while ample liquidity keeps deposit rates subdued.

Mongolia

Dynamism in services and a milder than expected winter helped the economy move out of stagnation in 2002, while a contained fiscal deficit and low inflation contributed to macroeconomic stability. However, the vital agriculture sector remains vulnerable to severe weather and suffers from a lack of investment. In the medium term, growth is expected to strengthen somewhat as mining—aided by promising new mineral deposits—and labor-intensive industries become important sources of economic expansion.

Macroeconomic Assessment

After 2 years of stagnation, prospects for the economy improved in 2002. In spite of unfavorable conditions in the world market for its exports, the economy grew by 3.9%, after 1.1% growth in the previous year, largely due to the robust performance of services. A milder than expected winter helped cushion losses in the livestock subsector, and agricultural output declined by a less steep 10.5%, after an 18.5% contraction in 2001.

Despite strong manufacturing activity, principally in textiles and meat processing, industrial output grew moderately by 4.7%, down from 11.9% growth in 2001, reflecting the impact of the poor performance of the mining sector. Lower copper production, triggered by falling prices in international markets, depressed both industrial output and exports receipts. Construction expanded by 11.0% as a result of the ongoing real estate boom in Ulaanbaatar. Services grew by 12.0%, propelled by the solid outcome in financial services, transport and communications, and wholesale and retail trade.

Improved economic performance had a favorable impact on the labor market. Actual unemployment is much higher than suggested by the official estimate of 3.6%, with high job losses in rural Mongolia driving migration to Ulaanbaatar. Moreover, employment estimates are also distorted by the size of the informal sector (around 35%

of GDP). In this regard, the rapid development of informal gold mining is important, an activity helping counter the losses of employment in other sectors. This alternative source of income, involving an estimated 50,000–100,000 workers, has become a means of living for families who lost their herds in past harsh winters (*dzud*) and for individuals who failed to find employment in urban areas. Without any regulation, however, informal gold mining can contribute to environmental degradation of rivers and streams.

Growing efforts to restore macroeconomic stability are reflected in a fiscal deficit of 5.6% of GDP, which is below the IMF Poverty Reduction and Growth Facility (PRGF) target of 6.5%. Payments from the largest taxpayers—Erdenet copper mine, Gobi cashmere factory, and Mongol Telecom—fell short of estimates by midyear. The budget came under additional pressure when the Government committed to support herdsmen affected by the previous *dzud* and increased public sector pay by 20%. The budget was amended in late August, and revenue and expenditure targets for the 2002 budget were revised to meet the requirements of the PRGF. In the last quarter, however, an improved fiscal position resulted from higher than expected revenue collection and improved fiscal accountability and transparency, as well as from substantial privatization receipts from the sale of the Trade and Development Bank.

On the monetary front, rapid growth in the

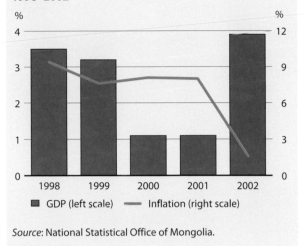

Figure 2.4 GDP Growth and Inflation, Mongolia, 1998–2002

Source: National Statistical Office of Mongolia.

money supply (42.0%) was a result of substantial financial deepening. It did not affect inflation, which was more responsive to falling food prices, particularly meat and meat products (together accounting for more than 50% of the consumer price basket). Inflation slowed to an annual rate of 1.6% from 8.0% in 2001 (Figure 2.4).

The Government has taken positive steps to deepen financial services and introduce international competition through the privatization of two important banks. The banking system is experiencing rapid growth in bank deposits, active lending, and a moderate level of NPLs (falling from 8.0% in 2001) that represented 7.2% of total outstanding loans.

In addition, the Bank of Mongolia (BOM) is planning to raise the minimum capital requirement for banks to $2 million. BOM is also paying attention to the maintenance of an appropriate structure of interest rates to foster investment and growth. Though still high, interest rates are coming down, as confidence grows and competition is triggered by the entry of new banking and nonbanking financial institutions. Commercial bank interest rates declined from 30–40% a year to 12–18% for dollar-denominated loans, and down to 15–30% for togrog debt. Mongolia maintains a flexible exchange rate regime and the togrog depreciated by 2.4% against the dollar to stand at MNT1,125:$1 at the end of the year.

Total trade amounted to $1.2 billion, or more than 100% of GDP. Exports declined by 3.9% and imports grew by 3.3% over the course of 2002, widening the trade deficit to about 14% of GDP. On the export side, copper concentrate sales, accounting for 40% of total exports, declined in volume and value terms due to falling international copper prices. The value of cashmere exports also fell as a result of a sharp slowdown in demand for luxury textile products in the US. However, rising meat and meat product exports after the lifting of the foot-and-mouth ban, and higher gold production and prices, helped partially offset these trends. Increased purchases of vegetables, machinery, and electrical appliances pushed up imports to $659 million. Excluding transfers, the current account deficit widened in absolute terms to $175.0 million but, given the higher rate of economic growth, declined slightly as a proportion of GDP to 16.0%. However, it remains a concern at this level. The overall balance of payments showed a $42.6 million surplus, reflecting large inflows of external assistance and growing remittances from overseas workers. The net foreign reserves at BOM reached $225.9 million by the end of the year, covering 17.8 weeks of imports.

Amendments to the Foreign Investment Law, improvements in the investment environment, and promising new gold and copper deposits in the south helped boost FDI inflows. Cumulatively, FDI inflows have amounted to $734 million since 1991, with inflows from the PRC accounting for 90% of the country's FDI stock. External debt stood at 88.3% of GDP in 2002, and debt service remains low at 4.9% of exports, partly due to the fact that most debt is concessional.

Policy Developments

Economic policy developments took place within the framework of the Action Program of the Government of Mongolia for 2000–2004, guided by the IMF PRGF targets and recommendations. In this context, macroeconomic stability, private sector-led growth, and more equitable income distribution remained the main pillars of the Government's overall development strategy.

Despite difficulties in early 2002, the Government made an effort to comply with these targets. This was shown by its willingness to amend the budget, and to desist from publicly announcing further wage and pension hikes for 2003, agreeing

Table 2.4 Major Economic Indicators, Mongolia, 2000–2004, %

Item	2000	2001	2002	2003	2004
GDP growth	1.1	1.1	3.9	5.0	5.2
Gross domestic investment/GDP	26.1	28.3	26.7	-	-
Gross domestic savings/GDP	32.4	26.0	23.7	-	-
Inflation rate (consumer price index)	8.1	8.0	1.6	5.0	5.0
Money supply (M2) growth	17.6	27.9	42.0	25.0	20.0
Fiscal balance/GDP	-6.8	-5.4	-5.6	-6.0	-6.0
Merchandise export growth	18.0	-2.4	-3.9	8.0	8.0
Merchandise import growth	19.2	2.5	3.3	6.0	5.3
Current account balance/GDP	-16.2	-16.6	-16.0	-13.4	-12.1
Debt service ratio	4.5	5.3	4.9	4.2	4.1

- Not available.

Sources: National Statistical Office; International Monetary Fund; staff estimates.

instead to limit future salary increases to the anticipated rate of inflation. To sustain a sound fiscal
strategy, the Government acknowledged the need
for a gradual reduction of the ratio of current
expenditures to GDP and to reduce the burden of
taxation on the private sector through a gradual
expansion of the tax base.

One of the major achievements in 2002 was
the approval of the long-delayed Public Sector
Management and Finance Law, a legal framework
to strengthen governance within the public sector.
The law should improve the efficiency of public
expenditures through comprehensive reforms of the
budget process for line ministries and other government agencies.

Because of financial deepening, rapid growth
in monetary aggregates did not push up inflation.
However, as the rate of deepening decelerates,
monetary growth must slow to sustain macroeconomic stability. Greater competition in the financial
sector generally and enhanced public confidence in
the banking sector specifically are leading to rapid
credit growth. As a result, the Government should
consider strengthening loan quality requirements,
credit risk analysis, and capital-adequacy ratios.

Other parts of the financial sector outside the
banking system remain, however, underdeveloped,
while the stock exchange has been moribund over
the last 2 years following a loss of public confidence

in its operations. Only a few private banks offer
modern payment services and sound lending practices are still being developed. Thus the population
still relies on cash for many domestic and international transactions, with cash accounting for about
80% of the supply of narrow money (M1).

Volatile prices for Mongolian exports have
resulted in both positive and negative effects.
Gold production and export revenues have soared
while copper and cashmere output and prices were
depressed. Mongolia's trade structure will necessarily be heavily influenced by developments in
the PRC and the Russian Federation, and it will be
a challenge for it to diversify its exports and find
a niche for its manufactured and services exports
in these markets. The overall balance-of-payments
surplus resulting from capital inflows is exerting
upward pressure on the real exchange rate. This
trend could erode the economy's competitiveness,
a situation that may be exacerbated by the growing
competition in manufacturing deriving from the
PRC's membership of WTO.

An ongoing initiative aims to help industries
develop and implement better business strategies,
specifically, to generate more value added through
improved productivity and quality improvement.
The initiative is focused on cashmere and fine
fibers, processed meat products, tourism, and the
public sector.

Outlook for 2003–2004

The Government will be confronted with the challenges of meeting its targets under the Action Program for 2000–2004 and the PRGF, namely GDP growth of 6.0% and significant poverty reduction. Prospects for achieving these objectives in 2003–2004 are mixed. The industry sector, led by textiles and food processing, along with mining and construction, is expected to perform very well and will provide the growth momentum and resources for development over the medium term.

In contrast, the primary sector is likely to struggle. The deteriorating performance of the agriculture sector has been one of the factors hindering economic growth, and, in fact, GDP growth excluding agriculture grew by 9.4% in 2002. The primary sector is vital for the economy and accounts for 23% of GDP and 30% of the labor force. Highly vulnerable to climatic conditions, the sector is still recovering from the losses sustained during two *dzud*, an outbreak of foot-and-mouth disease, and a severe drought affecting 70% of the country. Furthermore, a poor harvest and meager reserves of hay and fodder might delay the recovery of the sector, which is plagued by an array of shortcomings ranging from overgrazing and desertification to the deterioration in the supply of critical support services. A significant improvement in agricultural output is critical to accelerate growth and poverty reduction, and resources have to be marshaled to deal with the challenges that the primary sector faces.

Concerns are growing over debt sustainability in the short to medium term. Despite the concessional nature and long-term structure of the debt, the debt service burden is increasing. This is particularly worrisome given Mongolia's vulnerability to external price shocks. Hence, prudent external debt management policies need to be maintained. This will be a challenge since domestic savings rates are low. In addition, the capital market is underdeveloped and the banking system lacks the capacity for large-scale lending. Although FDI could represent a means to overcome these limitations, successful efforts to attract significant FDI inflows demand long-term planning as well as an innovative and more liberalized regulatory framework.

Macroeconomic stabilization therefore remains a priority for the Government. In the fiscal area, the Government's strategy will need to focus on the rationalization of both the expenditure and revenue structures of the budget, while aiming to improve social coverage and to reduce the tax burden on the private sector. Fiscal stability will facilitate the development and conduct of monetary and exchange rate policies to enhance private sector development and export-led growth, goals that will equally benefit from further development and liberalization of the financial system.

Given the vulnerability and narrow base of the economy, growth estimates must be tentative. PRGF projections show a rising rate of targeted growth for the next 2 years (5.0% and 5.2%), sustained by a more stable macroeconomic environment. Official estimates for 2003–2004, under the PRGF commitments, target inflation at below 5.0% and the fiscal deficit at 6.0% of GDP (both indicators are currently below these targets).

Growing demand for capital goods to fuel expansion of manufacturing, mining, and construction in the private sector will keep the current account under pressure and generate a deficit of about 13% of GDP during the forecast period. It is expected that this will be covered by inflows from international donors and growing FDI, particularly in mining. Increasing capital inflows should lift foreign exchange reserves to a comfortable level of 19 weeks of imports in 2003. Increasing worker remittances, foreign aid inflows, and FDI will strengthen the overall balance-of-payments surplus.

In the fight against poverty, encouraging progress has been made in meeting many of the social sector millennium development goals, an achievement facilitated by the already high level of education established under socialism. Nevertheless, improvements in the key area of poverty reduction are lagging due to low rates of economic growth. To promote a more even distribution of income, the Government should consider paying special attention to improving public goods delivery, intensifying the pro-poor focus of social expenditures, and developing social protection for the very poor.

Sustainable economic growth and poverty reduction will be possible only if concerted efforts are made to develop and strengthen the private sector within the context of a stable macroeconomic environment. However, the accompanying legal framework for the rapidly growing private sector is still weak and needs strengthening.

Taipei,China

The economy gradually recovered in 2002 from its worst recession in three decades, helped by robust export and industrial performance, which in turn stemmed from the mild recovery of the global economy. High unemployment, however, remains one of the major challenges to the economy in the short and medium run, while a prolonged epidemic of SARS would impact the economy, especially tourism.

Macroeconomic Assessment

In 2002, the economy steadily recovered. The monitoring indicator compiled by the Council for Economic Planning and Development in Taipei,China signaled "stable" since April that year, after 15 months of a "weak" signal. GDP grew by 4.8% and 4.2% in the third and fourth quarters, respectively, compared with the same periods in 2001, for an outturn of 3.5% GDP growth for the whole year. Much of the recovery was based on the growth of exports and industrial production, in particular among electronics and information technology (IT) products. However, this was to a large extent offset by weak consumer sentiment arising from job insecurity, falling earnings, and the negative wealth effect that falling stock prices had already caused.

Private consumption expanded by only 1.9% in 2002, and private investment remained moderate due to the uncertainty of both the global and domestic economic recoveries. Private investment started to strengthen in the third quarter of 2002, ending seven consecutive quarters of contraction, and resulted in a small increase of 1.6% for the whole of 2002. Government consumption and investment contracted further in 2002 by 0.9% and 10.9%, respectively, from the previous year's level. Consequently, gross fixed investment continued to shrink, by 2.0% in 2002. As a result, domestic demand strengthened by only 1.3%.

Services sector growth was a modest 2.7%, but the industry sector strengthened more rapidly due to increased exports. Value added in industry improved by 5.4% in 2002 over the 2001 level, driven largely by a 6.6% broad-based expansion in manufacturing: production in electronics and IT rose by 11.4%, basic metals by 10.3%, machinery by 5.8%, and chemicals by 4.4%. Production related to the food industry contracted by 4.5%. Construction declined by 2.9%.

Compared with 2001, the employed labor force rose by 0.8% in 2002, but the unemployed labor force increased by 14.5%, resulting in an unemployment rate of 5.2%, the highest in the past three decades (Figure 2.5). The major factor was the closure or downsizing of enterprises in response to sluggish economic performance and ongoing structural transition. Accordingly, average monthly earnings for manufacturing workers fell by 1.2% over the year. The slow growth in domestic demand contributed to a continuation of downward price pressures with the general level of consumer prices, as measured by the CPI, declining by 0.2%. However, the core CPI (excluding fresh vegetables, fruit, aquatic products, and energy) rose by 0.7% due to surcharges on goods such as wine, cigarettes, and other products that were imposed as a result of agreements between Taipei,China and other WTO members after the island's entry into WTO. The wholesale price index increased marginally in 2002 both due to the depreciation of the New Taiwan

Figure 2.5 GDP Growth, Inflation, and Unemployment, Taipei,China, 1998–2002

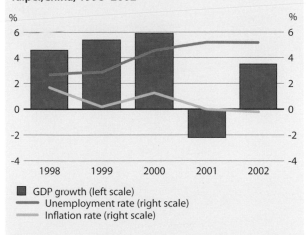

GDP growth (left scale)
Unemployment rate (right scale)
Inflation rate (right scale)

Source: Directorate-General of Budget, Accounting, and Statistics, Executive Yuan, available: www.stat.gov.tw.

dollar against the US dollar and to higher prices of raw materials (such as petrochemicals and metal products) in the global market.

Exports strengthened by 6.4% in 2002 as external demand conditions improved throughout the year, particularly the second half, with the global economy recovering further. Exports started to increase in April and began growing at double-digit rates from July. Strong demand from the PRC, particularly for IT-related goods, provided support for exports, offsetting soft demand from the US and Japan. The high volume of transit trade to the PRC resulted in Hong Kong, China replacing the US as the primary destination for exports, accounting for 23.6% of the total. Exports to Hong Kong, China consisted mainly of supplies to firms from Taipei,China that relocated production facilities to the PRC, indicating the increasing importance of indirect trade between Taipei,China and the PRC. The US (20.5%), EU (13.0%), and ASEAN countries (10.1%) were the other major export markets.

Total export orders improved by 11.2% in 2002. By category, orders for information and communications products showed the largest gain, followed by basic metals, machinery, and other electronics products. Textile products recorded a small contraction. In terms of destination, orders from Hong Kong, China strengthened the most (up 25%), followed by Japan, EU, and US.

Imports rose by 3.2% compared with 2001, due largely to higher levels of imported intermediate

goods and higher oil prices; this was despite the fact that household spending remained weak. Capital goods imports declined in both 2001 and 2002, by 31.6% and by 3.5%, respectively, as a result of weak private and public investment. Consequently, the trade surplus increased to $24.7 billion in 2002, or 22.4% higher than in the previous year.

Reflecting the rather uncertain and slow recovery of the global economy, stock prices fluctuated and interest rates fell. The stock market was volatile in 2002, growing by 11% in the first quarter, and then falling back both in price and volume terms in the second and third quarters. In November, the stock market began rising again, but overall its value fell by 11.2% during the year. The weak domestic investment climate and the negative impact of the turbulence occurring in the US stock market—particularly in the second half of 2002—contributed to domestic stock market weakness. At the end of December 2002, the Taiwan Stock Exchange Weighted Index stood at 44% of its peak in February 2000.

The Central Bank of China (CBC) continued its accommodative monetary policy in 2002. To stimulate the slowly recovering economy, CBC cut its official rediscount rate twice (in June and November), and has cut interest rates 14 times since December 2000. The rediscount rate was reduced from 2.125% in December 2001, to 1.875% in June 2002, and further to 1.625% in November. Average lending rates offered by commercial banks and rates on commercial paper and government bonds also declined. However, despite the reduction in the rediscount rate, commercial banks remained reluctant to lower their lending rates. CBC responded with a series of measures aimed at improving the transmission mechanisms of monetary policy. For example, an adjustable rate mortgage was introduced, which linked loan rates to benchmark interest rates both to bring the former more into line with prevailing interest rates set by CBC and to make rates more transparent to borrowers.

The demand for liquidity remained moderate due to the subdued nature of the economic recovery. M2 grew by only 3.6 % in 2002, compared with 5.8% in the previous year. Nevertheless, the continuous decline in interest rates has made bank deposits less attractive to investors. As a result, liquidity has been transferred from bank deposits into the bond market. The combined growth rate of M2

Table 2.5 Major Economic Indicators, Taipei,China, 2000–2004, %

Item	2000	2001	2002	2003	2004
GDP growth	5.9	-2.2	3.5	3.7	3.9
Gross domestic investment/GDP	22.6	17.4	16.8	18.1	18.6
Gross domestic savings/GDP	25.4	23.9	25.4	25.7	25.8
Inflation rate (consumer price index)	1.3	0.0	-0.2	0.4	0.6
Money supply (M2) growth	7.0	5.8	3.6	4.0	4.3
Fiscal balance/GDP	-1.3	-2.5	-3.0	-2.5	-2.5
Merchandise export growth	21.8	-17.3	6.4	7.4	7.8
Merchandise import growth	25.9	-23.7	3.2	11.5	10.0
Current account balance/GDP	2.9	6.4	9.2	7.9	8.0

Sources: Central Bank of China, available: www.cbc.gov.tw; Directorate-General of Budget, Accounting, and Statistics, Executive Yuan, available: www.stat.gov.tw; staff estimates.

and bonds was 5.6% in 2002 compared with 6.5% in 2001. Overall, CBC's relatively loose monetary stance has been a significant factor in promoting the revival of economic activity in Taipei,China. Given the efforts of both the authorities and the banking system, the NPL ratio among domestic banks declined from 8.04% in March to 6.12% in December 2002.

Policy Developments

In 2002, the relatively high levels of NPLs and of public debt remained the two pressing issues for the authorities. On the first point, some long-term measures have been taken to address the problem. The Legislative Yuan, the law-making body, passed the Financial Institution Merger Law and Financial Holding Company Law in 2001 to allow financial institutions to have greater flexibility to merge and to provide a wider range of financial services. It also passed the Financial Assets Securitization Statute in June 2002 to reinvigorate the financial and real estate market and to boost liquidity.

In 2002, the authorities used the Financial Restructuring Fund of NT$140 billion, established in 2001, to restructure 44 problematic financial institutions, and assisted in the establishment of 16 asset management companies (AMCs) to start the reduction of NPLs. AMCs are designed to serve as an intermediary for the authorities to deal with NPLs, since the ultimate goal is to develop the

secondary market, through which NPLs can be traded. The plan is to use financial asset securitization to accelerate the reduction of NPLs. AMCs in Taipei,China started operations in 2002, buying NPLs amounting to NT$211 billion. To expedite efforts to reduce NPLs, the Ministry of Finance proposed an increase in the size and scope of the Financial Restructuring Fund, including allowing the authorities to become directly involved in NPL trading. The Ministry's proposal is still under debate in the Legislative Yuan.

On the second point, the public debt-to-GDP ratio has worsened as a result of the continued large central government budget deficit in 2002. The weak economy, combined with accumulated tax incentives offered by the authorities, caused tax revenues to decline by 2.6% in 2002. The ratio of the central government deficit to GDP widened slightly from 2.5% in 2001 to 3.0% in 2002. In financing the rising budget deficit, the ratio of outstanding public debt to GDP rose from 12.0% in 1993 to 28.5% in 2001, and to 29.8% in 2002.

Further stimulus through additional public spending has been hindered by the sluggish economy, while the president's promise not to raise taxes in the next 2 years has made the widening of the tax base difficult. Instead of tax cuts, reform of the tax system has been directed to rationalizing the tax system, such as reducing some of the tax breaks that used to be enjoyed by high-tech companies, and improving the overall efficiency of the tax system. The Legislative Yuan is still reviewing the proposal to eliminate tax exemptions for teachers in the primary and secondary school system and for military personnel.

The war in Iraq has created uncertainty regarding external demand. To sustain the economic recovery, but after much debate due to the levels of spending involved, the Legislative Yuan passed two laws in 2002 to expand domestic demand in case there is a shortfall in external markets. One was to allow the authorities to have a supplementary budget of NT$50 billion to increase infrastructure construction in 2003, and the other was to allow them to make supplementary budget appropriations of NT$20 billion to create short-term jobs for the unemployed in 2003. In 2002, the authorities also launched a medium- to long-term program, Challenge 2008, aimed at upgrading the structure of the economy; the Legislative Yuan passed the first year's budget (2003) of the initiative, for NT$150 billion.

Outlook for 2003–2004

The slow but steady recovery in 2002 is expected to continue in 2003 and to improve in 2004 as the global economy strengthens further. Given that the PRC, through Hong Kong, China, has become the largest export market for Taipei,China, and that the rapid growth of the PRC economy is expected to continue, exports are expected to be buoyant, remaining the driving force in sustaining economic recovery. In addition, the laws passed by the Legislative Yuan could inject a substantial amount of funding into the economy. This would support the anticipated pickup of private investment and consumption in 2003–2004. The implementation of Challenge 2008 would also help adjust Taipei,China's economic structure, so as to accelerate economic recovery.

Monetary policy is likely to remain accommodative over the next 2 years. The threat of deflation in 2003 should be minimal due to higher industrial raw material prices in the global market and continuing recovery in the domestic economy. Nevertheless, consumer price inflation will remain subdued in 2003 as structural and cyclical unemployment restrains wage growth and as deregulation of the economy increases competitive pressure.

However, these forecasts must be considered against the backdrop of the recent outbreak of SARS. In light of the close links between the PRC; Hong Kong, China; and Taipei,China—especially in tourism—GDP growth in Taipei,China may be affected if the epidemic is prolonged.

ASIAN DEVELOPMENT
Outlook
2003

Economic Trends and Prospects in Developing Asia

Southeast Asia
Cambodia
Indonesia
Lao People's Democratic Republic
Malaysia
Myanmar
Philippines
Singapore
Thailand
Viet Nam

Cambodia

Growth slipped in 2002, despite a recovering global economy. Fiscal and monetary policies remained prudent and, on the reform agenda, substantial progress was achieved in terms of expenditure and tax policies, the trade regime, and financial sector restructuring—though further efforts are still needed. Prospects are favorable as the world economy strengthens and as domestic reforms raise economic efficiency.

Macroeconomic Assessment

GDP growth slowed to 4.5% in 2002 from 6.3% in 2001 (Figure 2.6). Nevertheless, annual growth during 2001–2002 was similar to the average of 5.3% over the previous 4 years. Expansion of agricultural output, which accounts for nearly 40% of GDP, has been hampered in the past by deep-seated structural problems. In 2002, a combination of drought and floods also had an adverse impact as growth slowed to 0.9%. Low soil quality in some areas, unclear land ownership, insufficient irrigation, and high transaction costs contributed to the decline in agricultural growth and low productivity. Industrial expansion, led by garments, also slowed relative to 2001, but the sector still grew by 11.8%. The services sector, led by tourism, grew by 3.9%.

Wages of skilled workers, who are in comparatively short supply, continued to improve while those of unskilled workers declined due to the difficulty of the labor market in absorbing new entrants. Open unemployment does not appear to be significant, but underemployment is. Based on the 2000 Labor Force Survey, 31% of employed respondents indicated that they were available for extra work.

The fiscal deficit in 2002 at 5.9% of GDP, down slightly from the previous year, was fully financed by grants and external borrowings. Revenues accounted for 13.6% of GDP and total expenditures for 19.5%. The share of current expenditures in 2002 for priority sectors (health, education, agricul-ture, and rural development) was 32.9%, up from 30.3% in 2001.

Inflation rose to 3.0% in 2002 due to price increases early in the year in major food items, housing, and utilities, but still remained below the Government's target ceiling of 5.0%. In a context of low inflation, the nominal exchange rate remained stable. The spread between the official and market exchange rates remained within 1.0%.

The trade deficit widened to an estimated $262 million in 2002 from $240 million in the previous year. At 6.5%, imports rose slightly faster than exports, which increased by 6.0%. The current account deficit of 8.1% of GDP was financed through official transfers and capital inflows in the form of concessional loans and FDI, the latter of which amounted to an estimated $60 million in 2002. Foreign exchange reserves stood at about 3.5 months of imports.

Around 80% of external debt is owed to the Russian Federation and the US, and, pending ongoing negotiations on rescheduling, this is not currently being serviced. Excluding this, external debt is estimated at about 12% of GDP. The debt service ratio, again excluding the debt to the two main creditors, was an estimated 3.3% of goods and services exports in 2002.

Policy Developments

The incidence of poverty remains high. The number of people below the poverty line is in the range of

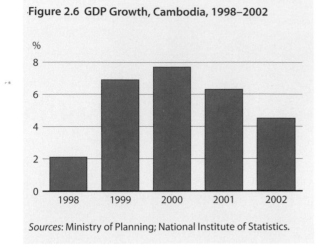

Figure 2.6 GDP Growth, Cambodia, 1998–2002

Sources: Ministry of Planning; National Institute of Statistics.

35–39%. To tackle poverty in a more focused and coordinated manner, the Government finalized its first National Poverty Reduction Strategy in 2002. However, given its limited resources, action plans should be further prioritized and better linked to the budget and the medium-term expenditure framework. Access to health and education for the poor also needs to be further improved. In addition, implementation of the land titling system, to provide the poor with formal land rights, requires acceleration, while the Government should specify and implement its policy on social land concessions, which reallocates underused state land to the poor.

Macroeconomic stability is a prerequisite for growth and poverty reduction and, to achieve it, continued fiscal and banking reform is essential. The Government has committed to maintain fiscal stability in the coming years, with an overall fiscal deficit of around 6% of GDP. The share of recurrent expenditures in the budget is expected to rise. Government expenditures on health, education, agriculture, and rural development are also expected to increase, while spending for military and defense purposes is projected to decline. The overall deficit will continue to be financed by foreign borrowings (mostly concessional) and grants.

Reforms in the banking sector started in 2000, following the adoption of the Banking and Financial Institutions Law in 1999. The number of banks fell, due to the closing of nonviable operations. ADB's Financial Sector Blueprint for 2001–2010 for the country proposes a long-term vision and policy reform agenda for all areas in the financial

sector over the 10-year period, while its Financial Sector Program Loan supports the implementation of the Blueprint, focusing on banking, insurance, interbank/money markets, and financial infrastructure. Banking supervision procedures and regulations are also being strengthened, with technical assistance from donors.

The restructuring of the Foreign Trade Bank, in preparation for privatization, is also making progress. However, despite recent improvements, banks still cannot fully perform their role as financial intermediaries and the banking system remains underdeveloped. At present, the economy is highly dollarized, with the ratio of foreign currency deposits to broad money amounting to nearly 70%. In addition, the financial system remains quite weak. Therefore, the scope of the central bank to pursue monetary policy is limited.

In the agriculture sector, further reforms are called for, especially in the areas of land, forestry, and fisheries concessions, as well as land ownership. Much good land is tied up in public land concessions, which are not fully utilized and, as a result, small farmers do not have access to enough farmland. Furthermore, access to common forestry and fisheries resources is important to the poor. Therefore, it is crucial to find a balance between granting concessions to use common resources and letting the poor use these resources.

In addition, the Government might consider making more effort in the area of securing land ownership, as only 10% of rural households hold legal land titles. Consequently, farmers have few incentives to make agricultural investment that would improve productivity. Finally, the implementation of forestry sector reforms is slow and needs to be expedited, even though 2002 saw progress made in the areas of legislation, curtailing illegal logging, monitoring forest crime, and reviewing concessions.

The quality of governance is an impediment to reform in Cambodia. Improved governance and greater efforts in combating corruption could make a significant impact on poverty reduction, and political commitment as well as legal and judicial reform are very important elements in this. The Government should therefore do more to ensure successful implementation of the Governance Action Plan, approved in 2001, in which the main commitments are reforms to improve public sector performance, the drafting of key legislation governing public

Table 2.6 Major Economic Indicators, Cambodia, 2000–2004, %

Item	2000	2001	2002	2003	2004
GDP growth	7.7	6.3	4.5	5.0	5.5
Gross domestic investment/GDP	13.5	17.9	16.2	16.6	17.0
Gross domestic savings[a]/GDP	10.7	10.2	10.0	9.7	9.4
Inflation rate (consumer price index)[b]	0.5	-0.5	3.0	3.5	4.0
Money supply (M2) growth	26.9	20.4	22.0	20.0	18.0
Fiscal balance[c]/GDP	-5.3	-6.0	-5.9	-6.1	-5.7
Merchandise export growth[d]	53.2	9.8	6.0	7.0	6.5
Merchandise import growth[e]	37.1	6.2	6.5	6.0	6.0
Current account balance[f]/GDP	-7.6	-6.3	-8.1	-8.9	-9.3
Debt service ratio	3.8	3.8	3.3	3.1	2.9

[a] Derived as gross national savings less net factor income from abroad. [b] Final quarter of the year. [c] Excluding grants. [d] Domestic exports. [e] Retained imports. [f] Excluding official transfers.

Sources: Ministry of Economy and Finance; National Institute of Statistics; National Bank of Cambodia; International Monetary Fund; staff estimates.

access to land and natural resources, and public finance reform and audit.

In 2002, trade reform made significant progress. On the multilateral front, the Government outlined some measures required before its accession to WTO, including improvements in infrastructure and telecommunications and more open laws and regulations to permit easy access to Cambodian markets. The Government also expressed the hope that the country would join WTO in 2003.

Overall growth in Cambodia has not been broad based, but is concentrated primarily in exports of garments—its main export product line—and tourism. The elimination of garment quotas under WTO rules in 2005 will put part of this growth at risk. A strategy to develop an environment conducive to private investment is therefore needed, and must be matched by concrete actions, such as strengthening capacity in customs administration and enhancing customs efficiency, as well as reducing the cost of transport by improving quality and reducing unofficial fees and charges.

Outlook for 2003–2004

The outlook is favorable, provided that developing Asia as well as the wider global economy continue to recover. In 2003, growth is projected to improve to 5.0%, and further in 2004 to 5.5%, supported mainly by garment exports and tourism.

Exports generally should be buoyed by stronger external demand as the world economy maintains its recovery. Nevertheless, the country will face tougher competition in foreign markets, especially in garments. Exporters are often at a disadvantage, despite low domestic wages, from high nonlabor costs and poor infrastructure. Tourism will continue to be a major source of income, contributing to the current account and the economy generally. Inflation—forecast to remain below 5.0%—and the exchange rate are expected to be stable.

The maintenance of macroeconomic stability and implementation of reforms in various sectors will be the main factors in an improved investment climate and sustainable economic growth.

Indonesia

Modest economic growth was sustained in 2002, driven largely by private consumption spending, while the Government made progress in improving both macroeconomic stability and fiscal sustainability. However, declining investment and limited advances in overcoming underlying impediments to investor confidence constrain near-term growth potential. The immediate economic disruption of the terrorist attacks in Bali in October 2002 has been generally contained, but the tragedy will negatively impact growth, which is expected to remain at modest levels in 2003 and 2004.

Macroeconomic Assessment

Following political changes in 2001, the economy benefited from macroeconomic stability and recorded modest growth of 3.7% in 2002, marginally higher than the previous year. Political stability, sound macroeconomic policies, and progress on structural reforms strengthened the currency and stock market, and later permitted interest rates and inflation to decline. However, this improving macroeconomic performance was offset by a slower recovery of the world economy, and a continuing decline in the level of investment in Indonesia. Accordingly, growth was largely sustained by consumption expenditures, which were supported by large formal sector wage increases and expansion of bank credit.

While growth accelerated over the first three quarters of 2002, it was then set back by the attacks in Bali in October. The currency and stock market reacted sharply, but quickly recovered as confidence returned when the Government took well-publicized and effective steps to ensure security. Nevertheless, the decline of visitor numbers in the aftermath of the bombings is impacting the Bali tourism industry specifically and the economy more broadly.

Manufacturing recorded growth of 3.7% in 2002. However, a slowdown was already evident by

the end of the third quarter, reflecting the impact of floods early in the year and continuing softness in investment spending. Utilities and some services subsectors showed strong growth, albeit slowing somewhat over the year. Agriculture grew by 2.3%, substantially up from the recent 0.7% annual growth trend. The growth was remarkable given the flooding in the early part of the year and the dislocation to markets, including those for agricultural inputs, due to heavy rainfall. The total production of paddy (wetland and dry land) for 2002 was up by 1.8% from the 2001 level with a 0.3% increase in the harvested area and a 1.6% increase in productivity. Nonfood production benefited from increases in the prices of palm oil, rubber, and robusta coffee.

Private and government spending grew strongly in 2002, providing the major stimulus to GDP growth during the year (Figure 2.7). Private spending was relatively stronger than overall income growth, partly in a delayed response to the ending of the long recession since the Asian financial crisis. Private spending, equivalent to more than 70% of GDP, grew by 4.7%, a slightly slower pace than in 2001. Public spending in 2002 was 12.8% above the level in 2001.

Based on national accounts data, both exports and imports declined in 2002. On balance, however, net exports contributed to growth as imports fell more heavily than exports. However, on a balance-

Figure 2.7 Growth of Domestic Demand Components, Indonesia, Q1 1998–Q4 2002

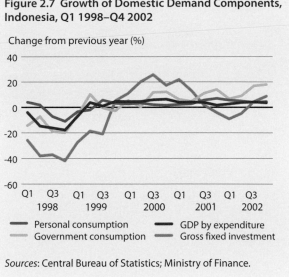

Change from previous year (%)

Personal consumption
Government consumption
GDP by expenditure
Gross fixed investment

Sources: Central Bureau of Statistics; Ministry of Finance.

of-payments basis, data show marginally positive growth for both merchandise exports and imports, following a very sharp drop in 2001. The trade account and the current account surplus increased somewhat in 2002, thus contributing positively to growth.

A poor investment climate has resulted in a continued decline in investment since the third quarter of 2001. The level of government approvals for foreign and domestic investment provides a guide to future investment trends. In the first 8 months of 2002, such approvals were more than 60% lower than in the equivalent period in 2001—a clear negative indicator of business and investment sentiment. The Manulife case in 2002, which saw the future of a sound insurance company threatened by corruption in the judicial system, gained widespread international attention. This was one of a number of incidents reflecting weak governance that discouraged investment by both domestic and foreign firms.

The latest data on employment have not been officially confirmed, but from preliminary analysis, the level of open unemployment rose from 8.1% in 2001 to 9.1% in 2002. The labor survey, carried out in August 2002, showed that the number of unemployed increased from 8.0 million to 9.1 million over the previous 12 months. However, the data did not represent the whole national situation because security concerns prevented effective employment

surveys in Aceh, Maluku, and Papua. Anecdotal evidence suggests that those working in conditions of underemployment could be triple the number of those officially unemployed.

The employment situation reflects generally the modest growth of GDP as well as the return of hundreds of thousands of illegal Indonesian workers from Malaysia during the year. Annually, in excess of 2 million young people graduate or leave school in search of employment, but the rate of economic growth achieved since the financial crisis has failed to create sufficient new jobs for them. Before the crisis, unemployment was about 4.0% and annual GDP growth was 6–7%. Unemployment has now more than doubled, with growth falling by nearly half. The previous government survey, in February 2002, indicated that more than 60% of the unemployed were young men aged 15–24 and more than one third were senior high school graduates.

Despite the generally rising level of unemployment and underemployment, formal sector wages have risen rapidly. In the first semester of 2002, workers in large and medium industrial firms received wages 15% above those of the same period in 2001. In the second semester of the year, their wages were 9% higher than in the same semester of 2001. This reflects a succession of steep rises in minimum wages, including a 30% increase in 2002. Higher wages are having a negative impact on the competitiveness of labor-intensive industries, such as textiles and electronics. Moreover, almost two thirds of the labor force are in the informal sector and do not directly benefit from minimum wage increases. The wage gap is widening between the two groups. For example, real wages of agricultural workers remain below precrisis levels, with only a 2.2% increase in the year to August 2002, while real wages in manufacturing were 35% higher in mid-2002 than in 1996.

The 2002 estimate of the incidence of poverty of 17.9% shows a continuing ebb from the peak 1998 level of 24.2%. The small decrease in the last 2 years broadly reflects the combined impacts of the moderate growth rates, especially in agriculture, an increase in population, and the appreciation of the rupiah. In the short term, the incidence of poverty in Indonesia is quite sensitive to movements in food prices.

The authorities have managed to sustain fiscal consolidation, as reflected by a progressive reduc-

Table 2.7 Major Economic Indicators, Indonesia, 2000–2004, %

Item	2000	2001	2002	2003	2004
GDP growth	4.8	3.3	3.7	3.4	4.0
Gross domestic investment/GDP	15.8	17.5	14.3	15.2	16.1
Gross domestic savings/GDP	25.1	24.9	21.1	20.1	19.7
Inflation rate (consumer price index)	3.7	11.5	11.9	10.0	8.5
Money supply (M2) growth	15.6	13.0	4.7	12.0	12.0
Fiscal balance/GDP	-1.6	-2.3	-1.7	-1.8	0.0
Merchandise export growth	27.6	-12.3	1.1	3.0	5.5
Merchandise import growth	31.9	-14.1	0.4	1.0	4.5
Current account balance/GDP	5.0	4.7	4.1	3.0	3.3

Sources: Bank Indonesia; Central Bureau of Statistics; Ministry of Finance; staff estimates.

tion in the planned budget deficit from 4.8% of GDP in 2000, to 2.5% in 2002, and to 1.8% in 2003. Moreover, the actual outcome has been a consistently lower deficit than budgeted: for example, in 2002 an estimated 1.7% actual deficit was lower than the original plan of 2.5%. A major contributor to the reduction in the fiscal deficit has been the progressive lowering of fuel subsidies that have been paid primarily to SOEs. In 2000, they accounted for more than 6% of GDP, but they are targeted to fall to under 1.0% in 2003.

The 2002 fiscal outturn shows tax revenues below target due to lower than projected growth, but this is more than offset by higher than planned oil revenues, lower expenditures on subsidies, and delayed development expenditures.

The fiscal burden of servicing government debt has been a major feature of the budget in the postcrisis years. Interest payments were equivalent to about 5.3% of GDP in 2002 and represented one of the major expenditure items in the budget. Nevertheless, an appreciating exchange rate against the dollar and increases in nominal GDP resulted in a rapid decline in government debt-to-GDP ratios from 98% in 2000 to about 72% at end-2002. The Government also made progress in 2002 with arrangements to make future repayment of both its external and domestic debt more manageable.

Inflation rose sharply in early 2002 in response to the impact of floods and hikes in electricity and transport prices. Thereafter, inflation rates fell from roughly 15% in early 2002, stabilizing at about 10% for most of the remainder of the year. Inflation for the year was slightly higher than in 2001. Further anti-inflation efforts may well have to contend with inflationary expectations on the basis of 10% as the annual price rise over the past 2 years.

An appreciating rupiah has enabled the monetary authorities to lower interest rates. The rate on 3-month central bank certificates declined to 12.9% in the fourth quarter of 2002, a fall of 4.7 percentage points from the comparable period in 2001. The rupiah appreciated in nominal terms during 2002 by 15% against the dollar and from January to October in real terms by 22%. The appreciation in 2002 reflected the balance-of-payments surplus, improved political stability, and the movement of other regional currencies.

The stock market responded to improving macroeconomic stability in early 2002, with the Jakarta composite stock price index rising by 44% in the first 4 months. Much of this gain was lost in the following 4 months in the face of negative sentiment on international markets, reflecting international accounting and corporate scandals, and domestic security and corruption concerns. However, the market recovered quickly and for the year as whole the index rose by 10%. The Jakarta Stock Exchange also saw growth in the number of firms listed (from 318 to 329), and in average daily trading value (up 24%) compared with the previous year.

Notwithstanding ongoing vulnerability,

the banking system continued to recover and strengthen. Bank credit has risen, albeit from a limited base. Outstanding bank credit increased by 16% in the first 11 months of the year, with growth focused on consumer credit. This growth in credit is reflected in the rise of the overall loan-to-deposit ratio for the banking system from 37.6% to 43.2% over 2002. The capital-adequacy ratio for nearly 150 reporting banks in the third quarter of the year was just over 23%, significantly higher than the minimum required 8.0%. However, the ratio is deceptively high, due to a large volume of government bonds and a corresponding low volume of lending that characterize most recapitalized banks. While consumer credit has expanded, the banking system provides only modest lending support for business spending. The reduction of banks' NPLs has slowed, with the gross ratio at 10.2% in November 2002. Indonesian banks are nevertheless reasonably provisioned for bad debts.

Following the sharp decline in exports experienced during the global downturn in the latter half of 2001, some recovery took place in 2002. With higher oil prices in the second half of 2002, imports of oil and gas were 32% larger than in 2001. However, with a reduction in non-oil and gas imports of 5.6%, total imports for the year were virtually the same as in 2001. The trade balance for 2002 turned in a surplus of $23.1 billion compared with $22.7 billion 2001. The impact of the terrorist attacks in Bali on tourism inflows and revenues is still to clearly emerge, but the possible drop in visitors could depress service revenues by perhaps $1 billion in 2003 and reduce export sales as well.

Private capital outflows have slowed since the fourth quarter of 2001. By the third quarter of 2002, outflows may have been running at roughly one quarter the pace seen in 2000–2001. This reflects inflows stimulated by state-asset sales and lower debt repayments on foreign private debt. FDI remains limited, discouraged by a poor investment climate (Box 2.4). Official net capital flows were slightly negative in 2002. However, this masked substantial support from Paris Club rescheduling agreements. Official reserves rose by 9% to $31.6 billion at the end of 2002.

External debt outstanding as of September 2002 was $131.3 billion, or some 13% less than at the end of 1998 after the exchange rate shock of the financial crisis. The fall in the debt level generally reflects declining enterprise (including SOE) debt. Public sector debt, at 56% of total external debt, has changed little from its end-of-year peak in 1999. The ratio of external debt to GDP declined to 77% by end-2002, down from almost 159% in 1998. The decline stems primarily from a growing nominal GDP and stronger currency rather than a smaller debt stock. The external position thus remains vulnerable: any adverse exchange rate movement could raise debt-burden indicators and reverse the trends seen in the past few years. Moreover, short-term debt continues to be a significant fraction of gross reserves—and external debt amounted to 226% of exports in 2002.

Policy Developments

The new Government of President Megawati Soekarnoputri, formed in August 2001, carried forward and developed Indonesia's economic and structural reform program agreed with IMF under a 3-year Extended Fund Facility that had been approved in early 2000. The Government's macroeconomic program for 2002 focused on fiscal consolidation in the difficult environment of managing the major public debt burden arising from the financial crisis. At the same time, structural reforms continued to address areas that impact macroeconomic stability, such as financial sector reforms, privatization and asset recovery, and legal and governance issues.

In 2002, the framework targets underlying the budget were substantially achieved. Interim results indicate that economic growth of 3.7% was within the 3–4% target range, and a fiscal deficit outturn estimated at 1.7% was well below the target 2.5% deficit. However, inflation at 11.9% was above the target range of 9–10% and the interest rate on Bank Indonesia Certificates hovered at the top of the intended target.

The Government has made considerable progress in making both external and domestic debt more manageable. In April 2002, bilateral creditors agreed to the third Paris Club rescheduling, under which $5.4 billion of interest and principal due between April 2002 and December 2003 were rescheduled. This paved the way for agreement with commercial creditors under a London Club rescheduling of syndicated loans on equivalent terms. These measures have significantly reduced

Box 2.4 Consultative Group for Indonesia Focuses on Investment

The 12th Meeting of the Consultative Group for Indonesia (CGI) was held in Bali in January 2003 with the theme "Promoting Equitable Growth, Investment and Poverty Reduction". The CGI noted the importance of encouraging investment. With current modest GDP growth rates, there is little room for improving the standard of living, especially of the poor.

Business investment—the spending on new plant and equipment—has been virtually absent since the crisis began in 1997. Weak investment reduces GDP immediately, but also lowers the longer-term potential for growth and higher-income employment.

Indonesia's experience is not unique. Investment-to-GDP ratios in most economies in East and Southeast Asia are lower now than in the mid-1990s. There are many reasons as the world economy is a different place now than a decade ago. In particular, there is generally now less FDI and a smaller volume of cross-border portfolio flows.

But there are local factors that have undermined investor sentiment—factors that reflect the policy and performance of Indonesia itself. First has been the tremendous political change, replacing decades of authoritarian rule from the center with very determined moves toward a market-oriented economy and democratic political institutions. These fundamental changes have been accompanied sometimes by uncertainty with respect to decision making, which discourages new commitments by businesses. Decentralization, for example, has not clarified key business concerns such as certainty of franchises or what levels of taxes or fees businesses might face.

There have also been security concerns. The latest threat, triggered by the terrorist attacks in Bali, has surely discouraged business investment. Long-standing civil strife in a number of regions such as Aceh and the Moluccas has also discouraged local investment.

Investment has also been hindered by the continuing weakness of the banking sector, much of which is still effectively nationalized. Banks rely upon government bonds for income and do not aggressively seek out corporate borrowers. Government efforts to return banks to the private sector, to strengthen supervision, and to reduce the scope for money laundering are crucial to providing the context for business investment to grow.

Finally, in Indonesia and across developing Asia, investment has been hindered by a growing awareness of the costs of poor governance—especially corruption. The financial crisis was partly a bursting of a speculative investment bubble and has prompted a reassessment of the nature of investment in this region. This has meant less investment in those economies that are considered to have more serious governance problems.

President Megawati has declared 2003 "Investment Year". However, improvements to the investment climate will not come before the Government seriously addresses widespread problems. Moreover, investors may well postpone decisions until the global economic and political situation improves and the 2004 national election is over.

To encourage investment commitments, on a priority basis, in addition to working to improve security conditions, the Government should (i) create a more consistent and conducive business environment in the regions, (ii) continue with the restructuring and re-privatization of the banks taken over by the state after the crisis, and (iii) strengthen law enforcement and the judicial system.

---

the impact of external debt servicing on the 2003 budget. However, the Government continues to face very large external repayment obligations in 2004–2005. A key policy issue will be the possible resort to further Paris Club rescheduling over this period, which would require an ongoing IMF program for Indonesia, and public debate is now addressing the implications of not extending the present program on its completion at end-2003.

In terms of domestic debt, important measures were taken in 2002 that provide new capacity to manage debt more effectively. First, enactment of the Sovereign Debt Securities Law in November 2002 provides the basis for the issue of domestic government bonds. This new capacity was utilized with the successful auction in December of Rp2 trillion of new bonds with an 8-year maturity. Regular ongoing auctions are planned as part of the development of an active market for domestic public debt. This will provide the Government with valuable flexibility to meet maturing domestic debt obligations. Second, in 2002 the Government negotiated an extension of maturities on Rp172 trillion of recapitalization bonds held by state banks. This will reduce bond redemptions by Rp35 trillion in 2004–2005. Third, arrangements have also been put into place regarding Rp160 trillion of Bank Indonesia Liquidity Credit (BLBI) bonds with the central bank arising from the liquidity credits provided to the banking system during the financial crisis. These bonds are being exchanged for a perpetual promissory note to the central bank, addressing long-outstanding uncertainty over liabilities relating to BLBI. The interest burden on the budget is effectively reduced by this action, while the financial soundness of the central bank is preserved. The overall impact of these steps has been to more than halve the scheduled domestic debt repayment in 2004–2005.

The Government also made significant progress in implementing structural reforms in 2002. Important legislation enacted during the year included the Anti-Money Laundering Law, the Sovereign Debt Securities Law, and the Law on the Anti-Corruption Commission. Despite delays and some opposition, the Government succeeded in privatizing two large banks, Bank of Central Asia and Niaga. These banks had been taken over in the crisis; the recent sales have resulted in more than 50% of equity ownership in each being returned to the private sector. While the sales proceeds are important to the budget, the transactions also represent important milestones toward the goal of reducing the Government's dominant ownership role in the banking sector stemming from the extensive bank recapitalization and nationalization undertaken during and following the crisis. The Government is planning further disposals or dilutions of bank ownership in 2003, including an initial public offering for state-owned Bank Mandiri, the country's largest bank.

Substantial progress has been made in planning and drafting legislation for a consolidated supervisory regulatory agency for the financial sector. Planning for a self-funding deposit insurance protection scheme is also under way. This is expected to play an important role as the present blanket deposit guarantee by the Government is to be progressively phased out.

The Indonesian Bank Restructuring Agency has moved significantly forward in accelerating the sale of assets accumulated during crisis-related corporate rescue operations. The privatization of SOEs has made limited progress in the face of public and political challenges. However, privatization revenues met targets after the sale of equity shares in the state satellite telecommunications firm, Indosat, at the end of 2002.

Investment remains weak, though several of the reforms noted above will contribute to improving the investment environment. Further steps are necessary if investment is to recover and a return seen to the higher economic growth that can sustain greater employment generation. Key areas for improvement are strengthening the judicial system and addressing policy uncertainties—particularly those related to labor laws and regulations, and to decentralization.

Outlook for 2003–2004

Although the pace of private spending is expected to weaken somewhat, modest increases in overall GDP growth are expected in the next 2 years as the external environment improves and as some expected pickup in investment spending materializes. GDP growth in 2003 is expected to be 3.4%, strengthening to 4.0% in 2004. The 1.8% budget deficit for 2003 incorporates a 0.5% fiscal stimulus to mitigate the negative impact of the Bali bombings, but nevertheless maintains the declining trend in the planned budget deficit.

Financial sector reforms will strengthen the banking system, supporting an increase in GDP growth. Credit expansion will be based particularly on household borrowing, sustaining consumer spending. However, a tight monetary policy is expected to be able to contain price increases and inflation should moderate from 11.9% in 2002 to 10.0% in 2003 and to 8.5% in 2004.

Although the external environment will contribute to the projected recovery, exports are likely to face stiffer international competition in the region, especially from the PRC and Viet Nam. Recent moves to increase minimum wages and uncertainties over the enforcement of labor regulations threaten to reduce Indonesia's international competitiveness. Continued efforts to reduce budget subsidies for energy and utilities will lead to rising administered prices and some cost pressures, also reducing export industry prospects. On balance, the current account surplus is expected to fall in the near term, but to rise as international markets recover further in 2004.

Investment spending is expected to slowly

improve, largely for cyclical reasons. However, any increased business spending is unlikely to be in response to changes in long-term prospects. Robustly higher levels of plant and equipment expenditures over the long term will have to await the resolution of issues that have discouraged investment. A stronger legal and judicial system, lower business costs due to reduced corruption, and improved certainty in the policy environment, especially at the local level, will be needed to see substantially higher levels of business investment.

The monetary authorities face a considerable challenge in working to lower inflation while meeting broader stabilization goals. Average inflation over 1998–2002 was 19.8% and the Government has targeted less than 10% over the next few years. The central bank faces a dilemma, particularly in the use of the rate of interest on its short-term bills (1- and 3-month Bank Indonesia Certificates), the primary tool available for influencing monetary policy. In the past, the central bank has maintained high interest rates to ease currency depreciation pressure and to lower inflation. However, in the future, this might weaken growth and raise public debt service needs, complicating fiscal policy. Higher interest rates might be especially discouraging for new investment. Conversely, the central bank is concerned with the health of the commercial banks and lowering interest rates will lower the profitability of some of them significantly.

The national elections scheduled for mid-2004 may involve increasingly politicized debate on economic policy. This may make it harder for the Government to take steps involving politically sensitive issues, such as privatization or increases in administered prices. In early 2003, the Government has already faced vocal opposition to planned increases in administered prices—for petroleum products, electricity, and telephone services—that had been agreed in Parliament. Nevertheless, there seems an increasing awareness of the value to Indonesia of prudent fiscal policy and it is likely that policies in this area, once agreed, will be implemented.

The country remains vulnerable to external shocks. Continued improvement in debt indicators and the capacity to service existing debt are dependent upon rupiah stability. Higher oil prices during the first quarter of 2003 provided some short-term windfall profits for the budget, but also exacerbated the political difficulties of moving administered energy prices to market levels. Stronger security measures have provided some confidence to the international community that the Government is taking what steps it can to improve security. Continued efforts may find a pay-off in a return of tourists to the country, although the SARS epidemic will affect the tourism industry in the first half of 2003.

Similarly, the Government has taken significant steps to improve regional security, in the Moluccas, but most notably in Aceh. The signing of a peace accord in early December 2002 may well bring about the conditions to allow for this rich region to meet its potential, with positive spillovers in neighboring regions and the country as a whole.

Lao People's Democratic Republic

The country maintained relatively stable macroeconomic conditions in 2002, although the Government's revenue collection was lower than target. Several reform efforts have moved forward, particularly in the financial sector, though more are needed. Economic growth in 2003 is expected to be favorable due to an expected significant rebound in FDI.

Macroeconomic Assessment

The pace of economic growth in the Lao People's Democratic Republic (Lao PDR) remained broadly stable in 2002. GDP growth was 5.8%, little changed from the previous year (Figure 2.8). Agriculture, which employs an estimated 80% of the workforce and accounts for about half of GDP, expanded by 4.0%. Industry remained the fastest growing sector—with construction and garments playing a key role—expanding by 9.8%. The services sector, which accounts for a quarter of the economy, grew by 5.8%. Tourism continued to play a major role, contributing both to GDP growth and the balance of payments. Income from tourism has increased steadily since the mid-1990s.

In FY2002 (ended 30 September 2002), the Government had an overall budget deficit of 8.3% of GDP, mostly financed by grants and external concessional loans. Revenue collection fell short of its target by about 10%. Fiscal decentralization, in a context of insufficient institutional capacity, impeded revenue mobilization. More public sector resources were allocated to the social sector, with the share of expenditures for education and health increasing from 11.4% in FY2001 to 19.1% in FY2002.

The acceleration in inflation in the second half of 2002 is of some concern. For the year as a whole, inflation increased to 10.6%, from 7.8% in 2001. The kip depreciated by 13% against the dollar. The spread between the official and market exchange rates remained at about 2%.

On the external front, electricity from hydro-power plants, garments, and wood products were the leading exports. The trade deficit decreased to $198.7 million from $217.0 million in 2001, while the current account deficit decreased to about 5.6% of GDP from 6.9% over the same period. Foreign exchange reserves strengthened in 2002 and were sufficient to cover 3.5 months of imports of goods and services at year-end.

The value of new foreign investment projects approved in FY2002 rose, attributed largely to a gradual recovery in developing Asia and improved investment conditions domestically. In terms of external debt, approximately half of it is owed to the Russian Federation. This debt is on the books at an unrealistic exchange rate and is not currently being serviced. The governments of the two countries have been negotiating rescheduling terms of the debt since 2000 and it is expected that this will lead to a significant reduction of the book value of the debt. The debt service ratio was still a manageable 16.6% in 2002.

Policy Developments

In recent years, the Government has made concerted efforts to reduce its fiscal deficit. It has had some success and inflation rates have fallen as a consequence. However, the fiscal deficit remains substantial, but is now almost entirely financed

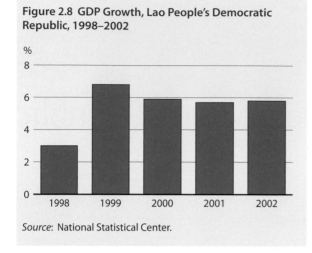

Figure 2.8 GDP Growth, Lao People's Democratic Republic, 1998–2002

Source: National Statistical Center.

through grants and external borrowings, rather than through credit creation by the Bank of the Lao PDR (BOL), as happened in the past. The Government hopes to contain the fiscal deficit through enhanced revenue mobilization efforts, but current targets are still modest and more could be done to improve revenue performance in three main areas: tax and customs administration, cutting exemptions, and adopting a VAT. To be effective, these measures need a commitment to sustained implementation by the Government. Tight constraints on expenditures are needed to control the size of the fiscal deficit. In terms of the components of the budget, there has been an imbalance between capital and recurrent expenditures, as the latter have not been allocated sufficient resources. Continuing efforts have been made to address this imbalance, as seen by the declining share of capital expenditures, which used to account for more than 60% of total expenditures.

There was also an increase in social sector spending as a share of expenditures, in particular, health and education. However, there is still room for improvement to address recurrent expenditures and social sector priorities. In addition, further reform measures in public expenditure management are needed, including the improvement of budget planning and execution, treasury operations, and auditing.

The principal objectives of monetary policy are to limit inflation and to stabilize the exchange rate. BOL monetized the Government's budget deficit and this created inflationary pressure in 1998 and 1999. Consequently, as part of the program to

reduce inflation, BOL stopped purchasing government bonds as a way to finance the budget deficit. Starting in mid-2002, BOL also strengthened control of credit growth at state-owned commercial banks (SOCBs).

Financial sector reform remains a priority for the Government, and it is in the process of undertaking these reforms with the support of ADB, IMF, and the World Bank. Although foreign banks and joint ventures operate in Vientiane, the financial system is now dominated by three SOCBs and the Agricultural Promotion Bank (APB). In the past, SOCBs focused on lending to SOEs, and a high proportion of these loans became nonperforming. Reforms will help the financial sector direct its lending to projects on the basis of commercial and credit considerations. It will also force SOEs to further commercialize their operations, reducing their reliance on easy credits from the SOCBs.

To prepare for restructuring the SOCB operations, the Government has implemented several measures. These include strictly applying regulations on loan classification and provisioning, ensuring external auditing, prohibiting lending to borrowers in default, and applying sector-wide ceilings on SOCB credit growth. Furthermore, bank supervision is being strengthened through on-site examinations and independent assessments of SOCB prudential reports. The Government is also committed to the improvement of rural and micro finance, as seen by the restructuring of APB to enable it to operate on a sustainable commercial basis. An operational diagnostic study and external audit for APB were conducted, and a corporate vision to guide the restructuring has been adopted.

Reforms are also under way in the SOE sector, including restructuring as well as tariff hikes for electricity and water. Domestic airline fares are also to be increased. The Government has plans to develop and implement specific action plans for each SOE, including sales of noncore assets.

In the area of private sector development, reforms to the foreign investment framework were carried out in 2002, including streamlining approval procedures for the establishment and operation of foreign investment and simplifying the regulations and procedures for establishing businesses. During the Foreign Investment Forum held in Vientiane in May 2002 and attended by more than 300 foreign investors, the Government stated its commitment

Table 2.8 Major Economic Indicators, Lao People's Democratic Republic, 2000–2004, %

Item	2000	2001	2002	2003	2004
GDP growth	5.9	5.7	5.8	6.0	6.5
Gross domestic investment/GDP	20.5	21.0	21.2	22.2	22.6
Inflation rate (consumer price index)	27.1	7.8	10.6	8.0	7.0
Money supply (M2) growth	45.5	20.2	20.0	19.0	18.0
Fiscal balance[b]/GDP	-8.3	-7.5	-8.3	-8.6	-8.7
Merchandise export growth	2.6	-0.3	2.7	5.2	5.6
Merchandise import growth	2.7	-0.4	-1.6	4.7	7.5
Current account balance[c]/GDP	-8.3	-6.9	-5.6	-5.7	-7.1
Debt service ratio	15.4	15.6	16.6	17.5	16.8

[a] Derived as gross national savings less net factor income from abroad. [b] Excluding grants. [c] Excluding official transfers.

Sources: National Statistical Center; Bank of the Lao PDR; Ministry of Finance; International Monetary Fund; staff estimates.

to expand the private sector, including facilitating SME development and attracting FDI to assist in the sustainable development of natural resources.

In 1998, 39% of the population lived below the poverty line. Poverty is not evenly distributed, tending to be higher and more concentrated in the northern region. Although evidence suggests that economic growth has had a positive effect in reducing poverty, the gains that the poor might have expected to receive from economic growth have been diluted due to increased inequality. The National Poverty Eradication Program and the Poverty Reduction Strategy Paper, to be completed in 2003, are expected to include specific policies to tackle poverty. Prioritized action plans and implementation of these plans are critical if the Program is to be successful.

Outlook for 2003–2004

The outlook is generally favorable due to an expected significant rebound in FDI. New regulations to promote it and the strong government commitment to support private sector development should contribute to a more conducive environment for private investment. GDP growth is expected to pick up, reaching 6.5% in 2004. Exports are likely to be supported by growth of external demand over the forecast period, as developing Asia continues to recover. Imports are forecast to rise due to higher capital goods requirements. With higher imports, it is expected that the trade and current account balances in 2003–2004 will deteriorate. Tourism will continue to contribute positively to the economy and the current account, but not enough to bring the current account into surplus.

Inflation is expected to fall to 7.0% by 2004 and the exchange rate to remain broadly stable. The maintenance of macroeconomic stability and the continued implementation of reforms in various sectors are likely to contribute to sustainable economic growth in the country.

In the medium term, government revenues are expected to rise modestly, provided that reforms in tax collection continue and coordination with provincial tax authorities improves.

Malaysia

The economy saw a recovery in 2002, led by strong consumption demand and a recovery in exports, though it is still performing below capacity. Whether the economy will realize its full potential will depend on both global economic recovery and domestic policy response to the need to diversify industry and export products, raise labor productivity, and upgrade technology.

Macroeconomic Assessment

A moderate economic recovery took hold in 2002, after low growth of only 0.4% in the previous year. At 4.2%, GDP growth represents a notable achievement given the many uncertainties and challenges on the global front that dampened both global trade and domestic investor confidence. Growth was driven by public and private consumption, which in turn was boosted by a series of fiscal measures. The economy began to show some signs of a rebound in the first quarter of the year when it grew by 1.1% year on year. The pace of the recovery accelerated further in the second quarter and the second half of the year, when growth averaged over 5% year on year.

On the production side, manufacturing and services played a lead role in strengthening output growth in 2002. After a sharp decline of 6.2% in 2001, manufacturing output grew by 4.1% in 2002, boosted largely by resilience of consumption demand and a turnaround in manufacturing exports. The growth of export-oriented industrial production gained strength through the year whereas domestic-oriented industrial production slowed. Overall, industrial production was still in the process of recovery in 2002, and it may be some time before it resumes more rapid growth. Electronics outperformed other subsectors and recorded the highest growth, followed by chemicals and vehicles. Agriculture, which accounted for about

8% of GDP, continued with low growth of 0.3% in 2002. Palm oil production registered lower yields, but good weather conditions led to increases in the production of rubber and cocoa. The services sector sustained its strong performance, recording robust growth of 4.5%. Construction maintained its 2001 growth rate of 2.3%. A greater number of government investment projects and of civil engineering activities contributed to the subsector's performance.

Since the Asian financial crisis that began in 1997, the Government has maintained a fiscal pump-priming policy to boost domestic demand, aimed at preventing recession and keeping unemployment down, in the wake of volatility and uncertainty in the global economy. In 2001 and 2002, the Government continued its expansionary fiscal policies to stimulate investment and production (Figure 2.9). Reflecting this, public consumption (accounting for about one fourth of total consumption) grew by 17.6% and 13.8% in 2001 and 2002, respectively, while private consumption increased by lower rates of 2.8% and 4.2% over the same period.

The growth rate of gross fixed capital formation for the whole of 2002 was 0.2%, after a contraction of 2.8% in 2001; it pushed into positive territory in the third quarter of 2002 after continued declines over the previous four quarters. Public investment, which accounted for 58.0% of gross fixed capital formation in 2001, continued to provide the major impetus, growing by 5.0% in 2002, though this was

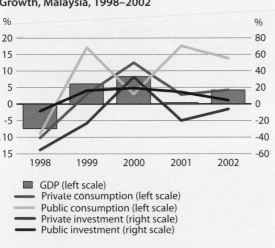

Figure 2.9 Role of Fiscal Pump Priming in GDP Growth, Malaysia, 1998–2002

Sources: Malaysian Institute of Economic Research, available: www.mier.org.my; Bank Negara Malaysia.

much lower than in the previous 2 years. Private investment, which decreased by nearly 22% in 2001, remained subdued, though Bank Negara Malaysia maintained an accommodative monetary policy and the Government increased its development expenditures. Uncertainty regarding the international political and economic outlook appears to have forestalled a resurgence in investment by the private sector.

On the external front, both exports and imports rebounded in 2002. Thanks to a significant recovery of major items such as palm oil, semiconductors, textiles, chemicals, and furniture in the latter half of the year, annual merchandise exports grew by 6.1% in 2002, compared with a fall of 10.6% in the previous year. Exports to ASEAN countries, PRC, and US increased, while markets in the EU and Japan remained weak.

Imports rose beginning in the second quarter of 2002 as domestic demand and component inputs for exports began to pick up. Import growth was led by intermediate and consumption goods, reflecting improved manufacturing activities and growing personal consumption. For the whole of 2002, imports rose by 8.1%, after a contraction of 10.3% in 2001.

Reflecting these developments, the trade account recorded a surplus of $18.1 billion in 2002, lower than in 2001. Increases in the services

deficit and income outflows from direct investments, coupled with a lower trade account surplus, resulted in a decrease in the current account surplus from $7.3 billion in 2001 to $7.2 billion in 2002. Applications for FDI have rebounded, implying that investor confidence may be gradually recovering. In 2002, FDI applications for manufacturing projects were up by 13.7% compared with the previous year. The top three applicants during the period, based on investment value, were Germany, UK, and US. Malaysia's reserve position strengthened in 2002 due to sustained current account surpluses and continued inflows of FDI. Net international reserves rose to $34.6 billion from $30.8 billion in 2001.

Monetary policy was accommodative in 2002. Ample liquidity was available and interest rates remained low in the financial markets. As a result, bank lending to the business sector remained strong. Major recipients of loans were manufacturing, wholesale and retail trade, construction, insurance, and businesses. Small businesses benefited significantly from bank lending: loans below RM100,000 rose by 17.8% from a decline of 15.7% in 2001. Loans to consumers also picked up sharply as housing and car loans increased rapidly. The commercial bank lending rate of 6.39% remained the same as in 2001.

The health of the banking sector continued to improve, with the NPL ratio on a 6-month classification basis falling to about 7%. With the economy operating below its long-term potential and with excess capacity, the CPI rose by only 1.8%, despite the accommodative monetary policy stance.

The unemployment rate was 3.6% in 2001 and declined to 3.5% in 2002. The foreign exchange rate remained fixed at RM3.8 to the US dollar, and, following the dollar down, depreciated generally against other major currencies.

The 2002 federal government budget accorded priority to supporting economic growth, while aiming at improved fiscal consolidation by targeting a lower deficit of 4.7% of GDP, compared with a 5.5% outturn in 2001. The deficit outturn for 2002 is estimated at 5.6%. To stimulate private sector activities, the budget included many important tax measures, including a reduction in personal income tax rates, lower import duties on certain intermediate goods, adjustments in investment allowances and depreciation, and changes to tax holiday coverage for enterprises.

Table 2.9 Major Economic Indicators, Malaysia, 2000–2004, %

Item	2000	2001	2002	2003	2004
GDP growth	8.3	0.4	4.2	4.3	5.1
Gross domestic investment/GDP	27.1	23.8	24.4	25.3	27.1
Gross domestic savings/GDP	47.1	42.2	41.8	42.1	43.0
Inflation rate (consumer price index)	1.6	1.4	1.8	1.9	2.2
Money supply (M2) growth	5.2	2.2	5.8	7.5	8.1
Fiscal balance/GDP	-5.8	-5.5	-5.6	-4.0	-2.5
Merchandise export growth	17.0	-10.6	6.1	8.1	10.2
Merchandise import growth	26.3	-10.3	8.1	8.8	11.3
Current account balance/GDP	9.4	8.3	7.6	6.3	5.7
Debt service ratio	5.4	6.1	6.0	5.8	5.6

Sources: Malaysian Institute of Economic Research, available: www.mier.org.my; Ministry of Finance, available: www.treasury.gov.my; Bank Negara Malaysia, available: www.bnm.gov.my; staff estimates.

Policy Developments

Although the focus of fiscal policy in 2002 was on boosting domestic demand in the short term, it also aimed at enhancing long-term industrial competitiveness and labor productivity through spending on infrastructure development and education, and training for human resources development. Public sector consumption and investment expenditures are estimated to have contributed 1.4 percentage points to overall GDP growth in 2002, or nearly a third of the total.

The 2003 budget aspires to fiscal consolidation in line with the government goal of achieving a balanced budget by the end of the Eighth Malaysia Plan (2001–2005). The target budget deficit in 2003 is 3.9% of GDP, based on projections of an improved economic outlook both domestically and globally. To support the private sector as the engine of economic growth, the budget increases expenditures for education and training, labor productivity improvement, R&D and technology, SMEs, and services in the areas of agriculture, finance, and computer software. Fiscal deficits have not come down much in the last 2 years and efforts need to be made to lower them further. The rate is much higher than in other economies in the region affected by the financial crisis.

Reflecting the sustained fiscal deficits, government debt had risen to 47.2% of GDP at the end of

2002. The Government should be able to rationalize fiscal expenditures and augment tax revenue collections to manage and reduce the debt, and needs to lower the fiscal deficit and the debt level within a reasonable time. However, assuming that global economic recovery takes place gradually, fiscal pump priming will remain a tool in the hands of the Government to boost consumption demand and, to a lesser extent, physical investment and construction activities in 2003–2004. It is widely expected that the Government will announce another major stimulus package in the first half of 2003, covering a range of initiatives aimed at raising government spending and encouraging private investment and consumption. The package may include an increase in construction projects on a modest scale to ensure rapid completion, a cut in the employee's contribution to the Employees' Provident Fund by 1–2 percentage points, a cut in the income tax rate, and greater support for SMEs and for attracting FDI. Therefore, the Government's attempt to pursue simultaneously the two goals of growth stimulation and fiscal stabilization is a major challenge.

Bank Negara Malaysia is likely to continue its accommodative monetary policy to support private sector activities but without creating substantial inflationary pressures, given the large amount of underutilized industrial capacity. The banking sector is generally strong and NPLs are no longer a key financial issue. Consequently, the central bank will be able to conduct a more flexible monetary policy in the future. Since Malaysia is a small, open economy, the Government has to take steps to minimize any deflationary pressure arising from an external shock that causes a slowdown in external demand globally. This reinforces the likelihood that Bank Negara Malaysia will favor an accommodative monetary policy over the next 2 years.

Outlook for 2003–2004

The economy, which has relied heavily on domestic demand over the last several years, will see external demand playing an increasingly important role in 2003–2004 since OECD economies are likely to grow faster than in 2002. Private investment is also expected to improve further as confidence builds and demand continues to strengthen. In view of this, economic growth in the forecast period should be more balanced, with significant contributions from consumption, investment, and exports. On the supply side, manufacturing, which experienced a modest recovery in 2002, is expected to be the main engine of economic growth, with the services sector continuing to play an important role.

Private consumption is projected to expand by 5.6% and 6.5% in 2003 and 2004, respectively, boosted by rising disposable incomes, continued accommodative monetary and fiscal policies, and improving consumer confidence. The growth rate of public consumption may fall to about 6%, reflecting the government policy stance to focus its expenditures on physical investment and construction activities, rather than on direct government consumption. Private investment is likely to improve further at a moderate rate of 5.3% in

2003, accelerating to 8.5% in 2004, while FDI will contribute to the growth of private investment over 2003–2004.

On the external front, merchandise exports are projected to grow by 8.1% in 2003 and by 10.2% in 2004 as a result of improving external market conditions for electronics, chemicals, and some agricultural products such as palm oil and rubber. Reflecting the growing consumption demand and recovering private investment, imports are expected to increase by 8.8% and 11.3% over the forecast period. Taking all these developments into account, GDP growth is forecast at 4.3% in 2003 and 5.1% in 2004. Manufacturing and services, which together account for about 85% of total GDP, will likely grow by 6–7% and 3–4%, respectively, in this period.

Inflation is projected to remain low, at its current level of about 2%, over the next 2–3 years, because of excess industrial capacity and low import prices. The unemployment rate should decline to 3.4% and to 3.1% in 2003 and 2004, respectively, due to higher GDP growth and improving business confidence in the private sector. The current account surplus is projected to decrease, primarily because of the expected higher growth in merchandise imports, which will exceed the increased rate of merchandise exports in this period. The current account surplus is forecast to drop to 6.3% and 5.7% of GDP in 2003 and 2004, respectively.

However, several downside risks are present that may adversely affect the economy and undermine the above projections. They include the effects of the conflict in Iraq, the outbreak of SARS in the region, and any further delay in the recovery of the US and Japanese economies and consequent weak electronics demand.

Myanmar

Growth in FY2001 was recorded at 11.1%. However, there are reasons to be concerned about prospects. Macroeconomic imbalances persist, and there are growing signs of problems at a structural level. The country faces a complex development agenda. In the short run, priority should be given to reducing fiscal deficits and realigning expenditure priorities. Agricultural liberalization offers potentially large benefits.

Macroeconomic Assessment

An objective assessment of economic developments in Myanmar is made difficult by poor quality data. Often, information is available only with a long lag, is incomplete, and is difficult to reconcile. Furthermore, many indicators are based on application of outdated statistical standards. The use of an official parity for the domestic currency (the kyat), which carries a vast premium over the market rate, to value public sector foreign exchange transactions, including those of state economic enterprises (SEEs), creates further interpretive difficulties.

The official estimate of GDP growth for FY2001 (ended 31 March 2002) is 11.1%. Strong economic performance in FY2001 follows on 3 years of rapid expansion. In FY2001, strong agricultural growth was complemented by fast industrial growth (including agroprocessing and gas production). On the demand side, royalties from gas production supported increased capital expenditures by SEEs. After the expansion of gas exports with major gas projects coming on stream in FY2000, exports continued to grow in FY2001.

The general picture of vigorous economic growth is, however, qualified by some other indicators. These point to falling yields for some key crops (including rice), reduced fertilizer production, continuing power shortages, and a reduction in cement production.

In FY2001, the fiscal deficit narrowed from FY2000's outcome. The deficit is estimated to be 6.6% of GDP, compared with 8.4% in FY2000. The improvement in the deficit position was entirely a consequence of reduced expenditures. Public sector revenues did not even keep pace with the expansion of income and fell below 5% of GDP. By the end of FY2001, total public sector debt as a proportion of GDP had risen to about 95%.

After a brief respite in FY2000, when consumer price inflation dipped below 4%, it accelerated to 56.8% by end-December 2002. In part, the acceleration can be traced to the large increase in public sector wages awarded in FY2002 that, to a large degree, was financed through central bank credit creation. In nominal terms, public sector credit grew by about 40%, and broad money by just over 45%, in both FY2000 and FY2001.

Historically, the dollar value of the kyat in the parallel market has been closely and inversely correlated with domestic inflation. By the close of FY2001, the parallel market exchange rate had depreciated by about 70% relative to its value at the start of the year. Interest rates, which are administratively determined, remained unchanged over the period.

Myanmar's balance-of-payments position remained weak in FY2001. The current account slipped into deficit after returning to a surplus in FY2000. At the same time, public sector imports increased as foreign exchange constraints were relaxed with the inflow of gas export revenues. Private capital inflows to Myanmar have all but evaporated in the face of international sanctions and domestic economic uncertainties. It is estimated that gross international reserves at the end of FY2001 were sufficient to cover about 2.3 months of imports. Total external debt was estimated to be just over $6 billion in FY2001 or about 73.4% of GDP, and, of this, $2.5 billion is in arrears following the suspension of payments to multilateral and bilateral creditors in 1997.

Policy Developments

Prospects for sustained reductions in poverty and broad-based improvements in the quality of life for the people of Myanmar are impaired by macroeconomic imbalances and impediments to structural adjustment. Despite recorded growth, there has been little change in the structure of the economy for more than a decade. There is also persuasive anecdotal evidence that, for a large number of people living in Myanmar, hardships are becoming more acute. A necessary if not in itself sufficient condition for pro-poor growth is the presence of a macroeconomic environment that allows markets to work efficiently, and that avoids the unfair and arbitrary redistributions of income that accompany high inflation.

Large fiscal deficits have underpinned perennially high inflation in Myanmar and the steep declines in the parallel market value of the kyat. The deficits are fueled by, on the one hand, large military expenditures and inefficient SEEs that receive direct budgetary support, and, on the other, by a poor track record in mobilizing public sector revenues. A pervasive system of implicit subsidies and taxes as well as the dual exchange rate system also contribute to fiscal stress.

The Government has now declared the objective of paring public sector deficits over a 5-year period. However, to achieve this, improved systems to plan coherently, and monitor and control expenditures must be put in place. Line ministries, SEEs, and other agencies must increasingly face the discipline of hard budget constraints. Equally important, in a context where real expenditures for the provision of basic social services are grossly inadequate, expenditure priorities need to be systematically realigned with development needs.

On the revenue side, revenue mobilization could be improved within the prevailing structure of taxes and levies, though efforts at revenue mobilization would be more likely to be successful if they were accompanied by structural reforms. In particular, the removal of administrative and other impediments to private sector activity and enterprise could generate large supply-side gains. In a context where comprehensive reforms are needed but implementation capacity is limited, efforts should initially focus on areas where the short-run costs of reform are likely to be small and benefits quick to materialize. This suggests that priority might be given to liberalizing the agriculture sector. In formulating and sequencing a longer-term reform program, Myanmar could usefully draw on the experience of other DMCs, particularly Viet Nam and the PRC.

Outlook for 2003–2004

The Government has targeted 6% GDP growth over the latest 5-year planning period. However, the immediate prospects for fast economic expansion are uncertain. Widespread flooding in 2002 is likely to have had an adverse impact on agricultural activity, which still accounts for over 40% of GDP. Also, yields of important agricultural crops have fallen recently against a backdrop of shortages of imported fertilizers and other inputs. Political and economic sanctions limit prospects for exports and FDI, and any significant easing of foreign exchange constraints is unlikely in the near future.

Over the medium term, the prospects for growth will, of course, depend crucially on policy choices. If macroeconomic imbalances and structural distortions persist, growth will undoubtedly suffer. If, however, a credible and sustained effort at reform were to begin, the prospects for sustainable economic expansion and poverty reduction would be good.

Philippines

In 2002, GDP grew faster than in 2001, supported by strong growth in industry and by increased services sector activity. However, the fiscal deficit deteriorated sharply, and measures to increase revenues are needed urgently. The passage of the Special Purpose Vehicle Act offers a promising start to reducing banking NPLs. While governance needs to be improved, peace and order (especially in the south) are also crucial to attract investment and facilitate economic development.

Macroeconomic Assessment

In 2002, GDP growth strengthened to 4.6% from 3.2% in 2001, while GNP growth accelerated to 5.2% from 3.4% over the same period. Industrial growth strengthened to 4.1% from 1.3% in 2001, largely as a result of a recovery in manufacturing, in turn due to stronger external demand for electronics and garments. The services sector, which grew strongly by 5.4%, remained the main pillar of economic growth, driven by the transport and communications subsectors. While agricultural growth decelerated, to 3.5% from 3.7% in 2001, it picked up strongly toward the end of the year.

On the demand side, personal consumption expenditure continued to be the main driver of rising GDP. Propelled by strong demand for household furnishing, transport, and communications, personal consumption expenditure rose by 3.9%. Investment grew by 2.1, after a 2.2% decline in 2001. Benefiting from the gradual recovery of the world economy, exports and imports increased in 2002, by 12.2% and 4.6%, respectively, after a contraction in 2001. In spite of budget constraints, government consumption expenditures grew by 1.8%, compared with 0.3% in 2001.

The total labor force in 2002 of 33.9 million rose by 3.4% from the prior year's level. Employment growth, though, was only 3.1%, compared with 6.2% in 2001. With employment growing slowly, unemployment remained high at 11.4% in 2002, edging up from 9.8% in the previous year. The unemployment rate remains one of the highest among ASEAN members, and has been exacerbated by the rapid growth in the labor force and by relatively slow economic growth in recent years. This has led to fewer job opportunities in urban areas, despite additional jobs created by the services sector.

In 2002, the fiscal deficit deteriorated sharply to reach P212.7 billion, or 64% above the revised full-year target of P130 billion and equivalent to 5.4% of GDP. In 2001, the budget deficit of P147 billion (4.0% of GDP) only slightly exceeded the fiscal deficit target of P145 billion. The principal reason for the wider deficit was a shortfall in tax collections. The lack of incentives for tax officers to monitor and follow up with taxpayers, a complicated tax system, the effect of unexpected low interest rates on withholding tax, and a noninflation-indexed rate for excise tax were among the main reasons for the revenue shortfalls.

However, efforts to improve tax revenues were made in the last quarter of 2002. The performance of the Bureau of Internal Revenue (BIR) improved as reflected in the higher tax collections on net income and profits as well as in VAT, which increased by 12.5% and 21.0%, respectively, compared with the corresponding period of the previous year. Measures to enhance tax revenues by BIR included tightening collection measures; setting

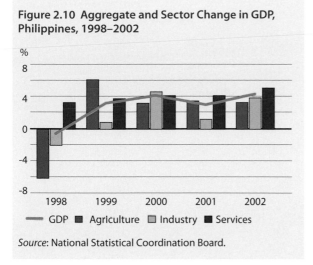

Figure 2.10 Aggregate and Sector Change in GDP, Philippines, 1998–2002

Source: National Statistical Coordination Board.

up a tax payment warning system; charging VAT on professionals; and sanctioning some firms once the expiration of the 5-day VAT compliance notice takes effect. An electronic filing and payment system was expanded for all types of tax payments at BIR. A rise in revenues in the last quarter of 2002 showed that the enhancement measures were taking effect, but not enough to reduce the sizable deficit accumulated in the first three quarters of the year.

Disbursements of the central Government for the whole of 2002 grew by 8.2% from the 2001 level. Public expenditures are estimated to have remained at about 19.0% of GDP during 2002, with the wage bill and other mandated expenditures, such as interest payments and allocations to local government units (LGUs), accounting for a large part of total central government expenditures. However, personal services and maintenance expenditures in general contracted in 2002 due to government expenditure-reduction measures. During the year, internal revenue allotment to LGUs grew by 16.4%, largely due to the need to support LGUs in their poverty reduction and peace and order programs. Capital outlays likewise continued to increase, by 29.9%, as a result of the faster implementation of foreign-assisted projects. The disbursement rate of foreign loans against the target disbursement rate rose to 80% in 2002, compared with 74% in 2001.

Growth in the money supply slowed somewhat in 2002 as a result of weak credit demand and an increase in the reserve requirement. Domestic liquidity (M3) grew by 9.5%, compared with 6.8%

growth in 2001. Growth was especially slow in the first half of 2002, but accelerated during the second half, largely due to an increase in net foreign assets in the banking system The sale of dollars by the nonbanking sector, including remittances from overseas workers during the Christmas holiday season, helped boost the net foreign asset position of banks in the second half of the year.

Interest rates remained generally stable over 2002. At the beginning of the year, Bangko Sentral ng Pilipinas (BSP) reduced the overnight borrowing rate and overnight lending rate by 75 basis points to 7.0% and 9.25%, respectively, from 7.75% and 10.0% in 2001; these interest rates remained unchanged until the end of 2002. Following the repeated downward adjustment in interest rates by the US Federal Reserve in 2001, Philippine interest rate policy was calibrated carefully, to maintain price stability while taking into account the risks associated with exchange rate movements and their impact on inflation. Treasury bill rates also fell during the year, to an average of 5.5% from 9.9% in 2001. With BSP's reduction of its policy rates to the lowest levels since 1995, the benchmark 91-day treasury bills fell to a historical low of around 4.0% in December 2002.

In 2002, the Government issued P109.3 billion in treasury bonds in the domestic market, as against P80.6 billion issued in the previous year. The Government also issued P2,850 billion (about $57 billion) in international bonds, compared with P420 billion in 2001. The main reasons for the sharp increase of domestic and international bonds were the Government's requirement to finance the fiscal deficit.

With the growing fiscal deficit and an unstable security situation, the peso depreciated to P53–54 to the dollar by end-2002 from about P50 in mid-2002. The real effective exchange rate has been declining since 1999. Regional currency weakness in 2002 also contributed to peso depreciation. Domestic inflation was not a major factor. Indeed, inflation in 2002 was the lowest since 1988, averaging 3.1%. This was well below the Government's full-year target of 4.5–5.5%, and the 6.1% seen in 2001. Inflation in December 2002 was 2.6%, compared with 4.1% 12 months earlier. The deceleration in inflation during the year resulted mainly from a slowdown in food price increases, mild domestic demand, and prudent monetary policy.

The Philippine financial system is dominated by

Table 2.10 Major Economic Indicators, Philippines, 2000–2004, %

Item	2000	2001	2002	2003	2004
GDP growth	4.4	3.2	4.6	4.0	4.5
Gross domestic investment/GNP	17.4	16.6	15.6	17.5	18.5
Gross national savings/GNP	24.8	17.0	17.3	19.5	21.0
Inflation rate (consumer price index)	4.4	6.1	3.1	4.5	4.5
Money supply (M3) growth	4.6	6.8	9.5	10.0	10.0
Fiscal balance/GDP	-4.1	-4.0	-5.3	-4.5	-4.0
Merchandise export growth	9.0	-16.2	12.2	6.0	7.0
Merchandise import growth	14.5	-4.5	4.6	5.0	5.8
Current account balance/GNP	7.4	0.4	1.6	2.0	2.5
Debt service ratio	12.5	16.0	17.0	17.0	16.5

Sources: National Statistical Coordination Board; Bangko Sentral ng Pilipinas; staff estimates.

the banking sector, in which 44 major commercial banks account for the major part of the market. Since the Asian financial crisis, the banking sector has become cautious about extending new credits to commercial borrowers. Together with a lack of investor confidence, this kept lending levels in 2002 low. Since 1997, the banking sector has weakened, as characterized by low profitability, a steady increase in the level of NPLs and nonperforming assets (NPAs, defined as NPLs plus properties owned or acquired), and stagnation in credit growth. Banks with excess liquidity have been a major source of demand for government securities at public auctions, helping drive interest rates down. At the same time, mainly due to reclassification of NPLs, the nominal NPL ratio in commercial banks declined to 16.4% of the total loan portfolio in 2002, from 17.4% in 2001. It is hoped that the passage of the Special Purpose Vehicle Act at the end of 2002 will encourage private asset management companies to acquire, turn around, and resell the financial sector's NPLs and NPAs.

After a contraction of 16.2% in 2001, merchandise exports rose by 12.2% in 2002, boosted by some recovery in global demand for electronics, which account for half total exports. Exports were also helped by improved markets for garments and agricultural products. On the back of stronger domestic demand, merchandise imports also swung into growth, at 4.6%, from a 4.5% contraction in 2001.

As a result, the trade balance registered a surplus in 2002. Remittances of overseas workers for the year of $6.9 billion also helped bring the current account into surplus at 1.6% of GNP, slightly higher than the 0.4% surplus in 2001. The overall balance-of-payments surplus was about $750 million in 2002, compared with a deficit of $1.3 billion in 2001. This development was mainly the result of the improvement in the current account.

The country's gross international reserves at the end of 2002 stood at $16.2 billion or 5 months of imports of goods and services, up slightly from the $15.7 billion recorded at the end of 2001. Reserves rose following the deposit by the National Power Corporation (NPC) of the proceeds of the flotation of its zero coupon notes and the Power Sector Assets and Liabilities Management Corporation's bond issuance in Japanese yen to fund the NPC's 2003 foreign exchange requirements. The increase in reserves was partly offset, however, by the debt service requirements of the central Government.

At the end of December 2002, outstanding external debt amounted to about $54.0 billion, up from $52.4 billion at the end of 2001. The increase in debt arose largely from government borrowings to meet its financial requirements during the year and from the upward revaluation adjustments of liabilities and net obligations by nonbank borrowers from the public and private sectors. The structure of the external debt has shifted toward longer maturities in recent years—long-term debt now accounts for 89% of total debt. The debt service ratio was 17.0% in 2002. Public sector obligations (including official public debts and debts of government-owned and controlled corporations) made up 64.6% of total external debt and official public debts accounted for 48.7% of total external debts. The bulk of the country's external debt is denominated in dollars (56.2%) and yen (26.0%).

Policy Developments

Since 1998, the fiscal deficit has been large and increasing. The main problem lies with the shortfalls in tax revenues, and indeed the Government has focused on reforms directed at improving the revenue base and tax effort, mainly in the following four areas: rationalization and simplification of tax systems (which are currently complicated and difficult to implement and monitor); using ICT to make the tax system more streamlined and offer transparency for tax collection; organizational reform to restructure BIR into a taxpayer-focused organization; and capacity building and human resources development at BIR. Despite these measures, the enhancement of certain administrative actions is needed to improve revenue collection, including strengthening the monitoring of large taxpayers, more intensive audits on tax payments, indexation of excise taxes to inflation, redefinition of automobiles to remove tax loopholes (i.e., classification of vehicles for tax purposes), improvement of VAT collection, and rationalization of fiscal incentives to encourage investment.

Policy measures and incentives need to be formulated to minimize tax evasion, particularly to minimize underdeclaration of income taxes by companies and self-employed professionals. In this regard, a legal framework to prevent tax evasion already exists, but implementation has been poor. In the short term, the Government will need to strengthen its efforts to enhance tax revenues through a review in excise taxes, which requires legal support, and the imposition of a limit on taxpayers' expenses that are deducted from taxable income.

The current monetary policy stance remains supportive of noninflationary economic growth. In the near term, the Government will need to take account of pending increases in user charges (such as those for electricity, transport, and water), and the impact of the conflict in Iraq on international oil prices as well as the challenges on the fiscal front.

The approval of the Special Purpose Vehicle Act at the end of 2002 is an encouraging move to solve the problem of NPLs and NPAs in the banking sector. The Act provides for the creation of private sector asset management companies (AMCs) to acquire commercial banks' NPLs and NPAs; it stresses an approach toward the resolution of bank's NPLs with adequate safeguards. Compared with other Asian countries hit by the financial crisis, the amount of banks' NPLs and NPAs in the Philippines is moderate, and estimated at roughly P500 billion. While the Government is keen to attract foreign companies specializing in asset management, it expects local companies to take the lead in purchasing the bad loans. The sale of NPLs and NPAs may trigger banking sector consolidation in the long run because banks will face more competition and higher turnover costs. The key challenge is the recovery of lending activities in the banking sector, which has been saddled by these NPLs and NPAs. Further reducing NPLs and NPAs must remain the focus of financial policy, while BSP's capability to detect, avert, and respond to potential bank failures should be strengthened.

The Government's commitment to maintain structural reforms and promote good governance, as well as its pursuance of sound macroeconomic policies should encourage capital inflows. The Anti-Money Laundering Act (AMLA), which was passed in September 2001, will improve the business climate. Under the law, an Anti-Money Laundering Council was set up to monitor banks and suspicious accounts. However, a subsequent assessment of the law by the OECD's Financial Action Task Force (FATF) identified several deficiencies, which were addressed in amendments to the AMLA approved by congress in March 2003. To help stamp out corrupt practices, a new procurement law was enacted in January 2003, which led to the computerization of government procurement transactions and processes.

Peace and order are among the primary prerequisites for sustaining economic growth and development, as they remain a major concern for investors in the country. Conflicts in Mindanao, the second-largest island in the south of the country, have contributed to a loss of business confidence.

This has had a negative impact on economic growth and development prospects, as well as on investment. However, in a difficult environment, the Government is taking the steps it can to help restore investor confidence, including proposing an Anti-Terrorism Act.

Outlook for 2003–2004

The following forecasts are based on the assumption that the conflict in Iraq will have only short-term negative impacts on the world economy, and that the SARS epidemic can quickly be brought under control. In 2003, GDP is expected to grow by 4.0%, driven by domestic consumption, improved exports, and public investment. Agricultural growth is expected to moderate because of continuing effects from El Niño, while growth in the industry sector should remain at the same level as in 2002, due to an expected moderate strengthening in the global economy, somewhat offset by continued weakness in domestic industry and sluggish investment demand.

Growth in services should continue at a higher rate than the other sectors, following a trend established in recent years of the economy moving slowly toward greater services orientation featuring more high-technology services, including computer software and other ICT elements. Imports will likely rise more slowly than exports, and thus net exports will contribute more strongly to GDP growth. In spite of higher oil prices at the beginning of the year, inflation should remain at a low level.

In 2004, GDP growth is expected to accelerate to about 4.5%. Agricultural growth is expected to pick up slightly, moving toward historical rates of growth while investment is projected to strengthen as the external climate improves further, offsetting contractionary forces resulting from a reduced fiscal deficit. The services sector will continue to do well.

On the demand side, consumption and net exports will likely continue to lead aggregate demand. The trade and current account balances should improve further as export growth continues to outpace import growth. Without a stronger recovery in investment, though, unemployment is likely to remain at around 10% in 2003–2004.

Inflation is projected to be higher than in 2002, reflecting partly the effect of the weaker peso on import prices, though the Government's target of 4.5% should be met. Domestic liquidity is expected to grow faster over the next 2 years if inflation remains moderate.

It is expected that the budget deficit will be contained to around 4.5% of GDP for 2003, in view of forceful measures to be taken by BIR and the Bureau of Customs in raising tax revenues. For 2004, with more reforms in the tax system and tax collection to be implemented, the budget deficit is projected to fall slightly to 4.0% of GDP.

The overall balance of payments is forecast to be in surplus in 2003. An increase in the current account surplus will more than offset capital outflows. In 2004, the current account surplus is expected to rise to 2.5% of GNP. Capital outflows are likely to reverse direction as the effect of higher investment incentives and financial reforms starts to be felt.

Singapore

The economic recovery in 2002 was slower than expected, mainly due to a persistent depression in private sector consumption and investment. In contrast, external demand, which experienced a turnaround from a sharp decline in 2001 to a modest strengthening in 2002, played a major role in reviving growth in manufacturing. Private consumption and investment are expected to gradually pick up in 2003–2004 thanks to an improvement in global economic conditions and supportive domestic policies.

Macroeconomic Assessment

After a sharp downturn in 2001, the economy recovered somewhat in 2002, though much less quickly than expected and expanding by only 2.2%. Growth was generally lower than in most other countries in East and Southeast Asia. The main factor was subdued domestic demand, particularly a decrease in fixed capital investment and private consumption. In contrast, external demand picked up in 2002 (Figure 2.11).

On the production side, manufacturing experienced high growth across a broad spectrum of industries, due to improved external demand. The subsector grew by 8.3% in 2002, with recoveries in electronics, rubber and plastic products, and instrumentation equipment. Electronics grew by 4.1%, after a decline of 21.3% in 2001, due to increased production of semiconductors and of data storage and office automation equipment. The growth was boosted by a modest recovery in the global electronics market. The personal computers and communications segments, however, saw lower output on the back of weak corporate ICT spending. Rubber and plastic products expanded by 9.6%, pushed by production of plastic precision components, industrial rubber parts, and pipes and tubes. Instrumentation equipment grew by 10.1%, bolstered by strong demand from the US and EU for medical instruments and measuring devices.

The construction subsector, which declined by 3.2% in 2001, fell by a further 10.8% in 2002. Both public and private construction activities remained weak. Nearly all segments in public investment declined, but the shrinkage in private construction was largely attributed to weak levels of commercial, industrial, and civil engineering works.

Finance, one of the economy's key industries, fell by 4.8% in 2002, compared with modest growth of 3.7% in 2001. The performance of various segments in the financial industry was mixed. While commercial banking, investment advisory services, and foreign exchange trading showed modest growth, this was outweighed by a sharp decline in insurance and stockbroking. In contrast, the wholesale and retail trade sector grew by 2.7%, a significant improvement from a decline of 3.3% in 2001. The rebound was aided by better performance in entrepôt trade, with a substantial increase in non-oil reexports.

In 2002, total domestic demand fell by 2.3%, led by a continued drop in gross fixed capital formation, increased inventory cutbacks due to less favorable business conditions, and persistent sluggishness in private consumption, which posted slower growth of 0.9%. The poor outcome occurred across a number of categories, including motor vehicles, recreational goods, and financial services. However, public consumption increased by 4.4% as a fiscal stimulus was introduced to boost aggregate

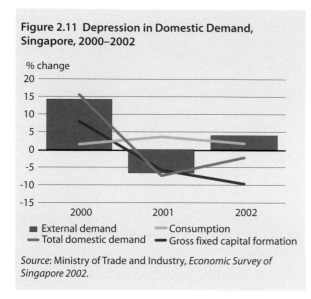

Figure 2.11 Depression in Domestic Demand, Singapore, 2000–2002

% change

- External demand
- Total domestic demand
- Consumption
- Gross fixed capital formation

Source: Ministry of Trade and Industry, *Economic Survey of Singapore 2002.*

demand. Battered by flagging business conditions and underlying global uncertainties, gross fixed capital formation continued to fall in 2002. Both private and public investment slumped. The main factor in the poor private investment was a significant drop in investment in nonresidential buildings due to substantial excess capacity.

In contrast, external demand, which had continued to decline sharply until the first quarter of 2002, switched to growth in the remainder of the year. Merchandise exports expanded by 3.2% in 2002, a significant improvement from a decline of 11.0% in 2001. Exports of manufactured goods, in particular electronics, recorded a swift improvement in the latter half of 2002, though services exports remained sluggish. Contributing to this healthy expansion were key items, such as integrated circuits, personal computer parts, and disk drives. Among nonelectronics items, exports of pharmaceuticals and petrochemicals recorded healthy growth, particularly to regional markets such as Hong Kong, China; Korea; Malaysia; and Thailand.

Imports overall increased by only 0.1% in 2002, with non-oil imports contracting by 0.3%, though key electronics items, pharmaceuticals, measuring instruments, and petrochemicals rose significantly. Mineral fuel imports registered an increase of 4.1%, after a decline of 6.7% in the previous year. As a result, the current account surplus improved from 19.0% of GDP in 2001 to 21.5% in 2002.

Maintaining currency stability remained the single most important goal of monetary policy.

Within this context, the Monetary Authority of Singapore (MAS) has followed a neutral policy stance since July 2001, with a stable, trade-weighted, Singapore dollar nominal effective exchange rate. The policy band was widened in October 2001 to allow greater flexibility in exchange rate management, but was restored to a narrower one in January 2002 as market and economic conditions became more stable. Domestic interest rates declined steadily in 2002 in tandem with easing monetary conditions. Inflationary pressures remained subdued, with the CPI falling by 0.4%.

The key initiatives in the budget for FY2002 (beginning 1 April) included reductions in corporate and personal income tax rates, enhanced tax incentives for the financial sector, and the introduction of employee stock option incentive schemes. The budget also prescribed that, to offset the loss of revenues from the reduction in income taxes, the goods and services tax rate should be raised from 3.0% to 4.0%, effective 1 January 2003. In FY2002, the budget deficit narrowed to S$94 million, or 0.1% of GDP, from S$2.7 billion, or 1.8% of GDP, a year earlier.

The employment situation deteriorated in 2002, with the number of those employed falling by 39,500 and the seasonally adjusted unemployment rate rising to 4.4% in December 2002, from 3.3% 12 months earlier; this was even higher than the 4.3% recorded during the financial crisis. The deterioration occurred across most sectors, with construction the hardest hit.

Policy Developments

The Government established the Economic Review Committee (ERC) in October 2001 to assess its development strategy and formulate a blueprint to restructure the economy. The ERC recommendations announced in early 2003 can be divided into two parts: more immediate measures to deal with current uncertainties, and longer-term strategies to restructure the economy. It identified lowering costs and staying competitive as immediate issues to address, while long-term national objectives should be expanding external ties, maintaining competitiveness and flexibility, encouraging entrepreneurship, promoting the twin growth engines of manufacturing and services, and developing human resources. These strategies aim to make Singapore a

Table 2.11 Major Economic Indicators, Singapore, 2000–2004, %

Item	2000	2001	2002	2003	2004
GDP growth	9.4	-2.4	2.2	2.3	4.2
Gross domestic investment/GDP	32.3	24.2	20.6	25.0	28.2
Gross domestic savings/GDP	47.9	43.6	44.2	47.1	47.3
Inflation rate (consumer price index)	1.3	1.0	-0.4	0.5	1.0
Money supply (M2) growth	-2.0	5.9	-0.3	3.1	7.3
Fiscal balance/GDP	2.5	-1.8	-0.1	-0.6	2.5
Merchandise export growth	20.0	-11.0	3.2	7.5	10.2
Merchandise import growth	24.1	-15.5	0.1	9.8	11.6
Current account balance/GDP	14.5	19.0	21.5	21.5	19.3

Sources: Singapore Department of Statistics, available: www.singstat.gov.sg; Ministry of Trade and Industry, available: www.mti.gov.sg; Ministry of Finance of Singapore, available: www.mof.gov.sg; staff estimates.

leading global city, as a hub of talent, diversification, enterprise, and innovation in the next 15 years.

The ERC has several subcommittees, including one on services. The share of services has assumed somewhat greater importance over the past decade and a half, rising from 61% of GDP in 1986 to 67% in 2001, while their share of total employment has increased from 64% to 74% over the same period. However, while Singapore's world ranking as an exporter of services was 16th in 2001, its rank in services productivity was only 23rd. Consequently, the services subcommittee has made major recommendations in an attempt to improve productivity in the sector and to make Singapore Asia's leading provider of world-class services. The subcommittee has also made recommendations on how to address issues of overregulation, corporatization, and privatization of public suppliers to introduce competition, institutional support, and training of human resources. The ERC's initiatives are intended to provide major inputs to the various line ministries in policy making to develop the sector.

As one of the key financial centers in the region, Singapore has stepped up its efforts to enhance its financial system, its institutional and regulatory framework, and its market structure. Two issues are of prime importance. First, it is essential to create a more conducive regulatory environment to foster market dynamism and innovation, while ensuring financial sector stability and soundness. For this, MAS is shifting its policy focus from regulation to

risk-focused supervision, disclosure and market discipline, and higher standards of corporate governance. Second, financial liberalization needs to be accelerated to promote competition and discipline. Several major steps have already been taken, to deregulate the banking and capital markets in particular. Local banks have upgraded risk management systems and introduced new products and services, while some of them have been consolidated through mergers and acquisitions. Further opening up of the banking sector is expected. In the capital markets, more government securities have been issued to increase market liquidity and to create a benchmark yield curve, while internationalization of the capital markets has received increased attention. These policy efforts should pave the way for revitalizing and upgrading the financial sector, which has generally registered only average performance over the last few years.

The FY2002 budget, released on 3 May 2002, aimed to address the need for fiscal incentives to encourage domestic demand, improve Singapore's international competitiveness, and attract global talent. To this end, major measures on both the tax and expenditure sides were announced. Tax measures include (i) the reduction of the corporate income tax rate to 22% in FY2003 from 24.5% in FY2002, with further reductions to 20% by FY2004; (ii) enhanced tax incentives for the wealth- and asset-management industries, derivatives market, equity capital market, and general insurance companies; (iii) tax deduction for approved R&D expenses of all services companies; and (iv) cuts in the top marginal personal income tax rate from 26% in FY2002 to 20% by FY2004. At 44.1% of the total, the largest share of government expenditures goes to social development. The income tax cuts and the tax incentive schemes are expected to be generally conducive to economic activity in the private sector, and should help boost the ongoing economic recovery.

Outlook for 2003–2004

In 2003–2004, MAS is likely to maintain the current monetary policy centered on the management of the exchange rate, recognizing that stability of the Singapore dollar is critically important for economic recovery through supporting financial activities and entrepôt trade. Market liquidity should continue to be abundant and interest rates in the international financial markets are likely to remain low in this period. Along with a stimulative fiscal policy, these moves will support recovery efforts in the country. Taken together with the Government's firm policy stance to develop and upgrade service industries in which the economy has a comparative advantage, the domestic economic environment will be highly private sector-friendly in 2003–2004. However, external developments will remain the key drivers of growth.

Assuming that the world economy will continue to recover, GDP growth is forecast at 2.3% and 4.2% in 2003 and 2004, respectively. The reduction in income tax rates will boost disposable incomes and private consumption over these 2 years. In contrast, the increase in the goods and services tax, continued high unemployment, and slow real wage growth could all dampen consumption growth. Falling residential property prices will also have a negative wealth effect on consumption. As a result, private consumption is likely to record only modest growth in this period, and is forecast at 3.3% in 2003 and 4.7% in 2004. Public consumption will likely maintain 5–5.5% growth rates in both years.

Gross fixed investment is projected to grow by 3.5% in 2003 and by 5.7% in 2004. This reflects the recent increase in new FDI commitments in manu-

facturing and services and the improving prospects for global demand. Noteworthy is the sharp increase in FDI commitments from the EU for petrochemical products and chip design services in the second half of 2002.

Merchandise exports are forecast to pick up by 7.5% in 2003 and by 10.2% in 2004, with growth led by strong demand for chemicals, instrumentation equipment, and pharmaceuticals, while ICT-related products are likely to expand moderately. Prices of ICT products will probably remain weak in 2003–2004, due to a modest recovery of global demand. Exports to the PRC should continue to increase rapidly, contributing to a further diversification of export destinations. The trade and current account balances are forecast to deteriorate slightly as import growth exceeds export growth. The services balance is likely to remain in surplus to the tune of about $2 billion–$3 billion over the next 2 years. The current account surplus of 21.5% of GDP in 2002 is projected to remain unchanged in 2003 and to fall to 19.3% of GDP in 2004.

Industry (i.e., manufacturing, construction, and energy), which started to pick up in the second half of 2002, will likely expand further in 2003–2004, by 4.3% in 2003 and 5.6% in 2004. Growth in the services sector will slow, largely due to the adverse impact of SARS on the sector. The unemployment rate is unlikely to drop rapidly because of continued modest economic growth, economic and political uncertainties on the global front, and the private sector's determination to streamline operations to decrease unit labor costs and increase international competitiveness. The unemployment rate is expected to increase slightly to 4.5% in 2003, before falling to 4.1% in 2004. With modest GDP growth, the CPI is forecast to increase marginally by 0.5%–1.0% each year, against a backdrop of low international prices, projected low wage growth, and excess residential capacity.

Several downside risks have become important recently and these may undermine the base-case scenario. The outbreak of SARS, over a prolonged period of time, would significantly affect Singapore's important tourism industry. A further delay in the recovery of global ICT demand would negatively impact growth.

Thailand

A rebound in exports and robust private consumption produced a return to strong growth in 2002. With a comfortable current account surplus, growing international reserves, and declining foreign debt, external vulnerability has also fallen considerably since the Asian financial crisis. As long as oil prices remain stable, growth in 2003–2004 should remain healthy.

Macroeconomic Assessment

Despite a subdued global economic environment, the economy posted solid growth of 5.2% in 2002 (Figure 2.12). This is a significant improvement from the 1.9% expansion recorded in 2001. Growth also accelerated through the four quarters, increasing from 3.9% to 5.1%, to 5.8%, and to 6.1%, year on year. With this rebound, Thailand has been able to recoup almost all the losses in per capita income (measured in constant local currency prices) sustained after the start of the financial crisis in 1997.

During the first half of 2002, most of the expansion was driven by strong private consumption spending, facilitated by government measures to ease access to credit. Fiscal pump-priming in the first half of the year, in an overall environment of low inflation and interest rates, also aided growth. In addition, the Government provided a stimulus through various nonbudgetary measures, such as a "village fund" project.

While private consumption spending remained vigorous in the second half of 2002, a strong increase in exports and private investment spending produced a more broad-based growth outcome. Private investment rose by 13.3% in 2002, compared with only 4.7% growth in 2001. This sharp rebound is encouraging, given that investment has been the most sluggish demand component to recover since the crisis. However, a significant portion of this increase appears to be related to housing construc-

tion rather than productive capacity. Exports too rebounded well, led mainly by electronics.

From a sector point of view, the main contributor to stronger growth was manufacturing, which expanded by 7.7% in 2002. Manufacturing output also accelerated through the four quarters, from 4.2%, to 6.8%, to 9.1%, and to 10.6%, year on year, due to improvements in both domestic and external demand. While output of iron and steel products and cement was boosted by greater domestic construction activity, production of electronic goods and electrical appliances rose in line with the measured upturn in the global electronics cycle.

The agriculture sector did not contribute to the overall economic expansion, with zero growth in 2002 compared with 3.3% in 2001. A major underlying factor was a 4.8% drop in fisheries output resulting from a slump in frozen shrimp exports to European markets stemming from food safety concerns. Major crops continued to perform well, however, despite somewhat erratic weather conditions—droughts in the first half of the year and floods in the second. Output of major crops grew moderately by 0.8% in 2002, led by rubber. Prices of major crops also rose, by 6.5%, due mainly to higher demand for agricultural products and the Government's price intervention measures.

The services sector grew by 4.1% in 2002. This sector is dominated by tourism, which accounts for almost 5% of GDP. The tourism industry has recovered from the sharp drop-off in tourist arrivals felt in the immediate aftermath of the September 11

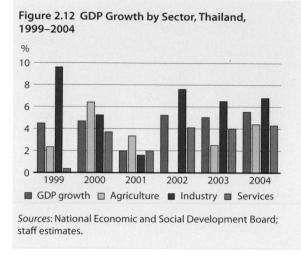

Figure 2.12 GDP Growth by Sector, Thailand, 1999–2004

■ GDP growth   □ Agriculture   ■ Industry   ■ Services

Sources: National Economic and Social Development Board; staff estimates.

attacks, and performed well in 2002. Tourist arrivals improved by 7.3% in 2002, with a significant rise in the number of tourists from nearby countries, such as Korea and Malaysia. Despite the new regional security concerns that emerged in October 2002 with the bombings in Bali, indications so far are that the tourism industry has not been adversely affected. However, it is too early to assess the potential long-term effects on tourism of these security concerns.

Unemployment continued to trend downward, falling to a 5-year low of 1.4% in December 2002, compared with 1.7% a year earlier. In 2002, it averaged 2.4%, as against 3.3% in 2001. Employment increased by about 1.3%, with the majority of jobs created in the wholesale and retail trade, construction, and tourism. At these levels, unemployment is no longer a major policy issue for the Government, though poverty incidence is. Based on consumption of $2 per day, the World Bank estimates that poverty rose significantly from 28.2% in 1996 to 35.6% in 2000, but that its incidence declined slightly to 32.5% in 2002. The incidence is much lower when poverty is measured on consumption of $1 per day.

Thailand still has some way to go in bringing poverty down to the levels seen prior to the financial crisis. The Government has, indeed, been trying to address this issue, mainly through its fiscal spending program. For instance, a substantial package of farm, village, and small enterprise-oriented programs designed to expand productive opportunities for low-income groups has been introduced. In addition, a low-cost universal health scheme has been brought in to cover the uninsured.

Furthermore, the rapid increase in farm income recorded in 2002, if it were to continue, would help in reducing the incidence of poverty in rural areas.

The budget deficit for FY2002 (ended 30 September 2002) was significantly lower than the target rate of 3.8% of GDP: it came in at B116.6 billion, or 2.2% of GDP. This was mainly the result of buoyant tax receipts, accruing from higher than expected economic growth. Government revenues for the fiscal year totaled B845.4 billion, up by 10.5% from the previous year, and B46 billion above target. Government spending continued to provide a stimulus to the economy, particularly in the first half of the year. Government expenditures for the fiscal year totaled B973.2 billion, 11.1% higher than the prior year's level.

Inflation remained subdued in 2002. Consumer price inflation averaged only 0.7%, while "core" inflation (excluding food and energy items) averaged 0.4%. The effects of rising world oil prices have begun to show however, with consumer price inflation increasing by 1.6% in December. Nevertheless, underlying inflationary pressures remain very weak, with excess capacity in many sectors. The main threat to the current low inflation environment lies in the possibility of a sharp rise in oil prices as a result of the conflict in Iraq.

The baht firmed in 2002, with the baht reference rate averaging 43.0 to the dollar in 2002, slightly stronger than the 44.5 recorded in 2001. With the rebound in exports and return to strong economic expansion, the baht could strengthen in 2003.

The Bank of Thailand (BOT) has an official policy of inflation targeting, and monetary policy is aimed at keeping core inflation within the 0–3.5% range. In 2002, BOT continued its accommodative monetary policy stance. Faced with low inflation and uncertainty over the pace of domestic economic recovery, in November it cut its benchmark 14-day repurchase rate by 25 basis points, to 1.75%. Money market interest rates declined even before this announcement, as the market had widely anticipated the move and priced it in. At these levels, interest rates are already at 30-year lows. These moves were also facilitated by the downward trend set by the US Federal Reserve, which cut its repurchase rate by 50 basis points in October to 1.25%.

The Stock Exchange of Thailand (SET) index reached a high of 426 in mid-June, up by nearly 50% in dollar terms since the end of 2001. Expectations

Table 2.12 Major Economic Indicators, Thailand, 2000–2004, %

Item	2000	2001	2002	2003	2004
GDP growth	4.6	1.9	5.2	5.0	5.5
Gross domestic investment/GDP	22.7	23.9	23.8	24.0	24.5
Gross domestic savings[a]/GDP	31.0	30.0	30.5	28.7	29.6
Inflation rate (consumer price index)	1.6	1.6	0.7	1.3	1.6
Money supply (M2) growth	2.2	4.6	-0.1	6.0	7.0
Fiscal balance[b]/GDP	-2.4	-2.1	-2.2	-2.2	-2.0
Merchandise export growth	19.5	-6.9	5.8	6.6	7.5
Merchandise import growth	31.3	-2.8	4.6	7.0	8.0
Current account balance[c]/GDP	7.6	5.3	6.0	4.1	4.5
Debt service ratio	15.4	20.7	18.0	15.5	16.5

[a] Derived as gross national savings less net factor income from abroad. [b] Includes national Government's budgetary and nonbudgetary accounts. [c] Excludes official transfers.

Sources: National Economic and Social Development Board; staff estimates.

of improved economic growth and better corporate profitability underscored the recovery. The sharp declines in US markets, which reverberated throughout Europe and Asia, were also felt in Thailand; by end-September 2002, the SET had slumped to about 332. Since then, it has recovered somewhat, and passed the 370 mark by mid-January 2003.

After dropping by 1.5% in the first half of 2002, exports rebounded strongly in the third and fourth quarters, rising by 11.4% and 15.2%, respectively. This resulted in an overall rise of 5.8% in 2002. Recent growth has been driven by improved demand conditions for electronics and related products, although improved world agricultural prices have also helped boost export income. Imports also turned up, growing by 2.1% in the second quarter after declining in the four previous quarters. The pickup in domestic demand was reflected in a surge in imports in the second half of 2002 as well. Import growth in the third and fourth quarters came in at 12.9% and 14.8%, respectively. This produced an overall increase in imports of 4.6% in 2002, and a merchandise trade surplus of $3.5 billion.

With surpluses in income and services, the current account surplus totaled $7.6 billion in 2002. The balance-of-payments surplus widened to $4.2 billion by the end of the year, increasing international reserves to $38.9 billion. This is more than

twice the level of short-term debt, and equivalent to more than 7 months of imports.

External debt totaled $59.3 billion at end-2002, down from $67.5 billion at end-2001. The debt stock has been trending downward since 1997. The ratio of public sector debt to private sector debt has also been falling, from 41.7% at end-2001 to 38.5% at end-2002. This drop is in line with government efforts to repay loans from multilateral agencies such as IMF, World Bank, and ADB. The Finance Ministry recently announced that it plans to lower the country's public debt target to 54.6% of GDP in 2003. In setting this, the Ministry cited better than expected growth outcomes, as well as the repayment of more than B37.4 billion in government debt—of which more than B32 billion was foreign denominated. Some of these repayments have been financed by the issuance of short-term paper (e.g., euro commercial paper), and this raised the ratio of short- to long-term debt from 19.8% at end-2001 to 23.2% at end-2002. The Government plans to continue with prepayment of loans from multilateral agencies in 2003 through the issuance of sovereign bonds. With a comfortable current account surplus, growing international reserves, and declining foreign debt levels, particularly private sector short-term debt, external vulnerability has fallen considerably since the financial crisis.

Policy Developments

In a context where external demand had been expected to be anemic, the authorities pursued accommodating fiscal and monetary policies in 2002. Deficit-spending measures included a public health program, a village and urban revolving fund, a debt suspension program for farmers, and housing credit support for government officials. Overall, expenditures rose by 11.1%. Tax breaks were also provided for business startups, home purchases, and stock exchange listings. But, in a context of stronger than expected economic growth, buoyant tax and nontax revenues helped contain the actual deficit. The central Government's deficit for FY2002 was 2.2%, as against a targeted deficit of 3.8% of GDP.

In a move toward greater fiscal transparency, arrangements were worked out in 2002 for the amortization and servicing of Financial Institutions Development Fund debts. The Fund's debts will be amortized using BOT profits. It may take 20–30 years to accomplish the write-off, however. In the meantime, interest payments will be met by the Ministry of Finance and will be directly "fiscalized". Other significant developments during the year included the postponement (for a second time) of the increase in VAT from 7% to 10%, until 30 September 2003.

The budget for FY2003 signals a shift toward fiscal consolidation. The ratio of public sector debt to GDP has risen from 16% in 1996 to around 54% at end-November 2002. Also, the need for fiscal priming is now less pressing as the external environment is expected to be more supportive in 2003. The Government is planning to pare the total public sector deficit, which includes local government, extrabudgetary, and off-budget activities, and public enterprise financing needs, by about 1.4% of GDP relative to 2002's outcome. Expenditures on special programs will decline, and the financial position of state enterprises is expected to improve. The expected reduction in the public debt ratio to 55% reflects not only a commitment toward fiscal consolidation but also a more optimistic assessment of growth prospects. If such prospects fail to meet expectations, the ratio of public debt to GDP could resume its upward trajectory, and narrow the Government's latitude for fiscal discretion.

In a benign inflationary environment, BOT lowered its repurchase rate twice in 2002, broadly maintaining the differential between domestic and (falling) international rates. As core inflation is expected to remain at the bottom end of the target range, and the output gap remains large, there is unlikely to be any departure from the current low interest rate environment. In the conduct of monetary policy, BOT is anxious to ensure that any changes in the value of the domestic currency are orderly, but it no longer targets a value for the exchange rate.

In 2002, several measures were taken to stimulate credit expansion, including some relaxation of loan provisioning and classification requirements for banks. In particular, consumer credit and the home mortgage market showed signs of revival. Indeed, strong growth in credit card use led to the reinstatement of minimum income regulations on credit card issuance that had been earlier relaxed, and BOT has now introduced a cap on credit card cash advances. These measures are intended to take some of the heat out of consumer credit expansion and to limit the rise in personal debt. However, provided that interest rates remain low and inflation favorable, these measures are unlikely to seriously constrain private consumption growth.

The completion of banking and corporate sector restructuring remains vital for the recovery of business investment and the medium-term prospects for the economy. The Thailand Asset Management Corporation has now acquired $17 billion of NPLs, largely from public sector banks. By December 2002, just over $11 billion of these NPLs had been resolved. The Corporation, which acquired assets at an average cost of 33.3% of their book value, expects to recover 45% from repayments by debtors. During the course of 2003, the Corporation will turn its attention to the acquisition of debts of less than B20 million from state-owned financial institutions and will acquire the debts of the Industrial Finance Corporation of Thailand.

Since details about individual cases are not readily available, it is difficult to make judgments about the quality and possible sustainability of the resolution process. One risk of emphasizing an approach that gives distressed businesses another chance is that some unviable debtors will remain in business, and that could pose a renewed threat to bank balance sheets. Also, many of the bad loans of the private banking sector still need to be resolved and it is possible that further losses and a concomitant need for fresh capital injections will occur in the future. Steps are also needed to strengthen the leverage of creditors in bankruptcy and foreclosure processes. Under current arrangements, debtors can often obstruct and delay resolution.

Outlook for 2003–2004

GDP growth is expected to remain strong in 2003 at 5.0%, and to increase to 5.5% in 2004. A number of factors underpin these projections. As an open economy, Thailand's prospects will depend heavily on world demand conditions. Exports are expected to continue to perform strongly over the forecast period. This is based on the expectation that growth in the US will pick up in the second half of 2003 and strengthen in 2004. A similar outcome is expected for the euro area in 2003–2004. Additionally, the electronics cycle should also turn up over this period, providing a boost to electronics exports. With capacity utilization rates still relatively low in manufacturing, the economy should be able to respond effectively to improved demand conditions in its major export markets.

Private consumption spending is expected to remain relatively robust in 2003–2004. The sharp pickup in consumer spending has been a major factor underlying the return to strong growth in 2002, and this is likely to continue. The low interest rate environment will probably continue to stimulate private consumption spending. Higher consumer confidence resulting from falling unemployment and rising farm and nonfarm incomes is also likely to boost consumption expenditures. It seems unlikely that government measures to rein in rising consumer debt, particularly on credit cards, will significantly dampen overall private consumption spending.

Investment spending is expected to come off its highs but remain strong over the forecast period, having shot up in 2002 from a relatively low base. Unless restructuring of corporate debt is accelerated to reactivate credit flows, the contribution of investment to growth is unlikely to return to the strong levels seen before the financial crisis.

The budget deficit is forecast to continue narrowing, especially in 2004, in line with buoyant tax collections driven by strong growth and a possible increase in VAT. This assumes that the Government does not pursue any new and expensive spending programs. Government spending is expected to remain relatively stable over the next 2 years. With robust growth probable, largely due to continued good export performance, and with private consumption spending remaining healthy, the need for fiscal pump priming over the forecast period will abate.

Even with such levels of economic performance, inflation is likely to stay relatively subdued. As interest rates are already very low, BOT has plenty of room to maneuver and could tighten monetary policy to stave off any significant threat to the low inflation environment. This would be in line with its stated objective of inflation targeting. The flexibility to manipulate interest rates to contain inflationary pressures would still exist even if interest rates were to edge up over the next 2 years, as they likely will, due to strong economic growth.

For the first time since the financial crisis, against a background of strong economic expansion in 2002 and its projected continuation over the next 2 years, the Government may be able to make inroads into reducing some of the poverty that resulted from the crisis itself. The country's experience with poverty reduction from the mid-1980s to the onset of the crisis suggests that rapid economic development can work to significantly reduce poverty. Strong growth, coupled with government programs targeting the poor should result in the poverty incidence falling appreciably over the next few years.

Several risks could significantly affect the projected base-case scenario. The main one relates to global demand conditions, and in particular growth in the US. Given the economy's heavy reliance on exports, any major delay in the economic recovery in the US could impinge significantly on export income and dampen domestic expansion. Another major risk relates to the possible impact on the country's large tourism industry of a spread in SARS, though such impact appears limited at the time of writing. With moderate oil price rises, Thailand's growth in 2003 would be adversely affected, perhaps by 0.5%. As a major net importer of oil, it would be one of the hardest hit of all ASEAN countries, although oil accounts for only 11% of imports. Its low inflation environment is also likely to be affected somewhat if oil prices rise sharply.

Table 2.13 Major Economic Indicators, Viet Nam, 2000–2004, %

Item	2000	2001	2002	2003	2004
GDP growth	6.1	5.8	6.4	6.9	7.1
Gross domestic investment/GDP	23.9	25.9	32.0	32.0	31.0
Gross domestic savings/GDP	25.5	27.4	29.2	28.3	25.8
Inflation rate (consumer price index)	-0.6	0.8	4.0	5.0	5.0
Money supply (M2) growth	39.0	25.5	23.2	21.0	21.4
Fiscal balance/GDP	-4.8	-3.7	-3.5	-5.3	-4.6
Merchandise export growth	25.2	6.5	7.4	9.1	8.4
Merchandise import growth	34.5	6.0	19.5	13.1	12.0
Current account balance/GDP	1.7	1.5	-2.8	-3.7	-5.2
Debt service ratio	10.5	10.6	10.2	8.8	8.1

Sources: General Statistics Office; State Bank of Viet Nam; International Monetary Fund; staff estimates.

of rural-urban migration. Strong industry sector growth, with further expansion of private domestic enterprises in the provinces, would probably help reduce underemployment in rural areas, which is high and a major problem there. This, however, will require intensifying the implementation of the new Enterprise Law, enacted in 2000, at the provincial and district levels.

Policy Developments

The reform process in Viet Nam is accelerating, which itself is an important variable in sustaining rapid and steady economic growth rates. Changes to the 1992 Constitution in 2001 to strengthen "rule by law", the enactment of the new Enterprise Law, the signing of the BTA, and the support enunciated for the private sector at the March 2002 Fifth Party Plenum have been important recent political milestones. Decentralization decrees including fiscal, licensing, and FDI approvals, and grassroots democracy (a mechanism to enhance people's participation and transparency in decision making) were other important policy developments. This all contrasts with the belief among policy makers in the 1990s that policy change was not urgent, since large FDI inflows and 20%-plus annual export growth rates had been achieved without much reform.

Since the financial crisis and subsequent period of slower growth, Viet Nam has entered a new phase of economic development. With increased market orientation and regional and global integration, it is in a better position now to exploit its full development potential which, in the past, was unnecessarily constrained by the centrally planned system. The BTA could also help pave the way to WTO accession. In addition, Viet Nam must prepare for AFTA commitments over the next 3 years and free trade arrangements with ASEAN by 2010. The PRC's entry into WTO also creates challenges and competition in export markets. All of these developments highlight the urgency of further reform.

The liberalization of interest rates on lending in domestic currency is potentially a significant move, although other formal and many informal controls over commercial banks still restrict their scope and flexibility. Banks were also permitted to increase their dollar holdings from 15% of total capital to 30%, and the required reserve ratio on foreign-currency deposits was lowered from 8.0% to 5.0%. All these moves have stimulated lending activity, but they also raise questions about the foreign exchange vulnerability of lending portfolios.

Trade reforms in 2002 included publishing the tariff reduction schedule under AFTA, issuing the implementing decision for the BTA, and starting working sessions for WTO accession. The foreign-exchange surrender requirement for exporters was reduced again from 40% to 30%. By the end of 2003, all quantitative restrictions on imports will be abolished with the exception of sugar (to be kept until 2005) and petroleum products. The shift toward tariffs from nontariff barriers has led to an increase in the average tariff rate from 13.4% in 1997 to 15.7% in 2002. However, this has resulted in an overall decrease in trade restrictions since the implicit cost of nontariff barriers was very high.

Driven by political and economic concerns, the momentum and depth of trade reform commitments are impressive. If the trade reform agenda to 2010 is followed, it will precipitate structural change that will improve competitiveness and focus resources in activities where the economy has a comparative advantage.

Private domestic manufacturing is still relatively small, accounting for less than 4.0% of GDP and 6.0% of manufacturing output. It accounts for about 3% of total employment. The nonstate sector, which includes collective households, mixed, private domestic enterprises (fully Vietnamese owned), and FIEs, accounted for about 61% of GDP in 2001. Its growth has been slow but positive over the 1996–2001 period.

Furthermore, over 2000–2002, some 53,000 new private domestic enterprises with a total capital of $5.3 billion were registered. In 2002 alone, 20,745 new enterprises having a total capital of about $2.4 billion were registered. This was higher than new FDI commitments, which amounted to $1.3 billion. More than half these new enterprises are registered as limited companies (57.5%), about one third are sole proprietorships, and the rest are joint-stock companies. With 20 workers on average, most of the new enterprises are concentrated in food processing, wood products, garments, and ceramics and glass products, and are usually located in Hanoi or Ho Chi Minh City.

In addition to the improved access to credit and other related improvements in the business environment, the implementation of the new Enterprise Law, and the resolution reaffirming the rights of people to do business by the Fifth Party Plenum appeared to be the major factors in a surge in private domestic enterprise registrations. Clearly many obstacles and biases remain, but signs point toward a period of rapid growth led by private domestic enterprises.

FIEs can now hire workers directly, and the tax on profit remittances from FIEs has been removed. A more profound move, however, has been the decentralization of FDI approvals and regulations to the provincial level. This is part of a general trend to give provincial and city governments greater control over development in their areas. It will allow the more progressive provinces to open up and attract foreign investors directly.

In 2002, to steer the transition to a socialist-oriented market economy and the implementation of the Government's twin aims of economic development and poverty reduction, a Comprehensive Poverty Reduction and Growth Strategy, a plank of the Socioeconomic Development Strategy (2001–2010), was completed. The Government has also published a Public Investment Program (2001–2005). These initiatives, with some refinements to ensure policy consistency and operational links, could provide further impetus as well as sustainability to further growth in the coming years.

Viet Nam has made substantial achievements in securing robust economic growth and in reducing poverty. However, the excessive bureaucracy, opaqueness, and inefficiencies in public administration could fetter the economy in various ways, including competitiveness, further development, and sustainability. The public administration also has to answer the needs of a growing private sector and respond to a population that is beginning to expect greater participation, transparency, and accountability from its public officials. For this reason, the Government aims to build a professional, modern, and efficient public administration system through its Public Administration Reform Master Program (2001–2010). This will be consistent with, as well as helpful to, Viet Nam's transition from a centrally planned to a socialist-oriented market economy. It should also help the economy (i) deal more effectively with emerging challenges and opportunities from its increasing openness, both regionally and internationally; (ii) remain attractive to foreign investors by reducing transaction costs; (iii) and improve public service delivery to the poor by cutting down on red tape and inefficiency.

In addition, with a view to bringing Vietnamese laws up to international standards, particularly in the context of the country's increasing international integration, a comprehensive legal needs assessment was completed in 2002, and a strategy for legal system development up to 2010 is being formulated.

To support private sector development, the Government introduced several reforms in 2002:

the number of special business licenses was reduced (five were revoked and 10 were modified; 194 remain); local government responsibilities in implementing the new Enterprise Law were clarified; and the use of land-use rights certificates was extended. In addition, a one-stop shop scheme for administrative service delivery was replicated in several provinces, and a registration system for secured transactions was established for the first time. To improve the corporate sector and its governance, clearer rules were promulgated for the equitization process; new accounting standards were approved (and will be issued in 2003); and the formulation of a competition law and bankruptcy law began. With regard to foreign trade, customs valuation and other customs administration reforms moved ahead, some of the few remaining dual prices were abolished, and nontariff barriers to trade were reduced. These are all small but important steps in the direction of a more market-oriented economy and, while their individual impacts may be modest, taken together they are stimulating domestic demand, improving economic efficiency, and boosting growth.

On the state-owned front, some progress has been made in the reform of SOCBs and SOEs. Recapitalization of SOCBs has started, but increasing their competitiveness is still a challenging task. The pace of equitizing small and medium SOEs is gaining momentum. Some of the positive steps taken in 2002 included drawing up various legal documents regarding many of the details for equitizing enterprises. For example, SOEs were classified (as to eligibility for equitization); rights to buy shares were clarified; guidelines for enterprise valuation were issued; and instructions on how SOEs were to settle outstanding debts were given. It is likely that the Government will retain ownership of the larger SOEs for some time, though it recently announced that only nine out of 78 of the smaller SOEs met the criteria to remain in state hands. Four of the largest corporations are being restructured into holding companies that will be encouraged to compete across a broad product range.

On the external front, there is concern that inherent structural weaknesses have the potential to undermine competitiveness in external markets. The high level of tariff and nontariff protection on many manufacturing and assembly activities will soon decline or vanish once Viet Nam starts complying with its regional and international obli-

gations, such as AFTA and BTA in the short run and WTO in the long run. Domestic labor costs are low, even in comparison with the PRC's, but utility and infrastructure costs are higher, and productivity in general is low. Transaction costs are also believed to be high due to administrative inefficiencies, while policy and institutional weaknesses are inherent in the economy.

The high costs of doing business in Viet Nam imply the need to (i) introduce greater competition into certain sectors such as telecommunications, power, and shipping (to help reduce costs); (ii) ease restrictions on the transfer of technology; (iii) make business policies and regulations more transparent (to enhance predictability for investors); (iv) broaden the tax base; (v) accelerate deregulation and implement the Enterprise Law aggressively outside the main urban areas; and (vi) correct the misconceptions on the role of the private sector and enhance its role.

To improve external competitiveness, Viet Nam needs to reduce transaction costs by removing structural weaknesses and by improving the business environment. Consequently, the Government should ensure speedier implementation of already announced reforms regarding SOEs, the banking sector, public administration, and legal system development. For long-term productivity and economic growth, as the country reaches higher stages of economic development, it will have to adopt more knowledge-intensive technology and take advantage of global production and distribution chains. This, however, will require timely and carefully designed investment in human capital formation.

Outlook for 2003–2004

The immediate outlook for the economy is good. It is estimated that GDP will grow by 6.9% in 2003 and by 7.1% in 2004, a slightly higher rate than achieved in 2002. The outlook predicts that growth will be underpinned by ongoing strong domestic demand driven by the Government's policy and institutional reform process and by expansionary fiscal policy. The industry sector's contribution to GDP will rise modestly and the shares of the agriculture and services sectors will likely remain substantially as before.

On the demand side, GDP growth is expected

to be led by domestic consumption and investment. The Government is expected to maintain its expansionary fiscal stance in 2003, partly to fund both the increase in the minimum salary of public officials, which amounts to a total of $780 million extra annually, and reforms in SOEs and SOCBs. Gross fixed investment should also continue to rise.

In the external sector, crude oil revenues will likely strengthen on average, partly because of higher oil prices in the first quarter of 2003. The conflict in Iraq could, however, have a negative impact on Vietnamese rice exports since Iraq was a significant importer of Vietnamese rice in 2002—nearly 1 million metric tons, or equivalent to one third of the country's rice exports. Iraq also imported one third of Viet Nam's total tea exports in 2002. Any fall in these two exports will have a direct bearing on the poorer sections of the population. To overcome any likely problem of this nature, officials are discussing contracts with Iran and other Middle Eastern countries as alternative markets.

Exports, particularly of garments, footwear, and seafood products, are forecast to increase by 9.1% in 2003 and by 8.4% in 2004, in response to the BTA and to likely improvements in global markets. Viet Nam's exports to the US will probably continue to grow due to the impetus created by the BTA. The Government's target for exports to the US in 2003 is $3.2 billion. Higher growth will be accompanied, however, by increased concern over conventional macroeconomic variables. First, it is likely that the trade deficit will widen, to over 3% of GDP in 2003 and to over 5% in 2004. This is grounded in the fact that imports are projected to continue growing more rapidly than exports because of a positive response to further reductions in import tariffs. Second, the fiscal deficit is estimated to be substantially higher at around 5.3% of GDP in 2003. AFTA commitments will compel significant tariff reductions, resulting in declining customs revenues. VAT has the potential to compensate for revenue losses from tariff reductions on imports, though it requires administrative strengthening and policy fine-tuning. If oil prices fall and other sources of customs revenues decline, a shortfall in projected government revenues may lead to a further buildup in debt as the Government will probably have to issue bonds.

Third, inflation will probably be around 5% in 2003. In general, food prices will continue to rise, but less markedly. Cash crop prices will also likely increase, except coffee and sugar where world stocks are high. Prices of imported consumer goods will fall somewhat as a result of lower tariffs, and this will exert downward pressure on the CPI.

Increases in resources will come from tourist and FDI inflows. The regional tourism market now regards Viet Nam as one of its safest tourist destinations; about 3.6 million tourists were (prior to the SARS outbreak) expected in the country in 2003. However, as in the other countries of Southeast Asia, the outbreak of the SARS epidemic will significantly affect tourism for some part of the year. Depending on the duration of the epidemic, slower growth in the tourism sector and in the services sector in general could result in lower GDP growth.

Net FDI inflows are forecast to reach $764 million in 2003. Remittances from Vietnamese overseas are also expected to grow. Gross official reserves are forecast to rise to $4.3 billion.

ASIAN DEVELOPMENT
Outlook
2003

Economic Trends and Prospects in Developing Asia

South Asia
Afghanistan
Bangladesh
Bhutan
India
Maldives
Nepal
Pakistan
Sri Lanka

Afghanistan

After two decades of war, an opportunity for peaceful development in the country emerged with the fall of the Taliban regime in late 2001, the creation of the Afghan Interim Administration, and in June 2002, the selection of an Afghan Transitional Administration by a special Loya Jirga (or traditional Afghan Grand Council). While much was accomplished during 2002, the tasks ahead in rebuilding the country are enormous and cannot be achieved without the strong support of the international community.

Macroeconomic Assessment

Analysis of the economy continues to be problematic as official economic statistics are almost nonexistent. Rough estimates suggest 2002 GDP at about $4.4 billion, with per capita GDP at $170. Observations in cities, especially Kabul, indicate a strong recovery in 2002, mainly in certain sectors such as services and construction, driven by the international community's spending and emergency assistance efforts. Given the deteriorated economic base, a rebound in real economic growth was expected.

The economy is primarily agriculture based (crops, livestock, and horticulture), supporting about 85% of the total population and accounting for about 50% of GDP by 1993 estimates. The annual food assessment of the Food and Agriculture Organization of the United Nations (FAO) and the World Food Program estimated 2002 agricultural production to be 82% higher than in 2001. The sharp gain was attributed to somewhat better rainfall than in 2001 and the increased availability and higher quality of seeds, fertilizers, and other key inputs. Rainfed wheat, in particular, recovered significantly in major growing areas of the north and western provinces from the levels of the previous 3 drought-affected years. Despite the recovery, aggregate 2002 cereal production is never-theless estimated at 4% below the 1998 crop. Livestock provides a major source of cash income from the sale of dairy items, mutton, wool, animal hides, and the skins of karakul sheep in both domestic and export markets. A March 2002 FAO survey reports that the total livestock population in Afghanistan had declined by about 60% from 1998 levels due to continued distressed selling of animals, especially during the summer and autumn drought of 2001. Improved rainfall in 2002 is expected to have helped the situation a little.

According to a United Nations Office for Drug Control and Crime Prevention survey, estimated opium production in 2002 was 3,400 tons, similar to levels reached during the mid- to late 1990s. The Afghan Interim Administration issued a strong ban on opium poppy cultivation, processing, trafficking, and consumption in January 2002, though its ability to suppress production, which at the farm may have a gross value of as much as $1 billion, is limited.

The population of Afghanistan is estimated at 23–26 million. Almost 2 million refugees had returned by end-September 2002. Return rates have dropped from a peak of 20,000 a day in May 2002 to around 4,000 a day toward late 2002. While there are no reliable labor force or employment statistics, unemployment is clearly very high in all age groups, for both men and women. UN agencies and nongovernment organizations have supported employment programs and food- or cash-for-work programs.

In April 2002, the interim administration adopted an ordinary (recurrent) budget for FY2002 with $483 million in expenditures—$460 million for the fiscal year plus $23 million for clearance of wage arrears for the previous fiscal year. (FY2002 covers 21 March 2002 to 20 March 2003, the Solar Year SY1381.) With domestic revenues budgeted at $83 million, this left a financing requirement of $400 million. It is estimated that FY2002 expenditures would reach almost 90% of budgeted amounts in afghani terms. In dollar terms, this would be equivalent to $325 million, given that the afghani depreciated compared with the accounting exchange rate of Af34/$ used in the budget. Domestic revenues were estimated to reach about $100 million, leaving an estimated financing requirement of $225 million, which was fully met (i.e., there would be no remaining aid requirement).

In October 2002, the Central Statistics Office released its first CPI data since 1987 (the CPI covers only Kabul). After recording average monthly increases of about 1% in the early months of 2002, the CPI increased by 16% in September, 12.4% in October, and 22.7% in November 2002. These significantly higher inflation rates were mainly due to the depreciation of the exchange rate caused by speculation surrounding the introduction of unified new currency notes in October 2002 and by high food prices resulting from the drought and the end of the growing season. However, in December 2002 and January and February 2003, the CPI decreased by 4.4%, 3.8%, and 1.4%, respectively, reflecting turnaround appreciation of the new afghani currency by December 2002.

Trade statistics have not been published by the Afghan authorities since FY1992. A survey sponsored by the World Bank puts Afghanistan's total trade in 2000 at $2.5 billion, comprising about $1.2 billion in imports and about $1.3 billion in exports. However, about 90% of the estimated total exports were reexports of commodities to neighboring countries. Trade has since fallen sharply, except for emergency food aid and other imports. The Government announced in September 2002 that it would temporarily forgo customs tariffs to boost trade. In January 2003, the US made Afghanistan a beneficiary of the Generalized System of Preferences, eliminating US tariffs on approximately 5,700 Afghan products.

Policy Developments

Perhaps the most significant economic policy action in 2002 was the introduction of the new afghani currency, which exchanged 1,000 old afghani for one new afghani. The new currency replaced a mixture of notes in circulation. There were at least three versions of the domestic currency. It is not known how many reruns of the same series of the official banknotes were issued. The total amount of old afghanis collected was Af19 trillion; Af14 trillion in regular old notes were exchanged at face value and Af3.4 trillion of notes were converted at 50% of value. An additional Af1.8 trillion were absorbed through the foreign exchange auction during October–January. All in all, Af15.6 billion in new afghanis were issued through the conversion process.

By early March 2003, the amount of currency in circulation was somewhat over Af20 billion, reflecting both the currency conversion and government payments in the new currency during the period October–March. The new currency is a substantive symbol of national sovereignty and sets the stage for Da Afghanistan Bank (DAB), the central bank, to provide an attractive alternative to increased use of foreign currency. After an initial speculative depreciation up to Af70/$, around the time of the introduction of the new currency in October, the exchange rate came back to around Af45/$ in December (similar to the preconversion rate in mid-September), although the rate deteriorated slightly to Af51/$ by early March, possibly reflecting the uncertainty in the Middle East.

This favorable development reassured the international community to step up its delivery of the $5.2 billion pledged assistance at the International Conference on Reconstruction Assistance to Afghanistan in Tokyo in January 2002. In October 2002, the pledge was revised to $2.1 billion for 2002 and $1.5 billion for 2003.

DAB is not yet fully operational and there are no operating commercial banks. With government policy of no DAB financing of the budget, changes in the amount of afghani currency in circulation are determined by changes in DAB's net foreign assets. Since the Government needs to convert the donor foreign exchange assistance that it receives to finance the budget into local currency to cover expenditures (mostly for wages), the amount of such donor assistance would essentially determine the expansion in the money supply. Since at present the size of such assistance is necessarily very large, implying about a doubling of the money supply within a year, the money supply mechanism carried the potential for excessive expansion. To prevent this and control money growth, DAB has engaged in foreign exchange auctions. Participants in these auctions are the larger money traders who constitute the foreign exchange market and provide a larger import capacity. Deciding on targets and implementing policy in the present circumstances must necessarily be flexible and adaptive.

Without functioning commercial banks, the country depends on the traditional *hawala* system for money transfer, the only effective payment system in place, and the informal credit market meets the demand for liquidity. The National Development Framework (April 2002) highlights the importance of strengthening DAB in monetary control and banking supervision and in establishing a commercial banking sector and modern payments system. The pending Central Bank Law and Banking Law will facilitate the establishment and operation of banks and modernize the banking sector. A joint initiative by the Aga Khan Fund for Economic Development, the International Finance Corporation, and ADB aims to find a foreign private bank to establish a local institution to handle trade financing and microfinance, facilitating the emergence of a formal banking sector. In parallel, reforms are being undertaken to improve the functioning of the banking sector and support private activity.

In March 2003, the Government announced a comprehensive government budget for FY2003—comprising an ordinary (recurrent) budget of $550 million, of which $350 million will have to be financed by external assistance, and a development budget of about $1.7 billion. This formulation of the budget will facilitate keeping the reconstruction process as coordinated and controlled as possible. Notwithstanding this, the implementation of a responsible fiscal policy requires the central Government to quickly develop its capacity for

managing the budget, especially increasing and streamlining revenue collection. The Government should also develop effective control measures for expenditures, accounting, and auditing. The Ministry of Finance is expected to receive substantial external assistance in developing tax administration capacity, especially in customs administration accounting, development of databases and a management information system, training needs assessment, and improvement in tax law. Already, the Ministry of Finance has made considerable progress in improving financial management with the help of international contractors. Besides, the Government's confirmed commitment to a no-overdraft rule, as well as the customs tariff and administration reforms currently in preparation, will help achieve and maintain fiscal and monetary balance.

Significant reconstruction efforts are required to establish basic administrative procedures and systems of accountability in the Afghan public service. Data on the size of the public sector are very poor, but estimates suggest a staff of about 240,000 (excluding military personnel) with a large proportion located in Kabul. Staff distribution is uneven with an imbalance between professional and administrative staff. Wages and salaries are very low and pensions negligible. The Transitional Administration has started working on improved payroll processes, staff capacity building, a merit basis for recruitment and promotion, an enhanced policy management process, a pay and grading review, and improved monitoring of staffing totals. The newly established Civil Service Commission has the overall responsibility for this.

Outlook for 2003–2004

Important challenges facing the Transitional Administration include writing a new constitution, preparing for the 2004 elections, and ensuring domestic security. Security and stability will remain problematic as long as the local power holders retain their own armed forces. Also, remnants of terrorist groups appear to be operational in pockets of the country and across borders. Efforts are under way to establish the rule of law, bring provincial and local authorities under central control, build a national army and police force, and extend the tenure and expand the role of the International

Security Assistance Force. The Government is keen to root out corruption, as reflected in President Karzai's October 2002 announcement to sack a number of influential provincial officials on charges of corruption. The new Investment Law will go a long way to improve the overall business and investment environment.

It is very difficult to predict with any confidence how the macroeconomic picture will develop in 2003–2004 and beyond, as the prediction crucially depends on the improvement in the security situation, the Government's commitment to sound economic management (especially reasonable progress in revenue mobilization), and continued donor support for reconstruction. Provided that these preconditions are met, there are positive factors indicating strong economic growth. First, following such a long war, a sharp economic rebound can be expected once investments flow in. Second, while the return of large numbers of Afghan refugees puts an added burden on the urban infrastructure and environment, they bring with them skills and entrepreneurship. Third, reconstruction activities will generate substantial demand and provide business opportunities. Given these factors, provided that the international support to reconstruction sustains— the conflict and its aftermath in Iraq distracting donor commitment is a concern—annual economic growth in 2003–2004 could be well above 10%, with inflation kept in reasonable check.

Bangladesh

GDP growth in FY2002 moderated due to a contraction in agriculture and a slowdown in exports. The Government has taken steps to improve the macroeconomic environment by reducing the fiscal deficit and by moving toward a more market-oriented economy. Economic growth should pick up in the next 2 years, with a recovery in both domestic and external demand.

Macroeconomic Assessment

The Government recently revised its GDP growth estimate for FY2002 (ended 30 June 2002) to 4.4% from 4.8%. Lower growth was primarily attributed to a contraction in agriculture and a slowdown in export-oriented manufacturing activity.

Total production of foodgrain in FY2002, at 25.9 million tons, represented a 3.2% (0.9 million ton) decline over the previous year. Lower production stemmed mainly from adverse weather, which more than offset the increased use of high-yielding variety seeds, fertilizer application, and extended irrigation. Despite this setback, net availability of foodgrain from domestic sources at 23.3 million tons represented a surplus in excess of 1 million tons over domestic consumption.

Industry sector growth moderated to 6.6% in FY2002 from 7.4% in the previous year, due mainly to weaker manufacturing output. Decreasing to 4.5% growth, from 6.6% in FY2001, the setback to medium- and large-scale manufacturing resulted largely from a significant slowdown in the export-oriented garment, processed food, and chemical industries. Notwithstanding subdued manufacturing growth, industrial activities that are less dependent on global demand—such as small-scale industry, electricity generation, and gas production—have experienced relatively robust growth. Growth in construction activity, however, slowed marginally to 8.4% from 8.7% in FY2001 due to an ongoing oversupply of commercial buildings and apartments. The subdued level of export-oriented manufacturing and a relatively flat level of foodgrain production depressed wholesale and retail trade, and transport, storage, and communications activities. As a result, growth in overall services sector activity moderated to 5.3% from 5.5% in FY2001.

Based on the findings of the 1999/2000 Labor Force Survey, which was published in August 2002, the annual average growth rate of the labor force increased by 1.9% in the 1990s, and by 2000 had reached 60.3 million people, compared with 51.1 million people in 1991. Relatively higher economic growth during this period did not, however, result in a significant creation of new jobs, with the annual employment growth rate increasing by only 1.6%. According to the Survey, the unemployment rate in FY2000 was only 3.7%. If, however, day laborers working less than 15 hours a week are included, in addition to the number of unemployed, the unemployment rate would increase to 11%. Further, inefficiency of the Bangladeshi labor market is revealed by the underemployment rate, which is as high as 35% of the employed population. Recently, the number of people who leave to work abroad has declined, with a particularly steep drop evident from FY2001 to FY2002, reflecting the global economic fallout following the September 11 attacks.

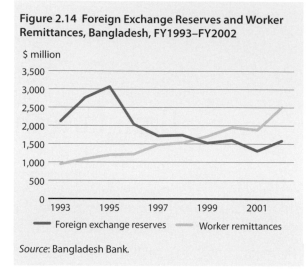

Figure 2.14 Foreign Exchange Reserves and Worker Remittances, Bangladesh, FY1993–FY2002

$ million

Source: Bangladesh Bank.

Despite the high incidence of unemployment, for those employed, increases in real wages have been maintained in recent years. This partly reflects relatively low inflation and a high demand for certain skills in the formal labor market.

Revenue collection in FY2002 rose to 10.2% of GDP from 9.5% a year earlier. Though falling short of the target by 2.0%, the revenue performance was impressive given the slowdown in imports, moderate growth in industrial production, and the political changes arising from the general election that took place during the year. Progress in revenue mobilization was possible because of a renewed emphasis on administrative initiatives and close monitoring and supervision. Despite revenues falling below target, the fiscal deficit declined sharply to 4.4% of GDP from 6.1% in the previous year. This was due to containing current expenditures and a substantial pruning of the Annual Development Program. Actions taken by the Government to reduce pressure on the budget, such as cancellation of a Non-Aligned Movement summit, freezing government recruitment, and upward adjustment of energy prices mainly accounted for the lower growth in current expenditure. Cutting back low-priority and unproductive projects and keeping in abeyance contracts under suppliers' credit substantially reduced expenditure under the Annual Development Program. These developments generally led to an improvement in the quality of budgetary allocation.

Despite the sharp decline in the fiscal deficit,

given the increasing domestic debt-to-GDP ratio, there is some concern over its sustainability. In terms of financing the fiscal deficit, external resources accounted for 2.3% of GDP and domestic resources 2.1%. A notable feature of the fiscal deficit financing sources was the reduced reliance on more expensive domestic borrowing, which dropped from 57.6% of total financing in FY2001 (3.5% of GDP) to 47.2% during FY2002. As a result, the ratio of interest payments on domestic debt to revenue, an indicator of debt-servicing capacity, declined from 13.6% in FY2001 to 12.9% in FY2002.

During FY2002, the increase in domestic credit slowed to 12.9% from 17.7% in the previous year. This was mainly due to a sharp deceleration in credit growth to the public sector, and reflected increased efforts to contain the central government fiscal deficit and the imposition of financial discipline on SOEs. During the year, private sector credit growth also experienced a moderate slowdown, reflecting both a lack of access to and appetite for credit as a result of sector-specific profitability issues, a more cautious attitude toward lending, an uncertain economic environment, a poor law-and-order situation, and relatively high interest rates due to a high level of NPLs. At the same time, net foreign assets of the banking system rose sharply as a result of increased migrant worker remittances (Figure 2.14). However, these higher asset levels could not offset the slowdown in domestic credit expansion, and the rate of increase in broad money (M2) moderated to 13.1% in FY2002 from 16.6% in FY2001. Slower money supply growth was, however, accompanied by a significantly higher (24.3%) increase in reserve money due mainly to a sharp rise in net foreign assets of Bangladesh Bank. Excess reserves of the banking sector accounted for the resulting decrease in the money multiplier.

The annual average rate of inflation edged up to 2.4% in FY2002 from 1.6% a year earlier. On a point-to-point basis, inflation picked up at a slightly higher pace from 1.7% in June 2001 to 2.6% in June 2002. Low inflation stemmed mainly from depressed food prices (which have a weight of over 60% in the overall index), which increased by 1.4% in June 2002, up from 0.9% in June 2001. Nonfood inflation, however, climbed more sharply to 6.1% from 3.1%, due mainly to a rise in administered prices after December 2001. Despite only a modest 1.6% devaluation of the taka in January 2002,

Table 2.14 Major Economic Indicators, Bangladesh, 2000–2004, %

Item	2000	2001	2002	2003	2004
GDP growth[a]	5.9	5.3	4.4	5.2	5.8
Gross domestic investment/GDP	23.0	23.1	23.2	24.0	25.5
Gross national savings/GDP	22.1	20.8	23.6	22.7	23.0
Inflation rate (consumer price index)	3.4	1.6	2.4	3.8	4.5
Money supply (M2) growth	18.6	16.6	13.1	12.8	14.2
Fiscal balance/GDP	-6.2	-6.1	-4.4	-3.9	-5.2
Merchandise export growth	8.2	11.4	-7.6	9.5	10.5
Merchandise import growth	4.8	11.3	-8.7	3.5	7.5
Current account balance/GDP	-0.9	-2.3	0.4	-1.3	-2.5
Debt service ratio[b]	8.0	8.2	8.7	8.6	8.4

[a] Based on constant 1995/96 market prices. [b] Represents the ratio of debt service to total foreign exchange earnings from exports of goods and nonfactor services plus worker remittances.

Sources: Bangladesh Bureau of Statistics; Bangladesh Bank; Export Promotion Bureau; Ministry of Finance; staff estimates.

the competitiveness of exports was not adversely affected during the year. After appreciating slightly in January and February 2002, because of inflation differentials with its trading partners, the real effective exchange rate of the taka subsequently eased back due to a weaker dollar. By November 2002, the real effective exchange rate had depreciated by 1.7% over the level of November 2001.

Balance-of-payments data for FY2002 indicate that merchandise exports and imports at $5,929 million and $7,697 million, respectively, declined by 7.6% and 8.7% from the prior year level. These trends reflected the global slowdown, the economic fallout from September 11, and the import-dependent nature of exports. Given that the decline in imports was larger than that of exports, and that imports constituted a higher initial base, the decline in imports more than offset the decline in exports and led to a narrowing of the trade deficit to $1,768 million in FY2002 from $2,011 million in FY2001.

The decline in export earnings was broad based, affecting all major export categories, excepting jute goods and agricultural products. Particularly large declines (in terms of value) were recorded for frozen foods and readymade garments. While the export of frozen foods was affected by a combination of higher freight and insurance costs (after the September 11 attacks), the decline in readymade

garment exports has been attributed to subdued global demand and the earlier granting of duty- and quota-free access to the US for garment exports from Caribbean and Sub Saharan countries, which undermined garment exports from Bangladesh during the year.

The decline in imports was also broad based. Significant falls were evident in foodgrain (rice in particular), sugar, cement, petroleum and petroleum products, and raw materials and other inputs for the garment industry. Imports of inputs to the garment industry were affected by the more subdued export sales for this industry.

During FY2002, the lower trade deficit was accompanied by a 32.9% increase in overseas worker remittances due, in large measure, to government efforts to encourage the flow of remittances through official channels (Figure 2.14). As a result of these developments, the current account balance (excluding official grants) moved to a surplus of $171 million (0.4% of GDP) from a deficit of $1,090 million (2.3% of GDP) in FY2001. The substantially improved current account more than offset a somewhat weaker capital and financial account arising from lower inflows of official grants, FDI, and supplier credits. This led to an overall balance-of-payments surplus of $365 million in FY2002, compared with a deficit of $226 million in the previous year. Following improvement in the overall balance, foreign exchange reserves increased to $1,583 million at the end of June 2002 from $1,307 million a year earlier.

Policy Developments

As FY2002 progressed, regaining and maintaining control over public finances, and moving toward a more market-oriented economy, became central to efforts by the Government to maintain macroeconomic stability. In addition to the measures taken to tighten budgetary discipline, the Government has set up a Public Expenditure Review Commission and a Revenue Reform Commission, and has planned a midterm review of the budget to ensure that it remains within sustainable limits and is no longer a source of instability to the economy. Both commissions have now submitted their interim reports, and the Government is expected to take account of their recommendations in revising the FY2003 budget and in framing the budget for the following year. The FY2003 budget also introduced major reforms in the import duty structure, restarting the tariff liberalization process that had been stalled since the mid-1990s.

During FY2002, greater efforts were made to use market-based instruments to manage liquidity and bring about a more realistic structure of interest rates. Toward this end, in February 2002 the Government made it mandatory for commercial banks to meet their cash reserve ratio only through local currency and not through their foreign currency balances, as the latter weakens monetary control and constitutes an expansionary device in the event of devaluation. Bangladesh Bank also increased the size of its treasury bill auctions during the year in a bid to contain the expansion in base money. This had the effect of progressively increasing the treasury bill rate to a more realistic level. Although the introduction of repurchase (repo) operations during the year was also meant to enhance the ability of the Government to control liquidity, due to the prevalence of excess liquidity in the market for much of the year, this facility was only used sparingly. The Government also appears to have agreed in principle to move toward a flexible exchange rate. However, timing remains an issue. There is agreement that a more flexible exchange rate system would require improving the institutional capacity of Bangladesh Bank and devel-

oping a more market-based monetary framework to control domestic inflation. With this in mind, the cabinet recently agreed to a number of major amendments to existing legislation to give greater autonomy to Bangladesh Bank to conduct monetary policy. Much effort has also been expended to prepare, on the basis of broad public consensus, the Government's National Strategy for Economic Growth, Poverty Reduction and Social Development, which would provide the basis for future development planning.

Notwithstanding these reform measures and the closure of a major loss-incurring state-owned jute mill and a number of loss-making branches of nationalized commercial banks, more remains to be done. Inadequate progress in governance as well as in institutional and structural policy reforms continues to adversely affect the investment environment.

Outlook for 2003–2004

GDP growth for FY2003 is likely to accelerate to 5.2% on the back of steady growth in agriculture and stronger demand in the US and EU for the country's major exports. While there are some indications of a shortfall in the *aman* rice crop due to adverse weather, the resulting high prices have led to renewed interest in the cultivation of the forthcoming *boro* crop. Overall, no major shortfall is expected in foodgrain production over the year.

Data for the first 3 months of FY2003 indicate a broad-based rebound in manufacturing. GDP growth is likely to strengthen further to 5.8% in FY2004 due to a further recovery in the major OECD markets and a pickup in private sector economic activity as the Government makes progress on structural and economic reforms. Although growth of this magnitude will be insufficient to make a major dent in reducing poverty in Bangladesh (currently estimated at close to 50% of the population on the basis of a cost of basic needs approach), the measures taken in FY2002 should nevertheless provide the basis for sustaining economic growth and poverty reduction in the future.

The fiscal deficit for FY2003 is likely to meet the target of 3.9% of GDP due to strong government commitment to contain low-priority expenditures, and a renewed effort at mobilizing revenue. Data for the first 6 months of FY2003 indicate that revenue collection has exceeded its target by 1.8%. The fiscal deficit is, however, likely to widen to 5.2% of GDP in FY2004 as revenue growth remains stable and as the Government increases both current and Annual Development Program expenditures, given the greater availability of concessional aid.

The annual average rate of inflation is likely to edge up to 3.8% in FY2003 due to relatively higher food prices and an increase in nonfood prices on account of a rise in administered prices. In FY2004, inflation is expected to increase to 4.5%, reflecting more buoyant domestic demand and a depreciation in the external value of the taka to increase the competitiveness of the country's exports. This is likely to increase the price of imports.

Preliminary balance-of-payments data for the first 4 months of FY2003 indicate that merchandise exports increased by 9.2% compared with the same period of the previous year. This was mainly due to large increases in exports for jute and jute goods, frozen foods, and knitwear and hosiery products, partly reflecting a pickup in global demand. This was, however, partly offset by continuing declines for tea, leather goods, and readymade garments, despite an increase in the volume of garments. This is perhaps an indication of the extent of competition facing the country's garment industry. Imports continue to show no clear sign of recovery with year-on-year imports declining by 7.1% during the first 4 months of FY2003. Such a low level of imports is, however, most unlikely to be sustained as the year progresses. Although large increases were evident for rice imports (perhaps reflecting a somewhat subdued domestic *aman* crop), this was more than offset by large decreases in imports of crude oil, textiles and textile articles, and capital goods. While the decline in textiles does not augur well for garment exports, the decline in capital goods reflects continued uncertainty on the part of the private sector over domestic economic prospects.

The current account balance in FY2003 will once again revert to a deficit in the order of 1.3% of GDP, as import growth recovers and growth in remittances remains stable. Foreign exchange reserves could come under some pressure with the worsening current account balance. Notwithstanding a further recovery in the global economy in FY2004, and an increase in exports, the current account deficit is likely to widen to 2.5% of GDP as import growth picks up strongly. Given the greater availability of concessional aid with the implementation of the National Strategy for Economic Growth, such a deficit level, which is historically high for Bangladesh, should nevertheless be manageable.

Bhutan

Prudent macroeconomic management over many years has resulted in rapid economic growth and low inflation. Given the potential for growth in power generation, and continued donor support, the medium-term prospects are favorable, though efforts are needed to foster private sector growth and competition, and to broaden the economy to generate much-needed employment opportunities.

Macroeconomic Assessment

Consistent with the trend of recent years, economic activity remained buoyant with an estimated GDP growth of about 7.7% in 2002, higher than the 6.6% recorded in 2001. Strong expansion in the construction and power generation subsectors remained the main drivers of growth. Construction output has grown rapidly since 1996 and now accounts for some 15% of GDP, reflecting the activities related to the phased construction of major hydroelectric projects including Tala (1,040 megawatts), Kurichhu (60 megawatts), and Basochu (62.2 megawatts), as well as other construction works of the private and public sectors. Growth in the agriculture sector, which accounts for about one third of GDP, continued to be moderate at 2.5% in 2002, as the opportunities for expansion were limited by natural circumstances.

The Government maintained a prudent macro-economic management stance during FY2002 (ended 30 June 2002), and at 3.4% of GDP posted a higher current fiscal surplus than the prior year's 2.6%. The estimated overall fiscal deficit narrowed to 6.8% of GDP in FY2002 from 11.8% in the previous year, and is attributed to lower capital expenditures associated with the phasing in of construction of hydropower stations and other public infrastructure works. The revenue ratio (excluding grants) remained strong at 22.9% of GDP in FY2002, slightly lower than the 23.5%

recorded a year earlier, as a decline in nontax revenues (mainly public corporation dividends) limited the impact of a strong increase in tax revenues.

Monetary conditions remained moderate with broad money supply (M2) accelerating to 17.6% growth in FY2002 from 5.5% in the previous year. As in the past, the surplus on the balance of payments and the consequent rise in banking system net foreign assets were the dominant factors of the expansion of M2. However, in a welcome development, lending to the private sector has picked up substantially in the last 2 years after a couple of years of slow growth.

As measured by the CPI, annual inflation moderated to 2.7% in June 2002 from 3.6% a year earlier. Almost all the major components in the CPI basket are goods imported from India, and given the parity link between the ngultrum and the rupee, the low inflation rate prevailing over the border has contributed to price stability at home.

The trade deficit narrowed to 18.3% of GDP from 21.2% in FY2001, reflecting an increase in power exports to India as several major hydro-power projects neared completion, and a decline in imports from that country. However, the current account turned from a surplus of 0.2% of GDP in FY2001 to a deficit of 1.7% in FY2002, due in rough equal measure to a fall in current transfers and a substantial decrease in interest income on financial sector assets held abroad. Capital inflows in the form of loans and grants, as in previous years, substantially exceeded the current account deficit in 2002. As a result, Bhutan's foreign exchange reserves, as of end-June 2002, stood at $317 million, equivalent to 20.2 months of merchandise imports, compared with $294 million a year earlier, when they were equivalent to 18 months of merchandise imports. Total external debt amounted to $291.8 million in June 2002, comprising 45% in convertible currencies and 55% in rupee loans. The debt, mostly in the form of official concessional loans, rose to 58.4% of GDP from 52.1% a year earlier. The debt service ratio increased slightly from 4.6% in FY2001 to 5.0% in FY2002.

Policy Developments

With the completion of the Eighth Five-Year Plan (1 July 1997 to 30 June 2002), the Ninth Plan was launched on 1 July 2002 with an emphasis on strengthening infrastructure, improving the quality of social services, and preserving and promoting culture and the environment. A feature of the Ninth Plan distinguishing it from earlier plans is the decentralization program, under which all development plans are to be framed at the local level with local communities determining the plans' priorities and strategies.

As a step toward strengthening institutional capacity, planning, and legal infrastructure, in July 2002 the Government separated the Department of Power into three entities, namely, the Bhutan Power Corporation, the Department of Energy, and the Bhutan Power Authority. The Bhutan Power Corporation, with about 1,200 employees, is now the largest company in Bhutan. The Government has also approved the establishment of industrial estates, and an FDI policy has been adopted. It allows foreigners to own up to 70% of joint-venture companies and specifies a minimum investment of $1 million in manufacturing sector projects and $0.5 million for services sector investments.

The 2003 budget announced various tax incentives aimed at boosting exports and employment. A personal income tax system was implemented in January 2002 as a basis for increasing revenues over the longer term. To strengthen the financial system, new prudential regulations have been introduced, including risk-weighted capital-adequacy requirements, rules specifying the qualifications of

directors of financial institutions, and regulations preventing interlocking membership of boards of directors. The trade regime has been strengthened by a rationalization of import tariffs and export duties. Greater emphasis on rural infrastructure and wider coverage of social services form essential elements of the Government's strategy for reducing rural poverty.

Given the low employment elasticity of power, construction, and transport, the labor market's task of absorbing an estimated 70,000 educated young people over the next 5 years is quite challenging and adds urgency to the promotion of private sector activity.

The failure to date of excess liquidity to translate into new lending stems from conservative practices prevalent in the banking sector, coupled with a dearth of investment opportunities. Implementation of planned financial sector reforms would likely increase competition and enhance corporate governance, while externally, expanded existing and planned subregional economic cooperation activities are expected to lead to export diversification and a widening of the economic base.

Outlook for 2003–2004

The Government has maintained a prudent macroeconomic stance resulting in high, noninflationary GDP growth, and the outlook over the medium term appears quite favorable. The Ninth Plan aims to achieve average annual GDP growth of 8.2%, higher than the Eighth Plan's achieved 6.7%. Continued current fiscal surpluses, boosted by higher tax and nontax revenues, would facilitate progressive reduction in the existing heavy reliance on external resources to finance the capital budget.

The country's major power project, Tala, has crossed its halfway mark and is expected to be operational in mid-June 2005, and the Kurichhu and Basochu projects are largely complete. Significant additional power generation will not only boost revenues and exports, but is also expected to create new business opportunities in the country, and benefit rural communities through expansion of rural electrification. Over the medium term, power, construction, and transport are likely to maintain their lead role as the primary drivers of continued high growth.

India

Economic growth slowed in 2002, largely due to a drought-induced drop in agriculture. Large food stocks kept inflation in check. Official reserves rose to record levels, mainly built by large capital inflows. The outlook is for a robust recovery based on resumption of trend agricultural performance and continued buoyancy in industry and services. Nevertheless, sustaining rapid growth will require action to reduce the large fiscal deficit and reinvigorate the economic reforms.

Macroeconomic Assessment

The comprehensive market-oriented reforms pursued in India through the 1990s aimed to rationalize resource allocation, improve productivity and competitiveness in all spheres of economic activity, and move the economy to a sustained rate of higher growth. The reforms ranged from macroeconomic stabilization and fiscal reforms, trade liberalization, and industrial deregulation, to financial sector reforms, disinvestments, and privatization. The economy did in fact attain higher rates of growth in the 1990s, led by services, which is now the largest sector of the economy. However, the trend was not sustained. Compared with an average growth of around 6% through the 1990s, GDP growth was disappointing, at an average of 5.0% in FY2000 and FY2001 and is now estimated to have further declined to 4.4% in FY2002 (ended 31 March 2003).

The slowdown in the initial years of the new millennium is quite evident in the services sector. After growing at an average rate of about 8% in the latter half of the 1990s, the sector's growth rate declined to 7.1% in FY2002. Growth rates in other sectors have fluctuated. Industrial growth slumped from 6.6% in FY2000 to 3.3% in FY2001 and then recovered to 6.1% in FY2002 (Figure 2.15). The agriculture sector recovered from a contraction of 0.4% in FY2000 to an impressive growth

rate of 5.7% in FY2001 and then suffered another contraction of 3.1% in FY2002. The primary factors contributing to lower growth in recent years include exogenous effects, such as global recession and drought, as well as the impact of a large and persistent fiscal deficit and slow progress of reforms in some sectors. The Government can help guide the economy back to a high growth path through an aggressive fiscal adjustment program and other reforms. This will revive business confidence as well as public and private investment, including FDI.

The decline in growth in FY2002 is primarily on account of a supply shock in agriculture, resulting from insufficient rainfall. By the end of the monsoon season, 21 out of 36 meteorological subdivisions in the country, covering more than 55% of the total land area, had received less than normal rainfall, with 19 of them in the "deficient" category. During June–November 2002, the shortfall in total rainfall was 20%.

The fall in overall growth in FY2002 masks a recovery in industry, where manufacturing growth at 5.4% during April–December 2002 was higher than the 2.7% growth registered during the same period in the previous year (Figure 2.15). Improved performance was seen across all subsectors. The turnaround in capital goods, especially in transport equipment, occurred despite the high growth in imports of capital goods. The growth rates of nondurable consumer goods, such as food prod-

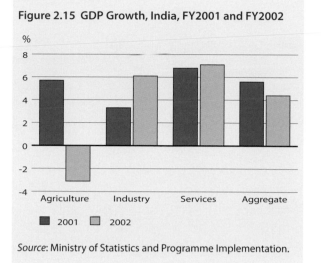

Figure 2.15 GDP Growth, India, FY2001 and FY2002

%

■ 2001   □ 2002

Source: Ministry of Statistics and Programme Implementation.

ucts, beverages, tobacco and other products, and textile products, especially wearing apparel, also rose during FY2002. The upturn in the basic goods sector is attributable to a sharp rise in construction activities. The recovery was also evident in six "core" infrastructure industries, namely, cement, steel, coal, electricity, crude oil, and petroleum products. These infrastructure industries registered a combined growth rate of 5.4% in April–December 2002 as against 2.5% in the corresponding period of 2001. The industrial recovery is mainly attributable to lower real interest rates, a revival of merchandise export growth, large foreign exchange reserves, and the large foodstocks that have contained inflation despite the supply shock in agriculture. These factors have triggered an upturn in the industrial business cycle. According to the National Council of Applied Economic Research, its index of business confidence, which stayed flat between June and October 2002, showed a marked improvement in January 2003.

Employment data are currently available only up to FY2001. While overall employment grew at a yearly rate of about 1% from FY1993 to FY2001, organized sector employment grew at an even slower rate of only about 0.3%. Employment in the private sector grew at about 2% a year during the period, but public sector employment registered an absolute decline over the same period, due to rightsizing reforms in government. With ongoing restructuring, public sector employment is likely to fall further. The prospects of private sector employ-

ment growth are also modest until the economy shifts to a higher growth trajectory. The avenues of future employment growth in the economy lie mainly in the labor-intensive services sector. Employment creation is a major goal of the recently finalized Tenth Five-Year Plan (Box 2.5).

Apart from temporary shocks, the recent slowdown in growth is attributable to structural constraints, arising from fiscal imbalances, which have adversely impacted investment. Recent average investment and savings rates of around 24% and 23%, respectively, are lower than the peak rates of around 27% and 25% achieved in 1995. In the past, economic growth was led by public investment. However, the situation changed significantly during the late 1990s with declining rates of public investment. The growing burden of servicing a burgeoning public debt, a large volume of subsidies, and a sharp increase in the government salary bill following the recommendations of the Fifth Pay Commission eroded public savings, thereby crowding out public investment in infrastructure. The share of public sector investment in GDP declined from 11.2% in FY1986 to 8.2% in FY1993 and further to 6.6% in FY1998, and has now settled at 6.3% of GDP. Private investment failed to fully replace public investment since it was also crowded out by a large transfer of private savings for public expenditures through the financial sector. Private savings amount to about 26.5% of GDP, while private investment amounts to only 16% of GDP, implying that the deficit-prone public sector has effectively siphoned off almost 40% of private savings. The effect of this crowding out has been further exacerbated by policy uncertainties and slow progress of reforms in some sectors.

On the fiscal front, the central government deficit showed a small narrowing to 5.9% of GDP in FY2002 from 6.1% in the previous year; the budgeted target was 5.3%. The deficit would have been higher but for the increase in net tax revenues, which registered an impressive 23% rise in FY2002. In addition to the central government deficit, the estimated combined deficit of the state governments is 4.2%, resulting in a consolidated (net) deficit of 9.3% in FY2002. Though slightly lower compared with the 10% level in FY2001, the overall fiscal deficit remains very large and a major challenge for macroeconomic management. Excessive public borrowing has led to rapid growth of public

Table 2.15 Major Economic Indicators, India, 2000–2004, %

Item	2000	2001	2002	2003	2004
GDP growth[a, b]	4.4	5.6	4.4	6.0	6.3
Gross domestic investment/GDP[c]	24.0	23.7	23.9	24.0	25.0
Gross domestic savings/GDP[c]	23.4	24.0	24.5	24.1	25.2
Inflation rate (wholesale price index)[d]	7.2	3.6	2.8	5.0	5.0
Money supply (M3) growth[e]	16.8	14.2	15.7	16.0	16.0
Fiscal balance/GDP[c, f, g]	-9.5	-10.0	-9.3	-9.5	-9.0
Merchandise export growth[h]	19.6	0.1	11.4	15.1	16.6
Merchandise import growth[h]	7.0	-2.8	6.3	11.8	12.2
Current account balance/GDP[c]	-0.6	0.3	0.6	0.1	0.2
External debt/GDP[c]	22.4	20.9	19.5	18.0	16.0

[a] Based on constant 1993/94 factor cost. [b] Advance estimate for 2002. [c] Projected data for 2002. [d] Data for 2002 are for April–December.
[e] Data for 2002 are as of 10 January 2003. [f] Includes combined fiscal deficit of the central Government and all state governments. [g] Fiscal data for 2002 are based on budget estimates. [h] Data for 2002 are for April–September.
Sources: Ministry of Finance; Ministry of Statistics and Programme Implementation; Reserve Bank of India; staff estimates.

debt. The combined outstanding public debt of the central and the state governments is estimated at 72.6% of GDP in FY2001; consolidated data are not yet available for FY2002. However, net market borrowings of $23.3 billion or approximately 5% of GDP by the central Government in FY2002 exceeded the budget estimate by 17.7%.

Turning to money and prices, money supply (M3) growth in FY2001 was in line with the projected trajectory at 14.2%. In the following year, money supply grew by 15.7% up to January 2003. Inflation, as measured by the wholesale price index (WPI), declined from 7.2% in FY2000 to 3.6% in FY2001, and further to 2.8% in April–December 2002. This is despite the setback in agriculture, high international oil prices, and a transition to market-determined prices in the hydrocarbon sector. Annual inflation as measured by changes in the CPI for industrial workers was somewhat higher at 4.0% in April–December 2002. The easing of the price situation despite adverse factors is primarily due to the large surplus stock of foodgrains in the country and global deflationary trends.

Through 2001 and 2002, the Reserve Bank of India (RBI) progressively eased its monetary policy stance in an attempt to revive growth. It has also been encouraging commercial banks to reduce their spreads. This was reflected in the Monetary and

Credit Policy for 2002 and the midyear review of credit policy. The RBI reduced the cash reserve ratio from 5.0% to 4.75% and the bank rate from 6.5% to 6.25% from 16 November 2002. With a cut in the bank rate, commercial banks lowered both deposit and lending rates. Most banks reduced their prime lending rates by 0.25–0.5 percentage points. The prime lending rates of the major banks were in the range of 10.75–11.5% as of 22 November 2002. This is still very high in real terms, given an inflation rate of less than 3.0%. Commercial banks continued to maintain relatively steep interest rates mainly on account of significant provisioning for NPLs. Also, the cost of money remains very high for nonprime borrowers.

Financial sector reforms, including interest rate deregulation, entry of commercial banks into term lending, and lack of concessional funds have increased the competitive pressure on development financial institutions (DFIs). Consequently, many DFIs are being restructured, following RBI guidelines, to enter retail banking. Thus, for example, the Industrial Credit and Investment Corporation of India has transformed itself into a bank.

On the external front, export growth is showing signs of revival after a poor performance in FY2001. The global slowdown, exacerbated by the events surrounding September 11, had resulted in a slump in exports, which averaged marginal growth of 0.1% in FY2001. Despite this, with imports contracting by 2.8% in FY2001, the trade deficit declined to 2.6% of GDP. The growth of merchandise exports and imports at 11.4% and 6.3%, respectively, in April–September 2002 is a marked improvement over the contraction witnessed in the corresponding period of 2001. The trade deficit narrowed to $6.9 billion in this period from $7.5 billion during April–September 2001. The turnaround in exports was largely due to a partial recovery of global demand, with an upturn in GDP and final consumption expenditures in the US, and a revival of growth in many Asian countries. The rise in consumer expenditures in the US in particular has pushed growth in exports of consumer items, such as textiles and garments, as well as gems and jewelry, to high rates. The growth in imports mainly reflects the recovery of domestic industrial activity. While capital goods imports have revived, those of consumer goods continued to decline. Moreover, with international crude oil prices hardening, the import value of petroleum and its related products has risen sharply.

The current account realized a small surplus of 0.3% of GDP for the first time in 23 years in FY2001, and it continued to improve during the first half of FY2002 with a surplus of $1.7 billion, mainly due to a surplus on the invisibles account. There is a risk that the recent appreciation of the nominal exchange rate might reverse this trend, and lower the current account surplus. Net capital inflows in FY2001 were led by a 67% increase in FDI inflows. However, total foreign investment inflows declined to $1.1 billion during April–September 2002 compared with $2.6 billion during the same period in 2001. This is the result of a drop in FDI inflows to $1.7 billion from $1.8 billion in April–September 2001 and a reversal in net portfolio investment by foreign institutional investors to a net outflow of $0.4 billion in April–September 2002, from a positive net inflow of $1.2 billion during the same period in 2001.

Despite the deceleration of foreign investment inflows, foreign exchange reserves continued to increase steadily from about $40 billion at the end of 2000 to around $51 billion at the end of 2001 and further to nearly $70 billion as of 31 January 2003. The recent accretion of foreign exchange reserves is mainly attributed to banking capital and other capital account transfers induced by a weak

dollar and India's positive interest rate differential compared with international rates. Such large increases in reserves caused the exchange rate of the Indian rupee to appreciate by about 0.4% against the dollar in January 2003 over the same month in 2002. Armed with large foreign exchange reserves, the RBI has recently liberalized the foreign exchange market. Moreover, since late FY2002 the Government has embarked on prepayments of high-cost external debt. These moves notwithstanding, India is yet to achieve the conditions for capital account convertibility laid down by the Tarapore Committee on Capital Account Convertibility in 1997, i.e., fiscal consolidation and a strong domestic financial system.

Policy Developments

There were several important policy developments in FY2002 covering tax, the financial sector, trade, and industry.

The Task Forces on Direct and Indirect Taxes recommended wide-ranging reforms in tax policy as well as tax administration. The budget for FY2003 initiated a phased implementation of some of these proposals, starting with a major reform of tax administration for both direct and indirect taxes. Among the important revenue proposals, the taxation of services has been extended to cover a larger number of items, and the tax rate has been revised upward to 8.0%. Moreover, a constitutional amendment has been proposed that will empower state governments to levy a tax on services.

The most important expenditure consolidation measure announced in the FY2003 budget is debt restructuring. High interest public debt will be prepaid to take advantage of the recent decline in nominal interest rates. About $3 billion of external debt to ADB and the World Bank has also been prepaid in this way. Moreover, the Government has announced a $21 billion debt swap scheme for the states to restructure their debt to the central Government over a period of 3 years. Under the scheme, states will borrow from the market at low interest rates to repay high-cost old debt to the central Government. These measures should significantly reduce the debt-servicing burden of the Government. However, India's basic macroeconomic problem of a large fiscal deficit has not been fundamentally addressed. The projected central

Box 2.5 Tenth Five-Year Plan

The recently finalized Tenth Five-Year Plan: 2002–2007 articulates the Government's development strategy. The Plan sets a target of 8.0% annual growth, especially in employment-intensive sectors, to ensure that there is rapid and well-distributed growth of income to sustain the pace of poverty reduction accomplished during the past decade. The Plan underscores that development cannot be measured in terms of increased GDP or per capita income alone, but should take into account human well-being, i.e., the reduction in both "income poverty" and "human poverty". Consequently, the Plan sets out specific monitorable targets for a few key indicators of human development. These are:

- Reduce the poverty ratio by 5 percentage points by 2007 and by 15 percentage points by 2012.
- Provide gainful employment and high-quality employment to at least the additional workforce over the Plan period.
- All children to be in school by 2003; all children to complete 5 years of schooling by 2007.
- Reduce gender gaps in literacy and wage rates by at least 50% by 2007.
- Reduce the decade rate of population growth to 16.2% between 2001 and 2011.
- Increase literacy rates to 75% within the Plan period.
- Reduce the infant mortality rate to 45 per 1,000 live births by 2007 and to 28 by 2012.
- Reduce the maternal mortality ratio to 2 per 1,000 live births by 2007 and to 1 by 2012.
- Increase forest and tree cover to 25% by 2007 and 33% by 2012.
- Improve sustained access to potable drinking water in all villages within the Plan period.
- Clean all major polluted rivers by 2007 and other notified stretches by 2012.

In its elaboration of the Government's development strategy, the Plan indicates that the role of the Government in the production of goods and services through public undertakings will continue to decline. Instead, its role will increase in providing a better regulatory and policy environment for private enterprises.

Poor infrastructure, especially in roads, railways, and power are seen as major impediments to growth. In this context, the Plan emphasizes the importance of improving existing infrastructure, and finishing incomplete projects, rather than investments in ambitious new projects. The Plan also focuses on the need to step up reforms, especially in the power sector, to improve cost recovery and restore the financial viability of the sector.

The financial sector can play a key role in providing better financial intermediation. The Plan notes that the organized financial sector is either unable or unwilling to provide adequate and timely financing, especially for small industries and agriculture. This gap has to be met without compromising prudential concerns. Moreover, there is a serious shortage of long-term risk capital in the domestic capital market, which must be addressed for the private sector to play an active role in long gestation infrastructure projects. The Plan notes that higher growth of 8.0% will entail a more rapid growth of imports, and assumes that this will be mainly financed by exports. It recognizes that greater integration with the global economy will require continuous efforts to reduce tariffs and quantitative restrictions on trade.

To ensure that the quality of growth is equitable and that the fruits of growth are better distributed, the Tenth Plan introduces two approaches. First, it decomposes its broad development targets into consistent state-level targets, to be reflected by corresponding plans at this level, to contain regional imbalances. Second, it lays special emphasis on agriculture and other employment-intensive sectors, which are most effective in ensuring equity in the quality of growth.

Source:
Government of India. 2002. *Tenth Five Year Plan: 2002–2007.* New Delhi: Planning Commission.

government fiscal deficit for 2003 is 5.6%. Since the actual deficit usually overshoots the projected deficit by at least 0.5%, it is likely that 2003 will end with a central government deficit of about 6%. After adding the combined deficit of the state governments, the total fiscal deficit in FY2003 is likely to exceed 9.5%.

Reducing the deficit has to focus on both raising revenues and better management of public expenditures. On the revenue side, using the average of Asia-Pacific countries as a benchmark, there is a potential for increasing tax revenues by around 3–5% of GDP. At the central level, there is significant scope for broadening the tax base, especially through taxation of services and reduced exemptions. Improved tax administration and better tax compliance will also help in this direction. Expenditure reforms at the center should aim at a phased reduction of subsidies, rationalization of government staff, and reduction of budgetary support to public enterprises. Finally, keeping in view the burgeoning debt stock of the Government, the associated crowding out of private investment, and the recent decline in interest rates, the Government should examine options for further debt restructuring to reduce the debt service burden.

With regard to fiscal consolidation at the state level, a Medium-Term Fiscal Reform Program for States was negotiated between the central Government and several state governments, which offers incentives for state fiscal reforms through performance-linked transfers from the central Government. However, this scheme needs to be rationalized and considerably strengthened. Also at the level of the states, it is essential to shift expenditures toward better provision of social services, and raise revenues to contain the revenue deficit. The transition to VAT and its effective administration is the crux of tax reforms at the subnational level. States also need to seriously consider untapped revenue sources, such as taxation of agriculture and enforcement of rational user charges for water and power. Restructuring of public expenditures at the state level should attempt to reduce unproductive and poorly targeted expenditures, while making sufficient provision for investment in infrastructure and human capital. Accelerating the pace of reforms of the state electricity boards, road transport corporations, and other public enterprises should be a high priority.

In the financial sector, the Government enacted the landmark Securitisation, Reconstruction of Financial Assets and Enforcement of Security Interest Act, 2002 that provides a comprehensive legislative framework for foreclosure of assets by lenders, formation of private asset reconstruction companies (ARCs), and securitization of assets with an emphasis on foreclosed assets to address the problem of a high level of NPLs. The new Act empowers banks to foreclose collateral assets for NPLs and it is expected to lead to a significant reduction in NPLs. The Act also creates a framework for ARCs, including capital ownership and issue of securities; regulation under RBI; transfer of ownership and management rights to the ARCs; and creation of a centralized depository for registering securities. In another important development, the Unit Trust of India, the largest mutual fund in the country and hitherto controlled by the Government, has been restructured into two entities, one dealing only with schemes based on net asset values, and the other dealing with assured return schemes. Another major policy development in the financial sector is legislation on money laundering. Parliament has approved a law that allows confiscation of property derived from or involved in money laundering. The law also makes it mandatory for banking companies, financial institutions, and intermediaries to maintain a record of all transactions exceeding a prescribed value and to furnish information to authorized government agencies whenever sought within a prescribed time period.

In foreign trade, the medium-term prospects of merchandise export growth will depend to a large extent on the removal of infrastructure bottlenecks, reduction in transaction costs arising from procedural delays or other bureaucratic impediments, and, most importantly, improvements in competitiveness by exports moving up the value chain to high-value capital goods. The Medium-Term Export Strategy for 2002–07 has attempted to address most of these issues. The Strategy aims at a compound growth rate of 11.9% for exports to achieve a 1% share of world exports by 2007. The Strategy identifies products and markets for potential export growth and suggests product-wise strategies that are beneficial for overall export growth. The instruments discussed in the Strategy include tariffs, FDI, and exchange rate policies, as well as measures for reducing transaction costs and setting up an appropriate environment for export growth. The last point includes special economic zones, marketing support, free trade agreements with potential trade partners, and participation of the states in export promotion.

Improved corporate governance is a major priority in industrial policy. The Competition Bill is an important step in that direction. The Bill is designed to replace the existing Monopolies and Restrictive Trade Practices Act, which has been a barrier to investment by large corporations. The Bill redefines anticompetitive trade practices, such as abuse of a dominant position, cartels, predatory pricing, bid-rigging, and boycotts. The Bill seeks to promote competition by abolishing the requirement to register business agreements, regulating mergers and acquisitions, and prohibiting both horizontal and vertical agreements between firms that affect competition, in accordance with internationally accepted practice. A competition commission has been proposed to ensure effective implementation.

Outlook for 2003–2004

The industry sector is on the upswing of a business cycle, which is expected to continue in FY2003 and lead a moderate revival in GDP growth. Assuming normal monsoon conditions, the economy is projected to grow by 6.0% in FY2003 with agriculture and services growing at average rates. Exports are expected to grow at over 15% in 2003, based on a moderate revival in world demand. The current account surplus should be maintained, assuming fairly stable oil prices, a positive net trade balance in invisibles, and a marginally appreciating currency due to large foreign exchange reserves. However, projections for the external account, especially for oil prices, as well as macro projections, will have to be reviewed to take into account impacts of the conflict in Iraq. Inflation will likely remain moderate at around 5%. Tax measures in the FY2003 budget are expected to enhance buoyancy and raise the revenue-to-GDP ratio. However, in the absence of strong measures to contain the rapid growth in expenditures, the consolidated fiscal deficit is expected to remain at the average level of 9.5% of GDP.

The projected macroeconomic trends of FY2003 are likely to continue through the following year with expected GDP growth of 6.3%. Inflation should remain at around 5%. The current account balance will likely remain positive, despite a higher rate of import growth (again, depending on the effects of the conflict in Iraq).

Strong fiscal consolidation is expected during the postelection phase of the political cycle in the latter half of FY2004, leading to a decline in the consolidated fiscal deficit to 9.0% of GDP. In the medium to long term, sustained high growth will require higher investments in capacity creation for infrastructure development as well as technology development for improvements in competitiveness, removal of various rigidities in labor laws and, especially, strong fiscal consolidation.

Maldives

The Maldives prospered in the 1990s due to a rapid expansion in tourism and modernization in traditional fishing, with rapid annual GDP growth of about 8%. The economy was hard hit by the September 11 events and returning to a rapid growth path will depend on a favorable external environment and careful macroeconomic management.

Macroeconomic Assessment

The economy staged a modest recovery in 2002 with GDP growth estimated at 4.3%, up from 3.5% a year earlier, driven by a gradual recovery in tourism and a larger fish catch. Tourism faltered after the September 11, 2001 events through the first half of 2002, though arrivals picked up in the second half to record an increase of 5.1% for the year. Consequently, tourism, which accounts for about one third of GDP, grew by 2.4% during the year, after zero growth in 2001.

Fisheries expanded by 13.7%, based on a recovery in international tuna prices that led to greater fishing and a strong export performance. The recovery in tourist arrivals and reform measures in the telecommunications sector that resulted in lower tariffs spurred demand for transport and communications services, resulting in a 6.2% increase in subsector output.

The Government's fiscal position for 2002 was marked by a 15% increase in expenditures and a sharp increase in the overall deficit to 7.4% of GDP from 4.7% of GDP in 2001. The major contributing factor to the jump in expenditures was the Government's Hulhumalé project, a large-scale infrastructure development initiative to create a land mass and develop a new town on an island near to the capital city of Malé. The deficit was mainly financed by larger foreign borrowing, including more commercial borrowing, while domestic financing (from the Ways and Means Account of the Maldives Monetary Authority) was contained at 0.4% of GDP.

Monetary conditions in 2002 were characterized by a large increase in net foreign assets and an 11.5% expansion in domestic credit, largely due to increased credit to the private sector. Broad money (M2) increased by 19.3% during 2002. Nevertheless, and despite the July 2001 8% devaluation of the rufiyaa, inflation in 2002 remained low at 0.9%.

The performance of the external sector in 2002 was positive. Total exports in 2002 surged by 18.1% over the 2001 level, mainly reflecting the recovery of international fish prices and stimulus provided by the lagged effects of the currency devaluation in 2001.

In contrast, total imports decreased by 2.4%, despite the modest pickup in the economy, and the trade deficit decreased to $208.0 million from $236.1 million in 2001. Receipts from tourism fell slightly (by 2.6%) because a decline in tourist unit spending more than offset the increase in the number of arrivals.

The current account deficit for 2002 narrowed to $46.9 million, or 7.4% of GDP from 9.2% a year earlier. In terms of the capital account, there was a significant increase in disbursement of official assistance and an expansion of private sector capital inflows to record a surplus of $73.5 million. Accordingly, the overall balance of payments posted a surplus of $26.6 million, a significant improvement from the deficit of $21.4 million in 2001. Official reserves reached $134.5 million at end-2002, providing cover for about 4.1 months of imports. External debt rose by $45 million to $227 million at end-2002, equivalent to about 36% of GDP. With most debt contracted on concessional terms, the debt service ratio was 4.5%.

Policy Developments

The Government's fiscal balance has been deteriorating in recent years and warrants close monitoring, but positive factors are coming into play that should help improve the fiscal position.

First, a new public accounting system to be introduced will enable more comprehensive and updated control over public expenditures. Second, the Government is committed to introducing new tax regimes to expand the tax base. Third, the Government aims to introduce a program budgeting approach in formulating the budget. In contrast, the trend toward greater capital expenditures, mainly in association with the Hulhumalé project, is a source of uncertainty. However, government policy to introduce a mechanism for cost recovery under the project is encouraging as it will ease pressure on the fiscal position.

Aware of financing constraints on private sector development, the Government recently undertook several measures. HSBC, a major international bank, was allowed to enter the local market. A leasing company was established during the year with assistance from the International Finance Corporation; this now allows private sector companies, particularly those in tourism, air transport, and shipping, to take advantage of a new financing option for their investments. In addition, with a view to long-term financial development, a stock trading floor was opened in April 2002. Nevertheless, the Maldives' financial market is still underdeveloped and major industries, particularly tourism, must depend heavily on foreign financing. While deregulation of the interest rate spread requirement in 2001 has led to greater bank lending to the private sector, further action needs to be taken to facilitate the greater mobilization of domestic financial resources for economic development.

Outlook for 2003–2004

Economic performance remains reliant on tourism. A gradual recovery in tourist arrivals is expected to continue in 2003–2004 due to a better outlook for the EU, the main market for tourism. In the domestic economy, the Government's Hulhumalé project and regional development programs will spur domestic demand for local construction and transport. Together, these elements suggest potential for further recovery in 2003 and onward. An initial projection of GDP growth for 2003 is 4.2%. However, the outlook is highly subject to external factors, especially the effects of the conflict in Iraq and the security situation in South Asia.

The 2003 budget envisages a nearly 12% expansion in expenditures and an increase in the overall deficit to 8.5% of GDP. The continued rise in the budget deficit indicates that fiscal developments need to be closely monitored in the medium term, particularly the increasing trend for capital expenditures, to keep the overall deficit as well as domestic and external borrowing requirements within prudent limits. The recent rapid rise in domestic credit and money supply has not had an adverse effect on price stability or the balance of payments. However, as the authorities take further steps to liberalize banking and to move to indirect means of monetary control, it will be important for them to ensure that monetary expansion is within a macroeconomic framework that guards against excessive pressures on prices and the fixed exchange rate.

The expected recovery of the world economy, particularly in the US, the largest export market, should have a continued positive impact on exports, though this cannot be certain given the large fluctuations in the international price of tuna. Favorable developments in tourism over the next couple of years will be an important contributory factor to keeping the current account deficit at the present manageable levels. The strengthening of the capital account in 2002 was encouraging; nevertheless, the increase in outstanding external debt, especially borrowing on commercial terms, underlines the need for careful monitoring and management of the country's external position.

Nepal

The economy contracted for the first time in two decades in FY2002, mainly due to escalation of the insurgency, an irregular monsoon, and weak external demand. A ceasefire announcement in January 2003 offers hope that the economy may strengthen, as well as an opportunity for the Government to undertake key economic reforms and to begin implementing a program targeted at poverty reduction.

Macroeconomic Assessment

The economic performance of Nepal was exceptionally weak in FY2002 (ended 15 July 2002). GDP contracted by 0.6% compared with growth of 4.6% in FY2001. A series of domestic and external shocks, especially an intensification of the insurgency, but also an irregular monsoon and weak external demand, combined to produce a broad downturn in production and external trade. Agricultural growth slipped to 2.2% in FY2002 from 5.5% a year earlier, while industrial output fell by 3.3%, largely due to a nearly 10% drop in manufacturing production. Tourist arrivals fell by 40%, resulting in an estimated 34% fall in tourism receipts and a 1.8% decline in services sector output.

Labor market conditions, characterized in FY2000 by a 47% underemployment rate, likely deteriorated during the year, given the high rate of annual population growth of 2.3% and the economic downturn. The downturn had a major negative impact on the FY2002 budget; however, the overall deficit including grants was contained at 3.3% of GDP, although domestic financing of the deficit was higher than planned (Figure 2.16). Budgetary adjustment was achieved by a large 40% cut in planned development expenditures.

Revenues increased by only 4.5%, after a 13.2% increase a year earlier, but this figure would have been lower had it not been for intensified collection measures, including the introduction of a voluntary

disclosure of income scheme and the raising of special fees on imports and income tax surcharges to fund higher security expenditures.

The growth of broad money (M2) slowed sharply to 6.3% in FY2002, from 15.2% in the previous year. This reflected the weaker economy and deposit withdrawals prompted by the verification efforts of the tax and anticorruption authorities associated with the voluntary disclosure of income scheme. Given the exchange rate peg to the Indian rupee and active trade across the relatively open border, inflation in Nepal generally follows that of India. In FY2002, consumer prices rose by 2.9%, or slightly faster than 2.4% in the previous year.

The current account deficit widened significantly to 7.0% of GDP in FY2002 from 5.4% in FY2001. (The value of officially recorded remittances from abroad is known as a significant underestimate of the total value of remittances. It is estimated that the current account would be in surplus at 2.5% of GDP in FY2002 if informal remittances were taken into account.) The increase in the deficit was due to a drop in net services receipts, stemming from the plunge in tourism receipts, as recorded net transfers and remittances from workers abroad rose and the trade deficit narrowed somewhat, to 14.1% of GDP from 14.7% in FY2001.

Despite this narrowing, the external trade sector suffered as both exports and imports sharply declined. Exports fell by 18.0% with most

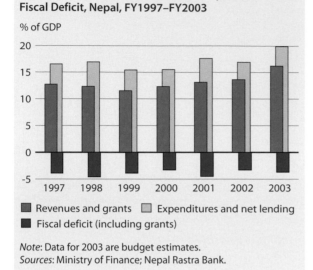

Figure 2.16 Government Revenues, Expenditures, and Fiscal Deficit, Nepal, FY1997–FY2003

% of GDP

■ Revenues and grants   ☐ Expenditures and net lending
■ Fiscal deficit (including grants)

Note: Data for 2003 are budget estimates.
Sources: Ministry of Finance; Nepal Rastra Bank.

of the decline due to the sharp drop in exports of readymade garments, woolen carpets, and pashmina shawls. Production disruptions, weak external demand, and intensified competition were factors in the weak performance.

Imports fell by 11.4% during the year, reflecting the decline in manufacturing activity, sluggish development activities, and lower aid inflows. Foreign exchange reserves at the end of FY2002 stood at about $1 billion, sufficient to cover about 8 months of imports of goods and services. External debt at that time amounted to $2.8 billion, or about 51% of GDP. While the debt is mostly on concessional terms, the debt service ratio increased to 9.7% in FY2002 from 6.8% in the previous year due to a sharp drop in foreign exchange receipts.

Policy Developments

The Tenth Plan (2003–2007), approved by the Planning Commission in December 2002, aims to reduce poverty from 38% to 30% of the population by 2007, with a strategy focused on broad-based and sustainable economic growth, social sector development, targeted programs for the poor and disadvantaged, and good governance. The poverty reduction objective is to be focused through a rolling 3-year medium-term expenditure framework, designed to anchor the Plan to a realistic resource estimate and the annual budgets.

To expedite and monitor the implementation of the core elements of the Tenth Plan, the Government prepared and implemented the Immediate Action Plan 2002. This focused on improving public expenditure management, basic service delivery, and governance.

The FY2003 budget focuses on addressing security issues and implementing an "immediate action plan" to prioritize and expedite reform programs. The overall deficit including grants is projected to be limited to 3.7% of GDP, with even heavier reliance on financing from the banking system. Domestic revenues are envisaged to be 13.0% of GDP, or 14.0% stronger than in FY2002; the budget proposes total expenditures of 20.0% of GDP (a 21.0% increase), of which regular expenditures are about 11% of GDP and development expenditures about 9% of GDP.

Security expenditures associated with the insurgency are planned at about 16% of total expenditures. While the FY2003 development expenditure program has been significantly restructured by dropping or amalgamating 160 low-priority projects and prioritizing the remaining projects based on poverty-reduction selection criteria, the development budget is still ambitious: it calls for a 25% increase in development expenditures, and needs to be further streamlined to maximize the development impacts and to ease the fiscal burden. Although the budget incorporates several reforms, domestic revenue estimates appear optimistic, as do the projected grant disbursements of 3.4% of GDP.

With the likely shortfalls in domestic revenue collection and external financing, and the increased expenditures, the budget deficit including grants in FY2003 is likely to widen to about 4.0%. It would therefore require a strong fiscal adjustment effort.

A new Nepal Rastra Bank Act granting the central bank greater autonomy and duties was passed in 2002; new banking regulations were also issued. Nepal Rastra Bank is now reengineering itself to cope with its expanded responsibilities, especially improving its supervision capabilities. In the financial sector, after considerable delays, external management contracts to manage and develop restructuring plans for the two largest commercial banks—Rastriya Banijya Bank and Nepal Bank Limited—have been completed. These state-owned banks account for about 52% of banking system assets and because of a very large

Table 2.16 Major Economic Indicators, Nepal, 2000–2004, %

Item	2000	2001	2002	2003	2004
GDP growth[a]	6.0	4.6	-0.6	1.5	3.5
Gross domestic investment/GDP	24.2	23.8	24.4	22.0	22.0
Gross domestic savings/GDP	18.8	19.0	17.4	17.0	17.0
Inflation rate (consumer price index)	3.5	2.4	2.9	5.0	5.0
Money supply (M2) growth	21.8	15.2	6.3	12.0	12.0
Fiscal balance[b]/GDP	-3.3	-4.5	-3.3	-4.0	-4.0
Merchandise export growth	37.5	4.6	-18.0	5.0	10.0
Merchandise import growth	22.0	-0.2	-11.4	5.0	10.0
Current account balance/GDP	-5.3	-5.4	-7.0	-5.0	-5.0
Debt service ratio[c]	6.0	6.8	9.7	7.0	7.0

[a] Based on constant 1994/95 factor cost. [b] Includes grants. [c] As percent of exports of goods and nonfactor services.
Sources: Ministry of Finance; staff estimates.

amount of NPLs are technically insolvent, with a combined estimated negative net worth of 7–9% of GDP. External audit and operational review of the Agricultural Development Bank and Nepal Industrial Development Bank are under way to address similar issues. Although SOE finances have continued worsening in recent years, little progress in reforming their operations is evident.

Various governance reform measures have been introduced. Installation of the computerized civil service personal information system to improve accountability and transparency of the service has been completed, and some 7,500 of 17,500 vacant posts have been eliminated.

In the area of decentralization, progress was mixed. While a decentralization implementation plan was approved and responsibility for key services (primary education, agricultural extension, and health service delivery) was devolved to local bodies, the suspension of the locally elected bodies in July 2002 significantly undermined these decentralization efforts. With no system for civil servants to declare their assets annually, the accountability and transparency of the civil service have been frequently questioned.

To contain corruption, the Government passed four anticorruption bills in April 2002, requiring the declaration of property and income by all senior public officials.

Outlook for 2003–2004

Economic performance will depend heavily on the domestic security and political scenario, the vagaries of the weather, and developments in the global economy—and India's particularly. While the announcement of a ceasefire on 29 January 2003 is clearly a welcome breakthrough, any positive impact on the economy will likely take some time to be felt. The underlying assumptions of the economic projections are that (i) law and order will be restored to allow some expansion in both private and public sector investment, (ii) the global economic recovery will continue, (iii) India's economy will grow by about 5–6% over the forecast period, and (iv) the weather will be normal. On this basis, GDP is projected to grow by about 1.5% in FY2003 and by about 3.5% in FY2004.

Agricultural growth may slow to about 2% in FY2003, but recover to about 3% in FY2004. The irregular monsoon in July–August 2002 will adversely affect summer crop production in FY2003. The industry sector is likely to grow by only 0.2% in FY2003 and then may recover to 3.5% in FY2004. The extent of the recovery will be largely determined by export growth and domestic political stability. A major upturn in the services sector is unlikely unless the ceasefire leads to a significant improvement in the security situation. The services sector is projected to show no growth in FY2003 but to expand by 3.5% in FY2004. Despite a possible increase in the prices of agricultural imports from India in FY2003 and the likely hike in domestic fuel prices, inflation is projected to be moderate at about 5% over the next 2 years.

Monetary policy is geared to supporting the exchange rate peg with the Indian rupee. Consequently, interest and inflation rates need to be kept in line with those in India. Given the projections for real growth and inflation, targets for broad money growth need to be in the range of 12–14% over the medium term. Given the optimistic estimates of revenues and grants in the FY2003 budget, it is important that central bank finance of the deficit be within monetary program limits.

The current account deficit is projected to return to around 5% of GDP, as seen in recent years, but this will require economic recovery in the country's major export markets, no major domestic security problems, a quick revival in tourism, and continued high levels of worker remittances. It will be crucial to accelerate export diversification and increase competition.

The insurgency has seriously exacerbated the daunting challenges that the country already faces. While the recent ceasefire announcement holds good prospects for social and economic development, it is still uncertain if this will eventually lead to a credible peace process, an end to the insurgency, and lasting peace. Addressing the insurgency—in large part a consequence of continued rural poverty and the failure to spread the benefit of development more widely—is critical for development.

Pakistan

The medium-term prospects for the economy greatly improved in FY2002 as macroeconomic indicators remained stable, the external account improved, and the Government's ambitious reform program remained on track. Economic growth is thus expected to pick up significantly in the medium term, provided that the internal and external security situations do not deteriorate.

Macroeconomic Assessment

The economy experienced several external shocks in FY2002 (year ended 30 June 2002), generated by the post-September 11, 2001 conflict in the subregion, tension on the border with India, continuing drought, and slow growth in the global economy. However, due to improvement in macroeconomic fundamentals achieved through stabilization policies pursued in the preceding 2 years, closer relations with the Group of Seven leading industrial countries after the September 11 events, and some fortuitous developments such as increased remittances and larger foreign grants, the economy was in a better position to absorb the external shocks. The signing of the Poverty Reduction and Growth Facility with IMF and the rescheduling of the country's bilateral debt by the Paris Club in December 2001 further reduced the economy's vulnerability.

Overall performance improved in FY2002: the GDP growth rate is estimated at 3.6% compared with 2.5% in FY2001. With the population rising by 2.2% a year, per capita income increased by 1.4% after negligible growth in the previous year. The revival of the economy started in the second half of the fiscal year, as a number of developments boosted demand in the period. Total consumption expenditures rose by 5.0% in FY2002, compared with 1.2% in FY2001. Public expenditures increased sharply, mainly because of large salary hikes for civil servants that came into effect on 1 January

2002. They also increased because of tension on the border with India. While general government consumption registered a substantial increase of 18.2%, private consumption expenditures rose by 3.3%, partially due to aggressive marketing of consumer credit by financial institutions and to sharp increases in private inflows of funds from abroad.

The net contribution of the external sector also rose by over 30%, as exports picked up sharply in the second half of FY2002. However, investor sentiment remained weak throughout the fiscal year because of the uncertainty generated by the post-September 11 events and tensions with India.

Expenditures on domestic fixed capital formation declined by 3.1% in FY2002, compared with a 0.9% increase a year earlier. According to provisional estimates, total investment declined to 13.9% of GDP in FY2002 from 15.9% in the previous year (though these figures may not reflect additional investment in the textile sector, and may be revised by the end of FY2003.) National savings rose to 15.4% of GDP in FY2002 from 13.9% in FY2001, largely due to a significant increase in net factor incomes from abroad.

In terms of supply-side sectors, the improvement in GDP growth performance was driven mainly by agriculture, which expanded by 1.4%, despite the continuing effects of drought, after a contraction of 2.6% in FY2001. There was a marginal decline of 0.5% in the value added of major crops, but the robust growth of 3.4% in the

remittances and official transfers in the post-September 11 period. The capital account balance, however, worsened in FY2002, primarily because of SBP's deliberate policy to pay off expensive debt and short-term liabilities.

The sharp improvement in the balance of payments observed in the last three quarters of FY2002 also continued in the first quarter of FY2003, with the current account remaining in surplus by $1.2 billion, in contrast to a deficit recorded in the corresponding quarter of FY2002. Pakistan's external debt stock and liabilities also declined in FY2002 as SBP retired its expensive, short-term liabilities, from $37.1 billion at the end of FY2001 to $36.5 billion at the end of FY2002. Foreign exchange reserves held by SBP closed at $4.3 billion at the end of the fiscal year, and subsequently rose to $7.6 billion by December 2002.

Policy Developments

The Government's fiscal policy agenda for the medium term has been effectively articulated in the federal budget for FY2003. The vision of the tax policy is based on four principles: (i) simplification of the tax regime by gradually eliminating withholding taxes, withdrawing exemptions, and reducing the number of statutory regulatory orders; (ii) reform of income tax; (iii) expansion of the general sales tax base; and (iv) continuation of trade reform through tariff reduction. Some of the key reforms announced in the budget included the initiation of a universal self-assessment scheme for income tax, the progressive reduction of the tax rate for banks and private companies over the next 5 years to 35% (the existing rate for public companies other than banks), and the continued progressive elimination of withholding taxes. In general, the taxation structure has changed significantly over the last 5 years, with a clear shift from trade taxes to taxes on domestic production and income. Among domestic taxes, a VAT-type sales tax has emerged as the largest revenue generator (Figure 2.17).

Since the announcement of the budget, the process of Central Board of Revenue (CBR) reforms has gathered momentum and various initiatives for structural reform in tax administration have been undertaken. These include setting up a Large Taxpayers Unit and a Model Income Tax Unit in Karachi and Lahore, respectively, where tax administration is organized along functional lines, thereby breaking with traditional practice. In addition, the CBR has initiated a Sales Tax Automated Refund Repository facility both to expedite the process of verification of invoices submitted with sales tax refund claims and to reduce the chances of spurious refunds. Other reforms include the Customs Administration Reform Plan, which envisages computerization of all customs refund applications, and a new recruitment and promotion policy. These measures aim at improving services for taxpayers through reorganization of the CBR along functional lines and automation of processing of tax returns and applications for tax refunds, as well as improving the skills-mix incentives of CBR staff through merit-based recruitment and training, and market-based salaries.

The Government has drafted a Fiscal Responsibility and Debt Limitation Ordinance. This requires it to eliminate the revenue deficit by 30 June 2007; reduce the outstanding public debt to 60% of GDP by 30 June 2012; reduce the outstanding public debt by 2.5% of GDP in every year, while ensuring that social- and poverty-related expenditures do not fall below 4% of GDP; and not to issue guarantees for any amount exceeding 2% of GDP. The bill is to be presented in Parliament for debate later in the year.

In September 2002, the federal cabinet approved an order granting full autonomy to SBP in the formulation of monetary, credit, and exchange rate policies as well as in the management of foreign exchange reserves. This should reduce policy uncertainty and encourage private sector development. Monetary policy is constrained by the conflicting demands of containing inflation and promoting economic growth. Given the relatively benign inflationary environment in 2002, SBP gradually eased monetary policy. It also removed restrictions on nationalized commercial banks for consumer financing, to boost economic growth.

The other policy issue faced by SBP in 2002 was that the large current account inflows into Pakistan were exerting upward pressure on the local currency. Given the uncertainty associated with these flows, and to protect exporters from large changes in the exchange rate, SBP has followed a policy of allowing only a gradual appreciation of the Pakistan rupee, by reducing excess liquidity in the interbank foreign exchange market. However, to prevent the buildup of foreign exchange reserves from expanding liquidity, SBP at the same time followed a policy of sterilization through treasury-bill auctions used to retire SBP holdings of government paper. However, the policy had substantial costs, as the domestic treasury-bill rate was significantly higher than that available to SBP on its foreign currency placements.

The Government has undertaken a series of banking sector reforms over the past year, with a strong emphasis on improving corporate governance through implementation of directives to regulate appointments of board members and chief executive officers of commercial banks, as well as more stringent review of audit procedures. In addition, minimum paid-up capital requirements of banks have been raised from PRs500 million to PRs1 billion, and banks have been authorized to issue term finance certificates as subordinated debt to raise their capital. SBP is also working with the Corporate Industrial Restructuring Corporation and the Committee on the Revival of Sick Units to effect financial restructuring of banks and reduce the proportion of NPLs in bank portfolios.

The Securities and Exchange Commission of Pakistan continued with reform of the stock markets. This included reconstitution of the boards of directors to include directors nominated by the Commission (a move toward demutualization of the stock exchanges with a view to preventing conflicts of interest on the part of individual members), prescription of an adequate capital base for each brokerage house, permission for futures trading in selected shares, and the prescription of a code of corporate governance for listed companies.

The Government also continued with the process of trade and foreign exchange system reforms. The main thrust of the Government's trade policies over the past 2 years has been to reduce the anti-export bias through trade and tariff liberalization. In addition to reducing the maximum tariff rate from 30% to 25% in 2002, the number of statutory regulatory orders governing tariff exemptions was further reduced; procedural requirements for imports were simplified; and exports and imports of wheat and its milling products and petroleum products were completely liberalized, in addition to imports of textiles, mobile phones, gold, and silver. From 1 July 2002, SBP put an end to the practice of purchasing foreign exchange from the kerb market. To remove segmentation in the foreign exchange

market, and to facilitate the move toward a unified exchange rate, the Government announced a plan to allow the establishment of foreign exchange companies from August 2002. Some companies have started operations.

Privatization picked up momentum in 2002, with one nationalized commercial bank, United Bank Ltd., privatized in September 2002, and 20% of the Government's stake in the National Bank of Pakistan having been divested through the stock market. A number of public sector mutual funds have also been privatized. The Government has privatized its working interests in nine petroleum concessions, and in noncore assets of the two gas transmission and distribution companies, Sui Southern Gas Company and Sui Northern Gas Pipelines Ltd. Appreciable progress has been made in the privatization of the country's largest oil company, Pakistan State Oil, and largest commercial bank, Habib Bank Ltd. The Government also set up the Oil and Gas Regulatory Authority in 2002 to encourage competition and private sector growth in the oil and gas sector.

The Government approved a new labor policy in September 2002, which is aimed at reconciling national laws governing industrial relations with international labor and trade union laws. The policy revamps and consolidates over 30 existing laws into six. Similarly, a new power generation policy was announced in October 2002, the main objective of which is to encourage the private sector to invest in hydropower and indigenous fuels-based electricity generation projects.

Outlook for 2003–2004

Prospects of realizing and possibly surpassing the government-projected growth rate of 4.5% in FY2003 are quite bright. This optimism is based on an improved outlook for the agriculture and industry sectors. Both supply and demand factors are expected to boost domestic economic activity. With regard to the former, increased availability of water should boost agriculture and hydropower generation. The textile industry is also better placed for increased production after heavy investment in the past 2 years. Demand factors include larger remittances (of $2.1 billion in the first half of FY2003, which are expected to increase to over $3.5 billion by the end of the fiscal year) and the associated increase in construction activity, as well as aggressive marketing of consumer credit by financial institutions. The growth rate is expected to improve further to 5.0% in FY2004 with acceleration in the agriculture sector, and more robust expansion in large-scale manufacturing led by the textile and consumer durables industries. The services sector is expected to maintain a growth rate of about 5.5%.

Economic uncertainty has been greatly reduced by Pakistan's improved macroeconomic fundamentals. Political uncertainty has been reduced by the smooth transfer of power to elected federal and provincial governments in October 2002 and the new Government's commitment to the reform program of the last 3 years. Total investment is thus expected to show marked improvement in the medium term, rising to 16.0% of GDP by FY2004.

It is anticipated that an easy monetary policy will continue through at least FY2003. The rate of inflation has shown an upturn in the first quarter of FY2003 due to an increase in prices of food items and an upward adjustment in domestic oil prices. The trend is likely to continue over the medium term, and inflation may rise to 5.0% in FY2004.

The modernization of the textile industry that has been under way for the last couple of years has started showing results in the form of a substantial increase in the industry's output and in export volumes.

Both for this reason, as well as a greater level of activity in the domestic economy and better access to EU markets, exports are likely to grow significantly in the medium term, registering increases of about 12% and 10% in FY2003 and FY2004, respectively. Exports and imports strengthened by 16.6% and 18.7%, respectively, in the first half of FY2003, compared with the corresponding period of FY2002.

Increased domestic activity, particularly higher growth in manufacturing, together with a reduction in import tariffs and a strong local currency, is likely to lead to strong growth in imports, which are likely to rise by about 14% in FY2003. The trade deficit is thus expected to almost double from FY2002 levels, to over $600 million in the medium term. The surplus on the current account, which is the result of fortuitous developments since September 11, 2001, is expected to fall to about $638 million

in FY2004. Some exceptional current transfers like grants will not be available in FY2003, but remittances are likely to exceed the high level achieved in FY2002.

FDI is expected to pick up significantly in the medium term provided that the domestic political situation remains stable, and that there is no recurrence of subregional tensions. The planned major privatizations, such as that of Pakistan State Oil and Habib Bank Ltd., are likely to be major factors in increasing FDI during the next 2 years. FDI was $570 million in the first half of FY2003, and is projected to rise slightly to about $600 million by the end of the year.

The outstanding external debt stock is expected to be maintained at about $32 billion over the medium term, with further improvement in the debt profile, as expensive, short-term debt is replaced by long-term concessional borrowings. External debt servicing is therefore projected to fall to some 20% of foreign exchange earnings by FY2004.

The Government's success in maintaining macroeconomic stability over the last year—in the face of unprecedented domestic and international shocks such as the prolonged drought, internal insecurity, and tensions on both its western and eastern borders—has greatly improved the medium-term prospects for the economy. This optimism is reflected in the new Five-Year Economic Vision recently articulated by the Government, which underlines the shift in policy focus from macroeconomic stabilization to a more broad-based focus on growth and poverty reduction. If the Government continues to pursue sound macroeconomic policies and to implement the planned economic and governance reforms, it should be possible to achieve the goals in the vision statement.

Although the outlook is generally positive, the above scenario is subject to risks, such as the possibility of renewed tensions on the border with India, political uncertainties that may unfold given that coalition governments are in place in the center and two provinces, and the ambiguities surrounding the future course of the global economy. In the immediate future, Pakistan's economy faces challenges arising from the conflict in Iraq and its consequences, as well as possible social and political instability and a loss in investor confidence in the medium term.

Sri Lanka

With the year-long ceasefire providing much-needed stability at home, the country achieved a moderate economic recovery in 2002. The Government needs to build on this foundation by pursuing the necessary structural reforms for sustained higher growth rates in the medium term.

Macroeconomic Assessment

Sri Lanka entered 2002 with an economy in serious difficulty, battered by both global and domestic events. The previous year had seen the country's worst macroeconomic performance since independence, with the economy contracting by 1.4%, inflation accelerating, and the fiscal position deteriorating. From this perspective, although the 2002 recovery may have been modest, the Government's progress in stabilizing the economy provides a firm foundation for more rapid growth in the medium term.

The Government and the Liberation Tigers of Tamil Eelam (LTTE) entered into a ceasefire to begin negotiations to settle the civil conflict that has ravaged the north and east for nearly 20 years. By midyear, tourism (Figure 2.18) and shipping had recovered to the monthly levels achieved prior to the LTTE attack on the international airport a year earlier, and during the second half of the year posted substantial gains. The ceasefire also opened up opportunities for internal trade and transport services, even though external trade was lagging. For the year, services were the leading growth sector, expanding by 4.6%.

In aggregate, GDP expanded by 3.0% in 2002. The end of the drought brought relief to the agriculture sector, which grew by 2.4% during the year, compared with a decline of 3.0% in the previous year. The one area of continued weakness was the industry sector, where the level of output remained largely unchanged from the previous year, growing by only 0.5%. Power cuts, of up to four hours a day, due to system failures and low water levels in the reservoirs, led to an almost 10% reduction in output from utilities in the first half of the year. Even once this power crisis had subsided, the sector had still not fully recovered lost ground by year-end. The power cuts, combined with weaker than expected global recovery, led to lackluster performance in manufacturing, with this subsector contracting over the first 6 months of 2002 and growing by a mere 1.5% for the whole year. Although an improvement from the 4% contraction in 2001, there is still excess capacity in manufacturing.

Savings and investment rates recovered somewhat in 2002, but significantly higher savings rates will only materialize as fiscal consolidation progresses. The private sector did not generate many new investments, despite the stability from the peace process, because of the excess capacity following the 2001 recession.

The labor market was weak in 2002 despite the recovery in production. The unemployment rate rose by a percentage point to 9.0% for the year. More than 60% of the unemployed have at least a middle school education and nearly 32% have at least a high school education. While conscious of the need to create jobs, the Government is reluctant to turn to the short-term solution of expanding public sector employment, which already accounts for nearly one fifth of the total. A public sector hiring freeze has been in place for more than a year,

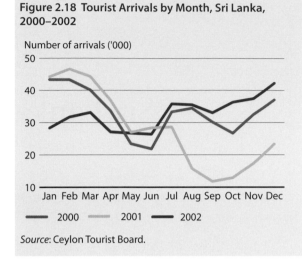

Figure 2.18 Tourist Arrivals by Month, Sri Lanka, 2000–2002

Number of arrivals ('000)

Jan Feb Mar Apr May Jun Jul Aug Sep Oct Nov Dec

—— 2000   —— 2001   —— 2002

Source: Ceylon Tourist Board.

and some key overstaffed public enterprises have offered voluntary retirement packages.

The primary goal of the 2002 budget was to stabilize the macroeconomy. Unsustainable deficits in the past had led to the depletion of foreign reserves, rising interest rates, and an expanding debt burden. The Government has had some success in reining in the budget deficit. The overall fiscal deficit, excluding grants and privatization proceeds, of 9.0% of GDP is a substantial improvement from the deficit of 10.9% in 2001. Although the main innovations under the budget were on the revenue side, current revenues of 16.5% of GDP were very similar to the performance in 2001. Total expenditures, on the other hand, fell by about 2 percentage points of GDP to 25.5%, about half of which was due to better control of recurrent expenditures.

The budget deficit is financed mainly through domestic borrowing, but the composition of that borrowing in 2002 included a welcome use of longer-term debt instruments: the Government reduced its outstanding balance on overdraft from SLRs38 billion at the beginning of the year to SLRs5 billion at the end. While privatization was budgeted to bring in SLRs21 billion, the largest deal—the sale of the Sri Lanka Insurance Corporation—was deferred to 2003, with the result that less than SLRs5 billion was actually received. The Government has shown flexibility in pursuing its privatization agenda. When no acceptable offers were received for its remaining shares in Sri Lanka Telecoms, it chose to sell a percentage of its shares

through an initial public offering on the Colombo Stock Exchange instead. The move had the added benefit of increasing the depth of the stock exchange.

Broad money supply increased by 13.4% in 2002, at a rate similar to the previous year. About half of this was due to a rise in domestic credit to the private sector. Net foreign assets also increased, as the central bank raised its holdings of foreign reserves to bolster the exchange rate. The Government, for its part, has relied on nonbank financing of the fiscal deficit to avoid putting pressure on the money supply. Domestic credit to the public sector accounted for less than 5% of broad money growth. Despite the higher growth in real output, inflation moderated only slightly to an average of 10.2% for the year, in part because of higher world oil prices and adjustments locally in some administered prices, but inflation slowed in the last half of the year. After a slight depreciation in the first quarter, the exchange rate hovered around SLRs96 to the dollar from April 2002, adding stability to traded goods prices. In response to declining trends in inflation and international interest rates, the central bank reduced its interest rates three times during the year, lowering the repurchase rate from 12.0% to 9.75% and the reverse repurchase rate from 14.0% to 11.75%; the interest rates in the secondary market for treasury bonds followed these rates down.

With the sluggish global economy, exports continued to flounder, declining by 2.4% to $4.7 billion, after falling by 12.8% in 2001. Textiles and apparel, which are heavily dependent on demand from the US and EU, were particularly hard hit. Imports expanded somewhat to $6.1 billion, due mainly to increasing imports of intermediate goods. Consequently, the trade deficit widened from 7.4% of GDP in 2001 to 8.5%. Trade in services—benefiting from recoveries in tourism and shipping—and remittances helped offset the gap in merchandise trade such that the current account deficit was at a manageable level of 2.5% of GDP. The overall balance of payments was in surplus, increasing official reserves from $1.3 billion (2.2 months of import cover) to $1.7 billion (2.9 months of import cover).

Policy Developments

The Government's initiative toward solving the civil conflict augurs well for the country's develop-

Table 2.18 Major Economic Indicators, Sri Lanka, 2000–2004, %

Item	2000	2001	2002	2003	2004
GDP growth[a]	6.0	-1.4	3.0	5.0	5.5
Gross domestic investment/GDP	28.0	22.0	23.0	24.5	26.0
Gross domestic savings/GDP	17.4	15.3	15.8	16.5	17.0
Inflation rate (consumer price index)	1.5	12.1	10.2	8.5	7.0
Money supply (M2B)[b] growth	12.9	13.6	13.4	13.5	12.5
Fiscal balance[c]/GDP	-9.9	-10.9	-9.0	-7.5	-6.5
Merchandise export growth	19.8	-12.8	-2.4	6.5	9.0
Merchandise import growth	22.4	-18.4	2.2	9.0	12.0
Current account balance/GDP	-6.5	-1.4	-2.5	-3.5	-4.5

[a] Based on constant 1996 factor cost. [b] M2 plus time and savings deposits held by commercial banks' foreign currency banking units.
[c] Excludes foreign grants and privatization proceeds.
Sources: Central Bank of Sri Lanka; Ministry of Finance; staff estimates.

ment and has received favorable responses from the international community, including donors. On 24 December 2001, the LTTE declared a unilateral ceasefire, which was reciprocated by the Government. Facilitated by the Norwegian Government, the two parties signed a formal ceasefire agreement on 22 February 2002 that included several confidence-building measures as precursors to formal peace negotiations. In September 2002, the Government lifted its ban on the LTTE to pave the way for face-to-face talks. During the year, three rounds of peace talks were held: two in Thailand and one in Norway. Both parties have agreed to seek a federal solution within a united Sri Lanka to end the country's long-standing civil conflict. Although the talks have not yet reached the stage for large-scale reconstruction to begin, a year without serious fighting between the two sides has allowed economic activity to blossom in the north and east and opened the door for internally displaced persons to move back to the area.

The Government's 2002 budget—approved only in April due to Parliamentary elections—focused on stabilization through fiscal consolidation. The deficit target of 8.5% of GDP, excluding grants and privatization proceeds, was to be achieved mainly through revenue reforms. Wide-ranging changes were made to simplify tax administration and widen the tax base, the cornerstone of which was the replacement of the goods and services tax

and national security levy with a two-tiered VAT. However, slow growth in trade led to shortfalls in customs receipts and changes in other taxes caused temporary shortfalls during the adjustment period. In the third quarter of 2002, the Government initiated some additional cuts in recurrent expenditures to achieve a revised deficit target of 8.9% of GDP. The 2003 budget announced in November will continue the process of fiscal consolidation, aiming to reduce the deficit further to 7.5% of GDP. Revenue reforms are still high on the agenda, most notably expanding the coverage of VAT to include wholesale and retail trade, thus bringing the complete supply chain under this tax. To bring interest expenditures down, the Government has been paying off expensive overdraft borrowings and floating longer-term debt.

Underutilization of foreign aid is a chronic problem in Sri Lanka. In 2002, the Government introduced a "pool fund" for capital expenditures, through which projects that disbursed more quickly than expected could draw on these counterpart funds without having to wait for a supplementary budget passed by Parliament. However, many agencies were not fully aware of the operations of the pool and so it was not widely used. In 2003, the pool arrangements will be refined and information on them more broadly disseminated among spending agencies. While the pool fund should ensure that adequate counterpart funds are readily available for ongoing projects, it does not address the systemic problems in project management and inefficient tender procedures that prevent more effective use of aid resources in the country.

Since the floating of the Sri Lanka rupee in January 2001, the monetary authorities have been accumulating foreign reserves, both through official sources such as IMF and direct purchases from the foreign exchange market. The increase in reserves has allowed the restrictions on foreign exchange transactions that were instituted at the time of the float to be relaxed.

With the passage of the 2002 budget, the Government was able to revive the IMF standby arrangement, which had been suspended the previous year, receiving $60 million in balance-of-payments support in April. Moreover, Sri Lanka successfully completed the final review of the facility and the final tranche of $64 million was released in September 2002. IMF is now discussing with the Government a possible Poverty Reduction and Growth Facility (PRGF) for the country, the basic parameters of which were outlined in the 2003 budget. The Government has prepared its poverty reduction strategy paper, in consultation with various stakeholders, to provide an overall framework for poverty reduction efforts in the country. The PRGF will likely focus on needed structural reforms in the labor and financial markets. The World Bank is planning a poverty reduction support credit to complement the PRGF.

Outlook for 2003–2004

Now that progress has been made in establishing macroeconomic stability, Sri Lanka is expected to enjoy rising GDP growth in 2003, particularly during the second half. Rising external demand from industrial countries, mainly in the second half of 2003, should provide a much-needed boost to the export sector. Tourism and shipping have shown the strongest recoveries as a consequence of the ongoing peace negotiations, and they are very likely to continue expanding in 2003. Investment as well should improve due to the cessation of hostilities and lower interest rates.

High oil prices would act as a damper on industrial growth, but the end of the drought that plagued the country over the last several years should help keep electricity prices in check, as generation need

not rely as much on expensive thermal plants. Moreover, electricity supply should become more reliable with the commissioning of an additional 165 megawatts of generation capacity in the first half of 2003. Agricultural production has also shown resurgence in recent months and should perform well in the first half of 2003. With continued favorable weather, the economy is expected to grow by 5.0% in 2003 with somewhat higher growth of 5.5% in 2004. This forecast is a bit more conservative than the Government's projection of 5.5% growth in 2003 and 6.5% in 2004, reflecting uncertainty in the strength of the global environment.

Geopolitical events notwithstanding, international oil prices, while high at the start of 2003, should stabilize at a lower level and so reduce the pressure on prices. Local prices should also have fully adjusted to the tax reforms implemented in 2002 such that inflation will be on a downward trend over 2003. The inflation rate should fall to 8.5% for the year; however, money supply growth needs to be kept in check for this to happen. In this respect, the Government's progress in bringing the fiscal deficit down to a sustainable level is a notable achievement. The target budget deficit of 7.5% of GDP in 2003 is ambitious, but feasible. As recurrent expenditures—which are dominated by wage and pension payments and interest charges—have limited scope for short-term reductions, the Government needs to make a concerted effort to increase tax receipts if further deficit reductions are to be attained.

As the world economy strengthens, the dollar value of Sri Lanka's exports is forecast to rise by 6.5% in 2003, with most of the improvement occurring in the second half of the year. However, because of the increase in investment, high oil prices in the early part of the year, and rising consumption, merchandise import growth will be even more rapid, expanding by 9.0% over the whole year. The widening trade gap will be offset somewhat by increased services income—due to the recoveries in shipping and tourism—and the rise in private remittances. However, overall the current account deficit will widen over time in the medium term, a reflection of the rising investment needs outstripping the gains in public-sector saving.

Much of the country's ability to achieve these projections hinges on external factors. Slower recovery in the US and EU—Sri Lanka's main export markets—would have a negative impact on manufacturing. Failure in either of the monsoons would limit agricultural output and cause the power sector to rely more on thermal generation.

The economy is also vulnerable to volatility in oil prices stemming from the conflict in Iraq, and the effect on shipping and global tourism could handicap Sri Lanka's recovery. The level of remittances, which are the country's largest source of foreign exchange earnings, may also be adversely affected by the aftermath of the conflict, given the large number of Sri Lankans who are working in the Gulf.

On the domestic front, the stability arising from the ongoing peace process is a key element for sustaining development. While a breakthrough is unlikely in the near term, steady progress needs to be made in the peace talks to target the needs of the poor in the north and east and to foster investor confidence in the country generally. At this point, the macroeconomic forecasts do not include the impact of major relief and rehabilitation works, the financing of which will need to come from abroad given the tight constraints on domestic resources.

The projections assume relative political stability during the period, but the cohabitation between the Government and the president, who is a member of the main opposition party, is very insecure. Moreover, the president can now dissolve Parliament at her discretion as a year has passed since the last Parliamentary elections. Holding elections at this point would pose risks for the peace process, in addition to the usual pressure on government spending and delays in public investment. In this context, it is important for the Government to bring inflation under control, as this has been one of the main criticisms from the opposition.

The Government eliminated load shedding of power in mid-2002, but system instability still causes occasional outages. Therefore, ensuring sufficient and reliable power supply is also a priority for maintaining higher rates of growth. The Government has also begun to address some of the structural impediments hindering more rapid economic growth. It passed legislation in early 2003 that will make the labor market more flexible and reduce delays in arbitrating in disputes between workers and employers. Work has also begun on developing a social safety net for displaced workers as a precondition for further labor reforms.

The groundwork has been laid for utilities to be regulated by an independent commission to eliminate political interference in these commercial activities, and the vertically integrated state-owned electricity company will be unbundled and corporatized for greater competition and efficiency in the power sector. The petroleum sector has been liberalized, and competitors to the state-owned petroleum company began operations in 2003. The Government's progress on its structural reform agenda is promising, but a clear set of priorities needs to be in place to better manage the process.

ASIAN DEVELOPMENT

Outlook
2003

Economic Trends and Prospects in Developing Asia

Central Asia
Azerbaijan
Kazakhstan
Kyrgyz Republic
Tajikistan
Turkmenistan
Uzbekistan

Azerbaijan

The economy maintained strong growth momentum in 2002, mainly due to a rebound in FDI inflows into the oil sector. Growth is expected to remain buoyant in 2003–2004, underpinned by a continuing investment boom in that sector, though this oil-driven expansion will have only a limited impact on employment and poverty. The Government needs to maintain sound macroeconomic policies and speed up market-oriented reforms, if broad-based growth and a considerable reduction in poverty are to be achieved.

Macroeconomic Assessment

GDP growth accelerated slightly to 10.6% in 2002 from 9.9% in 2001, driven by increased FDI in the oil sector. Reflecting the launch of several large-scale investment projects, including the construction of the Baku-Tbilisi-Ceyhan (BTC) oil pipeline, gross FDI inflows into the oil sector surged from $821 million (15% of GDP) in 2001 to $1,521 million (25% of GDP) in 2002. This pushed the ratio of fixed investment to GDP to about 30% and provided a major impetus to the economy (Figure 2.19).

Manufacturing and services related to oil development, such as construction and the production of construction materials, expanded rapidly, although oil production itself increased by a modest 1.8% to 0.3 million barrels a day due to capacity constraints. A bumper grain harvest led to a 6.4% expansion in agricultural production and contributed to GDP growth.

Since output growth resulted primarily from an increase in productivity, wages and salaries rose substantially, while employment increased only marginally. According to official statistics, the average wage rose by 20.3% in nominal terms (17.1% in real terms), while the unemployment rate is reported to have increased from 1.2% at end-2001 to 1.3% at end-2002. However, official statistics considerably underestimate the true unemployment

level. Results of recent labor market and household budget surveys suggest that, despite the impressive economic growth of the last 7 years, the actual unemployment rate in Azerbaijan remains well above 10%, while about half the population still lives in poverty.

The general government budget, which does not include the Oil Fund, recorded a deficit of AZM645 billion or 2.2% of GDP in 2002, compared with a 2001 deficit of 2.1% of GDP. Revenue performance improved from 18.0% of GDP in 2001 to 19.2% of GDP in 2002 but this was more than offset by an increase in expenditure. Similarly, while revenues of the Oil Fund continued to grow, the Government started utilizing its assets to finance social and investment projects. As a result, the Oil Fund's surplus fell to 3.5% of GDP in 2002 from 4.0% in the previous year.

Money supply increased by 13.1% during 2002. The level of financial intermediation, as measured by the ratio of broad money to GDP, remained low at about 13% of GDP, and the high degree of dollarization persisted, with foreign currency deposits accounting for about half of broad money. Average annual consumer price inflation accelerated slightly from 1.5% in 2001 to 2.8% in 2002. The nominal exchange rate of the national currency (the manat) depreciated by 4.4% against the dollar, and the real rate depreciated by 1.6%. Azerbaijan has so far avoided the excessive appreciation of the real

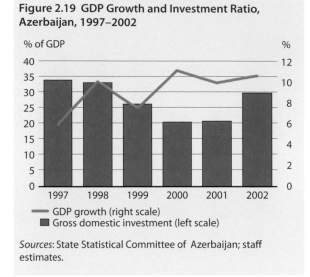

Figure 2.19 GDP Growth and Investment Ratio, Azerbaijan, 1997–2002

— GDP growth (right scale)
■ Gross domestic investment (left scale)

Sources: State Statistical Committee of Azerbaijan; staff estimates.

exchange rate that is often associated with a natural resource boom.

The external current account deficit widened substantially from $73 million (1.3% of GDP) in 2001 to $768 million (12.6%) in 2002, as imports related to oil development increased sharply. This was fully financed by inflows of FDI and other capital flows such that the overall balance of payments recorded a surplus of $230 million. Accordingly, gross official reserves, including Oil Fund assets, grew from $1,194 million at end-2001 to $1,373 million at end-2002. Reflecting the Government's cautious approach to external borrowing, the stock of public and public-guaranteed foreign debt increased by a modest $94 million to $1,356 million (22.3% of GDP), consisting mostly of concessional loans from multilateral and bilateral donors.

Policy Developments

Macroeconomic policies remained fairly tight in 2002. Although the general government deficit increased slightly from 2001, it was much smaller than the deficit of 4.0% of GDP envisaged in the 2002 budget. The refinance rate of the National Bank of Azerbaijan was lowered from 10.0% to 7.0% a year, but remained positive in real terms. However, in a worrisome development, several ad hoc decisions were made regarding the use of Oil Fund assets, including financing the state oil

company's equity participation in the BTC pipeline project. Such use of Oil Fund resources threatens to undermine the coherence and consistency of financial policies and entails the risk of destabilizing the macroeconomic situation over the medium term.

On the structural side, the Government took a number of measures to curtail implicit energy subsidies, enhance transparency and accountability of budget management, and improve the business environment. In particular, a program of strengthening financial discipline in the energy sector was adopted, and management of four electricity distribution networks, covering most of Azerbaijan's territory, was transferred to private firms, resulting in a significant improvement in tariff collection rates. In addition, all extrabudgetary funds, with the exception of the Oil Fund and the Social Protection Fund, were integrated into the state budget. In another major step toward greater fiscal transparency, implicit subsidies to the electricity and gas sectors, in the form of unpaid fuel deliveries to these sectors, were included in the 2003 budget. Furthermore, the number of business activities subject to licensing was reduced from 240 to 30 and licensing procedures were streamlined.

However, little progress was made in other areas of structural reform. The implementation of the second privatization program launched in 2001 was slow, and privatization of the International Bank of Azerbaijan, whose dominance of the banking system hinders competition in the financial sector, was delayed. Administrative reform, involving modernization of the Ministry of Taxes and the State Customs Committee as well as separation of regulatory and commercial functions of SOEs in the energy and transport sectors, was in effect stalled. Corruption remains a serious problem and much needs to be done to create an enabling environment for the development of a vibrant private sector in the non-oil economy.

The Government reaffirmed its commitment to foster broad-based and equitable growth, and to reduce poverty in the State Programme on Poverty Reduction and Economic Development for 2003–2005, which was unveiled at a high-level conference in Baku in October 2002. The Programme was prepared in a participatory process involving the donor community and civil society. Reflecting the multidimensional nature of poverty and development, the Programme pursues a broad agenda and

Table 2.19 Major Economic Indicators, Azerbaijan, 2000–2004, %

Item	2000	2001	2002	2003	2004
GDP growth	11.1	9.9	10.6	9.5	8.0
Inflation rate (consumer price index)	1.8	1.5	2.8	3.2	2.9
Money supply (M2) growth	26.2	30.5	13.1	-	-
Fiscal balance/GDP	-2.2	-2.1	-2.2	-	-
Merchandise export growth	83.1	9.0	12.7	9.8	-5.9
Merchandise import growth	7.4	-4.8	24.5	7.5	3.8
Current account balance/GDP	-2.4	-1.3	-12.6	-15.0	-18.0

- Not available.

Sources: State Statistical Committee of Azerbaijan; National Bank of Azerbaijan; staff estimates.

includes a wide range of policy measures aimed at reducing poverty and promoting sustainable development. However, it does not properly prioritize nor cost these measures, and neither does it set specific poverty reduction targets.

Outlook for 2003–2004

The economic outlook for 2003–2004 is positive, as the ongoing oil investment boom is expected to continue. GDP is projected to grow by 9.5% in 2003 and by 8.0% in 2004. FDI inflows into the oil sector, which are expected to reach $1.7 billion in 2003 and $1.8 billion in 2004, will remain the engine of growth. Manufacturing and services related to investment in the oil sector will continue to expand rapidly. Growth in oil production will likely accelerate to 3.0% in 2003 and to 8.6% in 2004 as capacity restraints are gradually removed. Growth in agriculture, however, will moderate to 3–3.5% as slow progress in sector reform and continuing deterioration of rural infrastructure impede productivity growth. Since GDP growth will be concentrated in capital-intensive sectors, a major fall in unemployment is unlikely, although wages are expected to continue rising.

Under the base-case assumption that fiscal policy remains sound and monetary policy sufficiently tight to preserve macroeconomic stability, annual consumer price inflation is forecast to remain within the range of 2.5–3.5%. The nominal exchange rate is expected to continue to depreciate moderately at about 3.0% a year, with the real exchange rate staying largely unchanged. Exports

of goods and nonfactor services are expected to increase from $2.7 billion in 2002 to $2.9 billion in 2003, due to a combination of higher world oil prices and larger exports volumes, but to decline to $2.8 billion in 2004 as the anticipated fall in world oil prices more than offsets a continuing rise in oil export volumes. At the same time, imports of goods and nonfactor services will increase, from $3.1 billion in 2002 to $3.5 billion in 2003 and to $3.6 billion in 2004, driven by increasing investment in the oil sector. Consequently, the current account deficit will widen further to 15.0% of GDP in 2003 and to 18.0% of GDP in 2004 and continue to be financed by inflows of FDI.

However, there is a risk that the Government will considerably increase budgetary and Oil Fund expenditures ahead of the presidential elections scheduled for autumn 2003. This will lead to a larger budget deficit and higher foreign exchange inflows from the Oil Fund, and will put upward pressure on the nominal exchange rate. With its net domestic credit equivalent to less than 1% of GDP and little room for sterilization of interventions in the foreign exchange market, the National Bank of Azerbaijan will have to make a difficult choice between, on the one hand, letting the nominal exchange rate appreciate and, on the other, absorbing additional foreign exchange inflows, which will increase money supply and fuel inflation. In either case, the real exchange rate will appreciate, which will adversely affect competitiveness of the non-oil traded goods sector. Consequently, output growth will be lower and the current account deficit higher than under the base-case scenario.

Kazakhstan

Overall economic performance remained strong in 2002, and the medium-term prospects are good, though they continue to depend heavily on the oil sector and thus remain vulnerable to external shocks. Effective management of large government oil revenues and continued structural reform will be necessary to ensure long-term sustained rapid growth, economic diversification, and employment creation.

Macroeconomic Assessment

In 2002, the economy continued its strong performance, despite weak world commodity markets; GDP growth of 9.5% exceeded the 7.0% government target. Fueled by past large investments and an improved transport infrastructure, production of crude oil and gas condensate expanded by 17.3% to 47 million metric tons in 2002, resulting in a 9.8% increase in industrial output (which accounts for about 30% of GDP). Growth in the manufacturing subsector slowed to 7.7% from 14.8% in 2001, mainly due to moderation in external demand. Agriculture sector output grew by 2.7%; growth in the livestock subsector was strong, but the grain subsector recorded only a modest rise due to a decline in crop productivity. Construction output rose sharply by 19.3%, largely as a result of rapid infrastructure development for the new capital, Astana, and rapid continued growth (at over 9%) in the services sector, mainly due to large rises in transport and telecommunications.

Fixed capital investment at 19.0% of GDP remained high, though somewhat below the 21.0% of GDP peak recorded in 2001. Investment in oil and gas activities increased to 53.0% of total investment from 41.0% in 2001. Transport and communications and manufacturing were also important investment destinations, accounting for 11.0% and 8.4%, respectively, of total investment. Domestic private investment continued to be the largest source of investment at 67% of the total, while foreign and public sector investment accounted for 25.0% and 8.0%, respectively, of the total.

Living standards improved as continuing economic growth helped raise real incomes by 7.4% from the year earlier level. In 2002, average monthly wages reached T20,305 (equivalent to $131), a 16.6% increase over the 2001 figure in nominal terms and 10.0% in real terms. However, regional income inequality remained, with wages in oil-rich regions double the country-wide average wage. Sustained economic growth and targeted poverty interventions helped reduce the proportion of the population living below the subsistence minimum of T4,734 ($31) per month from 28.4% in 2001 to 27.0% in 2002. The state law on targeted social assistance became effective on 1 January 2002, providing allowances for those with incomes below T1,853 ($12) per month. The unemployment rate declined from 10.4% to 9.4% in 2002, mainly due to greater employment in construction and services (Figure 2.20). However, unemployment is still a major problem, especially in rural areas and among women. While GDP growth has averaged over 10% in the past 3 years, employment growth has averaged only about 3%, largely because of the capital-intensive nature of the oil sector-led expansion.

The fiscal position continued to strengthen in 2002, aided by faster than expected economic growth. The general government (central and local) budget was essentially balanced (with a negligible surplus), compared with a small deficit of 0.4% of GDP in 2001. While tax revenues substantially

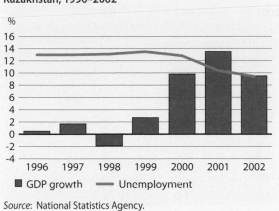

Figure 2.20 **Change in GDP and Unemployment, Kazakhstan, 1996–2002**

■ GDP growth   —— Unemployment

Source: National Statistics Agency.

exceeded budget targets, the revenue-to-GDP ratio fell as expected by about 1 percentage point to 21.9% of GDP, mainly because, in a classification improvement, privatization proceeds were treated as a financing item in 2002, rather than revenues as in 2001. Similarly, the expenditure-to-GDP ratio fell to 21.9% of GDP from 23.4% in 2001, mainly reflecting reduced allocations to the road and transport subsector after large increases and under-budget expenditures during the year.

While this presentation of the budget includes net balances of nonbudgetary accounts, it does not include revenues of the National Fund of the Republic of Kazakhstan (NFRK), which recorded a surplus of 1.4% of GDP in 2002; with this, the inclusive overall government surplus would have been 1.4% of GDP. The NFRK, which was established in 2001, accumulates a part of the Government's oil and mineral revenues for future investment to achieve economic diversification. While the mechanism used to calculate allocations of government revenues between the budget and the NFRK is complex, use of conservative baseline oil and mineral prices in planning, as well as provision for stabilization payments from the NFRK in case of lower than expected prices, works to assure that budget revenue assumptions are achieved. General government debt, including both external and domestic debt, was reduced to 15.0% of GDP from 17.3% in 2001, due to early repayments.

National Bank of Kazakhstan (NBK) monetary policy was generally accommodative during 2002. Broad money supply (M3) rose by about

33% in response to continued economic growth and financial deepening. A 36% surge in bank deposits in 2002 reflected rising public confidence in the banking sector, though the bulk of deposits continued to be held in foreign exchange-denominated accounts. NBK policy action during the year was evident in the easing of the refinance rate to 7.5% from 9.0% in 2001. This led to a reduction in the average weighted interest rate for the corporate sector from 16.3% in 2001 to 15.5% at end-2002, and helped boost credit to the economy by 37.0% from the year earlier level.

Strengthened central bank control over reserve money and monetary growth kept the exchange rate stable and reduced annual inflation, measured by the CPI, to 5.9% from 8.4% in 2001. The tenge depreciated by 3.2% and 0.1% against the dollar, in nominal and real terms, respectively, in 2002; the average exchange rate was T153.5 to the dollar. The tenge also depreciated in real terms by 5.5% against the Russian ruble, thus helping keep domestic industry competitive vis-à-vis the country's main trading partner.

Kazakhstan's external position improved in 2002. The trade surplus increased to $2.1 billion from $1.2 billion in the previous year. Merchandise exports grew by 12.0%, after a 2.8% decline in 2001, mainly due to the marked increase in production and export volume of oil and metals that offset weaknesses in their international market prices. Imports rose by only 2.0%, following the large increase of 14.6% in 2001.

Reflecting the improved trade balance, the current account deficit narrowed sharply to $200 million (around 1% of GDP) from $1.2 billion in 2001. Although net FDI inflows were substantially less than the exceptionally high amount recorded in 2001, a capital account surplus continued to ensure an overall payments surplus. Gross international reserves (including assets held by the NFRK) increased over the year by $1.3 billion to $5.1 billion at end-2002. The NFRK's assets increased by about $700 million to $1.9 billion, while NBK's official reserves rose by about $600 million to $3.1 billion, a level equal to 3.5 months of imports of goods and services. Total external debt is estimated at about $18 billion at end-2002 (about 74% of GDP); public sector debt accounted for only $2.9 billion of the total. The fact that official reserves exceed public sector external

Kyrgyz Republic

A contraction in the economy, stemming from an accident at the country's largest gold mine, exposed the narrow economic base and vulnerability of the economy to external and domestic shocks. Consequently, medium-term prospects depend largely on rapid diversification of the domestic production base and exports. Debt relief from Paris Club members has provided some additional resources and time to carry out the necessary structural reforms.

Macroeconomic Assessment

GDP is estimated to have fallen by 0.5% in 2002, as against 5.3% growth in 2001. This is mainly due to a 26% drop in gold production caused by an accident at the Kumtor gold mine in July—the mine contributed 9% of GDP and 40% of industrial output in 2001. Industry declined by 11.2% during 2002 on account of the steep fall in gold production and a downturn in electricity generation, which resulted from low export demand. However, a few sectors showed a strong turnaround: textiles, glass, leather products, and food processing. Late sowing due to adverse weather conditions delayed the agricultural harvest and affected crop yields, but sector output is expected to have risen by 3.3%, somewhat below the target of 4.0%. The services sector is estimated to have grown by about 4.2%. The output of hotels and restaurants rose by 28.5% and retail trade by 8.2%, mainly because of the foreign troops now based in the country and higher numbers of tourist arrivals.

Gross domestic capital formation declined from 20% of GDP in 2000 to about 18% of GDP in 2001 due to a fall in the Public Investment Program (PIP) as a result of budgetary pressure. This trend appears to have continued in 2002 and PIP disbursements are expected to fall short of target by over 10%, which might reduce the overall capital formation rate in 2002 to about 17% of GDP.

The incidence of poverty fell from 52% in 2000 to 47.6% in 2001. Despite the economic contraction in 2002, the potential impact on poverty is likely to be limited because of a 10.5% increase in average monthly wages in the year to September 2002, coupled with low inflation and continued growth in the agriculture sector, which employs about half the workforce. The level of unemployment is not officially available; however, it was likely little changed from the 7.8% estimate for 2001.

In 2002, the estimated fiscal deficit of 5.9% of GDP, higher than the target of 5.1%, is attributed to the fall in GDP and the consequent loss of revenues. The Government succeeded in eliminating pension arrears, and in reducing arrears in counterpart financing of externally assisted projects and payments to the medical insurance fund. The debt service burden eased with the decision of Paris Club members in March 2002 to reschedule repayments due between December 2001 and December 2004. They also agreed to consider providing more enduring long-term debt relief in the form of concessional stock treatment if the ongoing IMF-supported Poverty Reduction and Growth Facility (PRGF) is successfully implemented (Figure 2.21).

Broad money expanded by 34.1% in 2002, mainly due to the rise of foreign assets held by the central bank. This rapid expansion did not, however, cause a rise in inflation, on account both of increased demand for domestic currency spurred

Figure 2.21 External Debt, Kyrgyz Republic, 1994–2002

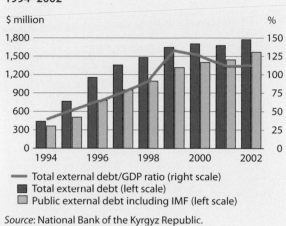

— Total external debt/GDP ratio (right scale)
■ Total external debt (left scale)
□ Public external debt including IMF (left scale)

Source: National Bank of the Kyrgyz Republic.

Policy Developments

The Government undertook several structural reform measures in 2002 to stabilize the economy, raise the quality of public resource management, and improve governance to create an environment in which the private sector can function efficiently. It has successfully implemented the policy benchmarks stipulated for 2002 under the PRGF. A draft of the National Poverty Reduction Strategy, which provides the blueprint for development for 2003–2005, has been prepared and was submitted to donors at the Consultative Group meeting held in October 2002 in Bishkek.

The Government made significant progress in fiscal reforms in 2001 and continued the momentum in 2002. Effective July 2002, it cut the business profit tax rate to 20% for all entities except natural monopolies where the tax cut was deferred until 2003 on revenue considerations. Personal income tax rate slabs (previously from 5% to 30%) were consolidated into two slabs of 10% and 20% to reduce the tax burden and simplify administration. Other revenue measures included removing many VAT exemptions, increasing the retail sales tax rate, and raising the nonagricultural land tax. The rate of employers' contribution to the Social Fund was reduced, aiding both business profitability and lowering employment costs. In an effort to improve revenue administration, the Government decided in September to merge the State Tax Inspectorate, the Customs Committee, the Financial Police, and the revenue-collecting division of the Social Fund into a single independent revenue-collecting organization under the Ministry of Finance. Moreover, it initiated steps to reform and strengthen the customs administration and to create a special unit to monitor and collect taxes from large taxpayers. Energy tariffs were increased by 20% to reduce the quasi-fiscal deficit, and further adjustments will be required. The Government, however, made little progress in privatizing four large SOEs in the electricity, gas, airlines, and telecommunications subsectors.

by the strong som, and of increased monetization of the economy. Expansion of credit unions in rural areas and improved availability of microcredit contributed significantly to the monetization process. Indeed, inflation continued falling with consumer prices rising by only 2.0% on average for the year (2.3% in the year to end-December 2002). Weighted average interest rates fell slightly during the year but were high at 36.4% for domestic currency loans and 22.7% for foreign currency loans in October 2002. Bank lending rates are very high due to large default risks and problems arising from the difficulties in enforcing claims against collateral.

Foreign trade increased in 2002 for the first time since 1998; it is estimated to have grown by about 14%, aided by a 25.4% increase in imports. The trade deficit is expected to exceed $50 million, as exports grew by only 3.7%. Imports of petroleum products for the foreign troops stationed in the country and strong domestic demand contributed to the surge in imports. Exports of precious metals (which accounted for 47% of total exports in 2001) fell by over 27% and the sale of electricity to neighboring countries declined. This would have caused a considerable drop in exports but for the notable export performance of agriculture and light industry products. The current account deficit for 2002 is expected to widen to 2.0% of GDP, from 2001's level of 1.3%. The inflow of FDI was a meager $1.6 million during the first 11 months. Foreign exchange reserves are sufficient to cover about 7 months of imports.

The primary objectives in the monetary area are to contain inflation and to improve financial intermediation through financial sector reforms. In 2002, the Government submitted amendments to the Law on Licensing of Banks to impart more authority to the central bank to revoke or suspend licenses of delinquent banks and to adjudicate disputes relating

Table 2.21 Major Economic Indicators, Kyrgyz Republic, 2000–2004, %

Item	2000	2001	2002	2003	2004
GDP growth	5.4	5.3	-0.5	5.2	4.5
Gross domestic investment/GDP	20.0	18.0	17.0	19.3	-
Inflation rate (consumer price index)	18.7	6.9	2.0	-	-
Money supply (M2) growth	12.1	11.3	34.1	13.0	-
Fiscal balance/GDP	-9.2	-5.0	-5.9	-4.7	-4.3
Merchandise export growth	10.4	-6.0	3.7	13.9	-
Merchandise import growth	-8.0	-13.1	25.4	10.6	-
Current account balance/GDP	-5.6	-1.3	-2.0	-3.4	-5.6
Debt service ratio	28.1	30.8	-	-	-

- Not available.

Sources: National Bank of the Kyrgyz Republic; National Statistics Committee; staff estimates.

to bank liquidation. The central bank has approved a strategy for reforming the banking sector and initiated measures to improve the payments system in the country with a view to encouraging banking system payments rather than cash in settling transactions. The Government is carrying out background work to introduce legal reforms for enforcing creditor rights, quickly resolving business disputes, improving corporate governance in the banking sector, and protecting depositor rights. Other notable structural reform measures include the phased introduction of international accounting standards, preparation of a blueprint and a time-bound implementation plan for judicial reforms, and initiation of steps to facilitate the early implementation of SOE reforms. Many of these measures are expected to be undertaken in 2003.

Outlook for 2003–2004

The Kumtor accident demonstrated the extent of the economy's vulnerability to internal and external shocks. It is difficult to insulate a small economy like that of the Kyrgyz Republic completely from such shocks. However, diversification of domestic production and foreign trade, rapid implementation of structural reforms, and continued pursuit of solid macroeconomic policies are needed to reduce such risks in the medium term. With revival of gold production in early 2003, GDP is expected to grow by about 5% in both 2003 and 2004. The Govern-

ment intends to reduce the fiscal deficit to 4.7% of GDP in 2003 by mobilizing additional revenues, which will also allow increased spending on social services. According to a recent survey, business confidence is high but business people cited expensive credit, intrusive regulations, and corruption as their most important constraints.

Medium-term economic prospects for maintaining 5% GDP growth will depend on the resolution of two inexorable trends during the next few years: a gradual reduction in foreign funding of the PIP to around 3% of GDP after 2005, and the beginning of a decline in gold production at Kumtor. These two developments underscore the immediate need for enhancing private investment, identifying new sources of production and exports to compensate for the fall in gold output, and raising domestic resources for maintaining the required levels of public investment. These can be accomplished only with further progress in financial sector reforms, improvement in governance, implementation of legal reforms, and removal of remaining impediments to private business.

The rescheduling of debt service payments by the Paris Club creditors and the promise to provide further debt relief through stock treatment in 2004–2005 have provided an opportunity and appropriate environment for the Government to pursue these goals. However, it will need to secure domestic resources and external grants to fund increasingly more of the PIP.

Tajikistan

Overall economic performance was strong in 2002. Macroeconomic management improved as Tajikistan continued in the effort to rebuild its economy and institutions shattered by civil war. A Poverty Reduction Strategy Paper was finalized and presented to Parliament. Implementation of its stabilization and structural reform policies is necessary to sustain economic growth and move toward a reduction in poverty.

Macroeconomic Assessment

GDP grew by 9.1% in 2002, the fifth consecutive year of strong economic growth. As in the past, growth was driven by the post-conflict recovery of output in aluminum, electricity, and agriculture. Aluminum output increased by 6.1% (total industrial growth was 8.2%), electricity was up by 5.0%, and cotton production rose by 13.9% (total agricultural growth was 15.0%). The end of a drought in 2002 also pushed up production of wheat, which is rain fed and not irrigated and, for the first time in many years, the country produced enough wheat to avoid dependence on foreign aid to supplement domestic production. Light industry, mostly textiles, and cotton processing grew markedly by about 27%. Construction was another major growth area, up 30%, but its 4% share of GDP somewhat limited its impact on overall growth. Domestic demand and economic growth were boosted by worker remittances, estimated at $120 million or about 10% of GDP. It is estimated that up to 1 million Tajiks, almost 17% of the population, live abroad either permanently or temporarily, and mainly in the Russian Federation.

Fixed capital investment amounted to only 7.0% of GDP in 2000, the latest year for which data are available, and it is unlikely to be any higher in 2002. The Public Investment Program (PIP) was equal to 2.8% of GDP in 2002, a slight increase from 2001. The PIP is financed by foreign aid, and most expenditures are directed toward the rehabilitation of agriculture, transport, and social infrastructure. After a trough in 2001, when the signing of several FDI contracts was delayed because of the crisis in Afghanistan, FDI inflows in 2002 picked up, doubling to $21.0 million. FDI continued to be concentrated in textiles and mining.

Reliable statistics on poverty trends since 1999 are not yet available, but anecdotal evidence and regional surveys suggest that incomes, both cash and noncash, increased substantially since the finalization of the peace agreement in 2000. This is mainly due to growth in informal, service-oriented activities. Most people's wages are substantially below the minimum consumption basket, and only a small share of the labor force is engaged in formal sector employment—an area that has shown little growth. While the official unemployment rate rose only slightly from 2.3% to 2.7% in 2002, unofficial estimates place unemployment or underemployment much higher, at over 30% of the labor force. For many Tajiks, informal activity, agricultural labor, and jobs abroad are the most likely sources of employment.

Under IMF economic programs, Tajikistan managed to improve revenue collection rates steadily from 12% of GDP in 1998 to over 15% in 2001. In 2002, fiscal performance was better than anticipated: faster than expected economic growth, an increase in cotton exports (leading to an increase of cotton sales tax collection), and a more system-

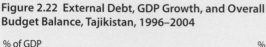
Figure 2.22 External Debt, GDP Growth, and Overall Budget Balance, Tajikistan, 1996–2004

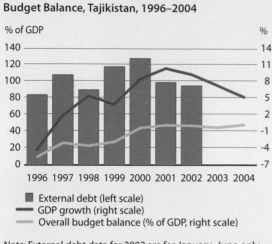

Note: External debt data for 2002 are for January–June only.
Sources: Government of Tajikistan; *Asian Development Outlook 2002*; International Monetary Fund; staff estimates.

atic implementation of the new VAT regime based on the destination principle meant that revenue collection was stronger than budgeted. After VAT, the cotton and aluminum sales tax, at 10% and 2%, respectively, are the largest revenue sources for the Government (together providing 20% of revenues). On the expenditure side, revenue performance allowed a 25% increase in civil servants' wage rates; these are very low and have been heavily eroded by inflation. Social expenditures accounted for about 43% of revenues. Excluding the foreign-financed PIP, the budget deficit was 0.2% of GDP (up slightly from 0.1% in 2001) and is among the lowest in Central Asia.

Public external debt is very high at over 87% of GDP (a total of $962 million, with about one third owed to the Russian Federation). The debt is a major obstacle in fiscal management: in 2002, total scheduled debt service amounted to 5.3% of GDP (Figure 2.22). In early 2002, the Government renegotiated concessional terms on debts with Kazakhstan and Uzbekistan, and a major breakthrough was achieved by the restructuring of debt to the Russian Federation on concessional terms in December (this lowered debt service due in 2002 from 41% to 18% of fiscal revenues).

The central bank, the National Bank of Tajikistan (NBT), in general pursued a tight monetary policy, which, with moderation in food price increases (due to the end of the drought) helped

pull down inflation to 14.5% in 2002 from 38.6% a year earlier. Implementation of monetary policy, however, was uneven. During 2002, the exchange rate depreciated by 14% against the dollar.

Recent movements of commercial interest rates have become more market oriented, have fluctuated less, and indeed became positive for the first time in many years. However, as there is a high degree of credit rationing, interest rates are not significant determinants in lending.

The health of the banking sector has not improved significantly. Two of the four major banks have effective negative net capital, and two are severely underprovisioned. Only five (out of 14) banks meet the minimum capital requirements. As part of the reform effort, improved banking regulations were issued during the year and supervision capacities of NBT were improved. Two regulations that stifled banking activities—a tax on remittances and the ability of the tax authorities to freeze accounts without a court order—were removed in 2001 and 2002, respectively. Reflecting these changes and an improving economy, household deposits increased by 85% in 2001 and by 22% in the first quarter of 2002. Nevertheless, deposits amount to little over 4% of GDP, representing a somewhat lower degree of mobilization than in most other transition economies.

The external sector performed significantly better in 2002 than a year earlier. Exports grew by 11.0% (to $723 million) while imports rose by only 6.0% (to $819 million). This reduction in the trade deficit and an improved surplus in invisibles narrowed the current account deficit to 4.1% of GDP from 7.1% in 2001. Exports and imports have been growing strongly since 1998 (except in 2001). However, export growth is not only highly dependent on world market prices—especially for cotton and aluminum, which weakened in the previous 2 years—but also on political relations with neighboring countries. Exports in 2001 suffered heavily because of the closure of the only railway line through Kazakhstan to Tajikistan's main export markets. In 2002, rail transport resumed, but export and import levels are still somewhat below their 2000 levels.

The current account deficit is financed almost entirely by external assistance. Capital flows, however, have been sufficient to increase gross international reserves and keep import cover stable

Table 2.22 Major Economic Indicators, Tajikistan, 2000–2004, %

Item	2000	2001	2002	2003	2004
GDP growth	8.3	10.2	9.1	7.1	5.0
Inflation rate (consumer price index)	32.9	38.6	14.5	10.0	6.0
Fiscal balance/GDP	-0.6	-0.1	-0.2	-0.5	-
Merchandise export growth	18.3	-17.3	11.0	11.3	10.5
Merchandise import growth	20.3	-7.3	6.0	4.0	3.7
Current account balance/GDP	-6.5	-7.1	-4.1	-4.0	-4.0
Debt service ratio	17.5	25.6	21.0	22.6	-

- Not available.

Sources: Ministry of Finance; National Bank of Tajikistan; State Statistical Committee; International Monetary Fund; staff estimates.

at approximately 2 months since 2000. Total debt service due in the first 6 months of 2002 increased to 20.0% of exports, from 16.0% over the same period in 2001, due to the expiry of loan grace periods. Because of Tajikistan's high level of exports (over 70% of GDP), the debt service ratio appears to understate the magnitude of the problem of managing a debt burden at nearly 100% of GDP.

Policy Developments

The Poverty Reduction Strategy Paper (PRSP) that was presented to Parliament in June 2002, finalized after 2 years of deliberation and consultations with civil society, outlines the major issues that the Government intends to address in the next 3 years. Identified reforms cover all major sectors and aim to promote the transition to a market economy and to combat poverty. The next steps are arguably even more difficult for the Government than producing the PRSP: to prioritize and implement the identified reforms and find necessary international concessional funding.

The healthy economic and fiscal performance in 2002 gave the Government some scope to plan for the 2003 budget to include an average 15% civil service wage increase and for social expenditures to rise to around 46% of the budget. Larger spending in the context of a balanced budget for 2003 was aided by the successful 2002 debt relief negotiations. Renegotiation of the Russian debt, which includes a 3-year grace period, considerably reduced the debt service burden. It fell to 18% of revenues in 2002 (it would have been 41% without restructuring) and

will remain low at approximately 12% until 2004. However, because of the heavy debt service and lack of counterpart funds for projects, the Government needs to limit the PIP to the availability of concessional funds and keep disbursement at approximately 3% of GDP.

During the next 2 years, the Government plans to reduce the quasi-fiscal deficit, mainly subsidies to the energy sector, that are estimated at about 5% of GDP. Plans include some increase in tariffs and increasing collection rates by cutting off commercial customers who fail to pay.

The Government's plans call for a continued tight monetary policy to reduce inflation to about 6% by 2004, which is very ambitious. One of the main contributors to inflation has been an excessive volume of loans directed almost exclusively to the cotton sector. Pressure on NBT to grant such loans might lessen, however, as more private finance by cotton investors and banks becomes available. Plans are in the pipeline to introduce a proper functioning interbank credit market in 2003 and this should facilitate a more efficient credit system. It is planned to allow banks to hold their capital in foreign exchange, a step intended to encourage them to increase their capital. No changes were made in the floating exchange rate regime during the year.

Ongoing bank restructuring will continue and the Government is committed to enforcing all prudential requirements in the first half of 2003. By end-September 2003, noncomplying banks (other than those currently being restructured) will be either closed or merged. Minimum capital requirements will increase to $2.0 million in December

2003 for existing banks, while for new banks the requirement is $3.0 million.

Agriculture sector restructuring is high on the reform agenda as it offers strong prospects for growth and poverty reduction. Ongoing farm privatization has created 14,500 *dekhan* (private) farms, which are either privately owned or operated by collectives. The proliferation of household plots as well as plots granted by the president means that private and *dekhan* farming has taken over the larger share of agricultural production (in volume terms) in all categories except cotton and silk. The Government plans to privatize all remaining farms by 2005. Some 225 very large farms are yet to be privatized, but they are burdened with large debts that make them unattractive to private investors; the Government is exploring options to deal with this problem. Other important agricultural reforms include removing government interventions in production and marketing decisions of producers and improving producers' access to finance and markets.

Since the economy is still very much in the process of recovering from civil war, it is crucial to physically rehabilitate infrastructure and utilities, particularly in power. With donor assistance, the Government has committed to unbundling and corporatizing utilities and to privatizing transport. The large aluminum smelter, TADAZ, is currently undergoing an international audit, as a first step toward restructuring in this crucial firm.

Outlook for 2003–2004

The outlook for the next few years is uncertain. International attention focused on the country and grant aid (mostly from the US) increased substantially after the events of September 11. Assuming that the goodwill of the international community persists, the inflow of additional funds and grants may well continue, significantly relieving pressure on the budget and current account. Increasing regional stability following the elimination of the Taliban in Afghanistan and subsequent regional integration will also contribute to the positive effect of economic reforms by reinforcing diversification and stabilizing the prospects for economic growth.

Nevertheless, Tajikistan's economic development remains extremely vulnerable to various constraints, including remnants of the monolithic culture of industrial and agricultural production, weak institutions and administrative capacities to carry out reforms, a high debt burden, and a narrow export base subject to volatile price swings.

In the period ahead, the economic policy framework is based on the PRSP, which focuses on enhancing macroeconomic stability and structural reform to reduce poverty. Key components of the strategy are reducing inflation, achieving modest fiscal strengthening while reducing quasi-fiscal energy subsidies, improving NBT operations, continuing agricultural privatization, and improving governance.

Aided by further diversification of agricultural production and expansion of light industry, GDP growth is expected to decline to about 7% in 2003 and then to about 5% in 2004, as aluminum production reaches capacity limits. It is expected that domestic demand will continue to be supplemented by substantial worker remittances from abroad. Assuming that NBT continues its tight monetary stance, inflation is expected to fall to about 10% in 2003 and to 6% in 2004. The budget, excluding the PIP, is expected to be kept in near balance.

The current account deficit is not expected to change much over the next 2 years. Stagnant or even slightly decreasing prices of the major exports (due to slower global demand for aluminum and large global stocks of cotton) are expected to lead to slow export growth. Two opposite pressures will influence import growth: on the one hand, demand for imported consumer goods will increase, financed in part by remittances, while on the other, this will be kept in check by slower growth of PIP-related capital goods imports. The immediate pressure on the budget to service external debt will be substantially reduced through 2004; however, further debt restructuring may be required to keep the subsequent debt service burden manageable.

Whether Tajikistan fully succeeds in implementing the measures outlined in the PRSP will depend on a host of uncertainties. That a political consensus has emerged to set out such a detailed plan is, however, a basis for some optimism.

Turkmenistan

With cotton output falling sharply, GDP growth in 2002 slowed. The growth was based primarily on further increases in natural gas production and exports. However, the prevailing macroeconomic and education sector policies need to be urgently reviewed to sustain industrial growth and diversification and avoid adverse long-term consequences.

Macroeconomic Assessment

GDP growth in 2002 slowed significantly on account of an extremely poor cotton harvest, which declined to a mere 0.5 million tons from 1.1 million tons in 2001, and against an official target of 2.0 million tons for the year. Performance in the agriculture sector, which accounts for some 25% of GDP and provides a livelihood for over one half of the population, was boosted by expansion of wheat and rice output bringing grain production up by 15% for the year to meet its official target.

According to preliminary official estimates, GDP growth was an impressive 14.9% in 2002, based primarily on a further increase in the export of natural gas, oil, and oil products and an increase in output of food processing and light industry. These official growth estimates are based on a 25.0% increase in industry sector output that in turn is reportedly derived from a 41.0% and 66.0% increase in the output of light industry and food processing subsectors, respectively. These estimates, however, do not appear to reconcile with other officially reported economic indicators such as consumption of electricity, which remained stagnant in 2002, an 11.0% decline in imports from already low levels in 2001, and continuing high levels of unemployment. Moreover, there are hardly any signs of increased private sector activity, except for the continuing boom in construction of luxury housing in Ashgabat.

The officially estimated shares in GDP for 2001 are about 35% for industry, 25% for agriculture, 32% for services, and 6% for construction. Official 2002 growth estimates of 9.5% in agriculture and services and 6.5% in the construction sector look plausible. However, keeping in view the performance in electricity output and the decline in imports, industrial growth estimates seem highly exaggerated. The natural gas subsector is estimated to account for nearly three quarters of the industry sector value added (official estimates state this to be much lower at 45% of the sector). Its output increased by 4.0% in 2002. Based on these observations, it appears that industry sector growth can be more realistically estimated at about 7–8%, even allowing for some growth in the light industry and food processing subsectors. This yields an estimate of GDP growth of about 8.6% for 2002, a substantial drop from the 20.5% increase recorded in 2001, and well below the preliminary official estimates.

Inflation increased to 8.8%, from 6.0% in 2001. However, changes in the official price index reflect a controlled and repressed price structure that is largely determined by the government policy of providing utility supplies like gas, power, and water almost free of cost and heavily subsidizing other necessities such as housing, bread, and transport and by the use of price controls. Monetary policy is not geared to macroeconomic considerations as the Central Bank of Turkmenistan (CBT) and the operations of the largely state-owned commercial banking sector are almost entirely oriented

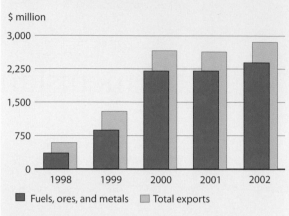

Figure 2.23 Share of Fuels, Ores, and Metals to Total Exports, Turkmenistan, 1998–2002

$ million

■ Fuels, ores, and metals   □ Total exports

Source: National Institute of State Statistics and Information of Turkmenistan.

to directed lending to meet the needs of SOEs. Frequent management changes at CBT during the year appear to have further limited its effectiveness, while the banking sector continued to stagnate because of extensive controls and restrictions. The large differential between the market and official exchange rates remained virtually unchanged during 2002, although the market rate appreciated by about 2% to TMM22,300 to the dollar. The official rate remained pegged at TMM5,200 to the dollar.

The 2002 state budget was essentially balanced, with expenditures exceeding revenues by only TMM500 billion or about 0.1% of GDP. The overall fiscal position of the Government, however, is difficult to assess because of large off-budget accounts including the foreign exchange reserve fund that is managed by the President's Office. Indeed, nonbudget funds managed by various ministries and government agencies received about TMM40.5 trillion, or more than three times the budget revenues.

Foreign trade turnover in 2002 stagnated, reflecting an 11.0% fall in imports and an 8.9% increase in exports. The trade surplus almost doubled to $1 billion from $535 million in 2001 with the $465 million improvement about equally due to the export gain and the import decline. The decline in imports is worrisome as it reflects, perhaps, Turkmenistan's growing disengagement from global trade and investment flows and a

slowdown in industrial expansion and diversification. With exports of cotton fiber declining by nearly 46%, the export increase was mostly due to a 9.4% rise in unit value for natural gas (as well as some increase in volume). The predominance of hydrocarbons in total exports increased from 82.8% to 84.0% in 2002 (Figure 2.23). Data on other accounts—services, capital, and reserves—of the balance of payments are not available and this would be necessary to better understand recent economic developments. However, Bank for International Settlements data indicate an over $200 million increase in Turkmenistan deposits in banks abroad in the 9 months through September 2002 and this would suggest an overall surplus on the balance of payments.

The Government's policy of heavily subsidizing consumption of basic necessities, combined with an increase in average nominal wages by about 20% during 2002, has ensured maintenance of welfare levels. However, this masks the increasing gap in living standards in urban centers like Ashgabat compared with provincial capitals and rural areas. Moreover, the worsening state of education and health facilities in rural areas, which is a result of a decline in their share of budgeted expenditures, is a further area of concern in growing welfare disparities. Growth and income prospects in the longer term are being undermined by education policies that have cut the number of years of education to nine and generally caused deterioration in educational facilities and standards. This issue is emerging as a source of discontent within the professional and educated urban population.

Policy Developments

The macroeconomic policy regime remained unchanged—to the extent that it did not regress—during 2002. The most deleterious aspect of this policy regime is the more than 300% spread between official and market exchange rates, which effectively translates to a regime of arbitrarily determined multiple exchange rates. This is a severe impediment for private sector growth and inhibits FDI. The policy of heavily subsidizing consumption of utilities and basic necessities needs to be reviewed and gradually moved toward approaching full cost recovery. This would allow self-financing in these sectors and restrain wasteful consumption.

Moreover, the policy of maintaining nonbudget funds under independent charge of individual ministries needs review. These funds, which financed 24.0% of total fixed investment in 2002, also accumulate as unspent balances.

Integrating nonbudget funds and their balances with the budget, if transparently managed and audited, would be a substantial improvement in fiscal management and enhance fiscal stability. Finally, there is a growing emphasis on directing education to vocational training in the belief that higher education and advanced skills are not at present needed for the economy. This policy and experimentation with the curriculum is resulting in dilution of education standards and, if not corrected urgently, is likely to result in a de-skilling of the workforce, adversely affecting productivity and management over the longer term.

Outlook for 2003–2004

Reconstruction of Afghanistan and trade expansion with neighboring Iran could provide new sources of external demand for Turkmenistan's hydrocarbon, energy, textiles, and light industry exports. There are reports also of new, larger contracts under negotiation for natural gas exports with the Russian Federation and Iran that will help improve utilization of existing production capacities. Domestic demand is unlikely to show significant improvement in a policy regime characterized by strict price controls, a pervasive industrial licensing system, and tight control of banking and foreign transactions. Cotton production and exports should also do better in 2003 after their dismal performance in 2002. Based largely on external demand for hydrocarbons, cotton, and textiles, as well as some strengthening of domestic demand, arising mainly from an improved agricultural performance, GDP growth is expected to be an annual 7–8% in 2003 and 2004, subject to risks of adverse global price fluctuations and transport bottlenecks. With the continuation of the existing price control and subsidy policies, inflation may be expected to continue to remain within single digits during 2003–2004.

The completion of a feasibility study for the trans-Afghan natural gas pipeline, designed to export 30 billion cubic meters of the country's gas to Pakistan and other Asian markets, is likely by October 2003. The study's findings may result in heightened investor interest yielding substantial benefits, improving growth prospects for 2004 and beyond. Nonetheless, growth based primarily on capital-intensive extractive sectors is unlikely to generate sufficient employment to absorb the existing pool of unemployed and new entrants to the work force. Therefore, unemployment and social stress may well increase in the next few years unless a more active policy is pursued both to stimulate private sector-led growth and to diversify exports.

Uzbekistan

GDP growth in 2002 remained slow and, with unchanged policies, the medium-term outlook is for continued sluggish expansion. The Government wants to attract greater investment inflows to accelerate development, but this would require action to carry out far-reaching economic and structural reforms.

Macroeconomic Assessment

Growth in GDP, according to official estimates, slowed to 4.2% in 2002 from 4.5% in 2001 and was below the official 5.0% target. Agriculture and industry recorded moderately improved performance, though expansion in other sectors, mainly services (accounting for about 50% of GDP), slowed markedly to about 1.5% from 14.2% in 2001. Value added in agriculture, the largest employer and exporter, rose to 6.1% growth from 4.1% in 2001. Productivity and area increases raised grain production by 38% to 5.3 million tons, exceeding domestic consumption needs. Adverse weather lowered the cotton harvest by 80,000 metric tons to 3.2 million tons, but most of it was of premium quality. The industry sector reportedly grew by 8.5%, up from 8.1% growth in 2001, though the data are unclear on what drove it. Intensified import restrictions and a weaker exchange rate boosted domestic manufacturing but hurt import-dependent enterprises and retail trade.

Oil production rose for the second consecutive year, by 2.4%, and natural gas production increased by 1.8%. The transport and communications subsector posted stronger performance, of 6.8% compared with 3.3% in 2001, driven mainly by the operations of Uzbekistan Airways. Retail trade output contracted by 0.5%, against 8.6% growth in 2001, as the impact of intensified trade restrictions on imports disrupted trade. The number of private SMEs continued to rise during the year with most new entrants in the agriculture sector.

Regional disparities in incomes persist. Per capita incomes in Tashkent were the highest at $40 per month (at the official exchange rate) and the lowest were in Samarkand at just $10 per month. Official unemployment data at 0.4% of the labor force continue to mask hidden unemployment as they do not include the unregistered unemployed. Actual unemployment remains high, especially in poorer regions, and mirrors regional variations in SME growth. No sustained migration out of depressed regions has been observed.

The fiscal deficit in 2002 was 0.8% of GDP according to official sources, with about one half of the deficit financed by privatization revenues, mainly equity sales to foreign investors, and the balance by credit from the Central Bank of Uzbekistan (CBU). Most government expenditures, 38% of the total, were on welfare and social programs, while subsidies and investment took up 7% and 20%, respectively, of the total, with most of this directed to state-owned industry and infrastructure.

While a tightening stance was adopted in January 2002 when CBU raised its monthly benchmark refinancing rate from 2.0% to 2.5% (for an annual compounded rate of 34.5%), monetary operations remained largely oriented to financing the credit needs of SOEs and the budget. Accordingly, little progress was made during 2002 in reducing inflation with the official CPI indicating an average annual rate of 27.6%, against a target of 18.0% and virtually unchanged from the previous year. Moreover, price controls, an artificial exchange rate, and methodological issues cause the official

CPI to underestimate true inflation. Devaluation of the official exchange rate and a rise in fuel prices, pensions, and public sector wages were the main sources of pressure on prices, as were import restrictions that led to shortages of consumer goods.

The official exchange rate was devalued in steps by about 30% against the dollar over the course of 2002 and the spread between the official and black-market rates was markedly narrowed. However, the 35% spread at year-end failed to achieve the 20% government target. The black market exchange rate appreciated by about 12% by year-end; however, since such strong action was taken to repress private import trading during the year, the appreciation may not reflect a fundamental improvement in the exchange market. At end-2002, the dollar was trading at 1,320 sum on the black market compared with the official rate of 970 sum. A secondary official rate, at which the public may buy limited amounts of foreign exchange, traded at 1,020 sum.

The trade surplus rose to $276.4 million from $35.0 million in 2001, due to import compression. Exports fell by nearly 6%. Cotton export earnings were lower than in 2001, as were exports to Commonwealth of Independent States (CIS) countries; however, higher global gold prices boosted gold earnings. Cotton, gold, and energy products, and for the first time, services were large foreign exchange earners. Imports fell by more than 13% from the 2001 level. Machinery and equipment and foodstuffs accounted for most of the import bill. The Russian Federation remained the main trade partner.

The estimated current account surplus of $47 million was around 0.6% of GDP, a turnaround from a deficit of about 0.5% of GDP in 2001. Estimates of the capital account are highly tentative, though it appears that FDI was substantially lower than in 2001 and the capital account was in deficit. Bank for International Settlements deposit data suggest that reserves have declined during the year. External debt is estimated at $4.4 billion (about 56% of GDP) at end-2002, and the debt service ratio for the year was 29.0%. The ratio of debt service costs to hard currency exports was over 40%.

Policy Developments

The Staff Monitored Program (SMP) agreed between the Government and IMF dominated macroeconomic policy in 2002. The Government stated its intention to accelerate the transition to a market economy and achieve macroeconomic stability by reducing the role of the state in the economy and adopting tight fiscal and monetary policies. Government policies in 2002 were consequently aimed at establishing an economic structure in line with SMP objectives while implementing safeguards against outcomes unwanted by the Government and ensuring government monitoring and control. However, progress in transition was far from satisfactory. The Government was especially sensitive to possible outflows of international reserves. Monetary and fiscal policies were broadly in line with agreed benchmarks through mid-2002.

In 2002, the Government was under particular pressure to show progress in three key areas of the SMP: (i) liberalization of the foreign exchange regime, (ii) trade liberalization, and (iii) reform of the state procurement system for cotton and grain. On the first, the Government devalued the official foreign exchange rate and liberalized over-the-counter foreign exchange transactions that are conducted at the secondary market rate. At the same time, wary of the possibility of large foreign exchange outflows and with a view to controlling imports, it enforced trade and exchange restrictions that allowed it to ration and reduce demand for foreign exchange. These restrictions adversely affected private business. Multiple exchange rates continued to be applied and a substantial spread between the secondary official rate and the market rate reemerged after its elimination in May.

The Government's policy measures were designed to redirect unofficial transactions to the more liberalized official channels. This was done to protect local industry and curb illegal trading. These regulations were accompanied by incentives to domestic producers of consumer goods. But cumbersome industrial licensing procedures restricted the growth of private enterprises. In addition, restrictions aimed at curbing imports adversely affected private retail trade.

The Government gradually moved to liberalize the agriculture sector, but needed reforms are so numerous that a gradual approach is, indeed, required. The Government has achieved successes in areas such as livestock, fruits and vegetables, and farm restructuring. However, as with other reforms, the Government has been careful to ensure that any changes do not cause disruptions that it considers unacceptable. Grain self-sufficiency remains a particularly sensitive matter: government efforts to stabilize grain production have ensured input and credit availability as well as a working marketing channel but have, in some cases, crowded out private rural enterprises.

Reforms have also been tempered by the importance to government finances of the foreign exchange earnings from cotton. While the general rationalization of regulations that apply to private enterprises and the liberalization of certain subsectors encouraged the development of agricultural SMEs, state ownership and control, as well as marketing restrictions, prevent the potential benefits of rural enterprise development from being realized fully. Export bans on certain products have been used to foster development of the domestic agroprocessing industry.

Government cotton procurement accounts for 50% of total production. However, despite being permitted to do so, farmers find it difficult to sell the remaining 50% on the free market because of inadequate private marketing channels. Ambiguities in the interpretation of resolutions and persistence with old practices by local leaders have impeded reform of the procurement system. Government procurement prices for wheat and cotton were increased to adjust for inflation and international price increases in 2002, but not for exchange rate changes.

Banking sector reforms were prominent in the Government's reform agenda. CBU officially reduced its directed lending and other interference in the operations of commercial banks. Informal control, however, persisted. Low deposit interest rates and regulations limiting private cash withdrawals from bank accounts continued discouraging savings, and inadequate domestic deposit mobilization has resulted in a large exposure of the banking system to external borrowing. During 2002, the Government made efforts to withdraw cash from circulation to reduce unmonitorable cash transactions and this adversely affected private business activity. In these circumstances, the population generally continues to show distrust of the banking sector.

Overall, the Government has been hesitant to make substantial changes to existing economic policies because it weighs the potential benefits of liberalization against in its view potential serious problems, including reduction in state direction and the adverse impact on the budget of unification of the exchange rate, especially on the state system of consumer subsidies and the domestic cost of external debt service.

Outlook for 2003–2004

Growth in 2003 is likely to remain at 2002's level or to fall slightly. Government steps to shore up its foreign exchange position and to avoid foreign exchange volatility are likely to continue to adversely impact private sector growth in the period ahead. GDP growth in 2003 is expected to be 3.5% with a moderate increase in 2004 to 4.0%.

Industrial growth is likely to remain slow in the forecast period and, without substantial foreign exchange reforms, state enterprises and private firms are unlikely to be able to attract significant FDI. Agriculture will probably continue on its present course with the slow pace of reforms unlikely to have any substantial impact on growth unless policies are adopted to substantially improve the incentive structure facing farmers. Indeed, if the Government persists with its plan to increase the grain crop area by 12% in 2003, it will probably be faced with a poor harvest as it fails to finance the input needs of this additional acreage. The services sector, particularly retail trade and restaurants, is likely to continue feeling the adverse effects of government trade controls in 2003.

Medium-term developments on the balance of payments are difficult to assess given the limited information available and the recent policy actions that have mixed exchange market reforms with strong administrative action to restrict trade activity. Barring introduction of comprehensive economic reforms, it appears that exports would grow by perhaps 4–5% in the medium term, bolstered by an improvement in cotton prices, as expansion in export volume is limited. Growth in imports would continue to be affected by restrictions on consumer goods so as to limit the bulk of spending on capital goods in support of the Government's investment program. In these circumstances, the recorded trade surplus is likely to remain at about $250 million, essentially the 2002 outcome, unless a stronger degree of import compression than was seen in 2002 leads to a further decline in imports.

ASIAN DEVELOPMENT

Outlook 2003

Economic Trends and Prospects in Developing Asia

The Pacific
Cook Islands
Fiji Islands
Kiribati
Republic of the Marshall Islands
Federated States of Micronesia
Nauru
Papua New Guinea
Samoa
Solomon Islands
Democratic Republic of Timor-Leste
Tonga
Tuvalu
Vanuatu

Cook Islands

Economic growth virtually stopped in FY2002, reflecting a decline in visitor arrivals following the September 11 events. Medium-term forecasts, however, suggest that economic activity should improve, if the expected expansions in tourism, pearl exports, and construction are realized.

Macroeconomic Assessment

Economic growth slowed to 0.3% in FY2002 (ended 30 June 2002), following 2 years of strong momentum. In the aftermath of the events of September 11, visitor arrivals fell by nearly 9% in FY2002 (Figure 2.24), with the largest decline occurring in the January-March quarter, leading to a 6.2% fall in visitor spending. International air services were curtailed for some airlines, though tourist growth resumed in the second half of 2002. Total merchandise exports fell from US$9.5 million in FY2001 to US$5.8 million in FY2002, largely due to an almost 50% drop in sales of pearls, which constitute around 90% of commodity exports. Due to bad weather condition, crops were reduced and many small farmers experienced difficulties with marketing their produce and remaining cost competitive. The tourism-related subsectors of hotels, restaurants, bars, transport, and communications experienced weaker sales. However, construction, trade, and community and personal services recorded modest to strong growth.

Consistent with the general slowdown, average inflation declined to 3.9% in FY2002 from 9.4% in the previous fiscal year. Price trends of various categories of goods and services showed different dynamics, with the index for the food group—with a 32% weight in the CPI—rising by 9.4% and that for gasoline falling by 18%. Inflation was low or negative in most other categories.

In FY2002, the budget was in surplus by NZ$0.53 million, equivalent to 0.3% of GDP, a steep drop from the surplus of NZ$2.7 million in FY2001. Total revenues and grants rose by 3.6%, due to a 4.9% increase in tax revenues and a 10.4% rise in grants; nontax revenues declined by 10.5%. On the expenditure side, the 6.6% increase in total expenditures was driven by a 9.2% rise in expenditures on goods and services, while capital expenditures fell by 9.0%. Net debt declined to 69.0% of GDP, with the Government maintaining a small reserve for future debt repayment. This compares with a debt stock of 76.0% of GDP in FY2000.

The steep fall in total merchandise exports stemmed largely from a 60% drop in pearl exports in the January-March quarter of the fiscal year. Also in FY2002, imports declined by 8.8% to US$46.3 million from the year earlier level, primarily because of decreases in imports of minerals and fuels, beverages and tobacco, and machinery and transport equipment. The trade deficit narrowed slightly from US$41.2 million in FY2001 to US$40.5 million in FY2002.

Net foreign assets in the banking system at end-June 2002 were down 7.0% compared with the level 12 months previously. Net domestic credit grew at a rate of 24.0%, reflecting higher claims on the private sector. Broad money supply at end-June 2002 was 3.2% higher than a year earlier. Nominal interest rates on deposits ranged from 1% to 3.25%, while nominal lending rates ranged between 9.75% and 16.50%. The Bank of the Cook Islands has been adopting a higher interest rate structure

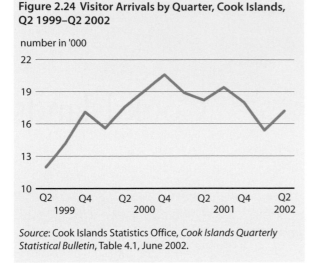

Figure 2.24 Visitor Arrivals by Quarter, Cook Islands, Q2 1999–Q2 2002

number in '000

Source: Cook Islands Statistics Office, *Cook Islands Quarterly Statistical Bulletin*, Table 4.1, June 2002.

than Westpac and the Australia and New Zealand Banking Group, the two commercial banks present in the country.

Policy Developments

Following a period of political instability in the second half of 2001, a new Government came to power in early 2002. The new budget policy statement presented in March 2002 focused on achieving national goals in six areas: social cohesion, economic sustainability, good governance, infrastructure development, outer island development, and environmental management. These priorities are similar to those that were already in place with the exception of environmental management, which was a new concern. One notable policy direction was the decision to reverse the devolution of political and economic responsibilities to local governments. However, repeated changes of key political figures in the later part of the year and early 2003 may affect the direction and actual outcomes of government policy.

Although the FY2003 budget continues to target a small operating surplus of about 2.6% of GDP, an overall deficit of about 2.5% of GDP is likely, reflecting higher capital expenditures and a new superannuation scheme for members of parliament. Recent budgets have helped consolidate the fiscal position. However, fiscal sustainability is fragile since debt is still considerable, principal repayments will increase in the coming years, and the economy

is small and heavily reliant on tourism. Any weakening of economic growth quickly impacts government revenues and the fiscal position.

Government debt reached unsustainable levels in the mid-1990s, culminating in a fiscal and economic crisis. A comprehensive economic reform program was initiated in 1996 with an emphasis on restoring fiscal discipline and transforming the economy to become more open and market friendly. External debt was restructured with the signing of the Manila Agreement in September 1998. Although the book value of external debt is still very high, much of it is at concessional rates and so servicing is currently manageable, provided that the fiscal stance remains prudent and economic growth continues. These, in turn, depend on ensuring that the public investments financed by the debt earn adequate economic returns and that the Government continues to pursue policies that support private sector development.

Current debt service commitments are close to the ceilings calculated when the debt restructuring agreement was put in place, so that there is currently little scope for increased borrowing. However, there will be some room to maneuver in the next few years to finance public infrastructure investments, of which the Government has identified several that it considers important in facilitating economic growth. These programs include lengthening the main airport runway on Rarotonga, sealing the runway on Aitutaki, and expanding port facilities to cater to the potential growth of offshore fishing. In relation to the last, there may be scope for negotiating arrangements with potential operators to have them pay for part of the capital costs upfront in return for usage rights.

Reform of the tax regime with the introduction of a VAT and reductions in company and income tax rates has been successful in improving economic efficiency and revenue generation. The FY2003 budget announced the raising of the income tax-free threshold from NZ$6,000 to NZ$10,000 for equity reasons, though there is still room to reduce import tariffs to be more consistent with economic efficiency. The Cook Islands has signed the Pacific Island Countries Trade Agreement (PICTA) and the Pacific Agreement on Closer Economic Relations between PICTA signatories and Australia and New Zealand. These agreements are expected to provide the impetus for further tariff reform.

With tourism the key driver of economic activity, environmental sustainability is an important issue. The expenditure allocation for environmental management was increased by 34% in the FY2003 budget. This will support environmental services on the outer islands. Options will also be developed for addressing environmental pressures on the Avaraua foreshore in Rarotonga.

The outer island communities are greatly disadvantaged. The new Government has identified social cohesion and outer islands development as priorities, and the latter received the largest single expenditure allocation in the FY2003 budget. However, the reversal of the devolution policy for agriculture, education, health, and justice has caused some confusion in terms of responsibilities and resource allocation. The outer islands were particularly hard hit by outward migration in the wake of the economic crisis of the mid-1990s and improving the delivery of economic and social services to them will continue to be an important challenge to the Government.

The Government is committed to facilitating the development of a longline tuna fisheries industry, constituting an important diversification as well as boosting growth over the longer term. There are no imminent developments but in the FY2003 budget the Government announced a loan to the Bank of the Cook Islands for NZ$2 million to support investors in commercial longline fishing.

Several major tourism projects to increase capacity are currently being considered by the Government. It is likely that these projects, as well as larger-scale fisheries industry development, will require significant foreign investment and manage-ment. A liberal approach to foreign investment was evident during the economic reform program under the authority of the Development Investment Board, but in its budget policy statement for FY2003 the Government noted that more emphasis is required both to protect business areas reserved for Cook Islanders and to ensure that major foreign investments have local partners.

A new draft investment code was in preparation in 2002 and early 2003. In developing and implementing the new code, it will be important to establish a transparent, consistent, and friendly foreign investment regulatory regime. Requirements that restrict the scope of foreign investment may result in less competition and a slower rate of economic development. The benefits of foreign investment to the local economy occur through employment, tax revenues, and skills transfer.

Outlook for 2003–2004

GDP is forecast to grow by 1.5% in FY2003 and by 3.2% the following fiscal year. These projections assume modest to strong growth in tourism and pearl exports as well as public and private construction activity, and are in line with the long-term performance of the economy. Inflation is forecast to stay in the 3–4 % range in FY2003. Pearl exports are expected to increase steadily to nearly NZ$9 million (or US$4 million) in 2005. However, total imports will continue to exceed exports, resulting in persistent trade deficits. The large surplus on the services trade account will help achieve a sustainable current account balance, with tourism receipts forming the bulk of services income.

Fiji Islands

Economic growth stayed on course in 2002 with tourism continuing to recover from the low of 2000 but with the sugar industry remaining depressed. Key issues that need to be resolved include the long-standing problems of low levels of private investment, insecurity of land tenure, and restructuring of the sugar industry. The outlook is for growth to continue in the medium term, but maintenance of sociopolitical and macroeconomic stability remains critical for this.

Macroeconomic Assessment

GDP increased by 4.4% in 2002, following growth of 4.3% in the previous year. This encouraging performance followed a weakening in the economy in 2000 associated with the effects of political instability and civil disorder. The tourism subsector again grew strongly, with visitor arrivals on a par with the record year of 1999. Several major conferences and sporting events were hosted. The perception in the global tourism market that the country was a safe location due to global and regional security concerns also appeared to have benefited the country.

Growth was broad based, weakened mainly by the poor performance of the sugar, forestry, and financial subsectors. The fisheries subsector grew by 8.0% following a 25.0% surge in 2001, supported by new export markets in Asia. As a whole the agriculture, forestry, and fisheries sector recorded modest growth of 1.1%. Manufacturing grew by 3.9%, while construction activity expanded by 8.0%, mainly as a result of public investment projects. The trade, restaurant, and hotel subsector grew by 8.6% supported by both tourism and resilient local demand. The transport and communications subsector also continued to perform well, expanding by 7.3%. On the other hand, the sugar industry continued to be beset by land lease, quality, and transportation problems and mill inefficiencies.

Labor market conditions improved in 2002, reflecting the overall economic expansion. This represents a significant improvement over 2000 and 2001 when a large number of workers (some 9,000 in the period from May 2000 to end-2001) were laid off as a result of the political instability and civil disorder. The Inland Revenue Department reported a substantial increase in registered taxpayers in 2002 and results from employment surveys indicate improved conditions. Firms' recruitment intentions remained optimistic in several services subsectors. However, skilled professionals are still emigrating and this is creating difficulties for some subsectors, such as education and health.

Notwithstanding overall expansion, private investment continued to be weak, prolonging the trend of the last decade although there were signs that investor confidence was improving in 2002. Many private sector projects remained in the pipeline. Infrastructure constraints and uncertainty related to an important court case about constitutional aspects of the Government seem to be holding back these projects.

For 2002 as a whole, exports increased by 3.6%, reflecting a rise in gold exports. This is a continuation of a recovery that started in the previous year. Total merchandise imports increased by about 9.8%, due largely to increased imports of minerals and fuels, and machinery and transport equipment. The merchandise trade deficit worsened and, together

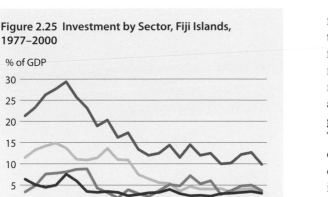

Figure 2.25 Investment by Sector, Fiji Islands, 1977–2000

% of GDP

— Total   — Private   — Government   — Public enterprise

Source: Reserve Bank of Fiji, *Quarterly Review*, September 2002.

with higher private services and investment income outflows, contributed to a widening of the current account deficit to 5.0% of GDP from 3.6% a year earlier. The capital account surplus contracted significantly, reflecting higher statutory debt payments, lower short-term private capital inflows, and a sharp decline in the short-term credit balance. As a result, foreign reserves declined in 2002. However, at end-2002, reserves were still able to cover 3.4 months of imports of goods and nonfactor services or 5.1 months of imports of goods alone.

During 2002, the Fiji dollar depreciated slightly against the basket of trading partner currencies. The real effective exchange rate index fell by 0.6%, implying a slight improvement in international competitiveness. The inflation rate for 2002 was low, with the yearly average falling to 0.9% from 4.3% for 2001. This outcome reflects the low inflation rate of trading partners as well as the absence of oil price pressures in the domestic market.

Monetary policy continued to focus on maintaining low inflation and ensuring adequate foreign exchange reserves but, with a favorable outlook for these variables, remained accommodative to help stimulate aggregate demand. In December 2001–November 2002, broad money increased by 10.2%. In the same period, total domestic credit expanded by 9.4%. Liquidity levels in the banking system remained high and interest rates declined slightly.

The authorities maintained a highly expansionary fiscal stance in 2002, as seen in a net budget deficit (including asset sales) of 7.0% of GDP

following a deficit of 6.5% in 2001. This was higher than expected, reflecting both higher expenditures for public service remuneration and lower tax revenues, particularly from direct taxes. While total revenues (excluding asset sales) changed marginally, total operating expenditures rose by 5%. Total government capital investment increased by 40.0%. The deficit (excluding asset sales) amounted to 8.5% of GDP in 2002 and, as a result, the government debt widened from 43.8% of GDP in 2001 to 46.0% in 2002.

Policy Developments

The developments described above imply that the Government has achieved success in addressing the macroeconomic consequences of the political instability and civil disorder of 2000. Growth has recovered and most macroeconomic parameters have improved. However, the strengthened performance partly reflects the strong fiscal stimulus and accommodative monetary policy of the past 2 years. This raises the issue of growth sustainability.

In this respect, the theme of the 2003 budget, "Securing Sustained Growth", is closely focused on the key issues. A medium-term strategy has been developed to support the theme, and has identified priorities to be addressed in the period 2003–2005. These include maintaining macroeconomic stability, raising investment, promoting security and national unity, implementing structural reforms to promote competition and efficiency, reducing poverty, implementing affirmative action and ensuring social justice, and improving governance.

In an attempt to secure greater macroeconomic stability, the Government is targeting a net deficit of 4.0% of GDP for 2003. The medium-term target for the debt-to-GDP ratio is 40.0% by the end of 2005. The 2003 budget contains measures to both strengthen revenues and restrain expenditures. The major revenue-raising measure announced was an increase in VAT from 10% to 12.5%. Together with some excise tax and tariff increases, this will mean an increase in indirect tax revenues of 30%. Operating revenues are estimated to increase by 15.8% in 2003, constituting the major element in the estimated deficit reduction. The previously proposed reduction in corporate and personal income tax rates from 32% to 30% was postponed. On the expenditure side, total expenditures are estimated

Table 2.23 Major Economic Indicators, Fiji Islands, 2000–2004, %

Item	2000	2001	2002	2003	2004
GDP growth	-3.2	4.3	4.4	5.7	3.6
Inflation rate (consumer price index)	1.1	4.3	0.9	3.0	3.6
Money supply (M2) growth	-2.1	-3.1	10.2	-	-
Fiscal balance/GDP	-3.4	-6.5	-7.0	-4.0	-
Merchandise export growth	-4.2	-8.4	3.6	9.2	8.3
Merchandise import growth	-8.7	-4.2	9.8	10.4	4.9
Current account balance/GDP	-6.3	-3.6	-5.0	-3.7	-1.6
Debt service ratio	3.0	2.0	-	-	-

- Not available.

Sources: Reserve Bank of Fiji, *Quarterly Review,* September 2002; Ministry of Finance and National Planning, *Economic and Fiscal Update, Supplement to the Budget Address;* Fiji Islands Bureau of Statistics, *Fiji Key Statistics,* December 2000; staff estimates.

to increase by 2.2%, comprising a 3.1% increase in operating expenditures and a 9.1% reduction in capital expenditures from a relatively high base of 22.1% of total expenditures in 2002.

To help meet its medium-term target for increasing overall investment to 25% of GDP, the government medium-term fiscal strategy includes raising public investment to 30% of total government expenditures. To help support such investment, the Fiji Investment Corporation is being established to provide capital to start up eligible ventures that have difficulty in raising funds. With ample liquidity in the banking system, the main issue is one of investor confidence in viable investment opportunities, rather than a shortage of funds.

In relation to the investment approval process, the Fiji Trade and Investment Board has attempted to act as a one-stop shop but anecdotal evidence suggests the approval process is still too lengthy. The Foreign Investment Act and investment approval process were reviewed in 2002 and the Government has indicated that it will pursue options to streamline the approval process. The 2003 budget also announced that proposals will be developed to deregulate the superannuation industry and an export credit guarantee scheme is to be established. In the financial sector, the Reserve Bank will add the National Provident Fund to the list of enterprises under its supervisory responsibility. The Bank will strengthen its supervision of the insurance subsector and develop an appropriate super-

visory framework for the superannuation industry as a whole. The Government has also re-engaged Moody's Investors Service to undertake sovereign credit ratings for the Fiji Islands.

To help promote the development of small businesses, the Government has established a National Centre for Small and Micro Enterprise Development. The Centre serves as an umbrella organization and integrates different functions previously carried out by various other departments. In relation to land leases, a formal consultative mechanism will be established on native land to promote efficiency, security, and fairness.

Other key structural reforms relate to the sugar industry, the labor market, competition policy, land reform, and the public sector. A sugar industry task force has been established to identify and pursue reform measures, and a plan to restructure the Fiji Sugar Corporation was endorsed by the Cabinet in 2002. The costs of the restructuring plan are considerable and include F$126 million to upgrade the mills, F$40 million for transport and handling systems, and F$40 million for adjustment assistance for small farmers to leave the industry. There is also the long-term prospect of losing preferential access to the EU market or, at the least, retaining access on less favorable terms. A related issue is the commercial exploitation of the maturing mahogany crop.

In the labor market, reforms will focus on the improvement of linkages between wages, productivity, and skills. Work on a draft National Productivity Plan is under way and a draft Industrial Relations Bill, covering all aspects of employment conditions, will be presented to Parliament in June 2003. In 2002, it was agreed that price controls would be lifted on 146 items and that other price and rent controls would be reviewed in 2003. The institutional arrangements for competition and consumer protection policy as well as the institutional framework for regulation of monopolies would also be reviewed.

Public enterprise reform has been an important government focus for some time. According to the 2003 budget documents, the overall performance of public enterprises improved slightly in 2002. The Government also divested part of its shareholding in Amalgamated Telecom Holdings in 2002 with an initial public offering that was successful in raising F$64.5 million. The Public Enterprise Act is also to be reviewed to ascertain if improvements can be made to the governance framework for public enterprises. The Government confirmed in the 2003 budget that it will continue to support various initiatives to provide for the basic needs of the poor and those living in rural areas.

Outlook for 2003–2004

Since 1987, there has been a trend decline in the ratio of fixed investment to GDP. By 2000, the investment ratio had fallen to about 10%, with the private sector ratio standing at only 3% (Figure 2.25). The economy has experienced an average growth rate of about 2.5% over the past 10 years, and 1.5% since 1985, but this average rate has been characterized by sharp contractions associated with both internal and external shocks. There is a strong relationship between the economy's expansion and that of its major trading partners, highlighting the importance of trade and other economic linkages. Monetary policy has only a marginal influence and fiscal policy an unpredictable impact on GDP growth. Adjustment to short-term supply-side shocks has been relatively quick. The relatively low long-term average growth rate suggests that the government target of sustainable annual overall economic growth of 5.0%, which is well above the trend level, is a challenging task, though the target appears achievable in the short to medium term.

Growth is forecast to accelerate to 5.7% in 2003, reflecting expected good performance by the tourism industry and its flow-on effects. The number of visitor arrivals is anticipated to reach a record level of 426,000, boosted by the South Pacific Games in June 2003, and is projected to stimulate rapid expansion in the trade, restaurant, and hotel subsector, as well as the transport subsector. Construction activity is projected to increase by 9.5%, as construction of major projects continues and as facilities are established for the South Pacific Games. Sugarcane production is projected to decline by 6.4% in 2003 before recovering modestly in 2004. The outlook for nonsugar, agro-based industries, and forestry and fisheries remains favorable. The mining subsector is projected to be very buoyant.

Growth for 2004 is expected to weaken to 3.6% with most sectors recording modest expansion. Tourism is projected to maintain its role as a key source of economic activity, though it is expected to strengthen less rapidly than in 2003. Mining is expected to continue to expand very strongly, and the fisheries and construction subsectors are also projected to register good improvements. Slow growth is projected in the community, personal, and business services subsectors, reflecting the expenditure restraints planned by the Government.

Inflation is projected to increase slightly to 3.0% in 2003 and 3.6% in 2004, partly reflecting the impact of the higher VAT announced in the 2003 budget. The relatively slow global recovery and modest inflation in trading partner countries are expected to help contain inflationary pressures.

Export growth is projected to be 9.2% and 8.3%, respectively, in 2003 and 2004, due to higher receipts from the key export commodities, except sugar and copra. Imports are expected to grow by 10.4% in 2003, largely driven by higher expected domestic demand due to the South Pacific Games. The current account deficit is likely to narrow to 3.7% in 2003 due to the strong anticipated growth in tourism earnings and higher inflows from transportation services; it is then forecast to narrow significantly further in 2004 with a small contraction in the trade deficit and a significant increase in net income from services. Higher direct investment inflows are expected to lead to a widening of the capital account surplus in 2003 and 2004.

Kiribati

GDP growth accelerated in 2002, supported by consumer spending stemming from increases in public sector wages, pre-election government spending, and employment at large development projects. The forecast is for growth to continue, but at a slower rate. A moderate relaxation of the country's fiscal stance will help ensure this outcome.

Macroeconomic Assessment

GDP grew by about 3% in 2002, double the previous year's level. It was supported by consumer spending, which in turn resulted from recent increases in the public sector wage bill, expenditures in the run-up to the national elections in late 2002, and the employment provided by construction work at large development projects. Much of the rise in activity took place on the main island of South Tarawa where most public servants work and where recent development projects have been concentrated.

Tourism continued to be active in the Line Islands and consisted of cruise ship vacationers visiting Fanning Island and sports-fishers flying in from Hawaii to Kiritimati. In the construction sector, the Government funded the building of a power station in South Tarawa, the replacement of much of the water and sanitation facilities in South Tarawa, the completion of smaller sanitation works on the outer islands, and a rural electrification project.

The Government also constructed a $2 million copra mill with state funds, junior secondary schools with funding from the Australian Agency for International Development, and a $5.5 million national sports complex in South Tarawa with financing from the PRC. These infrastructure projects were supplemented by new churches and schools built with church funding and a Japanese-

funded commercial satellite tracking project on the outer islands.

The Bank of Kiribati, under the majority ownership of the Australia and New Zealand Banking Group, went into its first full year of operation, raising service standards and improving internal procedures. In contrast, the establishment of a new power generating plant in South Tarawa failed to produce the expected additional electricity output. A fire damaged the major existing facility and, despite the new plant, most of South Tarawa was subject to power cuts during the day in late 2002.

The private sector was stimulated by consumer spending emanating from these activities and from the national elections held in late 2002. Over the first half of the year, both the country's only commercial bank, the Bank of Kiribati, and the government-run Development Bank of Kiribati reported strong demand for credit for the start-up and expansion of small businesses.

Consumer prices rose by 5.1% during the year, slightly below the previous year's 6.0%. The rise was the result mainly of an increase in the prices of food, beverages, and transport. Kiribati uses the Australian dollar as the local currency and does not operate an independent currency system.

Central government revenues amounted to 119.1% of GDP during the year, lower than the previous year's 148.2% (Figure 2.26). Fishing revenues typically account for half of internal revenues. Income from the overseas investments of the

Figure 2.26 Government Revenues and Expenditures, Kiribati, 1996–2003

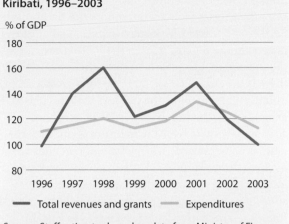

% of GDP

— Total revenues and grants   — Expenditures

Sources: Staff estimates based on data from Ministry of Finance and Economic Planning and the Kiribati Statistics Office.

Government's Revenue Equalization Reserve Fund (RERF), valued at $325 million, and local taxes and duties (mainly on wages and salary income, company profits, and imports) provides the other half.

The expenditure side of the national budget, on the other hand, was 125.0% of GDP in 2002, also lower than the 133.2% of the previous year. Many expenditures went into increases in the public sector wage bill. In fact, the recurrent budget, of which wages form the largest part, had risen by more than 20% in real terms over the period 2001–2002. The overall budget ended with a deficit equal to 5.9% of GDP, against the previous year's surplus of 15.0%.

Merchandise exports expanded to $4.2 million during the year, from $3.8 million in the previous year. Export products consisted of copra, live fish for aquariums, and seaweed. The price of copra, the country's main export, rose during the year, although production levels have been down since 2000, to about 7,000 tons, from a high of 12,500 tons in 1999. Live fish for aquariums as well as seaweed sold into healthy markets during the year, though the former is now facing a trend decline in stocks in some areas.

In 2002, merchandise imports rose to $35.9 million, from $31.5 million in the previous year, due to imported infrastructure components and materials, as various government projects moved from the planning to the construction phase. Improved consumer demand accounted for addi-

tional imports. With the substantial deficit in the balance of trade, along with a substantial deterioration in the net transfers balance, the current account turned negative for the first time in 8 years to reach a deficit of 6.5% of GDP.

Policy Developments

Fiscal management in Kiribati has historically been prudent and has provided for a large buildup in external reserves. During the 1990s, the only deficit was in 1996 and this was attributable to a shortfall in revenues arising from a large but temporary drop in fishing license fees. The value of the Government's overseas investments in its RERF has declined slightly in recent years as returns have eased on world stock markets, but remained high at approximately $325 million or $3,700 per person as of the end of 2002. This RERF provides both an important buffer against fluctuations in revenues and a source of funding for development expenditures. One of the major issues facing economic management is the future use of the Fund's reserves, with a good case existing for additional expenditures to improve infrastructure, and health and education services.

There are indications of the adoption of a more expansionary fiscal stance. In particular, the 2002 budget provides for substantial increases in the public sector wage bill additional to the 15% rise mandated in the 2001 budget. There is also evidence of government willingness to accept significant fiscal risks, as shown notably in the development of the copra mill and the extension into international routes of the government-owned airline.

The appointment of a new president and installation of a new Government is expected to be completed before mid-July 2003, and this resulted in the deferral of the release of the 2003 budget to early August. In this context, it will take some time for the fiscal stance of the new Government to become clear, and this is the key development to monitor over the medium term.

Concern has been expressed for some time that the absence of a second commercial bank is leading to some abuse of market power by the existing bank, with adverse consequences for service standards and interest rates. The problem is reflected in recent rates of return on equity in the order of 100%. Steps were taken during 2002 to provide the legislative framework required to allow the entry of competition. The completion of this regulatory package could do much to provide for either the entry or threat of entry of new competition. Either way, this should lower charges and/or increase deposit rates and raise the contribution of the financial sector to the economy.

Outlook for 2003–2004

The forecast is for GDP to grow at around 2.5% in 2003 and 2.3% in 2004, both lower than the 2002 growth rate. The attainment of these goals rests heavily on developments in the public sector, whose expenditures typically rise to 130% of GDP. Projections for 2003, based on official data, imply a fall in revenues to 99.7% of GDP as well as a reduction in expenditures to 112.6% of GDP. This would give rise to a fiscal deficit of 12.9% of GDP. These projections notwithstanding, recent developments suggest that internal revenues are likely to remain high, or at least not fall sharply from recent levels.

Development expenditures are also expected to remain firm over the medium term as the work on the various infrastructure projects begun in 2002 continues. Some of the activities on these projects, including those on the new national sports complex and the water and sanitation works in South Tarawa, are scheduled to last beyond 2004 and there is the prospect that work will commence on outer island rural electrification and water supply projects. This suggests that a substantial economic contraction is unlikely over the medium term. However, to minimize the impact of any contraction, the fiscal stance needs to be relaxed. This may require regular drawings from the savings held in the RERF (and not just the income that is generated from the Fund). While there is the risk that over time this may result in an undue enlargement of the public sector, increased expenditures would have a beneficial effect on economic activity over the medium term. Unfortunately, the Government's investment revenues are likely to diminish in 2003 as world stock markets weaken in reaction to risks associated with the conflict in Iraq, implying that the Government must find other, perhaps domestic, sources to sustain revenue collection.

The outlook for foreign trade is somewhat brighter than it has been. Exports are expected to increase to $5.1 million in 2003, though achieving this forecast rests heavily on developments in the copra industry. The recent improvement in world copra prices and the scheduled completion of the new copra mill in mid-2003 should help provide a somewhat improved outlook for copra in the medium term.

Imports are forecast to rise slightly to $36.6 million in 2003, with many imports related to the various infrastructure projects initiated in 2002. Still, the current account balance should post a surplus of $0.5 million, or equal to 1.1% of GDP, because of expected receipts from services.

Republic of the Marshall Islands

The economy continued to recover in 2002 after a long period of weakness. It benefited both from a tempo-rary boost in Compact funding (while negotiations were under way for new Compact arrangements) and much lower debt service commitments. The outlook for 2003 is similar to the outcome for 2002, but prospects will be driven by the level and nature of future Compact funding.

Macroeconomic Assessment

Economic growth accelerated somewhat to 4.0% in FY2002 (ended 30 September 2002) from around 2.0% in FY2001 (Figure 2.27). This followed a period of weakness related to fiscal contraction in 1996 1997 and adverse weather conditions. Copra production increased with the support of higher prices and significant subsidies. The primary sector also benefited from higher income from fish exports generated from a tuna processing plant. Construction was supported by sizable public investment projects. Government expenditures rose by around 4.0% of GDP in FY2002 (ended 30 September 2002), reflecting a much stronger fiscal position and providing general support to the economy. With a general wage freeze in place, the rise in such expenditures reflects the filling of vacant positions, creation of new positions, and capital spending. The transport, communications, and trade subsectors benefited from a general strengthening in economic activity. Inflation increased slightly to about 2%.

The fiscal position improved substantially in FY2002 as debt service commitments were greatly reduced following the repayment of outstanding commercial loans and bonds in FY2001. Principal repayments peaked in FY1999 but still amounted to around $25 million in FY2001. Debt service commitments relative to exports of goods and net services and net income receipts declined to

a manageable 8.0% in FY2002. The high level of these commitments in recent years has meant that the Government had to achieve substantial budget surpluses and draw down on its financial assets to meet the principal repayments. The fiscal position also benefited from a temporary boost in Compact of Free Association funding while a new agreement was being negotiated.

The Government receives considerable direct budget support and other forms of assistance from US federal government programs under Compact provisions. In FY2002, for example, grant funding amounted to 70.4% of total government revenues and grants. Nearly a third of the annual funding is earmarked for development spending on Kwaja-lein atoll and for rent payments to landowners on the atoll, in return for land use by the US. Separate compensation payments related to past US activities are made to families and communities of several atolls from a US-financed trust fund. The trust fund has dwindled in recent years, reflecting a combina-tion of mounting claims and low returns.

The first 15-year phase of the Compact expired in September 2001 and the provisions for the next phase were being negotiated in FY2002 with expectation of finalization by September 2003. The Compact provides for 2 years of interim financing. These funds, known as "bump-up" funds, are equiv-alent to the average of funding for the first 15 years and will be available for both FY2002 and FY2003.

Local revenue generation has been relatively

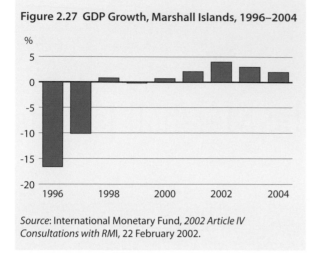

Figure 2.27 GDP Growth, Marshall Islands, 1996–2004

Source: International Monetary Fund, *2002 Article IV Consultations with RMI*, 22 February 2002.

poor in recent years, reflecting the weak state of the economy. However, FY2002 saw some recovery with total domestic revenues strengthening by 7.8%. Income taxes declined but revenues from gross revenue taxes, import duties, and fees from fishing rights rose significantly. Total expenditures increased from around 65% to 70% of GDP but, as the Government met its commitment to contain wage rises, an overall surplus of about 9% of GDP was realized. The Government used the surplus, plus some financial assets, to make a significant contribution to the Marshall Islands Intergenerational Trust Fund of $15.5 million, or around 14% of GDP in FY2002, and made a commitment to allocate a similar amount to the Fund in FY2003.

Local conditions are the major factors in determining interest rates, despite the use of the US currency and absence of exchange controls. Interest rate margins have been around 7–12% for many years. Real interest rates for loans continued to be very high in 2002 at around 17% for consumers and 9% for businesses. The Bank of Hawaii closed its operations in late 2002, leaving only the Bank of Guam and the Bank of the Marshall Islands providing commercial banking services.

The country's export base is very limited, with estimated exports of only $10 million in FY2001 compared with imports of nearly $50 million. In addition, reexports of diesel fuel associated with Majuro's fishing base constitute the single biggest export and accounted for 70% of total exports in FY2000. Proximity to a major tuna fishing area, good harbor facilities, duty-free fuel supplies,

reliable power and airline services, and ready availability of supplies in Majuro have led to the establishment of a fishing transshipment base in the town. In 1999, the facilities were expanded with the opening of a local tuna processing plant. Net income receipts, including fees from fishing rights, generate a significant income amounting to about 20% to 22% of GDP and, together with external transfers, have meant that the overall current account has been in substantial surplus for the past 3 fiscal years. Copra still provides the main source of export income on the outer islands.

The country joined the African, Caribbean, and Pacific States grouping and is receiving assistance under the Cotonou Agreement from the EU Center for Development Enterprises. In 2002, it was one of the main beneficiaries of the EU program in the Pacific with support for several activities to establish and promote exports.

In April 2002, OECD designated the country an uncooperative tax haven along with several other jurisdictions. The country was also on FATF's List of Non-Cooperative Countries and Territories. Later in the year, however, the country was removed from the list when the authorities took various steps to improve the transparency of the financial and monetary system.

Policy Developments

In the initial 15-year phase of the Compact, the Government and the economy became very dependent on US funding. However, public investments failed to deliver expected returns and the public sector became bloated and inefficient. The Government also borrowed heavily, using all future funds from the initial phase of the Compact as collateral. This led to a major financial crisis in 1996.

The new Compact provisions are reported to include measures to link funding to fiscal and public sector performance and long-term sustainability. It is also likely that the new Compact will stress accountability. An Intergenerational Trust Fund is supposed to receive Compact and government contributions with the aim of eventually replacing Compact budgetary support.

As a result of the financial crisis in 1996, a major public sector reform program was implemented with the support of ADB. Under the program, the civil service was reduced by about 35% between

1995 and 2000 and other measures were put in place to try to prepare for the possibility of lower assistance under a new Compact. In 2001, another reform program was agreed with ADB with a focus on fiscal and financial management, economic strategy advice, and improvement in the policy environment for private sector development. Budget reforms include the introduction of performance-oriented budgeting, which should start in the Ministry of Education and in the Ministry of Health and Environment in FY2003. In addition, a medium-term budget and investment framework has been developed in conjunction with the preparation of the FY2003 budget.

The reform program is also addressing a number of deficiencies in the structure and administration of the tax system. The income, social security, and health insurance tax systems are highly regressive. With social security and health insurance taxes only applying up to an income level of $20,000 or higher, the overall effective tax rate peaks at around 20% at that income level and then declines. In addition, nonwage incomes and fringe benefits are untaxed. A gross revenue tax of 3% on sales above $10,000, a separate wholesale sales tax of 4% levied by local governments, and a general tariff of 8% all need to be recognized as part of the overall tax system. There are also major enforcement and tax collection problems and anomalies associated with these taxes, including a lack of coordination among various bodies in identifying taxpayers and sharing information. This has led to a public perception of inequity in enforcement and the development of widespread incentives to evade taxes.

In response to these weaknesses, significant efforts were made to strengthen the administrative and enforcement capacity in the Tax Division of the Ministry of Finance in 2002 with more staff, computers, and new accounting systems. In addition, legislation is being drafted to reduce the highly regressive nature of the existing tax system. With nonwage income and fringe benefits not being taxed there is scope to raise more income tax revenues while meeting equity and economic efficiency objectives. The adoption of a broad-based sales tax also offers the potential to increase local revenues. This option is worth considering, particularly in light of the eventual adoption of PICTA.

Outlook for 2003–2004

Economic growth is forecast to slow slightly to 3.0% in FY2003, reflecting the impact of government spending restraint.

Total government expenditures are expected to rise as a proportion of GDP by 1.4 percentage points in FY2003; however, with total domestic and grant revenues to increase by a similar proportion, an overall surplus of 8.8% of GDP is projected. A freeze on general salaries remains in place but an increase has been approved for teachers; they have been left far behind in the pay league as they have been outside the Government's wage-setting regime since 1994.

The future level of Compact funding will continue to drive the economy over the medium term. Negotiations over the level of US funding beyond FY2003 are currently under way and due for completion by September 2003. Should Compact and other external funding be maintained in FY2004 at a similar or slightly lower level than the current one, some weakening in economic growth might be seen. The opportunity to emigrate to the US under the Compact provides an important adjustment mechanism for the economy.

The new Compact funding arrangements are considered to be more performance oriented than in the past and direct the Government's level and pattern of expenditures. However, continued long-term reliance on external funding represents a risk, unless the fundamentals for private sector development are greatly improved. Besides fiscal stability and tax system reform, key structural changes needed to facilitate private sector development are improving general access to land and adopting a more open and streamlined approach to foreign investment. Although actions have been taken to address these constraints, continued efforts are required to ensure that the regulatory environment is as attractive as possible for foreign investors.

Federated States of Micronesia

The economy grew in FY2002, albeit more slowly than the past 2 years. Growth was supported by increased government spending using "bump-up" Compact funds. The consolidated fiscal position conceals the need for the national and all four state governments to make significant fiscal adjustments in view of lower Compact funding expected from FY2004. Growth is projected to pick up in FY2003.

Macroeconomic Assessment

GDP increased by 0.8% in FY2002 (year ended 30 September 2002), following growth of 1.1% in FY2001. With the exception of FY2000, growth has been very weak since the mid-1990s following reductions in Compact of Free Association funding. As the private sector and public enterprises did not expand in FY2002, yearly growth was driven by consolidated government expenditures, which increased by 2.3%. Based on employment data, the manufacturing, distribution, financial, and business services were the only sectors to expand.

At the state level, GDP growth performance varied considerably. The respective growth rates were 6.8% for Kosrae and 3.0% for Pohnpei, and contractions of 1.8% for Chuuk and 2.3% for Yap.

Economic growth in recent years has been driven by high government spending that follows a period of adjustment to the reduction in Compact funds. The governments of the Federated States of Micronesia (FSM) and the US have been negotiating the extent and nature of continued Compact funds since 1999.

The commitments for the first 15 years ended in FY2001 and additional transitional funds (in excess of transfers for FY2001) became available for a further 2 fiscal years while negotiations continued. This transitional funding level is equivalent to the average of funding for the first 15 years—resulting

in an increase equal to $17 million or 7.3% of GDP in FY2002, known as "bump-up" funds.

High government spending continued in FY2002 financed by the contribution to government revenues from bump-up funds and some drawing down of reserves. Despite the fiscal boost, growth has remained weak, reflecting greater fiscal problems in Chuuk and a cautious attitude in the private sector as the Compact is renegotiated.

The consolidated accounts for FSM show an overall budget surplus of 2.4% of GDP in FY2002, following a series of sizable deficits that have averaged 6.8% of GDP since FY1998 (Figure 2.28). Total revenues and grants increased significantly to 69.1% of GDP in FY2002. Tax and nontax revenues (other than grants and fishing access fees) also increased. Total consolidated government expenditures were up to 66.7% of GDP in FY2002, reflecting the dominant role of the public sector in the formal economy.

The Government plays a major role in all states and in the FSM as a whole, though the exact importance of the public sector and its fiscal position vary considerably across the national and state governments. Pohnpei is the only state government where the economy is not dominated by public expenditures, as state government expenditures were 28.7% of total GDP in FY2002. On the other hand, the Government is particularly dominant in Kosrae where total public expenditures were 78% of GDP in the same fiscal year. The private sector continues to be generally characterized by small-

Figure 2.28 Fiscal Balance, Federated States of Micronesia, FY1996–FY2003

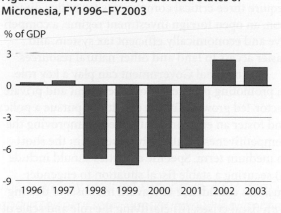

% of GDP

Sources: Department of Economic Affairs, Economic Management Policy Advisory Team, *FSM Economic Review*, October 2002; staff estimates.

scale activities focused on the local market. All four state governments continue to be heavily reliant on grants, although the national Government and Yap have been relatively more successful in raising local revenues.

Exports stagnated in FY2002 and imports declined by about 10%, leading to a narrower trade deficit. The services account also improved slightly, reflecting higher travel receipts and lower payments for freight and insurance. Tourist arrivals increased by 6.7%, following a decline of 18.8% in FY2001. However, fishing access fees (the single most important external income source apart from transfers and travel receipts) declined by 6.7% in FY2002, the third year in a row that a decline has been recorded.

The balance of payments is dominated by official transfers, primarily in the form of Compact receipts, which account for about 70% of all current account payments and indicate the high dependency of the economy on external aid. Official transfers rose by 16.8% in FY2002. Reflecting these developments, the overall current account moved into surplus of 3.7% of GDP, from a deficit of 7.6% of GDP in FY2001. The overall balance of payments also moved into a fairly strong surplus position. Net external debt (adjusted for offshore investments) declined from 17.0% to 15.0% of GDP, continuing a trend that started in FY1993 when net debt peaked at 35.0% of GDP. Debt service costs as a proportion of exports decreased from 36.0% to 8.0%.

Inflation for the country as a whole was negli-

gible in FY2002. Domestic items recorded an overall price decline of 1.4% while imported items showed a rise of only 0.7%. Inflation varied across states with Yap recording a yearly increase of 2.8%, Pohnpei a decrease of 0.5%, and Kosrae a decrease of 4.5% (no data were available for Chuuk). FSM uses the US dollar as its currency, which gives it the advantage of avoiding currency crises and, with its high import dependency, helping keep inflation low.

The Bank of Hawaii closed its operations in the country on 30 November 2002, as part of a broader corporate restructuring. The transfer of the customer base to the other two commercial banks (Bank of the FSM and Bank of Guam) appears to have occurred in an orderly fashion. However, the exit of what was regarded as the most profitable commercial bank in the country could only have impacted adversely on business confidence in 2002 and may raise concerns about future competitive influences.

Policy Developments

The budget surplus for FY2002 masks a deterioration in consolidated government finances reflected in sizable deficits since 1998 and variation in fiscal performance across states. The national Government alone has recorded fiscal deficits in the range of 4–6% of GDP in each year from FY1997 to FY2001 and a smaller but still sizable deficit is expected in FY2003 despite the boost from bump-up funds. The deficits have been financed by using reserves of the national Government. However, unreserved balances are now near zero or negative for the national Government and all state governments, except Yap, where unreserved balances were about $41 million in FY2002, equivalent to about 105% of state GDP. In recent years, Yap, the only state government in a strong fiscal position, has been able to achieve an impressive fiscal record and high standard of public sector management.

According to official government reports, part of the arrangements to secure further Compact funding is for FSM to establish a Compact Trust Fund and contribute $30 million of the additional $34 million in bump-up funds to this Trust Fund. The national Government, as well as the states of Pohnpei and Yap, have set aside adequate funds though Chuuk and Kosrae have failed to do this, with the result that there is currently a net short-

tional standards. The Government has relied heavily on the issuance of the Bank's checks to help fund its budget deficits and royalty payments to landowners, though a lack of liquidity suggests there is very little capacity for the Bank to honor these checks. Needless to say, weak fiscal management is constraining the country's ability to obtain external assistance.

Policy Developments

Attempts to achieve sound economic management are severely hampered by poor-quality planning and budget systems. Budget planning and implementation are haphazard, basic administration is impeded by the breakdown in computing capacity, and public accountability is extremely weak. Budget documents are usually treated as confidential and are not made available to the general public, while the accounts of public enterprises and trusts are typically out of date or nonexistent.

As time progresses, the Government has fewer options to fund its continuing budget deficits. In the past, loans have been acquired from official external sources, overseas corporations, the local bank, and drawdowns from the NPRT. However, the ability to secure new funds is seriously impaired by the absence of adequate collateral, local liquidity, or future revenue sources. In FY2002 (ended 30 June 2002) a deficit of as much as $20 million was budgeted, but it was unclear how this was to be funded. The actual budget outcome is unknown. In addition, the FY2003 budget was deferred with supply bills issued to cover government operations.

Both ADB and AusAID have given assistance to the Government to lay the groundwork for improved performance. More recently, assistance has been provided for economic management, the reform of the budget system, the reestablishment of banking services, and the restructuring of the NPRT. However, this assistance has had little impact due to a lack of political commitment to change and the very limited technical capacity available in the bureaucracy. The latter is mostly attributable to a shortage of Nauruans with appropriate skills, frequent and extended absence from work of senior bureaucrats, and a shortage of funding for government positions.

Outlook for 2003–2004

The medium-term outlook for the economy has recently improved. In December 2002, the Government of Australia agreed to provide a further $9.0 million in development aid. Of this amount, approximately $6.4 million is to be directed to essential infrastructure, including power and water supplies, as well as to health and education. The Government also agreed to continue activities in the camps for asylum-seekers. While the international community welcomed the installation of a new administration in January 2003, the growth path will depend on the new Government's ability to adopt major fiscal improvements and effect structural changes in the economy.

Immediate priorities for the new Government include: (i) reducing large budget deficits, principally by restructuring the public sector wage bill and containing the high cost of overseas representations; (ii) establishing a mechanism to reorganize the Nauru Phosphate Company, achieve the company's financial viability, and extract its remaining resources; (iii) improving management and restructuring the portfolio of the NPRT; (iv) introducing appropriate legislation to encourage the operation of a reputable commercial bank and to restructure Air Nauru; and (v) repaying existing arrears to government suppliers and lenders.

With a new Government, international confidence has gradually reemerged, partly because the new president was a supporter of previous reform efforts. However, his sudden death in early March 2003 has heightened uncertainties with regard to the future of the country, including the possibility of securing additional financial and technical support from external agencies. Elections for a new government are scheduled for May 2003.

Papua New Guinea

Outside the mining and oil sectors, economic activity increased in 2002 as improved conditions in the agriculture sector, election campaigning, and a relaxation of fiscal policy boosted consumer spending. Continued expansion will rest heavily on the Government's ability to reduce structural constraints and risks to macroeconomic stability, as well as on renewed international support.

Macroeconomic Assessment

GDP fell by 0.5% in 2002, in the prolongation of a recession from 2000 and 2001, when GDP contracted by 1.2% and 3.4%, respectively (Figure 2.29). The fall in 2002 stemmed mainly from the continued contraction of the mining and oil sector, which accounts for above 20% of GDP. However, the nonmining sector grew by 2.4%, after contractions of 0.5% in 2000 and 4.2% in 2001. The improvement in the nonmining sector is in part a result of a turnaround in the prices of key agricultural commodities, notably palm oil, cocoa, and, to a lesser extent, coffee. Construction shrank by 2.1% in 2002. Overall, the decline in economic activity occurred despite both a rise in consumer demand in the nonmining sector due to political campaigning in the lead-up to the national election of June–July 2002 and the stimulus provided by a large budget deficit.

As of end-June 2002, the recorded budget deficit was equal to the budgeted deficit for the full year. High government expenditures in the first half of 2002 were accompanied by the release of considerable funds held over from previous years in the trust funds of parliamentarians. Stronger domestic expenditures lifted manufacturing output by an estimated 7.5% over the year, as it did the transport and services sectors to a degree. This surge in activity, however, was largely met with existing capacity. Consequently, business investment outside the mining and oil sector remained subdued, with business lending from commercial banks declining by approximately 4% as of September 2002 over the year earlier level. In August 2002, the new Government announced an impending budget deficit for 2002 of 7.7% of GDP and brought in a supplementary budget to correct the fiscal position. The supplementary budget set a revised deficit target of 3.4% of GDP, which was subsequently revised to 3.8% of GDP. The budget deficit was funded entirely by domestic resources. The need to repay extraordinary finance from previous structural adjustment programs and rising debt repayment obligations on concessional loans led to negative external financing for 2002 in the order of 0.7% of GDP.

The Bank of Papua New Guinea (BPNG) reacted to downward pressure on the local currency, the kina, by selling its international reserves and buying kina. The combination of selling reserves and the absence of a net inflow of external financing produced a marked decline in international reserves in the second half of the year, from US$490 million by end-June 2002 to less than US$350 million by end-December.

The central bank's intervention helped keep the kina reasonably steady against the US dollar for much of the year, but did little to stem a decline against the Australian dollar near the end of the year. The average value of the kina against the US and Australian dollar in 2002 was 13.6% and 18.2%, respectively, below the average value for 2001.

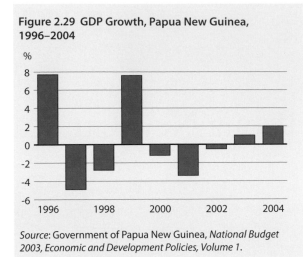

Figure 2.29 GDP Growth, Papua New Guinea, 1996–2004

Source: Government of Papua New Guinea, *National Budget 2003, Economic and Development Policies, Volume 1.*

BPNG tightened monetary policy over the second half of 2002 as improved demand conditions and downward pressure on the kina led to concerns of a prospective rise in inflation. Inflation rose to 11.8% in 2002 from 9.3% in 2001. The key official interest rate, the Kina Facility Rate, was unchanged during the first two quarters of 2002, but increased by 2 percentage points to approximately 14% in the final two quarters. The commercial banks made adjustments with a lag. The weighted average lending rate as of end-2002 was approximately 13.8%, below the 14.6% rate at the start of the year. The weighted average deposit rate was 5.6% as of end-2002, implying a large negative real interest rate.

The commercial banks faced weak private demand for lending in 2002, with private sector credit at year-end 2002 approximately 4.6% below the level at the start of the year. Official liquidity requirements for commercial banks were unchanged over the year, and the banking system remained characterized by high levels of excess liquidity. The money supply (M3) increased by approximately 9.4% over the course of 2002. With private sector credit declining during this period, the rise was attributable to a rise in net credit to government of more than 80% from January to December.

In 2002, total merchandise exports fell by 14.7% from the previous year's level. The decline was caused mainly by a 24.3% fall in oil exports, reflecting the natural decline in output of the major field of Kutubu. While landowner action cut production at one of the major gold producers

(Porgera), and drought reduced shipments from the second major producer (Ok Tedi), gold exports rose by 6.5%, reflecting higher international prices. Agricultural exports rose by 35.5% from the 2001 level, helped by higher world prices for major agricultural commodities. Log exports increased by 16.5%, largely as a consequence of a delayed wet season that improved access to logging areas.

Total merchandise imports fell by 12.8% in 2002, reflecting the depreciation of the kina and continued weakness in the economy. As a result, the trade surplus declined to US$591 million in 2002 from US$717 million in 2001. Combined with higher service payments, the current account deteriorated and turned to a deficit of 1.1% of GDP. The capital account also recorded a deficit, leading to an overall balance-of-payments deficit of K239 million in 2002 (or about US$61.5 million).

Policy Developments

Periods of weak fiscal management that trigger macroeconomic instability have been a feature of the economy since the 1990s, and the medium-term outcome has remained highly dependent on the fiscal stance. After the supplementary budget in the second half of 2002, the 2003 budget marked a further positive step toward fiscal consolidation. The budget announced a commitment to reduce the budget deficit to 2.3% of GDP in 2003 and 1.8% of GDP in 2004.

A small number of new revenue measures were announced in the 2003 budget to help correct the fiscal position, notably an increase in the company tax rate and an emphasis on improved tax compliance. But the improved fiscal stance was to be largely achieved through expenditure measures. Some expenditure cuts were made, notably in goods and services and the education subsidy. The recent growth in the public sector wage bill was to be curbed. In real terms, total expenditures were projected to fall over the medium term.

Whether the tight expenditure targets are achieved depends on the Government's ability to control a tendency to overspending, and great effort will be needed to improve expenditure administration. Initiatives to do this announced in the 2003 budget include the appointment of financial controllers in the larger agencies; a freeze on government engagement of casual and part-time

Table 2.24 Major Economic Indicators, Papua New Guinea, 2000–2004, %

Item	2000	2001	2002	2003	2004
GDP growth	-1.2	-3.4	-0.5	1.0	2.0
Inflation rate (consumer price index)	15.6	9.3	11.8	9.0	5.0
Money supply (M3) growth	7.1	4.2	9.4	9.3	-
Fiscal balance/GDP	-2.4	-3.7	-3.8	-2.3	-
Merchandise export growth	7.3	-13.7	-14.7	-	-
Merchandise import growth	-7.0	9.3	-12.8	-	-
Current account balance/GDP	10.2	9.6	-1.1	-	-
Debt service ratio	10.2	8.2	8.9	9.8	8.4

- Not available.

Sources: Government of Papua New Guinea, *National Budget 2003, Economic and Development Policies, Volume 1*; Bank of Papua New Guinea, *Monetary Policy Statement 31 January and July 2002* and *Quarterly Economic Bulletin*, September 2002; International Monetary Fund, *Staff Report for 2002 Article IV Consultation*, May 2002; staff estimates.

employees; tighter scrutiny of consultancies; more concerted action to contest court cases against the state; introduction of legislation to remove a state obligation to pay for unauthorized expenditures by civil servants; and an intention to take legal action against civil servants who make such expenditures.

Fiscal management is also to be enhanced by the proposed adoption of a medium-term fiscal framework, which is intended to help move the fiscal system from one based on a single-year perspective to one based on a multiple-year perspective, and provide for a smoother flow of resources over time, subject to a hard budget constraint. The fiscal framework is also to be linked to a new medium-term development strategy and, through this strategy, to the country's poverty reduction strategy.

The existing medium-term development strategy provides both a framework for government operations and an identification of high-priority budget areas focused on the delivery of basic services. The priority areas are basic education, primary and preventive health care, maintenance of transport infrastructure, law and order, and private sector development. The strategy provides a sound basis for development planning but effective implementation remains critical. Its success will rest heavily on priority areas of government receiving a preference in the budget process.

Against a background of an enhanced medium-term fiscal framework, the 2003 budget announced

a few new initiatives to help improve private sector confidence. These include the provision of funding for the Highlands Highway, the country's main road; support for small-scale agriculture through microfinance and extension services; and the provision of tax concessions to the mining and oil sector in an effort to promote exploration.

A recovery from the current difficult fiscal situation will also depend on the Government's ability to secure international support, which is important in allowing the central bank to rebuild reserves, in providing a focus for important technical support, and in helping build confidence among private sector investors. The 2003 budget foreshadowed action to secure external deficit financing to reduce the macroeconomic pressures created by the high level of domestic financing, and discussions with the international community have been initiated.

BPNG's own legislation limits it to buying treasury bills for monetary stabilization purposes only and not for deficit financing, but BPNG was, in fact, a source of such financing in 2002, when it breached legislative controls on the provision of short-term finance to the Government via a temporary advance facility. Further, the current status of compliance is obscured by a shortage of published data.

In 2002, BPNG frequently supported the kina with a view to stabilizing prices. The hard line taken on kina stability may be difficult to sustain over the medium term in the absence of any highly favorable economic developments or the early provision of international support. The management by BPNG of the trade-offs it faces will be the key monetary policy development to monitor over 2003.

The falling kina seen in recent years and continued external borrowing have been factors in the ratio of external debt to GDP rising from 31.0% to 46.4% over the 5 years to 2002. This, combined with high domestic interest rates, has raised debt service costs. However, the weaker kina has also boosted the domestic currency value of the large foreign grants and of mining and oil revenues received by the Government. This natural hedge characteristic of revenues and the concessional nature of most of the external debt provides some comfort that the debt position can be sustained in the medium term. However, the Government needs to remain cautious in accumulating additional debt.

Outlook for 2003–2004

GDP is projected to grow by about 1% and 2% in 2003 and 2004, respectively, on the basis of an improved outlook for commodity prices, a trend increase in the output of most agricultural commodities, and prospects of improved macroeconomic stability. These forecasts have been framed on the basis of a steady depreciation of the kina, but at a slower rate than seen in recent years. Consistent with the forecast improvements to the fiscal position, economic activity, and somewhat greater stability of the kina, the forecasts point to a decrease in inflation (to about 5% by 2004) and interest rates. The external current account is expected to remain in deficit in 2003 and turn into a small surplus in 2004. The overall balance of payments is projected to be in deficit both years.

Several important risks to these forecasts should be considered. The nonmining sector faces, in 2003, the contractionary effect of a reduction in the real value of government expenditures and the absence of the boost to private consumption provided by the 2002 election.

Increased private sector activity will rest on confidence in the ability of the Government to deliver on the commitments of the 2003 budget and the proposed medium-term fiscal framework. It also requires confidence that the structural problems, notably law and order problems and the deteriorating road network, will be addressed over the medium term. If BPNG intervenes in the foreign exchange market at the rate it did in the second half of 2002, its international reserves could be largely eroded by the end of 2003.

The increased competitiveness provided by the steady depreciation of the kina since 1994 has initiated some changes. There are some signs of local products displacing imports, particularly in fresh and processed foods, but also in new areas of economic activity (e.g., in oil refining, for which the country's first oil refinery is now being constructed.).

Also, new export-oriented ventures have been established in recent years to draw on the rich natural resource base and on increasingly competitive labor costs (e.g., a tuna factory employing 2,000 women, a slipway attracting ships from the region for maintenance works, and a new palm oil plant).

The most likely source of a favorable economic outcome is continued higher prices for gold and oil. This can provide a boost to government revenues and lessen macroeconomic pressures. The forecasts are based on the assumption that no major new projects, such as the proposed gas pipeline to Australia or the Ramu nickel project, begin construction over the medium term.

Samoa

Growth slowed sharply in 2002 as fishing, agriculture, and construction contracted and impacted the rest of the economy through flow-on effects. Macroeconomic and structural policies are focused on supporting a resumption of annual economic growth to 3–4%. Maintaining macroeconomic stability and deepening reforms remain critical for the long-term sustainability of economic growth.

Macroeconomic Assessment

After recording 2 years of rapid economic growth, the Samoan economy slowed considerably in 2002, especially in the first half of the year. The full-year outturn was 1.3% growth, down from 6.2% in the preceding year (Figure 2.30). There was a sharp contraction in economic activity in the first quarter of 2002, particularly in government-funded construction activity, fish exports, tourism earnings, and agricultural production. Overall economic activity picked up in the second quarter and through the second half of 2002, when fresh fish exports recovered, remittances strengthened, tourism expanded, and construction activity turned up, assisted by an increase in credit to the private sector.

CPI inflation rose from 3.8% in 2001 to 5.5% in 2002, largely reflecting a rise in the prices of local food components, transport, beer, cigarettes, and gasoline in the first half of the year.

The budget for FY2002 (ended 30 June 2002) closed with an overall deficit of 2.1% of GDP, which was better than expected, due to delays in the implementation of some public sector infrastructure projects and higher than expected tax revenues. In FY2002, tax revenues rose by 4.5% but nontax revenues declined by 29%, mainly due to lower cost recovery. External grants increased by 15.5%.

Current expenditures rose by 11.4%, mainly due to a 16% rise in the wage bill, which reflects the upgrading of positions as part of the economic and public sector reform program and the full-year effects of the 5% civil service wage hike implemented from 1 January 2001. Development expenditures declined in FY2002 by 15.3% such that overall expenditures increased by only 3.6%. Education and health continued to be priority sectors. The overall deficit was financed approximately 66% from external, concessional loans and the rest from domestic sources.

Total exports declined by 9.4% in 2002, mainly due to a fall of about 17% in the export value of the two main export commodities, fresh fish and garments. The fish harvest was lower than normal early in the year, and export values were also lower because of weaker prices. The decline in garment exports reflected weaker demand in international markets. Imports were 4.3% higher than in 2001, causing the merchandise trade deficit to widen by 6.1%. However, the current account deficit narrowed from 3.1% of GDP in 2001 to 0.7% of GDP in 2002, reflecting strong growth in remittances.

Tourism also expanded with the participation of visitors in various sporting competitions and the 40th anniversary of Samoa's independence. Net foreign assets increased during 2002 and were sufficient to cover about 4.5 months of imports by the end of the year.

The Samoan currency, the tala, is pegged to a trade-weighted basket of currencies that was reduced from six to five currencies in August 2002 and now consists of the Australian, Fiji, New Zealand, and US dollars as well as the euro. The

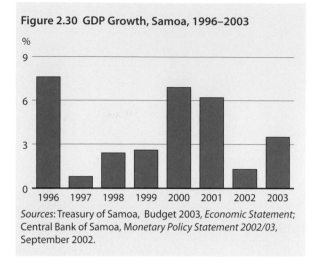

Figure 2.30 GDP Growth, Samoa, 1996–2003

Sources: Treasury of Samoa, Budget 2003, *Economic Statement*;
Central Bank of Samoa, *Monetary Policy Statement 2002/03*,
September 2002.

exchange rate may be changed within a 2% margin of the peg after approval by the central bank board. Between September 2001 and September 2002, the tala depreciated against all the currencies in the basket except the US dollar.

Broad money supply (M2) increased by 9.2% in 2002. Due to the slowdown in the domestic economy, an accommodative monetary policy stance was maintained throughout the year. With recent inflationary impulses related to local factors and expected to be temporary, this stance is appropriate. The weighted average interest rates on commercial bank loans fell by nearly 4 percentage points to 11.2%, while the average interest rate on commercial bank deposits remained at 4.5%, thus narrowing the interest rate spread. Growth rates of commercial bank lending decreased from 21% in the year ending September 2001 to 10% 12 months later.

Policy Developments

The major short-term policy challenge for the Government is to support a resumption of the high economic growth and strong inflation performance of recent years. Concerned about overheating in the economy, the Government deferred the implementation of some of its public investments in 2002, leading to a significant weakening in construction in the first half of the year. With expansionary fiscal and accommodative monetary policies, growth resumed in the second half of the year. The slight increase in the recurrent surplus and decrease in

the overall deficit in FY2003 is a move in the right direction.

While still relatively vulnerable, the Samoan economy has performed strongly in recent years. This performance can be attributed to a combination of growth-enhancing policies, the level of human capital development, natural resources, and some good fortune. Reforms introduced by the Government have made Samoa a more open economy and an easier place in which to do business. Tariff and tax reform and streamlining of business regulations have directly improved international competitiveness. Financial liberalization has made it easier for businesses to access finance and has generally boosted economic activity. Macroeconomic stability has created a more predictable and secure investment climate, while public sector reforms have helped alleviate the potential burden of taxation.

The implementation of the economic and public sector reform program continued making good progress in 2002. After several years of impressive overall economic growth, most policy makers now recognize the need to make greater efforts in redressing widening imbalances between the income levels of people in urban and rural areas. This concern is addressed in the Strategy for the Development of Samoa (SDS) 2002–2004, which emphasizes the theme of "opportunities for all". However, the achievement of macroeconomic stability and sustained economic growth still remains the primary strategic goal, and includes keeping the overall deficit to no more than 3.5% of GDP and the recurrent surplus to no less than 1.0% of GDP. Given the recent budget outcomes and likely prospect of more modest growth than seen in recent years, this will require rigorous control over expenditures, especially current expenditures, and a greater focus on the core functions of government.

In keeping with the Government's commitment to phase out tariffs and widen the tax base, many tax changes were announced in the budget for FY2003 (approved in May 2002). The changes include an increase in the value-added goods and services tax from 10.0% to 12.5%, reducing the import tariff on goods subject to a 10.0% duty rate to 8.0%, increasing excise rates and motor vehicle registration and license fees, and making the commercial fishing sector (above a certain scale) subject to corporate income tax. However, all commercial agriculture, small-scale commercial fishing, and ministers of religion are still exempt from tax, and the commercial fishing sector still does not pay any resource rent. The 2003 budget also announced that there would be duty exemptions for certain business inputs for hotels and for manufacturing. A budget deficit of 1.9% of GDP has been approved for FY2003, consistent with the target and strategies set out in the SDS.

In the area of financial sector reform, the central bank continued to develop its capacity to implement market-based monetary policy through the issue of new securities and improvements in forecasting liquidity in the banking system. With the introduction of 14-day paper in January 2002, six maturity options up to 365 days are now available. The central bank also created two facilities in 2002 that the commercial banks can use to borrow on a short-term basis—direct borrowing against collateral and a repurchase agreement facility.

To promote exports, a government export guarantee scheme, applying initially to goods, was established in 2002 to make it easier for exporters to obtain working capital from the local commercial banks and the Development Bank of Samoa.

The Government's vision of how to proceed with economic and social development goals emphasizes factors that will enhance short- and long-term international competitiveness. Key factors include macroeconomic stability, public sector efficiency, investment in human capital and relevant public goods, and specific interventions to address market failures that constrain key export activities. The Government is particularly concerned in the short to medium term with the role and efficiency of SOEs. Some have been a drain on public finances without providing commensurate benefits and some have high-cost operations that adversely impact the competitiveness of business. The effort launched in the second half of 2002 to develop and implement a program of corporatization and privatization for SOEs is likely to be continued. The Government will continue to develop a policy framework and implement an accountability framework to make a widespread and long-term impact on competitiveness.

Outlook for 2003–2004

Economic activity looks set to grow moderately in 2003–2004, largely reflecting continuing expansionary fiscal and accommodative monetary policies. Ongoing structural reforms and improvement in world economic conditions are also expected to support modest GDP growth in the medium term. Tourism and remittance income should continue to expand in line with expected economic growth in the main source countries. Tourism should also benefit from the perception of the Pacific region as a relatively safe tourist destination.

Agricultural production is expected to improve and the fishing sector should continue to expand as capacity increases. Further growth in construction activity will likely be seen, reflecting public infrastructure investment activity and private housing and other construction activities. All these should ensure the achievement of the SDS growth target of 3–4% in 2003–2004.

The central bank expects that bank credit to the private sector will grow less quickly than in recent years. The increase in VAT is also expected to be more than offset by lower tariffs, an increase in local food supplies, and the ongoing impact of low inflation in trading partners. Accordingly, inflation is forecast to decline to 3–4% in 2003. A small current account deficit of 1.4% of GDP is forecast for 2003, with the growth in imports outstripping the continued growth in commodity exports, tourism revenues, and remittances. The overall balance is expected to weaken slightly in 2003, reflecting lower private capital flows with foreign reserves declining slightly to less than 4.5 months cover for import goods. The main risk to the 2003 forecasts arises from possible deterioration in global conditions and higher oil prices.

In 2004, inflation is expected to rise to about 5% in light of the outlook at home and among the main trading partners. The current account deficit is forecast to remain below 4.0% of GDP and the overall balance of payments in surplus in light of the SDS commitments of the Government and the forecast for continued growth in remittances and tourism.

Solomon Islands

The country is still suffering from the after-effects of the ethnic tension that erupted in mid-2000. The fiscal situation is desperate, and quality of life has plummeted. Restoring the rule of law and achieving macroeconomic stability are the priorities to be tackled for the economy to recover and grow at a sustained rate.

Macroeconomic Assessment

Economic crisis continued to characterize the economy in 2002. GDP declined for the fourth year in a row, although the contraction of 4.0% was much lower than in 2000 and 2001. The economy has contracted by about 26% since 1998. With annual population growth of around 3%, GDP per capita in US dollar terms fell by about half over this period. The recent economic weakness reflects the damage to infrastructure, government functions, and private sector activity caused by the political crisis and violence associated with the coup in mid-2000. Disruption and economic weakness continued after a truce due to the Government's inability to initiate a rehabilitation and reconstruction program, prudently manage its finances, adopt a credible reform program, or restore law and order. The new Government that came to power, following generally peaceful elections in December 2001, has taken some steps to restore public security and stabilize the macroeconomy, but these have been grossly inadequate. The economy remains highly vulnerable to political developments and associated militant activity, social dissatisfaction, fiscal weakness, and problems of a general lack of confidence. The tax base has collapsed and business sentiment is weak.

Logging remains the main economic activity generating foreign exchange and tax revenue, though at a high cost to the environment. Log production, which contributed around 18% of GDP in 2001, was relatively weak in the first half of 2002 but strengthened in the second half with the harvesting of the Government's Alu plantation in Western Province. In the first 9 months of 2002, log production was 1.6% lower than in the same period in 2001. Cocoa production was around 28% higher than a year earlier, reflecting a rise in export prices and an improvement in the law and order situation in some parts of Guadalcanal. The fish catch was 14.2% higher than in the same period in 2001. Fishing exports have resumed with Solomon Taiyo (the only producer for export markets) operating at about 40% of capacity and supported by tax incentives. The financial difficulties faced by the Commodities Export Marketing Authority and Russell Island Plantation Limited have impacted adversely on copra production, which provides cash income for around 85% of the population. Copra growers experienced packaging, transport, and marketing problems, as well as weak prices, in 2002. Resumption of gold mining and of palm oil production is unlikely for at least 12 and 24 months, respectively. Most other sectors remained depressed.

Inflation was 9.0% in 2002, only slightly higher than in 2001. The modest rise, despite significant currency depreciation, reflects weak domestic demand.

Exports increased by 7.7% in 2002 but were still only about one third of their 1999 level. On the other hand, imports declined by 26.5%, the seventh consecutive annual decline, reflecting the general weakness in the economy. As a result, the trade deficit declined substantially and the overall current account recorded a small surplus of 3.0% of GDP. The overall balance of payments recorded a

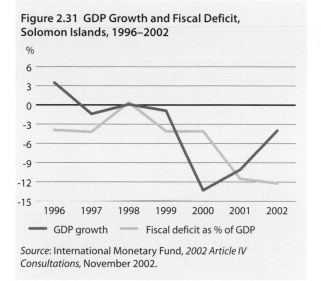

Figure 2.31 GDP Growth and Fiscal Deficit, Solomon Islands, 1996–2002

Source: International Monetary Fund, *2002 Article IV Consultations,* November 2002.

tiny surplus but gross official reserves remained at a level sufficient to cover only 1.5 months of imports of goods and services. By end-October 2002, the currency had depreciated over 12 months by 29.5% against the US dollar. In real effective terms and for 2002 as a whole, depreciation was about 19%.

The fiscal situation remains the most serious concern to macroeconomic stability (Figure 2.31). The overall deficit for 2002 was around 12.2% of GDP. Government arrears built up substantially, to around 19% of GDP at end-2002. In 2002, the public sector payroll was often up to three pay periods in arrears. Central government debt surged to about 110% of GDP in 2002, with external debt standing at 79% of GDP. The Government has generally been unable to meet its external or domestic debt service commitments for the past 2 years.

Restructured government bonds accounted for 27% of the total assets of the nation's commercial banks in mid-2002. The Government defaulted on its restructuring agreement with government bondholders, who included commercial banks, in 2001 and negotiations for a further agreement broke down in early 2002. Unilateral payments by the Government of interest of 3% resumed only in September 2002. As a result, the banks are faced with the prospect of being unable to recover the book value of the bonds or market interest on them.

The financial sector was under extreme stress in 2002, mainly due to the Government's inability to meet debt service commitments. The central bank had to confront a substantial negative equity

position following a write-off of government loans in 2002. The Development Bank of the Solomon Islands also continued to face capitalization problems. However, the situation at the National Provident Fund has improved somewhat with the Government resuming payment of its contributions in May 2002. It too has been significantly affected by the loss of income on restructured government bonds. The foreign partner in the National Bank of the Solomon Islands withdrew in 2002, underlining the seriousness of the country's banking situation.

In September 2002, the weighted average interest rate on commercial bank deposits was 0.6% while the weighted average lending rate on commercial bank loans was 15.6%. This implied an interest rate spread of 15%, and with inflation of around 9%, this represented a very large negative real interest rate. The money supply rose by 5.0%, after a contraction of 13.3% in 2001. The increase occurred toward the end of the year, with shrinkage a feature of the first half of the year. Following a sharp overall reduction in credit in 2001, domestic credit rose in 2002 by about 34.2%, with credit to the Government and private sector growing by 48.2% and 9.3%, respectively. Growth of credit to the private sector, albeit small, provides some sign that economic recovery may be under way.

Policy Developments

The budget for 2002, approved in April, provided for a sharp reduction in the overall fiscal deficit to 3% of GDP, to be achieved by cutting the public wage bill by 30% and only undertaking development spending when that was financed by concessional donor financing. However, public sector employment increased during the year, largely as a result of the recruitment of special constables, higher salaries and allowances for police and high-level officials, and a general lack of progress in achieving payroll reductions. Claims for compensation payments and extraordinary allowances continued to contribute to a compensation and rent-seeking culture in 2002.

Total revenues and grants were only 25.0% of GDP in 2002, compared with 44.4% in 1999, i.e., prior to the crisis. In contrast, total expenditures amounted to 37.2% of GDP, leading to a deficit of 12.2% of GDP for the year. The deficit was the outcome of problems on both sides of the budget. The recurrent budget target for wages and salaries for 2002 was exceeded by 42%. At the same time, external grants were well below their precrisis levels in 2002, although revenue targets of the government for 2002 were largely met through measures such as the revocation of duty and tax remissions, increases in import and excise duties on luxury goods, and improved tax administration. Although the management of government accounts improved, this was not enough to turn the budget around.

The 2003 budget proposed recurrent expenditures of SI$259 million with matching revenues. The budget proposed achieving a large reduction in the government wage and salary bill on the assumption that over 1,000 civil service redundancies would be made with redundancy payments financed by donors. However, in the event, donors appeared reluctant to commit. To improve expenditure management, the budget announced that all capital purchases would be subject to the discipline of the Central Tender Board. It also asserted that unauthorized spending by ministries and officers would not be paid. Compared with a large outstanding debt of above SI$2 billion, the budget proposed a modest effort by providing SI$39 million for debt repayments. The budget also proposed a significant amount for development; this, however, assumed donor support.

The ethnic tension in mid-2000 led to the suspension of a donor-sponsored economic reform program that was providing an important source of external financing. The disruption to civil order and government functions and the lack of agreement over an appropriate reform program meant that this program remained suspended in 2001–2002, adding to the Government's financing problems. In late December 2002, the Minister of Finance resigned. This development is likely to place the fiscal strategy at great risk in 2003.

The absence of corrective government action on the fiscal position can be expected to result in further deterioration in the financial sector, and continuing downward pressure on international reserves and the exchange rate. It will also lead to increasing discontent within the civil service and rising arrears in the business community as well as place further pressure on the financial stability of government entities.

Although progress has been made in improving personal security, there are reports of growing organized crime and continuing militant threats.

Restoring the rule of law and achieving macroeconomic stability are the major priorities that need to be addressed if economic recovery is to be seen and sustained. The pursuit of various structural reforms such as tax reform, public enterprise reform, and measures to streamline investment and business regulations, although important over the longer term, is unlikely to yield success until these short-term priorities are effectively tackled.

Outlook for 2003–2004

Lack of data constrains a credible analysis of future trends. A modest economic recovery of 2–3% is forecast for 2003 assuming reasonable progress in achieving fiscal stability. Continued growth of exports of timber, fish, copra, and cocoa are projected to be the mainstay of economic activity in 2003. Inflation is projected to moderate slightly to 8% as the supply position improves. The external current account is forecast to record a small surplus, but this also assumes substantial official transfers. Gross official reserves are forecast to remain at critically low levels. It will require strong political will and a remarkable turnaround in fiscal management to meet the projections made in the 2003 budget. However, central government external and domestic debt is forecast to decline slightly relative to GDP.

After contraction of overall economic activity of some 26% over the past 5 years, the complete loss of gold and palm oil exports, and a reduction in overall exports by about two thirds, it is unlikely that continued significant contraction will occur. However, the risks to growth are clearly on the downside given the precarious fiscal situation and the recent record of the Government, political instability, and the uncertain outcomes for public security. The more likely upshot is that the economy continues to experience a fiscal crisis in 2003 with the flow-on effects tending to offset gains made from growth of exports. Although there is obviously considerable uncertainty about the outlook for 2004, it is likely that the current weakness will continue.

Over the medium and longer term, the authorities will need to secure fiscal surpluses for a long period until arrears have been paid off and debt has reached more sustainable levels. Economic growth is unlikely without significant financial assistance from donors to restore infrastructure and recapitalize the financial sector.

Democratic Republic of Timor-Leste

As the international presence in the country continued to scale down in 2002, the economy contracted and public program implementation encountered difficulties. Weak conditions are expected to continue in 2003 before a possible turnaround in 2004. The main risks in the medium term come from continued delays in implementing public programs and, to a lesser extent, from a resurgence of civil unrest.

Macroeconomic Assessment

The country's GDP is estimated to have contracted anywhere between 1% and 3% in 2002 (Figure 2.32). The first figure is an estimate of IMF and the second of the Banking and Payments Authority of Timor-Leste. Statistical collection in Timor-Leste is extremely limited and making precise estimates is an almost impossible task. The contraction is inferred from the fact that domestic demand declined, following 2 years of high demand and high growth as the economy was rebuilt after the violence of 1999.

United Nations-funded activities and numbers of staff from international organizations were being progressively reduced and the implementation of development projects suffered severe delays during the year. These factors reduced the injection to the economy provided by the expenditure of individuals from international organizations present in the country and the contribution to demand from public programs.

The decline in activity in 2002 has been most marked in construction, where the slow pace of development project implementation and, to a lesser extent, the tapering off of reconstruction work in the private sector took its toll. The services sector, particularly the restaurant and hotel subsectors concentrated in Dili, was also adversely affected by the winding down of the international presence. However, the agriculture, commerce, and transport sectors are estimated to have expanded in 2002, stimulated by the infrastructure and transport systems, increased availability of seeds, and the major repairs to farming equipment. It is estimated that in 2002 output of important food crops (excluding rice) had returned to pre-violence levels.

With only 3.2% of the labor force employed in the public sector and only 6.1% in private, formal businesses, most people rely on the informal sector for their livelihood. The contraction in the formal sector is expected to have increased the unemployment rate, estimated at 16.8% in 2001. Unemployment among young people is particularly high and is estimated to be in the order of 40% in the main urban centers.

There are indications of a reduction in typical working hours over the year and a gradual downward adjustment in wage rates. Nonetheless, wage rates remain substantially higher than before the violence and than those prevailing in neighboring countries—a consequence of the large injection to demand provided by the international presence since 1999. This labor market situation, combined with a risky investment environment, has hindered expansion in the formal sector.

The inflation rate is estimated to have decelerated to around 1.0% in 2002, the fall attributable to the increased availability of locally produced food items and the easing in demand as the international sector contracted.

Gross investment is estimated to have fallen

Figure 2.32 GDP Growth, Democratic Republic of Timor-Leste, 1996–2004

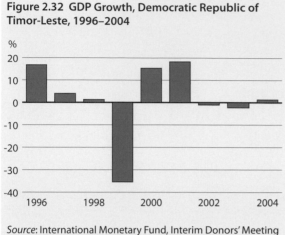

Source: International Monetary Fund, Interim Donors' Meeting on Timor Leste, *IMF Staff Statement*, 9–10 December 2002.

from 25% to 21% of GDP in 2002, with much of the decline explained by the contraction in donor-funded public sector investment.

Preparation for the adoption of normal central bank functions continued in 2002, focusing on the implementation of the financial and institutional autonomy of the Banking and Payments Authority (BPA) of Timor-Leste. Interim appointments have been made to the BPA's governing board. Bank deposits are estimated to have grown over the year by 15.4%, but the formal financial sector remains small and largely limited to two foreign-owned commercial banks and currency exchange bureaus. Given the limited local investment opportunities, most bank deposits are invested offshore. An ADB-administered project in microfinance is helping meet local lending needs.

Government internal revenue collections and grant funds that are provided as budget support are channeled through the Government's Consolidated Fund. Expenditures from this Fund were estimated at about 14% of GDP in FY2002 (ended 30 June 2002), and include 3.0% of GDP in capital expenditures. Additional funds are provided by the international community through the medium of the Trust Fund for East Timor (TFET) and bilateral development projects under the broad category of UN Assessed Contributions. The latter includes UN-funded activities that are not taken up by the Government, such as peacekeeping costs and commissions to the World Bank. In FY2002, Consolidated Fund expenditures accounted for

$53 million or 6.5% of the total estimated public expenditures of $810 million. A further $57 million was to be funded from the TFET, $110 million from bilateral development projects, with the remainder from the UN Assessed Contributions.

Consolidated Fund expenditures have steadily increased over time. However, in terms of the aggregate impact on GDP, this expansion has been neutralized by contraction in other sources of public expenditures. The Consolidated Fund was officially reported as having a deficit in FY2002 equivalent to 5.6% of GDP. However, this estimated deficit is calculated on the assumption that grants are a financing item. When the budget balance is defined according to standard international practice, the budget is seen to have been in surplus in FY2002, equivalent to 3.0% of GDP. This surplus is consistent with the accumulation over FY2002 of both cash reserves in the Consolidated Fund and assets in the Timor Sea Account, a trust fund in which royalties and interest income from oil developments are being accumulated.

Imports are estimated to have fallen by 28.6% in 2002 to $170 million as domestic demand contracted. While merchandise exports, excluding oil, are estimated to have risen by 25.0%, they are low at approximately $5 million, and largely limited to one crop—coffee. The lower level of imports led to a narrower deficit on the trade balance, though the current account deficit increased.

Policy Developments

The Government has been successful in achieving a prudent fiscal stance despite strong pressures to spend. Much of this success can be traced to the effort to keep the confidence of the international community that has provided a substantial commitment to funding over the medium term. The Government has secured foreign grants of about $20 million to $30 million per year, to be provided as direct budget support. These grants, combined with internal revenue collections, are projected to provide a substantial budget surplus on the Consolidated Fund over the medium term, when the budget balance is defined in accordance with standard international practice. An implication is that the Government is in the position of being a net saver, and will continue to accumulate assets in the Timor Sea Account over the medium term. This accumulation is expected to allow for a steady decline in foreign grant support.

The Government has also had significant success in managing the composition of expenditures, with a high share of its Consolidated Fund allocated to the priority areas of education and health. It is expected that in FY2003, 35% of the core budget will be allocated to these two sectors, with almost half the education budget going to primary education and some 45% of the health budget spent on hospital care.

The planning and budgeting system is still in the early stages of development and some problems are being faced in implementing the Government's policy framework, particularly in reducing high subsidies to the power sector. The power sector was restarted under the UN administration, prior to a mechanism for revenue recovery being put in place, and the sector has relied on large budget subsidies. This arrangement has proven strongly regressive and mainly benefits richer members of the community in the large urban areas. In FY2002, of the 20% of the government expenditures allocated to economic services, more than half went to power. Difficulties in implementing a cost recovery program and in introducing an external operator are expected to almost double the subsidies in FY2003 from $3.6 million to $6.1 million. This increased call on government funds is having the adverse effect of displacing expenditures on wages as well as goods and services (excluding those relating to health and education).

Difficulties are also being faced in the execution of the Government's expenditure programs. Over the first 4 months of FY2003, expenditures from the Consolidated Fund on goods and services and capital expenditures were 62% and 25% of expected levels, respectively. These shortfalls are attributed to expected delays in the preparation and presentation of capital expenditure plans, poor procurement planning, and an unsound understanding of procurement procedures. Increased training of line agency staff and technical support is planned for FY2003, so as to increase the rate of commitment.

Outlook for 2003–2004

While the continued phasing down in international presence is expected to induce a further contrac-

tion in economic activity in 2003 by about 2%, the medium-term economic outlook depends heavily on both the level and efficiency of public sector expenditures. Improved conditions are expected in 2004, with IMF-projected expansion in GDP of approximately 1% and an inflation rate of 2–3%.

The main risk to this outlook is the prospect of a shortfall in public expenditures. One potential cause will be any delay in the implementation of relevant public programs. Delays appear likely in government-funded activities, due to a lack of familiarity of government employees with expenditure systems and the reallocation of funds to the power sector subsidy. The finalization of donor country strategies is likely to take some months and to delay the execution of bilateral projects, which amount to close to 25% of GDP.

Revenue pressures may also lead to some reduction in expenditures. Some indications appeared in early FY2003 of a shortfall in domestic revenues arising from the slowdown in economic activity. In particular, indirect tax collections were adversely affected by the fall in import demand. To help correct for the shortfall, a supplementary allocation planned by the Government was cut by some 50% to $4 million.

A further risk to the medium-term outlook is the potential disruption to agricultural production caused by drought. The rainy season started late, in December 2002, and this may adversely affect the planting cycle for the main staples of maize and rice. Food shortages are widespread during the wet season, and delayed and low-quality planting may add to the seasonal difficulties. A decline in food production would also tend to raise inflation and exacerbate the expected contraction in GDP.

Long-term investment has been difficult to secure due to the economy's high cost structure and a poorly developed legal framework. Any recurrence of violence and sporadic public disturbances will further dampen prospects for investment. Civil unrest in early December 2002 saw a state of emergency declared, the deaths of several protestors, and the destruction of some property in Dili. Addressing the internal tensions that fueled this incident and providing a stable environment of law and order will be crucial in creating a business-friendly atmosphere in the country and in attracting the foreign investment needed to redevelop the economy.

Tonga

The macroeconomic situation remained difficult in 2002, with fairly weak growth, a surge in inflation, and a deterioration in the fiscal position. However, the squash season was exceptional, remittances rose signifi- cantly, and the Government made progress in implementing its comprehensive Economic and Public Sector Reform Program. Prospects are for economic performance to improve somewhat over the next 2 years.

Macroeconomic Assessment

The economy grew by only 1.6% in FY2002 (ended 30 June 2002), the second consecu- tive year of poor performance. The squash season was exceptional, though production of root crops was weak, a reflection of the damage inflicted by cyclone Waka. Fishing was hampered both by poor weather and by lack of transport capacity, though construction and mining expanded strongly due to infrastructure building related to cyclone damage. The tertiary sector grew by a meager 0.6%, reflecting a decline in the commerce, restaurants, and hotel subsector and low growth in government services. After an initial fall due to reduction in air access to and from the US and the cyclone, tourism recovered in the second half of the calendar year 2002, leading to a 2% rise over the preceding year.

Employment mirrored the weakness of the economy. Although around 2,000 young people leave school to look for work every year, only about 500 find jobs, mostly in the formal sector, and only a few can emigrate. Thus, the number of educated unemployed and underemployed is growing. This is contributing to a rise in crime and other social problems.

Inflation rose steeply to 10.4% in FY2002, up from 6.9% in the previous year (Figure 2.33). Infla- tionary pressures were the outcome of a combi- nation of factors, including local food shortages, higher wages, and the weakening of the currency by

20% in nominal effective terms (against a currency basket including the Australian, New Zealand, and US dollars, and the Japanese yen) since mid-2000.

The official budget is considered to have ended in a deficit of 1.5% of GDP in FY2002, or higher than the expected 0.6% of GDP. Total revenues (including grants) increased by 14.5%, driven largely by a 28.8% jump in trade taxes, while total expenditures rose by 15.7%, due to a sharp increase in the wage bill and expenditures on other goods and services. Subsidies for public enterprises also increased sharply, from 0.2% to 4.8% of total expen- ditures in FY2001 and FY2002, respectively. Current expenditures were slightly in excess of current reve- nues. Capital expenditures were a bit higher than in FY2001, amounting to only 3.5% of total govern- ment expenditures. The recent strain on the fiscal position reflects the continuing impact of 2001's 20% increase in public wages and the increase in subsidies to public enterprises.

In response to rising inflation and pressure on the balance of payments, the authorities tightened monetary policy in FY2002, with continued reliance on credit ceilings as the main instrument, as weak- ness in the central bank's balance sheet precluded the issue of short-term notes. Reflecting this tight- ening, growth of broad money slowed to 7.9% from the very rapid growth of 26.5% in FY2001. Expan- sion of domestic credit also decelerated, to 8.0%, but private sector credit growth remained strong at 14.6%. Net credit to government increased rapidly

Figure 2.33 GDP Growth and Inflation, Tonga, 1995–2002

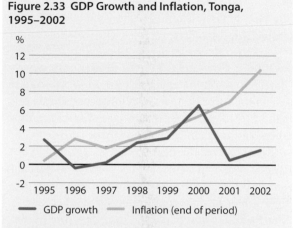

Sources: Ministry of Finance, *Budget Statement June 2003, Supplement 1: Review of the Tongan Economy and Outlook for 2002/03*; National Reserve Bank of Tonga, *Quarterly Bulletin, June 2002.*

in the first half of the fiscal year; however, by June 2002, the Government had become a net lender to the banking system as it deposited the first tranche of the Economic Public Sector Reform Program (EPSRP) loan from ADB. The weighted average deposit rate offered by commercial banks declined marginally to 4.6% in June 2002 and was negative in real terms. The base lending rate was stable at 9.0%, and has been unchanged since the mid-1990s.

Exports soared by 48.6%, reflecting the exceptional growth in squash and fish exports, and imports declined marginally. The trade deficit narrowed slightly to around 33% of GDP in FY2002, from 35% a year earlier. Remittances continued to be the major source of foreign exchange, and increased significantly in FY2002 to around 50% of GDP from around 40% in FY2001. Reflecting these developments, the current account recorded a surplus of 5.5% of GDP in FY2002, following 2 years of significant deficits. However, foreign reserves were under pressure due to capital outflows for most of the fiscal year but improved significantly in the last quarter, boosted by large official capital inflows related to the EPSRP loan. Reserves were boosted from 2.3 to 3.6 months of imports as of end-June 2002. However, the foreign reserves again came under pressure and represented less than 2 months of import cover by the end of the calendar year 2002. The official external debt (including that of public corporations) declined marginally to

45.7% of GDP. The debt service ratio dropped from 21.8% to 8.2% of exports of goods and services as of end-FY2002, largely reflecting a decline in scheduled principal repayments.

The pa'anga continued to depreciate in nominal effective terms by a further 9.2% at end-FY2002, after its 11.5% depreciation in end-FY2001. The surge in Tonga's inflation rate relative to that of its trading partners meant that the real effective exchange rate seems to have stabilized in 2002, despite the nominal effective depreciation.

Policy Developments

The government budget for FY2003 is expansionary. However, the projected deficit at 2.9% of GDP is to be financed entirely with external concessional funds. In addition, the budget proposes to start implementing a strategy to reduce wages to more sustainable levels, specifically to 50% of total current expenditures less interest payments in the medium term. In FY2003, 158 civil service posts are to be abolished and a further 425 vacant positions will remain unfilled.

The Government has embarked on a comprehensive EPSRP with the support of a loan and technical assistance from ADB. The reforms are intended to improve public sector governance and the investment environment for business. There is clear evidence of a commitment and progress with the EPSRP. New Public Service, Public Finance Management, Public Enterprise, Revenue Services Administration, Business Licensing, and Foreign Investment acts were passed in 2002. Proposals are being developed for a comprehensive tax reform. The distortionary Industrial Development Incentives Act was suspended in 2001 and is to be repealed as part of the tax reform. The resultant streamlining and improved transparency of the complex licensing system should help significantly in promoting private sector development.

The fiscal position remains difficult, inflation has escalated, and foreign reserves are still under pressure. Although inflationary, currency depreciation helped alleviate some of the macroeconomic pressure felt in the past 2 years. Export competitiveness improved, as reflected in the depreciation of the real effective exchange rate by 8.5% from mid-2000 to mid-2002 (although the real effective exchange rate seems to have stabilized in 2002).

Further exchange rate depreciation may be needed as the economy adjusts. The use of credit ceiling guidelines has had limited effectiveness in slowing credit growth to the private sector. At present, there are no penalties for banks that breach the guidelines. Given the current macroeconomic circumstances, more effective monetary control arrangements are called for. This would require a significant improvement in the balance sheet of the central bank.

Tax reform is a priority for the Government. The economy relies heavily on trade taxes and the current tax system has numerous economic distortions. The existing tax regime will also come under some pressure when PICTA, which Tonga has signed, is implemented. A recent World Bank study estimated that the potential revenue loss from trade diversion could easily range up to 15% of total tariff revenues, which equates to about 7% of total revenues and grants based on data for FY2003. There are also substantial capacity constraints in the administration of all major taxes, providing potential for considerable tax evasion and avoidance. Tax reform is a major component of the EPSRP. There are well-developed proposals for reducing the reliance on trade taxes, broadening the existing sales tax base, and improving the economic efficiency, equity, and revenue effectiveness of the tax regime. However, major efforts will be needed to improve administrative capacity if the tax reform program is to be successful.

The EPSRP includes civil service and public enterprise reforms aimed at reducing costs while improving both service delivery and the private sector regulatory environment. In addition to the new Public Enterprises Act (associated with EPSRP implementation), there is a need for complementary regulatory changes for monopoly public enterprises, guidelines for board appointments, and considerable resources to implement performance monitoring—since the reform of public enterprises in most jurisdictions has proven to be challenging. The EPSRP also contains a commitment to pass a new immigration act to make it easier for foreign investors and key staff to obtain visas.

Outlook for 2003–2004

GDP is forecast to grow by 2.5% in FY2003 and by 2.7% in FY2004 as the reform program gathers momentum. Inflation is expected to remain relatively high at around 10% in FY2003 but to gradually moderate in FY2004. The inflation rate reflects the recent expansionary pressures and the continuing flow-on effects of a weaker currency. The pressure on the external account is expected to ease in the medium term as reforms and improvement in fiscal management progress, and as remittances and tourism continue to grow.

Growth over the next 2 years is expected to be reasonably broad based, but tourism could perform well as Tonga has the potential to benefit from the diversion of tourists from other locations in the Asia-Pacific region perceived to suffer from public security risks.

The outlook for fishing is a concern, as is the heavy reliance of the economy on remittances from Tongans abroad. If 2002's high level of remittances does not continue, the economy could easily slump, jeopardizing efforts to improve the fiscal and external positions and placing further pressure on the currency. The downside risks for growth, the currency, and inflation are much greater than the upside risks and the authorities will need to be vigilant in their efforts to manage the macroeconomic situation.

The EPSRP is ambitious in scope and content, and will require sustained political commitment and significant resources to help ensure success. If measurable progress can be made on the urgent task of fiscal consolidation and the medium- to longer-term tasks of reforming the civil service, public enterprises, and the tax system, the result should be a more resilient economy and general improvements in the standard of living. In the medium to longer term, it should be possible to achieve a per capita growth rate of 2.5% over a sustained period.

The 2003 budget projects a rise in total revenues and grants of 15.5%, based on a projection of significant rises in both tax and nontax revenues, and of grants. The budget item on total expenditures and net lending is projected to increase by 23.0%, with subsidies and other transfers as well as capital expenditures surging.

However, the outcome could well be a higher deficit than budgeted, especially if economic growth and associated government revenues are weaker than projected and public enterprises increase their demands on the budget.

Tuvalu

GDP growth slowed in 2002, reflecting a significant reduction in government expenditures from the levels of 2001. It was sustained by the finalization of public infrastructure projects and a strong housing market. Major policy issues include adjustment to lower levels of government revenues and spending, and the need for improved budgetary processes and public sector management. The medium-term outlook is for modest growth.

Macroeconomic Assessment

Economic growth decelerated to about 2.0% in 2002, following several years of 3–4% expansion. The slowdown came in the wake of severely reduced government spending. Receiving little stimulus from the state sector, the country's production suffered in many sectors. The construction and retail sectors recorded marginal growth, with the primary sector faring slightly better.

Total government expenditures in 2002 were less than half the original estimate, as a result of lower special development spending, capital expenditures, and transfers. Special development spending was only A$3.8 million, against an original estimate of about A$11 million. The wage bill was some 8% lower than the original estimate. Maintenance expenditures were also only about half the original estimate, while spending on goods and services was also significantly reduced. The policy of increasing rents for government housing to close to their true economic value, introduced in February 2002, contributed to the restraining of economic activity.

This contraction of government expenditures can be understood in the context of the country's experience. In 2000, Tuvalu benefited from a huge windfall revenue from a leasing arrangement with the manager of Tuvalu's Internet domain address (".tv"). The windfall supported a dramatic rise in government spending that year, while still gener-

ating a large budget surplus (equal to 32.2% of GDP). Big spending continued in 2001 but the expected further windfall gain for that year did not materialize, giving rise to the country's first overall deficit (equal to 42.8% of GDP). In 2002, a substantial one-off boost to revenues came as a result of the sale of DotTV Corporation for A$20 million, but spending was curtailed in an effort to prevent a replication of the deficit of the preceding year. The combination of expanded revenues and a significant reduction in overall government expenditures led to a very large budget surplus of around 85% of GDP (Figure 2.34). Unfortunately, it also slowed economic growth.

Inflation rose slightly to 2.6%, largely reflecting developments in trading partner countries. Foreign trade statistics for Tuvalu are unavailable. It is a fact, however, that the country's nonmerchandise account is dominated by seafarers' remittances, estimated at about 20% of GDP a year. Another source of income is the Tuvalu Trust Fund (TTF). With the recent weakness in world equity markets, the market value of the TTF on 30 September 2002 was 10% less than the maintained value. Consequently, there was no distribution of earnings in 2002 and none is expected in 2003. In addition, the balance on the Consolidated Investment Fund (CIF)—a buffer account that takes government surpluses and is normally used to finance deficits—was half the minimum target balance.

Figure 2.34 Government Revenues and Expenditures, Tuvalu, 1996–2003

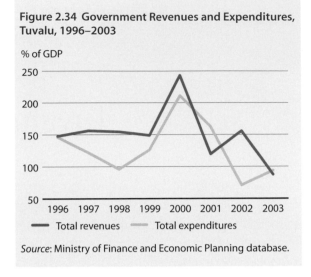

% of GDP

Source: Ministry of Finance and Economic Planning database.

The financial sector is dominated by the government-owned National Bank of Tuvalu, which continued to be highly profitable, reflecting its monopoly position. Real interest rates for deposits were slightly negative in 2001 and near zero in 2002. The spread between deposit and lending rates was maintained at around 8%, comparable to spreads in other small Pacific island economies.

The Australian dollar continues to serve as the domestic currency, so that fiscal policy effectively constitutes macroeconomic policy as a whole. Although it has been adversely affected by the impact of the downturn in world equity markets on the TTF investments, the Government's fiscal position has been boosted by the DotTV revenues and provides funds sufficient to cover some 5 years of imports.

A new Government came to power in mid-2002 and presented its first budget in November. This Government will continue to focus on human resources development, economic infrastructure, financial management, public sector reform, and private sector development. In addition, it allocated further funding to the Falekaupule Trust Fund to match extra contributions made by some outer islands.

Policy Developments

One of the main development issues is the devolution of administrative responsibilities to communities on the outer islands and the improvement of

infrastructure and services for them. Toward these ends, the Falekaupule Trust Fund was established in June 1999 as a key component of an Island Development Program with around A$16 million provided by the Government, an ADB loan, and the island communities themselves. The Fund's first distribution was made in June 2001 to finance development projects and maintain community assets. A policy of devolution and infrastructure development for the outer islands has been promoted since then.

Until recently, the country had a reputation for disciplined fiscal policy. A distinction is made between core and noncore revenues and expenditures. Surpluses in excess of the CIF buffer have been placed in the TTF, providing a sustainable fund to finance core expenditures. However, strong receipts from fishing license fees for several consecutive years and windfall revenues from the DotTV agreements in 2000 and 2001 raised public expectations for increased government spending. This led to a flouting of the ceiling on core expenditures for 3 years in a row and the creation of accountability and management problems associated with the budget, including improper use of advances.

The budget is formulated in a single-year framework which, together with the core/noncore distinction, leads to a number of adverse economic efficiency effects. The identification of expenditures as "core" creates a sense that they are essential. This has the effect of "protecting" most recurrent spending, which is classified as core. In addition, there is no integration between special development expenditures, extrabudgetary expenditures, and recurrent costs. In the 2002 budget, around 40% of special development expenditures were of a recurrent nature that could not be stopped without reducing government services.

A 3-year rolling public sector investment program is presented with the annual budget but it has no clear integration with the budget and has no policy strategy to guide its implementation. Recognizing this weakness, the Government intends to hold a national summit this year as part of the preparation for a medium-term economic development strategy.

Budget reform has been an important component of the public sector reform program since the mid-1990s. Performance-oriented "output" budgeting was introduced in 2000 and since then has guided budget preparation. However, reports consistent with effective output budgeting are yet to be prepared. There have also been long delays in complying with legislated reporting requirements. Audited government financial statements for 1997–1999 were prepared by a private auditing firm on behalf of the Auditor General and only submitted to Parliament in November 2002.

The 2003 budget announced that a new multi-year budget framework and improvements in the budget process will be introduced. However, consideration needs to be given to developing a more meaningful, usable, and effective performance-oriented framework and to ensuring that the framework matches institutional capacity. The 2003 budget has been formulated in recognition that there will be no windfall revenues and no distribution from the TTF in 2003.

The main civil service capacity issues are how to strengthen local capacity on the outer islands within existing budget constraints and to improve the capacity to develop and provide policy advice to the Ministry of Finance and Economic Planning and to the Cabinet. The civil service has been subject to considerable disruption in recent years with several changes of government and increased use of in-service scholarships. Poor record keeping is also a long-standing weakness in public administration. Various recommendations to improve accountability in the civil service and for public enterprises were endorsed by the Cabinet in 1999. However, apart from the drafting of a new Audit Act there has been very limited follow-up action.

Like budget reform, public enterprise reform has been under way since the mid-1990s. However, there is still a need to develop an effective governance framework to help improve financial accountability and operational performance. There have been clear failures to comply with legislation that requires timely annual reports and financial accounts. The 2003 budget announced that no operating subsidies will be paid to SOEs until they have signed operating agreements with the Government, and technical assistance will be sought to develop improved governance arrangements.

Tax and tariff reforms are issues for Tuvalu as it is a signatory to PICTA. Under this, all tariffs have to be gradually removed by 2016. The impact on revenues would also be intensified once tariffs on products from Australia and New Zealand are reduced under the framework Pacific Agreement on Closer Economic Relations. Import duties are currently around 14% of total non-grant, non-windfall revenues, so that the eventual removal of tariffs will create a need for new revenue sources. It should, though, not be too difficult to extend the existing sales tax and make use of selective excises on luxury products to replace import duties.

Outlook for 2003–2004

Growth in 2003 is projected to remain at about 2%, with inflation increasing to 3.0%. Revenues will be significantly lower in the medium term but expenditures will be higher. Restraint will be focused on capital and special development expenditures. An overall deficit of 6.5% of GDP is projected and will be financed from the CIF. The budget assumes a significant increase in grants and fishing license fees. However, with the CIF balance at half its recommended minimum target in late 2002 and a further drawdown anticipated in 2003, and the prospect of zero distribution from the TTF in 2003 and 2004, the Government's cash position will need careful management if it is to help ensure macroeconomic stability. The economy will continue to receive strong support from seafarers' remittances.

Vanuatu

The economy continued to suffer from recession in 2002 but modest recovery is projected over the medium term. The relatively high cost structure remains a factor in restraining growth, and competitiveness of the tourism industry has declined in recent years with the appreciation of the real exchange rate. Consequently, renewed efforts are needed to implement the Comprehensive Reform Program and to pursue further structural reforms so as to improve the economy's competitive position.

Macroeconomic Assessment

GDP fell further in 2002, by 0.3%, following a contraction of 2.7% in 2001 (Figure 2.35), reflecting the effects on agriculture and tourism of several major cyclones and weak demand. Agriculture as a whole strengthened modestly but the forestry subsector contracted by 34% following a similar drop in 2001. The cocoa subsector exhibited depressed conditions, though copra production grew by 7.1%, boosted by subsidized prices and, despite the cyclones, generally good weather conditions.

The construction sector expanded by 5%, stimulated by government expenditures on upgrading the airports on Efate and Santo, while the services sector as a whole contracted by 0.9%, with the hotels and restaurants subsector and government services leading the decline. Total visitors in 2002 were 7.4% lower than a year earlier, attributable to a decline in tourist arrivals due to a combination of greater competition from other destinations in the Pacific and, to a lesser extent, a relatively high real exchange rate.

Inflation moderated to around 2.0% in 2002, from 3.5% in 2001. Exports grew by 7.0% in 2002, following a steep fall in 2001; imports rose by 2.9%, following weak growth in 2001. The current account deficit narrowed slightly to 2.0% of GDP. Gross official reserves were slightly lower than in 2001 but still sufficient to cover around 6 months of imports of goods and services.

The Government's fiscal position improved in 2002, with an overall deficit of 2.1% of GDP, following 2 years of more sizable deficits. The improvement was mainly due to expenditure restraint and, in particular, to the impact of financial controls on personnel costs. A tight cash situation persisted in 2002 with the Government still using a system of monthly warrants to control spending. Revenues were also lower than originally estimated, reflecting the impact of weaker than expected economic growth. However, the impact of improvements in VAT and customs administration was also evident in 2002. Several privatizations that had been planned for 2002 (including Air Vanuatu, National Bank of Vanuatu [NBV], and Telecom Vanuatu) were delayed.

In mid-2001, the Government instructed the Vanuatu Commodities Marketing Board to pay substantial copra subsidies that had to be financed by direct advances from the Reserve Bank of Vanuatu (RBV). The price subsidy has continued and was estimated at about 1% of GDP in 2002. Supplementary budget support was also provided to the Asset Management Unit (AMU), amounting to about 0.9% of GDP in 2002. This was to repay the NBV for NPLs that had been transferred to the AMU.

Overall public debt declined slightly from 38.0%

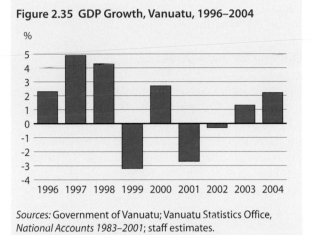

Figure 2.35 GDP Growth, Vanuatu, 1996–2004

%

Sources: Government of Vanuatu; Vanuatu Statistics Office, *National Accounts 1983–2001;* staff estimates.

to 37.0% of GDP in 2002. Around three quarters of it is external debt on concessional terms. The funding of substantial losses at the National Provident Fund contributed to a significant buildup of domestic debt in 1997–1998 but the Government currently has a cautious approach to borrowing. External debt service costs are relatively low but the main government focus is on total debt service requirements relative to government revenues, which stood at 6.2% in 2002, or below the target limit of 7.0%.

The money supply declined by 1.7% in 2002, largely reflecting a significant decline in net foreign assets. Domestic liquidity conditions eased for most of the year with currency and deposits increasing by 44.7%. Total domestic credit grew by 11.9%, driven primarily by strong credit growth for the Government, which itself was mainly in the form of a very large increase in the overdraft with RBV. Private sector credit expanded by around 7.9%. In 2002, commercial deposit interest rates eased slightly while commercial lending rates rose on average, and as a result, the average spread widened to 12.0% from 11.3% in 2001 and 10.1% in 2000. The effective spread is, however, considerably larger than this due to the common requirement for significant deposits as collateral, which are often financed by additional borrowing. Tight foreign exchange restrictions from early 2000 also contributed to the wider interest rate margins. Between mid-2001 and mid-2002, the vatu depreciated against the Australian dollar by 2.3% and against the euro by 6.8%, but appreciated against the US dollar by 8.1%.

The OECD designated Vanuatu as an uncooperative tax haven in April 2002, along with a handful of other jurisdictions. However, Vanuatu has taken steps to stay off the Financial Action Task Force list of uncooperative countries on money laundering. There have been concerns about the enforcement capacity of anti-money laundering regulations, but positive steps were taken in 2002. The introduction of "know-your-customer" guidelines in mid-2002 is expected to improve the effectiveness of anti-money laundering measures. A new International Banking Act was passed in November 2002, which will put offshore banks under the supervision of RBV from this year. Proposals are also being developed for more effective supervision in the nonbank offshore sector. Increasing global concerns about money laundering may have prompted recent actions; however, there is still much resistance and divided opinion in the offshore business community.

Policy Developments

Vanuatu is characterized by numerous long-standing structural weaknesses that raise costs relative to those of competitors, by fiscal limitations, and by vulnerability to external shocks and political developments. The Government has been implementing a Comprehensive Reform Program since 1998 to improve governance, particularly in the areas of parliamentary, judicial, and legal procedures, public sector efficiency, and financial management. Despite reasonably good progress, much more remains to be done.

Government expenditures on the wage bill, as a share of the total, continues to be relatively high, despite efforts made under the Comprehensive Reform Program to reduce them. The Government has recognized the need to strengthen the fiscal position through a broadening of the tax base, and a Revenue Strategy Committee has identified options to do this, though progress has been slow due to resistance from business. The need remains, however, to improve compliance with present taxes, and the Government's intention is to lift the ratio of taxes to GDP from the current 22–23% to 27%.

The prospective introduction of PICTA would place pressure on Vanuatu to establish new revenue sources, as it is still highly dependent on tariff revenues, despite the introduction of VAT in 1998. Tariff revenues constituted 35% of total revenues (including grants) in 2002 and are projected still to be 33% of total revenues in 2005. In 2002, the average implicit tariff was 24%. Under PICTA, all tariffs would have to be gradually removed by 2016. The impact would also be intensified once tariffs on products from Australia and New Zealand are reduced under the Pacific Agreement on Closer Economic Relations.

The 2003 budget announced an increase in import duty rates by 5 percentage points for various imported foods, medicines, insecticides, and textiles and an increase in the existing tariff from 20% to 40% for various timbers, from 30% to 40% for certain fruit juices, and from 25% to 40% for canned meat. As PICTA has not yet been ratified, there is no contradiction with the Agreement but some of these tariff increases are likely to entail adverse economic efficiency effects, which could be avoided by the use of excise taxes.

It has long been recognized that Vanuatu has a high cost structure relative to neighboring and competitor countries. For example, compared with the Fiji Islands, electricity tariffs are twice as high, the retail price of gasoline is 40% higher, and local telephone calls are three times as high. Internal and international transport costs are also much higher than in neighboring countries.

Part of the explanation for this relates to the geographic dispersion of the population across several well-separated islands and to the lack of appropriate regulatory arrangements for local monopolies. In addition, the heavy reliance on tariffs means that import duties on business inputs directly raise the cost of production. While a duty drawback scheme is in place, it does not extend to all business inputs or all businesses. The exchange rate also seems to undermine competitiveness: the real effective exchange rate has appreciated by nearly 10% over the last 6 years.

Outlook for 2003–2004

Modest economic recovery is forecast in the medium term with growth of 1.3% in 2003 and 2.2% in 2004. These growth rates are lower than the current population growth rate of around 2.6%, implying a decline in per capita income. Inflation is projected to continue to be moderate, at 2.5% in 2003 and 2004.

Agriculture is expected to lead the recovery. Tourism is also expected to pick up with the recent completion of two new hotels and ongoing advertising campaigns. A switch in the focus of the tourism market from certain other Asian locations as a result of security concerns, to the South Pacific and the flow-on effects of sporting events in this part of the world, will help support tourism in Vanuatu in 2003, but the cost aspect remains a consideration. The government sector is projected to decline in real terms by 5–5.7% in the medium term, contributing to relatively weak overall economic growth but helping secure a more sustainable fiscal position and facilitating longer-term private sector development.

The 2003 budget forecasts a modest overall surplus of 0.4% of GDP, which is projected to increase marginally in 2004. Much of the surplus will be realized from a reduction in development expenditures. The wage bill is projected to remain approximately constant in nominal terms but decline modestly as a share of total recurrent spending and relative to GDP in the medium term. However, this depends on the Government meeting the projected targets for these expenses.

ASIAN DEVELOPMENT
Outlook
2003

Part 3 Competitiveness in Developing Asia

Taking Advantage of Globalization, Technology, and Competition

ASIAN DEVELOPMENT

Outlook
2003

Competitiveness in Developing Asia
Taking Advantage of Globalization, Technology, and Competition

Competitiveness in Developing Asia

Taking Advantage of Globalization, Technology, and Competition

During the last decade, competitiveness has been brought into the discussion of the search for the panacea for growth almost as if it represented a pillar of economic development, similar to trade and openness or savings. However, competitiveness is not a panacea for development for Asia's developing countries. Nevertheless, the firm-level framework developed in Asian Development Outlook 2003 provides a pragmatic route for discussion about competitiveness by focusing on firms. The significance of competitiveness for firms and policy makers in developing Asia can be understood within the broader context of the constantly evolving environment created by the forces of globalization and technological progress, where knowledge is the most important resource. These factors have raised a whole spectrum of new challenges—and opportunities—that firms and policy makers in developing Asia should recognize. The key to success in the coming years is that governments and firms across Asia devise strategies to take full advantage of the potential benefits that globalization, technology, and competition offer. It will be necessary for them to understand what competitiveness means and how it fits in as a piece of the development process. Misconceptions of the nature and role of competitiveness in national economic development can be counterproductive. Understanding that it is firms that compete in an increasingly global market, both at home and abroad, and that the national policy environment can either constrain or improve their efforts, is critical.

This part of *Asian Development Outlook 2003* provides an analysis of competitiveness in developing Asia and shows how it is vital for productivity, national growth, and development. Competitiveness can be defined as a firm's ability to stay in business and achieve some desired result in terms of profit, price, rate of return, or quality of its products; and to have the capacity to exploit existing market opportunities and generate new markets.

During the last decade, there has been considerable interest in identifying the factors that can improve competitiveness, which is thought by many to be an important piece of the growth and development puzzle, perhaps the latest elixir in the quest for growth. Behind this quest is a complex interaction among a number of factors—or the "drivers of change"—which are globalization, technology, and competition. These factors are raising a whole spectrum of new challenges and opportunities in an irreversible process of rapid change. The Asian financial crisis that began in 1997 has added more variables to the equation. Although it brought serious disruption to the region, it demonstrated the need for an improvement in corporate and banking governance. Those countries that have learned the lessons will experience rapid growth again, while those that have not will stagnate. Recently, the emergence of the People's Republic of China (PRC) as an economic powerhouse, particularly in manufacturing, has come to be regarded with reservation among some East and Southeast Asian countries.

Governments and policy makers are especially interested in the issue of competitiveness, particularly the policies that can improve it. Governments have set up councils and competitiveness committees, have written white papers, and have organized conferences on the subject. In this way, the idea of national competitiveness has become one of the key themes in the current debate about national economic performance. Whether or not a country is seen as competitive depends on where it comes in the rankings of a variety of indicators used across countries. Unfortunately, national competitiveness has become something of a buzzword: in common parlance, competitiveness is used to cover almost any aspect of market performance and its overuse may detract from its importance. In fact, the key variable for the economic analysis of competitiveness is the growth of labor productivity since this, ultimately, is the main determinant in raising living standards. This is what competitiveness is about.

In this context, many developing Asian firms and governments alike feel the need to rethink how to achieve steady rapid growth. Although firms in the Asia-Pacific region are well positioned to succeed in the coming decades, it is crucial to provide a grounded explanation of the microeconomic foundations of competitiveness and growth of labor productivity. The consideration of the East Asian experience, in particular, provides useful insights for less developed countries in the Asia-Pacific region as they devise new strategies and approaches to promote higher rates of sustainable growth. The long-run growth prospects for the Asia-Pacific region, driven by the new opportunities offered by technological advances and globalization, are very positive, provided both that sound macroeconomic policies are implemented and that the necessary reforms in the financial sector continue.

The key to success in the coming years is that governments and firms across the region devise strategies to take full advantage of the potential benefits that globalization, technology, and competition offer. Governments will need to understand what competitiveness means and how it fits in the development process. Today's combination of the new industrial revolution and globalization is similar to that of the late nineteenth century when, for example, the United States (US) emerged as a major economic power; or earlier when the United Kingdom emerged as a colonial and manufacturing power. It can also be compared with the 1960s and 1970s, when Japan emerged as a leading industrial power, and with the 1980s, which saw the fast development of the Republic of Korea (Korea).

The rapid internationalization of world affairs during the last few decades has opened up many opportunities. The establishment of the World Trade Organization (WTO) has, through its policies, affected every level of economic activity. The lowering of tariffs and the dismantling of other restrictions to trade have generated intense competition and strong incentives for perceptive entrepreneurs. The result is that most domestic markets are being subjected to increased competition from foreign firms. At the same time, a collaborative world in which countries seldom make complete products from start to finish offers plenty of opportunities. World trade barriers are breaking down and economic instabilities are better understood than in the past. This way, states and markets have much room to develop a partnership to ensure growth and, above all, development, as manifested in the provision of basic needs in the fields of education and health, and, ultimately, in sustained increases in living standards. All these transformations demonstrate the need for policy makers to understand the constraints that markets place on governments and, conversely, those that governments place on markets. It is notable that these international developments are happening in a time of diminishing expectations about the effectiveness of government action (Stern 1997).

The analysis begins, in the section *Drivers of Change: Globalization, Technology, and Competition*, with an assessment of the drivers of change—i.e., globalization, technology, and competition—and of the emergence of the PRC as a major industrial powerhouse. It stresses that competitiveness is a firm-level issue, and that any understanding of the determinants of competitiveness must begin at that level.

The discussion then moves on, in *National Competitiveness: A Dangerous Obsession?*, to whether nations, per se, compete, in particular for shares in export markets, and whether the notion of "national competitiveness" makes sense. It is argued that nations do not compete in the way that firms do, and that the concept of national competitiveness is very elusive. The debate over whether national competitiveness has any meaning is rooted in the appropriate role and scope of government policy in enhancing firms' competitiveness. Government policies and actions can indeed greatly help firms' competitiveness; but they can also hamper it.

Despite the debate surrounding the term "national competitiveness," economists use several aggregate measures that try to capture some aspects of the issue. These are summarized and discussed in the section *Aggregate Measures of Competitiveness*. Likewise, there have been some attempts at constructing indices of national competitiveness by aggregating several variables. However, the construction of these indices is a rather problematic exercise and their usefulness might be very limited.

In the next section, *Institutions, The State, and The Market: A Partnership for Development,* it is argued that development requires a partnership between market and state with an appropriate division of responsibilities. The objective of this partnership is to create a competitive or *well-functioning* market economy, whose ultimate objectives are to raise living standards and, by implication, reduce the gap with the countries at the income and technological frontier. The production of private goods and services should be largely left to the market. Firms make the products and provide the services that consumers demand, and learn how to do business better by competing with other firms and by striving to improve their entrepreneurial capabilities. For its part, the role of government should be to enable firms to compete effectively. It can do this by ensuring a level playing field for all firms through the provision of the required institutional infrastructure, that is, the legal framework (emphasizing the importance of competition policies), macroeconomic stability, and the correction of market imperfections.

The role of industrial policy, which may have been successful in the past, is greatly diminished in the context of globalization. However, there are other areas, such as education, technology, and physical infrastructure, where responsibilities can be shared between the government and private sector. The other important component of this government-private sector partnership is the development of institutions, a difficult task since they cannot be transferred easily as they are country specific and have to be developed gradually.

In the following two sections, two important dynamic forces that can help firms in the Asia-Pacific region increase their competitiveness are discussed. The first is for firms to latch onto "global value chains" (GVCs), defined as the internationalization of the production process whereby firms located in different countries participate in the different stages of the process. (This is discussed in the section *Global Value Chains*.) GVCs offer many firms in the region an opportunity to take advantage of the potential benefits that globalization offers. Many firms in the newly industrializing economies (NIEs) of Hong Kong, China; Korea; Singapore; and Taipei,China used this approach not so long ago. The important question is why firms in some less developed countries have managed to enter GVCs but others have not, and many lessons can be learned from the firms in the NIEs that have successfully entered GVCs. The second force is education, the key production input in the knowledge society of the 21st century (assessed in the following section, *Education and Skills*). Knowledge, society's most important resource, has two main characteristics. First, it is a public good: many people can use it. Second, it is complementary with existing knowledge: the worth to society of an idea increases the more society already knows. This implies that investment in knowledge offers increasing returns. The objective for policy makers and firms is to identify the education and training policies and the institutions needed to respond to the economy's demands for more innovative and creative workers.

The final section prior to the conclusions, *Catch-Up Competitiveness: Some Lessons*, discusses lessons that can be drawn from the NIEs' experience in reducing the income and technological gaps with countries at the frontier—"catching up." It looks at what the nature of competitiveness is in countries that are not at the frontier, and the role of innovation in the catching-up process. Though very important lessons can be learned, the experience of countries at the frontier cannot, though, be replicated exactly.

Drivers of Change: Globalization, Technology, and Competition

The two most significant drivers of change in the world today are globalization and technological innovation. Both factors of growth are, in fact, the basis for a new division of labor between countries and firms that has emerged during the last few decades. Countries and firms are divided by their attitude toward globalization and by their capacity to innovate and/or adopt new technologies.

Globalization is defined as a process of economic integration of the entire world through the removal of barriers to free trade and capital mobility, as well as through the diffusion of knowledge and information. It is a historical process moving at different speeds in different countries and in different sectors. One of the results is that firms, whose output was previously significantly more limited by the size of their domestic market, now have the chance to reap greater advantages from economies of scale by "going global." The revolution in information and communications technology (ICT) in the last 10–15 years has also made communication much cheaper and faster. The transaction costs of transferring ideas and information have decreased enormously and the arrival of the Internet has accelerated this trend. This implies that countries with advanced technologies are best placed to innovate further. Moreover, unlike in the past when inventions and innovations were considered breakthroughs, today they are a regular occurrence. This implies that the transformation process is continuous, and this has important consequences both for the overall organization of firms and for policy making. Global firms rely on technological innovation to enhance their capabilities. In this sense, technology is both driven by and is a driver of globalization, so that it is possible to speak of the new "technologically driven character" of the global economy.

Two other factors of change have become significant in the Asia-Pacific region, especially after the financial crisis that began in 1997. The first is the rise of the PRC as a significant industrial powerhouse in the region. The second is the cyclical overcapacity that has arisen in several key electronics sectors, such as dynamic random-access memory (DRAM), personal computers, and mobile telephones. The combination of these two factors has led to fierce competition in the region, resulting in low profit margins and excess capacity in some industries.

Competition and Competitiveness

Figure 3.1 illustrates the relationship between globalization, technology, and competition. The main message is that the drivers are continuously creating a new competitive environment. Globalization manifests itself in intensified competition among firms and in the creation of new industry structures, so that, for example, today's GVCs are more integrated and technology-intensive than those in the past, forcing firms to be creative in terms of the responses and strategies to deal with emerging new scenarios (e.g., the need to create new products). The ultimate purpose is to compete, to gain advantage over and, if possible, to eliminate the competition in the industry and to dominate the market, generating both losers and winners in the process. The former have quickly to reinvent themselves, and can do this by merging with other companies, undertaking aggressive marketing campaigns, or launching totally new products. If they fail, they will soon be out of business. Those firms that seize new opportunities, on the other hand, are profitable and create value, as well as new products, services, and even industries, such as ICT (Box 3.1). The market system rewards them with extra profits, more resources, and greater economic power, with prices signaling to these entrepreneurs what to produce. The disappearance of some firms and the emergence of others inevitably leads to changes in the structure of competition. The important points to stress are, first, that this is a dynamic and iterative process, taking place constantly; and second, that the whole process is, overall, a positive-sum game for society, reflecting Schumpeter's idea of "creative destruction."

Competitiveness is primarily a firm-level concept. "A firm is competitive if it can produce products and services of superior quality and lower costs than its domestic and international competitors. Competitiveness is synonymous with a firm's

Figure 3.1 Globalization, Technology, and Competition: Drivers of Change

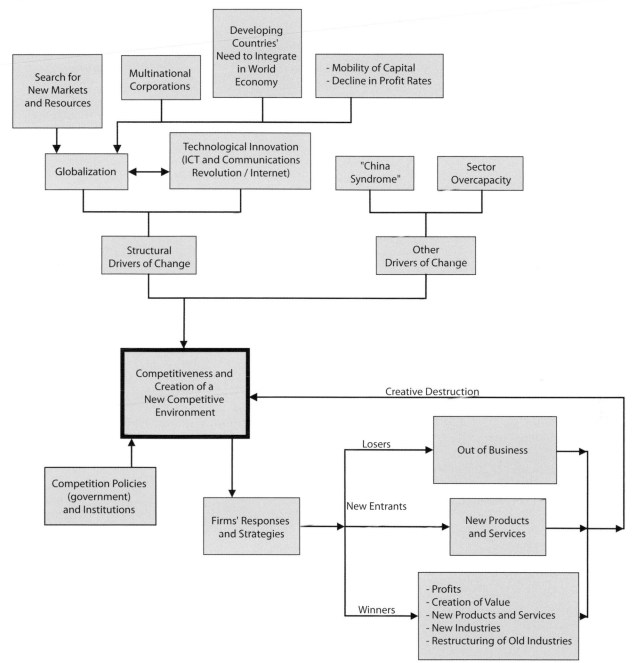

long-run profit performance and its ability to compensate its employees and provide superior returns to its owners" (Buckley et al. 1988, p.176). The ability to compete consists in doing better than comparable firms (i.e., rivals) in terms of sales, market share, and profitability, and is achieved through strategic behavior, defined as the set of actions taken to influence the market environment so as to increase a firm's profits, as well as by other marketing tools. It is also achieved through product quality improvement and product innovation—both very important aspects of the competitive process. McCombie and Thirlwall (1994, 1999), for example, argue and provide empirical evidence

Box 3.1 The Information and Communications Technology Industry in India

A decade after implementing major economic reforms, the Indian economy has entered a phase of dynamism and rapid growth. This is most evident in the information and communications technology (ICT) sector, which in India is predominantly a software-oriented industry. In a little over a decade, India has emerged as a major exporter of software. The Indian National Association of Software and Services Companies estimates that the software industry was valued at $15 million at the start of the 1990s, and climbed to $2.7 billion by the end of the decade. Between 1995 and 2000, Indian software expanded at a compound rate of 56% a year, nearly two thirds of which was due to exports. During this period, software exports grew by 57.4% in rupee terms, while the domestic software market grew by 48.3%. The share of software exports in total exports grew from a negligible amount in 1990 to 14% in 2000/01, most of which was accounted for by local rather than foreign companies. The National Association of Software and Services Companies estimates that by 2008, ICT software and services exports will account for 35% of India's total exports. Employment in the industry grew from about 160,000 ICT professionals in 1997 to an estimated 410,000 in 2000.

Today, some 40% of the Fortune 500 corporations are clients of the Indian software industry, while more than 25% of Indian software firms meet the requirements set by ISO 9000. Nearly all the world's major software producers have a presence in the country, and of the 19 companies worldwide that have a "capability maturity model" (a structured process for software development associated with the Software Engineering Institute at Carnegie Mellon University), which offers an indicator of global software excellence, 12 are Indian.

Part of this success is owed to the country's emphasis since the 1950s on training high-level scientific and technical personnel across a wide range of disciplines. In the 1960s and 1970s, many highly trained scientific personnel migrated to the US, a large proportion of whom were involved in the development of computers, in computer science, and in the communications industry. This provided a pool of skills that prompted the development of the Indian software industry, especially during the 1990s. Initially, Indian professionals provided services onsite in other countries, but as the ICT industry matured this allowed software subsidiaries to set up in India. Consequently, the links between Indian expatriates in industrial countries working in high-level technical positions and their local counterparts at home have allowed faster response to the growing demand for software services.

The requirements for software production are also particularly suited to the resource endowments of the Indian economy. Although it is still a labor-intensive country, India benefits from many fluent English speakers, the language for the major software producers. Scale economies are not a significant barrier to entry, and software is not heavily dependent on the existence of physical infrastructure such as roads and ports. The growth of the software industry was also facilitated by the "hands off" policies of the Government: by the late 1980s and 1990s, ICT-related equipment prices had fallen steadily, and the Government allowed liberal imports of both hardware and software tools.

The factors that constrain Indian ICT growth are the inadequate availability of power and quality of telecommunications. In 1996, for instance, India had only 15 telephone mainlines per 1,000 people, compared with Ireland's 395 and Israel's 446. There are also 1.5 computers per 1,000 people in India compared with 145 in Ireland and 117.6 in Israel. Costs of power are the second high-est expenditure for the industry and many software companies generate their own power. Low bandwidths are currently sufficient but will need to be upgraded if India is to move into higher-value software projects.

There are also concerns that the continued fast growth of the industry will lead to a shortage of ICT professionals. The Government has responded by increasing expenditures in engineering schools and placing greater emphasis on ICT teaching. Private firms have responded by investing more in software education and training for their employees. Using people from other disciplines besides engineering in providing software services might alleviate the labor shortage.

India's ICT sector will perform a critical role in the country's development process, as a major industry that is the country's largest single source of foreign exchange earnings. It will also serve as a critical input into the efficiency of the private sector, in terms of software applicability and management expertise. The ICT industry is also emerging as a model for management styles and attitudes, and will play a crucial role in the social process, as it supports the effective provision of public services, notably in governance, health, and education. This should help upgrade the public health and public school facilities as steps toward enhancing the country's human development.

Sources:
Arora, Ashish and Suma Athreye. 2001. "The Software Industry and India's Economic Development." WIDER Discussion Paper No. 2001/20. United Nations University; Prakash, Brahm. 2002. "Information and Communications Technology in Developing Countries of Asia." In *Technology and Poverty Reduction in Asia and the Pacific.* ADB/OECD; Sachs, Jeffrey D. and Nirupam Bajpai. 2001. "The Decade of Development: Goal Setting and Policy Challenges in India." CID Working Paper No. 62. Center for International Development, Harvard University.

that non-price competitiveness matters substantially more than price competitiveness,[1] i.e., it is more important in the long run for a firm to shift the demand curve for its product outward than to move the demand curve down through cutting costs and prices. A survey by the *Global Competitiveness Report* that asked firms in 59 countries about their main business strategy showed that, in all cases, "Low cost based on product or process technology," "Differentiate the product from the competitors' based on product design or image," and "Differentiate the product from the competitors' based on service" are the most important strategies. In only a few countries did a significant percentage of firms indicate that their main strategy was based on low wages (World Economic Forum 2000, p.227).

The underlying argument is that firms compete for markets and resources, measure competitiveness by looking at relative market shares, sales, or profitability, and use different strategies to improve their performance (Lall 2001a). Competitiveness, defined as a firm's ability to survive under competition, is the essence of a well-functioning market system, and being competitive implies succeeding in an environment where firms try to stay ahead of each other by reducing prices, by increasing the quality of their current products and services, and by creating new ones. A firm's competitiveness is a function of factors such as (i) its own resources (e.g., the human capital, its physical capital, and the level of technology); (ii) its market power; (iii) its behavior toward rivals and other economic agents; (iv) its capability to adapt to changing circumstances; (v) its capability to create new markets; and (vi) the institutional environment, largely provided by the government, including physical infrastructure and the quality of government policies.

At the expense of oversimplification, it is possible to distinguish at the firm level between short- and long-run elements of competitiveness. Short-run competitiveness is indicated by the product price, quality, and functionality; market share; profitability; return on assets; and share price. Some limited innovation for the improvement of the existing products (e.g., in terms of efficiency, cost, and quality) may be involved. In contrast, long-run competitiveness is concerned with how well a firm performs compared with other similar firms in developing new technologies to generate new products and processes and, ultimately, entirely new markets (Hamel and Prahalad 1994). This includes the advantages of product leadership and the benefits gained by the introduction of whole new families of products based on inventions and innovations derived from significant research and development (R&D).

Drivers of Change

Although globalization is driven by the same underlying factor as in the past—namely, the search for new markets and resources—specific factors and reasons today make it a process that differs from earlier periods. Indeed, the process of internationalization and the onset of global competition, along with the financial and monetary turbulence of the 1980s (e.g., Latin American debt crises) and 1990s (e.g., Asian financial crisis and Russian debt default), have played an important role in shaping and modifying the overall environment of firms. Competition has become increasingly international and, in many industries, completely global. The expansion of ICT, for example, has resulted in new production processes. Manufacturing activities and many services exhibit increasing returns to scale due to the presence of fixed costs (which globalization has reduced substantially) and learning effects. Furthermore, network externalities in the use of ICT goods often reinforce these supply-side effects (Box 3.2).

The way production at a global scale is undertaken today is very different from even a couple of decades ago. The difference lies in the complexity of the production process, together with the speed and size of the global movements of goods and information. Explaining how and where a manufactured good is "produced" is no longer an easy matter—design, production, distribution, and servicing are all divided into elements that are spread all over the world. Many products, including cars and computers, are made today by multinational corporations (MNCs) in highly competitive oligopolistic markets. While MNCs have existed for a long time, their presence is especially felt today. The peculiarity of today's MNCs is that they have production sites worldwide, with the consequence that production involves the logistical coordination of myriad functions. This allows MNCs to break up the chain of production of their products and to locate the

Box 3.2 Outsourcing and White-Collar Globalization: A Boon to Asia's Developing Countries

While globalization in the 1980s initially sent FDI and low-value added manufacturing to low-cost countries, the next round is sending white-collar jobs to these developing countries, ranging from basic research and chip design to engineering and financial analysis.

The PRC, for example, is becoming a key product developer for General Electric, Intel, Microsoft, Philips, and other electronics multinationals, for hardware design and embedded software. In the Philippines, more than 8,000 foreign companies source work in nine different information technology (IT) parks equipped with fiber-optic links. The country is known for its English-speaking workforce, college-educated accountants, software writers, architects, telemarketers, and graphic artists. In India, IT services, chip design, call centers, and back-office work for business generate $10 billion in exports. Indian providers such as Infosys, Tata, and Wipro are recognized global leaders in their fields, and many IT firms from the US are requesting their services.

With digitization, the Internet, and high-speed data networks as the driving forces, all kinds of knowledge-related work can now be done almost anywhere in the world.

Corporate downsizing in the US and Europe is also helping create more high-skilled jobs in developing countries. It is estimated that nearly 600,000 jobs will have moved from the US to low-wage countries by 2005, including 295,000 in office support and 109,000 in computer-related activities. This figure is estimated to rise to more than 3 million by 2015, including 1.7 million in office support and almost 500,000 in computer-related occupations. This covers a wide range of professions, such as life sciences, legal services, art and design, management, business operations, computing, architecture, sales, and office support.

The recipient countries, in turn, are helped by a large supply of an educated and highly skilled workforce, and the high rate at which they produce university graduates. The PRC, for instance, produces twice as many graduates in mechanical engineering as the US does. In the Philippines, which produces about 380,000 college graduates a year, there now exists an oversupply of accountants trained in US accounting standards, while India has more than 500,000 IT engineers.

The industrial countries are also likely to benefit from these develop-ments. They can reallocate their labor and capital to higher-value industries and cutting-edge R&D while sending more routine knowledge-related work overseas. This shifts the comparative advantage to activities with higher productivity, which in turn leads to a higher standard of living. It will also help keep prices of services competitive, as it did with garments, shoes, and appliances produced in developing countries.

In addition, industrial countries can find larger markets for their exports as a result of contributing to faster growth of developing countries. On the other hand, this could result in a loss of jobs. There is some evidence that there has been some reduction in pay for some IT jobs in the US, although to date the number of jobs affected has been insignificant. The future will determine the outcome of the emerging realignment in employment. For developing countries, however, the results will be beneficial for employment and the upgrading of skills.

Source:
Engardio, Pete, Aaron Bernstein, and Manjeet Kripalani. 2003. "The New Global Job Shift." *Business Week*, 3 February 2003.

links in different countries, depending on which provides the lowest unit costs. Finally, for MNCs to divide the production and distribution processes geographically, they have to be able to open plants, subsidiaries, offices, etc., easily where they are needed. This liberalization process, with a view to making the economy more efficient, is taking place everywhere. In the words of John Gray:

> The decisive advantage that a multinational company achieves over its rivals comes finally from its capacity to generate new technologies

and to deploy effectively and profitably. In turn, this depends to a considerable extent on the ways in which companies enable knowledge to be conserved and generated. In the late modern competitive environment, business organizations which do not capture and exploit new knowledge, which waste the stock of tacit understandings among their employees or discourage them from acquiring new knowledge, will soon go under (Gray 1998, p.76).

The above process has occurred on a huge scale

during the last few decades, and has been the result of a series of factors in developing and industrial countries. On the one hand, developing countries have tried a variety of policies since the end of the Second World War to encourage economic growth. By trial and error, they have reached the conclusion that the market system offers them the best possible solution, and that their firms have to compete in the world economy if they do not want to miss the opportunity for rapid development. Many developing countries, after decolonization, began by trying different combinations of import-substitution policies, government planning, and state-led industrialization in an attempt at "self-reliance." The failure of these approaches in many cases made leaders and policy makers think seriously about the opportunities provided by other options. The conclusion is that today, international trade, foreign direct investment (FDI), and the integration of firms across countries in GVCs are fundamental to any successful development strategy, and virtually all nations proclaim a commitment to global markets (Krueger 1997, Srinivasan and Bhagwati 1999, Coyle 2001).

On the other hand, economies of scale in research, product development, and manufacturing; the increasing mobility of capital; the differential in costs across countries, especially for labor; and the decline in profit rates in most industrial economies since the 1950s or early 1960s—all are pushing forward the globalization process.

The role of technology is very important in this context. Investing in new technology is necessary for firms to maintain, or increase, their competitive advantage. However, this requires considerable expenditure on both R&D and on the commercial exploitation of the results. Such investment also gives firms the opportunity to differentiate their products more clearly from those of their competitors. Often, only the already successful and profitable firms have access to the necessary finance, and only a few of the firms that invest in new technology will gain a sustainable advantage. Most will only achieve a brief competitive edge that will be quickly eroded by the response of their competitors, who will quickly adopt the same procedures.

In addition to globalization, technology, and competition, there are two other factors of change in Asia at present. These are the rapid growth of the PRC, and the existence of large, if cyclical,

overcapacity in certain key export sectors. On the first point, East and Southeast Asian firms are very concerned about their loss of price competitiveness with respect to enterprises in the PRC. The argument is that the PRC has built excess capacity in many of its industries and has flooded international markets with low-cost goods at the expense of East and Southeast Asia's exporters. Indeed, during the last decade, the PRC's impressive export performance and ability to attract substantial FDI have turned it into the "world's factory." The country now makes more than half of the world's cameras, about a third of its air conditioners, one fourth of its washing machines, and nearly one fifth of all refrigerators. This concern may be termed the "China syndrome," though the fear of losing out to the PRC is often overstated (Box 3.3).

On the second point, overcapacity is particularly seen in semiconductors, whose price experienced a sharp fall in 1996 and again in 2000 due to the decline in price of DRAMs, the largest selling semiconductor product group. In the second half of 2000, the price of DRAMs fell by 90%. As this product alone represents around 15% of total Korean exports, the fall in price presented severe problems for the country.

Enhancing Entrepreneurial and Technological Capabilities

Firms become more competitive by competing and slowly and patiently learning how to do business better. They accomplish this by both striving to enhance their entrepreneurial and technological capabilities—defined as the ability to use, generate, change, and add to the pool of the industrial arts—and by taking risks. In other words, firms become more competitive not only by reducing their costs of production, but also by developing their capability to create new, and more technology-intensive, products or new generations of existing products. This involves the firms moving into new areas, such as services, as well as taking risks and working through the process of trial and error.

Strong competition leads to the development of new markets, to the introduction of new technologies, and to the growth and transformation of existing markets. The exit of some firms that have lost the competitive struggle, despite the cost involved, is a desirable outcome for society, as it

Box 3.3 The Rise of the PRC: Threats and Opportunities

Many firms in East and Southeast Asia are concerned about losing their competitive position vis-à-vis the PRC in some labor-intensive exports (e.g., textiles and apparel) because of the low PRC relative wage rate. Indeed, the PRC remains a comparatively poor and labor-intensive economy with a large pool of reserve labor. Its manufacturing wages are about 5% of the US average, and 10% of those in some neighboring Asian economies As a result, about 70% of its exports consist of labor-intensive goods such as garments, toys, shoes, and furniture. It is mostly in these labor-intensive goods that PRC firms can potentially out-compete its neighbors. Further, the PRC has been able to maintain its low labor costs thanks to an abundant supply of labor from rural areas.

The PRC has thus been able to hold on to low-end industries (e.g., toys, textiles) and make inroads into the high-technology sectors (assembly). Likewise, last year the country surpassed the US as the world's largest recipient of FDI, with a value of $53 billion. Some countries fear that an important part of the FDI that could come to their countries is now being diverted to the PRC.

It is unlikely that the PRC will rapidly lose its cost advantage given that the large transfer of workers from rural to industrial areas will prevent wages from increasing faster than productivity (and hence prevent any large increases in unit labor costs). It is also doubtful whether there will be any marked appreciation in the currency that would reduce the economy's price competitiveness, while a move to full convertibility of the currency would expose the weak banking system to external shocks, as it did in countries affected by the Asian crisis. PRC price deflation and US dollar weakness suggest, if anything, that the yuan will depreciate in real terms.

While PRC firms have a comparative advantage in some labor-intensive sectors, and firms in Southeast Asia are being hurt, the evidence does not indicate that PRC firms are driving out of the market every single firm in the region in every single sector. To begin with, the PRC's gain in market share of manufactured exports to OECD countries since the 1980s has not been at the expense of ASEAN countries. In 1990–1995, ASEAN's share in total exports to OECD increased, while the share for NIEs declined slightly. As is well known, however, a large portion of the PRC's exports to OECD consists of goods produced by firms owned by investors from Hong Kong, China and Taipei,China. Moreover, as the PRC's exports have grown, so have its imports. Southeast Asian exports to the PRC have grown rapidly in recent years. Between 1999 and 2001, for instance, Singapore's exports to the PRC grew by an average of 14% per year. The PRC's imports from Japan have been increasing at an annual rate of 40–50%, and it has a substantial trade deficit with Korea, Malaysia, and Thailand. In 2001, the PRC's trade surplus increased to over $30 billion. This was 2.9% of GDP, larger than Japan's (1.7%) but lower than Korea's (3.2%). However, the PRC's trade surplus as a share of GDP has been declining since 1997.

What matters for a firm's competitiveness and the attractiveness of a country for FDI is not low wages but low unit labor costs. The PRC's low wages, moreover, are a threat to labor-intensive industries elsewhere. There is no significant statistical relationship between wage rates and FDI. For example, Singapore has higher wage rates than Malaysia but has not lost all its investment in labor-intensive industries to Malaysia because its higher productivity compensates for this. Other important factors influencing the level of FDI are macroeconomic stability, protection of intellectual property, and distance to suppliers and end markets.

The PRC's high level of FDI is partly a reflection of weaknesses in its financial system and its inability to utilize its high level of domestic savings. Indeed, it is questionable whether the PRC's FDI is, strictly speaking, foreign investment at all. Substantial profits of firms in the PRC are deposited in accounts in Hong Kong, China for tax purposes, which then return to the mainland as FDI.

Much of the PRC's production of capital-intensive goods (e.g., cars, semi-conductors, and computers) is reserved for the domestic market. Nearly all of the announced joint ventures in automobile assembly are destined for the domestic market, except one with Honda. This is because the PRC is still a long way behind other countries in its capability of producing these goods with the quality necessary for sale on world markets. The PRC has also disadvantages arising from its poor infrastructure, opaque government rules, and problematic business practices (e.g., bribery and corruption).

Not all PRC threats are supported by the evidence. From a different point of view, the PRC economy presents immense opportunities because of its large and growing domestic market. It is the second biggest market for Volkswagen after Germany. Ford anticipates that in 5 years it will become a bigger market for its cars than Japan or Germany. The PRC's accession to WTO will further open its markets to competition, and its importance as a source of demand will grow. Economist David Roland-Host estimates that the PRC will be the region's largest exporter by 2010. But it will also be the largest importer by 2005, offering unprecedented market opportunities to other Asian countries.

In November 2002, the ASEAN countries and the PRC signed an agreement to establish a free trade area by 2010 and by 2015 for the weakest ASEAN members. A crucial issue is whether the PRC's capacity to absorb the region's imports will require a significant overhaul of the production structures in East and Southeast Asia.

In the services sector, the PRC is one of the fastest-growing sources of tourists for Malaysia, Singapore, and Thailand. A rising PRC middle class also suggests strong potential for services industries in the region, such as higher quality education and health services, and more sophisticated financial services.

Sources:
Day, Philip. 2002. "China May Lose Shine As Manufacturing Base." *Asian Wall Street Journal.* 20 December 2002, pp.a1–a2; Roland Host, David. "China's Economic Prowess is not a Threat." *International Herald Tribune.* 4 March 2003; "China: Eating Your Lunch," pp.12–13, "Is the Wakening Giant a Monster?" pp.65–67. *The Economist.* 13 February 2003.

enables adjustment and change at the broader national level.

In their quest for profits, firms face the challenge of many competitors who are pursuing the same goals, and this competition forces the adoption of the cheapest methods of production and the improvement in the quality of products. Technological upgrading, in the form of introduction of new machinery and improvement of technological capabilities, provides a firm with the means to be successful in competition. In the process of introducing better technologies, new lower-cost methods become available, which allow the firm to increase labor productivity, i.e., the efficiency with which it converts resources into value. Firms will adopt these newer methods of production if they are more profitable than the older ones.

Why does raising firm-level labor productivity matter? Because this is how the profit motive is put into practice at that level. In order to increase profits, firms must increase labor productivity, and it is for this purpose that new machines and methods of production are introduced, leading to an increase in the capital/labor ratio. Increasing labor productivity is the key to ensuring survival and long-run growth both at the firm and national levels, and this is the essence of competitiveness. Figure 3.2 summarizes the two channels used by firms to increase labor productivity, i.e., technical and allocative efficiency, and technical progress. These two channels are, in practice, complementary and mutually reinforcing.

With regard to the first channel, a firm is said to be technically inefficient if it produces less than maximum possible output from any combination of inputs. A firm is said to be allocatively inefficient if the marginal rate of substitution between two inputs does not equal the corresponding factor price ratio.

With regard to the second channel—technical progress—a firm can raise labor productivity in two ways. One is through investment, which is a function of profit rates, profit shares, unit labor costs, expectations, the general investment environment, and risk. New investment leads to higher capital-labor ratios, or capital deepening. Giving workers more capital to work with raises their productivity. Investment has another role in raising labor productivity: most technological progress is embodied in new capital goods and so a high rate of investment will allow firms in developing countries to adopt, often through the imports of capital goods, new technology. Without new investment there can be little technological progress. There is also evidence that a high rate of investment allows firms to indigenously improve their products and processes through "learning by doing" (Kaldor 1957, Arrow 1962).

The ability of a firm to take advantage of technical progress is also enhanced if the firm improves its entrepreneurial and technological capabilities through two competitiveness strategies, namely (i) learning and adaptation, and (ii) innovation. The latter is a process of searching for, finding, developing, imitating, adapting, and adopting new products, new processes, and new organizational arrangements. Because rivals do not stand still, the firm's capacity to develop these capabilities, as well as its ability to compete, depends on the firm maintaining a steady pace of innovation. In addition, the country's general institutional infrastructure, discussed in *Institutions, The State, and The Market: A Partnership for Development*, is a key determinant of how firms develop these capabilities.

Figure 3.2 Entrepreneurial and Technological Capabilities and Labor Productivity

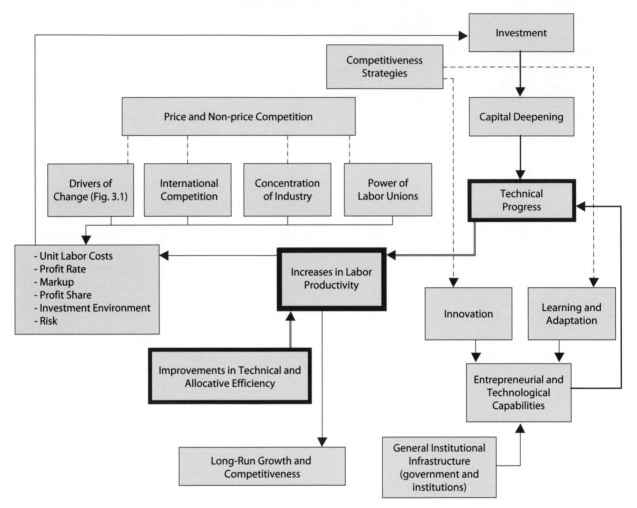

National Competitiveness: A Dangerous Obsession?

Today, many products in supermarkets and department stores carry the label "Made in PRC." Moreover, many markets in industrial countries, such as consumer electronics, have been dominated for years by products from previously less developed countries (e.g., Korea). This has led to the question as to whether nations themselves can be considered competitive or uncompetitive, analogously to firms. In other words, is the concept of "national competitiveness" a relevant issue? It could be argued that this is because the output of a country is the summation of the production of firms located there. Some authors therefore regard as legitimate, the discussion of the concept of national competitiveness, if only as a reflection of the competitiveness of the nation's firms.

National competitiveness has been defined as the "ability of a country to produce goods and services that meet the test of international markets and simultaneously to maintain and expand the real income of its citizens."[2] And again: "National competitiveness refers to a country's ability to create, produce, distribute and/or service products in international trade while earning rising returns on its resources" (Buckley et al. 1988, p.177). These definitions are consistent with the term "international competitiveness," which brings to mind the idea that each nation is viewed "like a big corporation competing in the global market place" (Krugman 1996a, p.4).

It is from this perspective that commentators in some Asian countries have voiced their concern over the consequences of the rapid development of certain industries in the PRC, such as textiles and electronics, as these industries are seen as posing a threat to existing domestic industries. Moreover, this alleged competition is often seen as unfair, to the extent that the PRC benefits from low wages and hence from low unit costs. The conclusion has often been drawn that unless governments take action, perhaps through some form of protection or public policies to increase the competitiveness of the threatened industries, the PRC poses a serious menace to the prosperity of these countries. The irony is that, while the benefits of competition are widely understood and accepted by most people,

it is competition from *abroad* that tends to cause concern among domestic firms and governments. This has led to discussion in terms of economic competition between countries, in much the same terms as competition between products, such as Coca-Cola and Pepsi-Cola (e.g., Thurow 1993).

However, the definition and use of the term competitiveness at the national level in this manner is far from uncontroversial, as some economists have expressed very serious reservations about its meaning as they believe the idea to be very elusive. In a series of papers, Paul Krugman (1994, 1996a, 1996b) argued that defining national competitiveness, in the specific context of trade (i.e., as export competitiveness), is a futile exercise, and is dangerous both because it implicitly proves a misunderstanding of the theory of comparative advantage and the benefits of free trade, and because it implies a mercantilist view of the world. Krugman contended that it is firms that compete for exports, not countries (although it is true that trade statistics are presented as an aggregate). National economies are not in direct competition with one another and nations do not go bankrupt in the way firms do. Krugman argued that the notion of competitiveness at the national level makes no sense, and claimed that the term was becoming, in fact, a "dangerous obsession."

While Krugman's argument has a great deal of validity, its limitations should also be appreciated. First, the conclusions of the neoclassical trade model depend on extremely restrictive and unrealistic assumptions, such as perfect competition with efficient markets, homogeneous products, universal access to technology with no learning costs, no externalities or scale economies, technically efficient firms, and, especially, fully employed resources.[3] A second limitation is put forward by Lall (2000), who argues that, contrary to received trade theory, in the real world, export structures are path-dependent and difficult to change. Trade patterns are much less responsive to changing factor prices than commonly assumed. They are the outcome of a long, cumulative process of learning, agglomeration, and increasing returns; institution building; and the overall business culture. This means that the world's pattern of specialization and trade is the result of history, accidents, and past government policies. It is not only dictated by comparative advantage, which is determined by tastes, resources, and technology. Moving from a low-technology (labor-intensive) structure to a high-technology (capital- and knowledge-intensive) one is a difficult and far from straightforward process, involving many policy interventions. In Lall's view, national competitiveness is, in fact, a real issue that can be defined and measured.

The above discussion clearly indicates that the very notion of national competitiveness is controversial, and, in the final analysis, the debate over whether the term has any meaning and substance has its roots in the appropriate role and extent of government policy. Given that it is firms that compete, the real question from the national point of view is: How can government policies ensure that firms are competitive? Despite the arguments about whether or not nations compete, governments, undoubtedly, play a critical role in shaping the competitive environment and behavior of firms through a variety of policies. The section *Institutions, The State, and The Market: A Partnership for Development*, addresses this issue.

Aggregate Measures of Competitiveness

Although the idea of competitiveness, understood as the capacity to compete with rivals, does not fit in well in terms of countries, at the national level, economists use several indicators (apart from labor productivity) that are referred to as measures of national competitiveness.

First, national competitiveness has been used to mean labor productivity. This is coherent with the argument that the key variable to achieve long-run growth is productivity. However, if productivity is used to measure competitiveness, then the term national competitiveness is simply "a poetic way of saying productivity without actually implying that international competition has anything to do with it" (Krugman 1996a, p.10).

Second, national competitiveness has been used to mean price competitiveness (Hooper and Larin 1989, Durand et al. 1992, McCombie and Thirlwall 1994, Turner and Golub 1997, Turner and Van 't dack 1993). The most widely used and best-known measures are the real effective exchange rate (REER) and unit labor cost (ULC).[4]

It is this view of "competitiveness," i.e., price competitiveness, that people often have in mind when making general statements about a country's competitiveness. From this perspective, it is correct to refer to the PRC as being competitive at the moment. The PRC's currency is undervalued, its wage rate is lower than that in many countries in Southeast Asia, and its labor productivity is about the same or higher. Hence, its products are competitive in terms of the REER and ULC.

For empirical purposes, however, there are several problems with the REER and ULC. First, obtaining reliable data on wages and productivity to construct ULCs, especially for developing countries, is not easy. Second, an issue concerning inter-country comparisons of ULCs is how to translate the costs calculated for individual countries into comparable or common-currency units. Third, a rise in a country's ULC relative to that in other countries should lead to a decline in its competitiveness, which would translate into a lower global market share. However, empirical evidence has shown that, over the long term, market share for exports and relative unit costs or prices, of indus-

trial countries especially, tend to move together—the "Kaldor paradox" (McCombie and Thirlwall 1994, Fagerberg 1996).[5] Likewise, it is clear from the historical evidence that the substantial exchange rate movements that have taken place since the early 1970s have not rectified balance-of-payments disequilibria. Speculative capital flows, rather than changes in economic fundamentals, have often driven these movements.

Fourth, a rise in either the REER or ULC can be accompanied by strong economic performance. For example, if firms in a country become more successful in terms of non-price competitiveness because they are innovative, flexible, produce high-quality goods, etc., then the REER would probably strengthen. Finally, both measures can be calculated in different ways, thus potentially leading to different results.

From a policy perspective and in pursuit of overall competitiveness, some economies may become price competitive by keeping their currencies undervalued through nominal depreciations. For short periods of time there can be important gains in price competitiveness due to exchange rate fluctuations, largely resulting from short-term speculative capital flows. These exchange rate changes are much more volatile than productivity. The result is that there can be sudden dramatic changes in price competitiveness without any change in the fundamentals. A strategy of keeping a currency undervalued, however, will most likely be unsuccessful in the long run since it may only mask and perpetuate a lack of productivity in the country's firms. It may also lead to competitive devaluations and beggar-thy-neighbor trade policies (UNIDO 2002, Box 6.3). Countries that systematically rely on devaluations to maintain competitiveness often fail to pay appropriate heed to quality and innovation.

Other economists have used Balassa's index of revealed comparative advantage (Drysdale 1988), defined as the share of a commodity group in the economy's total exports, divided by that commodity's share of world exports, so that the higher the ratio is above (below) unity, the stronger (weaker) that economy's comparative advantage in that commodity group, provided that government policies have not grossly distorted the composition of exports.

There is finally, another way of examining national competitiveness based on the construction of composite indices. In fact, the popularity of the idea of international competitiveness has been enhanced by the construction of a competitiveness index by the World Economic Forum (WEF), which is published in the *Global Competitiveness Report*. The 2001–2002 *Report* encompasses 75 countries, among them 13 in developing Asia. It produces two indices, the growth competitiveness index (GCI), and the current competitiveness index (CCI). The GCI aims to measure the capacity of the national economy to achieve sustained economic growth over the medium term (Table 3.1). It looks at the macroeconomic sources of GDP per capita growth, and generates predictions of the ability of a country to improve its per capita income over time.

The GCI is made up of three factors, namely technological capacity, quality of public institutions, and quality of macroeconomic environment. In each of these three factors, the *Global Competitiveness Report* constructs indices based on a combination of objective information and opinions of business leaders based on surveys (around 4,600 respondents).

The CCI, on the other hand, examines the microeconomic bases of a nation's GDP per capita and provides insights into the level of GDP per capita that is sustainable in the long term (Table 3.2). The CCI is made up of two subindices, the degree of company sophistication and the quality of the national business environment. The data used come primarily from a survey of senior business leaders and government officials. To compute an overall measure of the CCI, all the individual dimensions are combined using common factor analysis.

The CCI is largely based on Michael Porter's (1990) framework, known as the "competitiveness diamond," where the idea of competitive advantages—as opposed to comparative advantage—is introduced. These arise from firm-level efforts to develop new products, make improvements, develop better brands or delivery methods and so on, in other words, to innovate in a broad sense of the term. Innovation, in turn, is influenced by conditions given by four elements of the diamond: factor conditions, demand conditions, related and supporting industries, and the context for firm strategy and rivalry.

Although the rankings provided by the WEF are widely cited in some circles, and are taken seriously

Table 3.1 Growth Competitiveness Index and Components, 2001

Economy	GCI Rank	GCI Score	Technology Index Rank	Score	Public Institutions Index Rank	Score	Macro-economic Environment Index Rank	Score
Singapore	4	5.84	18	5.44	6	6.27	1	5.52
Taipei,China	7	5.59	4	6.19	24	5.30	15	4.69
Hong Kong, China	13	5.47	33	4.93	10	6.01	4	5.12
Korea	23	5.13	9	5.66	44	4.25	8	4.94
Malaysia	30	4.83	22	5.36	39	4.53	20	4.59
Thailand	33	4.53	39	4.54	42	4.36	16	4.68
China, People's Rep. of	39	4.40	53	4.05	50	4.10	6	5.04
Philippines	48	4.16	40	4.53	64	3.53	28	4.42
India	57	3.84	66	3.54	49	4.11	45	3.88
Viet Nam	60	3.77	65	3.56	63	3.58	37	4.15
Sri Lanka	61	3.74	59	3.82	58	3.84	60	3.56
Indonesia	64	3.69	61	3.76	66	3.35	41	3.96
Bangladesh	71	3.04	74	2.83	75	2.48	48	3.81

GCI = growth competitiveness index.
Source: World Economic Forum (2001).

Table 3.2 Current Competitiveness Index and Components, 1999–2001

Economy	Current Competitiveness Index Rank			Company Operations and Strategy Rank			Quality of National Business Environment Rank			2000 GDP Per Capita (ppp adjusted)
	2001	2000	1999	2001	2000	1999	2001	2000	1999	
Singapore	10	9	12	15	15	14	9	5	12	23,000
Hong Kong, China	18	16	21	21	23	24	16	14	18	24,448
Taipei,China	21	21	19	20	18	17	21	21	22	17,223
Korea	28	27	28	26	25	27	30	28	30	17,311
India	36	37	42	43	40	48	34	37	43	2,403
Malaysia	37	30	27	37	30	25	38	30	31	8,924
Thailand	38	40	39	42	47	43	39	40	39	6,489
China, People's Rep. of	47	44	49	39	38	31	47	45	50	3,953
Philippines	54	46	44	45	43	34	54	46	46	3,956
Indonesia	55	47	53	50	51	47	57	47	52	3,014
Sri Lanka	57	-	-	58	-	-	55	-	-	3,512
Viet Nam	62	53	50	64	50	41	64	52	49	1,974
Bangladesh	73	-	-	72	-	-	73	-	-	1,561

- Not available; ppp = purchasing power parity.
Source: World Economic Forum (2001).

by some governments, they have been questioned by many academic economists. Lall (2001a) put forward a very serious critique of the GCI and CCI on the basis that they take an oversimplified view of the constraints to structural change in developing countries. For example, Porter does not provide a theory of competitive advantages in economic terms. The discussion only gives a post hoc explanation, and even then in a rather general way, why certain activities have succeeded in certain countries. The link from competitive advantages at the firm level, where the approach is most useful, to the national level remains weak and unsubstantiated. Lall also points out that the indices are atheoretical as the "underlying model tends to lack rigor and clarity, with a propensity to use a large number of variables without theoretically justifying their causal relations to the dependent (and often without measuring them correctly)." Likewise, the weights applied to construct the indices are arbitrary, and the indices display an overly negative view of the role of government (Lall 2001a, p.1506) (e.g., free markets are good and positive for competitiveness while union power or pension benefits are bad). Finally, they rely extensively on qualitative data obtained through questionnaires

that are, at most, only tenuously related to the notion of competitiveness. Lall (2001a, p.1507) concludes: "Appealing as all this may be to the *Global Competitiveness Report*'s corporate audience, the economic validity of many of these propositions is debatable."

The *Industrial Development Report 2002/2003* of the United Nations Industrial Development Organization (UNIDO 2002) introduces a scoreboard in accordance with Lall's philosophy (2001a, 2001b), and thus differs from the WEF indices. This scoreboard provides important information on crucial aspects of industrial development and competitiveness. It has two parts: an index of a country's ability to produce and export manufactures—the competitive industrial performance index—and benchmarks of the structural drivers of industrial performance.

The competitive industrial performance index measures the ability of countries to produce and export manufactures competitively. It is constructed from four indicators: manufacturing value added per capita, manufactured exports per capita, share of medium and high-technology products in manufacturing value added, and share of medium- and high-technology products in manufactured exports.

The first two indicators provide information about industrial capacity, while the other two reflect the technological complexity and industrial upgrading of a country. The index is constructed as the average of the four indicators, and is calculated for a total of 87 economies with values for 1985 and 1998, including 14 economies in developing Asia (Table 3.3).

Industrial performance is the outcome of many social, political, and economic factors interacting in complex and dynamic ways. The second part of the scoreboard benchmarks economies on their key structural variables, called drivers, and focuses on five proxy variables: skills, technological effort, inward FDI, royalty and license payments abroad, and modern infrastructure (Tables 3.4 and 3.5).

UNIDO's work has the important advantage with respect to the WEF indices that it is much more simple. Likewise, all the variables considered by UNIDO's competitive industrial performance index and drivers of industrial performance, unlike many of the variables that constitute the WEF indices, are very appropriate. The major drawback

Table 3.3 Competitive Industrial Performance Index, 1998 and 1985

Economy	Rank 1998	Rank 1985	Index Value 1998	Index Value 1985
Singapore	1	6	0.883	0.587
Taipei,China	15	19	0.412	0.292
Korea	18	22	0.370	0.247
Malaysia	22	30	0.278	0.116
Philippines	25	45	0.241	0.044
Hong Kong, China	30	18	0.204	0.320
Thailand	32	43	0.172	0.058
PRC	37	61	0.126	0.021
Indonesia	49	65	0.054	0.012
India	50	50	0.054	0.034
Pakistan	60	55	0.031	0.028
Sri Lanka	69	71	0.017	0.008
Bangladesh	73	74	0.011	0.008
Nepal	79	79	0.006	0.001

Source: UNIDO (2002).

Table 3.4 Drivers of Industrial Performance, Ranking, 1998 and 1985

Harbison-Myers Index of Skills[a]			Tertiary Enrollments in Technical Subjects[b]			Financed Research and Development		
Economy	1998	1985	Economy	1998	1985	Economy	1998	1985
Korea	10	6	Korea	1	1	Korea	13	23
Taipei,China	23	21	Taipei,China	5	10	Singapore	14	19
Singapore	29	37	Philippines	26	28	Taipei,China	20	16
Philippines	32	23	Hong Kong, China	31	24	Malaysia	34	38
Hong Kong, China	39	39	Singapore	33	4	Hong Kong, China	40	46
Thailand	45	48	Indonesia	51	63	PRC	44	46
Malaysia	55	51	Thailand	54	49	Indonesia	45	41
Indonesia	56	57	Malaysia	59	62	India	46	36
Sri Lanka	58	53	India	62	51	Thailand	48	39
PRC	59	67	PRC	66	64	Philippines	57	40
India	69	60	Sri Lanka	68	61	Sri Lanka	60	0[c]
Nepal	71	66	Bangladesh	69	58	Bangladesh	61	0[c]
Bangladesh	76	72	Nepal	70	66	Nepal	61	0[c]
Pakistan	77	69	Pakistan	75	69	Pakistan	61	0[c]

[a] The Harbison-Myers Index is the average of the percentage of the relevant age groups enrolled in secondary and tertiary education, with tertiary enrollments given a weight of five. [b] Ranking is based on tertiary enrollment as percentage of the population. Technical subjects include pure science, mathematics and computing, and engineering. [c] All economies with negligible values are given the same rank. Data under 1998 are either for that year or for the latest available year.

Source: UNIDO (2002).

Table 3.5 Drivers of Industrial Performance, Ranking, 1998 and 1985

Per Capita Foreign Direct Investment			Royalty and License Payments Per Capita Abroad			No. of Telephone Mainlines per 1,000 People		
Economy	1998	1985	Economy	1998	1985	Economy	1998	1985
Singapore	1	1	Singapore	2	1	Singapore	10	16
Hong Kong, China	5	8	Hong Kong, China	4	2	Hong Kong, China	11	17
Malaysia	19	11	Malaysia	6	33	Korea	23	26
Taipei,China	35	36	Taipei,China	16	19	Taipei,China	24	23
Thailand	45	42	Korea	19	20	Malaysia	37	41
Korea	48	49	Thailand	28	37	Thailand	51	62
PRC	49	65	Indonesia	42	34	PRC	55	77
Philippines	52	62	Philippines	46	45	Philippines	64	66
Indonesia	53	59	PRC	57	64	Sri Lanka	67	70
Sri Lanka	64	53	India	60	58	Indonesia	68	73
Pakistan	72	64	Pakistan	61	54	India	69	72
India	77	71	Bangladesh	65	63	Pakistan	70	71
Nepal	81	75	Nepal	65	-	Nepal	76	86
Bangladesh	85	76	Sri Lanka	65	-	Bangladesh	83	85

- Not available.

Source: UNIDO (2002).

in the UNIDO approach is the aggregation of the four indicators into a composite number via a simple average. While the individual components of the index convey important information, their ad hoc weights in a single number can lead to a dubious ranking of countries, which is dependent on the exact weights chosen. Consequently, it is difficult to determine unambiguously the implications of such an index.

Summing up, these indices must be treated with caution. Much of the information provided in these reports through the individual variables (such as about innovation capacity) used to construct the indices can be very valuable for purposes of, for example, establishing priorities and policy responses. The Government of Singapore, for example, posts the results of the rankings in its web site (www.psb.gov.sg) and, for policy purposes, it focuses on those areas where it ranks poorly, and outlines steps to address these weaknesses. Nevertheless, as has been seen, the usefulness of the indices themselves is rather limited.

Institutions, The State, and The Market: A Partnership for Development

Firms do not operate in a vacuum; they cannot function successfully or be competitive in circumstances where appropriate institutions are lacking, where the role of government is not clearly defined, and where there is an inadequate investment environment. Figure 3.2 above showed that the general institutional infrastructure, largely provided by the government, affects how firms develop entrepreneurial and technological capabilities. Therefore, a development strategy requires a working partnership between the state and the market (Stern and Stiglitz 1997) as well as the building-up of institutions. The collaboration of the two parties, state and market, consists of a series of tasks and responsibilities assigned to each. This is particularly relevant in the context of developing countries, where markets and institutions are less developed. While the scope for government intervention may be greater in developing countries, government capacity to intervene may be more limited. Developing this partnership must be a synchronized process, since the tasks undertaken by the government and the market complement each other, and the smallest malfunction of one component puts the quality and efficiency of the entire system at risk. This is the essence of the "O-ring theory of economic development" (Box 3.4).

The objective of this partnership is to create a *well-functioning market economy*. This is, in fact, what is meant by a "competitive economy," and what the above definitions of national competitiveness amount to. Therefore, although "national competitiveness" remains a very elusive concept, in particular in the specific context of trade, it can be used as shorthand for well-functioning market economy, and this makes it a useful concept in the policy debate and for development purposes. The definition of a competitive economy as a well-functioning market economy is not readily amenable to empirical analysis, and to being expressed in terms of measurable indicators or a composite index. And it has nothing to do with rivalry and competition inherent in the definition of competitiveness at the firm level. However, the idea of a well-functioning market economy encapsulates nicely the objective of a nation, and the fact that being competitive is

not a state but a process. It is the general framework of analysis used here.

The question is, what is the appropriate mix between markets and state, and how does the partnership work? Figure 3.3 shows how the responsibilities of markets and state are linked so as to achieve the ultimate objective at the national level, namely, development. This consists not only of increasing GDP per capita, but also of improving the quality of life, i.e., reducing poverty, promoting health and education, maintaining a clean environment, creating an employable labor force, and so on. The key is to ensure fast long-run growth of output, the most important determinant of which is rapid productivity growth. (It should be noted that many Asian countries have specific programs and strategies to improve productivity [APO 2001].) Therefore, what needs to be understood are the determinants of productivity, and this is how international comparisons and rankings should be undertaken. An implication of this is that, as an economy develops, it will move further along the path toward catching up with the technological frontier.

Today there is widespread acceptance that private entrepreneurship and incentives do a better job than the government (Easterly 2001). Therefore, the initial premise is that the production and allocation of private goods and services should be left to the market, while the government performs the crucial role of providing the institutional infrastructure. Furthermore, markets on their own do not necessarily produce socially desirable outcomes (Stiglitz 2002). As market imperfections are more prevalent in developing countries than in industrial countries, developing-country governments have a critical role to play and can, potentially, improve the outcome by well-chosen interventions.

Finally, a third party is necessary for a well-functioning market economy—appropriate institutions. As seen above, the development of a firm's capabilities is affected by the general institutional infrastructure (see the subsection *Enhancing Entrepreneurial and Technological Capabilities*, above). Likewise, a firm's performance contributes to the development of a well-functioning market

Box 3.4 The O-Ring Theory of Economic Development

Why are wage and productivity differentials between industrial and developing countries so large? An O-ring is a donut-shaped rubber seal. The malfunctioning of one such seal caused the explosion of the Challenger space shuttle in 1986. The shuttle had cost billions of dollars, required the cooperation of several hundreds of teams, and combined a considerable number of components. All this joint effort was lost because one seal failed to function properly. In 1993, economist Michael Kremer applied the O-ring metaphor to explain why such large differences in income exist between industrial and developing countries. The implications of his theory are very important since they seem to contradict a great deal of conventional wisdom, especially regarding the implications of the theory of comparative advantage.

Kremer argued that production is often the result of a series of tasks, as for example, to be found on an assembly line. These tasks can be performed at different levels of "skills," where the latter refers to the probability of successfully completing the task. For the final product or service to be successfully made or delivered, every single task must be completed correctly. This implies that the value of each worker's efforts depends on the quality of all other workers' efforts. For example, a car that leaves the assembly line is, according to Kremer, a car if and only if brakes, transmission, etc., work properly. One of the most important implications of Kremer's theory is that it explains why workers of similar skills have strong incentives to match together, i.e., highly skilled workers will attempt to work with other highly skilled workers; likewise, low-skilled workers. The consequence is that highly skilled workers complement each other, giving rise to increasing returns to skills with the result that productivity will be even higher; likewise, unskilled workers lower each others' productivity even more.

The model has very important applications for both economic development and labor markets. It explains, for example, why highly skilled workers want to migrate to industrial countries, giving rise to the brain drain. They will be much more productive after they have migrated, even though their individual skills remain the same. Migration allows them to match up with the skilled labor force in the industrial country. Conventional economic theory would suggest that as surgeons are a scarce factor of production in, say, India, compared with, say, the US, their marginal products and pay would be commensurately higher than their US counterparts. In fact, their wage rates are much lower.

Financial capital will also flow to the richest countries since increasing returns imply that the rate of return is higher where it is already abundant. The model is also consistent with the evidence that rich countries specialize in the production of complicated products; that firms are larger in industrial countries; and that firm size and wages are positively correlated.

Differences in product quality are associated with differences in workers' skills, and explain why Italian bicycle manufacturers can compete with their PRC counterparts, despite the difference in labor costs. The matching story also offers an explanation of income differences among countries. A small difference in workers' skills leads to a proportionally larger difference in wages and output, so wages and productivity differentials among countries with different skill levels are huge.

Arguably, O-ring effects exist across firms. Suppose one firm builds roads and another cars. The additional value to drivers of an improvement in the quality of cars most likely will be smaller if the roads happen to be of poor quality, and vice versa. When tasks are performed sequentially (as in global value chains), highly skilled workers will perform the tasks at the later more complex stages of production, which explains why poor countries have higher shares of primary output in GDP, and why workers are paid more in industries with high-value inputs. Also, under sequential production, countries with highly skilled workers specialize in products that require expensive intermediate goods, and those with low-skill workers specialize in primary production. In other words, there is nothing natural about the international pattern of specialization: comparative advantage in primary goods, manufactures, and services is itself endogenously determined.

Finally, imperfect matching of workers due to imperfect information about worker skills leads to positive spillovers and strategic complementarity in human capital. Thus, subsidies to investment in human capital may be the optimal solution. Small differences between countries in such subsidies or in exogenous factors, such as geography or the quality of the educational system, lead to multiplier effects that create large differences in worker skills and hence in aggregate productivity and living standards.

Source:
Kremer, Michael. 1993. "The O-Ring Theory of Economic Development." *The Quarterly Journal of Economics* 108(3).

Figure 3.3 Achieving Development: Governments and Markets in Partnership

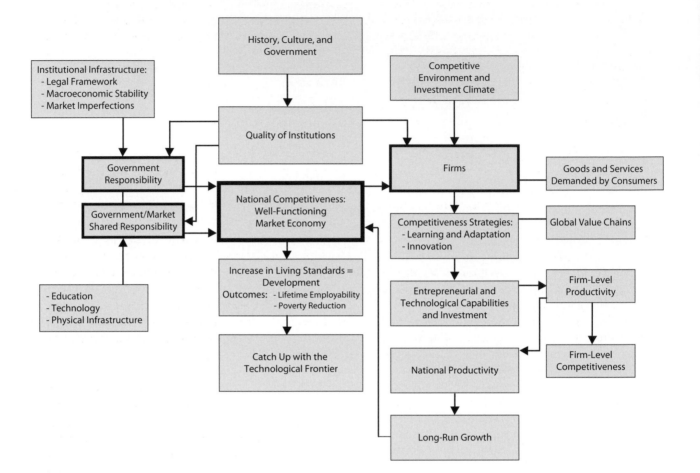

economy since the development of entrepreneurial and technological capabilities is a source of firm-level productivity, and the latter feeds into national productivity and long-run growth. The specific roles of institutions and governments to achieve this are discussed below.

Role of Institutions

Firms and governments operate in the context of an institutional setting, determined mostly by historical and cultural factors, and by the government itself. Institutions have been defined as a series of rules, norms, and organizations that coordinate human behavior (World Bank 2002), while their role is to enhance organizational incentives in situations where a monetary reward is not enough. According to Santonu Basu, the main task of institutions "is to provide support

to firms in exchange-related activities, such as marketing, communications, transport, the transfer of technology, credit and insurance" (Basu 2002). Successful institutions lower transaction costs, provide incentives, avoid or resolve conflict, and create the environment in which firms compete. The biggest differences between countries are in their institutions, and these differences are probably the most important bottleneck for development (Rodrik et al. 2002). In this sense, it can be argued that the quality of institutions ultimately determines the level of competitiveness of a country, if the latter is understood as a well-functioning economy.

The question arises as to what sorts of institutions are more conducive to achieving growth and enable firms to be more competitive. The answers are complicated, and can be considered under three heads.

First, the term "institutions" refers to a large "black box" that encompasses such diverse factors as political stability; the level of informal economic activity; public trust in politicians and the police; the level of organized crime and corruption; "bandit capitalism"; judicial and central bank independence; capacity to collect taxes and enforce the law; soundness of accounting systems; litigation costs; and protection of human rights.

Most economists acknowledge that a high degree of corruption constrains the development of a well-functioning market economy as it affects, for example, the credibility and integrity of the government both domestically and internationally (i.e., for potential investors). Letting markets work without excessive bureaucratic procedures and red tape is also a fundamental prerequisite for development.

Second, institutions evolve. In the words of Stern and Stiglitz "Institutions shape change and are shaped by change" (Stern and Stiglitz 1997, p.13), and whereas successful institutional arrangements usually take into account a country's history, a particular institution that worked at a certain time might not work later, even in the same country. For example, Korea in the 1960s and 1970s extensively subsidized private investment by controlling bank credit and rewarding successful companies (and penalizing poor performers) as a vehicle for sustained growth. Yet by the 1990s, the channeling of credit to favored companies had caused significant damage to the country's financial system. Broadly, "there is no single mapping between the market and the set of non-market institutions required to sustain it" (Rodrik 1999, p.13).

Third, institutions are, to a large extent, a very immobile factor of production, i.e., they are country specific. A country can import or copy a machine, imitate a production process, or attract skilled workers, but not the institutions that exist in a successful economy.

All this implies that the development of the institutions that suit the characteristics of each country is an organic, historical, and lengthy process that is subject to trial and error (Hausmann and Rodrik 2002). This process involves an element of domestic adaptation in so far as—although other countries' experiences might serve as a reference point—what works in one country might not work in another. If one looks across a broad spectrum of industrial countries, their institutions are very

different, despite having very general commonalities. Likewise, it is incorrect to infer that because there were some similarities in the stages of development of the NIEs, the institutions and government policies were the same in all of them. (These issues are considered further in *Catch-Up Competitiveness: Some Lessons*.)

Areas of State Responsibility

The key factor for developing countries is the creation of capability to specialize in those industries for which world demand is rapidly growing (in other words, for which there is a high income elasticity of demand for exports). This means developing high-value-added goods, and government policy has a definite role in facilitating this. The idea that nations compete as if they were big corporations derives from the notion that governments can implement policies that affect the competitiveness of firms. In fact, most government policies affect, more or less directly, the competitiveness of all firms by, for example, increasing the provision of basic education, or fostering the institutional change that will encourage innovation and the development of modern industries. The way in which the role of the state is defined and in which its services are delivered is probably the most important determinant of the standard of living of the community over the long term (Stern and Stiglitz 1997, p.27).

What is more controversial is how much further beyond these general responsibilities the state should go.[6,7] Despite the plethora of empirical studies, there seems to be no consensus.

According to Stern and Stiglitz: "Government has the central responsibility to provide an *institutional infrastructure* in which markets can function" (Stern and Stiglitz 1997, p.4; emphasis added). This definition may seem to assign a rather minimalist role to the government, but the opposite is true. Developing this institutional infrastructure represents a huge task for most developing countries. The objective is to level the playing field and provide the enabling conditions for all firms to operate efficiently. What constitutes this institutional infrastructure? The left-hand side of Figure 3.3 shows that the areas are, namely (i) the provision of a basic legal framework, (ii) the attainment of macroeconomic stability, and (iii) the correction of market imperfections. The first two areas encompass a series of major preconditions for a well-functioning market economy, and constitute a state's general responsibilities. Economists have come to a consensus over the importance of these policies at least and agree that, if governments perform these tasks well, they will be laying the foundations for rapid development.

In terms of the third area, when markets are imperfect due to the existence of noncompetitive market structures, public goods, or externalities, they tend to underprovide the goods and services that are desired by societies (or not provide them at all), or overprovide other goods and services that might not be desired by society (pollution). Governments should intervene to prevent both the formation of monopolies and, in general, any form of collusion, as well as stop consumer rights violations.

States' General Responsibilities

A general area of responsibility for the state is to establish a basic legal framework, which can be taken to encompass the following (Stern 1997, Stern and Stiglitz 1997): (i) rule of law, (ii) public administration, (iii) laws regarding contracts and the regulatory structure affecting key sectors such as telecommunications and financial services, (iv) intellectual property rights, and (v) competition laws and policies.

Klapper and Claessens (2002) have found a positive relationship between per capita GDP and judicial efficiency, and Klapper and Love (2002) have found that firm-level governance is lower in countries with weaker legal systems. The strength of firm-level governance is also inversely correlated with the extent of asymmetric information and contracting imperfections that firms face.

A particularly important issue with regard to the basic legal framework is that of competition law. There are two key issues. One is the prevention of the formation of monopolistic forms and collusion in general (e.g., antitrust laws and protection of consumer rights) since these reduce efficiency and consumer welfare. Many developing countries have a legal framework for competition policy, but the problem is that there is no real enforcement of competition law. The second key issue is that competition at the firm level requires a framework

that allows easy and quick entry and exit of firms. Competitive pressure is important for productivity growth and innovation. Empirical evidence suggests that the degree of product market competition may have significant effects on growth, and that barriers to entry and exit are positively correlated with lower productivity, greater corruption, and a larger informal economy (World Bank 2003b, pp.91–92). Thus, reducing policy-related barriers to competition is essential to raise the productivity of domestic firms.

The legal system should facilitate the entry of firms by, for example, reducing the number of applications and permits required to start a business.[8] Djankov et al. (2002) collected data on the regulation of entry of firms in 85 countries. Table 3.6 provides the data on the number of procedures and the cost of entry for the Asian countries included in their sample. It also includes, for reference, Canada (with the lowest number of procedures) and the Dominican Republic (with the highest). The authors concluded that official costs of entry are very high in most countries, and that, indeed, stricter regulation of entry is correlated with more corruption and a larger informal economy.

The legal system should also facilitate the exit of firms via well-defined bankruptcy and insolvency laws, as they are a fundamental part of a well-functioning market economy. For example, it would be contradictory to deregulate a sector so as to make it more competitive, and then bail out struggling firms. Exit is important because it releases resources that can be used in more productive activities. Often, unviable firms can stay in business by entering lengthy and costly rehabilitation periods. Governments tend not to recognize that firms' failures are an inescapable consequence of entrepreneurial risk taking, and often create a labyrinth of administrative obstacles to starting, operating, and shutting down businesses (Box 3.5).

Finally, the importance of a stable macroeconomic environment for economic growth, i.e., sound monetary, fiscal, and balance-of-payments policies, is very well understood. Macroeconomic stability, in particular the control of inflationary pressures, is essential for an effective working of the price mechanism, efficient firm-level decision making, investment, and growth.

Table 3.6 Cost of Entry of Firms

Economy	No. of Procedures	Safety & Health	Environ- ment	Taxes	Labor	Screening	Time	Cost	Cost & Time	GDP Per Capita 1999
Canada	2	0	0	1	0	1	2	0.0145	0.0225	19,320
Hong Kong, China	5	0	0	0	1	4	15	0.0333	0.0933	23,520
Mongolia	5	0	0	1	0	4	22	0.0331	0.1211	350
Singapore	7	0	0	1	2	4	22	0.1191	0.2071	29,610
Malaysia	7	0	0	1	1	5	42	0.2645	0.4325	3,400
Sri Lanka	8	0	0	1	1	6	23	0.1972	0.2892	820
Taipei,China	8	0	0	1	2	5	37	0.0660	0.2140	13,248
Pakistan	8	0	0	2	1	5	50	0.3496	0.5496	470
Kyrgyz Republic	9	0	0	1	1	7	32	0.2532	0.3812	300
Thailand	9	0	0	3	2	4	35	0.0639	0.2039	1,960
India	10	0	0	3	3	4	77	0.5776	0.8856	450
Indonesia	11	0	0	2	1	8	128	0.5379	1.0499	580
Kazakhstan	12	0	0	1	3	8	42	0.4747	0.6427	1,230
China, People's Rep. of	12	0	0	5	2	5	92	0.1417	0.5097	780
Korea	13	0	0	2	4	7	27	0.1627	0.2707	8,490
Philippines	14	0	0	5	1	8	46	0.1897	0.3737	1,020
Viet Nam	16	0	1	1	5	9	112	1.3377	1.7857	370
Dominican Rep.	21	0	0	2	3	16	80	4.6309	4.9509	191

Note: This table reports the total number of entry procedures required and their breakdown in the following five categories: safety and health, environment, taxes, labor, and screening. The table also reports the time, direct cost (as a fraction of GDP per capita in 1999) associated with meeting government requirements, and direct cost plus the monetized value of the entrepreneur's time (as a fraction of GDP per capita in 1999) as well as the level of GDP per capita in dollars in 1999. Countries are sorted in ascending order on the basis of the total number of procedures, time, and cost.

Source: Djankov et al. (2002).

States' Specific Interventions

In addition to making general interventions, governments can intervene in other, specific, situations to correct market imperfections resulting from inefficiencies in the market for information (e.g., asymmetric information problems). For example, it may well be that a location is very attractive but prospective investors are unaware of it. A review of the literature indicates that governments tend to be very active in three areas related to the investment environment. The government objective is to use a series of targeted interventions that aim to improve the investment environment and to support innovation and learning by firms. These areas are: (i) provision of tax incentives to encourage foreign direct investment (FDI); (ii) creation of export processing zones (EPZs); and (iii) promotion of industrial clusters. Government intervention in these areas is a controversial issue and there is less agreement among economists about the validity of this type of measure because

they are often not time-bound with sunset clauses. Also, some of these measures are no more than old-style industrial policies offering favorable treatment to some selected industries, though dressed up as "new competitiveness policies."

The underlying argument for intervention is that public policy in these areas can help overcome information failures that MNCs face in deciding where to locate, or in searching for a firm with which to link in a GVC (Moran 1998; UNCTAD 2001, 2002; OECD 2002). These interventions raise questions such as: Is host-country intervention needed to ensure the success of FDI? And, Would FDI flow to a given developing country without active government intervention?

Four reasons may justify government intervention. First, the potential investor has a problem in acquiring relevant information about the host country, such as the legal institutions and tax regime; thus there is a rationale for host governments to provide and subsidize information

Box 3.5 Exit Policies in Asian Countries

The Asian financial crisis has drawn attention to the importance of having efficient legal mechanisms to resolve situations of financial distress. While bankruptcy processes are a critical complement to other initiatives, they have played a limited role in the crisis. This is because of the magnitude of the problem, and because of the substantial amount of time required for bankruptcy rules and institutions to become effective in economies where they have only recently been introduced.

A study by Claessens et al. (1999) shows that out of a sample of 1,472 publicly traded firms in Indonesia, Korea, Malaysia, Philippines, and Thailand, 644 firms were identified as financially distressed. Of these, 83 filed for bankruptcy during 1997 and 1998—only 13% of the distressed firms used the formal, in-court bankruptcy process. There is a wide use of out-of-court resolution, market-based restructuring by facilitating mergers and acquisitions, and/or asset management companies and other forms of government support. This indicates a relative weakness of the bankruptcy systems (Claessens et al. 2001). Creditors in most crisis-affected countries, except Korea and Malaysia, regard court-supervised restructuring as an unattractive option because of the initial weakness in the bankruptcy regimes, with many having a long history of pro-debtor bias and poor creditor rights. This pro-debtor bias has often been aggravated by the limited efficacy of the judicial system.

Multinational agencies have been actively involved in providing technical assistance on insolvency reform, particularly in crisis-affected countries, and some of the deficiencies have been corrected. For instance, Indonesia revised its bankruptcy law in 1998 and set up special commercial courts to help in corporate restructuring. Thailand reorganized its bankruptcy law in 1999. And in Korea, amendments were made to the Corporate Reorganization Act, Composition Act, and Bankruptcy Law to improve the speed and efficiency of its relatively well-functioning system. In sum, creditor rights have been strengthened in all crisis-affected countries except for the Philippines where the judicial system is yet to be improved (see Box Table).

The ability to resolve insolvencies and bankruptcies efficiently allows an economy to operate more effectively, and is an essential part of a market economy. Improved bankruptcy regimes and the establishment of specialized courts have led to an increase in the use of bankruptcy to resolve financial distress cases in East and Southeast Asia. These improvements to the formal regimes, however, have not eliminated many of the institutional problems. It is important to recognize that bankruptcy reform should not be used in isolation: it may be necessary to combine it with legal and other reforms, e.g., the training of judges, improvements in corporate governance, and the strengthening of investor rights. Best practices must be continuously reviewed for better implementation.

Sources:

Claessens, Stijn, Simeon Djankov, and Leora Klapper. 1999. "Resolution of Corporate Distress in East Asia." World Bank Policy Research Working Paper 2133 (June); Claessens, Stijn, Simeon Djankov, and Ashoka Mody. 2001. "Resolution of Financial Distress: An International Perspective on the Design of Bankruptcy Laws." World Bank Institute Development Studies. May 2001; Asian Development Bank. Asia Recovery Information Center, available: www.aric.adb.org.

Box Table. Major Features of Bankruptcy Codes in Selected Asian Economies (mid-2001)

Economy	Legal Origin	Creditor Rights			Judicial Efficiency	
		Management Remains in Bankruptcy?	Automatic Stay on Assets?	Secured Creditors Get Priority?	Timetable to Render a Judgment	Specialized Bankruptcy Code?
Indonesia	French	No (Yes)	No (Yes)	Yes (Yes)	Yes (No)	Yes (No)
Korea	German	No (No)	No (No)	Yes (Yes)	Yes (Yes)	Yes (Yes)
Malaysia	English	No (No)	No (No)	Yes (Yes)	No (No)	No (No)
Philippines	French	Yes (Yes)	Yes (Yes)	No (No)	No (No)	No (No)
Thailand	English	No (No)	No (No)	Yes (Yes)	Yes (No)	No (No)

Note: Precrisis regimes are in parentheses.

networks. Second, there are market failures in terms of the credibility and willingness of host countries to fulfill the terms of long-term contracts; thus efforts to strengthen the credibility of the initial investment agreements are needed. Third, with FDI comes a know-how package that includes production methods, quality control techniques, and general management expertise. Host-country governments usually expect MNC investments to lead to an increase in employment and exports, as well as to knowledge spillovers—that is, to some externalities beyond the direct benefits reflected in market pricing, as technology is, to some extent, a public good. The MNC, however, does not include these benefits in its evaluation of the returns to foreign investment with the result that it tends to invest less than what is socially optimal. The role of policies to attract FDI is to bridge the gap between the private return (to the MNC) and the social return (to the host country). Fourth, developing countries face the problem that national and regional authorities in industrial countries are also targeting some of the same MNCs for FDI.

The three areas related to the investment environment in which governments are frequently very active are discussed in the following paragraphs.

Encouragement of FDI. FDI supplies a know-how package. Under appropriate conditions, this package can be a source for upgrading and learning in an effort at catching up with the frontier. When do these appropriate conditions contribute the most to the growth and development of the host country? According to Moran (2002, p.4) this will occur "when the parent has made the affiliate an integral part of the firm's strategy to maximize its corporate position in world markets. To accomplish this, the parent corporation almost always insists upon wholly owned status for the affiliate, combined with freedom to use inputs from wherever price, quality, and reliability are most favorable." Empirical evidence shows that arrangements such as mandatory joint ventures, export performance, or technology transfer mandates are not as beneficial as the host country might have hoped, to the extent that technology transferred in these cases tends to be older than that transferred to wholly owned affiliates. UNCTAD (2001, p.178) concurs that policies aimed only at inducing or encouraging foreign affiliates to transfer technology have generally not been very effective. For example, Korea used technology transfer requirements in the 1960s, but discontinued their application in 1989, as the measure began to produce disappointing results. The PRC has also stipulated technology transfer agreements in the automobile and automobile parts industry, though these arrangements will be phased out as part of its WTO commitments.

Wholly owned affiliates that are free to source from wherever is most advantageous have the incentive to develop a supplier base that gives the parent an edge. "The incentive of the foreign affiliates to invest in the performance of suppliers, moreover, turned out to be quite weak in comparison with the intense motivation to ensure low price, timely delivery, and high quality control when the parent investors used local firms as an extension of their international supplier networks" (Moran 2002, p.13). FDI projects with high domestic-content mandates have high costs, show a lag in both technology and management practices, and offer little hope of maturing from infant-industry status to internationally competitive operations. They generally operate within a protectionist environment, a fact that tends to retard hosts' efforts at liberalizing trade and investment. Likewise, FDI projects launched with joint-venture requirements show a high degree of conflict among the partners, suffer from instability, and exhibit older technology and slower rates of technology transfer, than FDI projects without the mandate for joint ownership (Moran 1998).

It should be added that local content requirements, together with other trade-related investment measures (TRIMs) are now being phased out as a result of the 1995 TRIMs agreement that emerged from the Uruguay Round.[9] The TRIMs agreement commits all countries to eliminate local content requirements, trade-balancing requirements, foreign-exchange balancing requirements, and restrictions on exporting.[10] In view of the empirical results summarized, "the more beneficial option might be to expand the TRIMs agreement to include a prohibition on joint venture and technology sharing requirements" (Moran 2002, p.24).

In this context, should governments compete for FDI? Governments often try to "lure" MNCs by offering them fiscal and financial incentives (e.g., tax breaks, loss writeoffs, accelerated depreciation, capital subsidies, subsidized loans) and business facilitations so that they set up operations in their country (UNCTAD 2001, p.171). The problem with these strategies is that, as various national and regional governments try to attract FDI with the same types of incentives, their effects tend to cancel each other out. This can lead to a race as countries each try to give the biggest incentives to investors, which merely ends up as a policy of beggar-thy-neighbor (World Bank 2003b, p.80; OECD 2002, p.177). Moreover, while these strategies may lead to higher investment levels, there is little evidence that such initiatives can be systematically successful. Investment incentives do not generally make up for deficiencies in the investment environment. Furthermore, within countries, these proactive policies discriminate against those sectors and projects not targeted by incentives. In deciding whether to build a factory, MNCs use a variety of indicators and variables such as labor costs, productivity, and distance to suppliers and end markets. The host country's financial incentives tend not to be particularly important (Villela and Barreix 2002).

UNCTAD (1996) and OECD (2002) conclude that fiscal and financial incentives can have an effect on attracting FDI, but only at the margin. Thus, when a firm has two approximately similar location alternatives for its investment, then incentives can tilt the decision. The problem is that many government officials seem to believe that these incentives work, because the benefits, such as jobs created or a new plant, are visible, while the wider costs are not obvious and hence overlooked. Often, the financial costs of the incentives far outweigh the benefits from faster growth and from increased employment and tax revenues (World Bank 2003b, p.82; OECD 2002, p.169).[11] The worst case is, perhaps, when the MNC beneficiary of the subsidy does not differ in any fundamental way from domestic firms. The subsidies simply distort competition.

Under some circumstances, though, targeted FDI incentives may have beneficial effects. Indeed, the case for public policy in attracting FDI rests on the argument that MNCs produce positive externalities derived from their specific knowledge about production or management. Knowledge has the nature of a public good, and therefore can spill over to local firms. OECD (2002) summarizes the empirical evidence based on case studies and statistical analysis as follows: "There is strong evidence pointing to the potential for significant spillover benefits for FDI, but also ample evidence indicating that spillovers *do not occur automatically*. Whether these potential spillovers will be realized or not depends on the ability and motivation of local firms to engage in investment and learning to absorb foreign knowledge and skills" (OECD 2002, p.176; emphasis added).

Despite the potential benefits derived from the presence of externalities (and hence a possible case

for investment incentives), the recent consensus is, however, that a government's efforts should be directed at convincing investors that the country is implementing sound economic policies. Policy makers should therefore remain cautious about the positive effect of granting incentives exclusively to foreign investors. Policy measures that focus on general forms of support available to all firms, foreign and domestic, tend to reduce rent seeking and corruption. Evidence shows that the effective enforcement of contracts, absence of red tape, adequate infrastructure, and trained and trainable workers act as a powerful force to attract FDI in sectors such as electronics, automobile parts, chemicals, industrial and medical equipment, and business services (Moran 2002).

To sum up, public policy to attract FDI to the Asia-Pacific region should aim at improving the macro- and microeconomic fundamentals of the economy, including infrastructure and education, and at strengthening institutions, such as the legal system. Attempts at incorporating domestic-content and joint-venture requirements into FDI agreements will have negative effects (see also Moran 1998, p.166). From a microeconomic point of view, governments must tackle the impediments to competition and entrepreneurship if they are to encourage FDI, and should direct efforts to reduce any excessively complex administrative procedures (e.g., business and tax registration, land access, site development, import procedures, and inspections) required to establish and operate a business. These discourage inflows of FDI (Morisset and Lumenga Neso 2002).[12]

Creation of Export Processing Zones. Countries have also tried to encourage industrial development by establishing EPZs (UNIDO 2002, pp.117–132). The argument for setting up EPZs is that they can be useful for countries that are trying to establish an export-oriented manufacturing sector but that lack the technical and/or administrative capacity to develop a countrywide system to allow exporters duty-free access to imported equipment and materials. However, the empirical evidence for (or against) the benefits of EPZs is inconclusive. While their immediate benefits—job creation, greater foreign exchange earnings, and higher real wages in the EPZ itself—have been documented, it is less clear whether EPZs simply cause firms that already export to relocate into the EPZ to benefit from the financial incentives, and whether they produce spillover effects to the rest of the economy and improve competitiveness (Schrank 2001). For example, Taipei,China's early EPZs in the 1960s provided basic infrastructure and freedom from red tape for firms in textiles and apparel, plastic products, and electrical appliances, and EPZs were very important initially since they helped in placing Taipei,China on the path toward export-led industrialization. However, as infrastructure facilities improved generally and as regulatory procedures were rationalized, the importance of EPZs diminished. Since the 1980s, little new investment has taken place in the EPZs, reflecting both their redundancy as infrastructure and the fact that duty-free procedures have improved outside these zones (UNIDO 2002, p.122).

Some authors argue that MNCs have used EPZs mainly for assembly operations, with the result that the envisaged backward and forward linkages with the rest of the economy tend to be minimal. For example, Noland (1990, p.61) indicates that in the 1980s, only around 3% of the material inputs used in the Penang free-trade zone in Malaysia were acquired domestically. The question is how to transform low-skill export enclaves, which is what EPZs tend to start from, into higher-skill and higher-productivity areas that are better linked to the rest of the economy, so triggering a sequence of beneficial changes throughout the economy.

Promotion of Industrial Clusters. An industrial cluster is a regional agglomeration of firms in related industries offering complementary infrastructure (e.g., roads, transport, and public utilities). The idea has been around for many decades, but it appeared again with strength in Michael Porter's (1990) work. More than a decade later, efforts to promote competitive clusters at both the national and regional levels represent an important component of development and investment policies in many countries. The objective of a cluster is to create a virtuous circle to attract new firms and help existing ones grow. Industrial parks are a particular type of cluster, which often go beyond physical infrastructure by providing a variety of common facilities and support services (e.g., finance, law, information, joint research facilities, and hotels). Their overall objective is to reduce

costs and risks. Science and technology parks are intended for technologically advanced industries—Suzhou Technology Park in the PRC, for example, is made up of three institutions: Suzhou New and High-Technology Service Centre, Suzhou International Business Incubator, and China Suzhou Pioneering Park for Overseas Chinese Scholars. The park now accommodates 300 firms, 90% of which were set up by overseas Chinese and 10% by R&D institutes and universities. Twenty percent are high-technology enterprises. UNIDO (2002) argues that the success of the park is due to the wide array of services it provides: banks, Internet access every 10 square meters, conference rooms, accounting and legal services, human resources support, and import-export services (UNIDO 2002, p.122).

By far the best-known cluster is Silicon Valley, in California. Every government wants to build a Silicon Valley without, however, realizing that it was not planned. Scientists and engineers moved there because the right conditions existed, e.g., patent laws, financial system, and an "informal creative culture" of inventing (Box 3.6). However, there is little evidence that efforts to create clusters are successful, especially when they are policy driven or little more than efforts to force the creation of a particular industry.[13] The reason is that it is difficult for governments to pick the winners (Hausmann and Rodrik 2002). While it is easy to see the industrial parks and clusters that have succeeded, there is little understanding about how to create them, and it is unlikely that governments have any great expertise in selecting the areas where clustering may be successful. In general, the effectiveness of these measures is largely context specific, predicated on the economic environment and institutional setting. If local firms operate in a well-functioning market environment, it is more likely that they will actively engage in some sort of linkage or cluster program anyway. Governments that have succeeded in supporting the emergence of competitive clusters have acted as mere catalysts or initiators in support of cluster development initiatives, and have sought to complement, rather than replace, private sector efforts to improve conditions for competitive performance. The government, in these cases, has set priorities, which involved making choices (e.g., budget allocation). But this was different from picking the winners.

The general conclusion about these specific

Box 3.6 The Origins of Silicon Valley: Meticulous Planning or Chance?

Today Silicon Valley is known as a center of scientific and technological innovation, with hundreds of companies operating from the Stanford Industrial Park to San Jose and beyond. Its name was first used in 1971, but its origins date back to the beginning of the 20th century. Its symbolic beginnings date back to 1909, when the Stanford University President David Starr Jordan put up the first venture capital of $500 for work on an invention called the audion tube, a device used to amplify electrical signals. This invention would later become commercially unviable due to the heat it generated, but it set the stage for the symbiotic relationship between academia and industry in the area, marked by technical innovation, risk taking, imagination, and entrepreneurship.

The development of Silicon Valley has been largely a private sector initiative, and was especially notable for the positive externalities from Stanford University. This is attributed greatly to Professor Frederick Terman, an engineering professor recruited to Stanford from the East Coast of the US in the 1920s to improve the prestige of the university. He was concerned that after graduation many students sought jobs on the East Coast. Now widely regarded as the "father of Silicon Valley," Professor Terman was instrumental in convincing many of Stanford's graduates to set up local businesses near the university. This included his students William Hewlett and David Packard, who started their company and produced their commercially viable audio-oscillator in 1937. This led to a contract with Walt Disney and the start of a long-term growth path for the company. Other students also founded small companies, and in turn other inventions were made, such as the klystron tube, which is used to generate and amplify ultra-high frequencies.

Stanford's policy of leasing part of its land to raise funds also contributed to the growth of Silicon Valley. This led to the development in 1951 of Stanford Industrial Park, which served as a center of high technology close to a cooperative university. Companies such as General Electric, Eastman Kodak, and others set up shop. The establishment of the industrial park strengthened the character of Silicon Valley as a conglomeration of interrelated, interbred companies.

During the 1950s, the government defense programs in air, space, and electronics meant large semiconductor procurements for the defense agencies. This strongly stimulated growth of companies in Silicon Valley, and further strengthened the ties between Stanford and private firms. Lockheed Aerospace Co., for instance, helped start a space and air department in the university while Stanford gave scientific advice and training for its employees. Other companies followed in setting up research centers in the area, such as IBM (1952), NASA (1958), and Xerox (1970). In other words, Silicon Valley is a story of clustering of related firms (matches) and increasing returns resulting from special agglomeration and concentration of skilled workers.

Now home to many successful companies including Intel, Sun, and Cisco, it was in Silicon Valley where private engineers in the 1950s first used silicon as a semiconducting material. Its long history has seen important legacies in the form of the rapid growth of high-technology industries, with important contributions in lasers, microprocessing, aerospace, office automation, high-energy physics, and biotechnology. These contributions have not been the result of any masterplan, but of Stanford's research support and firms' risk taking, and the variety of unexpected ways in which this has borne fruit, giving rise to what Silicon Valley is known for today.

Source:

http://people.deas. harvard.edu/
~jones/shockley/sili_valley.html,
downloaded 7 March 2003.

intervention policies is that they work best when they are implemented in conjunction with broad reform packages. In the final analysis: "Bigger payoffs are likely to come from interventions to improve the broader business environment" (World Bank 2003b, p.83). (Box 3.7 gives an example of this in the context of Ireland.)

There is, finally, another raft of microeconomic interventions that, though difficult to evaluate, are less controversial than the above three (UNCTAD 2001, pp.173–193). Experience with some programs suggests that the returns to well-conceived initiatives can be high, otherwise, they can be a waste of resources. Public initiatives can play a role in enhancing the availability of information about the host country. The provision of information, a public good, through seminars, web sites, maintenance of databases, commercial missions, or trade fairs and exhibitions is certainly useful. Also, industry associations and chambers of commerce can be valu-

Box 3.7 Success Elements of the Irish Miracle

From a country with relatively low per capita income in the 1960s, together with an outward migration of labor in search of better opportunities, Ireland emerged as a dynamic, productive, and fast-growing economy in the 1990s. GDP growth averaged about 9% a year during 1993–1999, while the number of people employed increased by over 60%, with the unemployment rate falling from 15.7% to a mere 3.6% over the period 1993–2000. Ireland also saw strong productivity growth, driven by the development of the high-technology sectors of the economy, particularly chemicals/pharmaceuticals, electronics, electrical engineering, and computer software.

Ireland's process of economic adjustment started in the 1980s. It included policies supportive of an open international framework to facilitate trade, investment, and capital flows. A high priority was also given to establishing an internationally competitive logistics sector, which includes infrastructure, a high level of services to firms engaged in international trade, and productivity-enhancing technology innovations in logistics.

The recent Irish "economic miracle" has been attributed to several factors, which include:

- Human resources and quality of education
- Favorable regulatory, tax, trade and investment policies, especially for foreign direct investment and new business start-ups
- Use of industry-clustering, technology transfer, and supply chains
- Stability of political and legal institutions
- Consensus and relative industrial calm through social partnership

- Subsidies from the European Union (EU)
- Use of the English language and proximity to the UK and continental European markets

It is important to stress that the various incentives attracting foreign investors, including low taxes, good infrastructure, access to the EU market, and continuously increasing labor skills, have also been available to local companies. That is, incentives have been on equal terms to all investors, regardless of nationality.

Ireland currently benefits from favorable demographic factors and a strong focus on education. It has a healthy supply of well-educated and highly skilled young people entering the labor force. The proportion of the population less than 25 years of age in Ireland is higher than in any other EU country.

Historically, the fast expansion in education in the 1960s and 1970s, based on the provision of free secondary education and reform at the tertiary level, helped lay the foundations for sustained growth in the 1990s, while throughout the 1980s and 1990s Ireland also experienced rapid growth in higher education.

There has also been a rapid expansion in non-university technical education with considerable EU funding that facilitated the availability of graduates for computing, science, and engineering. An international survey showed that, in 2000, Irish students at age 15 have higher reading, mathematics, and science skills than those of most other OECD countries.

It has been argued that Ireland's focus on education and information technologies was key to changing its once rural economy into Europe's largest exporter of computer

software. Early on, successive Irish governments identified the ICT sector as a key strategic industry. It was seen as ideal in utilizing the highly educated workforce without compromising environmental concerns. Ireland is currently Europe's major center for software production, and the world's electronic-business center. Its success has been attributed to a variety of policies: a strong base of significant investments in e-business-related activities, a proven high rate of return on investment through generous tax advantages, a high-quality telecommunications infrastructure with competitive prices, a highly supportive government and legislative framework, and high-specification R&D programs.

It has also been argued that social cohesion and political consensus are a crucial link that allows the right policies to be developed and implemented successfully. Healy (2002) notes that "while much of the international evidence is still very tentative, there is enough to suggest that some of the recent Irish 'economic miracle' may be attributable to historical accumulations of values, norms and networks which facilitated entrepreneurship, lowered transactions costs, and generally facilitated the impact of education, trade and investment on the domestic economy."

Sources:
Healy, Tom. 2002. "Miracles Do Happen: The Story of Recent Irish Economic Growth." Paper presented at a World Bank Conference on Using Knowledge for Development in EU Accession Countries. Paris. 21 February 2002; O'Mally, Desmond. 2002. "Technology and Growth: Ireland's Recent Experience." In *Technology and Poverty Reduction in Asia and the Pacific.* ADB/OECD.

able sources of information. Evidence shows that a proactive approach in terms of marketing a country through customized packages of information for specifically targeted industries yields high returns (Moran 2002). These packages include host-country web sites, with access to relevant legal texts and regulations, links to relevant ministries, and direct contacts to existing investors and industrial-park developers. The objective is to help foreign firms reduce their search costs and overcome market failures due to asymmetric information to avoid bad location decisions.

Areas of Shared Responsibility between the State and the Market

As Figure 3.3 showed, the state and the market have three areas of shared responsibility toward creating a well-functioning market economy: education, physical infrastructure, and technology and innovation/R&D.

Providing basic education (primary and secondary) is clearly the role of the state. Education plays the dual role of enhancing a person's quality of life as well as increasing his or her productivity. But beyond basic education, the question is how tertiary education should be supplied. (Education and science and technology policies are discussed further in the section *Education and Skills*.)

For a long time, many economists believed that the government alone should provide physical infrastructure, which includes bridges, roads, ports, railways, water, telephones, and electricity. Today, however, it is clear that this is an area of shared responsibility and that the private sector can also provide infrastructure. This eliminates the problems inherent with government monopolies, such as inefficiency and rent seeking, and increases competition among both domestic and foreign companies.

Technology and innovation/R&D policies are key to successful development.[14] A crucial point is that the government must put in place the institutional infrastructure necessary for an effective transfer of technology and for the development of indigenous technology (Chang 1996). This infrastructure refers to the bodies that support industrial technology, such as education and training, R&D, or export information. Successful innovation and building of technological capabilities cannot be undertaken without them. Some of these institutions, such as universities and public laboratories, may be funded by the government. Others are sponsored by the private sector, for example industry associations. In fact, most industrial countries have succeeded in developing cooperative interaction among them.

Summing up, the role of public policy in enhancing firms' competitiveness is multifaceted. There is no doubt that governments can positively affect the environment in which all firms operate. Guaranteeing the legal system (and making sure that it is enforced through appropriate institutions), providing macroeconomic stability, and correcting market failures are fundamental government-supported pillars in ensuring a well-functioning or competitive economy.

Education and infrastructure, also crucial to improving firms' competitiveness, are areas of responsibility that the government can share with the private sector. But beyond these areas, it is less clear what the role of public policy should be. The evidence at hand is inconclusive regarding governments' incentives to attract FDI, to create EPZs, and to promote clusters. Governments could, on the other hand, play an important role in providing information about their country.

Two related dynamic competitive factors that are making developing Asia a formidable producer and exporter of technology-intensive goods are having important consequences and are inducing a shift in the location of the world's knowledge-based work. The first factor is the shifting investment strategies of MNCs and the importance of GVCs, which has been facilitated by faster and cheaper transport and communications[15] (discussed further in the section *Global Value Chains*). The second factor is the availability of skilled labor (examined in the section *Education and Skills*).

Global Value Chains

Global value chains can be defined as the

> internationalization of a manufacturing process in which several countries participate in different stages of the manufacture of a specific good. The process is of considerable economic importance since it allows stages of production to be located where they can be undertaken most efficiently and at the lowest cost. Furthermore, if production sharing is increasing in relative importance this implies that countries are becoming more interdependent on each other (Yeats 1998, p.1).

For firms in less developed countries of Asia, being part of a GVC can be an important catalyst in learning and adapting advanced technologies. It can also enhance the development process in general. Estimates show that the benefits of trade liberalization that are accompanied by the establishment of international supplier chain arrangements between firms in industrial and less developed countries can be 10 to 20 times larger than those accruing from trade liberalization alone (Moran 2002).

International production chains are likely to benefit firms in countries where they can go into GVCs in sectors including furniture, footwear, textiles and garments, and electronics, in three main ways. First, by increasing the set of internationally traded goods, GVCs increase opportunities to benefit from the gains from trade by allowing the participants greater room for specialization in the labor-intensive stages of manufacturing processes (which overall might be technology or capital intensive). Second, by broadening the scope for gains from trade, GVCs render protectionist, import-substitution, or anti-foreign investment policies even less effective. Third, given that this kind of production and trade tends to occur in tightly knit "just in time" global networks, GVCs give added impetus to the need to improve the efficiency of transport and communications infrastructure and for a stable business environment (Yeats 1998, p.2).

GVCs can enable firms to enter global production networks more easily, allowing them to benefit from globalization, climb the technology ladder, and gain wider access to international markets. GVCs provide firms with a wide spectrum of options to operate in global markets with a view to staying competitive. In theory, GVCs offer a way for local enterprises in developing countries to engage in international markets at their own level of capability. In practice, however, it is often extremely difficult for a firm to secure an initial order, and only if a firm has a proven track record with a buyer is it likely to win a major contract. Entry into GVCs is easiest when an agglomeration of local buyers and manufacturers already exists, so that newcomers can learn from the established players. Sometimes, new entrants emerge as spin-offs from existing local firms or from MNC subsidiaries with whom they establish a new GVC linkage. For countries and groups of firms outside successful clusters, accessing GVCs can be difficult. For very poor countries with little engagement of or prior experience in GVCs (especially high-technology GVCs), entry can pose major developmental challenges to policy makers and business leaders alike.

Exploiting Global Value Chains for Economic Development: Ten NIE Entry Strategies

Firms in the NIEs have been participating in GVCs for several decades and their experience can be very useful for firms in other Asia-Pacific countries. GVCs encouraged local firms to learn technology and overcome the barriers to entry into export markets. Ten common GVC entry strategies for firms in the NIEs have been the following:
1. foreign direct investment (FDI)
2. joint ventures
3. foreign and local buyers
4. licensing
5. subcontracting
6. informal means (e.g., overseas training, hiring, returnees)
7. original equipment manufacture (OEM)
8. own design and manufacture (ODM)
9. strategic partnerships for technology
10. overseas acquisition of equity.
    Each of the 10 strategies enabled latecomer

firms to enter GVCs at progressively more advanced stages of development, though they had to expand both technological and market opportunities. Indeed, GVCs are not always easy to enter and it can be decades before the latecomer gains a strong position. These entry strategies are not new, although some have expanded greatly due to globalization of production. Numbers 1 to 7 represent early-stage strategies; 8 to 10 are highly advanced methods for latecomers to initiate their own GVCs. Each strategy has evolved through time as latecomers have acquired greater technological capabilities and marketing skills.

Foreign Direct Investment. Table 3.7 shows the significant expansion of FDI in the Asia-Pacific region, and that it is highly concentrated in the more advanced economies of East Asia as well as the PRC. This concentration worries the Southeast Asian countries, which have traditionally depended on FDI for their exports and for technology transfer. In less developed countries of the region, FDI has stagnated, except in India, where it is picking up.

Historically, FDI was an important export starting point for many firms in East and Southeast Asia, and sometimes led to joint ventures and OEM. As Schive (1990) and Fok (1991) show, foreign subsidiaries acted as "demonstrators" for local firms. Some foreign firms (e.g., the American Singer Company, which produced sewing machines in Taipei,China) directly assisted local firms to develop by training local subcontractors. Most MNCs trained local technicians, engineers, and managers in their subsidiaries, upgrading the capabilities and experience of the workforce.

While the overall contribution of FDI to capital formation in economies such as Korea and Taipei,China was very small, it accounted for a large share of exports and employment (James 1990, Dahlman and Sananikone 1990). For example, in Taipei,China, FDI contributed about 2.2% of total domestic capital formation between 1965 and 1968, rising to 4.3% between 1969 and 1972. This fell to 1.4% between 1977 and 1980, and again rose to 2.5% between 1984 and 1986. Foreign firms accounted for around 20% of the economy's total exports between 1974 and 1982, falling to 16% in 1985 as local firms assumed greater significance. MNCs accounted for around 16% of manufac-

turing employment in 1975, increasing to 17% in 1979, and declining to 9% in 1985 (Hobday 1995a, pp.108–109). In Taipei,China, individual MNC investments gave rise to a Schumpeterian process of "swarming" as local firms rushed to supply basic services and simple components.

Joint Ventures. In the early stages of Korean export development, the Government permitted firms such as Hyundai, Daewoo, Lucky Goldstar, and Samsung to form joint ventures with Japanese and US firms (Amsden 1989). Samsung Electronics began by assembling simple transistor radios and black-and-white televisions under a joint venture with Sanyo Electric in 1969. According to Bloom (1991), the Government later encouraged Japanese firms to leave, once local companies had acquired the necessary know-how. In electronics, now the largest GVC, of the 691 firms registered in Korea as producers back in 1977, 480 were Korean owned (mostly small companies), 167 were joint ventures, and 44 were wholly foreign-owned ventures.

Table 3.8 shows how leading Japanese firms formed joint ventures in the late-1960s and early-1970s with Korean partners. Samsung and the others diversified into electronics from other industrial areas. They offered low-cost finance and labor in exchange for know-how and export outlets. By 1976, around 50% of electronics employment was accounted for by foreign-owned or joint venture firms (Bloom 1991, p.9). Joint ventures first applied to consumer goods and later to telecommunications. Samsung Electronics, as indicated above, began as a joint venture with Sanyo. Its first step was to acquire overseas training, machinery, components, raw materials, and foreign management techniques from Sanyo. As wages rose in Japan, Samsung offered Japanese companies capacity for producing large-scale, low-cost, standardized goods. Korean overhead costs were pared to an absolute minimum to meet Japanese demands. In Taipei,China, Japanese firms tended to supply the local market through joint ventures. By 1963, at least seven major joint ventures had been agreed between firms there and Japanese electrical appliance manufacturers (Wade 1990), mostly producing transistor radios, black-and-white televisions, and simple components. In 1963, Sanyo formed a joint venture with the Taipei,China importer of its goods to supply the local market

Table 3.7 Gross Foreign Direct Investment Inflows, Selected Asian Economies, $ million, Selected Years

	1970	1980	1990	1995	2001
East Asia	178	939	8,881	45,407	77,050
East Asia (excluding China, People's Rep. of)	178	882	5,394	9,558	30,204
China, People's Rep. of	-	57	3,487	35,849	46,846
Hong Kong, China	50	710	3,275	6,213	22,834
Korea	66	6	789	1,776	3,198
Mongolia	-	-	-	10	63
Taipei,China	62	166	1,330	1,559	4,109
Southeast Asia	288	2,435	12,737	24,785	12,997
Cambodia	0	1	-	162	113
Indonesia	83	180	1,092	4,346	-3,277
Lao People's Dem. Rep.	0	-	6	88	24
Malaysia	94	934	2,611	5,816	554
Myanmar	-	0	161	277	123
Philippines	-25	-106	550	1,459	1,792
Singapore	93	1,236	5,575	8,788	8,609
Thailand	43	189	2,562	2,068	3,759
Viet Nam	0	0	180	1,780	1,300
South Asia	68	203	546	2,952	4,072
Afghanistan	0	9	-	0	2
Bangladesh	-	9	3	2	78
Bhutan	-	-	2	0	0
India	45	79	237	2,151	3,403
Maldives	-	0	6	7	12
Nepal	-	0	6	8	19
Pakistan	23	64	250	719	385
Sri Lanka	0	43	43	65	172
Central Asia	-	-	-	1,454	3,269
Azerbaijan	-	-	-	155	227
Kazakhstan	-	-	-	984	2,760
Kyrgyz Republic	-	-	-	96	40
Tajikistan	-	-	-	10	22
Turkmenistan	-	-	-	233	150
Uzbekistan	-	-	-	-24	71
The Pacific[a]	136	117	520	710	195
Fiji Islands	6	36	92	76	-3
Kiribati	-	-	0	0	1
Papua New Guinea	130	76	398	595	179
Samoa	0	0	7	3	1
Solomon Islands	-	2	10	2	-5
Tonga	-	-	0	2	2
Vanuatu	-	3	13	31	20
Total East Asia and Southeast Asia	466	3,374	21,617	70,192	90,047
Total Developing Asia	670	3,695	22,684	75,309	97,583

0 Negligible. - Not available or not separately reported. [a] Nonlisted Pacific DMCs have negligible amounts of FDI.

Notes: Some data are estimates and some 2001 data are preliminary.

Source: UNCTAD (2003).

and by 1970 the company began exporting. This venture initiated production of "white goods," air conditioners, audio products, television sets and, later, videocassette recorders (Chaponnière and Fouquin 1989).

Foreign and Local Buyers. Foreign and local buyers were a key entry point into GVCs for NIE firms and an essential source of marketing and technological knowledge. Hone (1974) shows that many Asian firms initially sold their goods to the large

Table 3.8 Early Joint Ventures and Technical Assistance from Japan

Year	Technology Activity and Firms
1961–1962	Matsushita and Sanyo provided technical assistance to Samsung and Goldstar to set up transistor radio factories in 1961 and 1962.
Late-1960s	Toshiba formed a joint venture and two major technical agreements to assemble consumer goods, cathode ray tubes (CRTs) and parts for CRTs, in Korea.
1969	Samsung Electronics Engineering began assembly of black-and-white televisions following technology transfer agreements with Sanyo. Joint venture (Samsung-Sanyo) formed to manufacture electronic parts.
1970	NEC formed two joint ventures, with Goldstar Electric and Samsung. Samsung-NEC produced electronic components for CRTs.
1973	Samsung Electronic Parts, a joint venture, was established in 1973 with Sanyo. Anam Industrial of Korea formed a jointly owned venture with Matsushita of Japan to produce color televisions. Samsung joined Corning of America to acquire technology to produce the glass for CRTs.

Sources: Bloom (1991, p.8) and Archambault (1992, p.8), cited in Hobday (1995a, p.66).

buying houses from Japan and the US. Foreign buyers would typically place orders of between 60% to 100% of the annual capacity of local firms in sectors such as clothing, electronics, and plastics. The Japanese buyers (e.g., Mitsubishi, Mitsui, Marubeni-Ida, and Nichimen) located themselves in the NIEs to purchase cheap goods as wages started rising in Japan in the early-1960s. In the late-1960s, these buyers purchased more than US$1.4 billion a year of low-cost East Asian manufactured goods, 75% of which were then sold to the US. This led to a host of Japanese manufacturers moving directly to Korea; Singapore; and Taipei,China; many American retail companies (e.g., J.C. Penney, Macy's, Bloomingdales, Marcor, and Sears Roebuck) also set up offices there (Hone 1974). The buyers enabled local firms to obtain the credit needed to expand.

Without these guaranteed forward export orders, many firms would not have been able to gain the necessary credit facilities.

Foreign buyers supplied technology in various forms. They provided information on product design and advice on both quality and cost accounting procedures. The larger buyers visited factories and supervised the start-up of new operations, assisting with the purchase of essential materials and capital equipment. Rhee et al. (1984) show that around 50% of a sample of 113 firms in Korea benefited directly from buyers through plant visits by foreign engineers. Buyers supplied latecomers with blueprints, specifications, information on competing goods, production techniques, and guidance on design and quality. About 75% of firms received assistance with product design, style, and detailed specifications. In electronics, American retail chains and importers were the most important buyers during the 1970s in Korea. As Moran points out:

> The number of cases in which foreign buyers helped local suppliers to penetrate international markets, selling first to sister plants and then to independent purchasers, grew rapidly. Over the course of the 1990s, the pattern of contract manufacturing became the new model for an authentic infant industry development strategy (Moran 2002, p.14).

Licensing. Under licensing contracts, local firms paid for the right to manufacture goods usually for the local market and the MNC would transfer the necessary technology for this to be undertaken. Usually, licensing required a higher level of technological capability on the part of the latecomer than say a joint venture, in which a "senior partner" would normally provide the necessary expertise for the local firm to undertake the production. In Taipei,China, between 1952 and 1988 the authorities approved more than 3,000 licensing agreements, many including formal technology transfer clauses (Dahlman and Sananikone 1990). Companies often secured licenses in the early stages to gain access to technology and markets, leading on to OEM. This continued into the 1970s and 1980s.

Subcontracting. Sometimes, MNCs trained local firms under long-term subcontracting relationships.

Under these, the latecomer firm would be granted access to training and engineering support and, in return, would produce a component or subsystem, which would then be incorporated into the final equipment by the purchaser. Subcontracting usually took place in lower-value products and systems and was mostly oriented toward the export market, via the MNC buyer.

Informal Means. Complementing the formal means for entering GVCs, firms often deployed informal or unofficial strategies, including the copying of products and reverse engineering. It was common to hire foreign engineers on short-term contracts, who were sometimes retired, and recruited local staff already trained by foreign MNCs located in the home economy. Also, many East Asian engineers were educated in foreign universities or worked abroad in foreign companies and some were employed by well-known R&D institutes, such as Bell Laboratories in the US. The flow of technically trained people from Taipei,China returning home rose from just 250 in 1985, to 750 in 1989, to more than 1,000 in 1991. Also, in Taipei,China, former Bell Laboratories employees began the Taipei,China Bell Systems Alumni Association. By 1992, this had 120 members, exceeding its rival Bell Alumni equivalent in Korea, which had around 80 members. Hundreds of other people returned from Caltech, Massachusetts Institute of Technology, and other leading US technology centers (Hobday 1995a).

Original Equipment Manufacture. OEM is a specific form of subcontracting that developed out of the joint operations of MNCs and local suppliers, becoming the most important channel for export marketing during the 1980s. This was especially true in electronics, the leading export sector in the NIEs. OEM, which began in semiconductors and computer products, is similar to subcontracting in other sectors, such as bicycles and footwear. The term OEM originated in the 1950s among people in the computer industry who used subcontractors to assemble equipment for them. In the 1960s, it was adopted by American semiconductor companies that used local firms to assemble and test semiconductors. Under OEM, the latecomer would produce a completed product according to an exact specification provided by the foreign MNC. The MNC

would then market the product under its own brand name, through its own distribution channels. This enabled the latecomer to avoid investing in export marketing and distribution channels. OEM often involved the foreign partner in the selection of capital equipment and the training of managers and engineers as well as advice on production and management. Sometimes (e.g., Hong Kong, China; Korea; and Taipei,China) OEM grew out of licensing deals, as the partners got to know each other. Initial success in OEM often led to long-term technological relationships between partner companies because the MNC depended on the quality, delivery, and price of the final output from reliable and trusted suppliers.

Own Design and Manufacture. ODM was first reported by Johnstone (1989) and applies mainly to the electronics sector. As the OEM system evolved during the early 1980s, Taipei,China companies such as Acer and RJP began to specify and design the electronic products purchased under OEM, usually beginning with simple products. In 1988 and 1989, this began to be called ODM in Taipei,China but the term was not used in Korea until a decade or so later. However, Korean firms also made equivalent progress in carrying out some or all of the product design, usually according to a general design layout supplied by the foreign buyer, which was often an MNC. In some cases the buyer cooperated with the latecomer on the design. In other cases the buyer was presented with a range of finished products to choose from. These were defined and designed by the latecomer firm based on its growing knowledge of the international market. As with OEM, the goods were then sold under the MNC's or buyer's brand name. ODM offered a means for latecomer firms to capture more of the value added while avoiding the risk associated with the launching of its own-brand products. In the early stages, ODM applied mainly to incremental changes to existing products, rather than to new products developed by the leading firms based on R&D.

Strategic Partnerships for Technology. Strategic partnerships for technology are non-equity joint ventures carried out by Asian firms on an equal basis with foreign MNCs. In recent years, this strategy has enabled the largest latecomer firms to enhance their position in GVCs by developing highly advanced new products and processes jointly with foreign companies. Samsung, for example, entered into an 8-year agreement with Toshiba of Japan in 1992 to develop flash memory chips and with Texas Instruments of the US to make semiconductors in Portugal in 1993. More recently, in 1999, Lucky Goldstar (LG) of Korea formed a joint venture with Philips of the Netherlands (LG-Philips). In this venture, LG provided Philips with advanced manufacturing process know-how for liquid crystal display monitors for desktop and notebook computers, while Philips provided financial capital and access to its basic research facilities in Eindhoven. The combination of LG and Philips enabled LG to recover quickly from the financial crisis in Korea in 1997, and then to forge ahead to become the world leader in the manufacture of thin-film transistor/liquid crystal display screens.

Overseas Acquisition of Equity. At their most advanced stage, former latecomer firms operate as "leaders" on the international stage, initiating their own GVCs. Companies such as Samsung and Hyundai have bought several high-technology firms in industrial countries to gain distribution channels, technology, and production facilities. For example, in 1986 Samsung acquired Micron Technology to enter the semiconductor market. In 1988, the same firm took an equity stake in Micro Five Corp to acquire computer technology and invested in Comport in the US to gain hard disk drive technology. Similarly, in 1986 Daewoo acquired a majority holding in Zymos to gain wafer fabrication capabilities. In 1986, Daewoo took over Cordata Tech to gain know-how in IBM-compatible personal computers, as well as manufacturing and marketing facilities. In 1986, LG acquired Fonetek, a radio communication company, to gain technology. These types of acquisitions enabled the most advanced latecomer firms to dominate their own GVCs and compete with GVCs dominated by US, Japanese, and European firms (Bloom 1989).

Marketing and Technology Upgrading Strategies

GVCs enabled firms to move beyond labor-intensive assembly into the production and export of advanced goods in areas such as computer products and electronics. However, these firms were not solely concerned with technology. To move up the GVCs, they also needed to acquire marketing knowledge and distribution skills to meet increasingly sophisticated customer demands in industrial countries. This would also enable them to capture a greater proportion of the post-production value added denied to them under GVC arrangements such as subcontracting, OEM, and licensing.

Table 3.9 presents a simplified "stages" representation of both marketing and technological progress under typical GVC arrangements, such as subcontracting and OEM. In reality, the process is far more complex and many firms do not follow this path. However, as a first-order approximation, the model is a useful starting point for assessing actual patterns of progress.

Marketing Strategies. According to the five-stage marketing model of Wortzel and Wortzel (1981), the local NIE firm progressively internalizes the marketing functions initially carried out by the foreign buyer or manufacturer. In stage 1, the latecomer is entirely dependent on local or foreign buyers for marketing, distribution, and quality control. The local firm simply delivers low-cost production capacity. As the model indicates, during stages 2–5, the latecomer firm assimilates more and more sophisticated marketing functions. Spurred on by the prospect of additional growth and profit and by competition from other local firms, the latecomer learns how to conduct its own sales and marketing. In doing so, it broadens its range of customers and improves the packaging and, eventually, the quality of its products.

Eventually, by stage 5 the latecomer firm develops its own brand and organizes its own sales either directly to overseas customers or through distributors. It no longer depends on the distribution channels of foreign buyers or manufacturers. In marketing terms, the latecomer is indistinguishable from leaders and followers in the industry. During the 1980s, most advanced Asian exporters had reached stages 3 and 4 in areas such as electronics, clothing, and footwear. However, although many firms had taken control of local marketing, product design, and quality, they had yet to establish their own brand names in the markets of industrial countries.

Wortzel and Wortzel (1981), writing when they

Table 3.9 Combining Marketing and Technology Strategies: Five Stages

Stage	Marketing Dimension	Technology Dimension
1	Passive importer (pull) Cheap labor assembly Dependent on buyers for distribution	Assembly skills, basic production capabilities Mature products
2	Active sales of capacity Quality and cost-based Foreign-buyer dependent	Incremental process changes for quality and speed Reverse engineering of products
3	Advanced production sales Marketing department established Overseas marketing started Own designs marketed	Full production skills Process innovation Product design capability
4	Product marketing (push) Sell direct to retailers and distributors overseas Build up product range Start own-brand sales	R&D for products and processes begun Product innovation capabilities
5	Own-brand (push) Market directly to customers Independent distribution channels, direct advertising In-house market research	Competitive R&D capabilities R&D linked to market needs Advanced product/process innovation

Sources: Marketing stages from Wortzel and Wortzel (1981); technology stages derived from Hobday (1995a).

did, believed that stage 5 was largely theoretical in the NIEs. By the early 1990s, however, some latecomer firms such as Samsung and LG of Korea and Acer and Tatung of Taipei,China had established well-known global brand names. Nevertheless, most latecomers remained dependent on foreign buyers and MNCs for their marketing outlets. For example, although Cal-Comp of Taipei,China was the world's largest producer of calculators and fax machines in 1991, it was virtually unknown in western industrial economies. Cal-Comp produced roughly 80% of Japanese Casio calculators under OEM. Similarly, Inventec of Taipei,China produced a significant share of the world's telephone handsets, including 60% of British Telecom's handset sales, but remained virtually unknown.

The marketing strategies deployed within GVCs involved investment and learning; they also involved considerable risk. In computers, Acer for example, experienced major problems in sustaining its own-brand sales (accounting for 60% of sales in 1988). The sheer scale of investment forced the company to retreat to OEM/ODM after sustaining heavy financial losses. Similarly, Hyundai

was forced to cease marketing its own brand of computers in the US, after consumers were puzzled as to why Hyundai, a car brand, should be selling computers.

Technology Strategies. The right-hand column of Table 3.9 above adds a technology dimension to the marketing model, suggesting how latecomer firms gradually learn the techniques of production. This sequence for the firm is broadly consistent with what has been found to occur empirically at the industry level (e.g., Dahlman et al. 1985, Westphal et al. 1985). By upgrading their capabilities, firms learn production skills, then investment know-how and, ultimately, innovation capabilities (as initially argued by Lall [1982]).

Successful early entrants to GVCs tend to begin with simple assembly skills and, later, incrementally assimilate process capabilities. At these early stages, firms are highly dependent on outside sources of technology from, most notably, the firms that buy their products. As their capacity expands and the number of customers increases, they need to control the quality and speed of production, so they invest in the technical skills required to internalize key production methods. Spurred on by export market opportunities and competition, firms invest in product and process engineering, and some establish an engineering department to coordinate these activities. This enables the firm to sell higher quality products to a larger base of customers and, most importantly, allows the firm to move up the value chain by bringing the advantages of low-cost engineering to the GVC.

Typically, the latecomer entrepreneur recognizes that, unless the firm acquires technology at least as rapidly as its competitors, it will remain trapped in the capacity export stage and low-value-added production. By stage 4, the firm's strategy is to strengthen the engineering capabilities needed to develop new processes and products. In these areas, the firm has overcome its technological dependency. By this stage, it is likely to have forged independent links with capital goods suppliers and may conduct some limited R&D into new products, enhancing its prospects and position within the GVC.

A firm that reaches the final phase, stage 5, is no longer a latecomer. It has reached the stage of being able to initiate its own GVC by acting as a leader in the chain, through its advanced marketing and R&D capabilities. At stage 5, firms are indistinguishable from world market leaders and compete at the technological frontier. However, the most advanced Korean and Taipei,China firms have only recently reached this stage, in a few product areas.

Links Between Marketing and Technology Strategies. The purpose of matching marketing with technology in Table 3.9 is to indicate how export marketing can pull forward the technology of latecomer firms. For example, through subcontracting and OEM relations, export demand acts as a focusing device for technological investments and forces the pace of learning. Local competition stimulates the process, as followers imitate the export leaders.

There may not always be a systematic interdependence between the marketing and technology dimensions. In principle, it is possible for a firm to acquire advanced technology but still remain at the early stages of marketing. However, if the firm does not focus closely on the type of products that the market demands, it runs the risk of investing in inappropriate technology. To avoid this problem, most Asian latecomers have developed strategies to improve both marketing and technology skills simultaneously. Marketing and distribution capabilities are needed for firms to capture the value added in packaging, distribution, and after-sales service, and eventually increase brand recognition. Improved marketing helps firms expand their customer base and provide better control of the direction they take. Similarly, technological know-how is needed to improve quality, punctuality, and flexibility in production.

In some of the five stages, marketing and technology have direct links. For instance, when shifting from stage 1 to stage 2, firms have to internalize process skills to expand production capacity, shorten delivery times, and improve product quality. Later, to achieve stage 4, firms will need sufficient R&D to convert market signals into new products.

Often, the channels for technology transfer and marketing in GVCs are one and the same, as in the case of subcontracting, OEM, and ODM. Within GVC arrangements, latecomer firms are presented with a technology transfer mechanism—and a requirement for strategy upgrading. In subcontracting, the local firm is often supplied with technical specifications that require training and advice on production engineering by the MNC. The strategy of the MNC is to ensure high quality and to control the delivery and price of the final output. Consistent with this, the strategy of the latecomer is to meet these demands via technological learning.

Difficulties, Risks, and Threats Within Global Value Chains

Up to this point, this section has stressed the potential benefits for enterprises engaging in GVCs. These include the ability of local enterprises to (i) begin production with its existing level of capability, (ii) access technological knowledge, (iii) access large export markets, (iv) exploit economies of scale, (v) progressively upgrade capabilities in manufacturing with the help of foreign enterprises, (vi) learn process and product innovation skills, and (vii) eventually catch up with advanced firms.[16] Within the GVC, there is pressure to adapt to market demand in industrial countries, resulting in more flexible and competitive enterprises. The willingness and ability of latecomers to learn rapidly from leading GVC players are essential.

However, firms also face many challenges and risks in taking part in GVCs. Under many GVC arrangements, the latecomer partner is often subordinated to the decisions of the buyer in the initial stages of the relationship, and often depends on the MNC for technology and components as well as market access. The MNC sometimes imposes restrictions on the activities of the latecomer firm by, for instance, preventing it from selling in other markets or to other customers. Profits tend to be severely squeezed and, without its own distribution outlets, the latecomer is limited in its post-manufacturing valued added. The heavy dependence on assembly can prevent firms from spreading the risks of production to other parts of the GVC. Also, the arrangement makes it difficult for latecomers to build up the international brand image needed to sell high-quality goods directly. This situation is often overcome, though, when the latecomer firm grows, finds new customers, and builds its capacity.

Summary

GVCs have clearly facilitated rapid industrial growth and permitted the assimilation of technology by developing countries. In some cases, latecomer firms have overcome or renegotiated restrictive clauses; for example, Korean firms managed to have some marketing restrictions set aside so that they could sell directly to third countries. GVCs have allowed many firms to achieve economies of scale in production and have justified investments in automation technology. Nonregional MNCs continue to benefit from the expansion of low-cost capacity in the region. GVCs therefore endure as arrangements valued by both MNCs and latecomer firms.

This section has outlined some of the key business strategies for exploiting GVCs, showing how latecomer firms can secure upgrading paths via technological learning and innovation. The latter not only increases the efficiency and profit of local firms, but also makes them even more attractive within the chain to buyers. Upgrading helps protect firms against lower-wage competition, allowing companies to move on to higher-value-added, and more complex, products. Investment strategies have enabled many firms to move from process innovation (i.e., making something more efficiently) to product innovation (i.e., creating a new product), as learning about processes also requires more knowledge about product design. Working closely with leading MNC product designers provides firms with the opportunity, eventually, to take over the design of the product. Within long-term relationships with MNC buyers, local firms have broadened their product ranges, moved beyond heavy reliance on single clients and, in some cases, developed their own-brand products.

Each firm and country must learn its own lessons from the successes of the NIEs in GVCs. These differ according to the firm's or country's particular level of development, resources, entrepreneurial capabilities, and existing and potential areas of dynamic comparative advantage. Firms in less developed Asian economies can draw no simple or mechanistic lessons, partly because the GVCs themselves changed when the NIEs joined them. However, it is clear that firms wishing to enter GVCs need to be operating in an environment in which the right institutional fundamentals are in place, including a stable macroeconomic environment for business investment, a reliable business infrastructure, and widely available basic and technical education. Policies are required to reward entrepreneurial risk taking, otherwise firms will not enter GVCs and clusters of suppliers will be unable to form.

Policy makers may wish to consider the barriers facing firms that wish to enter a GVC. Sometimes, it is overregulation of companies or high taxation; sometimes, bureaucratic rules concerning FDI, joint ventures, and company start-ups. Also, skilled workers and technicians may be lacking in some areas. Resolving these constraints may help provide a conducive environment for firms to join a GVC.

Education and Skills

As firms in developing Asia climb the GVC ladder, production becomes ever more knowledge and technology intensive. Therefore, it is important to assess how education and training policies and institutions need to respond to the demands for more innovative and creative workers. How is the longer-term progress toward a more knowledge-intensive economy likely to affect the demand for skilled labor? This is an area where governments can play a major role, as education is a shared responsibility between the state and the market. The provision of universal primary and secondary education, including bringing the level of female education up to that of males in countries and regions where it is lagging, has always been considered primarily the state's responsibility. Education plays the dual role of contributing to a person's quality of life and increasing that person's productivity. However, it is less clear how tertiary education should be financed and how the state's and individuals' responsibilities should be divided.

Since the 1980s, the labor market in industrial countries has shown a remarkable development in terms of the increase in demand for skilled labor relative to unskilled labor, accentuated by the creation of the knowledge society (Drucker 2001). Productivity growth, innovation, and product quality rest critically in the hands of skilled workers and, therefore, lack of educational opportunities and training has serious consequences for any economy, including high unemployment (or disguised unemployment), low growth, insufficient innovation, and poor product quality. A second labor market development, a product of the forces of technological change and international trade, is the continually changing nature of jobs and the appearance of new job categories. Consequently, skills become obsolete quickly.

These two developments have begun to be seen in developing Asia, where they reflect the skill bias of technological progress as well as the changes in the product demand mix toward more sophisticated goods and services. Three factors explain the phenomenon: (i) the "computer revolution" has raised the demand for highly educated workers; (ii) the rise in the demand for professional, manage-

rial, and technical services has raised the demand for skilled labor; and (iii) MNCs in industrial countries initially imported products intensive in unskilled labor from developing countries. Today, however, these firms have realized that many developing countries in Asia have a large pool of well-trained and highly skilled workers (engineers and scientists) that can perform jobs currently performed by substantially better-paid people in industrial countries. Different countries are being affected by these developments in different ways depending, among other factors, on their labor market institutions.

Yusuf and Evenett (2002) argue that both the supply and quality of education and skills underpin the long-term ability of countries to assimilate and master new technologies. Education helps increase the science and technology (S&T) "absorptive capacity" of a nation, enabling it to benefit from S&T inputs from a multitude of sources. (In GVCs, these sources include the spillover effects of MNC investment, licensing, the ability to learn within GVCs, and acquiring knowledge during the import of essential capital goods.) Local industries' S&T absorptive capacity is partly determined by the availability of high-quality human capital (Cohen and Levinthal 1989) and indeed, such human capital enabled the NIEs rapidly to assimilate and master new production processes; it also enabled them to innovate.

Basic Educational Achievements

The educational attainment of the East Asian economies and its relevance in contributing to the remarkable growth and development of the last 30 years have been well documented (World Bank 1993, Asian Development Bank 1997). Of particular importance is the provision of primary education to a large portion of the school-age population. Most NIEs have achieved high literacy rates, as reflected in the high secondary and tertiary enrollment rates in the more advanced developing Asian economies (Tables 3.10 and 3.11 give data for 12 selected countries in the region). These attainments reflect large allocations to educational spending.

In Korea, for example, total education expenditure increased from 8.8% of GDP in 1966 to 13.3% in 1998. Illiteracy declined to virtually zero by the late 1990s, primary school enrollment was 100%, and secondary school enrollment was almost universal.

Although countries such as the US, Australia, and Finland have higher enrollment rates than the NIEs, the more advanced developing countries in the region have moved quickly up the educational rankings: Korea has overtaken Japan and the UK in terms of tertiary enrollment rates (in 1998, the tertiary enrollment rate was 43.7% in Japan and 58.4% in the UK). Student performance has also improved in most countries in developing Asia, with Korean students in grade 4 outperforming the OECD average (Ihm 2002, p.3).

Most Asian countries in the table have achieved enrollment rates of virtually 100% at the primary school level (Table 3.10). For countries such as Bangladesh, Cambodia, India, or Lao PDR, this represents a very important achievement, as in 1970 this rate was very low. Secondary enrollment rates have increased substantially and in many cases have more than doubled since 1970. Some countries, such as Korea and Malaysia, have achieved virtually universal secondary education. (Tertiary enrollment rates in developing Asia are substantially lower than primary and secondary ratios, except in Korea.)

These high enrollment rates do not, however, indicate the length of time that children have actually attended school. Such data on the percentage of students reaching grade 5, although incomplete, indicate that drop-out rates among children entering school are not high in East Asia (Table 3.11). However, in some countries, they are very high. Neither do enrollment rates provide information about the quality of education offered. An indirect indicator of educational quality is the pupil/teacher ratio. Here there is a marked contrast among the countries in Table 3.11 between the East Asian economies and, for example, Bangladesh, Cambodia, and India, with the latter group still exhibiting very high ratios, though these are declining.

While India has achieved universal primary education, its educational attainment at the secondary level lags behind that of the East Asian economies (including the PRC). India also suffers from a very high drop-out rate, and rural households see a very low return on basic education,

Table 3.10 Indicators of Educational Attainment, Selected Asian Economies, Various Years

	1970	1980	1990	1998/99
School Enrollment, Primary (% gross)				
Bangladesh	54.3	61.1	71.6	106.1[a]
India	77.8	83.3	97.2	100.9
PRC	90.9	112.6	125.2	106.4
Cambodia	30.3	138.6	120.9	102.4
Lao PDR	57.1	113.5	105.0	115.3
Viet Nam	-	108.8	102.9	107.7
Indonesia	80.0	107.2	115.2	107.9
Malaysia	88.7	92.6	93.7	101.4
Philippines	108.3	111.9	111.3	113.2[a]
Thailand	81.4	98.9	99.1	93.5
Korea	103.4	109.9	104.9	98.6
Singapore	105.5	107.7	103.7	79.8
School Enrollment, Secondary (% gross)				
Bangladesh	-	17.5	19.0	53.7
India	24.2	29.9	44.4	49.9
PRC	24.3	45.9	48.7	62.8
Cambodia	8.2	-	32.1	17.3
Lao PDR	3.7	20.7	25.2	35.6
Viet Nam	-	42.0	32.0	64.6
Indonesia	16.1	29.0	44.0	54.9
Malaysia	34.2	47.7	56.3	98.8
Philippines	45.8	64.2	73.2	75.9[a]
Thailand	17.4	28.8	30.1	79.0
Korea	41.6	78.1	89.8	97.4
Singapore	46.0	59.9	68.1	-
School Enrollment, Tertiary (% gross)				
Bangladesh	1.9	2.8	4.2	5.2
India	4.9	5.2	6.1	-
PRC	0.1	1.7	3.0	7.5
Cambodia	1.5	0.1	0.7	2.7
Lao PDR	0.2	0.4	1.3	2.9
Viet Nam	-	2.1	1.9	9.7
Indonesia	2.5	3.8	9.2	-
Malaysia	-	4.1	7.3	23.3
Philippines	16.8	24.4	28.2	29.5[a]
Thailand	3.1	14.7	16.7	31.9
Korea	7.4	14.7	38.6	71.7
Singapore	6.1	7.8	18.6	-

- Not available. [a] 1998.

Source: World Bank, *World Development Indicators*, available: http://publications.worldbank.org/WDI.

Table 3.11 Indicators of Educational Attainment, Selected Asian Economies, Various Years

	1970	1980	1990	1998/99
Pupil/Teacher Ratio, Primary				
Bangladesh	46	54	63	59.3[a]
India	41	45	47	43
PRC	29	27	22	19.8
Cambodia	17	44	33	50.1
Lao PDR	36	30	28	30.1
Viet Nam	-	39	35	29.5
Indonesia	29	32	23	22.4
Malaysia	31	27	20	20
Philippines	29	31	33	-
Thailand	35	-	22	20.8
Korea	57	48	36	32.2
Singapore	30	31	26	25.3
Persistence to Grade 5, Total (% of cohort)				
Bangladesh	-	20.5	-	-
India	-	-	-	59.7[a]
PRC	-	-	86.0	97.3[a]
Cambodia	-	-	-	-
Lao PDR	-	-	-	54.2[a]
Viet Nam	-	-	-	82.8[a]
Indonesia	-	75.5	83.6	90.5
Malaysia	-	96.8	98.2	-
Philippines	-	-	-	-
Thailand	-	-	-	97.1[a]
Korea	96.3	93.9	99.5	-
Singapore	-	97.2	-	-

- Not available. [a] 1998.

Source: World Bank, *World Development Indicators*, available: http://publications.worldbank.org/WDI.

especially for women. The rest of South Asia faces the same structural problems as India but without having achieved the same relatively high levels of tertiary education. The tertiary education stock (defined as the mean number of school years spent at university by the working-age population) of India is very high to the point that one can speak of a "dualistic" nature of education. While large sections of the manufacturing workforce do not have even a basic education due to high drop-out rates, India has a large stock of students with university degrees (Agrawal et al. 2000, pp.121–122).

The PRC's situation is slightly different since it has had to make up for the time lost in "the Great Leap Forward" and the Cultural Revolution (OECD 1994, p.308), when the Government emphasized primary and secondary schooling but neglected university education. Despite the efforts made during the 1980s, in 1990 only 2% of the country's 20–24-year-olds were enrolled in universities (NSF 1993, Table A-2).

The Central Asian republics had developed excellent educational systems during the Soviet era. However, with the breakup of the Soviet Union and the political transition, educational provision in terms of both the curricula offered and the physical infrastructure collapsed. These countries need to invest in physical infrastructure and develop new curricula, especially in the social sciences.

It is not merely the volume of education that matters, especially as countries move up the development ladder into more knowledge-intensive activities. Indeed, Yusuf and Evenett (2002, p.40) argue that at the high school and tertiary levels education in much of East Asia is "mediocre and uncompetitive at best." They cite Lee (2001) who shows that, due to the poor environment of secondary and tertiary education in Korea, student performance and foreign language skills fall off sharply in the higher age groups. Lee argues that even Korea, a country highly committed to further education, suffers from a poor academic environment characterized by inadequate facilities and low teacher pay. Although Korea is second only to the US in the number of university graduates per head of population, educational quality remains a major concern.

As far as achievements in science and mathematics are concerned, Table 3.12 presents a mixed picture for Asia, with Korea; Singapore; and Taipei,China scoring well above the US, but with Indonesia, Philippines, and Thailand scoring substantially below the US and the international average. Clearly, there are major differences across East Asian economies and significant weaknesses in some of the Southeast Asian economies.

The importance of competitiveness in the context of globalization has brought to the forefront again the significance of the role of education. The reason is that, while the East and Southeast Asian economies did very well in providing basic education for their populations, they are now transiting

Table 3.12 Science and Mathematics Average Achievement Scores at Age 14, Selected Economies

Economy	Mathematics	Science
Singapore	604	568
Korea	587	549
Taipei,China	585	569
Japan	579	550
Netherlands	540	545
Canada	531	533
Finland	520	535
United States	502	515
United Kingdom	496	538
Thailand	467	482
Israel	466	468
Indonesia	403	-
Philippines	345	345
Hungary	-	552
International Average	487	488

- Not available.

Source: Science "Third International Mathematics and Science Study," 8 December 2000, cited in Yusuf and Evenett (2002, p.42).

from labor-intensive manufacturing to technology-intensive manufacturing—or have already made the transition. Those that have not will require new FDI inflows and the development of domestic R&D for which an educated workforce is required. In practical terms, this means that they need not only increase the volume of education, but also, and more importantly, raise the quality of the education. The latter particularly requires an emphasis on the relevance to the needs of a modern economy of the curriculum and style of education.

Correlating Inputs with Science and Technology Outputs

Understanding the relationship between educational inputs and S&T outputs is extremely difficult, as inputs take many years to become "outputs" and there are many other factors affecting S&T achievements, such as business investment in R&D. Table 3.13 suggests that educational investments have played a significant part in contributing to an increasing supply of professional skills as well as S&T advances, including patents granted in the

US and high-technology exports, especially from Korea and Singapore. However, once again, the table highlights the huge disparities among NIEs, with the PRC; Hong Kong, China; Malaysia; and Thailand scoring very low in terms of scientists and engineers engaged in R&D per million population and numbers of patents granted, compared with the Asian leaders such as Japan, Korea, and Singapore.

As seen in the section *Institutions, The State, and The Market: A Partnership for Development*, whenever markets are imperfect, there is potentially a role for the government to improve on the market solution. Subsidizing R&D and the development of an institutional infrastructure in S&T, due to the divergence between private and social returns, is one such case. Most Asian countries have well-defined S&T programs (OECD 1994, Chamarik and Goonatilake 1994, Asian Development Bank 1995, APO 2001). Evidence indicates that at the highest S&T level, the number of advanced publicly funded S&T institutions in East Asia is low, with only a few international players, including the Korean Institute of Science and Technology, the Korean Advanced Institute of Science and Technology, the Korean Aerospace Research Institute, and POSEK (an S&T institute modeled after MIT), also in Korea; the Industrial Technology Research Institute in Taipei,China; and Singapore's Institute of Molecular and Cell Biology.

The effectiveness of some S&T institutes in terms of their international S&T status and contribution to local industrial advance has been called into question (Rush et al. 1996). In countries such as the Philippines or Thailand, for example, there is a discrepancy between quantitative and qualitative progress in S&T. While improvements have been obvious in terms of new S&T and R&D institutions, more scientists and technologists with advanced degrees, and more research going on, the qualitative improvement has lagged behind. This refers to the process of "endogenization" of technology, which requires strong linkages between scientific and technological R&D and the country's production systems. In countries such as the PRC or India, the S&T system had a strong ideological emphasis until very recently, was geared toward import substitution, and was not demand driven, with the result that S&T did not generate spillovers into the industrial economy.

Overall, developing Asia has a strong base on

Table 3.13 Indicators of R&D Effort and Outcomes, Selected Economies, Various Years

Economy	Scientists and Engineers[a]	Number of Patents Granted[b]	High-Tech Exports (%)[c]
	1985–1995	1996	1997
PRC	350	46	21
Hong Kong, China	98	88	29
Indonesia	1	20	-
Japan	6,309	23,052	38
Korea	2,636	1,493	39
Malaysia	87	12	67
Philippines	1,299	4	12
Singapore	2,728	88	71
Taipei,China	1,897	-	-
Thailand	119	11	43
United States	3,732	61,107	44

R&D = research and development.
[a] Number in R&D, per million population. [b] By the US Patent and Trademark Office (utility patents). [c] As share of manufacturing exports.
Source: Cited in Yusuf and Evenett (2002, p.43).

which to build but suffers from several handicaps. While spending has tended to increase as a percentage of GNP per capita in primary and secondary education, tertiary educational increases have fallen behind. In addition, greater attention needs to be focused on the quality of education. In addition, there are few universities in Asia with highly effective S&T or business research capabilities. Furthermore, there is a need for a higher level of S&T education to enable firms to continue to climb the GVCs via local R&D and engineering efforts.

Science and Engineering Education

Some countries in Asia are now producing substantial numbers of scientists and engineers, and the high proportion of science and engineering graduates as a percentage of total degrees awarded is impressive. In Korea and Taipei,China, for example, in the late 1990s, the figures were about 45% and 40%, respectively, compared with around 33% in the US. Also, according to US National Science Foundation data, in 1999, universities in developing Asia produced 322,100 graduates with engineering

degrees (greater than the US, Japan, and the European Union combined). The PRC alone supplied nearly 200,000 engineering graduates in 1999. In the same year in India, 147,000 students graduated with a bachelor's degree in science, 3,000 more than in the US. It is notable that, together, India and the PRC generated around a quarter of the world's total graduates in science and engineering in 1999.[17] This has led some to believe that these two countries will become technological powerhouses in the 21st century as the world moves toward more knowledge- and research-intensive production. It is this emphasis on science and engineering that is attracting MNCs from industrial countries.

However, though impressive, the supply of S&T education and highly skilled labor is a necessary but not sufficient condition for increasing competitiveness and ascending GVCs. Such progress, as illustrated in Figure 3.3, also depends on other essential economic factors.

Also, these impressive S&T educational attainments are not true for all developing Asian countries and there are significant problems in tertiary education. Generally, the poorer Asian countries trail well behind. Less developed Asian economies need to avoid falling into a "low-skill, bad-job trap" (Snower 1996). While cheap, semiskilled labor may provide an important entry point into GVCs for firms in countries such as Indonesia, Philippines, and Viet Nam, they must quickly upgrade technologically in order to increase the value added of their production (as did Korea; Singapore; and Taipei,China before them). Otherwise, they may stay caught in a cycle of low skills, low wages, depressed productivity, and low levels of technology. Avoiding this vicious circle requires an upgrading of the educational base for several Asian countries and active government participation (Box 3.8).

Examples of this approach include East and Southeast Asian economies, in particular Korea and Singapore, that have undertaken a number of training programs since the 1970s. For example, in 1976, Korea introduced the Basic Law for Vocational Training that requires private firms with 150 or more employees to conduct in-house training for a portion of its employees, or to pay a training levy equivalent to no less than 6% of its wage bill. This levy is used to promote vocational training via government-sponsored vocational training schools.

Box 3.8 Low Skills, Vicious Circles, and Traps

Countries that try to exploit their comparative advantages based on low labor costs by restricting wages or through devaluations end up sucked into a vicious circle of low productivity, deficient training, and a lack of skilled jobs, preventing the sector in question from competing effectively in the markets for skill-intensive products. This situation is referred to as the "low-skill, bad-job trap." Bad jobs are associated with low wages and little opportunity to accumulate human capital. Good jobs, though, demand higher skills and command higher wages.

A second trap derives from the complementarities between capital and labor, referred to as the "low-skill, low-tech trap." If workers have insufficient skills to operate modern machines, the latter will be underutilized. Consequently, firms have little incentive to invest in the latest technology. This reduces workers' productivity even more.

A third problem emerges from the interaction between innovation and skills. Innovation is crucial for developing technological capabilities, but it requires well-trained workers. Economies can get caught in a vicious circle in which firms do not innovate because the labor force is insufficiently skilled, and workers have no incentives to invest in knowledge (so they do not train sufficiently) because there is no demand for these skills.

Therefore, the relatively low demand for and supply of skills in a country is seen as deriving from rational decisions made by both firms and individuals in the context of the particular legal and institutional framework in which they operate. Countries with a less skilled workforce have greater incentives to produce nontraded services rather than tradables, such as manufactured goods, because the former are relatively protected from foreign competition. This pattern of specialization creates and perpetuates the demand for less skilled labor.

One of the most important consequences of the deficiency in training is the effect on the composition of goods produced in the country: a lack of skilled workers adversely affects product quality. And skill deficiencies lead to producing and exporting relatively poor-quality and low-value products. A businessperson with only an unskilled labor pool available may well consider that any attempt to produce high-value goods will be subject to errors and poor quality. Thus, the labor force will be more suited to the production of a low-value rather than a high-value product, as it is better to risk ruining a low-value than a high-value one. The manufacture of products of high quality requires highly trained workers. But if the country does not generate enough of these workers, firms will be forced to produce low-quality goods; and likewise, workers will acquire little training because few high-quality goods are produced. This leads to a vicious circle because the choices made by employers reflect the availability of a skilled workforce. Different outputs require different types of training.

Why can the above happen? The reason is that the market does not lead to the best possible outcome because there are differences between private and social returns to knowledge. Individuals are not fully rewarded for the social contribution they make when they invest in knowledge by increasing the stock of knowledge available to everyone. They get no reward for this spillover, and so contributions to social knowledge will be underprovided. In the end, firms' decisions about what type of products to produce depend on the degree to which skilled labor is available. The result is that "in countries that offer little support for education and training and that contain a large proportion of unskilled workers, the market mechanism may reinforce the existing lack of skills by providing little incentive to acquire more; whereas in countries with well-functioning educational and training institutions and large bodies of skilled labor, the free market may do much more to induce people to become skilled" (Snower 1996, p.112).

Breaking out of such traps and vicious circles may require government intervention in subsidizing knowledge acquisition. People will have the incentive to go to school if the country already possesses a high average level of skills, but they will not if skills are still low. Thus a nation with low average skills will be stuck in this position because people do not find it worthwhile attending school.

But what can the government do to remedy the situation? It is difficult for it to know all the aptitudes needed by every single firm and worker. Likewise, government support for training is not cheap and it must finance it by imposing taxes or cutting other expenditures. In other words, substantial public investment will not enable the country to get out of a trap if this investment is financed by a punitive tax on private investment. This implies that the subsidies should be financed by taxes that do not discourage knowledge accumulation, such as taxes on consumption.

One measure that governments can adopt includes training vouchers, financed by government revenues and used to compensate both firms for providing training and workers for acquiring the resulting skills. Another measure is investment tax credits and depreciation allowances.

Source:
Snower, Dennis. 1996. "The Low-Skill, Bad-Job Trap." In Alison L. Booth and Dennis J. Snower (eds.), *Acquiring Skills: Market Failures, Their Symptoms and Policy Responses*, pp.109–24. Cambridge: Cambridge University Press.

Likewise, Singapore has a series of programs such as the Vocational and Industrial Training Board, set up in 1979 and financed with a levy of 1% on wages to subsidize efforts to upgrade the skills and expertise of employees or retraining of retrenched workers. Other initiatives are the Basic Education and Skills Development program to teach basic skills in arithmetic and literacy to workers, and the creation of the National Productivity Board (1972) and the National Productivity Council (1982) to promote productivity consciousness. In Malaysia, training costs can be subsidized, and the Penang Skills Development Center puts together training courses contributed by MNCs to upgrade their suppliers' skills. Thailand grants a 150% tax deduction for training expenses.

The educational implication of the necessity for GVC upgrading is that countries should consciously follow strategies to improve educational attainment. Wherever possible, they should emphasize S&T education that supports those industries that have a good potential for upgrading (e.g., consumer electronics, computer products, and telecommunications goods). The dual education–industry upgrading imperative therefore places a heavy burden on those at all levels who are responsible for basic and technical education.

Relevance of School and University Education

The modernization of the workplace places new demands on employee skills, which, in turn, place new demands on educational provision. The number of people acquiring a university education, especially in the natural sciences and engineering, affects the quality of the labor force and the economic development potential of a country. New technologies require workers to possess practical specialized knowledge in, for example, the areas of ICT and automated production processes. Given the need for constant upgrading within GVCs, workers need to be able to continuously improve their skills to match workplace needs. This places emphasis on the "trainability" of workers through on-the-job learning and formal training. But will the production of scientists and engineers in developing Asia be sufficient to meet the future needs of the region?

Firms need to be able to assess the level of trainability of prospective new entrants and their inherent ability to communicate and cooperate with others to keep up with organizational and technological changes. Trainability or individual "absorptive capacity" may well now be more important than the initial entry qualifications or professional skills of a worker in this kind of environment.

Once employed, workers have to become familiar with new methods of performance assessment and reward; again, the emphasis is on lifelong learning and teamwork. The standard skills (e.g., general clerical ability, problem solving, information processing, and teamwork) are still widely required. However, in advanced manufacturing, for example, modern Asian firms need to introduce management practices to improve quality control and error detection. Each worker is therefore expected to participate in a wider set of processes through multiskilling or by learning more about surrounding processes and how they fit together (Ihm 2002).

The changing demands within the workforce challenge the usefulness of traditional schooling and university education in many developing Asian countries. Individuals need to be sure that skills learned at school will be useful in the workplace. For example, computer and ICT skills need to be taught as well as English as a foreign language. The demand for mathematics, logical skills, and problem solving is increasing.

Many countries in the region are concerned about the adequacy of their supply of scientists and engineers, and indeed a mismatch is now evident between the type of education supplied and the skills demanded by firms. In Korea, for example, as Table 3.14 shows, both managers and workers perceive a significant mismatch between the skills acquired at university and those needed in the workplace. It is not clear how to remedy this situation regionally. There is a widely held concern around the region that university education is perhaps failing to produce the quality of skills, research, and talent needed to climb the development ladder. But when it comes to specific policies, it is very difficult to pinpoint what it takes to "build an MIT." It might be a matter of more competition among universities, or more linkages with foreign universities so as to facilitate the transfer of ideas and technology, or even more emphasis on research publications in universities. For example, since the 1950s, the NIEs have systematically assimilated the

Table 3.14 Deficiencies in Supply of Work-Related Competencies in Korea, %[a]

Respondents	1[b]	2	3	4	5	Number of Respondents[c]
Personnel Managers	2.2	13.4	43.6	34.5	6.2	417
College-Graduated Workers	1.6	9.5	23.5	53.4	12.0	442

[a] Based on personnel managers' and graduate workers' ranking of the difference between skills/competences acquired in universities and those required at worksites (% of respondents). [b] 1 indicates no mismatch, 5 indicates greatest mismatch. [c] Equal to 100% of respondents.
Source: Korea Research Institute for Vocational Education and Training. 2000. "A Study on the Business Firms' Satisfaction of University Education" (in Korean), p.105, cited in Ihm (2002).

benefits of foreign education. For a long time, Asia has sent more of its students in tertiary education to the US than any other region. In particular, the US higher education institutions are a significant source for doctoral education for Asian students, three quarters in the case of Taipei,China in natural sciences and engineering in 1990 (NSF 1993, Table 3.5). Hong Kong, China and Singapore have created new universities over the last decade—the Hong Kong University of Science and Technology in the early 1990s, and, very recently, the Singapore Management University. Both institutions have great expectations for their futures and have recruited faculty and researchers from institutions around the world (Box 3.9).

Unfortunately, there are no definite answers to these questions and more research and empirical evidence are needed. First, more work is needed on developing the methodologies and data necessary for estimating supply and demand for scientists and engineers. Second, more data are needed on the PRC's stock of scientists and engineers, in particular regarding the country's accomplishments in strengthening S&T education for economic development. Third, the degree of mobility among Asian countries and throughout the world for graduate degrees in S&T needs to be investigated, and employment possibilities in industry, government institutes, and universities studied. Fourth, analysis of the particular scientific strengths and the research niche of each country should be undertaken, given that many S&T initiatives in Asian nations are similar (e.g., ICT, biotechnology), with a view to boosting collaboration.

New policies are needed to support relevant, high-quality education, and technical training to meet production-upgrading needs, so that "upskilling" becomes an ongoing process. In some cases, policies may also be needed to enhance lifelong learning opportunities for workers. This might be done, for example, through new schemes of retraining and skill development that take place throughout employees' careers and that support firm-level efforts to upgrade.

Already, much of the focus of the discussion about education in Asia is on quality and the ability of education to contribute to innovation. New approaches to learning are being carried out in Japan, Korea, and Singapore, while many other countries are introducing young children to computer technology and the Internet. As Yusuf and Evenett (2002) show, Korea has proposed setting up special schools similar to the PRC's "key schools," to develop the scientific talent of gifted youngsters. The PRC now encourages competition between schools and has given legal recognition to the large number of private schools (which teach around 7 million primary and high school students), encouraging diversity in educational provision.

At the tertiary level, until universities in the region can produce the necessary supply of graduate students, in particular in science and engineering, many Asian countries could continue sending students to US universities. Here, Japan could play an important role in training students from the region, the same as the PRC and India in some cases. Japan's policy to attract foreign students has been successful: since the 1980s, good engineering schools sought to recruit foreign students from Asia. Efforts must also be made at attracting these students and well-established senior researchers and scholars back home with attractive salaries and living conditions. In the past, when students went abroad to earn an advanced degree, there was a high probability that they would remain

Box 3.9 Education Reform in Singapore: Toward Greater Creativity and Innovation?

Singapore's leaders appear to be overly worried about the apparent lack of creativity and thinking skills among the country's students and workers. Thus, schools are being encouraged to foster creativity and innovation to enhance national economic competitiveness. The authorities feel the need to upgrade education and training as prime sources of such competitiveness.

However, the tangible evidence that has led to this pessimism is not clear, unless the authorities want to blame the education system for the country's alleged lack of competitiveness. In fact, Singapore's students scored very well in the Third International Mathematics and Science Study in 1999, a test made up of questions that examined students' creative problem-solving skills and their ability to respond to open-ended questions. Moreover, examination results published by the University of Cambridge Local Examinations Syndicate reveal that Singaporean students do well in questions regarding the cultivation of higher-order thinking and analytical skills.

Nevertheless, the Government has implemented a series of policies with a view to enhancing the country's international competitiveness. There are two main initiatives. The first has been the growing "marketization" of education since the mid-1980s; the second has involved the curriculum.

The marketization of education has been manifested in increased school autonomy and greater interschool competition. In terms of autonomy, beginning in 1988, several well-established schools were allowed to operate largely independent of the Ministry of Education. They were given autonomy and flexibility in the recruitment, deployment, and reward of staff, as well as finance, management, and curriculum design. These schools charge higher fees (depending on the degree of autonomy) than regular schools, and their main attraction is that they tend to offer a wider range of subjects. Competition between schools is also emphasized, as it is believed that it will force schools to improve their programs and performance. To this end, all secondary schools and junior colleges have been publicly ranked on an annual basis since 1992 and the results have been published in local newspapers with a view to providing better information to parents and students so that they can make informed choices.

The second initiative, relating to the curriculum, has spurred three schemes to encourage the transition to a knowledge economy. The first of these is called Thinking Schools, Learning Nation, launched in 1997, and focuses on developing critical thinking skills. Its key strategies include the explicit teaching of critical and creative thinking skills, the reduction of subject content, the revision of assessment modes, and a greater emphasis on processes instead of outcomes when appraising schools. The second scheme is the Masterplan for Information Technology in Education. It attempts to incorporate information technology in teaching and learning in all schools. The target is to provide one desktop computer for every two students and one notebook computer for every two teachers. The third scheme focuses on university admission criteria. The idea is to broaden the criteria for acceptance at university by considering not only the results in the General Certificate of Education (Advanced) Level examination but also the results in the Scholastic Assessment Test (I), the results of project work at school, and the extent of students' participation in extracurricular activities.

What have been the results so far of these important steps and reforms? Even though the evidence about the need for such reforms is not convincing, any attempt at improvement should be welcomed. The results of increased school autonomy have been mixed. For example, the degree of choice and diversity is still limited and the government maintains a great deal of influence over the secondary school curriculum. The promotion of competition between schools has aroused a great deal of controversy and criticism, in particular the ranking of schools, which has been criticized even by the external review team commissioned by the Ministry of Education for two reasons. First, the less prestigious institutions are at a disadvantage and cannot compete with the well-established schools. Second, competition has led to a concentration of effort on those activities that will lead to a higher ranking and to attracting students and parents.

Source: Tan, Jason, and S. Gopinathan. 2000. "Education Reform in Singapore: Towards Greater Creativity and Innovation?" *NIRA Review* (Summer): 5–10.

abroad rather than return home; between one half and two thirds of these students chose to stay abroad (NSF 1993, Table 10).[18] Hong Kong, China; Korea; Singapore; and Taipei,China have been particularly successful at attracting them back.

Incentives for teacher retraining could help overcome some of the resistance to modern educational methods and topics. At higher levels, joint programs with industrial-country educational groups provide part of the solution, as these are able to import directly new educational techniques and adapt them to suit local circumstances. Many leading universities from Australia, France, UK, and US already have joint programs with universities in developing Asia.

To meet more advanced research needs, some universities in developing Asia and government-sponsored research institutes have begun to engage more intensively in commercially oriented research, taking on consulting, contract research, and collaboration with local industry and MNCs. For instance, several genome research institutes in the PRC have been spun off from government research institutes and have become more financially independent. There is also some evidence of private pharmaceutical company investment in university-based research in East Asia (Yusuf and Evenett 2002). However, although these programs will help develop new approaches to S&T education, much of developing Asia is still at the early stages of this transition, and educational systems will need to change more fundamentally and more quickly to support the S&T requirements of the region's leading businesses.

Summary

Given the recognition of the educational difficulties, governments in PRC, Korea, Malaysia, and some other Asian countries are increasing their expenditure on tertiary level education, encouraging university-based R&D, and increasing funding to government research institutes. Self-evidently, new policies for education need to be tailored to the specific needs, problems, and opportunities of each individual country.

The role of education policies in enhancing the productivity of labor is important in two ways. First, it facilitates and encourages the accumulation of human capital via direct investment by the government. Second, it makes investment in schooling profitable to households. For the countries that seek to exploit GVCs, there are perhaps five key policy messages arising from the trend toward higher value-added, knowledge-intensive production (Ihm 2002). First, while basic education needs to remain the bedrock of schooling at all levels, many schools need to shift the focus away from mere rote learning of facts toward a more critical understanding of analytical concepts and technical knowledge. Although national curricula need several core subjects, there may also be a need for

more discretion at the school level to teach work-related subjects relevant to the changing needs of industry. In many countries, this will require some deregulation and decentralization of curriculum policy.

Second, at the level of student assessment and teaching methods, pedagogy should encourage more experimental learning as well as group learning and teamwork, the cornerstone of skills in the modern workplace. More continuous evaluation of performance at the school level may also be needed. Governments should ensure that industrial needs are assessed regularly and provide incentives for schools and teachers to place greater emphasis on these areas in the curriculum. Teacher training provision may also need to be revised, as well as college admission procedures that have traditionally stressed basic cognitive achievements rather than the students' behavioral attributes and potential.

Third, the modern workplace requires employees who are inherently "trainable" and can learn rapidly. Policies may therefore be needed at the upper secondary education level. More vocational colleges and high schools may need to add relevant skills such as ICT, group working, English, and other foreign languages. Governments may wish to increase support and provide new incentives to vocational schools to introduce programs for the retraining and redeployment of teachers to help them cope with new work requirements.

Fourth, there may well be a case in several countries for increasing public investment in higher education to expand provision and make it more affordable to a greater number of students. In developing Asia, as in industrial countries, the demand for lifetime learning by workers and managers is likely to increase. Workers will need to be encouraged to undertake further education and training to keep up with competence and performance requirements. Nontraditional means of financing such training (e.g., student loans and other schemes) could be increased to encourage more adult workers to undertake new learning opportunities.

Fifth, governments in several less developed countries may need to improve the supply and quality of lifetime learning. The new capacities and skills needed in the workplace will require continuing investment in new learning and training programs. Schools, colleges, universities, and S&T institutes need to become more responsive to the needs of industry as well as to the specific skills that individuals need through different phases of their careers. Obviously, high-quality basic education is needed, but to reach more individuals, new learning methods such as distance education, electronic-learning, and group learning need to be considered by educational groups and government policy makers. Lifetime career requirements should play a greater part in deliberations between teachers, trade unions, government bodies, and firms.

Catch-Up Competitiveness: Some Lessons

Previous sections have emphasized that (i) competitiveness is a firm-level question, (ii) economy-wide, competitiveness is shorthand for a "well-functioning market economy," and (iii) at the aggregate level, the increase in national productivity is the result of these firm-level productivity improvements.

In this section, three important questions of particular relevance to firms in less developed countries of Asia are considered:

• What is the nature of competitiveness in a catch-up context?

• What is the nature and role of innovation in catch-up competitiveness?

• What policy lessons can less developed nations draw from the NIEs with respect to catch-up competitiveness in GVCs?

For a developing nation, long-run growth depends on the combined capabilities of all the main economic actors (e.g., firms, government bodies, educational suppliers, and providers of infrastructure) to implement effectively strategies for sustainable growth and development. To catch up, rather than merely keep up with (at a certain distance behind) the leaders, this combined capability must be sufficient to assimilate and improve on technologies created in the leading nations over sustained periods of time. The absorption of foreign technology is essential to create internationally tradable products that are competitive in terms of cost and quality. This points to an important difference between leadership and catch-up competitiveness. The former is centered on the creation of new markets through R&D and marketing investments. By contrast, catch-up competitiveness is based on "behind-the-frontier" innovation, involving constant improvements to process and products (and their interfaces), supported by various kinds of technical and engineering capabilities. Selective R&D may also be required to support these capabilities. Catch-up competitiveness depends on entrepreneurship and educational provision, as well as market-friendly institutions and sound macroeconomic management.

Therefore, catch-up competitiveness is a dynamic concept. Catch up cannot occur if a country does not create new resources or restructure its industries toward more productive, higher-value-added products. This is achieved by the country absorbing, adapting, and improving on the technologies that underpin new products, services, and processes. Dynamic competitiveness also relies on the infrastructure needed for sustained industrial development. Countries may be compared with their performance in each of these areas, as these will feed into the aggregate "transformational" performance of the economy.

In a catch-up context, an economy needs not only to build up the dynamic capabilities that underpin the absorption, adaptation, and generation of new technology. It also needs the institutions and policies required to ensure that a country's industry is sufficiently dynamic and outward looking, so that its firms are able and encouraged to compete successfully in the foreign markets of industrial countries. Failure to compete in these markets usually means falling behind in the technological race.

These catch-up conditions require a degree of innovation at the technological, institutional, and policy levels. Mere imitation is insufficient, because the more advanced countries will constantly be moving the technology frontier outward and generating new technologies and product types. In addition, other industrializing countries will be entering, competing, and changing the competitive landscape. This implies that each developing country needs to overcome its own particular disadvantages in terms of resources and its stage of development. But this is not sufficient. It also needs to build up its own distinctive advantages and resources to prevent itself from falling behind, and to go beyond merely keeping up in order to catch up.

Indeed, it is unlikely that any developing country ever has achieved, or could achieve, long-run competitiveness, i.e., a well-functioning economy, without a substantial degree of innovation in the policy, institutional, and technological arenas. On this basis, no single set of policies can be prescribed for achieving sustained competitiveness. On the contrary, each country must generate its own distinctive policies based on its individual

the competitive drive of local plants were essential for successful technology acquisition.[22] In Southeast Asia, as in East Asia, achieving competitiveness was neither automatic nor painless. The studies demonstrate that there were long periods of trial-and-error experimentation, and extensive training of local operators, technicians, and engineers. There was also a great deal of management ingenuity in the more successful cases of technology development within MNC subsidiaries. In this respect, Hobday (1995b) concluded that:

> East Asian latecomers did not leapfrog from one vintage of technology to another. On the contrary, the evidence shows that firms engaged in a painstaking and cumulative process of technological learning: a hard slog rather than a leapfrog. The route to advanced electronics and information technology was through a long difficult learning process, driven by the manufacture of goods for export (Hobday 1995b, p.1188).

Kim (1997) described Hyundai's efforts to produce a car after it had purchased the foreign equipment, hired expatriate consultants, and signed licensing agreements with foreign firms as follows:

> Despite the training and consulting services of experts, Hyundai engineers repeated trials and errors for fourteen months before creating the first prototype. But the engine block broke into pieces at its first test. New prototype engines appeared almost every week, only to break in testing. No one on the team could figure out why the prototypes kept breaking down, casting serious doubts even among Hyundai management, on its capability to develop a competitive engine. The team had to scrap eleven more broken prototypes before one survived the test. There were 2,888 engine design changes... Ninety seven test engines were made before Hyundai refined its natural aspiration and turbocharger engines... In addition, more than 200 transmissions and 150 test vehicles were created before Hyundai perfected them in 1992 (Kim 1997, p.129).

And in the case of Samsung:

> It took the team a year of 80-hour weeks to complete the first prototype (in 1976) but the plastic in the cavity melted in a test... Finally, in June 1978, after two years, the team developed a model that survived the test; but it was too crude to compete in the world market. Samsung incrementally improved the product and developed a makeshift production line, producing one over a day, then two, which it placed in local bakeries for feedback from users (Kim 1997, p.137).

The nature of catch-up competitiveness in the NIEs contrasts sharply with the traditional definition of technological innovation, namely the production of new (or improved) products, based on R&D. Instead, what occurred was behind-the-frontier innovation, including improvements to products, the changing of processes to become more efficient and flexible, improvements in "design for manufacture," and the introduction of new types of product imitating the designs of leading firms.

Furthermore, the stages model captures the fact that innovation occurs, not just in technological terms but also, and very importantly, in institutional terms. The technological change that took place in East Asia in electronics probably could not have occurred with such rapidity without the OEM and, later, ODM systems.

Similarly, the increase of MNC-led growth was also a critical development. MNC investment on such a large scale was new to Southeast Asia and allowed parent companies to transfer foreign technology to local subsidiaries. These were then able to systematically learn the technological arts of electronics production. MNC subsidiaries provided a route into international markets and enabled continuous, routine technological learning to occur within local plants. The "master-pupil" relationship described by Cyhn (2002) in case studies of East Asian OEM mirrors the relationships that developed between parent and subsidiary plants in Southeast Asia.

The exploitation of MNC investment began in Singapore (Goh 1996) and was imitated by other countries wishing to export to OECD countries. Although FDI occurred prior to 1960s, the electronics industry brought with it a huge expansion of FDI in Southeast Asia, leading to the development of several industrial clusters. For example, the computer disk-drive cluster in Thailand is the largest of its kind in the world. Similarly, in Penang, Malaysia, the semiconductor assembly and testing cluster is the largest exporter of semiconductors worldwide.

As a method for describing past developments, the stages approach is clearly quite useful, though it has a number of shortcomings. First, as with most historical summaries, there is a danger of over-generalization. The stages model only helps explain the evolution of low-cost, relatively simple electronics components and products. It is less useful in explaining more highly priced and more complex goods where the NIEs remain substantially weaker.

Second, the stages model conceals significant technological differences between exporters. For example, major Korean firms such as Samsung began investing in R&D very early on, and, in some product areas (e.g., microwave ovens) as early as the 1960s (Magaziner and Patinkin 1989). This was long before they progressed to OBM. Other firms (e.g., Acer of Taipei,China) "jumped in" at later stages, benefiting from the infrastructure developed previously.

Third, even at today's fairly advanced stage of catch up, many East Asian firms conduct a mixture of OEM, ODM, and OBM. It is not correct to imply that all firms have progressed to OBM. Indeed, even the most advanced producers such as Samsung of Korea still produce large quantities of output under basic OEM arrangements (e.g., in consumer electronics and microwave ovens) with Japanese and US firms.

Innovations in Policy and Variety in Industrial Structures

In addition to the difficulties in making generalizations, if viewed in isolation the stages approach can obscure the wide variety of government policies and industrial structures used to achieve competitiveness. One cannot assume, because of some similarities in the stages of development, that the government policies adopted, or the critical success factors for growth, were similar, let alone the same, across NIEs. On the contrary, policy and institutional innovation occurred in very different ways in the NIEs, and the stages model must be seen within this broader context of development.

Figure 3.4 illustrates some of the variety in policy and industrial structure within the electronics industry for Hong Kong, China; Korea; and Taipei,China (East Asia); and Malaysia, Singapore, and Thailand (Southeast Asia). The degree of direct policy intervention is on the vertical axis, while the degree of openness of each economy to FDI and imports is on the horizontal axis. The figure indicates a high degree of direct government

Figure 3.4 Diversity of Policy Approaches and Industrial Structures, Selected Asian Economies

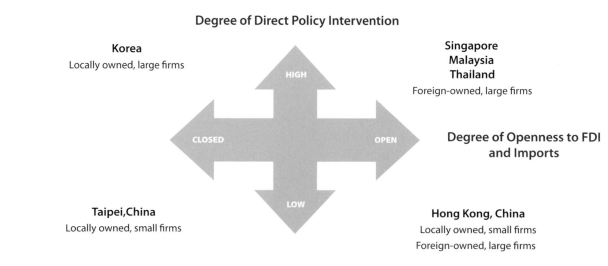

Source: Amended from Hobday (1995a, p.196).

intervention in the early stages of development of electronics (i.e., in the 1960s and 1970s) for Korea but shows a much lower degree of direct intervention in Taipei,China and a more or less laisser faire approach in Hong Kong, China. In Korea, for example, the Government directly supported the large *chaebol* with favorable finance, subsidies, and other privileges (Amsden 1989). Indeed, some authors suggest the Government helped create the *chaebol* (Jones and Sakong 1980).

In Southeast Asia, governments intervened mostly indirectly with support for large foreign firms that were encouraged to export. Large MNCs were attracted with incentives, infrastructure in the form of EPZs, and a degree of freedom rarely seen before in the developing world (Yue 1985).

In contrast to the "big firm" approach of Korea and Singapore, much of Taipei,China's early electronics manufacture relied on small and medium enterprises, linked to international markets through traders (Chou 1992). Many of these manufacturers operated in a more or less "underground" manner. Only later on, for example in scale-intensive semiconductors, did the Taipei,China authorities become more directly involved in supporting electronics producers (e.g., in Hsinchu and other industrial parks and with institutions such as the Information Technology Research Institute in semiconductors; see Mathews and Cho 2000).

The horizontal axis of Figure 3.4 indicates that both Korea and Taipei,China were fairly closed to FDI for much of the 1960s, 1970s, and 1980s. By contrast, Hong Kong, China; and Singapore received far higher volumes of FDI, despite their smaller economies. For example, taking the two largest investors, Japan and the US, in 1980–1988, total FDI amounted to US$14.3 billion in the four NIEs. Hong Kong, China received the largest amount of FDI (US$6.3 billion), Singapore US$3.6 billion, Korea received only US$2.3 billion, and Taipei,China US$2.1 billion (James 1990, p.15). Hong Kong, China and Singapore encouraged FDI whereas Korea and Taipei,China restricted and controlled FDI, protecting local industries from foreign competition and encouraging domestic firms to supplant foreign ones wherever possible.[23]

Figure 3.4 hints at important differences in the orientation of industrial policy. While Hong Kong, China and Singapore pursued conventional export-led policies, Korea and Taipei,China combined these policies with import substitution, controlling or banning imports to protect local firms and using government procurement to stimulate local enterprise. Korea was very restrictive, resisting imports of most consumer goods, including electronics and automobiles and many raw materials. Similarly, the Taipei,China authorities often negotiated the terms of the FDI and tied MNCs to local content rules and export targets.

Figure 3.4 points to important differences in company size and ownership in achieving competitiveness (Khader 2002, Tables 2 and 3). While Hong Kong, China and Taipei,China depended to a large extent on small (and a few large) locally owned family businesses, the Korean Government supported the *chaebol*. Korean policies resulted in a highly concentrated industrial structure, with the *chaebol* dominating electronics and many other industries. By contrast, in Hong Kong, China and Taipei,China, small firms proliferated and grew, resulting in a highly dispersed industrial structure.[24]

Government policies and company strategies were closely interconnected. In Taipei,China small and medium enterprises tended to rely on speed and flexibility, while the Korean *chaebol* focused on high-volume, process-intensive electronics manufacture. In the early stages, firms from Hong Kong, China and Taipei,China specialized in fast-changing market niches, whereas Korean companies emphasized scale and vertical integration. In terms of ownership, Korea and Taipei,China relied mostly on locally owned firms, while Singapore depended almost entirely on foreign MNCs. Hong Kong, China relied on a mixture of local and foreign firms to lead electronics exports.

Insights for Other Countries

Given the wide variety of paths that the NIEs have followed in catching up with the more advanced countries in terms of competitiveness, it is very difficult to draw any general conclusion. Each country must develop its own policies, based on its own resources and given its particular level of development. The stages of development are endogenously determined and not simply and automatically passed through. This qualification applies both to early developers who followed existing new paths and to latecomers. The latter respond, adapt, and act on the new conditions facing them as a result of new technology and market conditions created by earlier developers. Countries wishing to improve competitiveness need to focus on and develop their own distinctive capabilities and resources.

At a general level, experience in the NIEs suggests that innovation is at the heart of the process of economic development and catch-up competitiveness. Attempts to imitate earlier developers and follow established development paths and policies are not, and in most cases probably cannot be, sufficient to produce catch-up development. The NIEs revealed a wide variety of development paths, not only in terms of government policy and industry structure, but also in patterns of industrial ownership, firm size, and the mechanisms for acquiring technology. The evidence shows that the NIEs undertook a great deal of experimentation and innovation in the technological, institutional, and policy arenas.

Achieving long-run competitiveness depends on the combined capabilities and resources of all the main economic actors (firms, government, and institutions) in their efforts to generate and execute strategies for sustainable economic development. To catch up, rather than merely keep up with the leaders (and to prevent falling behind), this "dynamic" capability must be sufficient both to assimilate and to improve on technologies created by the leading nations over a long period of time.

Technological innovation is an essential part of catching up because it is crucial to the creation of internationally tradable products that are competitive in terms of cost and quality with those of more advanced nations. As has been noted, this kind of behind-the-frontier innovation, widely demonstrated in the NIEs, is not necessarily based on R&D but instead is concerned with continuous incremental improvements to existing production processes and products. Although these activities may lead eventually on to specific types of indigenous R&D-based innovations (e.g., for new product designs) that result from indigenous R&D expenditure, catch-up competitiveness is very different from the leadership competitiveness carried out by firms in industrial countries. The latter depends on substantial long-term R&D with respect to new materials, processes, and products that these firms undertake over long periods of time. The evidence also reveals considerable innovation in institutions and policies in the NIEs as they developed. This occurred because each NIE had to ensure that its industry was sufficiently dynamic and outward looking. The experience of the NIEs strongly suggests that the mere imitation of the paths followed by the leading countries would be unsuccessful because the latter group constantly moves the competitive frontier forward by generating new technologies and new markets.

Conclusions

Competitiveness is defined as the ability of firms to remain profitable by delivering to the market the products and services that consumers desire and demand. Firms become more competitive by competing with other firms and by slowly and patiently learning how to do business better. Consequently, it is unavoidable that many firms will fail and go out of business, yet others will emerge.

Governments and policy makers are particularly interested in the issue. This has given rise to the notion of "national competitiveness" and to the discussion of the topic as if it were the elixir for growth and development. However, competitiveness is not a panacea for development for the developing countries in Asia. Rather, a proper discussion of competitiveness can provide a framework for entrepreneurs and policy makers to analyze the best ways to achieve sustained growth.

For example, a consideration of competitiveness can help focus on ways to improve the environment for investment. Competitiveness should be best understood as a course of action, and not as a one-time event. It is a continuing process, a way of seeking a better future for individual firms, industries and, ultimately, national economies. The consideration of the East Asian experience, in particular, provides useful insights for firms and policy makers in less advanced countries in the Asia-Pacific region as they devise new strategies and approaches to promote higher rates of sustainable growth.

The main conclusions are as follows.

Globalization, technological progress, and competition are the main drivers of change in today's world, where knowledge is the most important resource. These three factors have raised a whole spectrum of new challenges and opportunities of which firms and policy makers in developing Asia should be aware. The discussion has shown that this environment offers substantial opportunities for the firms and countries in the region to achieve sustained growth. The key to success in the coming years is that governments and firms across Asia devise strategies so as to take full advantage of the potential benefits that globalization, technology, and competition offer. It will be necessary for them

to understand what competitiveness means and how it fits in the development puzzle.

Competitiveness is a firm-level issue and hence its analysis requires a firm-level approach. It is, therefore, essential to provide a grounded explanation of the microeconomic foundations of competitiveness. An important implication is that the term national competitiveness, especially if used in the context of nations competing for market shares in exports, as some scholars and governments have taken it, is elusive and even misleading. While nations are concerned about status and power, they do not compete for market shares in the same manner that individual firms do. Indices of national competitiveness have little theoretical foundation and thus must be treated with caution. Misconceptions of the nature and role of competitiveness in national economic development can be counterproductive.

Competition and the quest for profits are the driving forces of firms in a market economy. Competition among firms forces the adoption of the cheapest methods of production and the improvement in the quality of products. In the process of introducing better technologies, new lower-cost methods become available, which allows for increases in labor productivity. Increasing productivity is critical for firms because this is how the profit motive that drives them is put into practice. Labor productivity grows through the interplay of two complementary mechanisms—increases in efficiency and the rate of technical progress. The latter is the result of both investment and the development of entrepreneurial and technological capabilities. These capabilities are defined as the ability to use, generate, change, and add to the pool of the industrial arts. In other words: firms become more competitive not only by reducing costs but also by improving existing products and developing new technologically intensive products. This involves firms moving into new areas, such as services, as well as taking risks and engaging in trial and error.

The debate over whether national competitiveness has any meaning has its roots in the discussion about what the appropriate role for government policy to enhance firms' competitiveness is. Firms compete in an increasingly global market and government policies can either help or hinder their efforts. The goal of governments in this context can be summarized in the idea of creating a well-functioning market economy, which is what is meant by a competitive economy.

A well-functioning market economy is the result of a partnership between the state and firms. Although national competitiveness may be an elusive concept, as a shorthand for well-functioning market economy, it has a place in the policy debate. The ultimate objective of this partnership is for developing countries to increase living standards and to catch up with the countries at the income and technological frontier. Increases in labor productivity are the key to achieving sustained long-run growth in living standards. The other component of a well-functioning market economy is the development of institutions, which are determined by historical and cultural factors as well as by government actions. Institutions are an immobile factor of production and consequently each country has to experiment and set up the institutions that work in its particular context.

The role of firms in this partnership is to try to be as competitive as possible. Governments have a very important role to play with a view to building a well-functioning market economy, and toward enhancing firms' competitiveness. They have to provide the institutional infrastructure and make available myriad services to facilitate competition among firms by providing a level playing field. Specifically, governments' main functions are to provide macroeconomic stability; set up the necessary legal system, including competition and entry and exit laws; and address market failures. Likewise, there are three major areas where there is room for state and markets to share responsibilities: education, technology and innovation, and physical infrastructure.

Certain aspects of government intervention that aim to enhance competitiveness **are more controversial when they are used as competitiveness policies** and, in particular, if they cloak what is in effect industrial policy and an exercise in picking the winners. These are the provision of financial incentives to attract FDI, the creation of EPZs, and the creation of clusters and industrial parks. The empirical evidence to date indicates that government intervention in these areas might not yield significant benefits. Moreover, the evidence regarding technology transfer mandates, specific local content requirements, or mandatory joint ventures indicates that these approaches do not yield benefits as large as expected by the host country. The problem with the creation of clusters and EPZs is that they often appear packaged as "new competitiveness policies" when, in many cases, they are no more than discredited industrial policies that attempt to pick the winners.

Two related dynamic competitive factors are making developing Asia a formidable producer and exporter of technology-intensive goods. Among the variety of possibilities for firms to enhance their entrepreneurial and technological capabilities, **GVCs offer significant opportunities to many Asian firms to take advantage of the potential benefits of globalization.** There are many ways for a firm to enter a GVC and these largely depend on the firm's level of development. The NIE firms successfully entered GVCs three decades ago and it was in this way that they climbed the development ladder. Their experience can be very useful to the firms in less developed countries of the region.

The availability of skilled labor is another dynamic competitive force. Education is an area of shared responsibility between government and market, especially at the tertiary level. The East and Southeast Asian economies now provide basic education for all those who are eligible. However, in recent years they have realized that their educational systems need important reforms, in particular regarding the mismatch between the type of education supplied by universities and the skills demanded by the firms. There is no unique solution to this problem and countries in the region will have to experiment.

Finally, **firms in less developed countries in the region can learn a great deal from the experience of the firms in the NIEs,** which reduced substantially the technological gap with firms at the frontier during the last two decades. They did this not by undertaking R&D, but through behind-the-frontier innovation, which involved constant improvements to processes and products. This has been referred to as catch-up competitiveness, which depends on entrepreneurship, provision of education as well as market-friendly institutions, and sound macroeconomic management. The discussion has argued that exactly replicating the NIEs' experience will be impossible, mainly because the global economic environment has changed, and because the specific resources and capabilities of today's developing economies differ from those of the NIEs.

Thus, although the successful experience of many NIE firms has many important lessons, catch-up by the firms in less developed countries in the region will be impossible without a substantial degree of indigenous innovativeness at the entre-preneurial and technological levels, as well as at the policy and institutional levels.

Endnotes

1 Non-price competitiveness is determined by such factors as the degree of product innovation, the quality and reliability of products, their speed of delivery, and the extent and efficacy of the distribution network.

2 Cited by Haque (1995) and attributed to the US Commission of Industrial Competitiveness.

3 Only under global full employment does free trade increase the global wealth of nations by reducing each nation's aggregate supply constraints through the law of comparative advantage. If, on the other hand, unemployment were to arise in the process of specialization and resource allocation, the resource gains from specialization might be offset by resource losses from unemployment.

4 $$REER_j = \sum_i w_{ij} e_{ij} \cdot \frac{CPI_j}{WPI_i}$$, where $REER_j$ is the real effective exchange rate of home country j; WPI_i is the wholesale price index of partner country i; CPI_j is the consumer price index of home country j; e_{ij} is the exchange rate index between country i and j expressed in foreign currency per local currency; and w_{ij} is share of country i in the total trade of country j.

$$ULC = \frac{w}{(Q/L)}$$, where w is the nominal wage rate, Q is total real output, and L is labor.

5 If the growth of exports and imports were highly responsive to changes in relative prices, then we should expect that those countries that had a noticeable improvement in their relative prices would also experience, all other things being equal, the most rapid increase in their overseas market shares. In practice, and paradoxically, as Kaldor first pointed out, the converse holds for much of the postwar period, with those countries that experienced the greatest decline in their price competitiveness also having had the greatest increase in their market share.

6 For reasons of space, the theoretical debate about the appropriate role of government in fostering development and in enhancing competitiveness by targeting selected firms and industries is not discussed here. The interested reader can see Amsden (1989), Wade (1990), World Bank (1993), Page (1994), Lall (1994), Perkins (1994), Chang (1996), and Noland and Pack (2003), among others.

7 These are not all the areas of the government's responsibility. It is of the greatest importance that governments protect citizens (defense, law and order) as well as from basic deprivations, e.g., illiteracy, basic hunger, or homelessness, and meet fundamental requirements, e.g., education and basic health. What constitutes an adequate safety net and how it should be provided varies with each country, and attention must be paid to the adverse incentive effects of poorly designed safety nets and to the heavy costs of their provision (Stern and Stiglitz 1997, p.5).

8 Number of weeks to start a business: India: 14; PRC: 8; Philippines: 9; Thailand: 6; Malaysia: 8; Korea: 5 (World Bank 2003b, Figure 3.8). On the other hand, it takes 2 business days in Canada to start a firm (World Bank 2003b, p.91).

9 Trade and investment liberalization are currently under discussion. At the Fourth Ministerial Conference of WTO held in Doha in November 2001, ministers expressed their intentions to secure transparent, stable, and predictable conditions for long-term cross-border investment, particularly FDI. The Fifth WTO Ministerial meeting, to be held in Cancun (Mexico) in September 2003, will discuss whether investment measures will be further considered in the Doha Round of negotiations.

10 See also Noland and Pack (2003, pp.88–92).

11 There seems to be evidence that fiscal incentives given for export-oriented FDI affect location decisions, while fiscal incentives do not attract FDI geared to the domestic market (World Bank 2003b, p.81).

12 For example, according to their data, a foreign investor must follow nine administrative procedures to start up a business in India; it takes 39 days, at a cost of US$261 (Morisset and Lumenga Neso 2002, Table 2).

13 Thailand's recent competitiveness plan, promoted by the Government, identifies five sectors where the country can develop niches. These sectors and the objectives are: software (world center of graphic design), auto industry (the Detroit of Asia), fashion (world center of tropical fashion), food (kitchen of the world), and tourism (tourism capital of Asia). Singapore has recently published a document entitled "New Challenges, Fresh Goals" where the Ministry of Trade and Industry (2003) outlines a series of strategies to promote growth, development, and competitiveness over the next 15 years.

14 Today, all developed countries have such policies (Nelson 1993).

15 For example, between the early 1980s and the mid 1990s sea freight unit costs declined by nearly 70% (World Bank 2003b, p.57).

16 UNIDO (2002, Boxes 6.1, 6.2) provides examples of how firms latched onto GVCs. Box 6.1, for example, describes the case of the Ammar and Sarah knitwear group, from Pakistan; Box 6.2 provides the example of the Sinos Valley shoe cluster in Brazil. See also UNCTAD (2002, chapter V).

17 Detailed data until 1990 can be found in NSF (1993).

18 Asians accounted for more than half of all scientists and engineers migrating to the US between 1970 and 1985 (NSF 1993, p.44).

19 Singapore is now turning biotechnology into its next pillar of manufacturing and is making significant investments to nurture its development. By the middle of 2003, the Government will open Biopolis (http://www.biomed-singapore.com/bms/index/jsp), a S$500 million research park that will provide facilities for biotechnology activities as well as provide legal and laboratory support services.

20 For stages in general in Thai industry, see Intarakumnerd and Virasa (2002), for firm-level development stages see Chairatana (1997), for electronics in Thailand see Poapongsakorn and Tonguthai (1998).

21 See Ca and Anh (1998) for Viet Nam, and Thee and Pangestu (1998) for Indonesia.

22 See Ngoh (1994) for the case of Motorola and Lim (1991) for the case of Intel.

23 Note that recently this situation has changed with a huge influx of FDI into Korea.

24 For Taipei,China see Chaponnière and Fouquin (1989). Schive (1990) shows how small and medium enterprises from Taipei,China attracted more MNCs in the early stages, creating a series of backward and forward linkages; for Hong Kong, China's experience, see Berger and Lester (1997).

References

Agrawal, Pradeep, Subir V. Gokarn, Veena Mishra, Kirit S. Parikh, and Kunal Sen. 2000. *Policy Regimes and Industrial Competitiveness: A Comparative Study of East Asia and India.* Singapore: Institute of Southeast Asian Studies.

Amsden, A. H.1989. *Asia's Next Giant: South Korea and Late Industrialization.* New York: Oxford University Press.

Archambault, E.J. 1992. "Incremental or Radical in Semiconductor Manufacturing? Some Evidence from South Korea." Mimeo, Science Policy Research Unit, University of Sussex, United Kingdom.

Ariffin, N. and M. Bell. 1999. "Firms, Politics and Political Economy: Patterns of Subsidiary-Parent Linkages and Technological Capability-Building in Electronics TNC Subsidiaries in Malaysia." In K.S. Jomo, G. Felker, and R. Rasiah (eds.), *Industrial Technology Development in Malaysia.* London: Routledge.

Arrow, K.J. 1962. "The Economic Implications of Learning by Doing." *Review of Economic Studies* 29 (3): 153–173.

Asian Development Bank. 1995. *Technology Transfer and Development: Implications for Developing Asia.* Manila: Asian Development Bank.

——. 1997. *Emerging Asia: Changes and Challenges.* Manila: Asian Development Bank.

Asian Productivity Organization (APO). 2001. *APO Asia-Pacific Productivity Data & Analysis.* Tokyo: APO.

Basu, Santonu. 2002. "Financial Fragility: Is It Rooted in the Development Process? An Examination with Special Reference to the South Korean Experience." *International Papers in Political Economy*, Vol. 9, No.1.

Bell, M., M. Hobday, S. Abdullah, N. Ariffin, and J. Malik. 1996. "Aiming for 2020: A Demand-Driven Perspective on Industrial Technology Policy in Malaysia." Final report to Ministry of Science, Technology and Environment (Malaysia). World Bank/United Nations Development Programme.

Berger, S. and R.K. Lester (eds.). 1997. *Made by Hong Kong.* Hong Kong: Oxford University Press.

Bloom, M. 1989. "Technological Change and the Electronics Sector: Perspectives and Policy Options for the Republic of Korea." Paris: OECD.

——. 1991. "Globalization and the Korean Electronics Industry." Presentation to the EASMA Conference, The Global Competitiveness of Asian and European Firms, Fontainbleau, 17–19 October.

Buckley, Peter J., Christopher L. Pass, and Kate Prescott. 1988. "Measures of International Competitiveness: A Critical Survey." *Journal of Marketing Management* 4 (2): 175–200.

Ca, T.N. and L.D. Anh. 1998. "Technological Dynamism and R&D in the Export of Manufactures from Vietnam." In D. Ernst, T. Ganiatsos, and L. Mytelka (eds.), *Technological Capabilities and Export Success in Asia.* London: Routledge.

Chairatana, P. 1997. "Latecomer Catch-up Strategies in the Semiconductor Business: the Case of Alphatec Group of Thailand and Anam Group of Korea." MSc thesis, unpublished, SPRU, University of Sussex, United Kingdom.

Chamarik, Saneh and Susantha Goonatilake (eds.). 1994. *Technological Independence: The Asian Experience.* Tokyo: The United Nations University Press.

Chang, Ha-Joong. 1996. *The Political Economy of Industrial Policy.* London: Macmillan Press Ltd.

Chaponnière, J.R. and Fouquin, M. 1989. "Technological Change and the Electronics Sector: Perspectives and Policy Options for Taiwan." Paris: OECD.

Chou, T.C. 1992. "The Experience of SMEs' Development in Taiwan: High Export-Contribution and Export-Intensity." *Rivista Internazionale di Scienze Economiche e Commerciali* 39 (12): 1067–1084.

Cohen, W. and D.A. Levinthal. 1989. "Innovation and Learning: The Two Faces of R&D." *Economic Journal*, Vol. 99: 569–596.

Coyle, Diane. 2001. *Paradoxes of Prosperity: Why the New Capitalism Benefits All.* New York: Texere.

Cyhn, J. W. 2002. *Technology Transfer and International Production: The Development of the Electronics Industry in Korea.* Cheltenham: Edward Elgar.

Dahlman, C.J., B. Ross-Larson, and L.E. Westphal. 1985. "Managing Technological Development: Lessons from the Newly Industrializing Countries." Washington, DC: World Bank.

Dahlman, C.J. and O. Sananikone. 1990. "Technology Strategy in the Economy of Taiwan Province of China: Exploiting Foreign Linkages and Investing in Local Capability." Preliminary Draft, Washington, DC: World Bank.

Djankov, Simeon, Rafael La Porta, Florencio Lopez-de Silanes, and Andrei Shleifer. 2002. "The Regulation of Entry." *Quarterly Journal of Economics* 117 (1): 1–37.

Drucker, Peter. 2001. "The Next Society. A Survey of the Near Future." *The Economist*, 3 November 2001.

Drysdale, Peter. 1988. *International Economic Pluralism. Economic Policy in East Asia and the Pacific.* New York: Columbia University Press.

Durand, Martine, Jacques Simon, and Colin Webb. 1992. "OECD's Indicators of International Trade and Competitiveness." OECD, Economics Department, Working Paper No. 120. Paris.

Easterly, William. 2001. *The Elusive Quest for Growth: Economists' Adventures and Misadventures in the Tropics.* Cambridge, Massachusetts: MIT Press.

European Bank for Reconstruction and Development. 1995. *Transition Report 1995: Investment and Enterprise Development.* London.

Fagerberg, Jan. 1996. "Technology and Competitiveness." *Oxford Review of Economic Policy* 12 (3): 39–51.

Fok, J.T.Y. 1991. "Electronics." In *Doing Business in Today's Hong Kong.* American Chambers of Commerce, December, 4th Edition.

Goh, Keng Swee. 1996. "The Technology Ladder in Development: The Singapore Case." *Asian-Pacific Economic Literature* 10 (1): 1–12.

Gray, John. 1998. *False Dawn: The Delusions of Global Capitalism.* New York: The New Press.

Hamel, G. and C.K. Prahalad. 1994. *Competing for the Future.* Boston, Mass.: Harvard Business School Press.

Haque, I. ul. 1995. "Technology and Competitiveness." In I. ul Haque (ed.), Chapter 2, *Trade, Technology and International Competitiveness.* Washington, DC: World Bank.

Hausmann, Ricardo and Dani Rodrik. 2002. "Economic Development as Self-Discovery." National Bureau of Economic Research Working Paper 8952, November. Also available at: http://ksghome.harvard.edu/~.drodrik.academic.ksg/SelfDiscRev2.pdf.

Hobday, M. 1994. "Export-led Technology Development in the Four Dragons: The Case of Electronics." *Development and Change* 25 (2): 333–361.

———. 1995a. *Innovation in East Asia: The Challenge to Japan.* Aldershot, United Kingdom: Edward Elgar.

———. 1995b. "East Asian Latecomer Firms: Learning the Technology of Electronics." *World Development* 23 (7): 1171–1193.

———. 2002. "Innovation and Stages of Development: Questioning the Lessons from East and South East Asia." Paper prepared for SOM/TEG-Conference at the University of Groningen, The Netherlands: Empirical Implications of Technology-Based Growth Theories. August.

Hone, A. 1974. "Multinational Corporations and Multinational Buying Groups: Their Impact on the Growth of Asia's Exports of Manufactures: Myths and Realities." *World Development* 2 (2): 145–149.

Hooper, Peter and Kathryn A. Larin. 1989. "International Comparisons of Labor Costs in Manufacturing." *Review of Income and Wealth*, Series 35, No. 4. December: 335–355.

Huang, Yasheng. 2002. *Selling China: Foreign Direct Investment During the Reform Era.* Cambridge, United Kingdom: Cambridge University Press.

Ihm, C.S. 2002. "Part C: Skills that Matter in the Workplace." In *Korea: How Firms Use Knowledge.* Poverty Reduction and Economic Management Unit (East Asia and Pacific Region), draft paper, January. Washington, DC: World Bank.

Intarakumnerd, P., and T. Virasa. 2002. "Taxonomy of Government Policies and Measures in Supporting Technological Capability Development of Latecomer Firms." Science, Technology and Innovation Policy Research Department, National Science and Technology Development Agency (NSTDA), Thailand and College of Management, Mahidol University, Thailand, NSTDA Working Paper.

James, W. 1990. "Basic Directions and Areas for Cooperation: Structural Issues of the Asia-Pacific Economies." Asia Pacific Cooperation Forum, Session 2, 21–22 June, Korea Institute for International Economic Policy, Seoul.

Johnstone, B. 1989. "Taiwan Holds its Lead, Local Makers Move into New Systems." *Far Eastern Economic Review*, 31 August: 50–51.

Jones, L. P., and Il Sakong. 1980. "Government, Business, and Entrepreneurship in Economic Development: The Korean Case." Harvard East Asian Monographs No. 91. Cambridge, Mass.: Harvard University Press.

Kaldor, N. 1957. "A Model of Economic Growth." *Economic Journal* 67 (268): 591–624.

Khader, S.A. 2002. "Global Development and Small and Medium Enterprises." In *Enhancing SME Competitiveness in the Age of Globalization,* pp.11–29. Tokyo: APO.

Kim, Linsu. 1997. *Imitation to Innovation: Dynamics of Korea's Technological Learning.* Boston, Mass.: Harvard Business School Press.

Klapper, Leora F. and Stijn Claessens. 2002. "Bankruptcy Around the World: Explanations of its Relative Use." World Bank Working Paper 2865. July.

Klapper, Leora and Inessa Love. 2002. "Corporate Governance, Investor Protection, and Performance in Emerging Markets." World Bank Policy Research Working Paper 2818. April.

Kng, Chng Meng, Linda Low, Tay Boon Nga, and Amina Tyabji. 1986. T*echnology and Skills in Singapore.* Singapore: Institute of Southeast Asian Studies.

Krueger, Ann. 1997. "Trade Policy and Economic Development: How We Learn." *American Economic Review* 87 (1): 1–22.

Krugman, Paul. 1994. "Competitiveness: A Dangerous Obsession." *Foreign Affairs* 73 (2): 28–44.

———. 1996a. *Pop Internationalism.* The MIT Press.

———. 1996b. "Making Sense of the Competitiveness Debate." *Oxford Review of Economic Policy* 12 (3): 17–25.

Lall, Sanjaya. 1982. *Developing Countries as Exporters of Technology: The Indian Experience.* London: The Macmillan Press Ltd.

———. 1994. "'The East Asian Miracle' Study: Does the Bell Toll for Industrial Strategy?" *World Development,* Vol.22. April: 645–654.

———. 2000. "The Technological Structure and Performance of Developing Country Manufactured Exports, 1985–98." *Oxford Development Studies* 28 (3): 337–369.

———. 2001a. "Competitiveness Indices and Developing Countries: An Economic Evaluation of the Global Competitiveness Report." *World Development* 29 (9): 1501–1525.

———. 2001b. *Competitiveness, Technology and Skills.* Northampton, Mass.:Edward Elgar.

Lee, T. J. 2001. "Technological Capabilities and International Relations in Developing Countries: Case Studies of the Nuclear Fuel Cycle in South Korea." D. Phil thesis. Unpublished. Brighton: University of Sussex, United Kingdom.

Lim, P. 1991. *Steel: From Ashes Rebuilt to Manufacturing Excellence.* Pelanduk Publications: Petaling Jaya, Malaysia.

Magaziner, I. C. and M. Patinkin. 1989. "Fast Heat: How Korea Won the Microwave War." *Harvard Business Review,* January–February, pp.83–92.

Mathews, J. A. and D. S. Cho. 2000. *Tiger Technology: The Creation of a Semiconductor Industry in East Asia.* Cambridge, Mass.: Cambridge University Press.

McCombie, John S.L. and A.P. Thirlwall. 1994. *Economic Growth and the Balance of Payments Constraint.* St. Martin's Press.

———. 1999. "Growth in an International Context." In Johan Deprez and John T. Harvey (eds.), pp.35–90. *Foundations of International Economics: Post Keynesian Perspectives.* London: Routledge.

Ministry of Trade and Industry. 2003. *New Challenges, Fresh Goals.* Republic of Singapore.

Moran, Theodore H. 1998. *Foreign Direct Investment and Development: The New Policy Agenda for Developing Countries and Economies in Transition.* Washington, DC: Institute for International Economics.

———. 2002. *Strategy and Tactics for the Doha Round. Capturing the Benefits of Foreign Direct Investment.* Manila: Asian Development Bank.

Morisset, Jacques, and Olivier Lumenga Neso. 2002. "Administrative Barriers to Foreign Investment in Developing Countries." World Bank and International Finance Corporation. Policy Research Working Paper 2848. May.

National Science Foundation (NSF). 1993. *Human Resources for Science & Technology: The Asian Region.* Surveys of Scie–nce Resources Series. Special Report NSF 93-303. Washington, DC.

Nelson, Richard R. (ed.). 1993. *National Innovation Systems. A Comparative Analysis.* New York: Oxford University Press.

Ng, C.Y., R. Hirono and Robert Y. Siy, Jr. 1986. *Technology and Skills in ASEAN. An Overview.* Singapore: Southeast Asian Studies.

Ngoh, C. L. 1994. *Motorola Globalisation: The Penang Journey.* Lee and Sons: Kuala Lumpur. Malaysia.

Noland, Marcus. 1990. *Pacific Basin Developing Countries: Prospects for the Future.* Washington, DC: Institute for International Economics.

Noland, Marcus, and Howard Pack. 2003. *Industrial Policy in an Era of Globalization: Lessons from Asia.* Washington, DC: Institute for International Economics.

Organisation for Economic Co-Operation and Development (OECD). 1994. *Science and Technology Policy*. Paris: OECD.

———. 2002. *International Investment Perspectives*. Paris: OECD.

Osman-Rani, H., Toh Kin Woon, and Anuwar Ali. 1986. *Technology and Skills in Malaysia*. Singapore: Institute of Southeast Asian Studies.

Page, John M. 1994. "The East Asian Miracle: An Introduction." *World Development* 22 (4): 615–625.

Perkins, D.H. 1994. "There are at Least Three Models of East Asian Development." *World Development* 22 (4): 655–661.

Poapongsakorn, N. and P. Tonguthai. 1998. "Technological Capability Building and the Sustainability of Export Success in Thailand's Textile and Electronics Industries." in D. Ernst; T. Ganiatsos, and L. Mytelka, (eds.), *Technological Capabilities and Export Success in Asia*. London: Routledge.

Porter, Michael. 1990. *The Competitive Advantage of Nations*. New York: Free Press.

Rasiah, R. 1994. "Flexible Production Systems and Local Machine Tool Sub-contracting: Electronics Components Transnationals in Malaysia." *Cambridge Journal of Economics* 18 (3): 279–298.

Rhee, Y.W., B. Ross-Larson, G. Pursell. 1984. *Korea's Competitive Edge: Managing the Entry into World Markets*. Baltimore: Johns Hopkins University Press.

Rodrik, Dani. 1999. "Institutions for High-Quality Growth: What They Are and How to Acquire Them." Draft paper presented at the International Monetary Fund Conference on Second-Generation Reforms, Washington, DC. 8–9 November 1999.

———. 2002. "What is Wrong with the (Augmented) Washington Consensus?" John F. Kennedy School of Government, Harvard University. Manuscript.

Rodrik, Dani, A. Subramanian, and F. Trebbi. 2002. "Institutions Rule: The Primacy of Institutions over Integration and Geography in Economic Development," IMF Working Paper/02/189. Washington, DC.

Rush, H., M. Hobday, E. Arnold, J. Bessant and R. Murray. 1996. *Technology Institutes: Strategies for Best Practice*. London: International Thomson Business Press.

Schrank, Andrew. 2001. "Export Processing Zones: Free Market Islands or Bridges to Structural Transformation." *Development Policy Review* 19 (2): 223–242.

Schive, C. 1990. *The Foreign Factor: the Multinational Corporation's Contribution to the Economic Modernization of the Republic of China*. Stanford, CA: Hoover Institution Press.

Siamwalla, Ammar. 2002. "Globalization and its Governance in Historical Perspective, with Special Reference to Mainland Southeast Asia." Thailand Development Research Institute.

Snower, Dennis J. 1996. "The Low-Skill, Bad-Job Trap." In Alison L. Booth and Dennis J. Snower (eds.), *Acquiring Skills: Market Failures, Their Symptoms and Policy Responses*, pp.109–124. Cambridge: Cambridge University Press.

Srinivasan, T.N., and Jagdish Bhagwati. 1999. "Outward-Orientation Development: Are Revisionists Right?" Downloaded from www.columbia.edu/~jb38/papers.htm.

Stern, Nicholas. 1997. "Macroeconomic Policy and the Role of the State in a Changing World." European Bank for Reconstruction and Development. Working Paper 19 (April).

Stern, Nicholas and Joseph Stigllitz. 1997. "A Framework for a Development Strategy in a Market Economy: Objectives, Scope, Institutions and Instruments." European Bank for Reconstruction and Development. Working Paper 20 (April).

Stiglitz, Joseph. 2002. *Globalization and its Discontents*. Penguin Books.

Thee, K. W. and M. Pangestu. 1998. "Technological Capabilities and Indonesia's Manufactured Exports." In D. Ernst, T. Ganiatsos, and L. Mytelka (eds.), *Technological Capabilities and Export Success in Asia*. London: Routledge.

Thurow, Lester. 1993. *Head to Head. The Coming Economic Battle Among Japan, Europe and America*. New York, NY: Morrow.

Turner, Anthony G. and Stephen S. Golub. 1997. "Towards a System of Multilateral Unit Labor Cost-Based Competitiveness Indicators for Advanced, Developing, and Transition Countries." IMF Working Paper WP/97/151. November.

Turner, Philip and Jozef Van 't dack. 1993. "Measuring International Price and Cost Competitiveness." BIS Economic Papers, No.39. November.

United Nations Conference on Trade and Development (UNCTAD). 1996. *World Investment Report 1996: Investment, Trade and International Policy Arrangements.* New York and Geneva: United Nations.

———. 2001. *World Investment Report 2001: Promoting Linkages.* New York and Geneva: United Nations.

———. 2002. *World Investment Report 2002: Transnational Corporations and Export Competitiveness.* New York and Geneva: United Nations.

———. 2003. Foreign Direct Investment database, downloaded 21 January 2003, available: http://stats.unctad.org/fdi/eng/ReportFolders/Rfview/explorerp.asp

United Nations Industrial Development Organization (UNIDO). 2002. *Industrial Development Report 2002/2003: Competing Through Innovation and Learning.* Vienna: UNIDO

Villela, Luiz, and Alberto Barreix. 2002. "Taxation and Investment Promotion." Background Note for Global Economic Prospects 2003. Washington: Inter-American Development Bank.

Wade, R. 1990. *Governing the Market: Economic Theory and the Role of Government in East Asian Industrialization.* New Jersey: Princeton University Press.

Westphal, L.E., Kim, L. and Dahlman, C.J. 1985. "Reflections on the Republic of Korea's Acquisition of Technological Capability." In N. Rosenberg and C. Frischtak (eds.), *International Transfer of Technology: Concepts, Measures, and Comparisons.* New York: Praeger Press.

Wong, P. K. 1992. "Technological Development Through Sub-Contracting Linkages: Evidence from Singapore." *International Business Review* 1 (3): 28–40.

———. 1998. "Pattern of Technology Acquisition by Manufacturing Firms in Singapore." *Singapore Management Review* 20 (1): 43–64.

World Bank. 1993. *The East Asian Miracle: Economic Growth and Public Policy.* New York: Oxford University Press.

———. 2002. *World Development Report 2003: Sustainable Development in a Dynamic World.* Washington, DC: World Bank.

———. 2003a. *Global Development Finance. Striving for Stability in Development Finance.* Washington, DC: World Bank.

———. 2003b. *Global Economic Prospects and the Developing Countries: Investing to Unlock Global Opportunities: 2003.* Washington, DC: World Bank.

World Economic Forum. 2000. *The Global Competitiveness Report 2000.* New York: Oxford University Press.

———. 2001. *The Global Competitiveness Report 2001–2002.* New York: Oxford University Press.

Wortzel L. H. and Wortzel H.V. 1981. "Export Marketing Strategies for NIC and LDC-based Firms." *Columbia Journal of World Business,* Spring: 51–60.

Yeats, Alexander. 1998. "Just How Big is Global Production Sharing?" The World Bank. Policy Research Working Paper No.1871.

Yue, C. S. 1985. "The Role of Foreign Trade and Investment in the Development of Singapore." In W. Galenson (ed.), *Foreign Trade and Investment: Economic Development in the Newly Industrializing Asian Countries.* Wisconsin: University of Wisconsin Press.

Yusuf, Shahid, and Simon J. Evenett. 2002. *Can East Asia Compete? Innovation for Global Markets.* Washington, DC: World Bank.

ASIAN DEVELOPMENT
Outlook
2003

Statistical Appendix

ASIAN DEVELOPMENT
Outlook
2003

Statistical Appendix

Statistical Notes and Tables

The Statistical Appendix presents selected economic indicators for 41 developing member countries (DMCs) of the Asian Development Bank (ADB) in a total of 24 tables. These tables can generally be classified into the following accounts, namely: (i) national accounts, both production and demand sides; (ii) labor (unemployment); (iii) prices; (iv) money supply; (v) components of the balance of payments; (vi) external debt and debt service; (vii) exchange rates; (viii) international liquidity (gross international reserves); and (ix) government finance. The DMCs are grouped into five subregions: East Asia, Southeast Asia, South Asia, Central Asia, and the Pacific.

These tables contain historical data from 1997 to 2002. Forecasts for 2003 and 2004 are also provided in the following tables: Growth Rate of GDP (A1), Growth Rate of Per Capita GDP (A2), Growth Rate of Value Added in Agriculture (A3), Growth Rate of Value Added in Industry (A4), Growth Rate of Value Added in Services (A5), Gross Domestic Savings as Percent of GDP (A7), Gross Domestic Investment as Percent of GDP (A8), Inflation (A9), Changes in Money Supply (A10), Growth Rate of Merchandise Exports (A11), Growth Rate of Merchandise Imports (A13), Balance of Trade (A14), Balance of Payments on Current Account (A15), and Balance of Payments on Current Account as Percent of GDP (A16).

As much as possible, efforts were undertaken to standardize the data to allow comparability over time and across DMCs. However, limitations exist because of differences in statistical methodology,

definitions, coverage, and practices. A discussion of the sources, definitions, scope, and nature of data in the 24 tables, as well as methodology for regional averages follows.

Historical data are obtained from the ADB Statistical Database System, as well as official sources, statistical publications, secondary publications, working papers, and internal documents of ADB, the International Monetary Fund, and the World Bank. Projections for 2003 and 2004 are staff estimates. Data in the tables refer to either calendar year or fiscal year. For some countries, the majority of their accounts are reported on a fiscal year basis (see figure), but some of their accounts are recorded on a calendar year basis, as follows: GDP sector data, current account, and exchange rates for Cook Islands; prices and money for the Marshall Islands; and exchange rates for Tonga. Other DMCs record their data in calendar year except for government finance data, which are reported on a fiscal year basis: Hong Kong, China; Indonesia (1997–1999); and Singapore (fiscal year ending 31 March); Democratic Republic of Timor-Leste; Samoa; and Taipei,China; (fiscal year ending 30 June); and the Lao People's Democratic Republic (Lao PDR), and Thailand (fiscal year ending 30 September). External debt as well as debt service ratio data for Samoa are reported on a fiscal year basis.

Regional averages or totals for DMCs are provided for nine economic indicators tables. Data for Afghanistan, Myanmar, and Nauru are excluded in the computation of subregional averages due to measurement problems. For Inflation (Table A9),

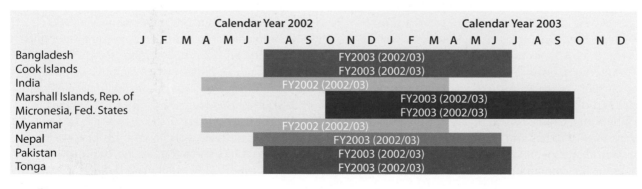

Timor-Leste is excluded in the computation of the averages for the Pacific and developing Asia.

Out of the nine economic indicator tables, six have regional averages (A1, A2, A9, A11, A13, and A16). Averages are computed on the basis of a consistent sum, which means that where there are missing data for a given year, corresponding data, if there are any, are also excluded in the other year that is also used to calculate the average. Totals are incorporated in three tables (A12, A14, and A5) except that in Table A12, subregional totals are represented in terms of percentage shares to developing Asia.

For four tables, growth rate of GDP (A1), growth rate of per capita GDP (A2), inflation (A9), and current account balance as a percentage of GDP (A16), levels of gross national income (GNI) at current US$ using the World Bank Atlas method were used as subregional weights to calculate the subregional and regional averages. Tables on growth rate of merchandise exports and imports (A11 and A13) do not use weights in the computation of averages.

The GNIs, in current US$, for ADB's DMCs from 1997 to 2001 were obtained from World Bank data query (http://devdata.worldbank.org/data-query/). The most recent data, 2001, are also used as weights for 2002 to 2004. GNIs for four of the DMCs are unavailable, namely: Cook Islands; Marshall Islands; Taipei,China; and Tuvalu. For these economies, weights are estimated.

Tables A1, A2, A3, A4, A5, A7, and A8: These tables refer to the national income accounts. They show output and sector rates, as well as the gross domestic savings and gross domestic investment as percentages of GDP. Definitions relating to output growth, production, and demand are generally based on the United Nations System of National Accounts.

Sector shares of agriculture, industry, and services for 2001 are, respectively, presented in Tables A3 to A5. In the case of Azerbaijan, Bangladesh, Cambodia, Kazakhstan, Lao PDR, and Turkmenistan, sums of sector shares do not add up to 100% because of some statistical discrepancies and differences in definitions (see below). For Hong Kong, China; Korea; Malaysia; and Singapore, import duties and taxes net of imputed bank service charges were added to the services sector only for the computation of the sector shares to

obtain a 100% sum for all sectors. However for Azerbaijan, Bangladesh, Kazakhstan, and Turkmenistan, where the sum is not equal to 100%, import duties and taxes less imputed bank service charges are excluded in the sector data but are not netted out in the total value of output or GDP. Otherwise, inconsistency in the sum of sector shares is due to statistical discrepancies and unavailability of data for certain sectors.

Sector shares are computed based on constant prices except for the Marshall Islands where shares are based on current prices. The growth rate of GDP (A1) for the Cook Islands is reported on a fiscal year basis while sector growth rates and shares (A3–A5) are on a calendar year basis.

Gross domestic investment is presented in Table A8. These amounts represent final expenditures on investment at purchasers' prices. Correspondingly, gross domestic savings are shown in Table A7. Both variables are presented as percentages of GDP and all are valued at current prices.

The following paragraphs examine the tables in closer detail.

Table A1: Growth Rate of GDP. This shows annual growth rates of GDP valued at constant market prices, factor costs, or basic prices. GDP at market prices is the aggregation of the value added of all resident producers at producers' prices including taxes less subsidies on imports plus all nondeductible value-added or similar taxes. Other valuations for GDP use gross payments to factors of production and amount receivable by the producer from the purchaser for a unit of a good or service exclusive of taxes payable and inclusive of subsidies receivable on products, excluding transport charges invoiced separately by the producer. These valuations respectively refer to factor costs and basic prices. Most DMCs use constant market price valuations. South Asian countries predominantly use constant factor costs, including Bhutan, India, Nepal, Pakistan, and Sri Lanka while Maldives' GDP valuation is at basic prices. Among the Pacific economies, Fiji Islands, Solomon Islands, Tuvalu, and Vanuatu employ constant factor cost valuation, though for the Fiji Islands, constant market price valuation is used from 2000 onward. For Hong Kong, China, the computations of real GDP and sector growth rates were based on volume indices.

Table A2: Growth Rate of Per Capita GDP. Real per capita GDP is obtained by subtracting the midyear population growth rate from real GDP growth.

Table A3: Growth Rate of Value Added in Agriculture. The table gives the growth rates of value added in agriculture and its corresponding share for 2001. The agriculture sector includes agricultural crops, livestock, poultry, fisheries, and forestry.

Table A4: Growth Rate of Value Added in Industry. The table gives the growth rates of value added in industry and its corresponding share for 2001. This sector includes the manufacturing and nonmanufacturing subsectors. Mining and quarrying, construction, and utilities fall under the latter subsector. For Kazakhstan, the industry sector does not include construction.

Table A5: Growth Rate of Value Added in Services. The table gives the growth rates of value added in services and its corresponding share for 2001. Subsectors include trade, banking, finance, real estate, public administration, and other services.

Table A6: Unemployment Rate. The unemployment rate is the percentage of the labor force that actively seeks work but is unable to find work at a given time. The age of the working population generally ranges from 18 to 65, though this may vary from country to country. In Bangladesh, for instance, the labor force includes those aged 10 and above. The unemployment rates of the PRC and Viet Nam refer to unemployment in urban areas only. For the Pacific, data are primarily obtained from the *Pacific Human Development Report 1999*; some figures are from country sources.

Table A7: Gross Domestic Savings (% of GDP). This table gives the ratio of gross domestic savings (GDS) to GDP. Gross domestic savings is derived as the difference between GDP and total consumption or gross national savings minus net factor income from abroad. For some countries, the concept of gross national savings is employed. Gross national savings (GNS) is computed as GNP minus total consumption, thus this value includes the net factor income from abroad. Most countries present GDS as a percentage of GDP except for the economies of Azerbaijan, Bangladesh, Kazakhstan, Nepal, Pakistan, Philippines, and Sri Lanka, which use GNS. For the Philippines, GNP is used as the denominator of ratio while for Nepal, GNS/GDP is valued at current market prices.

Table A8: Gross Domestic Investment (% of GDP). This table gives the ratio of gross domestic investment to GDP. Gross domestic investment is the sum of gross fixed capital formation plus changes in inventories. Gross fixed capital formation is measured by the total value of a producer's acquisitions, less disposals, of fixed assets in a given accounting period. Additions to the value of nonproduced assets, e.g., land, form part of gross fixed capital formation. Inventories are stocks of goods held by institutional units to meet temporary or unexpected fluctuations in production and sales. For the Lao PDR, investment approvals based on staff estimates were used as gross domestic investment while for Pakistan gross national investment data are used. As with Table A7, GNP is used as the denominator for the Philippines.

Table A9: Inflation. Except for India, which reports a wholesale price index and Solomon Islands, which uses a retail price index, the annual inflation rates presented are based on consumer price indices. For most DMCs, the reported inflation rates represent period averages except for Bhutan, Cook Islands, Timor-Leste, Tonga, and Viet Nam, which use end-of-period data. Cambodia uses the average CPI for the last quarter of the year, October to December. The data for Singapore is on a calendar year basis, yet the base year used for the computation of inflation rates is November 1997–October 1998. The inflation rate for India in 2002 is for April–December only. The consumer price indices of the following countries are for a given city or group of consumers only: Cambodia is for Phnom Penh, Marshall Islands is for Majuro, and Nepal is for urban consumers.

Table A10: Change in Money Supply. This table tracks the annual percentage change in the end-of-period broad money as represented by M2 (for most DMCs). M2 is defined as the sum of M1 and quasi-money where M1 denotes currency in circulation plus demand deposits and quasi-money consists of time and savings deposits including foreign currency deposits. For Sri Lanka, M2 includes time and savings deposits held by commercial banks' foreign currency banking units. For the Marshall Islands, broad money consists only of deposits, while for India, Kazakhstan, Micronesia, Papua New Guinea, and Philippines, broad money is represented by M3, defined as M2 plus other assets that are less liquid than what would be classified under M2 and M1. For India, M3 includes deposits with the Reserve Bank of India, and its FY2002 data are only until 10 January 2003.

Tables A11, A13, A14, A15, A16, and A17: Balance of Payments. This set of tables primarily contains items from the balance of payments (BOP). These items cover the annual flows recorded in the BOP account.

Tables A11 and A13: Growth Rates of Merchandise Exports and Imports. The annual growth rates of exports and imports, in terms of merchandise goods only, are shown in this table. Data are in million US$, primarily obtained from the BOP account of each DMC. Exports in general are reported on a free-on-board (f.o.b.) basis. In this case, exports are valued at the customs frontier of the exporting country plus export duties and the costs of loading the goods onto the carrier unless the latter is borne by the carrier. It excludes the cost of freight and insurance beyond the customs frontier. For Cambodia, exports refer to domestic exports. Import data are reported either on an f.o.b. or c.i.f. (cost, insurance, freight) basis. On a c.i.f. basis, the value of imports includes the cost of international freight and insurance up to the customs frontier of the importing country. It excludes the cost of unloading the goods from the carrier unless it is borne by the carrier. For Cambodia, imports only refer to retained imports, referring to total imports net of reexports and include project aid imports and an estimate of unrecorded imports. Retained imports are those goods that are kept in the country for domestic use.

For East Asia, all economies report imports on an f.o.b. basis except for Mongolia which records them on a ci.f. basis. Imports are valued on an f.o.b. basis for Indonesia, Malaysia, and Viet Nam while the rest of the Southeast Asian countries' imports are valued on a c.i.f. basis. Bhutan, India, and Nepal record imports on a c.i.f. basis while Bangladesh, Maldives, Pakistan, and Sri Lanka value them on an f.o.b. basis. For all the Central Asian economies, all imports are costed on an f.o.b. basis. Most of the Pacific countries report imports on an f.o.b. basis while imports of Cook Islands, Papua New Guinea, and Samoa are recorded on a c.i.f. basis. For the PRC, trade data for 2002–2004 are estimated using the customs basis concept. Based on available data for 2002, export and import growth rates for 2002 were estimated using the respective growth rates

covering the period April to September for India. For Hong Kong, China, BOP data are only available from 1997 onward, thus 1996 data, for the computation of 1997 growth rates, were derived from the national income accounts.

Table A12: Direction of Exports. Data from this table are sourced from IMF, *Direction of Trade Statistics*, CD-ROM (February 2003). This table shows the exports of ADB's DMCs, except Taipei,China. It shows the percentage share of exports of each DMC to developing Asia excluding the PRC, PRC only, US, Japan, European Union (EU), and others or rest of the world. The rest of the world is derived as total exports of DMCs to the world minus their exports among themselves and to US, Japan, and EU.

Table A14: Balance of Trade. The trade balance is the difference between merchandise exports and merchandise imports. Figures in this table are based on the export and import levels used to generate Tables A11 and A13.

Table A15: Balance of Payments on Current Account (US$ million). The current account balance is the sum of the balance of trade for merchandise, net trade in services and factor income, and net transfers. The amounts shown in this table are in million US$. In the case of Bangladesh, Cambodia, Lao PDR, Mongolia, Thailand, and Viet Nam, official transfers are excluded from the current account balance.

Table A16: Balance of Payments on Current Account (% of GDP). The values reported in Table A15 are divided by GDP at current prices in US$, except for the Philippines where GNP in current US$ is used.

Table A17: Foreign Direct Investment. Foreign direct investment refers to equity capital, reinvested earnings, and other capital associated with the transactions of enterprises. Amounts reflected are net of capital flows in the reporting home country except for Cambodia and Thailand where gross capital flows are presented. For Bangladesh, only those capital investments passing through banking channels are reported. For India, data for 2002 only refer to flows from April to November 2002. Data for the Pacific countries are derived from the United Nations Conference on Trade and Development (UNCTAD) *World Investment Report 2002* and refer to gross inflows.

Table A18: External Debt Outstanding. For

most DMCs, external debt outstanding includes long-term debt, short-term debt, and IMF credit. For Mongolia, outstanding external debt, based on IMF estimates, excludes unresolved claims owed to the Russian Federation. The external debt reported by Cambodia and Lao PDR also excludes that owed to the Russian Federation and the United States. For Taipei,China, the 2002 figure is at September 2002.

Table A19: Debt Service Ratio. This table presents the total debt service payments of each DMC as a percentage of exports of goods and services. Total debt service payments comprise of principal repayments and interest payments on outstanding external debt. For Taipei,China, the debt service refers to external public debt only. The exports of goods is used in the ratio for PRC, Kiribati, Mongolia, and Papua New Guinea.

Table A20: Exchange Rates to the US Dollar. The annual average exchange rates of the DMCs are quoted in local currencies per US dollar. Tonga reports end-of-period exchange rates. The 2002 average exchange rates reported by Cook Islands, Fiji Islands, Samoa, Solomon Islands, and Vanuatu cover months from January to September while Kiribati, Nauru, and Tuvalu are from January to November only. The 2002 data for Papua New Guinea are estimated using data from January to September.

Table A21: Gross International Reserves. Gross international reserves (GIR) are defined as the US$ value of holdings of the special drawing rights (SDR) reserve position in the IMF, foreign exchange, and gold at the end of a given period. Most DMCs report GIR without gold. However, for Southeast Asian countries except Singapore, gold is included in the computation of gross international reserves; a similar concept is used by Bangladesh and Bhutan. For India, GIR excludes gold and SDR and data reported for 2002 is as of 31 January 2003 while for the Maldives foreign assets of Maldives Monetary Authority are included in the definition of GIR. For Pakistan, GIR includes foreign reserves with the State Bank of Pakistan. Samoa's GIR refer to gross foreign assets. For Taipei,China, GIR refers to foreign exchange reserves only.

Tables 22, 23, and 24: Government Finance. This set of tables refers to the revenue and expenditure transactions as well as fiscal balance of the central government. For PRC, India, Mongolia, and Tajikistan, transactions are those reported by

both central and local governments or consolidated government while Azerbaijan and Kazakhstan transactions are those recorded by the general government. The shares of these major fiscal items as a percentage of GDP are calculated for this group of tables.

Table 22: Central Government Expenditures. Central government expenditures comprise all nonrepayable payments to both current and capital expenses. These amounts are computed as a percentage of GDP at current prices. For Bhutan, Cambodia, Lao PDR, Maldives, Pakistan, Nepal, and Sri Lanka, net lending is included in the computation of expenditures. Pakistan's expenditures do not include one-off expenditure items.

Table 23: Central Government Revenues. Central government revenues comprise all nonrepayable receipts, both current and capital , other than grants. These amounts are computed as a percentage of GDP at current prices. Grants are counted for countries such as Bhutan, Maldives, Kiribati, Nepal, Philippines, and Vanuatu. Grants in cash are added in the revenues of these Pacific countries. In some countries, other revenue items are included and excluded in the reported revenue figures: the social security fund is included for Korea, the Oil Fund is excluded for Azerbaijan, sales from assets are excluded for the Fiji Islands, and privatization proceeds are excluded for Sri Lanka.

Table 24: Overall Budget Surplus/Deficit of Central Government. This is the residual between central government revenues and expenditures. The difference is also computed as a share of GDP. Data variations may arise due to statistical discrepancies, e.g., balancing items for both central and local governments, and differences in the concept used in the individual computations of revenue and expenditure as compared with the calculation of the fiscal balance. For the Fiji Islands, the computation of budget balance includes the proceeds from the sale of assets. For Kazakhstan, privatization proceeds were treated as financing items rather than revenues in 2002. Some off-budget accounts are included in the computation of the fiscal balance for Turkmenistan.

Consistency with ADB Annual Report 2002. In general, *ADO 2003* figures are consistent with the ADB *Annual Report 2002* figures. However, moderate discrepancies maybe noted for some countries. One reason is that the *Annual Report* derives its numbers from official government sources. A number of *ADO 2003* figures were obtained through the respective ADB resident missions and from IMF documents as against the *Annual Report* numbers which were reported by the official statistical agencies or from *Annual Report* survey replies. In some cases, the concept and computational method used differ between *ADO 2003* and the *Annual Report 2002*. For instance, the average of period inflation rates are derived from the average index for the year for the *Annual Report*, as against the average based on a year-on-year computation of inflation rate using monthly data for *ADO 2003*. Differences in base years for the various time series also account for minor discrepancies between the same series used in both publications. There are also some imputed adjustments in the definition for GDS and exports, imports, and balance of trade.

Finally, there are cases where the *ADO 2003* independent assessment does not converge with the official view of the government. For these reasons, an artificial convergence between the *ADO 2003* and the *Annual Report 2002* numbers is not made.

Table A1 Growth Rate of GDP (% per year)

	1997	1998	1999	2000	2001	2002	2003	2004
East Asia	7.1	2.9	7.3	8.1	4.4	6.5	5.6	6.2
China, People's Rep. of	8.8	7.8	7.1	8.0	7.3	8.0	7.3	7.6
Hong Kong, China	5.1	-5.0	3.4	10.2	0.6	2.3	2.0	4.0
Korea, Rep. of	5.0	-6.7	10.9	9.3	3.1	6.3	4.0	5.3
Mongolia	4.0	3.5	3.2	1.1	1.1	3.9	5.0	5.2
Taipei,China	6.7	4.6	5.4	5.9	-2.2	3.5	3.7	3.9
Southeast Asia	4.4	-6.6	4.1	6.2	1.7	4.1	4.0	4.8
Cambodia	4.3	2.1	6.9	7.7	6.3	4.5	5.0	5.5
Indonesia	4.7	-13.1	0.8	4.8	3.3	3.7	3.4	4.0
Lao People's Dem. Rep.	6.5	3.0	6.8	5.9	5.7	5.8	6.0	6.5
Malaysia	7.3	-7.4	6.1	8.3	0.4	4.2	4.3	5.1
Myanmar	5.7	5.8	10.9	13.7	11.1	-	-	-
Philippines	5.2	-0.6	3.4	4.4	3.2	4.6	4.0	4.5
Singapore	8.5	-0.1	6.4	9.4	-2.4	2.2	2.3	4.2
Thailand	-1.4	-10.5	4.4	4.6	1.9	5.2	5.0	5.5
Viet Nam	8.2	4.4	4.7	6.1	5.8	6.4	6.9	7.1
South Asia	4.5	6.0	5.7	4.5	5.0	4.2	5.7	6.1
Afghanistan	-	-	-	-	-	-	-	-
Bangladesh	5.4	5.2	4.9	5.9	5.3	4.4	5.2	5.8
Bhutan	7.2	6.4	7.6	5.3	6.6	7.7	-	-
India	4.8	6.5	6.1	4.4	5.6	4.4	6.0	6.3
Maldives	10.4	9.8	7.2	4.8	3.5	4.3	4.2	2.8
Nepal	5.1	3.2	4.5	6.0	4.6	-0.6	1.5	3.5
Pakistan	1.7	3.5	4.2	3.9	2.5	3.6	4.5	5.0
Sri Lanka	6.3	4.7	4.3	6.0	-1.4	3.0	5.0	5.5
Central Asia	2.5	2.0	4.8	8.5	10.9	7.7	5.8	5.8
Azerbaijan	5.8	10.0	7.4	11.1	9.9	10.6	9.5	8.0
Kazakhstan	1.7	-1.9	2.7	9.8	13.5	9.5	6.0	6.2
Kyrgyz Republic	9.9	2.1	3.7	5.4	5.3	-0.5	5.2	4.5
Tajikistan	1.7	5.3	3.7	8.3	10.2	9.1	7.1	5.0
Turkmenistan	-11.3	7.0	16.0	17.6	20.5	8.6	7.5	7.5
Uzbekistan	5.2	4.4	4.4	4.0	4.5	4.2	3.5	4.0
The Pacific	-2.8	-0.8	5.1	-0.5	0.4	0.9	2.4	2.5
Cook Islands	-1.5	-3.5	0.7	7.9	5.1	0.3	1.5	3.2
Dem. Rep. of Timor-Leste	4.0	1.3	-35.4	15.4	18.3	-1.1	-2.3	1.3
Fiji Islands	-0.9	1.5	9.5	-3.2	4.3	4.4	5.7	3.6
Kiribati	5.7	5.0	6.2	0.2	1.5	2.8	2.5	2.3
Marshall Islands, Rep. of	-10.1	0.8	-0.2	0.7	2.1	4.0	3.0	2.0
Micronesia, Fed. States of	-4.6	-2.8	0.2	4.4	1.1	0.8	2.4	1.5
Nauru	-	-	-	-	-	-	-	-
Papua New Guinea	-4.9	-2.8	7.6	-1.2	-3.4	-0.5	1.0	2.0
Samoa	0.8	2.4	2.6	6.9	6.2	1.3	3.6	3.5
Solomon Islands	-1.4	0.1	-0.9	-13.3	-10.1	-4.0	2.0	3.0
Tonga	0.2	2.4	2.9	6.5	0.5	1.6	2.5	2.7
Tuvalu	3.5	14.9	3.0	3.0	4.0	2.0	2.0	1.8
Vanuatu	4.9	4.3	-3.2	2.7	-2.7	-0.3	1.3	2.2
Average	6.0	1.7	6.4	7.1	4.1	5.7	5.3	5.9

- Not available.

Table A2 Growth Rate of Per Capita GDP (% per year)

	1997	1998	1999	2000	2001	2002	2003	2004	Per Capita GNP, $, 2001
East Asia	6.1	2.0	6.5	7.4	3.8	5.9	4.8	5.6	
China, People's Rep. of	7.8	6.8	6.2	7.3	6.8	7.2	6.7	7.0	890
Hong Kong, China	4.2	-5.8	2.4	9.2	-0.3	1.3	0.7	2.8	25,920
Korea, Rep. of	4.1	-7.4	10.2	8.5	2.4	5.7	3.4	4.7	9,400
Mongolia	2.5	3.9	1.9	-0.2	-0.1	3.1	4.2	4.4	400
Taipei,China	5.8	3.6	4.6	5.0	-2.9	4.0	2.6	3.3	13,380
Southeast Asia	2.4	-8.6	2.5	4.6	0.0	3.4	3.0	3.9	
Cambodia	-1.1	-2.4	4.2	5.0	3.7	2.0	2.4	2.9	270
Indonesia	3.2	-14.6	-0.7	3.3	1.9	2.2	-	-	680
Lao People's Dem. Rep.	4.3	0.9	2.6	3.9	3.8	3.8	4.1	4.6	310
Malaysia	5.0	-9.7	3.7	4.9	-1.7	2.1	2.3	3.1	3,640
Myanmar	3.9	2.0	8.9	11.7	9.1	-	-	-	-
Philippines	2.9	-2.8	1.2	2.3	1.1	2.4	2.2	2.3	1,050
Singapore	5.2	-3.5	5.7	7.7	-5.2	5.4	2.3	4.2	24,740
Thailand	-2.3	-11.5	3.4	4.5	1.2	4.1	3.9	4.6	1,970
Viet Nam	4.1	2.2	2.3	5.1	4.8	5.3	5.8	5.9	410
South Asia	2.6	4.0	3.9	2.7	3.4	2.5	4.1	4.4	
Afghanistan	-	-	-	-	-	-	-	-	-
Bangladesh	3.5	3.4	3.6	4.6	5.8	2.8	3.8	4.2	370
Bhutan	4.2	3.5	4.4	2.4	3.0	4.6	-	-	640
India	2.9	4.5	4.2	2.6	3.8	2.6	4.4	4.7	460
Maldives	8.1	7.6	5.1	2.7	1.7	2.6	2.6	1.3	2,040
Nepal	2.7	0.8	2.2	3.7	1.5	-2.8	-0.6	1.4	250
Pakistan	-0.7	1.1	1.8	1.6	0.2	1.4	2.3	2.8	420
Sri Lanka	5.0	3.4	2.8	4.5	-2.8	1.8	3.8	4.3	830
Central Asia	2.3	2.0	4.3	7.6	13.2	9.1	6.6	6.7	
Azerbaijan	4.8	9.0	6.5	9.3	9.5	9.7	8.6	7.1	650
Kazakhstan	3.3	-0.2	3.7	10.2	13.8	9.6	6.1	6.6	1,360
Kyrgyz Republic	8.3	0.5	2.3	4.6	4.5	-1.3	-	-	280
Tajikistan	0.1	3.7	2.3	7.5	-	-	-	-	170
Turkmenistan	-14.1	4.0	12.4	13.9	16.9	-	-	-	950
Uzbekistan	3.3	2.8	2.9	2.6	-	-	-	-	550
The Pacific	-5.1	-3.0	3.5	-2.4	-1.9	-1.3	0.1	-	
Cook Islands	-	1.2	7.8	14.5	9.6	4.0	1.5	3.2	-
Dem. Rep. of Timor-Leste	2.8	0.0	-18.4	14.3	6.2	-8.8	-10.1	-	-
Fiji Islands	-2.6	0.3	8.2	-3.7	3.9	3.9	5.2	3.1	2,130
Kiribati	3.8	3.1	4.4	-1.1	-0.1	1.2	0.9	-	830
Marshall Islands, Rep. of	-11.3	-0.6	-1.5	-0.7	0.7	2.6	1.6	-	2,190
Micronesia, Fed. States of	-4.8	-3.1	0.0	4.2	0.8	0.6	2.2	-	2,150
Nauru	-	-	-	-	-	-	-	-	-
Papua New Guinea	-7.8	-5.8	4.2	-4.3	-6.4	-3.6	-2.1	-1.2	580
Samoa	0.3	1.9	2.1	5.0	4.1	-0.7	1.6	-	1,520
Solomon Islands	-4.3	-2.6	-3.6	-15.6	-12.6	-6.7	-0.8	-	580
Tonga	-0.6	1.7	2.4	6.2	0.1	1.3	2.1	2.2	1,530
Tuvalu	2.1	13.5	1.7	1.7	2.7	0.7	0.7	-	-
Vanuatu	2.2	1.7	-5.6	0.0	-5.3	-2.8	-1.3	-	1,050
Average	4.6	0.4	5.2	6.0	3.2	4.9	4.4	5.1	

- Not available.

Table A3 Growth Rate of Value Added in Agriculture (% per year)

	1997	1998	1999	2000	2001	2002	2003	2004	Sector Share 2001
East Asia									
China, People's Rep. of	3.5	3.5	2.8	2.4	2.8	2.9	2.8	2.9	11.3
Hong Kong, China	-	-	-	-	4.1	4.1	4.2	4.3	0.1
Korea, Rep. of	4.6	-6.6	5.4	2.0	1.9	-4.1	2.7	3.2	5.2
Mongolia	4.3	6.4	4.2	-16.8	-18.5	-10.5	-	-	26.8
Taipei,China	-1.5	-6.6	2.7	1.2	-2.1	1.6	1.6	1.7	2.5
Southeast Asia									
Cambodia	5.5	3.0	0.0	-0.3	3.9	0.9	1.8	2.4	39.6
Indonesia	1.0	-1.3	2.7	1.1	0.7	2.3	3.0	3.0	16.2
Lao People's Dem. Rep.	7.0	3.1	8.2	4.9	3.8	4.0	4.2	4.3	50.5
Malaysia	0.7	-2.8	0.5	2.0	1.8	0.3	1.5	-0.5	8.7
Myanmar	3.7	4.5	11.5	11.0	-	-	-	-	-
Philippines	3.1	-6.4	6.5	3.4	3.7	3.5	3.0	3.5	20.0
Singapore	0.1	-6.9	-1.1	-4.9	-5.9	-6.0	0.5	0.1	0.1
Thailand	0.7	-1.5	2.3	6.4	3.3	0.0	2.5	4.4	10.4
Viet Nam	4.3	2.8	5.2	4.0	2.3	3.0	2.9	3.0	22.7
South Asia									
Afghanistan	-	-	-	-	-	-	-	-	-
Bangladesh	6.0	3.2	4.7	7.4	3.1	0.0	2.6	3.1	24.1
Bhutan	3.0	2.8	5.2	4.5	3.2	2.5	-	-	32.9
India	-2.4	6.2	0.3	-0.4	5.7	-3.1	2.1	2.1	23.9
Maldives	2.1	7.0	3.5	-0.7	5.1	9.6	4.5	-1.9	9.5
Nepal	4.4	0.9	2.8	4.9	5.5	2.2	2.0	3.0	38.0
Pakistan	0.1	4.5	1.9	6.1	-2.6	1.4	2.8	4.0	24.6
Sri Lanka	3.0	2.5	4.5	1.8	-3.0	2.4	3.0	2.5	20.1
Central Asia									
Azerbaijan	-	-	-	12.1	5.0	6.4	3.0	3.5	15.2
Kazakhstan	-0.9	-18.9	28.0	-4.2	17.3	2.7	2.8	2.8	8.7
Kyrgyz Republic	12.3	2.9	8.2	2.6	7.3	3.3	-	-	50.2
Tajikistan	0.2	6.5	3.8	-	-	15.0	-	-	-
Turkmenistan	-	-	-	-	-	9.5	-	-	25.0
Uzbekistan	5.8	4.1	5.9	-	4.1	6.1	-	-	30.1
The Pacific									
Cook Islands	12.2	-17.2	-28.2	32.3	-24.0	-	-	-	11.9
Dem. Rep. of Timor-Leste	7.1	-	-	-	-	-	-	-	-
Fiji Islands	-13.0	-7.2	16.2	-0.9	1.7	1.1	1.6	3.2	16.6
Kiribati	-14.6	6.0	8.8	7.9	-	-	-	-	-
Marshall Islands, Rep. of	-9.0	-13.9	1.8	10.1	4.2	-	-	-	13.8
Micronesia, Fed. States of	-	-	-	-	-	-	-	-	-
Nauru	-	-	-	-	-	-	-	-	-
Papua New Guinea	-1.2	-11.3	4.3	9.1	-5.4	3.6	2.9	3.4	31.3
Samoa	-6.5	3.4	-3.5	0.3	-4.6	-10.2	-2.8	-	17.4
Solomon Islands	4.7	-7.5	-12.0	-25.1	-11.0	-	-	-	32.4
Tonga	3.8	-0.1	-3.2	10.6	-6.3	0.5	-	-	28.0
Tuvalu	5.8	0.7	-	-	-	-	-	-	-
Vanuatu	4.6	8.6	-12.2	7.4	0.5	1.7	3.4	3.2	17.9

- Not available.

Table A4 Growth Rate of Value Added in Industry (% per year)

	1997	1998	1999	2000	2001	2002	2003	2004	Sector Share 2001
East Asia									
China, People's Rep. of	10.5	8.9	8.1	9.4	8.7	9.9	10.0	11.0	64.5
Hong Kong, China	-	-	-	-	-4.6	-3.1	-5.2	-1.4	12.9
Korea, Rep. of	5.4	-7.5	12.8	11.9	2.9	6.1	6.0	5.3	44.8
Mongolia	-3.3	3.8	1.1	7.4	11.9	4.7	-	-	27.9
Taipei,China	6.1	2.7	4.7	5.7	-6.0	5.4	5.6	5.7	33.3
Southeast Asia									
Cambodia	21.3	7.3	13.2	34.6	15.5	11.8	11.7	11.7	24.0
Indonesia	5.2	-14.0	2.2	5.6	3.3	3.7	3.8	4.1	43.7
Lao People's Dem. Rep.	8.1	9.2	8.0	8.5	9.7	9.8	10.2	10.5	23.2
Malaysia	7.5	-10.6	-0.2	14.2	-4.2	4.0	4.6	5.4	41.1
Myanmar	8.9	6.1	13.8	21.3	-	-	-	-	-
Philippines	6.1	-2.1	0.9	4.9	1.3	4.1	4.0	4.2	34.0
Singapore	7.6	0.6	7.1	10.9	-9.2	4.0	4.4	5.0	31.3
Thailand	-1.8	-13.0	9.6	5.2	1.6	7.6	6.5	6.8	44.2
Viet Nam	12.6	7.3	7.6	9.6	9.7	8.9	9.6	9.8	36.9
South Asia									
Afghanistan	-	-	-	-	-	-	-	-	-
Bangladesh	5.8	8.3	4.9	6.2	7.4	6.6	6.9	7.9	25.2
Bhutan	3.5	8.6	11.6	2.2	13.4	12.1	-	-	30.7
India	4.3	3.7	4.8	6.6	3.3	6.1	6.4	7.4	26.7
Maldives	20.5	17.2	12.4	1.6	8.1	1.4	4.0	7.1	15.1
Nepal	6.5	2.3	6.0	8.7	2.7	-3.3	0.2	3.5	23.4
Pakistan	-0.3	6.1	4.9	1.3	3.1	2.8	4.0	5.0	25.2
Sri Lanka	7.7	5.9	4.8	7.5	-2.0	0.5	5.0	5.8	27.4
Central Asia									
Azerbaijan	-	-	-	6.9	7.7	4.2	6.7	4.5	35.3
Kazakhstan	4.1	-2.4	2.7	15.5	13.8	9.8	8.0	9.8	30.7
Kyrgyz Republic	19.8	-1.8	-3.8	8.9	5.2	-11.2	-	-	18.7
Tajikistan	-2.0	8.1	5.0	-	-	8.2	-	-	-
Turkmenistan	-	-	-	-	-	7.5	-	-	35.0
Uzbekistan	6.5	5.8	6.1	5.8	8.1	8.5	-	-	19.9
The Pacific									
Cook Islands	6.4	3.3	7.0	6.8	-0.8	-	-	-	8.1
Dem. Rep. of Timor-Leste	4.1	-	-	-	-	-	-	-	-
Fiji Islands	1.4	3.1	9.8	-7.4	7.4	5.1	5.5	4.8	26.6
Kiribati	17.4	32.9	38.0	-32.4	-	-	-	-	-
Marshall Islands, Rep. of	-4.7	28.4	1.3	5.4	0.8	-	-	-	16.0
Micronesia, Fed. States of	-	-	-	-	-	-	-	-	-
Nauru	-	-	-	-	-	-	-	-	-
Papua New Guinea	-17.0	9.7	5.7	-4.8	-3.3	-5.5	2.3	3.3	35.0
Samoa	-1.9	-9.2	1.4	11.4	10.3	-3.4	0.7	-	24.8
Solomon Islands	-17.5	-17.2	-6.9	-25.0	-24.1	-	-	-	7.2
Tonga	-11.7	6.6	12.3	3.7	2.3	5.5	4.0	-	15.0
Tuvalu	4.0	21.5	-	-	-	-	-	-	-
Vanuatu	-3.7	4.2	4.6	2.1	-4.2	0.4	1.2	2.3	9.1

- Not available.

Table A5 Growth Rate of Value Added in Services (% per year)

	1997	1998	1999	2000	2001	2002	2003	2004	Sector Share 2001
East Asia									
China, People's Rep. of	9.2	8.3	7.7	8.1	7.4	7.3	6.2	7.1	24.1
Hong Kong, China	-	-	-	-	1.4	3.2	2.2	4.8	86.8
Korea, Rep. of	5.7	-4.0	8.4	7.3	4.3	7.4	2.4	5.5	50.0
Mongolia	9.0	0.3	3.5	17.0	10.0	12.0	-	-	45.2
Taipei,China	7.4	6.2	6.0	6.1	-0.1	2.7	2.9	3.1	64.3
Southeast Asia									
Cambodia	-2.6	0.7	7.1	5.8	2.9	3.9	4.1	4.6	31.5
Indonesia	5.6	-16.5	-1.4	5.6	4.4	4.4	3.1	4.3	40.2
Lao People's Dem. Rep.	5.9	1.8	4.9	5.3	6.0	5.8	5.5	6.8	25.6
Malaysia	11.1	-1.1	11.9	5.7	5.7	4.5	4.4	5.6	50.2
Myanmar	6.7	7.0	9.2	13.4	-	-	-	-	-
Philippines	5.4	3.5	4.0	4.4	4.4	5.4	5.0	5.5	46.0
Singapore	9.5	-0.2	6.1	8.6	1.7	1.6	1.3	3.8	68.6
Thailand	-1.1	-10.0	0.4	3.7	2.0	4.1	4.0	4.3	45.4
Viet Nam	7.1	3.0	2.1	4.5	4.4	6.0	6.5	6.7	40.4
South Asia									
Afghanistan	-	-	-	-	-	-	-	-	-
Bangladesh	4.5	5.0	5.2	5.5	5.5	5.3	5.5	5.8	47.0
Bhutan	13.4	6.6	5.9	9.5	6.6	8.0	-	-	36.4
India	9.8	8.4	10.1	5.6	6.8	7.1	7.8	7.8	49.5
Maldives	10.0	8.9	6.8	6.0	2.4	4.3	4.2	2.6	75.4
Nepal	4.8	6.7	5.4	5.7	5.3	-1.8	0.0	3.5	38.6
Pakistan	3.6	1.6	5.0	4.2	4.8	5.1	5.5	5.5	50.2
Sri Lanka	7.1	5.1	4.0	7.0	-0.5	4.6	5.8	6.5	52.4
Central Asia									
Azerbaijan	-	-	-	8.7	5.4	20.7	13.9	11.9	40.2
Kazakhstan	-0.5	0.4	-1.5	8.5	12.1	9.3	4.1	6.3	49.2
Kyrgyz Republic	0.6	3.9	3.4	5.8	3.3	4.2	-	-	31.1
Tajikistan	-	-	-	-	-	-	-	-	-
Turkmenistan	-	-	-	-	-	9.5	-	-	32.0
Uzbekistan	21.3	9.5	12.6	13.0	14.2	1.5	-	-	50.0
The Pacific									
Cook Islands	-7.4	-0.8	13.9	6.6	0.6	-	-	-	80.0
Dem. Rep. of Timor-Leste	2.7	-	-	-	-	-	-	-	-
Fiji Islands	2.3	3.3	7.8	-1.8	3.6	4.9	6.8	3.1	56.8
Kiribati	8.1	6.5	3.4	2.1	-	-	-	-	-
Marshall Islands, Rep. of	-10.2	0.2	-0.5	-2.9	0.7	-	-	-	70.2
Micronesia, Fed. States of	-	-	-	-	-	-	-	-	-
Nauru	-	-	-	-	-	-	-	-	-
Papua New Guinea	6.1	-8.6	22.4	-7.0	1.9	1.3	0.7	1.8	33.8
Samoa	5.7	7.8	5.5	7.6	8.1	6.7	6.4	-	57.8
Solomon Islands	-1.7	5.7	-2.6	-6.7	-5.6	-	-	-	60.4
Tonga	1.5	2.8	4.0	5.2	3.4	0.6	2.4	-	57.0
Tuvalu	2.7	16.0	-	-	-	-	-	-	-
Vanuatu	5.3	3.8	-1.7	1.4	-3.2	-0.9	0.8	1.9	73.0

- Not available.

Table A6 Unemployment Rate (%)

	1997	1998	1999	2000	2001	2002	2003	2004
East Asia								
China, People's Rep. of	3.1	3.3	3.1	3.1	3.6	4.0	4.5	4.6
Hong Kong, China	2.2	4.7	6.2	4.9	5.1	7.3	7.4	6.2
Korea, Rep. of	2.6	6.8	6.3	4.1	3.7	3.0	-	-
Mongolia	7.7	5.9	4.7	4.6	4.6	3.6	-	-
Taipei,China	2.7	2.7	2.9	4.6	5.2	5.2	-	-
Southeast Asia								
Cambodia	-	-	-	-	-	-	-	-
Indonesia	4.7	5.5	6.4	6.1	8.1	9.1	-	-
Lao People's Dem. Rep.	-	-	-	-	-	-	-	-
Malaysia	2.4	3.2	3.4	3.1	3.6	3.5	3.4	3.1
Myanmar	4.1	-	-	-	-	-	-	-
Philippines	7.9	9.6	9.4	10.1	9.8	11.4	10.0	10.0
Singapore	2.5	3.2	4.6	4.4	3.3	4.4	4.5	4.1
Thailand	1.5	4.4	4.2	3.6	3.3	2.4	-	-
Viet Nam	6.9	6.9	7.4	6.4	6.3	-	-	-
South Asia								
Afghanistan	-	-	-	-	-	-	-	-
Bangladesh	-	-	-	3.7	-	-	-	-
Bhutan	-	1.4	1.4	-	-	-	-	-
India	-	-	7.3	-	-	-	-	-
Maldives	-	-	-	-	2.0	-	-	-
Nepal	-	-	1.8	-	-	-	-	-
Pakistan	6.1	5.9	6.8	7.8	8.5	9.0	-	-
Sri Lanka	10.5	9.2	8.9	7.6	7.9	9.0	-	-
Central Asia								
Azerbaijan	1.0	1.1	1.2	1.2	1.2	1.3	-	-
Kazakhstan	13.0	13.1	13.5	12.8	10.4	9.4	9.1	8.5
Kyrgyz Republic	5.7	5.9	7.2	7.6	7.8	-	-	-
Tajikistan	2.8	3.2	3.0	2.7	2.3	2.7	-	-
Turkmenistan	-	-	-	1.6	-	-	-	-
Uzbekistan	0.4	0.5	0.5	0.6	0.5	0.4	-	-
The Pacific								
Cook Islands	-	12.7	-	-	-	-	-	-
Dem. Rep. of Timor-Leste	-	-	-	-	-	-	-	-
Fiji Islands	6.5	7.4	7.6	12.1	-	-	-	-
Kiribati	-	0.1	-	-	-	-	-	-
Marshall Islands, Rep. of	-	12.2	30.9	-	-	-	-	-
Micronesia, Fed. States of	-	16.2	-	-	-	-	-	-
Nauru	-	-	-	-	-	-	-	-
Papua New Guinea	-	11.9	-	-	-	-	-	-
Samoa	-	2.1	-	-	-	-	-	-
Solomon Islands	-	-	-	-	-	-	-	-
Tonga	-	0.1	-	-	-	-	-	-
Tuvalu	-	9.0	-	-	-	-	-	-
Vanuatu	-	-	-	-	-	-	-	-

- Not available.

Table A7 Gross Domestic Savings (% of GDP)

	1997	1998	1999	2000	2001	2002	2003	2004
East Asia								
China, People's Rep. of	41.5	39.8	39.4	38.0	38.6	38.7	38.2	38.6
Hong Kong, China	31.6	30.5	30.9	32.9	31.6	33.9	34.0	33.5
Korea, Rep. of	33.7	34.4	32.9	32.4	30.2	29.2	28.0	29.0
Mongolia	-	-	20.0	32.4	26.0	23.7	-	-
Taipei,China	26.4	26.0	26.1	25.4	23.9	25.4	25.7	25.8
Southeast Asia								
Cambodia	10.2	8.3	9.7	10.7	10.2	10.0	9.7	9.4
Indonesia	31.5	26.5	19.5	25.1	24.9	21.1	20.1	19.7
Lao People's Dem. Rep.	8.8	13.6	13.2	15.1	15.4	16.1	19.6	18.3
Malaysia	43.9	48.7	47.4	47.1	42.2	41.8	42.1	43.0
Myanmar	11.8	11.8	13.0	12.3	-	-	-	-
Philippines	18.7	21.6	26.5	24.8	17.0	17.3	19.5	21.0
Singapore	50.5	51.7	48.8	47.9	43.6	44.2	47.1	47.3
Thailand	33.6	36.1	32.8	31.0	30.0	30.5	28.7	29.6
Viet Nam	21.4	17.8	26.3	25.5	27.4	29.2	28.3	25.8
South Asia								
Afghanistan	-	-	-	-	-	-	-	-
Bangladesh	18.6	20.4	20.8	22.1	20.8	23.6	22.7	23.0
Bhutan	21.3	12.5	12.9	16.8	20.2	20.0	-	-
India	23.1	21.5	24.1	23.4	24.0	24.5	24.1	25.2
Maldives	45.9	46.7	44.2	44.2	44.9	45.8	44.9	43.6
Nepal	16.0	16.2	17.1	18.8	19.0	17.4	17.0	17.0
Pakistan	11.8	14.7	11.7	14.1	13.9	15.4	15.2	16.0
Sri Lanka	17.3	19.1	19.5	17.4	15.3	15.8	16.5	17.0
Central Asia								
Azerbaijan	11.1	2.7	13.4	18.3	19.7	17.5	-	-
Kazakhstan	16.0	15.0	13.8	20.1	22.2	-	-	-
Kyrgyz Republic	14.3	-8.2	1.2	14.4	16.8	16.0	-	-
Tajikistan	-	23.3	19.4	-	-	-	-	-
Turkmenistan	-	-	-	-	-	-	-	-
Uzbekistan	14.9	9.9	10.5	16.5	-	-	-	-
The Pacific								
Cook Islands	-	-	-	-	-	-	-	-
Dem. Rep. of Timor-Leste	-	4.0	-13.0	-50.0	-49.0	-39.0	-29.0	
Fiji Islands	7.6	4.2	12.4	8.6	-	-	-	-
Kiribati	-	-	-	-	-	-	-	-
Marshall Islands, Rep. of	-	-	-	-	-	-	-	-
Micronesia, Fed. States of	-	-	-	-	-	-	-	-
Nauru	-	-	-	-	-	-	-	-
Papua New Guinea	21.5	22.6	13.3	25.3	-	-	-	-
Samoa	-	-	-	-	-	-	-	-
Solomon Islands	-	-	-	-	-	-	-	-
Tonga	-22.2	-29.6	-18.4	-10.6	-	-	-	-
Tuvalu	-	-	-	-	-	-	-	-
Vanuatu	19.5	21.3	19.2	19.3	19.1	-	-	-

- Not available.

Table A8 Gross Domestic Investment (% of GDP)

	1997	1998	1999	2000	2001	2002	2003	2004
East Asia								
China, People's Rep. of	38.2	37.7	37.4	37.1	38.6	38.5	38.2	38.5
Hong Kong, China	34.5	29.2	25.3	28.1	26.5	24.2	25.0	27.0
Korea, Rep. of	34.2	21.2	26.9	28.3	27.0	26.1	26.0	27.0
Mongolia	-	-	27.0	26.1	28.3	26.7	-	-
Taipei,China	24.2	24.9	23.4	22.6	17.4	16.8	18.1	18.6
Southeast Asia								
Cambodia	14.3	11.3	15.9	13.5	17.9	16.2	16.6	17.0
Indonesia	31.8	16.8	11.4	15.8	17.5	14.3	15.2	16.1
Lao People's Dem. Rep.	26.2	24.9	22.7	20.5	21.0	21.2	22.2	22.6
Malaysia	43.0	26.7	22.4	27.1	23.8	24.4	25.3	27.1
Myanmar	12.5	12.4	13.4	12.4	-	-	-	-
Philippines	23.8	19.3	17.8	17.4	16.6	15.6	17.5	18.5
Singapore	38.6	32.2	32.4	32.3	24.2	20.6	25.0	28.2
Thailand	33.7	20.4	20.5	22.7	23.9	23.8	24.0	24.5
Viet Nam	28.3	22.5	22.2	23.9	25.9	32.0	32.0	31.0
South Asia								
Afghanistan	-	-	-	-	-	-	-	-
Bangladesh	20.7	21.6	22.2	23.0	23.1	23.2	24.0	25.5
Bhutan	33.7	37.6	43.0	46.5	48.0	48.0	-	-
India	24.6	22.6	25.2	24.0	23.7	23.9	24.0	25.0
Maldives	33.2	30.1	33.6	26.3	28.1	24.1	23.4	22.5
Nepal	25.3	24.8	20.5	24.2	23.8	24.4	22.0	22.0
Pakistan	17.9	17.7	15.6	16.0	15.9	13.9	15.0	16.0
Sri Lanka	24.4	25.1	27.3	28.0	22.0	23.0	24.5	26.0
Central Asia								
Azerbaijan	34.2	33.4	26.5	20.7	21.0	30.1	-	-
Kazakhstan	15.6	15.8	17.8	18.1	26.9	-	-	-
Kyrgyz Republic	21.7	15.4	18.0	20.0	18.0	17.0	19.3	-
Tajikistan	-	15.4	17.3	-	-	-	-	-
Turkmenistan	-	-	-	-	-	-	-	-
Uzbekistan	18.9	10.2	11.8	15.9	20.2	-	-	28.0
The Pacific								
Cook Islands	-	-	-	-	-	-	-	-
Dem. Rep. of Timor-Leste	-	35.0	21.0	29.0	25.0	21.0	20.0	-
Fiji Islands	13.5	15.7	16.1	12.6	-	-	-	-
Kiribati	-	-	-	-	-	-	-	-
Marshall Islands, Rep. of	-	-	-	-	-	-	-	-
Micronesia, Fed. States of	-	-	-	-	-	-	-	-
Nauru	-	-	-	-	-	-	-	-
Papua New Guinea	21.3	17.9	16.4	13.0	-	-	-	-
Samoa	-	-	-	-	-	-	-	-
Solomon Islands	-	-	-	-	-	-	-	-
Tonga	18.8	19.9	22.0	21.8	-	-	-	-
Tuvalu	-	-	-	-	-	-	-	-
Vanuatu	18.3	17.0	20.3	22.3	21.0	-	-	-

- Not available.

Table A9 Inflation (% per year)

	1997	1998	1999	2000	2001	2002	2003	2004
East Asia	3.2	1.8	-0.9	0.6	1.1	-0.1	1.1	1.4
China, People's Rep. of	2.8	-0.8	-1.4	0.4	0.7	-0.8	0.5	1.0
Hong Kong, China	5.8	2.9	-4.0	-3.7	-1.6	-3.0	-1.5	0.5
Korea, Rep. of	4.4	7.5	0.8	2.3	4.1	2.7	4.0	3.5
Mongolia	36.6	9.4	7.6	8.1	8.0	1.6	5.0	5.0
Taipei,China	0.9	1.7	0.2	1.3	0.0	-0.2	0.4	0.6
Southeast Asia	-10.5	16.5	6.5	2.4	4.6	4.1	4.2	4.0
Cambodia	9.1	12.6	0.0	0.5	-0.5	3.0	3.5	4.0
Indonesia	-42.9	58.5	20.4	3.7	11.5	11.9	10.0	8.5
Lao People's Dem. Rep.	19.3	87.4	134.0	27.1	7.8	10.6	8.0	7.0
Malaysia	2.7	-12.8	2.8	1.6	1.4	1.8	1.9	2.2
Myanmar	-	25.3	21.3	-0.2	21.2	-	-	-
Philippines	5.9	9.7	6.7	4.4	6.1	3.1	4.5	4.5
Singapore	2.0	-0.3	0.1	1.3	1.0	-0.4	0.5	1.0
Thailand	5.6	8.1	0.3	1.6	1.6	0.7	1.3	1.6
Viet Nam	3.6	9.2	0.1	-0.6	0.8	4.0	5.0	5.0
South Asia	5.2	6.3	4.1	6.3	3.7	3.0	4.9	5.0
Afghanistan	-	-	-	-	-	-	-	-
Bangladesh	2.5	7.0	8.9	3.4	1.6	2.4	3.8	4.5
Bhutan	7.4	9.0	9.2	3.6	3.6	2.7	-	-
India	4.4	5.9	3.3	7.2	3.6	2.8	5.0	5.0
Maldives	7.6	-1.4	3.0	-1.2	0.7	0.9	-	-
Nepal	8.1	8.3	11.4	3.5	2.4	2.9	5.0	5.0
Pakistan	11.8	7.8	5.7	3.6	4.4	3.5	4.0	5.0
Sri Lanka	7.1	6.9	4.0	1.5	12.1	10.2	8.5	7.0
Central Asia	28.1	14.1	15.2	17.2	13.6	12.3	13.9	14.2
Azerbaijan	3.5	-0.8	-8.5	1.8	1.5	2.8	3.2	2.9
Kazakhstan	17.4	7.1	8.3	13.2	8.4	5.9	5.9	5.4
Kyrgyz Republic	23.4	10.5	35.9	18.7	6.9	2.0	-	-
Tajikistan	163.6	43.2	27.5	32.9	38.6	14.5	10.0	6.0
Turkmenistan	83.7	16.7	23.5	7.4	6.0	8.8	-	-
Uzbekistan	27.6	26.1	26.0	28.0	27.4	27.6	30.0	32.0
The Pacific	3.8	9.8	9.4	9.1	6.9	7.1	6.3	-
Cook Islands	-1.2	1.2	1.3	1.7	9.4	3.9	3.4	3.4
Dem. Rep. of Timor-Leste	-	80.0	140.0	3.0	0.0	1.0	2.0	2.0
Fiji Islands	3.4	5.7	2.0	1.1	4.3	0.9	3.0	3.6
Kiribati	1.9	3.7	1.8	0.4	6.0	5.1	-	-
Marshall Islands, Rep. of	4.8	2.2	1.7	1.6	1.7	2.0	2.5	-
Micronesia, Fed. States of	2.7	1.6	1.9	1.8	2.0	0.0	1.5	-
Nauru	-	-	-	-	-	-	-	-
Papua New Guinea	4.0	13.6	14.9	15.6	9.3	11.8	9.0	5.0
Samoa	6.8	2.2	0.2	1.0	3.8	5.5	3.5	5.0
Solomon Islands	8.1	10.0	10.4	8.6	8.0	9.0	8.0	-
Tonga	1.8	2.9	3.9	5.3	6.9	10.4	10.0	-
Tuvalu	1.4	0.9	3.8	5.3	1.8	2.6	3.0	-
Vanuatu	0.9	2.7	4.2	1.9	3.5	2.0	2.5	2.5
Average	0.8	5.6	1.6	2.2	2.4	1.4	2.5	2.7

- Not available.

Table A10 Change in Money Supply (% per year)

	1997	1998	1999	2000	2001	2002	2003	2004
East Asia								
China, People's Rep. of	19.6	14.8	14.7	12.3	14.4	16.8	15.5	16.0
Hong Kong, China	10.1	11.6	8.8	7.8	-2.7	-0.9	-1.0	2.0
Korea, Rep. of	14.1	27.0	27.4	25.4	13.2	10.4	15.0	15.0
Mongolia	32.5	8.8	31.7	17.6	27.9	42.0	25.0	20.0
Taipei,China	8.0	8.6	8.3	7.0	5.8	3.6	4.0	4.3
Southeast Asia								
Cambodia	16.6	15.7	17.3	26.9	20.4	22.0	20.0	18.0
Indonesia	23.2	62.3	11.9	15.6	13.0	4.7	12.0	12.0
Lao People's Dem. Rep.	65.8	113.3	78.4	45.5	20.2	20.0	19.0	18.0
Malaysia	22.7	1.5	13.7	5.2	2.2	5.8	7.5	8.1
Myanmar	28.9	36.5	-	45.0	45.0	-	-	-
Philippines	20.9	7.4	19.3	4.6	6.8	9.5	10.0	10.0
Singapore	10.3	30.2	8.5	-2.0	5.9	-0.3	3.1	7.3
Thailand	2.0	6.1	1.3	2.2	4.6	-0.1	6.0	7.0
Viet Nam	26.1	25.6	39.3	39.0	25.5	23.2	21.0	21.4
South Asia								
Afghanistan	-	-	-	-	-	-	-	-
Bangladesh	10.8	10.2	12.8	18.6	16.6	13.1	12.8	14.2
Bhutan	30.9	41.7	21.4	21.4	5.5	17.6	-	-
India	18.0	19.4	14.6	16.8	14.2	15.7	16.0	16.0
Maldives	23.1	22.8	3.6	4.1	9.0	19.3	-	-
Nepal	11.9	21.9	20.8	21.8	15.2	6.3	12.0	12.0
Pakistan	12.2	14.5	6.2	9.4	9.0	14.8	9.5	-
Sri Lanka	15.6	13.2	13.4	12.9	13.6	13.4	13.5	12.5
Central Asia								
Azerbaijan	33.6	-8.6	8.7	26.2	30.5	13.1	-	-
Kazakhstan	28.1	-0.1	84.4	44.9	45.1	33.0	22.4	16.6
Kyrgyz Republic	25.4	17.2	33.9	12.1	11.3	34.1	13.0	-
Tajikistan	110.7	53.9	33.5	64.5	33.4	32.5	20.0	17.5
Turkmenistan	107.2	67.7	23.6	68.3	-	-	-	-
Uzbekistan	36.0	28.0	31.5	17.1	16.4	-	-	-
The Pacific								
Cook Islands	31.2	12.1	16.7	4.8	14.4	3.2	-	-
Dem. Rep. of Timor-Leste	-	-	-	-	-	-	-	-
Fiji Islands	-8.7	-0.3	14.2	-2.1	-3.1	10.2	-	-
Kiribati	-3.1	11.1	0.3	5.0	-	-	-	-
Marshall Islands, Rep. of	-11.6	29.1	14.7	-1.9	25.0		-	-
Micronesia, Fed. States of	-2.7	9.8	-0.8	1.4	0.7	-5.8	-	-
Nauru	-	-	-	-	-	-	-	-
Papua New Guinea	13.3	3.6	9.0	7.1	4.2	9.4	9.3	-
Samoa	13.4	5.4	15.6	16.3	6.1	9.2	3.4	-
Solomon Islands	6.3	4.8	4.5	0.4	-13.3	5.0	11.8	-
Tonga	14.1	2.4	15.0	8.4	26.5	7.9	-	-
Tuvalu	-	-	-	-	-	-	-	-
Vanuatu	-0.3	12.6	-9.2	5.5	5.6	-1.7	6.2	-

- Not available.

Table A11 Growth Rate of Merchandise Exports (% per year)

	1997	1998	1999	2000	2001	2002	2003	2004
East Asia	10.1	-5.3	5.7	22.0	-5.8	12.0	8.3	9.2
China, People's Rep. of	20.9	0.5	6.1	27.9	6.8	22.3	10.0	12.0
Hong Kong, China	6.3	-8.5	-0.6	16.0	-5.8	4.9	6.5	6.2
Korea, Rep. of	6.7	-4.7	9.9	21.2	-14.0	7.5	8.0	8.0
Mongolia	34.5	-18.8	-1.7	18.0	-2.4	-3.9	8.0	8.0
Taipei,China	5.4	-9.5	9.9	21.8	-17.3	6.4	7.4	7.8
Southeast Asia	4.5	-7.4	9.2	19.5	-10.3	4.9	6.8	8.7
Cambodia	81.0	13.0	17.9	53.2	9.8	6.0	7.0	6.5
Indonesia	12.2	-10.5	1.7	27.6	-12.3	1.1	3.0	5.5
Lao People's Dem. Rep.	-1.4	6.4	1.5	2.6	-0.3	2.7	5.2	5.6
Malaysia	0.7	-7.3	17.2	17.0	-10.6	6.1	8.1	10.2
Myanmar	8.7	4.3	36.0	36.8	30.0	-	-	-
Philippines	22.8	16.9	19.1	9.0	-16.2	12.2	6.0	7.0
Singapore	-0.2	-12.0	5.4	20.0	-11.0	3.2	7.5	10.2
Thailand	3.8	-6.8	7.4	19.5	-6.9	5.8	6.6	7.5
Viet Nam	24.6	2.4	23.2	25.2	6.5	7.4	9.1	8.4
South Asia	4.8	-0.1	4.4	17.2	1.1	7.0	13.6	14.7
Afghanistan	-	-	-	-	-	-	-	-
Bangladesh	14.0	16.8	2.9	8.2	11.4	-7.6	9.5	10.5
Bhutan	1.7	12.1	-5.9	9.1	-12.9	-1.8	-	-
India	4.5	-3.9	9.5	19.6	0.1	11.4	15.1	16.6
Maldives	12.3	6.6	-4.3	18.8	1.4	18.1	-	-
Nepal	10.2	11.9	18.2	37.5	4.6	-18.0	5.0	10.0
Pakistan	-2.6	4.2	-10.7	8.8	9.1	2.2	12.0	10.0
Sri Lanka	13.3	3.4	-3.9	19.8	-12.8	-2.4	6.5	9.0
Central Asia	4.7	-17.1	6.4	45.2	-1.3	8.2	6.5	2.8
Azerbaijan	2.4	-16.2	51.3	83.1	9.0	12.7	9.8	-5.9
Kazakhstan	9.7	-14.9	2.0	55.1	-2.8	12.0	5.1	4.3
Kyrgyz Republic	18.8	-15.2	-13.5	10.4	-6.0	3.7	13.9	-
Tajikistan	-3.1	-21.4	13.7	18.3	-17.3	11.0	11.3	10.5
Turkmenistan	-54.2	-20.7	93.3	111.7	4.7	8.9	-	-
Uzbekistan	-4.4	-19.6	-8.3	0.9	-2.9	-5.7	-	-
The Pacific	-14.8	-14.2	9.8	-0.6	-12.6	-9.7	-	-
Cook Islands	-39.5	-10.0	41.2	38.6	100.9	-39.1	-	-
Dem. Rep. of Timor-Leste	17.1	27.1	-14.8	-90.4	-20.0	25.0	20.0	16.7
Fiji Islands	-21.1	-13.4	19.2	-4.2	-8.4	3.6	9.2	8.3
Kiribati	16.2	-6.0	55.3	-31.5	-38.2	9.0	20.8	-
Marshall Islands, Rep. of	-29.0	-47.2	-4.0	22.2	15.9	-	-	-
Micronesia, Fed. States of	-17.1	6.7	-9.4	-11.0	26.4	-1.2	-	-
Nauru	-	-	-	-	-	-	-	-
Papua New Guinea	-14.8	-16.1	9.1	7.3	-13.7	-14.7	-	-
Samoa	45.1	28.7	-3.5	-24.9	10.8	-9.4	-	-
Solomon Islands	-4.0	-9.7	6.5	-53.8	-32.6	7.7	7.8	-
Tonga	4.4	-10.1	1.6	-9.5	9.5	48.6	-	-
Tuvalu	-	-	-	-	-	-	-	-
Vanuatu	22.7	1.6	-24.0	2.0	-24.4	7.0	20.1	5.0
Average	7.7	-5.9	6.8	21.1	-6.9	9.4	7.9	9.3

- Not available.

Table A12 Direction of Exports (% of total)

From \ To	DMCs		People's Rep. of China		Japan		United States		European Union		Others	
	1990	2001	1990	2001	1990	2001	1990	2001	1990	2001	1990	2001
East Asia	24.3	21.1	9.6	14.6	12.5	12.0	20.9	21.2	14.8	14.5	17.9	16.6
China, People's Rep. of	52.2	30.9	0.0	0.0	14.7	16.9	8.5	20.4	10.0	15.4	14.7	16.4
Hong Kong, China	10.7	8.7	24.8	36.9	5.7	5.9	24.1	22.3	18.5	14.5	16.2	11.7
Korea, Rep. of	14.8	19.6	0.0	12.1	18.6	11.0	28.6	20.9	14.8	13.1	23.1	23.2
Mongolia	2.6	0.9	11.4	47.9	17.6	2.1	2.0	30.5	20.5	8.0	45.9	10.6
Taipei,China	-	-	-	-	-	-	-	-	-	-	-	-
Southeast Asia	29.1	34.1	1.9	4.5	18.3	13.4	19.6	18.2	15.8	15.0	15.3	14.9
Cambodia	82.9	6.3	0.4	1.3	7.6	1.0	0.0	64.2	5.0	24.8	4.1	2.3
Indonesia	18.4	28.9	3.2	5.5	42.5	20.9	13.1	15.3	12.0	13.8	10.6	15.7
Lao People's Dem. Rep.	69.0	45.0	9.1	1.6	7.1	1.5	0.1	0.9	9.4	25.6	5.3	25.4
Malaysia	40.0	35.5	2.1	4.3	15.3	13.3	16.9	20.2	15.4	13.6	10.3	13.0
Myanmar	49.0	48.4	8.1	4.4	6.9	3.4	2.3	16.6	6.9	14.5	26.8	12.7
Philippines	14.2	24.0	0.8	2.5	19.8	15.7	37.9	28.0	18.5	19.3	8.9	10.6
Singapore	34.7	43.4	1.5	4.4	8.8	7.7	21.3	15.4	15.0	13.4	18.7	15.8
Thailand	19.3	28.0	1.2	4.4	17.2	15.3	22.7	20.3	22.7	16.1	17.0	15.9
Viet Nam	25.3	20.0	0.3	6.8	13.5	17.5	0.0	7.6	6.8	26.8	54.1	21.3
South Asia	12.3	17.4	0.4	2.8	8.4	3.8	16.3	23.8	29.9	26.1	32.8	26.1
Afghanistan	14.3	48.5	0.4	0.2	1.5	0.2	3.4	0.8	61.7	26.9	18.7	23.4
Bangladesh	8.6	5.0	1.5	0.1	3.9	1.1	30.5	29.6	31.5	41.3	24.0	22.9
Bhutan	-	-	-	-	-	-	-	-	-	-	-	-
India	11.3	20.0	0.1	3.5	9.3	4.5	15.1	21.0	27.7	24.0	36.5	27.1
Maldives	38.5	24.9	0.0	0.1	8.5	2.8	24.2	54.4	26.2	11.6	2.6	6.2
Nepal	11.6	37.2	2.3	0.7	0.8	1.8	23.4	34.8	53.3	19.6	8.6	5.8
Pakistan	17.2	16.0	1.2	3.1	8.2	2.0	12.4	24.3	36.0	27.1	25.0	27.5
Sri Lanka	9.1	7.6	0.2	0.1	5.4	3.9	25.9	40.8	26.3	26.7	33.2	20.9
Central Asia	-	10.4	-	4.5	-	0.4	-	1.8	-	29.6	-	53.3
Azerbaijan	-	1.8	-	0.1	-	0.0	-	0.6	-	69.5	-	28.0
Kazakhstan	-	5.9	-	7.6	-	0.2	-	1.8	-	23.3	-	61.1
Kyrgyz Republic	-	21.4	-	4.1	-	0.1	-	1.5	-	24.7	-	48.2
Tajikistan	-	17.6	-	0.0	-	0.0	-	0.2	-	32.8	-	49.4
Turkmenistan	-	27.8	-	0.1	-	0.0	-	4.0	-	11.3	-	56.7
Uzbekistan	-	24.5	-	0.3	-	2.4	-	2.5	-	21.2	-	49.1
The Pacific	13.3	12.7	0.3	3.3	21.6	10.4	4.2	6.8	23.4	9.6	37.3	57.2
Cook Islands	-	-	-	-	-	-	-	-	-	-	-	-
Dem. Rep. of Timor-Leste	-	-	-	-	-	-	-	-	-	-	-	-
Fiji Islands	4.1	15.3	0.5	0.0	5.9	5.0	8.4	28.8	23.3	13.5	57.7	37.4
Kiribati	1.0	43.6	0.0	0.0	12.2	49.2	8.9	3.0	72.3	1.8	5.7	2.4
Marshall Islands, Rep of	-	-	-	-	-	-	-	-	-	-	-	-
Micronesia, Fed. States of	-	-	-	-	-	-	-	-	-	-	-	-
Nauru	11.5	31.7	0.0	0.0	0.0	6.9	2.0	0.0	0.5	1.4	86.1	60.0
Papua New Guinea	17.0	9.6	0.2	4.2	27.8	10.6	2.4	1.5	24.1	8.9	28.6	65.1
Samoa	6.8	12.4	0.0	0.0	0.9	1.4	6.9	11.2	20.5	2.0	64.9	72.9
Solomon Islands	19.4	54.7	0.0	6.9	43.1	21.9	3.9	3.4	22.6	5.3	10.9	7.8
Tonga	1.7	3.1	0.0	0.0	30.0	51.3	26.0	34.4	1.6	3.0	40.7	8.2
Tuvalu	0.0	14.3	0.1	0.0	0.0	0.0	0.0	0.0	12.6	79.0	87.3	6.8
Vanuatu	3.3	54.0	0.0	0.6	20.6	12.4	3.7	1.0	54.3	19.7	18.1	12.3
DMCs	25.1	25.4	6.0	10.1	14.4	11.8	20.0	19.9	16.3	15.6	18.1	17.2

- Not available.

Table A13 Growth Rate of Merchandise Imports (% per year)

	1997	1998	1999	2000	2001	2002	2003	2004
East Asia	4.5	-14.2	9.5	28.3	-6.6	10.2	9.6	10.5
China, People's Rep. of	3.7	0.3	15.9	35.2	8.1	21.0	12.0	14.0
Hong Kong, China	7.2	-12.3	-3.1	18.6	-5.5	3.1	5.9	6.7
Korea, Rep. of	-2.2	-36.2	29.1	36.2	-13.4	7.7	9.0	9.0
Mongolia	5.3	8.2	-2.6	19.2	2.5	3.3	6.0	5.3
Taipei,China	10.1	-7.4	6.2	25.9	-23.7	3.2	11.5	10.0
Southeast Asia	-0.2	-25.6	8.3	26.0	-10.0	4.1	7.8	9.6
Cambodia	5.8	1.6	27.1	37.1	6.2	6.5	6.0	6.0
Indonesia	4.5	-30.9	-4.2	31.9	-14.1	0.4	1.0	4.5
Lao People's Dem. Rep.	-6.0	-14.7	0.3	2.7	-0.4	-1.6	4.7	7.5
Malaysia	1.2	-26.6	13.5	26.3	-10.3	8.1	8.8	11.3
Myanmar	17.8	9.8	3.5	-10.9	17.8	-	-	-
Philippines	14.0	-18.8	4.2	14.5	-4.5	4.6	5.0	5.8
Singapore	0.7	-23.3	9.3	24.1	-15.5	0.1	9.8	11.6
Thailand	-13.4	-33.8	16.9	31.3	-2.8	4.6	7.0	8.0
Viet Nam	-0.2	-1.1	1.1	34.5	6.0	19.5	13.1	12.0
South Asia	3.3	-6.6	10.5	7.3	-1.8	2.5	11.0	11.5
Afghanistan	-	-	-	-	-	-	-	-
Bangladesh	3.1	-5.4	6.6	4.8	11.3	-8.7	3.5	7.5
Bhutan	18.4	3.7	19.2	14.0	6.1	-4.0	-	-
India	4.6	-7.1	16.5	7.0	-2.8	6.3	11.8	12.2
Maldives	15.6	1.5	13.6	-3.4	1.3	-2.4	-	-
Nepal	21.7	-12.4	-10.3	22.0	-0.2	-11.4	5.0	10.0
Pakistan	-6.4	-8.4	-6.7	-0.1	6.2	-6.9	14.0	10.0
Sri Lanka	7.8	0.4	1.5	22.4	-18.4	2.2	9.0	12.0
Central Asia	2.4	-7.9	-9.7	11.5	9.5	0.1	6.3	5.3
Azerbaijan	2.8	25.4	-16.9	7.4	-4.8	24.5	7.5	3.8
Kazakhstan	8.3	-7.0	-15.3	21.2	14.6	2.0	6.0	5.7
Kyrgyz Republic	-17.5	17.0	-27.1	-8.0	-13.1	25.4	10.6	-
Tajikistan	2.5	-10.0	-4.4	20.3	-7.3	6.0	4.0	3.7
Turkmenistan	-27.6	13.1	30.0	16.6	21.7	-11.0	-	-
Uzbekistan	-4.2	-27.3	-5.4	-5.2	6.4	-13.5	-	-
The Pacific	-1.2	-19.7	4.6	-3.2	3.6	-5.8	-	-
Cook Islands	-4.8	-10.2	-3.6	18.0	13.0	-8.8	-	-
Dem. Rep. of Timor-Leste	-	7.0	-21.7	72.3	16.1	-28.6	-15.9	0.0
Fiji Islands	-2.2	-25.2	25.1	-8.7	-4.2	9.8	10.4	4.9
Kiribati	1.6	-15.8	26.0	-3.9	-20.3	13.9	2.0	-
Marshall Islands, Rep. of	-10.0	2.9	4.2	-14.9	-3.6	-	-	-
Micronesia, Fed. States of	-4.4	0.4	-3.0	12.3	-3.5	-9.9	-	-
Nauru	-	-	-	-	-	-	-	-
Papua New Guinea	-1.6	-27.0	-0.1	-7.0	9.3	-12.8	-	-
Samoa	1.1	-3.2	19.3	-8.2	21.6	4.3	-	-
Solomon Islands	24.0	-0.1	-25.1	-16.0	-12.4	-26.5	6.2	-
Tonga	-9.5	29.7	-28.9	12.8	-1.6	-0.4	-	-
Tuvalu	-	-	-	-	-	-	-	-
Vanuatu	-3.6	-5.5	9.3	-7.3	0.5	2.9	10.2	5.0
Average	2.7	-17.4	8.9	25.5	-7.1	7.6	8.9	10.3

- Not available.

Table A14 Balance of Trade (US$ million)

	1997	1998	1999	2000	2001	2002	2003	2004
East Asia	39,657	90,604	76,124	57,032	59,090	78,211	75,302	71,346
China, People's Rep. of	46,222	46,614	35,982	34,474	34,018	44,621	43,647	42,393
Hong Kong, China	-17,299	-7,833	-3,158	-8,193	-8,331	-5,131	-4,233	-5,583
Korea, Rep. of	-3,179	41,627	28,371	16,872	13,392	14,180	13,830	13,320
Mongolia	31	-120	-113	-140	-170	-156	-156	-149
Taipei,China	13,882	10,316	15,042	14,019	20,181	24,698	22,213	21,366
Southeast Asia	-2,872	61,810	70,086	65,162	57,644	63,124	63,882	66,262
Cambodia	-231	-173	-276	-263	-240	-262	-265	-273
Indonesia	10,074	18,429	20,642	25,041	22,695	23,147	24,538	26,239
Lao People's Dem. Rep.	-331	-216	-212	-218	-217	-199	-206	-229
Malaysia	3,652	17,637	22,644	20,827	18,383	18,135	19,077	20,123
Myanmar	-1,280	-1,463	-1,172	-360	-186	-	-	-
Philippines	-11,128	-28	4,959	3,815	-743	1,595	2,025	2,589
Singapore	1,031	14,907	11,976	10,116	14,768	18,549	17,414	17,502
Thailand	-4,624	12,235	9,272	5,466	2,525	3,453	3,427	3,345
Viet Nam	-1,315	-981	1,080	377	473	-1,295	-2,129	-3,034
South Asia	-24,107	-19,039	-24,278	-20,545	-18,288	-15,818	-15,415	-14,609
Afghanistan	-	-	-	-	-	-	-	-
Bangladesh	-2,735	-1,600	-1,897	-1,809	-2,011	-1,768	-1,474	-1,390
Bhutan	-32	-25	-58	-71	-97	-91	-	-
India	-15,507	-13,246	-17,841	-14,370	-12,703	-11,213	-10,885	-9,678
Maldives	-217	-216	-262	-233	-236	-208	-	-
Nepal	-1,245	-995	-766	-852	-816	-773	-812	-893
Pakistan	-3,145	-1,867	-2,085	-1,412	-1,268	-360	-595	-650
Sri Lanka	-1,225	-1,091	-1,369	-1,798	-1,157	-1,406	-1,650	-1,998
Central Asia	-1,285	-2,290	-349	3,843	2,244	3,709	2,616	2,455
Azerbaijan	-567	-1,046	-408	338	581	482	570	345
Kazakhstan	-277	-801	341	2,440	1,175	2,101	2,137	2,105
Kyrgyz Republic	-15	-221	-88	4	40	-54	-44	-
Tajikistan	-60	-139	-27	-46	-121	-96	-47	6
Turkmenistan	-231	-323	-291	790	535	1,000	-	-
Uzbekistan	-136	240	125	317	35	276	-	-
The Pacific	-175	26	162	231	-223	-269	-	-
Cook Islands	-41	-37	-35	-40	-41	-40	-	-
Dem. Rep. of Timor-Leste	-94	-91	-67	-200	-234	-165	-137	-136
Fiji Islands	-374	-210	-294	-241	-255	-313	-352	-348
Kiribati	-33	-27	-32	-33	-28	-32	-32	-
Marshall Islands, Rep. of	-41	-50	-52	-42	-39	-	-	-
Micronesia, Fed. States of	-83	-83	-81	-94	-87	-77	-	-
Nauru	-	-	-	-	-	-	-	-
Papua New Guinea	662	717	881	1,099	717	591	-	-
Samoa	-85	-78	-97	-92	-114	-121	-	-
Solomon Islands	9	-6	40	-23	-34	-9	-9	-
Tonga	-47	-66	-43	-52	-50	-44	-	-
Tuvalu	-	-	-	-	-	-	-	-
Vanuatu	-47	-43	-58	-51	-58	-59	-63	-66
Total	11,218	131,111	121,745	105,722	100,468	128,956	126,385	125,454

- Not available.

Table A15 Balance of Payments on Current Account (US$ million)

	1997	1998	1999	2000	2001	2002	2003	2004
East Asia	30,542	79,571	65,898	50,619	56,058	72,571	63,113	59,445
China, People's Rep. of	36,963	31,472	21,115	20,518	17,405	23,441	21,220	21,406
Hong Kong, China	-5,319	4,426	12,046	9,108	12,284	17,483	18,819	14,195
Korea, Rep. of	-8,167	40,365	24,477	12,241	8,617	6,092	0	-1,759
Mongolia	14	-129	-124	-153	-169	-175	-160	-157
Taipei,China	7,051	3,437	8,384	8,905	17,921	25,730	23,234	25,760
Southeast Asia	-2,681	47,562	53,724	44,986	36,901	40,712	36,782	36,711
Cambodia	-268	-209	-258	-254	-213	-284	-324	-358
Indonesia	-5,001	4,097	5,783	7,991	6,900	7,262	5,818	6,573
Lao People's Dem. Rep.	-282	-130	-130	-145	-122	-99	-102	-133
Malaysia	-5,935	9,529	12,604	8,487	7,286	7,208	6,335	6,150
Myanmar	-397	-435	-217	-	-125	-	-	-
Philippines	-4,351	1,546	6,963	5,870	305	1,300	1,500	1,800
Singapore	18,123	19,706	15,185	13,281	16,138	18,704	19,212	18,189
Thailand	-3,128	14,262	12,423	9,251	6,133	7,571	5,446	6,401
Viet Nam	-1,839	-1,239	1,154	505	475	-950	-1,102	-1,911
South Asia	-10,911	-6,976	-8,117	-4,622	8	3,724	623	130
Afghanistan	-	-	-	-	-	-	-	-
Bangladesh	-909	-520	-656	-441	-1,090	171	-650	-1,296
Bhutan	-56	-47	-98	26	1	-8	-	-
India	-5,500	-4,038	-4,698	-2,579	1,351	1,666	728	1,956
Maldives	-35	-22	-79	-52	-57	-47	-	-
Nepal	-460	-422	-168	-294	-298	-383	-287	-304
Pakistan	-3,557	-1,701	-1,856	-217	326	2,744	1,450	638
Sri Lanka	-393	-227	-562	-1,066	-225	-419	-618	-864
Central Asia	-3,079	-4,138	-1,910	24	-1,457	-985	-1,363	-1,761
Azerbaijan	-916	-1,365	-600	-124	-73	-768	-979	-1,245
Kazakhstan	-799	-1,236	-236	675	-1,241	-200	-384	-516
Kyrgyz Republic	-138	-364	-180	-77	-19	-32	-	-
Tajikistan	-61	-120	-36	-62	-74	-32	-	-
Turkmenistan	-580	-952	-694	-572	-	-	-	-
Uzbekistan	-584	-102	-164	184	-50	47	-	-
The Pacific	-119	55	78	270	176	-123	-	-
Cook Islands	-4	-2	-2	-2	5	6	6	-
Dem. Rep. of Timor-Leste	-21	-21	6	53	-6	-59	-42	-26
Fiji Islands	35	-6	-84	-103	-68	-94	-77	-35
Kiribati	11	17	6	9	2	-3	0	-
Marshall Islands, Rep. of	2	-3	-8	21	39	32	-	-
Micronesia, Fed. States of	-21	-12	-1	-13	-17	9	-	-
Nauru	-	-	-	-	-	-	-	-
Papua New Guinea	-116	60	144	353	281	-31	-	-
Samoa	19	15	5	3	-8	9	-	-
Solomon Islands	-15	16	25	-44	-32	5	12	-
Tonga	-2	-18	-1	-10	-13	7	-	-
Tuvalu	-	-	-	-	-	-	-	-
Vanuatu	-7	8	-12	4	-5	-5	-1	-3
Total	13,753	116,074	109,674	91,277	91,686	115,898	99,156	94,525

- Not available.

Table A16 Balance of Payments on Current Account (% of GDP)

	1997	1998	1999	2000	2001	2002	2003	2004
East Asia	1.6	5.0	3.3	2.5	2.8	3.6	3.0	2.7
China, People's Rep. of	4.1	3.3	1.6	1.9	1.5	1.9	1.6	1.5
Hong Kong, China	-3.1	2.7	7.5	5.5	7.5	10.7	11.5	8.5
Korea, Rep. of	-1.7	12.7	6.0	2.7	2.0	1.3	0.0	-0.3
Mongolia	1.3	-13.2	-14.1	-16.2	-16.6	-16.0	-13.4	-12.1
Taipei,China	2.4	1.3	2.9	2.9	6.4	9.2	7.9	8.0
Southeast Asia	-0.2	10.2	10.5	8.1	7.0	7.2	6.3	6.0
Cambodia	-8.2	-6.9	-7.8	-7.6	-6.3	-8.1	-8.9	-9.3
Indonesia	-2.4	4.2	4.1	5.0	4.7	4.1	3.0	3.3
Lao People's Dem. Rep.	-16.2	10.1	-8.9	-8.3	-6.9	-5.6	-5.7	-7.1
Malaysia	-5.9	13.2	15.9	9.4	8.3	7.6	6.3	5.7
Myanmar	-0.2	-0.2	-0.1	-	0.0	-	-	-
Philippines	-5.1	2.3	8.7	7.4	0.4	1.6	2.0	2.5
Singapore	19.2	24.0	18.7	14.5	19.0	21.5	21.5	19.3
Thailand	-2.1	12.8	10.1	7.6	5.3	6.0	4.1	4.5
Viet Nam	-6.9	-4.6	4.1	1.7	1.5	-2.8	-3.7	-5.2
South Asia	-2.0	-1.3	-1.4	-0.8	0.0	0.8	0.0	0.0
Afghanistan	-	-	.	-	-	-	-	-
Bangladesh	-2.1	-1.2	-1.4	-0.9	-2.3	0.4	-1.3	-2.5
Bhutan	-17.6	-12.8	-25.9	6.1	0.2	-1.7	-	-
India	-1.3	-1.0	-1.1	-0.6	0.3	0.6	0.1	0.2
Maldives	-6.9	-4.1	-13.4	-8.2	-9.2	-7.4	-	-
Nepal	-9.4	-8.7	-3.3	-5.3	-5.4	-7.0	-5.0	-5.0
Pakistan	-5.7	-2.7	-2.9	-0.4	0.6	4.5	2.2	0.9
Sri Lanka	-2.6	-1.4	-3.6	-6.5	-1.4	-2.5	-3.5	-4.5
Central Asia	-7.4	-7.6	-3.7	1.6	-3.3	-2.1	-4.2	-5.1
Azerbaijan	-23.1	-30.7	-13.1	-2.4	-1.3	-12.6	-15.0	-18.0
Kazakhstan	-3.6	-5.5	-1.4	3.7	-5.6	-1.0	-1.5	-1.8
Kyrgyz Republic	-7.8	-22.2	-14.4	-5.6	-1.3	-2.0	-3.4	-5.6
Tajikistan	-5.2	-8.3	-3.4	-6.5	-7.1	-4.1	-4.0	-4.0
Turkmenistan	-32.7	-18.0	-13.0	-	-	-	-	-
Uzbekistan	-4.0	-0.8	-1.0	1.4	-0.5	0.6	-	-
The Pacific	-1.2	0.9	1.3	3.9	2.8	-1.9	-	-
Cook Islands	-3.7	-2.9	-2.2	-2.6	6.3	6.3	5.9	-
Dem. Rep. of Timor-Leste	-5.5	-5.4	2.2	16.5	-1.5	-16.0	-12.2	-7.3
Fiji Islands	1.9	-0.4	-4.5	-6.3	-3.6	-5.0	-3.7	-1.6
Kiribati	21.7	36.4	11.4	19.0	4.0	-6.5	1.1	-
Marshall Islands, Rep. of	1.7	-2.6	-7.9	21.4	38.2	29.7	-	-
Micronesia, Fed. States of	-9.8	-5.8	-0.7	-6.0	-7.6	3.7	-	-
Nauru	-	-	-	-	-	-	-	-
Papua New Guinea	-2.4	1.6	4.2	10.2	9.6	-1.1	-	-
Samoa	7.7	6.6	2.2	1.1	-3.1	-0.7	-1.4	-
Solomon Islands	-3.4	4.6	7.0	-15.9	-15.2	3.0	6.5	-
Tonga	-0.9	-11.2	-0.6	-6.1	-9.5	5.5	-	-
Tuvalu	-	-	-	-	-	-	-	-
Vanuatu	-2.6	3.2	-4.8	1.8	-2.3	-2.0	-0.3	-1.1
Average	0.4	4.6	3.5	2.8	2.9	3.6	2.9	2.6

- Not available.

Table A17 Foreign Direct Investment (US$ million)

	1997	1998	1999	2000	2001	2002
East Asia						
China, People's Rep. of	41,674	41,117	36,978	37,483	37,356	42,026
Hong Kong, China	-	-2,220	5,222	2,564	12,431	-3,976
Korea, Rep. of	-1,605	673	5,136	4,285	1,108	-703
Mongolia	25	19	30	54	63	58
Taipei,China	-2,995	-3,614	-1,494	-1,773	-1,371	-3,441
Southeast Asia						
Cambodia	168	121	144	112	63	60
Indonesia	4,525	-356	-2,745	-4,550	-2,914	-
Lao People's Dem. Rep.	-	-	52	34	24	41
Malaysia	6,788	2,708	2,473	1,762	600	3,200
Myanmar	419	275	212	-	-	-
Philippines	1,113	1,592	608	1,348	1,953	850
Singapore	1,281	5,594	7,848	6,402	1,402	2,015
Thailand	3,298	7,360	5,742	3,372	3,652	614
Viet Nam	1,900	669	358	459	273	397
South Asia						
Afghanistan	-	-	-	-	-	-
Bangladesh	16	249	198	194	174	65
Bhutan	0	0	1	0	0	2
India	3,557	2,462	2,155	2,339	3,904	2,146
Maldives	11	12	12	13	12	-
Nepal	28	11	9	0	0	0
Pakistan	700	572	428	473	285	484
Sri Lanka	430	193	177	176	172	-
Central Asia						
Azerbaijan	1,115	1,023	510	119	265	1,167
Kazakhstan	1,320	1,143	1,468	1,278	2,748	1,359
Kyrgyz Republic	83	87	38	-7	-1	7
Tajikistan	18	25	21	24	9	21
Turkmenistan	108	108	130	80	-	-
Uzbekistan	285	140	121	75	71	-
The Pacific						
Cook Islands	-	-	-	-	-	-
Dem. Rep. of Timor-Leste	-	-	-	-	-	-
Fiji Islands	-11	140	-79	-69	-3	-
Kiribati	1	1	1	1	1	-
Marshall Islands, Rep. of	-	-	-	-	-	-
Micronesia, Fed. States of	-	-	-	-	-	-
Nauru	-	-	-	-	-	-
Papua New Guinea	88	110	296	130	179	-
Samoa	20	3	2	-2	1	-
Solomon Islands	9	2	-19	1	-5	-
Tonga	3	2	2	2	2	-
Tuvalu	-	-	-	-	-	-
Vanuatu	30	20	20	20	20	-

- Not available.

Table A18 External Debt Outstanding (US$ million)

	1997	1998	1999	2000	2001	2002
East Asia						
China, People's Rep. of	130,960	146,040	151,830	145,730	170,100	180,000
Hong Kong, China	37,133	43,703	49,713	366,998	340,024	351,280
Korea, Rep. of	137,138	139,270	130,508	128,396	110,109	122,551
Mongolia	-	701	810	755	899	966
Taipei,China	33,545	30,021	38,628	34,757	34,336	42,390
Southeast Asia						
Cambodia	2,056	2,146	2,223	2,195	2,218	2,218
Indonesia	136,161	151,236	150,844	141,803	132,600	131,200
Lao People's Dem. Rep.	1,158	1,374	1,538	1,447	1,458	1,736
Malaysia	47,228	44,725	42,667	42,355	45,745	48,776
Myanmar	5,503	5,647	6,004	6,046	6,000	-
Philippines	45,683	48,266	53,019	50,063	52,355	54,000
Singapore	-	-	-	-	-	-
Thailand	109,276	105,062	95,051	79,715	67,511	59,252
Viet Nam	21,633	20,500	20,400	12,000	12,500	14,143
South Asia						
Afghanistan	-	-	-	-	-	-
Bangladesh	14,373	14,813	15,338	15,791	16,239	16,648
Bhutan	119	135	162	174	237	292
India	93,531	96,886	98,263	101,132	98,492	-
Maldives	165	185	186	178	182	227
Nepal	2,633	2,382	2,658	2,699	2,661	2,807
Pakistan	30,079	32,080	31,285	32,254	32,124	33,400
Sri Lanka	6,141	6,805	7,042	6,770	6,812	7,834
Central Asia						
Azerbaijan	548	661	964	1,162	1,262	1,356
Kazakhstan	7,750	9,932	12,081	12,685	15,078	17,950
Kyrgyz Republic	1,356	1,480	1,647	1,704	1,678	1,774
Tajikistan	1,106	1,179	1,233	1,226	1,024	962
Turkmenistan	1,771	2,259	2,015	-	-	-
Uzbekistan	4,665	3,467	4,237	4,449	4,600	4,360
The Pacific						
Cook Islands	31	65	64	58	53	54
Dem. Rep. of Timor-Leste	-	-	-	-	-	-
Fiji Islands	244	225	261	249	227	212
Kiribati	9	8	9	8	8	14
Marshall Islands, Rep. of	127	123	99	87	67	71
Micronesia, Fed. States of	98	94	84	67	58	53
Nauru	-	-	-	-	-	-
Papua New Guinea	1,258	1,298	1,348	1,394	1,483	1,307
Samoa	155	157	148	148	142	-
Solomon Islands	106	110	119	118	128	134
Tonga	61	60	67	62	58	61
Tuvalu	-	-	-	-	-	-
Vanuatu	42	53	56	77	70	69

- Not available.

Table A19 Debt Service Ratio (% of exports of goods and services)

	1997	1998	1999	2000	2001	2002
East Asia						
China, People's Rep. of	8.5	8.6	9.0	7.4	8.0	7.3
Hong Kong, China	-	-	-	-	-	-
Korea, Rep. of	8.2	12.9	24.6	10.9	13.9	9.4
Mongolia	-	7.3	9.3	4.5	5.3	4.9
Taipei,China	-	-	0.0	0.0	0.0	0.0
Southeast Asia						
Cambodia	1.2	2.1	1.6	3.8	3.8	3.3
Indonesia	-	-	-	-	-	-
Lao People's Dem. Rep.	7.3	9.6	14.2	15.4	15.6	16.6
Malaysia	7.4	7.0	6.3	5.4	6.1	6.0
Myanmar	-	-	-	-	-	-
Philippines	11.6	11.7	14.1	12.5	16.0	17.0
Singapore	-	-	-	-	-	-
Thailand	15.7	21.4	19.4	15.4	20.7	18.0
Viet Nam	12.8	13.9	12.8	10.5	10.6	10.2
South Asia						
Afghanistan	-	-		-	-	-
Bangladesh	7.9	7.7	8.0	8.0	8.2	8.7
Bhutan	8.5	6.8	10.2	4.8	4.6	5.0
India	19.0	17.8	16.2	17.3	14.1	-
Maldives	6.9	3.5	3.9	4.2	4.3	4.5
Nepal	4.5	6.1	6.1	6.0	6.8	9.7
Pakistan	62.7	55.4	35.3	36.5	37.3	44.1
Sri Lanka	7.3	8.3	9.3	7.6	8.7	9.8
Central Asia						
Azerbaijan	5.8	1.2	4.2	4.4	4.9	4.4
Kazakhstan	25.3	22.4	27.3	32.5	39.0	-
Kyrgyz Republic	12.0	21.8	26.0	28.1	30.8	-
Tajikistan	-	-	11.9	17.5	25.6	21.0
Turkmenistan	34.0	50.5	39.1	13.9	-	-
Uzbekistan	9.0	12.4	16.5	27.3	28.0	29.0
The Pacific						
Cook Islands	11.0	3.7	4.8	3.5	3.5	-
Dem. Rep. of Timor-Leste	-	-	-	-	-	-
Fiji Islands	2.9	4.1	3.2	3.0	2.0	-
Kiribati	7.1	9.5	7.6	9.3	7.9	-
Marshall Islands, Rep. of	44.2	78.6	109.0	50.7	-	-
Micronesia, Fed. States of	75.0	74.0	69.0	80.0	36.0	8.0
Nauru	-	-	-	-	-	-
Papua New Guinea	9.7	8.3	7.3	10.2	8.2	8.9
Samoa	13.1	12.9	11.8	12.7	11.7	-
Solomon Islands	1.6	3.7	4.5	8.2	-	-
Tonga	10.8	8.1	3.9	12.0	21.8	8.2
Tuvalu	-	-	-	-	-	-
Vanuatu	1.7	0.3	0.5	0.8	0.8	1.3

- Not available.

Table A20 Exchange Rates to the US Dollar (annual average)

	Currency	Symbol	1997	1998	1999	2000	2001	2002
East Asia								
China, People's Rep. of	Yuan	CNY	8.3	8.3	8.3	8.3	8.3	8.3
Hong Kong, China	Hong Kong dollar	HK$	7.7	7.7	7.8	7.8	7.8	7.8
Korea, Rep. of	Won	W	951.1	1,398.9	1,189.5	1,130.6	1,290.8	1,251.1
Mongolia	Togrog	MNT	790.0	840.8	1,021.9	1,076.7	1,097.7	1,125.0
Taipei,China	New Taiwan dollar	NT$	28.7	33.5	32.3	31.2	33.8	34.6
Southeast Asia								
Cambodia	Riel	KR	2,991.0	3,774.0	3,814.0	3,859.0	3,924.0	3,950.0
Indonesia	Rupiah	Rp	2,909.4	10,013.6	7,855.1	8,421.8	10,260.8	-
Lao People's Dem. Rep.	Kip	KN	1,260.0	3,296.0	7,108.0	7,846.0	8,871.0	10,069.0
Malaysia	Ringgit	RM	2.8	3.9	3.8	3.8	3.8	3.8
Myanmar	Kyat	MK	6.2	6.3	6.3	6.5	6.7	-
Philippines	Peso	P	29.5	40.9	39.1	44.2	51.0	51.6
Singapore	Singapore dollar	S$	1.5	1.7	1.7	1.7	1.8	1.8
Thailand	Baht	B	31.4	41.4	37.8	40.2	44.5	43.0
Viet Nam	Dong	D	11,706.0	13,297.0	13,944.0	14,168.0	15,050.0	15,200.0
South Asia								
Afghanistan	Afghani	AF	-	-	-	-	-	-
Bangladesh	Taka	Tk	42.7	45.5	48.1	50.3	54.0	57.4
Bhutan	Ngultrum	Nu	35.8	38.4	42.6	43.6	46.4	48.2
India	Indian rupee	Re/Rs	37.2	42.1	43.3	45.7	47.5	-
Maldives	Rufiyaa	Rf	11.8	11.8	11.8	11.8	12.2	12.8
Nepal	Nepalese rupee/s	NRe/NRs	57.0	61.9	67.9	69.0	73.7	76.7
Pakistan	Pakistan rupee/s	PRe/PRs	39.0	43.2	46.7	51.8	58.4	61.4
Sri Lanka	Sri Lanka rupee/s	SLRe/SLRs	59.0	64.5	70.6	77.0	89.4	95.7
Central Asia								
Azerbaijan	Azerbaijan manat	AZM	3,985.4	3,868.7	4,120.2	4,474.2	4,656.0	4,860.8
Kazakhstan	Tenge	T	75.4	78.3	119.6	142.1	146.9	153.5
Kyrgyz Republic	Som	Som	17.3	20.8	39.0	47.7	48.4	46.9
Tajikistan	Somoni	TJS	-	0.8	1.2	1.8	2.4	2.8
Turkmenistan	Turkmen manat	TMM	4,156.0	4,808.0	5,200.0	5,200.0	5,200.0	-
Uzbekistan	Sum	SUM	67.7	94.7	124.9	236.9	421.0	770.0
The Pacific								
Cook Islands	New Zealand dollar	NZ$	1.5	1.9	1.9	2.2	2.4	2.1
Dem. Rep. of Timor-Leste	US dollar	US$	1.0	1.0	1.0	1.0	1.0	1.0
Fiji Islands	Fiji dollar	F$	1.4	2.0	2.0	2.1	2.3	2.2
Kiribati	Australian dollar	A$	1.4	1.6	1.6	1.7	2.0	1.8
Marshall Islands, Rep. of	US dollar	US$	1.0	1.0	1.0	1.0	1.0	1.0
Micronesia, Fed. States of	US dollar	US$	1.0	1.0	1.0	1.0	1.0	1.0
Nauru	Australian dollar	A$	-	-	-	-	-	-
Papua New Guinea	Kina	K	1.5	2.1	2.6	2.8	3.4	3.9
Samoa	Tala	ST	2.6	2.9	3.0	3.3	3.5	3.4
Solomon Islands	Sol. Islands dollar	SI$	3.7	4.8	4.9	5.1	5.3	6.8
Tonga	Pa'anga	T$	1.2	1.3	1.6	1.6	1.9	2.2
Tuvalu	Australian dollar	A$	1.4	1.6	1.6	1.7	2.0	1.8
Vanuatu	Vatu	Vt	115.9	127.5	129.1	137.8	145.7	140.3

- Not available.

Table A21 Gross International Reserves (US$ million)

	1997	1998	1999	2000	2001	2002
East Asia						
China, People's Rep. of	139,890	144,960	154,675	165,574	212,165	286,400
Hong Kong, China	92,823	89,625	96,256	107,583	111,159	111,921
Korea, Rep. of	20,369	51,974	73,987	96,130	102,753	121,343
Mongolia	138	125	157	188	207	226
Taipei,China	83,502	90,341	106,200	106,742	122,211	161,656
Southeast Asia						
Cambodia	262	390	422	485	548	629
Indonesia	17,396	23,762	27,054	29,394	28,016	31,571
Lao People's Dem. Rep.	136	112	106	127	134	191
Malaysia	21,016	23,042	30,854	29,879	30,843	34,577
Myanmar	250	315	265	223	-	-
Philippines	8,768	10,806	15,107	15,024	15,658	16,180
Singapore	71,289	74,928	76,843	80,132	75,375	79,706
Thailand	26,968	29,536	34,781	32,661	33,048	38,924
Viet Nam	1,857	1,995	2,947	2,831	3,540	3,815
South Asia						
Afghanistan	-	-	-	-	-	-
Bangladesh	1,719	1,739	1,523	1,602	1,307	1,583
Bhutan	176	217	259	293	294	317
India	25,976	29,522	35,058	39,554	51,049	69,888
Maldives	100	120	129	124	94	135
Nepal	647	712	791	942	1,020	1,052
Pakistan	1,195	932	1,672	966	1,685	4,333
Sri Lanka	2,028	1,981	1,636	1,044	1,338	1,700
Central Asia						
Azerbaijan	468	447	673	680	699	664
Kazakhstan	2,291	1,964	2,003	2,096	2,508	3,134
Kyrgyz Republic	194	189	249	261	285	298
Tajikistan	30	65	58	87	96	92
Turkmenistan	-	-	-	-	-	-
Uzbekistan	1,167	1,168	1,242	1,273	1,358	-
The Pacific						
Cook Islands	11	10	14	13	16	-
Dem. Rep. of Timor-Leste	-	-	-	-	-	-
Fiji Islands	386	385	420	422	370	369
Kiribati	352	379	404	394	-	-
Marshall Islands, Rep. of	-	-	-	-	-	-
Micronesia, Fed. States of	-	-	-	-	-	-
Nauru	-	-	-	-	-	-
Papua New Guinea	381	186	204	296	424	340
Samoa	65	64	68	65	58	61
Solomon Islands	32	48	51	31	21	13
Tonga	27	16	22	16	13	18
Tuvalu	-	-	-	-	-	-
Vanuatu	40	45	43	41	38	38

- Not available.

Table A22 Central Government Expenditures (% of GDP)

	1997	1998	1999	2000	2001	2002
East Asia						
China, People's Rep. of	13.6	15.1	17.2	17.8	20.0	21.5
Hong Kong, China	14.5	18.7	17.9	18.1	18.7	19.1
Korea, Rep. of	22.1	26.0	25.1	24.8	24.8	22.8
Mongolia	34.5	41.9	39.4	41.4	43.9	44.0
Taipei,China	14.1	14.1	13.1	16.5	17.9	16.8
Southeast Asia						
Cambodia	13.0	13.8	14.5	16.3	17.5	19.5
Indonesia	17.4	18.1	21.1	17.2	23.8	19.4
Lao People's Dem. Rep.	19.8	22.7	19.5	21.5	20.7	21.6
Malaysia	21.0	21.8	22.7	23.8	29.3	28.7
Myanmar	-	-	-	-	-	-
Philippines	19.4	19.2	19.8	19.6	19.5	19.6
Singapore	16.9	20.0	18.2	17.7	18.0	17.6
Thailand	20.1	17.9	17.8	17.6	17.2	18.2
Viet Nam	20.0	19.9	19.3	20.4	21.4	20.8
South Asia						
Afghanistan	-	-	-	-	-	-
Bangladesh	13.5	13.4	13.8	14.7	15.6	14.5
Bhutan	43.5	34.3	44.9	46.5	52.8	43.5
India	25.8	26.6	28.2	28.3	29.5	30.3
Maldives	31.9	32.3	36.1	36.7	37.7	41.1
Nepal	16.5	16.9	15.4	15.5	17.6	16.9
Pakistan	22.3	23.7	22.0	23.6	21.3	22.0
Sri Lanka	26.4	26.3	25.2	26.7	27.4	25.5
Central Asia						
Azerbaijan	20.7	22.9	23.6	20.8	20.1	21.3
Kazakhstan	20.4	26.2	23.2	23.1	23.4	21.9
Kyrgyz Republic	25.3	28.8	30.4	24.9	22.8	25.6
Tajikistan	17.0	15.8	16.6	14.2	15.3	19.7
Turkmenistan	25.0	24.6	19.4	-	-	-
Uzbekistan	32.5	34.5	32.0	30.2	28.3	31.0
The Pacific						
Cook Islands	38.1	40.2	35.5	38.2	42.5	43.2
Dem. Rep. of Timor-Leste	-	-	-	-	13.7	20.1
Fiji Islands	32.4	26.2	25.2	27.1	28.2	27.0
Kiribati	115.0	120.1	112.6	118.0	133.2	125.0
Marshall Islands, Rep. of	65.5	59.2	56.8	65.8	65.2	69.9
Micronesia, Fed. States of	66.0	80.5	78.7	73.2	65.8	66.7
Nauru	-	-	-	-	-	-
Papua New Guinea	31.4	31.9	31.9	33.7	36.1	33.3
Samoa	39.8	34.1	39.5	35.2	34.0	35.5
Solomon Islands	33.2	41.6	48.5	38.6	34.0	37.2
Tonga	36.7	32.9	26.9	26.9	28.5	32.1
Tuvalu	121.9	95.9	126.2	211.0	162.3	70.9
Vanuatu	23.7	31.2	23.6	27.8	25.3	23.8

- Not available.

Table A23 Central Government Revenues (% of GDP)

	1997	1998	1999	2000	2001	2002
East Asia						
China, People's Rep. of	12.1	13.0	14.3	15.3	17.4	18.5
Hong Kong, China	20.9	16.9	18.7	17.5	13.7	13.6
Korea, Rep. of	20.6	21.8	22.4	26.0	26.1	26.6
Mongolia	25.5	27.6	27.2	34.6	38.5	38.4
Taipei,China	12.4	14.1	11.8	15.3	15.4	13.8
Southeast Asia						
Cambodia	9.0	8.3	10.6	11.0	11.4	13.6
Indonesia	17.9	16.4	18.6	16.0	20.1	17.8
Lao People's Dem. Rep.	11.0	9.8	10.5	13.2	13.2	13.3
Malaysia	23.3	20.0	19.5	18.1	23.8	23.1
Myanmar	-	-	-	-	-	-
Philippines	19.4	17.4	16.1	15.6	15.5	14.3
Singapore	38.4	31.3	22.2	21.4	19.6	18.7
Thailand	18.0	15.6	15.4	15.4	15.0	15.9
Viet Nam	24.8	22.1	22.5	25.2	25.2	24.3
South Asia						
Afghanistan	-	-	-	-	-	-
Bangladesh	9.2	9.3	9.0	8.5	9.5	10.2
Bhutan	40.8	35.4	43.0	42.4	41.0	36.7
India	17.8	16.5	17.7	18.0	18.5	20.0
Maldives	30.5	30.4	32.1	32.3	33.0	33.7
Nepal	12.7	12.3	11.5	12.3	13.1	13.6
Pakistan	15.8	16.0	15.9	17.1	16.0	16.9
Sri Lanka	18.5	17.2	17.7	16.8	16.5	16.5
Central Asia						
Azerbaijan	20.2	20.3	19.1	18.6	18.0	19.2
Kazakhstan	16.7	22.0	19.8	23.0	23.0	21.9
Kyrgyz Republic	16.2	18.0	17.7	15.1	17.0	19.2
Tajikistan	13.7	12.0	13.5	13.6	15.2	20.8
Turkmenistan	24.9	22.0	19.4	-	-	-
Uzbekistan	30.1	31.1	29.3	28.0	25.9	29.0
The Pacific						
Cook Islands	37.9	37.7	33.1	36.3	44.0	43.4
Dem. Rep. of Timor-Leste	-	-	-	-	8.0	11.5
Fiji Islands	25.8	25.4	24.6	23.7	21.7	20.1
Kiribati	139.6	160.0	121.6	130.3	148.2	119.1
Marshall Islands, Rep. of	74.6	74.7	67.3	74.7	82.4	79.0
Micronesia, Fed. States of	66.4	73.6	71.2	66.4	59.9	69.1
Nauru	-	-	-	-	-	-
Papua New Guinea	31.5	29.5	29.3	31.3	32.4	29.5
Samoa	40.0	36.1	39.8	34.4	31.6	33.4
Solomon Islands	29.0	42.1	44.4	34.5	22.5	25.0
Tonga	36.7	32.9	26.9	26.9	28.5	32.1
Tuvalu	156.1	154.4	148.7	243.2	119.5	155.6
Vanuatu	23.1	21.8	22.5	20.8	21.6	21.7

- Not available.

Table A24 Overall Budget Surplus/Deficit of Central Government (% of GDP)

	1997	1998	1999	2000	2001	2002
East Asia						
China, People's Rep. of	-1.5	-2.1	-2.9	-2.8	-2.6	-3.0
Hong Kong, China	6.5	-1.8	0.8	-0.6	-5.0	-5.5
Korea, Rep. of	-1.5	-4.2	-2.7	1.3	1.3	3.9
Mongolia	-9.0	-14.3	-12.2	-6.8	-5.4	-5.6
Taipei,China	-1.6	0.1	-1.3	-1.3	-2.5	-3.0
Southeast Asia						
Cambodia	-4.0	-5.5	-3.9	-5.3	-6.0	-5.9
Indonesia	0.5	-1.7	-2.5	-1.6	-2.3	-1.7
Lao People's Dem. Rep.	-8.8	-12.9	-9.0	-8.3	-7.5	-8.3
Malaysia	2.4	-1.8	-3.2	-5.8	-5.5	-5.6
Myanmar	-	-	-	-	-	-
Philippines	0.1	-1.9	-3.8	-4.1	-4.0	-5.3
Singapore	11.8	3.4	3.5	2.5	-1.8	-0.1
Thailand	-1.9	-2.5	-2.9	-2.4	-2.1	-2.2
Viet Nam	-4.8	-2.2	-3.2	-4.8	-3.7	-3.5
South Asia						
Afghanistan	-	-	-	-	-	-
Bangladesh	-4.3	-4.1	-4.8	-6.2	-6.1	-4.4
Bhutan	-2.6	1.0	-1.9	-4.1	-11.8	-6.8
India	-7.3	-9.0	-9.5	-9.5	-10.0	-9.3
Maldives	-1.4	-1.9	-4.1	-4.4	-4.7	-7.4
Nepal	-3.9	-4.6	-3.9	-3.3	-4.5	-3.3
Pakistan	-6.4	-7.6	-6.1	-6.6	-5.3	-5.1
Sri Lanka	-7.9	-9.2	-7.5	-9.9	-10.9	-9.0
Central Asia						
Azerbaijan	-0.4	-2.6	-4.5	-2.2	-2.1	-2.2
Kazakhstan	-3.7	-4.2	-3.5	-0.1	-0.4	0.0
Kyrgyz Republic	-9.2	-9.5	-11.9	-9.2	-5.0	-5.9
Tajikistan	-3.3	-3.8	-3.1	-0.6	-0.1	-0.2
Turkmenistan	-0.2	-2.7	0.9	0.3	-	-0.1
Uzbekistan	-2.0	-3.3	-2.9	-2.4	-2.2	-1.7
The Pacific						
Cook Islands	-0.2	-2.5	-2.4	-1.9	1.5	0.3
Dem. Rep. of Timor-Leste	-	-	-	-	-5.6	-8.6
Fiji Islands	-6.7	-2.4	-0.6	-3.4	-6.5	-7.0
Kiribati	24.6	40.0	9.0	12.3	15.0	-5.9
Marshall Islands, Rep. of	9.1	15.6	10.5	8.9	17.2	9.1
Micronesia, Fed. States of	0.4	-6.9	-7.5	-6.7	-5.9	2.4
Nauru	-	-	-	-	-	-
Papua New Guinea	0.1	-2.4	-2.6	-2.4	-3.7	-3.8
Samoa	0.3	2.0	0.3	-0.7	-2.3	-2.1
Solomon Islands	-4.2	0.4	-4.1	-4.1	-11.5	-12.2
Tonga	-4.9	-2.5	-0.2	0.7	-0.2	-0.6
Tuvalu	34.2	58.6	22.5	32.2	-42.8	84.7
Vanuatu	-0.5	-9.4	-1.2	-7.1	-3.7	-2.1

- Not available.